Rebel Voices: An I.W.W. Anthology

Rebel Voices

An I.W.W. Anthology

Edited, with introductions, by

Joyce L. Kornbluh

Ann Arbor: The University of Michigan Press

Dedicated to the memory of
James Chaney, Andrew Goodman, and Michael Schwerner—
Philadelphia, Mississippi, 1964

Second printing 1972
First edition as an Ann Arbor Paperback 1968
Copyright © by the University of Michigan 1964
All rights reserved
ISBN 0-472-06139-9
Published in the United States of America by
The University of Michigan Press and simultaneously
in Don Mills, Canada, by Longman Canada Limited
Manufactured in the United States of America

Preface

"We have been naught, we shall be all," sang the delegates to the founding convention of the Industrial Workers of the World in Chicago in 1905. The socialists, anarchists, trade unionists, and revolutionaries who met to lay the groundwork for One Big Union formed one of the first social movements in this country to develop an extensive literature and lore all its own. The Wobblies sang their songs of savage mockery and sardonic humor. They laughed grimly at the evils of the world. They used their songs, poems, stories, anecdotes, skits, language, and visual symbolism to transmit their own values within the structure of a society they wished to change.

Combining elements of Marxian and Darwinian thought, the I.W.W. ideology envisaged a utopian society consisting of one big industrial union which would abolish capitalism and the wage system and create a social order in which all good things of life would be meted out to workers with complete justice. "The I.W.W. was a fighting faith," wrote Wallace Stegner in the preface to his novel *The Preacher and the Slave* (Boston, 1950). "Its members were the shock troops of labor. . . . It existed for the prime purpose of making the first breaches in the resistance of entrenched industry so that later organizations could widen and deepen them."

Yet, as Stegner also pointed out, "no thoroughly adequate history of the I.W.W. exists. The standard histories are factual and doctrinal summaries, valuable for the record of the I.W.W.'s organization and activities . . . but lacking in the kind of poetic understanding which should invest any history of a militant church."

This anthology is an attempt to bring together the history of the I.W.W. as told by the Wobblies themselves. It is a story of their strikes, free-speech fights, trials, and riots, of militancy and martyrdom, of sacrifices and suppression, of epic struggles for a One Big Union and a Cooperative Commonwealth which would be free of class and nationality distinctions.

The I.W.W. message was spread through tracts and pamphlets, newspapers, and magazines, and thousands of copies of the "little red songbook"—started by the Wobblies about 1909. In 1920 historian Paul F. Brissenden listed close to sixty official and semiofficial I.W.W. periodicals which had been published by that date. Many of them were in foreign languages—Swedish, Finnish, Hungarian, Lithuanian, Russian, Flemish, Yiddish, Italian, and Spanish—published in American cities to meet the needs of the ethnic groups whose members carried Wobbly red membership cards. One of the newspapers was published in London, another in Australia, another in South Africa—countries where I.W.W. branches had been started by sailors and marine transport workers who spread the O.B.U. message to other lands.

Through the dedicated efforts of Jo Labadie and Miss Agnes Inglis, many of the I.W.W. newspapers, pamphlets, and songbooks have been collected in the Labadie Collection of Labor Materials in the University of Michigan Library. In 1911 Charles Joseph Antoine Labadie, of French and American-Indian descent, gave the University of Michigan a remarkable accumulation of pamphlets, periodicals, leaflets, and other material dealing chiefly with anarchism but including information on labor unions and various economic and political reform movements. Labadie, whose great great grandfather was a Potawatomie chief and whose father for many years served as interpreter for the Jesuits among the Indian tribes of Michigan and Indiana, was then sixty-one. He had been a printer, editor, and publisher, an early organizer for the Knights of Labor, and Greenback-Labor Party candidate for mayor of Detroit. He was one of the original founders of the Detroit Council of Trades, helped to form the Michigan Federation of Labor, and served two terms as its president. Drawn to anarchism in the 1880's, he became known throughout Michigan as "the gentle anarchist," about whom R. C. Stewart, a University of Michigan librarian, wrote: "He was first and foremost a good neighbor, a humanitarian, who despised man's cruelty to man and fought it with such moral and intellectual resources as he had in his keeping" (*Michigan Alumnus Quarterly Review*, May 10, 1947).

In 1917 Miss Agnes Inglis, who was born in Detroit in 1870 of wealthy and socially prominent parents, learned that the Labadie Collection was lying in boxes in the University of Michigan Library. Although she was not a trained librarian, Miss Inglis, who had worked at Chicago's Hull House and Detroit's Franklin Settlement, volunteered to put the collection in order. Over the years Miss Inglis added to the scope and value of the collection, acquiring many rare historic items through her extensive correspondence with individuals and institutions around the world.

The material for this anthology was taken from over twenty I.W.W. and socialist periodicals in the Labadie Collection, as well as from the files of clippings, scrapbooks, songbooks, and boxes of pamphlet materials. Although the I.W.W. organized among many trades in the United States and abroad, the material in this book focuses on four groups of I.W.W. members: textile, agriculture, lumber, and mining workers who were active in different geographic areas of this country. All of the items are by I.W.W. members or by writers whose work was published in the I.W.W. press.

Finding biographical material about the writers has been an extremely difficult task, and many of them remain unknown except for the names with which they signed their songs, poems, stories, and articles. For most Wobblies, the Movement was more important than the record of the lives of individual members. Also, as Nels Anderson pointed out in *The Hobo* (Chicago, 1923), most migratory workers made a point of not inquiring into the background and past life of a new acquaintance or associate. This cult of anonymity extended to the manner in which many Wobblies signed their contributions to the I.W.W. press: "J.H.B., The Rambler," "Card No. 34528," "Denver Dan," "Red," or simply, "A Wob." When I asked Ben Williams, the first editor of the I.W.W. newspaper *Solidarity* about I.W.W.-poet August Wahlquist, whom he had met several times, Williams could describe Wahlquist only as "a big Swede" who frequently dropped into the I.W.W. editorial office in Cleveland about 1913, helped address and mail out copies of *Solidarity* during his visits, and rolled out his bedding at night in the small back room.

It is hoped that this collection will be a starting point for additional research into the literature and lore of the I.W.W. that will explore its impact on American society. In addition, I hope that it may serve as a long overdue tribute to Jo Labadie and Agnes Inglis, as well as attract additional materials of interest and importance to labor history archives that have been started at several universities in different areas of the country.

I owe a debt of gratitude to many persons in many cities who have helped with this anthology. My thanks go also to the many librarians who helped at various stages of research: Edward Weber and Miss Marjorie Putnam in the Labadie Collection, Mrs. Louise Heinze at the Tamiment Institute Library in New York City, Mrs. Hazel

Mills of the Washington State Library, Miss Margaret Brickett of the U.S. Department of Labor Library in Washington, D.C., and Dr. Philip Mason, Dr. Stanley Solvick, and Mrs. Roberta McBride at the Labor Archives at Wayne State University in Detroit.

I owe a great debt of appreciation to several persons who read the manuscript and made knowledgeable and insightful suggestions: Dr. Sidney Fine of the University of Michigan, my Washington friends Henry Fleisher and Henry Zon, Carl Keller, the present editor of the I.W.W. *Industrial Worker*, and Fred Thompson, author of *The I.W.W.: Its First Fifty Years* (Chicago, 1955).

My debt to folklorist Archie Green cannot be measured. Professor Green generously shared with me many items from his own collection, suggested material that I might otherwise have overlooked, put me in contact with many persons who were of help in providing information, patiently read the manuscript, and made many valuable suggestions. His work with me has made a major contribution to this book. My thanks go also to Page Stegner, who permitted me to quote from his unpublished manuscript, "Protest Songs of the Butte Mines," to Peter Stone, Richard Brazier, Ben and Rose Williams, Carlos Cortez, Chuck Doehrer, Ted Frazier, John Forbes, Aino Thompson, Herb Edwards, Phyllis Collier, and Olga Winstead Peters, who provided additional help and information about persons and events.

My appreciation is also due the Institute of Labor and Industrial Relations, the University of Michigan–Wayne State University, which offered me office space during the writing phase of this book, and to Mrs. Esther Van Duzen who competently and cheerfully typed most of the manuscript. My profound thanks go also to the Rabinowitz Foundation whose financial help at a critical time enabled this work to be completed.

I am especially grateful to *School Arts* magazine for permission to reprint "Modern Hieroglyphics," to Mr. Alex Hillman for permission to reprint the section from Fred Beal's *A Proletarian's Journey* (New York: Hillman-Curl, 1937), to E. Clemente Publishers for permission to reprint the poems by Arturo Giovannitti from *The Collected Poems of Arturo Giovannitti* (Chicago: E. Clemente, 1962), and to the editors of *Western Folklore* for permission to reprint the version of "Fifty Thousand Lumberjacks" which appeared in *California Folklore Quarterly,* I (1942).

A very special debt of gratitude goes to my husband, Hy Kornbluh, and our own three rebels, Peter, Jane, and Kathe, whose intense interest, encouragement, and enthusiasm made this book very much a part of our family life during the past two years.

Contents

Chapter 1

One Big Union:
The Philosophy of Industrial Unionism

At 10 A.M. on June 27, 1905, William D. Haywood, then secretary of the Western Federation of Miners, walked to the front of Brand's Hall in Chicago, picked up a piece of loose board and hammered on the table to silence the whispers in the crowded room.

"Fellow Workers," he said to the delegates and spectators in the room, "This is the Continental Congress of the Working Class. We are here to confederate the workers of this country into a working-class movement in possession of the economic powers, the means of life, in control of the machinery of production and distribution without regard to capitalist masters."[1]

In the audience were nearly 200 delegates from thirty-four state, district, and national organizations—socialists, anarchists, radical miners, and revolutionary industrial unionists. They were united in opposition to what they called "the American Separation of Labor's" craft unionism, conservative leadership, and nonclass-conscious policies, and by their desire to establish an industrial labor organization that would ultimately overthrow the capitalist system and create a "cooperative commonwealth" of workers.

On the speakers' platform were Eugene Debs, leader of the American Socialist Party, Haywood, and Mother Mary Jones, a little lady of seventy-five with curly white hair and gray eyes, who had been a labor agitator for almost half a century. Other well-known delegates were Daniel De Leon, the sharp-tongued, erudite leader of the Socialist

Labor Party; A. M. Simons, editor of the *International Socialist Review;* Charles O. Sherman, general secretary of the United Metal Workers; William E. Trautmann, editor of the United Brewery Workers' German-language newspaper; Father Thomas J. Hagerty, a tall, black-bearded Catholic priest who edited the American Labor Union's *Voice of Labor;* and Lucy Parsons, widow of one of the anarchists condemned to death following the 1886 Chicago Haymarket riot.

Rapidly expanding machine technology, the growth of large-scale corporate enterprise, and the class-war character of many industrial struggles west of the Mississippi had led to several previous attempts to organize workers into industrial unions and to oppose the conservative orientation of the American Federation of Labor. Shaken by crushing strikes in Colorado and Idaho, leaders of the Western Federation of Miners which broke from the A.F.L. in 1897, formed first the Western Labor Union, then the American Labor Union to strengthen their organization and broaden their base of support.

Late in 1904, W.F.M. leaders initiated a meeting in Chicago of six radical spokesmen to consider plans for a new national revolutionary union. They invited thirty prominent socialists and labor radicals to meet for a secret conference in the same city on January 2, 1905. The invitation expressed hope that the working classes if correctly organized on both political and industrial lines were capable of successfully operating the country's industries.[2]

The January Conference, as it came to be known, was held for three days in a hall on Lake Street often used by the Chicago anarchists. Most of those invited were present. They drafted a manifesto, an analysis of industrial and social relations from the revolutionary viewpoint, which spelled out labor's grievances, criticized existing craft unions for creating a skilled aristocracy, and suggested "one big industrial union" embracing all industries" and "founded on the class struggle."[3]

Printed in great quantities, the Industrial Union Manifesto was sent around the country. All workers who agreed with the document's principles were invited to attend a convention in Chicago's Brand's Hall on June 27, 1905, to found a new, revolutionary working-class organization.

The Western Federation of Miners was the most important organization represented in this founding convention. Others were the Socialist Trades and Labor Alliance; the American Metal Workers Industrial Union; and a few former A.F.L. locals. Individuals came from the Socialist Labor Party and Socialist Party.

"Big Bill" Haywood, chairing the sessions, a massive, stoop-shouldered man, had been a cowboy, homesteader, and miner. Blinded in one eye in a mine accident, Big Bill left the Silver City, Utah, mines at the turn of the century to become an organizer for the Western Federation of Miners and the Socialist Party. He was, as historian Foster Rhea Dulles has phrased it, "a powerful and aggressive embodiment of the frontier spirit." From the start of the convention Haywood expressed his interest in organizing the forgotten unskilled workers, those without votes and without unions.

"I do not care a snap of my fingers whether or not the skilled workers join the industrial movement at this time," Haywood shouted at the meeting. "We are going down into the gutter to get at the mass of workers and bring them up to a decent plane of living."[4]

Speaker after speaker rose to elaborate the theme that since machinery was rapidly eliminating the craftsman's skill, it was necessary to organize workers made unskilled by advancing technology into integrated industrial unions paralleling the integrated structure of modern industry. This was vital to wage effective war on the great combinations of capital. To the philosophy of industrial unionism, an essentially American contribution to labor theory and practice, the I.W.W. added a new concept: that industrial unions would become the basis for a new social order.

For ten days the delegates debated issues and voted on resolutions and a constitution. Although they were united in opposition to capitalism and craft unionism, they were divided as to the tactics of bringing about an end to capitalism and the wage system.

Secretary to the constitution committee was Father Thomas J. Hagerty, a Catholic priest from New Mexico who had been converted to Marxism even before his ordination in 1892. Suspended by his archbishop for urging Telluride miners to revolt during his tour of Colorado mining camps in 1903, his formal association with the church ended at this time, although he insisted that he was still a priest in good standing. Hagerty, who helped frame the Industrial Union Manifesto and composed the chart of industrial organization ("Father Hagerty's Wheel"), is also credited with authoring the famous Preamble to the I.W.W. constitution with its provocative opening sentence, "The working class and the employing class have nothing in common."[5]

For much of the convention, debate focused on the political clause of the Preamble whose second paragraph, as presented by the constitution committee, read: "Between these two classes [capital and labor] a struggle must go on until all the toilers come together on the political as well as the industrial field, and take and hold that which they produce by their labor through an economic organization of the working class without affiliation with any political party."

For the most part, the western delegates were against "political action at the capitalist ballot box"; as itinerant workers, many had never voted in a public election. In addition to their antagonism to all types of politicians, they feared that the Socialist Labor Party and the Socialist Party would dominate the new organization and ultimately use the I.W.W. as a political adjunct.

Daniel De Leon, making the longest speech in favor of the political clause, argued that political action was "a civilized means of seeking progress." He emphasized the Marxist position that "every class struggle is a political struggle." It was necessary, however, he stated, "to gather behind that ballot, behind that united political movement, the Might which alone is able, when necessary, 'to take hold.'"[6]

When the political clause came to a vote, it was

The Employers' Pipe Organ

Solidarity, November 5, 1910.

The constitution provided that the structure of the I.W.W. would prepare for the eventual establishment of the trade-union state. Thirteen centrally administered industrial departments composed of unions of closely related industries were proposed. In this way, when the "one big strike" was called, and won, the I.W.W. would have control of each of the major industries of the country. Socialism would be established through action by workers at the point of production, and thus, "the army of production [would] be organized, not only for the every-day struggle with capitalists, but to carry on production when capitalism shall have been overthrown."[8]

An I.W.W. poet was to make this philosophy enduring with his famous stanza from the labor hymn, "Solidarity Forever":

In our hands is placed a power greater than
    their hoarded gold;
Greater than the might of armies magnified a
    thousand fold.
We can bring to birth a new world from the
    ashes of the old,
For the Union makes us strong.[9]

sustained by a sizeable majority, yet the controversy over direct vs. political action led to major cleavages in the I.W.W. which came to a head three years later at the 1908 convention.

The constitution and resolutions passed during the first convention attempted to link the immediate struggles of workers with a class-conscious, revolutionary aim. Any wage earner could be a member of the new organization regardless of occupation, race, creed, or sex. To the I.W.W. it "did not make a bit of difference if he is a Negro or a white man . . . an American or a foreigner."[7] An immigrant with a paid-up union card in his own country was eligible for immediate membership. Initiation fees and dues were set very low.

Labor-management contracts were viewed as an interference with labor's only weapon—the strike. Contracts were also rejected because they hampered workers from declaring strikes at the most critical times for employers. The "social general strike" was recommended as the most effective weapon to overthrow the capitalist system, and May 1 adopted as the Labor Day of the new organization. Militarism was condemned, and membership could be denied anyone who joined the state militia or police.

Less than six months after the first I.W.W. convention Frank Steunenberg, the anti-union, ex-governor of Idaho, was killed by a bomb as he opened the gate to his house during the Christmas holidays. Within a few days after Steunenberg's murder, police arrested a man who called himself Harry Orchard (born Albert E. Horsley) and turned him over to James McParland, head of the Denver Pinkerton Agency and a "consultant" to the Colorado Mine Owners' Association. Orchard confessed to the murder, as well as twenty-six other crimes which he claimed had been plotted by a radical "inner circle" of the Western Federation of Miners. Several weeks later, Idaho officials without warrants, seized Charles Moyer, W.F.M. president; Bill Haywood, W.F.M. secretary; and George Pettibone, a blacklisted miner turned small businessman. The men, arrested individually at night, were taken by a special railroad car to Boise, Idaho, charged with the murder of Steunenberg, and put in the death cells of the federal penitentiary.

The Haywood-Moyer-Pettibone case outraged the I.W.W., other labor organizations, and the labor and radical press. Frantic activity focused on raising thousands of dollars to defend the prison-

ers. Rallies in large cities netted enough money
to engage Clarence Darrow and other prominent
attorneys. Agitation in labor and radical newspapers resulted in improved treatment for the
prisoners, including their transfer to cells in the
county jail.

Fifteen months after his arrest, the trial of Haywood began in Boise on May 9, 1907. Defense
lawyer Darrow was matched against prosecuting
attorney William Borah, the Idaho attorney who
was later to become a powerful senator from that
state. In a brilliant courtroom performance, Darrow exposed Harry Orchard as a perjurer, produced witnesses to contradict his statements, and
charged that McParland of the Pinkerton Agency
had deliberately "fixed" Orchard's confession to
throw blame for the murder on the W.F.M. The
jury found Haywood, the first to be tried, not
guilty. Moyer and Pettibone were later acquitted
and released. Orchard was sentenced to be hanged,
with a recommendation for clemency.

Haywood left Idaho a popular hero. Turning
down lucrative offers from theater managers to
lecture about his prison experiences, he toured
the large cities, preaching the gospel of industrial
unionism to hundreds of thousands of workers.

However, despite the emergence of Haywood
as a national labor figure, the Idaho trial was a
paralyzing blow to the newly organized I.W.W.,
which had invested tremendous funds and energy in contributing to the defense. Ideological
factionalism and personality disputes split the
new organization in the tense first years of its
existence. Dissension developed almost immediately between the members who favored the tactics of direct economic action and those who
advocated political action. Describing his views,
direct-actionist Vincent St. John wrote:

> The first year was one of internal struggle for
> control by these different elements. The two
> camps of socialist politicians looked upon the
> I.W.W. only as a battleground on which to set-
> tle their respective merits and demerits. The
> labor fakirs strove to fasten themselves upon
> the organization that they might continue to
> exist if the new union was a success.[10]

Quarrels erupted in a chaotic 1906 convention
held while Haywood and Moyer were in prison.
The "wage slave delegates" led by Daniel De
Leon, William Trautmann, and Vincent St. John
opposed the "conservative" faction, which included I.W.W. president Charles Sherman and
most of the delegates from the Western Federation of Miners. In the process Sherman was
charged with misdirected use of funds, removed
from office, and the office of president was abolished. W.F.M. delegates bolted the convention
and control of the organization remained with the
"revolutionists."[11]

At their 1907 convention, the Western Federation of Miners voted overwhelmingly to withdraw
from the I.W.W., whose revolutionary views had
tinged the national newspaper publicity of the
Idaho trials. Growing increasingly more conservative, the miners' federation was to rejoin the

Masthead of Solidarity—*letters are formed from tools.*

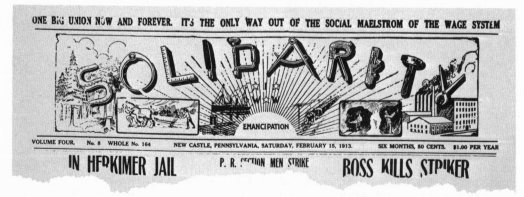

Mr. Block

He Learns Something About Craft Jurisdiction

A.F.L. four years later. Meanwhile, it fired Bill Haywood who had been going around the country agitating for class solidarity, militant direct action, and a new social order. Vincent St. John, a W.F.M. executive board member, stayed with the I.W.W. in spite of the withdrawal of the miners' federation. The stage was set for the final clash between the direct and political actionists.

Despite organizational schisms, across the country from Tacoma, Washington, to Skowhegan, Maine, the message of "One Big Union" stimulated strikes among loggers, miners, smeltermen, window washers, paper makers, silk workers, and streetcar men. Wobblies staged the first sitdown strike in America at the Schenectady, New York, plant of the General Electric Company in December 1906. In the frontier town of Goldfield, Nevada, where Vincent St. John had been a zealous organizer, an I.W.W. strike won a minimum of $4.50 a day for most of the cooks, waiters, and bartenders. In Portland, Oregon, the I.W.W. helped win a nine-hour day and a wage increase for sawmill workers and dramatized itself as a new force on the industrial scene of the Pacific Northwest.

Led by Jack Walsh, a former Socialist Party soapboxer, some twenty of these vigorous Westerners—loggers, sawmill workers, and seasonal harvest hands—beat their way across country to Chicago, to attend the 1908 I.W.W. convention. Traveling in freight cars, and camping in hobo jungles, these men, who were dressed in denim overalls, black shirts, and red bandanna neckerchiefs, held I.W.W. propaganda meetings along the way, selling I.W.W. pamphlets and song cards to finance their expenses.

In Chicago members of the "Overalls Brigade" numbered about twenty of the twenty-six delegates in a convention whose delegate strength was reduced because of membership splits and the 1907 financial depression. De Leon was offended by their lack of sophistication and little knowledge of socialist theory. He dubbed them the "rabble" and the "bummery" because of their singing of "Hallelujah, I'm a Bum" at convention sessions and accused them of trying to make the I.W.W. a "purely physical force body." "Most of them," he noted soon after the convention, "slept on the benches on the Lake Front and received from Walsh a daily stipend of 30 cents. This element lined the walls of the convention."[12]

In turn, the Westerners joined Trautmann and St. John in ousting De Leon from the convention on the parliamentary technicality that he was a delegate to the convention from a union other than his own. De Leon and his followers withdrew to set up a rival I.W.W. with headquarters in Detroit, which became a propaganda arm of the Socialist Labor Party. In 1915 it changed its name to the Workers International Industrial Union and was finally dissolved in 1925. As editor of the S.L.P. newspaper, *The Weekly People*, De Leon continued until his death in 1914 to attack the anarcho-syndicalists, "labor-fakirs," craft unionism, and Samuel Gompers.

One of the first actions of the 1908 convention delegates after De Leon's ouster struck out all reference to political activity from the Preamble. Detached from both the Socialist Party and Socialist Labor Party influence, the pragmatic Westerners helped in the next few years to shape the fundamental long-range policies of the I.W.W. The goal was industrial democracy in a worker-controlled, cooperative commonwealth. The basic tactic to achieve it would be the weakening of the capitalist system through "action at the point of production" which would form "the structure of the new society within the shell of the old."[13] The vehicle would be the One Big Union which, when strong enough, would carry through a general strike of all workers in industry to abolish the wage system, take over the means of production, and establish the new social order.

"We have been naught, we shall be all," sang the delegates to the 1905 founding convention.[14] Inspired by the social idealism of the Manifesto and Preamble and the militant spirit of the Western rank-and-filers, the radical documents, slogans, songs, and poems by Wobblies in the years to come reflected the antiauthoritarian, anarchistic thrust set in that epochal 1908 convention.

> They have taken untold millions that they never
>   toiled to earn,
> But without our brain and muscle not a single
>   wheel could turn;
> We can break their haughty power, gain our
>   freedom when we learn—
> That the Union makes us strong.[15]

A NOTE ON SOURCE CITATION

The source cited in the note to each selection is the earliest date I have found the item in print in an I.W.W. publication. Many of the items were frequently reprinted in the I.W.W. press and a large number of the songs have been included in other editions of the I.W.W. songbook after their first appearance. The latest edition of the I.W.W. songbook is the twenty-ninth. It was issued in 1956 in commemoration of the fiftieth anniversary of the organization. I have marked with an asterisk those songs and poems which were selected for inclusion in the twenty-ninth edition. The addition and deletion of various songs and poems from the songbooks over the years would make an interesting, and valuable folklore study.

1

In January 1905 about thirty prominent socialists and labor radicals met in Chicago to lay the groundwork for a new industrial union. They included Eugene Debs, A. M. Simons, and Ernest Untermann from the Socialist Party; Charles Moyer, Bill Haywood, and John O'Neil from the Western Federation of Miners; Clarence Smith and Daniel McDonald from the American Labor Union; and Frank Bohn representing the Socialist Labor Party and Socialist Trade and Labor Alliance. The meeting drafted a Manifesto, spelling out labor's grievances and calling for an organization that would help overthrow the capitalist system. Father Thomas Hagerty, a Catholic priest who shortly before the Manifesto conference had become the editor of the Voice of Labor, *the publication of the American Labor Union, is credited with taking a leading role in writing the Manifesto. The Manifesto was signed by those present at the January meeting and sent to all unions in the United States and to the industrial unions in Europe. A discussion of the "Origin of the Manifesto" was printed in the* Proceedings of the First Convention of the Industrial Workers of the World *(New York, 1905).*

MANIFESTO

Social relations and groupings only reflect mechanical and industrial conditions. The *great facts* of present industry are the displacement of human skill by machines and the increase of capitalist power through concentration in the possession of the tools with which wealth is produced and distributed.

Because of these facts trade divisions among laborers and competition among capitalists are alike disappearing. Class divisions grow ever more fixed and class antagonisms more sharp. Trade lines have been swallowed up in a common servitude of all workers to the machines which they tend. New machines, ever replacing less productive ones, wipe out whole trades and plunge new bodies of workers into the ever-growing army of tradeless, hopeless unemployed. As human beings and human skill are displaced by mechanical progress, the capitalists need use the workers only during that brief period when muscles and nerves respond most intensely. The moment the laborer no longer yields the maximum of profits, he is thrown upon the scrap pile, to starve alongside the discarded machine. A *dead line* has been drawn, and an age-limit established, to cross which, in this world of monopolized opportunities, means condemnation to industrial death.

The worker, wholly separated from the land and the tools, with his skill of craftsmenship rendered useless, is sunk in the uniform mass of wage slaves. He sees his power of resistance broken by craft divisions, perpetuated from outgrown industrial stages. His wages constantly grow less as his hours grow longer and monopolized prices grow higher. Shifted hither and thither by the demands of profit-takers the laborer's home no longer exists. In this helpless condition he is forced to accept whatever humiliating conditions his master may impose. He is submitted to a physical and intellectual examination more searching than was the chattel slave when sold from the auction block. Laborers are no longer classified by differences in trade skill, but the employer assigns them according to the machines to which they are attached. These divisions, far from representing differences in skill or interests among the laborers, are imposed by the employers that workers may be pitted against one another and spurred to greater exertion in the shop, and that all resistance to capitalist tyranny may be weakened by artificial distinctions.

While encouraging these outgrown divisions among the workers the capitalists carefully adjust themselves to the new conditions. They wipe out all differences among themselves and present a united front in their war upon labor. Through employers' associations, they seek to crush, with brutal force, by the injunctions of the judiciary, and the use of military power, all efforts at resistance. Or when the other policy seems more profitable, they conceal their daggers beneath the Civic

Solidarity, April 28, 1917.

Federation and hoodwink and betray those whom they would rule and exploit. Both methods depend for success upon the blindness and internal dissensions of the working class. The employers' line of battle and methods of warfare correspond to the solidarity of the mechanical and industrial concentration, while laborers still form their fighting organizations on lines of long-gone trade divisions. The battles of the past emphasize this lesson. The *textile* workers of Lowell, Philadelphia and Fall River; the *butchers* of Chicago, weakened by the disintegrating effects of trade divisions; the *machinists* on the Santa Fe, unsupported by their fellow-workers subject to the same masters; the long-struggling *miners* of Colorado, hampered by lack of unity and solidarity upon the industrial battle-field, all bear witness to the helplessness and impotency of labor as at present organized.

This worn-out and corrupt system offers no promise of improvement and adaptation. There is no silver lining to the clouds of darkness and despair settling down upon the world of labor.

This system offers only a perpetual struggle for slight relief within wage slavery. It is blind to the possibility of establishing an industrial democracy, wherein there shall be no wage slavery, but where the workers will own the tools which they operate, and the product of which they alone will enjoy.

It shatters the ranks of the workers into fragments, rendering them helpless and impotent on the industrial battle-field.

Separation of craft from craft renders industrial and financial solidarity impossible.

Union men scab upon union men; hatred of worker for worker is engendered, and the workers are delivered helpless and disintegrated into the hands of the capitalists.

Craft jealousy leads to the attempt to create trade monopolies.

Prohibitive initiation fees are established that force men to become scabs against their will. Men whom manliness or circumstances have driven from one trade are thereby fined when they seek to transfer membership to the union of a new craft.

Craft divisions foster political ignorance among the workers, thus dividing their class at the ballot box, as well as in the shop, mine and factory.

Craft unions may be and have been used to assist employers in the establishment of monopolies and the raising of prices. One set of workers are thus used to make harder the conditions of life of another body of laborers.

Craft divisions hinder the growth of class consciousness of the workers, foster the idea of harmony of interests between employing exploiter and employed slave. They permit the association of the misleaders of the workers with the capitalists in the Civic Federations, where plans are made for the perpetuation of capitalism, and the permanent enslavement of the workers through the wage system.

Previous efforts for the betterment of the working class have proven abortive because limited in scope and disconnected in action.

Universal economic evils afflicting the working class can be eradicated only by a universal working class movement. Such a movement of the working class is impossible while separate craft and wage agreements are made favoring the employer against other crafts in the same industry, and while energies are wasted in fruitless jurisdiction struggles which serve only to further the personal aggrandizement of union officials.

A movement to fulfill these conditions must consist of one great industrial union embracing all industries,—providing for craft autonomy locally, industrial autonomy internationally, and working class unity generally.

It must be founded on the class struggle, and its general administration must be conducted in harmony with the recognition of the irrepressible conflict between the capitalist class and the working class.

It should be established as the economic organization of the working class, without affiliation with any political party.

All power should rest in a collective membership.

Local, national and general administration, including union labels, buttons, badges, transfer cards, initiation fees, and per capita tax should be uniform throughout.

All members must hold membership in the local, national or international union covering the industry in which they are employed, but transfers of membership between unions, local, national or international, should be universal.

Workingmen bringing union cards from industrial unions in foreign countries should be freely admitted into the organization.

The general administration should issue a publication representing the entire union and its principles which should reach all members in every industry at regular intervals.

A *central defense fund,* to which all members contribute equally, should be established and maintained.

All workers, therefore, who agree with the principles herein set forth, will meet in convention at Chicago the 27th day of June, 1905, for the purpose of forming an economic organization of the working class along the lines marked out in this Manifesto.

Representation in the convention shall be based upon the number of workers whom the delegate represents. No delegate, however, shall be given representation in the convention on the numerical basis of an organization unless he has credentials —bearing the seal of his union, local, national or international, and the signatures of the officers thereof—authorizing him to install his union as a working part of the proposed economic organization in the industrial department in which it logically belongs in the general plan of organization. Lacking this authority, the delegate shall represent himself as an individual.

Adopted at Chicago, January 2, 3 and 4, 1905.

A. G. SWING
A. M. SIMONS
W. SHURTLEFF
FRANK M. MC CABE
JOHN M. O'NEIL
GEO. ESTES
WM. D. HAYWOOD
MOTHER JONES
ERNEST UNTERMANN
W. L. HALL
CHAS. H. MOYER
CLARENCE SMITH
WILLIAM ERNEST TRAUTMANN
JOS. SCHMIDT
JOHN GUILD
DANIEL MC DONALD
EUGENE V. DEBS
THOS. J. DE YOUNG
THOS. J. HAGERTY
FRED D. HENION
W. J. BRADLEY
CHAS. O. SHERMAN
M. E. WHITE
WM. J. PINKERTON
FRANK KRAFFS
J. E. FITZGERALD
FRANK BOHN

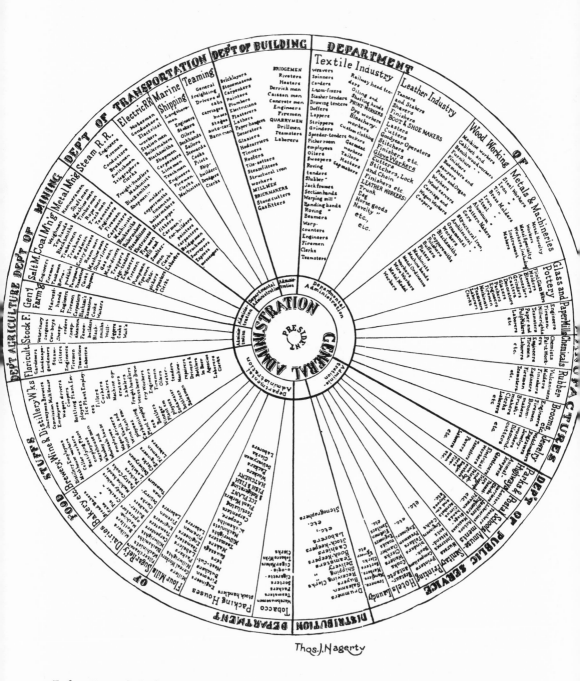

Father Hagerty's "Wheel of Fortune"

2

In the Voice of Labor (*May 1905*) *Father Thomas J. Hagerty graphically illustrated the structure of the new organization that would eventually become the basis of a new industrial society. The chart which was shaped in the form of a wheel, included every wage earning occupation then in existence. Hagerty divided them into eight departments: Manufacture, Public Service, Distribution, Food Stuffs, Agriculture, Mining, Transportation, and Building. The major departments formed the periphery of the wheel and their subdivisions constituted the spokes which led to a hub titled General Administration. School teachers, librarians, nurses, chambermaids, salesmen, and landscape gardeners were included in the chart. In his article on "Thomas J. Hagerty, the Church, and Socialism" in* Labor History (*Winter 1962*), *Professor Robert E. Doherty called the chart the most comprehensive scheme of labor organization ever envisaged. A.F.L. President Samuel Gompers dubbed it "Father Hagerty's Wheel of Fortune."*

FATHER HAGERTY'S "WHEEL OF FORTUNE"

The Structure of the Industrial System

A labor organization to correctly represent the working class must have two things in view.

First—It must combine the wage-workers in such a way that it can most successfully fight the battles and protect the interests of the working people of today in their struggle for fewer hours, more wages and better conditions.

Secondly—It must offer a final solution of the labor problem—an emancipation from strikes, injunctions, bull-pens and scabbing of one against the other.

Study the Chart and observe how this organization will give recognition to control of shop affairs, provide perfect Industrial Unionism, and converge the strength of all organized workers to a common center, from which any weak point can be strengthened and protected.

Observe, also, how the growth and development of this organization will build up within itself the structure of an Industrial Democracy— a Workers' Co-Operative Republic—which must finally burst the shell of capitalist government, and be the agency by which the workers will operate the industries, and appropriate the products to themselves.

One obligation for all.

A union man once and in one industry, a union man always and in all industries.

Universal transfers.

Universal emblem.

All workers of one industry in one union; all unions of workers in one big labor alliance the world over.

3

As secretary to the constitution committee of the first I.W.W. convention in June 1905, Father Hagerty was influential in framing the original Preamble to the I.W.W. constitution. Dissension arose at the meetings over the sentence, "Between these two classes a struggle must go on until all the toilers come together on the political, as well as on the industrial field, and take and hold that which they produce by their labor through an economic organization of the working class, without affiliation with any political party." Hagerty was among the group which opposed political socialism. In a convention speech he said, "The Ballot Box is simply a capitalist concession. Dropping pieces of paper into a hole in a box never did achieve emancipation of the working class, and in my opinion it never will."

Although the Preamble, with its controversial political clause was adopted at the 1905 convention and published in the Proceedings of the First Convention of the I.W.W. (New York, 1905), subsequent additions and changes were made in it at the 1906 and 1908 conventions. In 1906, the clause, "we are forming the structure of the new society within the shell of the old," was inserted, and in 1908, following the split with Daniel De Leon's group which favored political action, the controversial sentence was dropped from the Preamble. In its place was substituted, "Between these two classes a struggle must go on until the workers of the world organize as a class, take possession of the earth and the machinery of production and abolish the wage system."

Hundreds of thousands of copies of the 1908 Preamble were printed over the years by the I.W.W. and distributed throughout the world. The Preamble is printed in every I.W.W. publication and songbook. With its provocative first sentence, "The working class and the employing class have nothing in common," it has been one of the organization's most influential propaganda pieces. In his autobiography, Wobbly: The Rough and Tumble Story of an American Radical (Chicago, 1948), Ralph Chaplin wrote, "The Preamble came first in our affections. It was at once our Declaration of Freedom and the Tablets of the Law. Exploited, homeless, voteless, frequently jobless, and always kicked about from pillar to post, the American migratory worker nailed the I.W.W. Preamble to the masthead and took his stand against the great and powerful of the earth to work out his economic and social destiny without benefit of respectability or law. . . . That was what the unrestrained exploitation and injustice of the early decades of the Twentieth Century did to us."

PREAMBLE
as adopted by the 1905 I.W.W. Convention

The working class and the employing class have nothing in common. There can be no peace so long as hunger and want are found among millions of working people and the few, who make up the employing class, have all the good things of life.

Between these two classes a struggle must go on until all the toilers come together on the political, as well as on the industrial field, and take and hold that which they produce by their labor, through an economic organization of the working class without affiliation with any political party.

The rapid gathering of wealth and the centering of the management of industries into fewer and fewer hands make the trades unions unable to cope with the ever-growing power of the employing class, because the trades unions foster a state of things which allows one set of workers to be pitted against another set of workers in the same industry, thereby helping defeat one another in wage wars. The trades unions aid the employing class to mislead the workers into the belief that the working class have interests in common with their employers.

These sad conditions can be changed and the interests of the working class upheld only by an organization formed in such a way that all its members in any one industry, or in all industries, if necessary, cease work whenever a strike or lockout is on in any department thereof, thus making an injury to one an injury to all.

4

The Preamble to the Constitution of the Industrial Workers of the World as amended appeared in the Proceedings of the 1908 I.W.W. Convention in the I.W.W. Industrial Union Bulletin (November 7, 1908).

PREAMBLE
of the Industrial Workers of the World

The working class and the employing class have nothing in common. There can be no peace so long as hunger and want are found among millions of working people and the few, who make up the employing class, have all the good things of life.

Between these two classes a struggle must go on until the workers of the world organize as a class, take possession of the earth and the machinery of production, and abolish the wage system.

We find that the centering of management of the industries into fewer and fewer hands makes the trade unions unable to cope with the ever growing power of the employing class. The trade unions foster a state of affairs which allows one set of workers to be pitted against another set of workers in the same industry, thereby helping defeat one another in wage wars. Moreover, the trade unions aid the employing class to mislead the workers into the belief that the working class have interests in common with their employers.

These conditions can be changed and the interest of the working class upheld only by an organization formed in such a way that all its members in any one industry, or in all industries if necessary, cease work whenever a strike or lockout is on in any department thereof, thus making an injury to one an injury to all.

Instead of the conservative motto, "A fair day's wage for a fair day's work," we must inscribe on our banner the revolutionary watchword, "Abolition of the wage system."

It is the historic mission of the working class to do away with capitalism. The army of production must be organized, not only for the every-day struggle with capitalists, but also to carry on production when capitalism shall have been overthrown. By organizing industrially we are forming the structure of the new society within the shell of the old.

5

"Workingmen, Unite," and the following song, "The Banner of Labor," were first published in the I.W.W. press in the Industrial Union Bulletin (*October 24; 1908*) *under the headline, "Songs Sung by the Industrial Union Singing Club on Their Trip Across Country to Convention." The Industrial Union Singing Club, no doubt, was made up of the men, led by J. H. Walsh, who traveled by freight trains from Portland to the 1908 I.W.W. convention in Chicago.*

E. S. Nelson, who wrote "Workingmen, Unite," was a Swede who was active in the Northwest in

the eight-hour day campaign. He wrote two popular I.W.W. pamphlets, The Eight Hour Day, *and* An Appeal to Wage Earners: A Statement of I.W.W. Principles and Methods. *The author of "The Banner of Labor" is unknown. Both songs were included in the first edition of the I.W.W. songbook.*

WORKINGMEN, UNITE!*

By E. S. NELSON

(*Tune: "Red Wing"*)

Conditions they are bad,
And some of you are sad;
You cannot see your enemy,
The class that lives in luxury.
You workingmen are poor,—
Will be forevermore,—
As long as you permit the few
To guide your destiny.

Chorus:

Shall we still be slaves and work for wages?
It is outrageous—has been for ages;
This earth by right belongs to toilers,
And not to spoilers of liberty.

The master class is small,
But they have lots of "gall."
When we unite to gain our right,
If they resist we'll use our might;
There is no middle ground,
This fight must be one round,
To victory, for liberty,
Our class is marching on!

Workingmen, unite!
We must put up a fight,
To make us free from slavery
And capitalistic tyranny;
This fight is not in vain,
We've got a world to gain.
Will you be a fool, a capitalist tool?
And serve your enemy?

6

THE BANNER OF LABOR

(*Tune: "Star Spangled Banner"*)

Oh, say, can you hear, coming near and more near
The call now resounding: "Come all ye who labor?"

The Industrial Band, throughout all the land
Bids toilers remember, each toiler's his neighbor.
Come, workers, unite! 'tis Humanity's fight.
We call, you come forth in your manhood and
    might.

Chorus:

And the *Banner of Labor* will surely soon wave
O'er the land that is free, from the master and
    slave.

The blood and the lives of children and wives
Are ground into dollars for parasites' pleasure;
The children now slave, till they sink in their
    grave—
That robbers may fatten and add to their treasure.
Will you idly sit by, unheeding their cry?
Arise! Be ye men! See, the battle draws nigh!

Long, long has the spoil of labor and toil
Been wrung from the workers by parasite classes;
While Poverty, gaunt, Desolation and Want
Have dwelt in the hovels of earth's toiling masses.
Through bloodshed and tears, our day star
    appears,
Industrial Union, the wage slave now cheers.

7

*"Union Scabs" appeared as an article in the
I.W.W. Industrial Union Bulletin (March 14,
1908) and was made into a pamphlet by the organization around 1910. It was advertised in the
January 22, 1910, issue of* Solidarity *as a "red-hot
satire on the Craft Union methods."*

*Oscar Ameringer (1870–1943) was a socialist
writer and editor who had come to the United
States from Germany at age fifteen. A member
of the American Federation of Musicians, he organized for the Knights of Labor before editing
a series of publications which included* The Labor
World, *the* Voice of the People, *the* Oklahoma
Pioneer, *the* Illinois Miner, *and the* American
Guardian. *He was active in Socialist Party politics, and in 1912 was the Socialist Party candidate
for governor of Wisconsin. He was the author of
many colorful and earthy pamphlets and articles,
including* Socialism: What It Is and How to Get
It (Chicago, 1908) *and* The Life and Deeds of
Uncle Sam (1909).

*Ameringer included "Union Scabs" in his auto-
biography,* If You Don't Weaken (New York,
1940).*

UNION SCABS

By Oscar Ameringer

There are three kinds of scabs: the professional,
the amateur and the union scab.

The professional scab is usually a high-paid,
high-skilled worker in the employ of strikebreak-
ing and detective agencies. His position is that of
a petty officer's in the regular scab army.

The amateur scab brigade is composed of bums,
riff-raff, slum dwellers, rubes, tramps, imbeciles,
college students and other undesirable citizens.

The last, and by far the most important class is
the union scab.

Professional scabs are few and efficient. Amateur scabs are plentiful and deficient, and union
scabs both numerous and capable.

The professional scab knows what he is doing,
does it well and for the sake of the long green only.

The amateur scab, posing as a free-born American citizen, who scorns to be fettered by union
rules and regulations, gets much glory (?), little
pay and when the strike is over he is given an
honorable discharge in the region where Darwin
searched for the missing link.

The union scab receives less pay than the professional scab, works better than the amateur scab
and don't know that he is a scab.

He will take a pattern from a scab pattern-
maker, cast it in a union mold, hand the casting
to as lousy a scab as ever walked in shoe leather,
and then proudly produce a paid-up union card
in testimony of his unionism. Way down in his
heart he seems to have a lurking suspicion that
there is something not altogether right in his action, and it is characteristic of the union man who
co-operates with scabs that he is ever ready to
flash a union card in the face of innocent by-
standers.

He don't know that the rose under any other
name is just as fragrant; he don't know that calling
a cat a canary won't make the feline warble, and
he don't know that helping to run the shop while
other workers bend all their energies in the opposite direction is scabbing. He relies on the name
and seeks refuge behind a little pasteboard card.

When a strike is declared it becomes the chief
duty of the organization to effect a complete shut-
down of the plant. For that purpose warnings are
mailed, or wired, to other places, to prevent working men from moving to the afflicted city.

Pickets are stationed around the plant or factory, or harbor, to stop workers from taking the places of the strikers. Amateur scabs are coaxed, persuaded, or bullied away from the seat of the strike. Persuasion having no effect on the professional strikebreaker, he is sometimes treated with a brickbat shower. Shut down that plant, shut it down completely, is the watchword of the striker.

Now while all these things are going on and men are stopped in ones and twos, a steady stream of dinner pail parades pours through the factory gate. Why are they not molested? Oh! they're union men, belonging to a different craft than the one on strike. Instead of brickbats and insults it's "Hello, John; hello, Jim; howdy, Jack," and other expressions of goodfellowship.

You see, this is a carriage factory, and it's only the Amalgamated Association of Brim Stone and Emery Polishers that are striking, the Brotherhood of Oil Rag Wipers, the Fraternal Society of White Lead Daubers, the Undivided Sons of Varnish Spreaders, the Benevolent Compilation of Wood Work Gluers, the Iron Benders' Sick and Death Benefit Union, the Oakdale Lodge of Coal Shovelers, the Martha Washington Lodge of Ash Wheelers, the Amalgamated Brotherhood of Oilers, the Engineers' Protective Lodge, the Stationary Firemen, the Portable Firemen, the F. O. O. L., the A. S. S. E. S. Societies have nothing to do with the Amalgamated Association of Brimstone and Emery Polishers.

At the next regular meeting of those societies, ringing resolutions endorsing the strike of the Amalgamated Association of Brimstone and Emery Polishers will be passed. Moral support is pledged and five dollars' worth of tickets are purchased for the dance given by the Ladies' Volunteer and Auxiliary Chore for the Benefit of the Amalgamated Association of Brimstone and Emery Polishers.

The whole thing is like beating a man's brains out and then handing him a headache tablet.

During a very bitterly fought molders' strike in a northern city the writer noticed one of the prettiest illustrations of the workings of plain scabbing and union scabbing.

A dense mass of strikers and sympathizers had assembled in front of the factory awaiting the exit of the strikebreakers. Out they came, scabs and unionists in one dark mass. Stones, rotten eggs and other missiles began to fly, when one of the strikebreakers leaped on a store box and shouted frantically: "Stop it, stop it, for C——'s sake, stop it; you are hitting more unionists than scabs; you can't tell the difference."

That's it. Wherever scabs and union men work harmoniously in the strike-breaking industry all hell can't tell the difference.

To the murky conception of a union scab, scabbing is only wrong when practiced by a non-union man. To him the union card is a kind of scab permit that guarantees him immunity from insults, brickbats and rotten eggs.

After having instructed a green bunch of amateur scabs in the art of brimstone and emery polishing all day, he meets a striking brother in the evening and forthwith demonstrates his unionism by setting up the drinks for the latter.

Union scabbing is the legitimate offspring of craft organization. It is begotten by ignorance, born of imbecility and nourished by infamy.

My dear brother, I am sorry to be under contract to hang you, but I know it will please you to hear that the scaffold is built by union carpenters, the rope bears the label, and here is my card.

This is union scabbing.

8

In The Call *(May 6, 1920), a British Socialist Party weekly, Jim Connell (?–1929) recalled how he had written "The Red Flag" in 1889. He said that he had been inspired by the London Dock Strike of 1889, the work of the Irish Land League, the Russian Nihilist movement, and the hanging of the Chicago anarchists following the Haymarket bombing of 1887. He wrote most of "The Red Flag" on a fifteen-minute train ride between Charing Cross and New Cross. It was first published in the 1889 Christmas issue of* Justice, *a British socialist publication. Connell, who was secretary of the Workmen's Legal Friendly Society, described himself in* Who's Who *as "sheepfarmer, dock labourer, navvy, railwayman, draper, lawyer (of a sort), and all the time a poacher."*

"The Red Flag" became the official anthem of the British Labour Party and has continued to be popular in England until the present time. On August 1, 1945, it was sung in the British House of Commons following the Labour Party victory in the Parliamentary elections.

Connell composed the verses to the tune of "The White Cockade," a Jacobite song. It was later sung to the tune of "Maryland" ("Tannen-

baum") which, Connell wrote, is really an old German Roman Catholic hymn. "The Red Flag" was first published in the I.W.W. press in the Industrial Union Bulletin (July 25, 1908) and was included in the first edition of the I.W.W. songbook. It is one of the most popular and well-known radical songs in this country.

THE RED FLAG °

By Jim Connell

The People's flag is deepest red,
    It shrouded oft our martyred dead;
And ere their limbs grew stiff and cold
    Their life-blood dyed its every fold.

Chorus:

Then raise the scarlet standard high
    Beneath its folds, we'll live and die,
Though cowards flinch and traitors sneer,
    We'll keep the red flag flying here.

Look 'round! the Frenchman loves its blaze,
    The sturdy German chants its praise;
In Moscow's vaults, its hymns are sung,
    Chicago swells its surging song.

It waved above our infant might
    When all ahead seemed dark as night;

It witnessed many a deed and vow,
    We will not change its color now.

It suits today the meek and base
    Whose minds are fixed on pelf and place;
To cringe beneath the rich man's frown,
    And haul that sacred emblem down.

With heads uncovered, swear we all,
    To bear it onward till we fall;
Come dungeons dark, or gallows grim,
    This song shall be our parting hymn!

9

B. L. Weber, the author of this song which first was printed in the Industrial Worker *(December 29, 1910) may have been Bertram Lester Weber, who was a member of the artistic Bohemian group of radicals and writers active in Chicago in the 1920's. Former I.W.W. acting secretary-treasurer, Peter Stone wrote: "He was a habitue of the 'Dill Pickle Club' and a friend of Dr. Ben Reitman under whose supervision he worked as a clerk in the Chicago Health Department. He had some local reputation for debates in Newberry Square and poetry in praise of the Walt Whitman philosophy" (letter to J. L. K., February 3, 1964).*

Solidarity, May 19, 1917.

A. F. OF L. SYMPATHY

By B. L. WEBER

(Tune: "All I Got Was Sympathy")

Bill Brown was a worker in a great big shop,
  Where there worked two thousand others;
They all belonged to the A. F. of L.,
  And they called each other "brothers."
One day Bill Brown's union went out on strike,
  And they went out for higher pay;
All the other crafts remained on the job,
  And Bill Brown did sadly say:

Chorus:

All we got was sympathy;
  So we were bound to lose, you see;
All the others had craft autonomy,
  Or else they would have struck with glee
But I got good and hungry,
  And no craft unions go for me.
Gee! Ain't it hell, in the A. F. of L.
  All you get is sympathy.

Bill Brown was a thinker, and he was not a fool,
  And fools there are many, we know.
So he decided the A. F. of L.
  And its craft divisions must go.
Industrial Unions are just the thing,
  Where the workers can all join the fight;
So now on the soap box boldly he stands,
  A singing with all of his might:

Chorus:

All we got was sympathy;
  So we were bound to lose, you see;
All the others had craft autonomy,
  Or else they would have struck with glee
But I got good and hungry,
  And no craft unions go for me.
Gee! Ain't it hell, in the A. F. of L.
  All you get is sympathy.

10

The first edition of the I.W.W. songbook included a "Song for 1910." This version, "A Song for 1912" appeared in the third edition. It was unsigned.

A SONG FOR 1912

Long in their bondage the people have waited,
  Lulled to inaction by pulpit and press;

Hoping their wrongs would in time be abated,
  Trusting the ballot to give them redress.
Vainly they trusted; a high court's decision
  Swept the last bulwark of freedom away;
The voice of the people is met with derision,
  But a people in action no court will gainsay.

Chorus:

Then up with the masses and down with the
    classes,
  Death to the traitor who money can buy.
Co-operation's the hope of the nation,
  Strike for it now or your liberties die.

Hark to the cries of the hungry and idle,
  Borne on the breezes from prairie to sea;
Patience their fury no longer can bridle,
  Onward they're coming to die or be free.
Hear and grow pale, ye despoilers of virtue,
  Corporate managers, masters of slaves.
Fools, did ye fancy they never could hurt you?
  Ye were the cowards and they the braves.

Hail to the birth of the new constitution—
  Laws that are equal in justice to all.
Hail to the age of man's true evolution,
  Order unfolding at Liberty's call.
Buried forever be selfish ambition,
  Cruel fomenter of discord and strife;
Long live the commonwealths, Hope's glad frui-
    tion,
  Humanity rises to news of life.

11

William Trautmann, former editor of the German language newspaper of the United Brewery Workers, was one of the six men who laid plans in 1904 for the organization of the I.W.W. At the 1906 and 1908 I.W.W. conventions he was a key figure in the expulsion of I.W.W. President Charles Sherman and in the factional fight with Daniel De Leon. At the 1908 convention, Trautmann was elected general organizer. In 1912 he withdrew from the Chicago I.W.W. to join De Leon's Detroit-based group, the Workers International Industrial Union. By 1923, according to historian Mark Perlman (Labor Union Theories in America, Evanston, 1958), he seemed to advocate works council and workers' education movements, endorsed Walter Rathenau's New Society, and Woodrow Wilson's concept of democracy in the shop. Trautmann was the author of several im-

portant I.W.W. pamphlets, including, Why Strikes
Are Lost, *published in Chicago about 1911.*

WHY STRIKES ARE LOST

By William Trautmann

After a tremendous epidemic of strikes a few
years ago, conflicts expressive of a general discontent finding its outlet in vehement eruptions, but
ending only with a pitiful exhaustion of vitality,
there seems to be at present a relapse all around.
"The workers have gone to sleep" thinks the super-
ficial observer and the uninformed outside world.

This seems, indeed, to be the truth. However, a
relapse in numerical strength would amount to
little: economic depression could be attributed as
the cause.

But deplorable would it be if there were in
reality a relapse in the aggressive attitude, in the
revolutionary feelings of the workers.

This spirit of revolt manifesting itself a few
years ago in somewhat rough actions and expressions seemed to mark the beginning of a general
awakening of large masses of workers, and yet
there seems to be nothing left of the spontaneous,
widespread tendency of revolt.

For this there must be reasons. Such powerfully
exploding forces cannot be destroyed altogether,
or be dammed in by repressive measures.

Time flies quickly; here and there one hears
again of rapid flaring up, of a volcanic eruption
of accumulated discontent, but in most of the
cases it is only a last flicker of a light before it
goes out altogether.

If occasionally larger bodies of workers become
involved in these demonstrations of revolt, politicians and labor (mis)leaders are quickly on
hand to suggest termination of the conflict, with
the promise of speedy arbitration. These leaders
of labor often even threaten to engage union
strikebreakers if the workers refuse to obey their
mandates. In some cases the places of striking
workers have been filled by other members of
these so-called unions so as to suppress any rebellion against the leaders and the capitalist class
whom they serve. But seldom is anything more
heard of the results of such conciliatory tactics, or
of any determined stand on the part of the workers to enforce the terms of such settlements. Their
power once crushed after having been exercised
with the most effective precision, also destroys

their confidence; and the organization through
which they were able to rally the forces of their
fellow workers for concerted action disappears.

After an apparent awakening of three or four
years' duration (1901 to 1905), during which some
of the largest conflicts were fought on American
soil, a general indifference superseded the previous activity. A lethargy prevails now, even to
the extent that many workers with eyes still shut
are marching into the pitfalls laid for them. Blind-
folded by false theories they are being prevented
from coming together into organization in which
the workers would be able to profit from the lessons of the past, and prepare for the conflicts
with the capitalist class with better knowledge of
facts and more thoroughly equipped to give them
better battle.

In the period mentioned the general clamor for
an advance in wages, and the shortening of the
workday, had to find its expression. Prices of the
necessities of life had been soaring up, as a rule,
before the workers instinctively felt that they, too,
had to make efforts to overcome the increased
poverty attendant upon increased prices for life's
necessities. Powerless as individuals, as they well
knew, they were inclined to come together for
more collective and concerted action. With great
displays and much oratory the beauties and the
achievements of such action on craft union lines,
as exemplified by the American Federation of
Labor and the eight independent national Broth-
erhoods of Railway Workers, were presented to
them.

Not knowing better, seeing before their eyes
immediate improvement of their conditions, or
at least a chance to advance the price of their
labor power in proportion to the increased cost of
living, the workers flocked into the trades unions
in large numbers. At the same time the relative
scarcity of available workers in the open market,
at a period of relative good times, forced the employers of labor to forestall any effort to cripple
production. Consequently, in the epidemic of
strikes following one another, the workers gained
concessions. Such concessions, however, were as
much the combined result of a decreased supply
of labor to an increasing demand, as to the spontaneously developed onrush into the trade unions.

One thing, also, contributed largely to the success of these quickly developed strikes. The workers would come together shortly before walking
out of the shops. In the primary stage of organiza-

tion thus formed they knew nothing of craft distinctions. Unaware of what later would be used as a barrier against staying together, they would usually strike in a body and win in most cases. Anxious to preserve the instrument by which alone they could obtain any results, they found in most cases that certain rules were laid down by a few wise men in bygone years, which were to govern the organizations and force them to admit to, or reject from membership, anyone who did not strictly fit into the measure of "craft autonomy."

What Is Craft Autonomy?

It is a term used to lay down restrictive rules for each organization which adheres to the policy of allowing only a certain portion of workers in a given industry to become members of a given trade union. Formerly, as a rule, a craft was determined by the tool which a group of workers used in the manufacturing process. But as the simple tool of yore gave way to the large machine, the distinction was changed to designate the part of a manufacturing process on a given article by a part of the workers engaged in the making of the same.

For instance, in the building of a machine the following crafts are designated as performing certain functions, namely:

The workers preparing the pattern are patternmakers.

The workers making cores are core makers.

The workers making molds and castings are molders.

The workers molding the brass bearings are brass molders.

The helpers working in the foundry are foundry helpers.

The workers preparing and finishing the parts of machines are machinists.

The workers polishing up the parts of machines are metal polishers.

The workers assembling the parts of machines are assemblers.

The workers putting on copper parts are coppersmiths.

The workers putting on the insulation parts are steamfitters.

This line of demarkation could thus be drawn in almost every industry.

Now these various crafts, each contributing its share in the production of an article, are not linked together in one body, although members of these crafts work in one plant or industry.

They are separated in craft groups. Each craft union zealously guards its own craft interests. The rule is strictly adhered to that even if the protection of the interests of a craft organization is detrimental to the general interests of all others no interference is permitted. This doctrine of non-interference in the affairs of a craft union is what is called "craft or trade autonomy."

Evil Effects of Craft Autonomy

Now, as observed in the beginning, a body of workers, only recently brought together, may walk out on strike, before they have learned to know what craft autonomy implies. In such cases they usually win. As soon as they begin to settle down to do some constructive or educational work, to keep the members interested in the affairs of the organization and prepare for future conflicts with the employers, they learn to their chagrin that they have done wrong in allowing all to be together.

They are told that they had no right to organize all working at one place into one organization. The splitting-up process is enforced, trade autonomy rules are applied, and what was once a united body of workers without knowledge of the intricate meaning of "autonomy" is finally divided into a number of craft organizations.

The result is that no concerted action is possible in the conflicts following. Many a time the achievements of one strike, won only because the workers stood and fought together, are lost in the next skirmish. One portion of workers, members of one craft union, remain at work, while others, members of another trade union, are fighting either for improved working conditions, or in resistance against wrongs or injustice done them by the employing class.

Take, for example, the first street car workers' strike in San Francisco, in the first year of Mayor Schmidt's administration. Not only were all motormen, conductors and ticket agents organized in one union, but the barnmen, the linemen and repairers, and many of the repair shop workers enlisted in the union, also the engineers, the firemen, the electricians, the ashwheelers, oilers, etc., in the power stations. They all fought together. The strike ended with a signal victory for the workers; this was accomplished because the workers had quit their work spontaneously. But hardly had they settled down to arrange matters for the future, and to make the organization still stronger, when they found themselves confronted with the clamor of "craft autonomy rules."

They were told that the electricians in the power houses, linemen and line repairers had to be members of the International Brotherhood of Electrical Workers. The workers heard to their amazement that the engineers had to be members of the International Union of Steam Engineers.

The firemen, ashwheelers and oilers were commanded to withdraw at once from the Street Car Employes' Union, and join the union of their craft. The workers in the repair shops were not permitted under trade autonomy rules to form a union embracing all engaged therein. They had to join the union of their craft, either as machinists, molders, polishers or woodworkers, and would not be permitted to be members of any other organization. *They are restrained by the rules of craft autonomy from being members of a union embracing all in the industry, even if they had chosen to remain members by their own free choice. They were not allowed to think that their place would be in such an organization through which the best results with the least of sacrifices for the workers could be obtained.*

In the second strike of street car workers in 1907 the absolute failure, the complete disaster, was solely due to the fact that the workers, separated in several craft groups, could not strike together and win together. Similar cases, by the hundreds, could be enumerated to show what grave injuries craft autonomy inflicts upon the workers. And if the investigator will follow the investigation of facts and underlying causes, he will be surprised to see how the employers take advantage of this dividing-up policy. He will see how the capitalist gleefully helped to pit one portion of the workers against others in the same or other industries, so that the latter, while kept busy fighting among themselves, had no time nor strength to direct their fights against the employers and exploiters.

The most striking example was given recently in the two strikes of street car workers in Philadelphia. In July 1909, they went on strike. Only a portion of them were then organized. But the workers all made the fight a common cause of all. Not only did workers on the subway lines begin to quit, but also the power house workers in several stations walked out, shutting off the power, thus forcing the company to make a settlement.

The Philadelphia street car lines are controlled by the same corporation that operates and owns the lines in San Francisco, in Pittsburgh, in Cincinnati, in Louisville, in Detroit, and other cities, the Elkins-Widener-Dolan Syndicate. The same trick was played in Philadelphia as in San Francisco after the first victorious contest. The separation process began. The power-house men, members of the National Union of Steam Engineers and the Brotherhood of Stationary Firemen, 1,800 of them, according to Tim Healy, one of the head labor fakirs of these organizations, and the electricians were tied down by contracts.

The street car company forced the second strike in February, 1910, and of course the craft union engineers, the union firemen, and the union electricians remained at work, protecting their craft union interests.

When, in the course of rapidly developed events, it was found necessary to call a general strike in all industries, what was the real result? The A. F. of L. unions who had declared the strike were the ones to ignore the strike orders. They had to protect their "contracts," by order from the national labor lieutenants. The Brewery Workers, the Printers, the Molders, later the Cigarmakers, and scores of other "union men" scabbed it on their own order, while the *big bulk of unorganized again responded nobly.*

Now that the real facts are known it is ascertained that out of approximately 320,000 wage workers in that city, 45,000 responded to the strike call, of whom there were 32,000 so-called "unorganized" workers, or partly organized in independent unions or in the Industrial Workers of the World. The balance, 13,000, were either building trades workers, who were not working anyway at the time of the strike order, or were members of radical, progressive unions.

But the body of approximately 45,000 workers, organized in the A. F. of L. unions, who had issued the strike call, remained at work, protecting their contracts. *The real union-made scabs*—the 1,800 union engineers, firemen, electricians, in the power houses—failed to respond; they *union-labeled scabs* by order of the labor lieutenants! And all other street car workers in other cities, where the same syndicate operates the street car service, remained at work, although a farcical general strike was pulled off, so as to discredit forever the general strike idea.

In the Baldwin Locomotive Works thousands

of so-called "unorganized" workers had gone out in response to the general strike call. They were ready to form an organization embracing all in that industry. First they were urged not to insist on having *one union*. Their reply was: "Either all into one, or none at all!"

Finally, in a meeting attended by most of the "great" leaders of the strike, they were promised a charter as "Baldwin Locomotive Workers' Association"; but at the moment that the promise was made, William Mahon, "president of the Amalgamated Association of Street and Electric Car Employes," A. F. of L., turned around and remarked: "They can be assorted to their respective craft unions after this strike is over." (Authentic reports, corroborated by editorials in the Philadelphia Tageblatt, the official organ of the German Trades Union Council of Philadelphia.)

What more is needed to convince the workers of the reason: "Why Strikes Are Lost"?

The Sacredness of Contracts

"Perhaps the workers, although compelled in most of the cases to adhere to the outlined plan of organizing in craft unions, would have made common cause with other crafts in any one industry in their conflicts with the capitalists, if they had realized that the defeat of one ultimately meant the defeat of all"—such may be said in rebuttal.

But with the separation from other groups of workers a craft or sectarian spirit was developed among members of each of the trade organizations. A spirit manifested itself, and does so now, in their relations to other groups of workers as well as to the employers of labor. "Gains at any price" even at the expense of others, has become the governing rule. The rule of "non-interference" made sacred by the decrees of those who blatantly pose as leaders of labor, permitted one craft union to ride roughshod over the others. "Let us go ahead; the devil take the hindmost," has drowned the old idea of the "injury to one is the concern of all." Woe to anyone who would try to throw himself against this current. He will be drowned and buried under mud thrown upon him by all the vultures and vampires.

A great victory is proclaimed in print and public when one or the other of such craft organizations succeeds in getting a contract signed with an individual employer, or, what is considered still better, if it is consummated with an association of employers in a given industry. But actu-

ated by that sectarian spirit these contracts are considered to be inviolable. Not so much by the employers, who will break them any time when it will be to their advantage; but by the workers who are organized in craft unions. Imbued with their sectarian ideas, by the terms of such a contract they are in duty bound to protect the interests of the employers if the latter should have controversies with other craft unions. Thus the workers consent to being made traitors to their class.

Small wonder, therefore, that in that period between 1901 and 1905, the time that these lessons and conclusions are drawn from, the employers were able to check first, then to retard, and finally to paralyze the workers in any efforts to secure by their organized efforts permanently improved conditions in their places of employment. The employers, supported by such lieutenants of labor as Gompers, Mitchell, Duncan and others (as they were rightly called by Marcus Aurelius Hanna when he organized the Hanna-chist Civic Federation), would harp continually on the sanctity of contracts with some of the craft unions, while at the same time slaughtering piece-meal other craft unions with whom they were in conflict.

Of the thousand and odd strikes that took place in that period and since, none bears better testimony of the impotency of the craft unions; not one has presented better proof of the shameless betrayal of working class interests than the gigantic strike of workers in the meat packing and slaughter houses in Chicago, Omaha and other places in the country.

A Horrible Example

The meat wagon drivers of Chicago were organized in 1902. They made demands for better pay and shorter hours. Unchecked by any outside influence, they walked out on strike. They had the support of all other workers in the packing houses. They won. But before they resumed work the big packing firms insisted that they enter into a contract. They did. In that contract the teamsters agreed not to engage in any sympathetic strike with other employes in the plants or stockyards. Not only this, but the drivers also decided to split their union into three. They then had the "Bone and Shaving Teamsters," the "Packing House Teamsters," and the "Meat Delivery Drivers."

Encouraged by the victory of the teamsters, the other workers in the packing houses then started to organize. But they were carefully advised not to organize into one body, or at the best into one National Trades Union. They had to be divided up, so that the employers could exterminate them all whenever opportunity presented itself.

Now observe how the dividing-up process worked. The teamsters were members of the "International Union of Teamsters." The engineers were connected with the "International Union of Steam Engineers." The firemen, oilers, ash-wheelers were organized in the "Brotherhood of Stationary Firemen." Carpenters employed in the stockyards permanently had to join the "Brotherhood of Carpenters and Joiners." The pipe and steam fitters were members of another "National Union." The sausage makers, the packers, the canning department workers, the beef butchers, the cattle butchers, the hog butchers, the bone shavers, etc., each craft group had a separate union. Each union had different rules, all of them not permitting any infringements on them by others. Many of the unions had contracts with the employers. These contracts expired at different dates. Most of the contracts contained the clause of "no support to others when engaged in a controversy with the stockyard companies."

The directory of unions of Chicago shows in 1903 a total of 56 different unions in the packing houses, divided up still more in 14 different national trades unions of the American Federation of Labor.

What a horrible example of an army divided against itself in the face of a strong combination of employers. This was best displayed in the last desperate and pitiful struggle of the stock yard laborers against the announced wage reduction from 17 to 16 cents an hour in 1904.

These oppressed workers, mostly Poles and Lithuanians, who have so often helped others when called upon, could have reasonably expected the support at least of those who were working with them in the same industry.

Nor would their expectations have failed of realization, if the other workers had been given a free hand.

No wage worker, if he has any manhood in him, likes to be a strikebreaker of his own free will. That there are thousands of strikebreakers in America is due to the discriminative rules of the American Federation of Labor unions. Due also to the high initiation fees, as high as $500.° But the history of strikes proves that where no restrictive measures are enforced, the workers in one plant instinctively make common cause; they stand together in every conflict with their employers.

Not so when the lash of a sacred contract is held over their head. The breaking of a contract, in most of the cases, means suspension from the union. It means that the union agrees to fill the places of men or women who suspend work in violation of contracts. This is so stipulated in most of the agreements with the employers. In more than one case labor leaders have helped the employers to fill the places of the rebellious workers.

Now in that strike of butcher workmen in the stock yards they looked to the engineers, the firemen and others to quit their jobs. They expected the teamsters to walk out in their support as the latter themselves had gained their demands only by the support of all. And really all the members of these craft unions were prepared and ready to lay down their tools. The strike would have been won within 24 hours if all had stood together. The employers realized that. They sent for their labor lieutenants. Over 25 labor leaders conjointly helped to force the workers back to their stations. Drivers already walking out were told to return or their places would be filled by other union men. The engineers were commanded to abide by their contract with the companies. Union printers, members of the Typographical Union, employed in the printing plants of the stock yards, were escorted every day through the picket lines of the poor strikers with permit badges pinned to their coats, issued by their union, so that the strikers' pickets would not molest these "licensed" strikebreakers. These aristocrats of labor even looked down with contempt on the men and women whom an ill fate compelled to be slaves of the magnates of

° This amount is charged by the National Association of Green Bottle Blowers. In August, 1908, there was held in the city of Paris, France, an international congress of delegates of the ceramic trades. Delegates from the Green Bottle Blowers' Association of America were present. They were requested to at least waive that initiation fee for union men from other countries, at the same trade. To this the delegates of the Green Bottle Blowers' Association replied with the withdrawal of their two delegates, and with the announcement that they would work for the increase of that initiation fee to $1,000 for anybody who wants to get work in that industry. (See records published in Paris.) Dennis Hayes, the General President of that Association, is fourth Vice President of the American Federation of Labor.

"Packingtown." All appeals to the manhood of these union strikebreakers were in vain. Stronger than their sense of duty and of solidarity in the struggle of members of their own class, was the "iron gag and chain of craft union non-interference." *The contracts* were the weapons in the hands of the capitalists, by which the craft unionists were forced to wear the stigma of strikebreakers. They were made union scabs at the moment when concerted action would have pulled down the flag of boastful, defiant triumph from the palaces of the bosses, and would have raised up the banner of working class victory on the miserable pest houses in which men and women and children are compelled to drudge for a pitiful, miserable existence. Yes! these were the weapons used by the meat barons of America to ultimately extinguish all unions of workers in their employ.

The capitalists could not defeat the workers, not they! The craft unionists, forced by the lieutenants of the employing class—because most of the craft union leaders are indirectly their servants—defeated themselves. They shattered not only their own hopes, but the hopes, the confidence, the aspirations of thousands and tens of thousands, who had thought, after all, that unionism meant: "Solidarity, Unity, Brotherly Support in Hours of Strike and Struggle."

This is why and how the workers lost! Not only in Packingtown, but in almost every industrial place of production in that period referred to. That was the way the employers did, and still do, rally their forces in their successful efforts to defeat labor. By slashing piecemeal the Giant, tied hand and foot by a paper contract, they throttled him, threw his members out of joint, so that his enormous strength could not be used against his oppressors. Oh, but they would not kill him, oh, no! He who is so useful to them to create everything, so that they who do nothing may abound in luxury and debauchery; he must only be kept in his cage, within his dungeon where he drudges in the sweat of his brow, bent over in blunt indifference, carrying stupidly his burden, the weight of a world that depends on him for its existence. Believing that he is eternally condemned to be a slave he perishes and falls by the wayside when his usefulness for the master class ceases. In "Organized Labor," John Mitchell, one of the "great leaders," begins his first sentence with the words: "The workers never hope to be more than wage earners."

Craft unionism, fostered by the American Federation of Labor, has made him the pathetic wage slave, always contented to be no more than a wage slave, with no higher ideals and sublime hopes for a better life on earth.

Can you hear the curses and condemnation, intermingled with the outcries of despair when the burdens become too heavy? Not so much hatred is expressed against those and their class who Shylock like, only ask for and take their good pound of flesh, as against the vampires who suck the life blood of the workers, destroy their hopes and energies, stultify their manhood! The labor traitors who live and dwell in debaucheries akin to the masters', whose pliant dirty tools they are, more than any other force are responsible that the workers have so often lost their battles for a higher station in life.

Labor Vultures

They, whether their names be Gompers, Mitchell, Duncan, Tobin, Golden, Grant Hamilton, or what else, are the vultures, because they exist only by dividing the workers and separating one from another. They have been and are doing the bidding of the master class. Upon them falls the awful curse of a world of millions. They have made America the land of the lost strikes—the land where from the mountains and the hills, and in the plains and vales resound the echoes of the curse of an outraged working class. They are the dark forces that the world should know as the traitors, the real malefactors, the real instigators of the appalling defeats and betrayals of the proletarians. The land in which the depravity of these vultures has driven thousands back into despair and distrust, and aroused their suspicion—thousands who only lost because they placed implicit confidence in those who were agents of their oppressors—thousands who never were shown what they had come together for—thousands who had confided, only to be betrayed—to be thrown back into the desert from where there is no escape from the penalty for blind confidence: all those hundreds of thousands have lost faith in the ability of their own class to release themselves from the grasp of the oppressors. But what does it concern the labor leaders? It is on these conditions that they are allowed to exist in their debaucheries, to continue their destructive work in the interests of the capitalists.

This great country furnishes the most valuable

object lesson to the working class movement of the universe. Let us hope, let us trust, that the workers everywhere may profit from the trage-dies of this land, so that, enlightened by such experiences, they may throw their efforts into one cause and so enable the proletariat to free them-selves from the chains of economic slavery and prepare themselves for the historic mission, for the real, final struggle, for their industrial free-dom, the only freedom worth while fighting for.

12

Although this poem frequently appeared in the I.W.W. press over Ralph Chaplin's name, in his autobiography, Wobbly (Chicago, 1948), Chap-lin claimed that it was written by a West Virginia miner, Elmer Rumbaugh. He wrote: "The only convert I made for the 'One Big Union' idea was Elmer Rumbaugh, a young, hard bitten miner, blind in one eye as the result of a mine accident. . . . 'Rummy' afterward joined the I.W.W. and remained true to the faith until his dying day. He was very much interested in writing labor songs. One of these, 'Paint 'Er Red,' in time be-came a proletarian classic."

"Paint 'Er Red" was first published in the Hun-tington, West Virginia, Socialist and Labor Star (January 24, 1913), while Chaplin was the edi-tor. On November 7, 1914, it was published in Solidarity. The song was used by the prosecution in several federal and state trials of I.W.W. mem-bers during World War I period as proof of the organization's revolutionary intent.

PAINT 'ER RED

By Ralph H. Chaplin

(*Tune: "Marching Through Georgia"*)

Come with us, you workingmen, and join the rebel
   band—
Come, you discontented ones, and give a helping
   hand,
We march against the parasite to drive him from
   the land,
With *One Big Industrial Union.*

Chorus:

Hurrah! hurrah! we're going to paint 'er red!
Hurrah! hurrah! the way is clear ahead—

We're gaining shop democracy and liberty and
   bread
With *One Big Industrial Union.*

In factory and field and mine we gather in our
   might,
We're on the job and know the way to win our
   hardest fight,
For the beacon that shall guide us out of darkness
   into light,
Is *One Big Industrial Union!*

Come on, you fellows, get in line; we'll fill the boss
   with fears;
Red's the color of our flag, it's stained with blood
   and tears—
We'll flout it in his ugly mug and ring our loudest
   cheers
For *One Big Industrial Union!*

"Slaves," they call us, "working plugs," inferior by
   birth,
But when we hit their pocketbooks, we'll spoil
   their smiles of mirth—
We'll stop their dirty dividends and drive them
   from the earth—
With *One Big Industrial Union!*

We hate their rotten system more than any mortals
   do,
Our aim is not to patch it up, but build it all anew,
And what we'll have for government, when finally
   we're through,
Is *One Big Industrial Union!*

13

"One Big Industrial Union" by George G. Allen appeared in the seventh edition of the I.W.W. songbook.

ONE BIG INDUSTRIAL UNION*

By G. G. Allen

(*Air: "Marching Through Georgia"*)

Bring the good old red book, boys, we'll sing
   another song.
Sing it to the wage slave who has not yet joined
   the throng
Of the revolution that will sweep the world along,
To One Big Industrial Union.

Solidarity, June 30, 1917.   The Hand That Will Rule the World—One Big Union.

Chorus

Hooray! Hooray! The truth will make you free.
Hooray! Hooray! When will you workers see?
The only way you'll gain your economic liberty,
Is One Big Industrial Union.

How the masters holler when they hear the
    dreadful sound
Of sabotage and direct action spread the world
    around;
They's getting ready to vamoose with ears close to
    the ground,
From One Big Industrial Union.

Now the harvest String Trust they would move to
    Germany.
The Silk Bosses of Paterson, they also want to flee

From strikes and labor troubles, but they cannot
    get away
From One Big Industrial Union.

You migratory workers of the common labor clan,
We sing to you to join and be a fighting Union
    Man;
You must emancipate yourself, you proletarian,
With One Big Industrial Union.

Chorus

Hooray! Hooray! Let's set the wage slave free.
Hooray! Hooray! With every victory
We'll hum the workers' anthem till you finally
    must be
In One Big Industrial Union.

14

John Brill set these verses to the hymn tune, "Take It to the Lord in Prayer." It was printed in the ninth edition of the I.W.W. songbook.

DUMP THE BOSSES OFF YOUR BACK*

By John Brill

(Tune: "Take It to the Lord in Prayer")

Are you poor, forlorn and hungry?
   Are there lots of things you lack?
Is your life made up of misery?
   Then dump the bosses off your back.
Are your clothes all patched and tattered?
   Are you living in a shack?
Would you have your troubles scattered?
   Then dump the bosses off your back.

Are you almost split asunder?
   Loaded like a long-eared jack?
Boob—why don't you buck like thunder
   And dump the bosses off your back?
All the agonies you suffer,
   You can end with one good whack—
Stiffen up, you orn'ry duffer—
   And dump the bosses off your back.

Ralph Chaplin.
Brown Brothers photo.

15

"Solidarity Forever," the best-known union song in this country, was composed by Ralph Chaplin (1887–1961), an artist, poet, pamphleteer, and one of the editors of Solidarity, *the* Industrial Worker, *and other I.W.W. publications. Chaplin, a commercial artist, joined the I.W.W. in 1913. In his autobiography he wrote that the idea for "Solidarity Forever" came to him while he was editing a labor paper in West Virginia during the Kanawha Valley coal mining strike. He wrote the stanzas in January, 1915, while lying on his living-room rug in Chicago. In Wobbly, he recalled, "I wanted a song to be full of revolutionary fervor and to have a chorus that was ringing and defiant."*

"Solidarity Forever" appeared in Solidarity *(January 9, 1915). Since that time it has become, according to Joe Glazer and Edith Fowke (*Songs of Work and Freedom, *Chicago, 1960), "in effect, the anthem of the American labor movement."*

Chaplin was one of the most prolific of Wobbly songwriters and poets. Some of his I.W.W. poems are collected in privately printed books: When the Leaves Come Out *(1917) and* Bars and Shadows *(1919).*

SOLIDARITY FOREVER!*

By Ralph Chaplin

(Tune: "John Brown's Body")

When the Union's inspiration through the workers'
   blood shall run,
There can be no power greater anywhere beneath
   the sun.
Yet what force on earth is weaker than the feeble
   strength of one?
But the Union makes us strong.

Chorus:

Solidarity forever!
Solidarity forever!
Solidarity forever!
For the Union makes us strong.

Is there aught we hold in common with the greedy
    parasite
Who would lash us into serfdom and would crush
    us with his might?
Is there anything left for us but to organize and
    fight?
For the Union makes us strong.

It is we who plowed the prairies; built the cities
    where they trade;
Dug the mines and built the workshops; endless
    miles of railroad laid.
Now we stand, outcast and starving, 'mid the
    wonders we have made;
But the Union makes us strong.

All the world that's owned by idle drones, is ours
    and ours alone.
We have laid the wide foundations; built it sky-
    ward stone by stone.
It is ours, not to slave in, but to master and to own,
While the Union makes us strong.

They have taken untold millions that they never
    toiled to earn.
But without our brain and muscle not a single
    wheel can turn.
We can break their haughty power; gain our
    freedom when we learn
That the Union makes us strong.

In our hands is placed a power greater than their
    hoarded gold;
Greater than the might of armies, magnified a
    thousand-fold.
We can bring to birth the new world from the
    ashes of the old,
For the Union makes us strong.

16

*Ralph Chaplin's song "The Commonwealth of
Toil" was printed in the fourteenth edition of the
I.W.W. songbook. It was composed to the popular
melody, "Nellie Grey."*

THE COMMONWEALTH OF TOIL°

By Ralph Chaplin

(*Air: "Nellie Grey"*)

In the gloom of mighty cities
    Mid the roar of whirling wheels,
We are toiling on like chattel slaves of old,
    And our masters hope to keep us
Ever thus beneath their heels,
    And to coin our very life blood into gold.

Chorus

But we have a glowing dream
    Of how fair the world will seem
When each man can live his life secure and free;
    When the earth is owned by Labor
And there's joy and peace for all
    In the Commonwealth of Toil that is to be.

They would keep us cowed and beaten
    Cringing meekly at their feet.
They would stand between each worker and his
    bread.
    Shall we yield our lives up to them
For the bitter crust we eat?
    Shall we only hope for heaven when we're
    dead?

They have laid our lives out for us
    To the utter end of time.
Shall we stagger on beneath their heavy load?
    Shall we let them live forever
In their gilded halls of crime
    With our children doomed to toil beneath their
    goad?

When our cause is all triumphant
    And we claim our Mother Earth,
And the nightmare of the present fades away,
    We shall live with Love and Laughter,
We, who now are little worth,
    And we'll not regret the price we have to pay.

17

*Titled "The Cry of Toil," this poem first appeared
in the I.W.W. press in the* Industrial Union Bulletin *(April 18, 1908). It was credited to Rudyard
Kipling. Following that date it was reprinted
many times in I.W.W. periodicals, titled "We*

Sheet music of "We Have Fed You All a Thousand Years."

Have Fed You All for a Thousand Years," and either signed "anonymous" or "by an unknown proletarian." About 1916 the verses were set to music by Rudolph von Liebich of the Chicago General Recruiting Union, and the sheet music was advertised in I.W.W. newspapers. The poem was included in John Mulgan's Poems of Freedom *(London, 1938), under the title "Labour," and is also printed in Marcus Graham's* An Anthology of Revolutionary Poetry *(New York, 1929) with the comment that it is a parody of a poem by Rudyard Kipling.*

WE HAVE FED YOU ALL FOR A THOUSAND YEARS*

Poem—By AN UNKNOWN PROLETARIAN

We have fed you all for a thousand years
And you hail us still unfed,
Though there's never a dollar of all your wealth
But marks the workers' dead.
We have yielded our best to give you rest
And you lie on crimson wool.
Then if blood be the price of all your wealth,
Good God! We have paid it in full!

There is never a mine blown skyward now
But we're buried alive for you.
There's never a wreck drifts shoreward now
But we are its ghastly crew.
Go reckon our dead by the forges red
And the factories where we spin.
If blood be the price of your cursed wealth
Good God! We have paid it in.

We have fed you all for a thousand years—
For that was our doom, you know,
From the days when you chained us in your fields
To the strike of a week ago.
You have taken our lives, and our babies and
wives,
And we're told it's your legal share;
But if blood be the price of your lawful wealth
Good God! We have bought it fair.

18

Harry Kirby McClintock (1883–1957), a pioneer radio hillbilly who was known to thousands as "Haywire Mac," is an important figure in hobo, Wobbly, and hillbilly folk tradition. In an interview with John Greenway reported on in his

American Folksongs of Protest (Philadelphia, 1953) McClintock claimed to have been a busker in the I.W.W. band of musicians organized about 1908 by J. H. Walsh in Portland to rival Salvation Army bands in attracting crowds to streetcorner propaganda meetings. During his long and colorful career, McClintock worked as a railroad switchman in South Africa and bummed his way to London to attend the coronation of Edward VII in 1902. He was a civilian mule skinner in the Spanish American War, and had also made his way to China at the time of the Boxer Rebellion.

In 1925 San Francisco radio station KFRC hired him for the "Blue Monday Jamboree." He then moved to the "Happy Go Lucky Hour" network show, worked for awhile in Hollywood, and returned to San Francisco's "Breakfast Gang" show on which he played and sang until 1955, two years before his death. He was a member of ASCAP and Local 6 of the Musicians' Union.

"Hymn of Hate" was printed in Solidarity *(January 1, 1916).*

HYMN OF HATE

By HARRY MCCLINTOCK

For the sailors that drown when your ill found
ships go crashing on the shore,
For the mangled men of your railroads, ten thousand a year or more,
For the roasted men in your steel mills, and the
starving men on your roads,
For the miners buried by hundreds when the fire
damp explodes,
For our brothers maimed and slaughtered for your
profits every day,
While your priests chant the chorus—"God giveth
—and God hath taken away."
For a thousand times that you drove back when
we struck for a living wage,
For the dungeons and jails our men have filled
because of your devilish rage.
For Homestead and for Chicago, Coeur D'Alene
and Telluride,
For your bloody shambles at Ludlow, where the
women and babies died,
For our heroes you hanged on the gallows high to
fill your slaves with awe,
While your Judges stood in a sable row and
croaked, "Thus saith the law."
For all of the wrongs we have suffered from you,
and for each of the wrongs we hate,

Solidarity, August 4, 1917.

With a hate that is black as the deepest pit, that is
    steadfast and sure as fate.
We hate you with hand, and heart, and head, and
    body, and mind, and brain.
We hate at the forge, in the mine and mill, in the
    field of golden grain.
We curse your name in the market place as the
    workman talks with his mate,
And when you dine in your gay cafe the waiter
    spits on your plate.
We hate you! Damn you! Hate you! We hate your
    rotten breed.
We hate your slave religion with submission for its
    creed.
We hate your judges. We hate your courts.
    We hate that living lie,
That you call "Justice" and we hate with a hate
    that shall never die.
We shall keep our hate and cherish our hate and
    our hate shall ever grow.
We shall spread our hate and scatter our hate 'till
    all of the workers know.
And The Day shall come with a red, red dawn;
    and you in your gilded halls,
Shall taste the wrath and the vengeance of the
    men in overalls.
The riches you reaped in your selfish pride we
    shall snatch with our naked hands,

And the house ye reared to protect you shall fall
    like a castle of sand.
For ours are the hands that govern in factory,
    mine and mill,
And we need only to fold our arms, and the whole
    wide world stands still!
So go ye and study the beehive, and do not quite
    forget,
That we are the *workers* of the world and we have
    not spoken—yet.

19

*"Dublin Dan" Liston who wrote "Dan McGann"
and "The Portland Revolution" was the proprietor
of the famous "Dublin Dan's" bar in Butte, Montana, the hangout for many colorful union personalities in that mining town. Liston was a
member of the I.W.W. as well as the A.F.L. Bar-
tenders' Union. On his death in 1942 in San Francisco, an obituary in the* Industrial Worker *(January 31, 1942) read:*

*"His song, 'The Portland Revolution,' is one of
the standbys of the I.W.W. songbook. Perhaps
he should be remembered for his gift of popu-
larizing some of the obscure phrases of his Dublin childhood and giving them world-wide cur-
rency. . . . The most apt way of describing the
economic level of the worker is the phrase by
Dublin Dan, 'he hasn't a pot in which to spit or
a window to throw it out.'"*

*"The Portland Revolution" refers to a water-
front strike in 1922 in Portland, Oregon, when the
I.W.W. Marine Transport Workers' Union, organized in 1913, and the A.F.L. International
Longshoreman's Union struck when waterfront
employers announced that hiring would be done
through a company employment agency rather
than through the union list system.*

*Sung to the tune, "The Portland County Jail,"
the verses were printed in the twenty-fifth edition
of the I.W.W. songbook. "Dan McGann" was
printed in the twenty-first edition of the I.W.W.
songbook.*

DAN McGANN

By DUBLIN DAN

Said Dan McGann to a foreign man,
    Who sat with him on a bench:
"Let me tell you this," and for emphasis,
    He flourished a Stillson wrench,

"Don't talk to me of the bourgeoisie,
　　Don't open your lips to speak
Of the socialist or the anarchist,
　　Don't mention the bolshevik.

"I've heard enough of your foreign stuff,
　　I'm as sick as a man can be
Of the speech of hate, and I'm telling you straight,
　　That this is the land for me;
If you want to brag, take a look at our flag,
　　And boast of its field of blue,
Boast of the dead whose blood was shed
　　For the peace of the likes of you.

"I'll have no more," and he waved once more
　　His wrench, in a forceful way,
"Of the cunning creed of the Russian breed,
　　But I stand for the U. S. A.
I'm sick of your fads and your wild-eyed lads,
　　Don't flourish your flag so red,
Where I can see—or at night there'll be
　　Tall candles around your head.

"So tip your hat to a flag like that
　　Thank God for its stripes and stars,
Thank God you are here, where the roads are
　　　clear,
　　Away from the kings and czars,
And don't you speak of the bolshevik,
　　I'm sick of that stuff, I am—
One God, one flag, that's the creed I brag,
　　I'm boosting for Uncle Sam."

Reply

The "foreign" man looked at Dan McGann,
　　And in perfect English, said:
"I cannot see, for the life of me,
　　What you have got in your head.
You boast and brag 'bout the grand old flag
　　And the foes you put to rout,
When you haven't a pot in which to spit,
　　Or a window to throw it out.
You howl and kick about the bolshevik,
　　The anarchist and Wob—

Industrial Pioneer, August 1924.

You defend this rotten system when
    You don't even own your job.

"Immigration laws would be 'jake' with you
    If they kept out the Russian Finn,
The German Jew, and the Frenchman too,
    And just let the Irish in;
You're full of that religious bunk
    And the priest on your life has a lease—
You're not even blest, like some of the rest,
    With the sense that God gave geese;
You're a rank disgrace to the human race,
    You're one of those grand mistakes,
Who came from the land, from which I under-
    stand,
    St. Patrick drove the snakes.

"The boss told you, and you think it's so,
    And I guess it is at that,
That your head is a place on the top of your face,
    Which is meant to hold your hat.
If a thought ever entered your ivory dome—
    Which I am inclined to doubt—
You would not rest till you'd done your best
    To drive the 'foreigner' out.
You kick about the strangers here,
    But you give no reason why—
And without these so-called 'foreigners,'
    How would you get by?

"You're working for an Englishman,
    You room with a French Canuck,
You board in a Swedish restaurant
    Where a Dutchman cooks your chuck;
You buy your clothes from a German Jew,
    Your shoes from a Russian Pole,
And you place your hope in a dago pope,
    To save your Irish soul.
You're an 18-carat scissorbill,
    You're a regular brainless gem—
But the time's at hand when you'll have to stand
    For the things you now condemn.

"So throw away your Stillson wrench,
    You booster for Uncle Sam,
For the language you use, when you're full of
    booze,
    Doesn't scare me worth a damn—
Go fight and be damned, for your glorious flag,
    And the boss who is robbing you;

One Union Grand, that's where I stand;
    I'm boosting the O. B. U."

20

THE PORTLAND REVOLUTION°

By Dublin Dan

The Revolution started, so the judge informed the
    Mayor,
Now Baker paces back and forth, and raves and
    pulls his hair,
The waterfront is tied up tight, the Portland news-
    boy howls,
And not a thing is moving, only Mayor Baker's
    bowels.

A call went out for pickets, you should see the
    railroad yards,
Lined up with honest workers, all displaying
    "Wobbly Cards,"
It made no difference to those boys, which
    industry was hit,
They all were fellow workers, and they meant to
    do their bit.

When they arrived in Portland, they went right to
    their hall,
And there and then decided a meeting they would
    call,
The chairman was elected, when a thing built like
    a man,
Informed them that they must finish up their
    meeting in the can.

They were ushered to the court room, bright and
    early Tuesday morn,
Then slowly entered "Justice," on his face a look
    of scorn,
Some "Cat" who had the rigging, suggested to his
    pard,
"Here a chance to line up "Baldy," so they wrote
    him out a card.

When he spied the little ducat, his face went white
    with hate,
And he said, "I'll tell you once for all," this court
    won't tolerate
You "Wobblies" coming in here, and he clinched
    his puny fists,

One Big Union Monthly, July 1920.

'Cause Mayor Baker has informed me that an
  emergency exists.

"Bring forth the prisoners, officer, we'll stop this
  thing right here.
You state your name, from whence you came, and
  what you're doing here.
You don't belong I. L. A. or M. T. W.
Now what I'd like to find out is, how this strike
  concerns you?

The One Ten Cat then wagged his tail, and smiled
  up at the "law,"
He said, "I am a harvest hand," or better known
  as "Straw,"
I'm interested in this wheat, in fact I'm keeping
  tabs,
I'm here, to see, twixt you and me, t'ain't loaded
  by no scabs.

The One Ten Cats were jubilant, the fur flew from
  their tails,
"His Honor" rapped for order, and the next man
  called was "Rails,"
I belong to old "Five Twenty," I'm a switchman
  in these yards,
And I'm here to state, we'll switch no freight,
'Cause we've all got red cards.

We're here to win this longshore strike, in spite of
  all your law,
That's all I've got to say, except, we're solid behind
  "Straw."

The logger then was next in line, he stood just six
  feet six,
"One Twenty," that's where I belong, the
  "Wobblies" call us "Sticks."

All red cards cut this lumber, also loaded it on
  flats,
And we won't see it handled by a bunch of
  "Legion Rats."

Old "Baldy" then was furious, I could see his
  pride was hurt,
When a Three Ten "cat" informed him, that his
  moniker was "Dirt."
He said, "Your honor, Listen, we have taken this
  here stand,
Because we all are organized in 'One Big Union
  Grand.'

"An injury to one, we say's an injury to all,
United we're unbeatable, divided, we must fall,
Your jails can't crush our spirit, you're already
  wise to that,"
When "Baldy" rapped for order, and cut off the
  Three Ten Cat.

He said, let me get straightened out, I'm in an
  awful mix,
For "Shorty" plainly says he's "dirt," and "Slim"
  belongs to "sticks."
Now "Blackie," he belongs to "rails" and "Whitey"
  says he's "straw,"
And all of you seem to have no respect for "law."

Now I can't send you men to jail, I can't find one
  excuse,
I'll wash my hands of this damn'd mess, and
  turned the whole bunch loose,
Then "dirt" and "sticks" walked arm in arm, with
  "flirts" and "skirts" and "rails,"
While the One Ten Cats brought up the rear, fur
  flying from their tails.

Chapter 2

With Folded Arms:
The Tactics of Direct Action

Vincent St. John, who called the fourth I.W.W. convention to order on September 21, 1908, had been a farm worker, printer, upholsterer, and miner. Experiences with the grim economic and social realities of Western frontier industrial life shaped his militant philosophy. His leadership in the Goldfield strike and his organizing ability in local situations won him the support and affection of the Western delegates who called him "Vint" or "The Saint."

St. John saw the class struggle as a brutal fact of everyday life. In 1914 he told the Senate Industrial Relations Commission:

[employers] take us into the mills, before we have even seen the semblance of an education, and they grind up our vitality, brain and muscular energy into profits, and whenever we cannot keep pace with the machine speeded to its highest notch, they turn us out onto the road to eke out an existence as best we can, or wind up on the poor farm or in potter's field.[1]

With De Leon barred from the convention, the "straight industrialists," who had considered De Leon a "pope" and an "intellectual," elected St. John general secretary-treasurer, a key position which he held until 1914. William Trautmann, who in 1904 was one of the six men instrumental in organizing the I.W.W., was elected general organizer.

The direct-actionists discounted working-class political action for a number of reasons. For one

thing, it had no meaning for a large portion of the working class—women, migrants, aliens, Southern Negroes—who were unable to vote. But more fundamentally, the direct-actionists questioned the value of reforms gained through the state, since the capitalist government, as St. John phrased it, "was a committee to look after the interests of the employers."[2] In a class war in which "all peace as long as the wage system lasts is but an armed truce,"[3] sheer economic power alone would decide economic and social questions between conflicting forces.

The tactics of direct action found expression during the next few years in various forms of pressure applied by I.W.W. members through strikes, free speech fights, boycotts, and demonstrations. An I.W.W. publication defined the term "direct action" this way:

Direct action means industrial action directly by, for, and of the workers themselves, without the treacherous aid of labor misleaders or scheming politicians. A strike that is initiated, controlled, and settled by the workers directly affected is direct action. . . . Direct action is combined action, directly on the job to secure better job conditions. Direct action is industrial democracy.[4]

On the industrial scene, these tactics were applied effectively in a number of stoppages during this period, especially in the 1909 strike at McKees Rocks, Pennsylvania, a Pittsburgh suburb.

Here, over 6000 employees of the Pressed Steel Car Company, an affiliate of the United States Steel Corporation, struck spontaneously for better working conditions and an end to a speed-up system. Most of them were immigrants from many countries. Ignored by the A.F.L. union officials, they readily accepted encouragement and leadership from I.W.W. organizers.

An unknown committee of strikers determined strike strategy. When the "Black Cossacks," as the club-wielding troopers of the Pennsylvania Constabulary were called, injured over 100 strikers in repeated charges on meetings and picket lines, the strike leaders warned that they would fight back. They threatened that a "Cossack" would be killed or injured for every worker killed or maimed.

When a striker was killed, 5000 sympathizers representing fifteen nationalities marched in the funeral procession, and the strikers made good their threat. Ten days later a fight broke out with troopers as the strikers returned home from a meeting; a brief gun battle left four strikers and three troopers dead.

In the first issue of *Solidarity*, an I.W.W. newspaper started in 1909 at Newcastle, Pennsylvania, in the heart of the steel district, general organizer William Trautmann reported: "Then the chief of the Cossacks called off his bloodhounds. After that, no striker or deputy was killed. Organized and disciplined 'physical force' checked violence and wanton destruction of life at McKees Rocks."[5] With the strikers freely picketing the factories, they finally won their demands.

The victory at McKees Rocks won better working conditions, brought an end to some of the notorious company abuses for the strikers, and enhanced the reputation of the I.W.W. In addition, the organization used the strike as a vehicle of agitation against the capitalist system and as a tactic to strengthen working class solidarity. Strikes were part of the guerilla warfare against the employer, which would eventually overthrow the capitalist system. In the words of one I.W.W. propagandist:

Strikes are mere incidents in the class war; they are tests of strength, periodic drills in the course of which the workers train themselves for concerted action. This training is most necessary to prepare the masses for the final "catastrophe," the general strike which will complete the expropriation of the employers.[6]

The general strike was viewed in the broadest sense as the peaceful taking over of the means of production, once the workers had been organized and capitalism had proved its inefficiency. It would be brought about, said Haywood and other I.W.W. organizers, by the "folded arms" of the workers. "When we strike now, we strike with our hands in our pockets," Haywood told a reporter for the magazine, *World's Work,* in 1913. "We have a new kind of violence, the havoc we raise with money by laying down our tools."[7]

This philosophy was eloquently voiced by I.W.W. organizer Joseph Ettor, addressing the Lawrence textile strikers at the Franco-Belgian Hall on January 25, 1912. He said:

If the workers of the world want to win, all they have to do is recognize their own solidarity. They have nothing to do but fold their arms and the world will stop. The workers are more powerful with their hands in their pockets than all the property of the capitalists. As long as the workers keep their hands in their pockets, the capitalists cannot put theirs there. With passive resistance, with the workers absolutely refusing to move, lying absolutely silent, they are more powerful than all the weapons and instruments that the other side has for attack.[8]

Until the time of the general strike, Ettor held, workers must be inspired with a sense of class solidarity and militancy.

In line with I.W.W. philosophy, no contracts would be recognized after a strike was won. Only temporary "truces" could be effected on the "battlefield of capital and labor." As St. John wrote in his much circulated pamphlet, *The I.W.W.: Its History, Structure, and Methods:* "There is but one bargain that the Industrial Workers of the World will make with the employing class—complete surrender of the means of production."[9]

This philosophy was forcefully expressed in one of the many Wobbly songs on the general strike:

Why do you make agreements that divide you
    when you fight
And let the bosses bluff you with the contract's
    "sacred right"?
Why stay at work when other crafts are battling
    with the foe;
You all must stick together, don't you know?

Tie' em up! Tie 'em up; that's the way to win.
Don't notify the bosses till hostilities begin.

Don't furnish chance for gunmen, scabs and
    all their like;
What you need is One Big Union and the
    One Big Strike.[10]

Wobblies "tied up" their bosses by assorted forms
of harassment on the job, undertaken when other
efforts proved ineffective. This was called "sabotage," or "conscientious withdrawal of efficiency."
It proved to be the most controversial concept
affecting the organization.

The tactics of direct action evolved from the
nature of working conditions of the I.W.W. membership. In many cases, unable to finance long-
term strikes, the unskilled laborers resorted to
short decisive actions. It was impossible to maintain a picket line across thousands of miles of
Kansas, Nebraska, and Dakota wheat fields. But
it was possible for the Wobblies to leave threatening signs: "$3.00 a day—shocks right side up; $2.00
a day, shocks upside down."[11] Intermittent strikes,
strikes on the job, and "sabotage" were means of
gaining practical concessions quickly, as well as
part of the long-term battle to weaken the capitalist system.

The word "sabotage" was first used officially by
French labor organizations in 1897, when anarch-
ist Emile Pouget reported to the Confédération
Générale du Travail (CGT) about the earlier
Scottish practice called "ca'canny," meaning to
"go slow" or "soldiering." The etymology of the
word has been summarized by Waldo Browne in
What's What in the Labor Movement (1921):

> Derived from the French word sabot, meaning
> a wooden shoe, this term is often supposed to
> have originally denoted the idea of stalling ma-
> chinery by throwing a wooden clog into it.
> Probably its more direct derivation is from the
> French verb saboter, meaning to bungle or to
> botch; while some find its origin in the French
> expression, "Travailler à coups de sabots," mean-
> ing to work as one wearing wooden shoes, often
> applied to lazy or slow-moving persons.[12]

I.W.W. historian Fred Thompson relates that
in France, long after the industrial workers had
started wearing leather shoes, the peasants, who
were frequently used as strikebreakers, still used
wooden sabots. The peasants were called "saboteurs" in much the same way as the word "hay-
seed" is used in this country. When the defeated
strikers returned to work, they expressed their

discontent by bungling their work in the same
manner as the inexperienced, clumsy strikebreakers. Their efforts were called "sabotage."[13]

Whatever its origin, sabotage in I.W.W. terms
aimed, as pamphleteer Walker C. Smith wrote,
"to hit the employer in his vital spot, his heart
and soul, or in other words his pocketbook."[14]
It included actions which would disable machinery, slacken production, spoil the product, or
reduce company profits by telling the truth about
a product. In her pamphlet *Sabotage* (1915),
Elizabeth Gurley Flynn, an I.W.W. organizer from
1906 to 1917, much later a leader of the Communist Party, wrote:

> Sabotage means either to slacken up and inter-
> fere with the quantity, or to botch in your skill
> and interfere with the quality of capitalist pro-
> duction so as to give poor service. It is some-
> thing that is fought out within the walls of the
> shop. Sabotage is not physical violence; sabo-
> tage is an internal industrial process. It is sim-
> ply another form of coercion.[15]

The word sabotage appeared in the I.W.W.
press for the first time in *Solidarity* (June 4, 1910)
in a report of a strike of 600 Chicago clothing
workers who had walked out of Lamm and Company when one of their coworkers was dismissed.
The article stated that when scabs were brought
into the clothing factory, "workers in other firms
where the material for the strike-bound firm was
made, 'sabotaged' their work to such perfection"
that the company yielded to almost all the strikers' demands.[16] Organizer Trautmann advised the
strikers to go back to work and use "passive resistance" methods of getting the discharged worker
rehired.[17]

The controversy over the term sabotage was
dramatized in the 1912 convention of the Socialist Party when a resolution was passed aimed
at disqualifying for Socialist Party membership
anyone who "opposes political action or advocates
crime, sabotage, or other means of violence as a
weapon of the working-class to aid in its emancipation."[18] The resolution was an outgrowth of
the schism between the right and left wing over
politics vs direct action, a rift which had been
growing since soon after the Party's organization
early in the century. It hit at Bill Haywood who,
as a Socialist Party executive board member, had
been a delegate to the 1910 congress of the Second International in Europe and had come home

to America to lecture on the need for "socialism with its working clothes on,"[19] militant direct action, and the general strike. In February 1913 Haywood was recalled from his post as executive board member and expelled from Socialist Party membership. He continued to be one of the best-known and most popular Wobbly leaders.

According to Haywood, literature dealing with sabotage was circulated in the I.W.W. from about 1913 to 1917, although translations of radical European articles had appeared in the I.W.W. press since 1910. Some of the pamphlets sold by soap-boxers or distributed at meetings were written by I.W.W. members, privately printed, and did not represent the official views of the organization.[20] The growing argument over the relation of sabotage to violence led the 1913 I.W.W. convention to adopt a resolution which stated in part: "The program of the I.W.W. offers the only possible solution of the wage question whereby violence can be avoided, or at the very worst, reduced to a minimum."[21] The following year, the I.W.W. convention resolved that its speakers recommend to all workers the curtailing of production "by slowing down and sabotage."[22]

However, bold rhetoric continued to dramatize industrial evils, and the wooden shoe symbol for sabotage appeared widely in Wobbly song, prose, and illustration between 1913 and 1918. Some editions of the Wobblies' little red songbook carried the verse:

> If Freedom's road seems rough and hard,
> And strewn with rocks and thorns
> Then put your wooden shoes on, pard,
> And you won't hurt your corns.[23]

Sabotage symbols of a wooden shoe and a black cat appeared constantly in Wobbly illustrations and cartoons. Stickers and circulars showed a hunched black cat showing its claws. The words "sab cat," "kitten," "fix the job," were used to suggest or threaten striking on the job, sabotage, and direct action.[24]

Whether or not I.W.W. members practiced lawlessness and violence would be difficult to determine at this time, but many investigators conclude that such reports were exaggerated. After spending several months in the West studying the I.W.W. for a series of articles which appeared in the New York *Evening Post* in February and March 1918, writer Robert Bruere found no evidence that the men in the lumber camps were guilty of sabotage as had been charged.

"Won't we be taking [the lumber camps] over one of these days, and what sense would there be in a destroying what is going to belong to us?" one Wobbly lumberjack asked him.[25]

Bruere reported on February 16, 1918, that western lumber owners admitted to the President's Mediation Commission in Seattle that "the peculiar reputation for violence and lawlessness which has been fixed upon the I.W.W. was largely the work of their own ingenious publicity agents."[26] The report of the President's Mediation Commission in 1917 declared that for many Wobblies, I.W.W. membership represented a "bond of groping fellowship" and the unrest in the lumber camps was "at bottom . . . the assertion of human dignity."[27]

In a 1919 memorandum regarding persecution of the radical labor movement in the United States the National Civil Liberties Bureau stated:

> The common charge of violence to achieve the organization's purpose has not been proved in a single trial. Not a single fact has been proved against the organization which could not have been proved with equal force against any aggressive A.F.L. union—with the single exception of the publication of radical literature expressing revolutionary ideas of the struggle of labor.[28]

An extensive 1300-page study of criminal syndicalism laws by E. F. Dowell at Johns Hopkins University in 1939 concluded:

> The evidence made available in the course of this study leads to the conclusion that from 1912, or earlier, until 1918, the I.W.W. undoubtedly advocated in its publications sabotage in the sense of disabling or injury of property to reduce the employers' profits or production, and then ceased this advocacy in 1918. Although there are contradictory opinions as to whether the I.W.W. practiced sabotage or not, it is interesting to note that no case of an I.W.W. saboteur caught practicing sabotage or convicted of its practice is available.[29]

Bold free speech fights which brought the impact of the organization to the doorstep of many communities across the country, militant strikes, revolutionary theories, and inflammatory propaganda resulted in legal and illegal attempts to suppress the organization. Its success in organizing rebellions of immigrant factory workers, the expansion of its membership in the mines, lumber

forests, and midwestern harvest fields led to a savage opposition in the press which made no attempt to separate rhetoric from reality and frequently exaggerated the "Wobbly menace" to create a dramatic news story and an eye-catching headline. Although the I.W.W. proved far less extreme in its actions than in its words and conducted strikes notably lacking in violence, the members were individually persecuted by federal and state governments, and the organization was violently condemned.

In the attack on all radicalism in the second and third decade of the twentieth century, the Wobblies were characterized first, as wild, bomb-throwing industrial terrorists, then as German saboteurs financed by the kaiser's gold, and, finally, as fanatic Bolsheviks plotting to sovietize the United States.

Communities across the country took literally the title and words to a vigorous Wobbly song, "Paint 'Er Red," offered by the prosecution in many courtroom trials as evidence of "revolutionary intent":

We hate their rotten system more than any
    mortals do,
Our aim is not to patch it up, but build it all
    anew,
And what we'll have for government, when
    finally we're through,
Is One Big Industrial Union.[30]

1

James H. Walsh, who wrote this account of the trip of twenty Westerners to the 1908 I.W.W. convention in Chicago, was a Socialist Party member who had worked in Alaska before becoming an I.W.W. soapboxer and organizer in the Portland area. The men whom he led to Chicago were dubbed "the Bummery" by Daniel De Leon from their singing of the ribald verses of "Hallelujah, I'm a Bum." Walsh was a leader in the I.W.W. campaign against employment "sharks," which led to the Spokane free speech fight in 1909. This article appeared in the Industrial Union Bulletin *(September 19, 1908).*

I.W.W. "RED SPECIAL" OVERALL BRIGADE

On Its Way Through the Continent.—Along the Campfires.—Great Success in Propaganda.—Thou-sands Listen to the Speakers.—The "Special" Leaving a Red Streak Behind It.—Contributions Liberal.—Gompers and His Satellites Furious with Rage!

Well, we're in the yards, gathered together at the water tank. In order to know if all are present, we have numbered ourselves. The numbers run from one to nineteen, Mrs. Walsh making twenty. A switchman is seen and he informs us where our "Special car" will be found. The train is late however, and we are delayed a few hours. "Fly Cops" are pretty busy in the yards. They are watching their master's property that some hobo may not break a sacred seal and pile into a car where valuable merchandise is stored.

Two blasts of the locomotive whistle are heard and the train is starting on its journey, and simultaneously nineteen men, all dressed in black overalls and jumpers, black shirts and red ties, with an I.W.W. book in his pocket and an I.W.W. button on his coat, are in a "cattle car" and on our way.

In a short time a glim (lantern) appears and the brakeman jumps into the car. His unionism is skin-deep. He belongs to the B. of R. T., but never heard of the class struggle. He is unsuccessful, however, in the collecting of fares, and we continue our journey.

Our first stop, where we expect to hold a meeting is Centralia, and when about half way there, "our car" is set out. There is only one now left in the train to ride on. It is an oil car, so nineteen men will be found "riding" on that car as soon as the train starts. Being delayed for a few hours again, while the train is being transferred across the ferry, we are hovered around the first campfire toward the wee sma' hours of morning. At last two short blasts of the whistle are heard, and all are aboard. It is only a short distance to our destination and the train is whirling along at passenger speed. The morning is turning cold and spitting a little rain, but all are determined to stick to the car, when again, appears the brakeman and tells us we cannot ride since daylight has come, but he is informed that we must get to Centralia. He insists we'll get off at the next stop, but we fail to get off, and in a few minutes we arrive at our first stop.

It is early Sunday morning, and we are off to get a cup of coffee, after which we will congregate around the camp fire in the "jungles." The morning is bright and all are sleeping on the jungle grass, with our arms for pillows, and coats for covers.

About noon we are all up and wending our way toward the depot; here we meet Mrs. Walsh and the whole "bunch" congregates. The rubber-necks of the little country city are all stretched on us. Later in the day the "To Night Bells" are distributed and at 8 P.M., we find a good crowd at the park to listen. They all like the songs and close attention is given to the lecture. The literature sales are fair, the collection fair and the songs sell like hot cakes.

We have finished our first propaganda meeting, and taking all in all, it is a grand success. Now, for the next date which is Tacoma. The train committee has ascertained that "our special car" will not leave until 2 A.M., so off to the camp fire again. The time has arrived for departure and we are again on our way. Another brakeman appears and after a conference he decides to let us ride. A few minutes later he appears again with two large watermelons. We are in an empty coal car, but the train is making passenger time. A long blast of the whistle tells us that we are near Tacoma. Now for a few blocks' walk and we are at the I.W.W. hall. The bills are being distributed and a big meeting is expected. The street is packed and a great meeting is the result. The sale of literature is good, the collection is fair, and again the songs sell like hot cakes. Four new members are secured for the Tacoma local.

Having finished our work here, we are ready for a start toward Seattle. On arrival in the yards,

Industrial Worker, February 13, 1913.

WHY SHOULD WORKERS PRODUCE FOR IDLERS?

we find a "train ready." We are off, but on arrival at Meaker Junction, we find a walk in store for us of eight miles, in order to catch a train that will land us in Seattle in time for a propaganda meeting. The eight miles is undergoing repair work, and the Italians are on strike, so you can imagine what a beautiful roadbed we have to "hike" over in the night.

The trip has been made and luckily we strike another train ready to land us in Seattle. We find "our special car," and several hobos are in it. They are telling of the bad "shack" (brakeman) on the train who packs a big gun and makes the "boes" get. The shack arrives with a big gun. He is a small man, but says in a gruff voice: "Get out of here! Every G—— d—— one of you," and the strangers in the car all pile out. Three of our bunch step up to him to tell him that we are all union men, and desire to get to Seattle. He is not a union man and again gives the command that we must get off. At this juncture the whole bunch is awakened and told that we must get off and that the shack has a gun. The command is given, "call the roll!" The roll is called, and as they sound their numbers from one to nineteen the brakeman turns white and meekly says: "I did not know this." He piles out and we are on our way. In Seattle we held several good meetings and then departed for the east. We met a very nice train crew apparently, out of Seattle. They claimed to all be union men, but they proved to be cheap dogs of the railroad. Fearing such a large bunch, they telegraphed ahead to Auburn Junction for a force to take us off. When we arrived at the junction we were surrounded by a band of railroad officials—the papers stated there were 25—when we were covered by guns and told to unload. We were marched to jail and held over night. In the morning the writer was separated from the bunch, but finally we were all turned loose. Being separated, we did not learn until evening where each and all were. However, all except the writer had gotten back to Seattle, and secured the services of Attorney Brown, to take up the case, should it become necessary. It was not necessary. The boys held a street meeting in Seattle, and part started from there for Spokane, over one road, and the rest over another road.

We continued our work of propaganda without missing a single date, and all re-united at Spokane, where we held several good meetings. Leaving Spokane, we took in Sandpoint, Idaho, and then rambled into Missoula, Montana, where we had some of the best meetings of all the places along the route.

We put the "Starvation Army" on the bum, and packed the streets from one side to the other. The literature sales were good, the collections good, and the red cards containing the songs sold like hot cakes.

At Missoula, Mont., we have completed two full weeks' work on the road. We left Portland with 20 members. We lost 4 of them, but we picked up one at Seattle, and two at Spokane, so our industrial band is practically the same as when we started.

There are "Mulligan Bunches" all along the road. We had scarcely gotten out of the city limits of Portland, when we saw the camp fires of the "boes" along the road, and we have never, as yet, been out of sight of those camp fires. In fact, the further east we get, the more numerous appear to be the "boes." On investigation, we find that the "Mulligan Bunch" is not composed of pick and shovel artists alone, but that all kinds of tradesmen can be found among them.

There is still three weeks between us and the Fourth Annual Convention, and we expect to be in Chicago by that time. So far we have made every place on schedule time, and we hope to keep up the record.

The receipts from the sale of literature and collections for the first week, were $39.02, and the second week was $53.66, a total of $92.68. Of course, do not imagine that this is all profit, for it's necessary to buy a passenger ticket for the wife of the writer, and as we are carrying 160 pounds of excess baggage—literature—these receipts are eaten into at a lively rate.

This may not be a "Red Special," but it is leaving a red streak behind it. All fellow workers can get a meal at our special car—the jungles—free of charge. Many a poor, hungry devil has been fed by the boys around the camp fires.

In the above money of literature and collections, the song sales are not counted. The boys in the bunch have that money to themselves. It runs from two or three dollars to eleven dollars per night.

It is time for another street meeting, and so I must close to join the revolutionary forces on the street, who are now congregating, after a big feed in the jungles.

Yours for the I. W. W.,
J. H. WALSH,
National Organizer.

2

Vincent St. John (1873–1929) was one of the founders of the Western Federation of Miners and a member of its general executive board until 1907, a founder of the I.W.W. and its general secretary from 1908 to 1914. Son of a Wells Fargo pony express rider, St. John had been president of the Telluride Miners Union (W.F.M.) during the epic Colorado miners strike of 1903–4; president of the Burke Miners Union during the struggles of the Coeur d'Alenes; and leader of the I.W.W. in the Goldfield, Nevada, miners' strike of 1907. Detectives of the Colorado Mine Owners' Association once said of him: "St. John has given more trouble in the past year than any twenty men. . . . If left undisturbed, he would have the whole district organized in another year."

St. John left the I.W.W. in 1914 to become a prospector in New Mexico, and as self-employed, automatically ceased to be a member of the I.W.W. A chronic bronchial condition which contributed to his death was said to be the result of a mine disaster at Telluride, Colorado, when St. John led a rescue party into a smoke-filled mine to bring out the wounded and the bodies of twenty-five miners who had choked or smothered to death. St. John was one of the best loved of the I.W.W. leaders. In a tribute to him published in Industrial Solidarity *(July 17, 1929) after his death, I.W.W. organizer Joseph Ettor wrote: "When the true story of labor's efforts across the past thirty years . . . is written, the Saint must be the heart of it."*

Political Parties and the I.W.W. *was a widely circulated pamphlet published by the organization's Publicity Bureau about 1910.*

POLITICAL PARTIES AND
THE I. W. W.

By VINCENT ST. JOHN

I am in receipt of many inquiries relative to the position of the I.W.W. and political action. One fellow worker wants to know, "How is this revolutionary body going to express itself politically?" and "is it going to hop through the industrial world on one leg?"

A little investigation will prove to any worker that while the workers are divided on the industrial field it is not possible to unite them on any other field to advance a working class program.

Further investigation will prove that with the working class divided on the industrial field, unity anywhere else—if it could be brought about—would be without results. The workers would be without power to enforce any demands. The proposition, then, is to lay all stress in our agitation upon the essential point, that is upon the places of production, where the working class must unite in sufficient numbers before it will have the power to make itself felt anywhere else.

Will it not follow that, united in sufficient numbers at the workshops and guided by the knowledge of their class interests, such unity will be manifested in every field wherein they can assist in advancing the interest of the working class? Why then should not all stress be laid upon the organization of the workers on the industrial field?

The illustration used by our fellow worker in which he likens the economic organization to a one-legged concern because it does not mention political action, is not a comparison that in any way fits the case. As well might the prohibitionist, the anti-clerical, or any other advocate of the many schools that claim the worker can better his condition by their particular policy, say that because the declaration of principles of the economic organization makes no mention of these subjects, the I.W.W. is short a leg on each count.

The Preamble of the I.W.W. deals with the essential point upon which we know the workers will have to agree before they can accomplish anything for themselves. Regardless of what a wage worker may think on any question, if he agrees upon the essential thing we want him in the I.W.W. helping to build up the organized army of production.

The two legs of the economic organization are *Knowledge* and *Organization*.

It is impossible for anyone to be a part of the capitalist state and to use the machinery of the state in the interest of the workers. All they can do is to make the attempt, and to be impeached—as they will be—and furnish object lessons to the workers, of the class character of the state.

Knowing this, the I.W.W. proposes to devote all of its energy to building up the organization of the workers in the industries of the country and the world: to drilling and educating the members so that they will have the necessary power and the knowledge to use that power to overthrow capitalism.

I know that here you will say: what about the injunction judges, the militia and the bull pens? In answer, ask yourself what will stop the use of these same weapons against you on the political field if by the political activity of the workers you were able to menace the profits of the capitalist?

If you think it cannot be done, turn to Colorado where in 1904 two judges of the supreme court of that state, Campbell and Gabbert, by the injunction process assumed original jurisdiction over the state election and decided the majority of the state legislature, the governorship and the election of the United States senator.

Turn to the Coeur d'Alenes where the military forces of the United States put out of office all officials who would not do the bidding of the mining companies of that region.

Turn to Colorado, where a mob did the same thing in the interest of the capitalist class.

The only power that the working class has is the power to produce wealth. The I.W.W. proposes to organize the workers to control the use of their labor so that they will be able to stop the production of wealth except upon terms dictated by the workers themselves.

The capitalists' political power is exactly the measure of their industrial power—control of industry; that control can only be disputed and finally destroyed by an organization of the workers inside the industries—organized for the every day struggle with the capitalists and to carry on production when capitalism shall have been overthrown.

With such an organization, knowing that an injury to one member of the working class is an injury to every member of that class, it will be possible to make the use of injunctions and the militia so costly that the capitalist will not use them. None of his industries would run except for such length of time as the workers needed to work in order to get in shape to renew the struggle.

A stubborn slave will bring the most overbearing master to time. The capitalists cannot exterminate a real labor organization by fighting it—they are only dangerous when they commence to fraternize with it.

Neither can the capitalists and their tools exterminate the working class or any considerable portion of it—they would have to go to work themselves if they did.

It is true that while the movement is weak they may victimize a few of its members, but if that is not allowed to intimidate the organization the employers will not be able to do that very long.

Persecution of any organization always results in the growth of the principle represented by that organization—if its members are men and women of courage. If they are not, there is no substitute that will insure victory.

The I.W.W. will express itself politically in its general convention and the referendum of its members in the industries throughout the land, in proportion to its power.

The work before us is to build up an organization of our class in the field wherein our power lies. That task must be accomplished by the workers themselves. Whatever obstacles are in the way must be overcome, however great they seem to be. Remember that the working class is a great class and its power is unbounded when properly organized.

The sooner all the members of the working class who agree with this program lend their efforts to bring it about—by joining the I.W.W.— the sooner will the struggle be ended in spite of all the machinations of the capitalist and his judges and armies.

We are forced, however, to point out the limitations of political action for the working class in order that the workers be not led into a cul de sac by the politician, and because of that lose all idea of ever being anything but slaves for generations to come.

This we can only do by devoting our entire effort in the work of organization and education to the industrial field.

To those who think the workers will have to be united in a political party, we say dig in and do so, but do not try to use the economic organization to further the aims of the political party.

3

Born in Salt Lake City, Bill Haywood (1869–1928) went to work in the mines at the age of nine. He joined the Western Federation of Miners in 1896 and was active as an executive board member and as secretary-treasurer of that organization until 1907. One of the founders and the best known of the I.W.W. leaders, he became its secretary-treasurer for 1916–18. In September 1917 he was arrested and convicted under the Federal Espionage Act. In 1920, while out of Leavenworth Penitentiary on bail, he fled to the Soviet Union where, for a time, he was a leader of the American Kuzbas Colony in Siberia. He died in Moscow in 1928 after writing his memoirs, which he titled Against the Current. *They were published as* Bill Haywood's Book *by International Publishers (New York, 1929).*

Haywood wrote several pamphlets and numerous articles. He was one of the I.W.W.'s most famous lecturers. In World of Labour *(London, 1913), G. D. H. Cole said: "Haywood could make himself understood by a crowd that did not know a word he said, merely by waving his arms and shouting." On Haywood's death, an obituary in the* Nation *(May 30, 1928) called him "as American as Bret Harte or Mark Twain."*

Haywood's pamphlet The General Strike *(Chicago, n.d.), published by the I.W.W., was a summary of a speech he gave in New York City on March 16, 1911.*

THE GENERAL STRIKE

By WILLIAM HAYWOOD

I came to-night to speak to you on the general strike. And this night, of all the nights in the year, is a fitting time. Forty years ago to-day there began the greatest general strike known in modern history, the French Commune; a strike that required the political powers of two nations to subdue, namely, that of France and the iron hand of a Bismarck government of Germany. That the workers would have won that strike had it not been for the copartnership of the two nations, there is to my mind no question. They would have overcome the divisions of opinion among themselves. They would have re-established the great national workshops that existed in Paris and throughout France in 1848. The world would have been on the highway toward an industrial democracy, had it not been for the murderous compact between Bismarck and the government of Versailles.

We are met to-night to consider the general strike as a weapon of the working class. I must admit to you that I am not well posted on the theories advanced by Jaures, Vandervelde, Kautsky, and others who write and speak about the general strike. But I am not here to theorize, not here to talk in the abstract, but to get down to the concrete subject whether or not the general strike is an effective weapon for the working class. There are vote-getters and politicians who waste their time coming into a community where 90 per cent of the men have no vote, where the women are disfranchised 100 per cent and where the boys and girls under age, of course, are not enfranchised. Still they will speak to these people about the power of the ballot, and they never mention a thing about the power of the general strike. They seem to lack the foresight, the penetration to interpret political power. They seem to lack the understanding that the broadest interpretation of political power comes through the industrial organization; that the industrial organization is capable not only of the general strike, but prevents the capitalists from disfranchising the worker; it gives the vote to women, it re-enfranchises the black man and places the ballot in the hands of every boy and girl employed in a shop, makes them eligible to take part in the general strike, makes them eligible to legislate for themselves where they are most interested in changing conditions, namely, in the place where they work.

I am sorry sometimes that I am not a better theorist, but as all theory comes from practice you will have observed, before I proceed very long, that I know something about the general strikes in operation.

Going back not so far as the Commune of Paris, which occurred in 1871, we find the great strike in Spain in 1874, when the workers of that country won in spite of combined opposition against them and took control of the civil affairs. We find the great strike in Bilboa, in Brussels. And coming down through the halls of time, the greatest strike is the general strike of Russia, when the workers of that country compelled the government to establish a constitution, to give them a form of government—which, by the way, has since been taken from them, and it would cause one to look on the political force, of Russia at least, as a bauble not worth fighting for. They gave up the general strike for a political constitution. The general strike could and did win for them many concessions they could gain in no other way.

While across the water I visited Sweden, the scene of a great general strike, and I discovered that there they won many concessions, political as well as economic; and I happened to be in France, the home of all revolutions, during the strike on the railroads, on the state as well as the privately owned roads. There had been standing in the parliament of France many laws looking toward the improvement of the men employed on the railroads. They became dissatisfied and disgruntled with the continued dilatory practices of the politicians and they declared a general strike.

242

C. Kesty

PALMIST: "There is a Man Following You With a Bludgeon."
CAPITALIST: "Yes, Yes! What Else Do You See?"
PALMIST: "Nothing But Your Finish!"   *Industrial Worker,* March 27, 1913.

The demands of the workers were for an increase of wages from three to five francs a day, for a reduction of hours and for the retroaction of the pension law. They were on strike three days. It was a general strike as far as the railroads were concerned. It tied up transportation and communication from Paris to all the seaport towns. The strike had not been on three days when the government granted every demand of the workers. Previous to this, however, Briand had issued his infamous order making the railroaders soldiers —reservists. The men went back as conscripts; and many scabs, as we call them over here (I don't know what the French call them; in England they call them "blacklegs"), were put on the roads to take the places of 3,500 discharged men.

The strike apparently was broken, officially declared off by the workers. It's true their demands had all been granted, but remember there were 3,500 of their fellow-workers discharged. The strikers immediately started a campaign to have

the victimized workers reinstated. And their campaign was a part of the general strike. It was what they called the "grève perlée," or the "drop strike" —if you can conceive of a strike while everybody is at work; everybody belonging to the union receiving full time, and many of them getting overtime, and the strike in full force and very effective. This is the way it worked—and I tell it to you in hopes that you will spread the good news to your fellow-workers and apply it yourselves whenever occasion demands—namely, that of making the capitalist suffer. Now there is only one way to do that; that is, to strike him in the place where he carries his heart and soul, his center of feeling— the pocketbook. And that is what those strikers did. They began at once to make the railroads lose money, to make the government lose money, to make transportation a farce so far as France was concerned. Before I left that country, on my first visit—and it was during the time that the strike was on—there were 50,000 tons of freight piled up at Havre, and a proportionately large amount at every other seaport town. This freight the railroaders would not move. They did not move it at first, and when they did it was in this way: they would load a trainload of freight for Paris and by some mistake it would be billed through Lyons, and when the freight was found at Lyons, instead of being sent to the consignee at Paris it was carried straight through the town on to Bayonne or Marseilles or some other place—to any place but where it properly belonged. Perishable freight was taken out by the trainload and side-tracked. The condition became such that the merchants themselves were compelled to send their agents down into the depots to look up their consignments of freight—and with very little assurance of finding it at all. That this was the systematic work of the railroaders there is no question, because a package addressed to Merle, one of the editors of *"La Guerre Sociale,"* now occupying a cell in the Prison of the Saint, was marked with an inscription on the corner, "Sabotagers please note address." This package went through posthaste. It worked so well that some of the merchants began using the name of "La Guerre Sociale" to have their packages immediately delivered. It was necessary for the managers of the paper to threaten to sue them unless they refrained from using the name of the paper for railroad purposes.

Nearly all the workers have been reinstated at the present time on the railroads of France.

That is certainly one splendid example of what the general strike can accomplish for the working class.

Another is the strike of the railroaders in Italy. The railroaders there are organized in one great industrial union, one card, taking into membership the stenographers, train dispatchers, freight handlers, train crews and section crews. Everyone who works on the railroad is a member of the organization; not like it is in this country, split up into as many divisions as they can possibly get them into. There they are all one. There was a great general strike. It resulted in the country taking over the railroads. But the government made the mistake of placing politicians in control, giving politicians the management of the railroads. This operated but little better than under private capitalism. The service was inefficient. They could make no money. The rolling stock was rapidly going to wreck. Then the railroad

organizations issued this ultimatum to the government, and it now stands: "Turn the railroads over to us. We will operate them and give you the most efficient service to be found on railroads in any country." Would that be a success for the general strike? I rather think so.

And in Wales it was my good fortune to be there, not to theorize but to take part in the general strike among the coal miners. Previous to my coming, or in previous strikes, the Welsh miners had been in the habit of quitting work, carrying out their tools, permitting the mine managers to run the pumps, allowing the engine winders to remain at work, carrying food down to the horses, keeping the mines in good shape, while the miners themselves were marching from place to place singing their old-time songs, gathering on the meeting grounds of the ancient Druids and listening to the speeches of the labor leaders; starving for weeks contentedly, and on all occasions acting most peaceably; going back to work when they were compelled to by starvation. But this last strike was an entirely different one. It was like the shoemakers' strike in Brooklyn. Some new methods had been injected into the strike. I had spoken there on a number of occasions previous to the strike being inaugurated, and I told them of the methods that we adopted in the West, where every man employed in and around the mine belongs to the same organization; where, when we went on strike, the mine closed down. They thought that that was a very excellent system. So the strike was declared. They at once notified the engine winders, who had a separate contract with the mine owners, that they would not be allowed to work. The engine winders passed a resolution saying that they would not work. The haulers took the same position. No one was allowed to approach the mines to run the machinery. Well, the mine manager, like the mine managers everywhere, taking unto himself the idea that the mines belonged to him, said, "Certainly the men won't interfere with us. We will go up and run the machinery." And they took along the office force. But the miners had a different notion and they said, "You can work in the office, but you can't run this machinery. That isn't your work. If you run that you will be scabbing; and we don't permit you to scab—not in this section of the country, now." They were compelled to go back to the office. There were 325 horses underground, which the manager, Llewellyn, complained about being in a starving condition. The officials of the union said, "We will hoist the horses out of the mine."

"Oh, no," he said, "we don't want to bring them up. We will all be friends in a few days."

"You will either bring up the horses now or you will let them stay there."

He said, "No, we won't bring them up now."

The pumps were closed down on the Cambria mine. 12,000 miners were there to see that they didn't open. Llewellyn started a hue and cry that the horses would be drowned, and the king sent the police, sent the soldiers and sent a message to Llewellyn asking "if the horses were still safe." He didn't say anything about his subjects, the men. Guarded by soldiers, a few scabs, assisted by the office force, were able to run the pumps. Llewellyn himself and his bookkeeping force went down and fed the horses.

Had there been an industrial organization comprising the railroaders and every other branch of industry, the mines of Wales would be closed down to-day.

We found the same condition throughout the West. We never had any trouble about closing the mines down; and could keep them closed down for an indefinite period. It was always the craft unions that caused us to lose our fights when we did lose. I recall the first general strike in the Coeur d'Alenes, when all the mines in that district were closed down to prevent a reduction of wages. The mine owners brought in thugs the first thing. They attempted to man the mines with men carrying sixshooters and rifles. There was a pitched battle between miners and thugs. A few were killed on each side. And then the mine owners asked for the soldiers, and the soldiers came. Who brought the soldiers? Railroads manned by union men; engines fired with coal mined by union men. That is the division of labor that might have lost us the strike in the Coeur d'Alenes. It didn't lose it, however. We were successful in that issue. But in Leadville we lost the strike there because they were able to bring in scab labor from other communities where they had the force of the government behind them, and the force of the troops. In 1899 we were compelled to fight the battle over in a great general strike in the Coeur d'Alenes again. Then came the general strike in Cripple Creek, the strike that has become a household word in labor circles throughout the world. In Cripple Creek 5,000 men were

on strike in sympathy with 45 men belonging to the Millmen's Union in Colorado City; 45 men who had been discharged simply because they were trying to improve their standard of living. By using the state troops and the influence of the Federal government they were able to man the mills in Colorado City with scab millmen; and after months of hardship, after 1,600 of our men had been arrested and placed in the Victor Armory in one single room that they called the "bull-pen," after 400 of them had been loaded aboard special trains guarded by soldiers, shipped away from their homes, dumped out on the prairies down in New Mexico and Kansas; after the women who had taken up the work of distributing strike relief had been placed under arrest—we find then that they were able to man the mines with scabs, the mills running with scabs, the railroads conveying the ore from Cripple Creek to Colorado City run by union men—the connecting link of a proposition that was scabby at both ends! We were not thoroughly organized. There has been no time when there has been a general strike in this country.

There are three phases of a general strike. They are:

A general strike in an industry;

A general strike in a community;

A general national strike.

The conditions for any of the three have never existed. So how any one can take the position that a general strike would not be effective and not be a good thing for the working class is more than I can understand. We know that the capitalist uses the general strike to good advantage. Here is the position that we find the working class and the capitalists in. The capitalists have wealth; they have money. They invest the money in machinery, in the resources of the earth. They operate a factory, a mine, a railroad, a mill. They will keep that factory running just as long as there are profits coming in. When anything happens to disturb the profits, what do the capitalists do? They go on strike, don't they? They withdraw their finances from that particular mill. They close it down because there are no profits to be made there. They don't care what becomes of the working class. But the working class, on the other hand, has always been taught to take care of the capitalist's interest in the property. You don't look after your own interest, your labor power, realizing that without a certain amount of provision you can't reproduce it. You are always looking after the interest of the capitalist, while a general strike would displace his interest and would put you in possession of it.

That is what I want to urge upon the working class; to become so organized on the economic field that they can take and hold the industries in which they are employed. Can you conceive of such a thing? Is it possible? What are the forces that prevent you from doing so? You have all the industries in your own hands at the present time. There is this justification for political action, and that is, to control the forces of the capitalists that they use against us; to be in a position to control the power of government so as to make the work of the army ineffective, so as to abolish totally the secret service and the force of detectives. That is the reason that you want the power of government. That is the reason that you should fully understand the power of the ballot. Now, there isn't any one, Socialist, S. L. P., Industrial Worker or any other workingman or woman, no matter what society you belong to, but what believes in the ballot. There are those—and I am one of them—who refuse to have the ballot interpreted for them. I know, or think I know, the power of it, and I know that the industrial organization, as I stated in the beginning, is its broadest interpretation. I know, too, that when the workers are brought together in a great organization they are not going to cease to vote. That is when the workers will *begin* to vote, to vote for directors to operate the industries in which they are all employed.

So the general strike is a fighting weapon as well as a constructive force. It can be used, and should be used, equally as forcefully by the Socialist as by the Industrial Worker.

The Socialists believe in the general strike. They also believe in the organization of industrial forces after the general strike is successful. So, on this great force of the working class I believe we can agree that we should unite into one great organization—big enough to take in the children that are now working; big enough to take in the black man; the white man; big enough to take in all nationalities—an organization that will be strong enough to obliterate state boundaries, to obliterate national boundaries, and one that will become the great industrial force of the working class of the world. (Applause.)

I have been lecturing in and around New York now for three weeks; my general topic has been Industrialism, which is the only force under which the general strike can possibly be operated. If there are any here interested in industrial unionism, and they want any knowledge that I have, I will be more than pleased to answer questions, because it is only by industrial unionism that the general strike becomes possible. The A. F. of L. couldn't have a general strike if they wanted to. They are not organized for a general strike. They have 27,000 different agreements that expire 27,-000 different minutes of the year. They will either have to break all of those sacred contracts or there is no such thing as a general strike in that so-called "labor organization." I said, "so-called"; I say so advisedly. It is not a labor organization; it is simply a combination of job trusts. We are going to have a labor organization in this country. And I assure you, if you could attend the meetings we have had in Philadelphia, in Bridgeport last night, in Haverhill and in Harrison, and throughout the country, you would agree that industrialism is coming. There isn't anything can stop it. (Applause.)

Questions by the Audience

Q.—Don't you think there is a lot of waste involved in the general strike in that the sufferers would be the workers in larger portion than the capitalists? The capitalist class always has money and can buy food, while the workers will just have to starve and wait. I was a strong believer in the general strike myself until I read some articles in *The Call* a while ago on this particular phase.

A.—The working class haven't got anything. They can't lose anything. While the capitalist class have got all the money and all the credit, still if the working class laid off, the capitalists couldn't get food at any price. This is the power of the working class: If the workers are organized (remember now, I say "if they are organized"—by that I don't mean 100 per cent, but a good strong minority), all they have to do is to put their hands in their pockets and they have got the capitalist class whipped. The working class can stand it a week without anything to eat—I have gone pretty nearly that long myself, and I wasn't on strike. In the meantime I hadn't lost any meals; I just postponed them. (Laughter.) I didn't do it voluntarily, I tell you that. But all the workers have to do is to organize so that they can put their hands in their pockets; when they have got *their* hands there, the capitalists can't get theirs in. If the workers can organize so that they can stand idle they will then be strong enough so that they can take the factories. Now, I hope to see the day when the man who goes *out* of the factory will be the one who will be called a scab; when the good union man will stay in the factory, whether the capitalists like it or not; when we lock the bosses out and run the factories to suit ourselves. That is our program. We will do it.

Q.—Doesn't the trend of your talk lead to direct action, or what we call revolution? For instance, we try to throw the bosses out; don't you think the bosses will strike back?

Another thing: Of course, the working class can starve eight days, but they can't starve nine. You don't have to teach the workingman how to starve, because there were teachers before you. There is no way out but fight, as I understand it. Do you think you will get your industrialism through peace or through revolution?

A.—Well, comrade, you have no peace now. The capitalist system, as peaceable as it is, is killing off hundreds of thousands of workers every year. That isn't peace. One hundred thousand workers were injured in this state last year. I do not care whether it's peaceable or not; I want to see it come.

As for starving the workers eight days, I made no such program. I said that they could, but I don't want to see them do it. The fact that I was compelled to postpone a few meals was because I wasn't in the vicinity of any grub. I suggest that you break down that idea that you must protect the boss's property. That is all we are fighting for —what the boss calls his "private property," what he calls his private interest in the things that the people must have, as a whole, to live. Those are the things we are after.

Q.—Do the Industrial Unionists believe in political action? Have they got any special platforms that they support?

A.—The Industrial Workers of the World is not a political organization.

Q.—Just like the A. F. of L.?

A.—No.

Q.—*They* don't believe in any political action, either, so far as that is concerned.

A.—Yes, the A. F. of L. does believe in political action. It is a political organization. The Industrial Workers of the World is an economic organization without affiliation with any political party or any non-political sect. I as an Industrialist say

that industrial unionism is the broadest possible political interpretation of the working-class political power, because by organizing the workers industrially you at once enfranchise the women in the shops, you at once give the black men who are disfranchised politically a voice in the operation of the industries; and the same would extend to every worker. That to my mind is the kind of political action that the working class wants. You must not be content to come to the ballot box on the first Tuesday after the first Monday in November, the ballot box erected by the capitalist class, guarded by capitalist henchmen, and deposit your ballot to be counted by black-handed thugs, and say, "That is political action." You must protect your ballot with an organization that will enforce the mandates of your class. I want political action that counts. I want a working class that can hold an election every day if they want to.

Q.—By what means could an Industrial Unionist propagate Industrial Unionism in his organization of the A. F. of L.? He would be fired out and lose his job.

A.—Well, the time is coming when he will have to quit the A. F. of L. anyway. And remember, that there are 35,000,000 workers in the United States who can't get in the A. F. of L. And when you quit you are quitting a caste, you are getting back into your class. The Socialists have been going along maintaining the Civic Federation long enough. The time has almost arrived when you will have to quit and become free men and women. I believe that the A. F. of L. won't take in the working class. They don't want the working class. It isn't a working-class organization. It's a craft organization. They realize that by improving the labor power of a few individuals and keeping them on the inside of a corral, keeping others out with initiation fees, and closing the books, and so on, that the favored few are made valuable to the capitalists. They form a little job trust. It's a system of slavery from which free people ought to break away. And they will, soon.

Q.—About the political action we had in Milwaukee: there we didn't have Industrial Unionism, we won by the ballot; and while we haven't compelled the government to pass any bills yet, we are at it now.

A.—Yes, they are at it. But you really don't think that Congressman Berger is going to compel the government to pass any bills in Congress? This Insurgent bunch that is growing up in the country is going to give you more than the reform Socialists ever asked for yet. The opportunists will be like the Labor party in England. I was in the office of the *Labor Leader* and Mr. Whiteside said to me: "Really, I don't know what we are going to do with this fellow, Lloyd-George. He has taken every bit of ground from under our feet. He has given the working class more than the Labor party had dared to ask for." And so it will be with the Insurgents, the "Progressives" or whatever they propose to call themselves. They will give you eight-hour laws, compensation laws, liability laws, old-age pensions. They will give you eight hours; that is what we are striking for, too—eight hours. But they won't get off the workers' backs. The Insurgents simply say. "It's cruel, the way the capitalists are exploiting the workers. Why, look! whenever they go to shear them they take off a part of the hide. We will take all the wool, but we will leave the hide." (Laughter.)

Q. (By a woman comrade)—Isn't a strike, theoretically, a situation where the workingmen lay down their tools and the capitalist class sits and waits, and they both say, "Well, what are you going to do about it?" And if they go beyond that, and go outside the law, is it any longer a strike? Isn't it a revolution?

A.—A strike is an incipient revolution. Many large revolutions have grown out of a small strike.

Q.—Well, I heartily believe in the general strike if it is a first step toward the revolution, and I believe in what you intimate—that the workers are damn fools if they don't *take* what they want, when they can't get it any other way. (Applause.)

A.—That is a better speech than I can make. If I didn't think that the general strike was leading on to the great revolution which will emancipate the working class I wouldn't be here. I am with you because I believe that in this little meeting there is a nucleus here that will carry on the work and propagate the seed that will grow into the great revolution that will overthrow the capitalist class.

4

Born in a slate-quarry town in Maine, Ben Williams (1877–1964) started working at the age of eleven in his older brother's print shop in Nebraska. As Williams wrote: "The Western farmers' revolt was in full swing with the Farmers' Alliance. My brother supported the movement in his paper,

and as a result, got all kinds of radical publications on exchange. Before my twelfth year, I was introduced to all the social philosophies—anarchism, socialism, communism, direct legislation, and Alliance programs . . . absorbing the idea of a New America and a better world" (letter to J. L. K., October 24, 1963).

Williams worked his way through college by typesetting and teaching in a one-room schoolhouse, joined the Socialist Labor Party in 1904, and became one of its lecturers and publicists. He became an I.W.W. member in 1905, shortly after the founding convention, and started soapboxing and organizing for the One Big Union idea. He edited several issues of the I.W.W. Industrial Union Bulletin before it failed for lack of funds in 1909. When a new I.W.W. publication, Solidarity, *started in Newcastle, Pennsylvania, during the 1909 McKees Rocks steelworkers' strike, Williams became its typesetter and then editor, continuing at this until 1917. Williams who read French fluently, translated many articles by French radicals and published them in* Solidarity *during this period.*

His article on sabotage appeared in Solidarity *(February 25, 1911).*

SABOTAGE

By BEN H. WILLIAMS

Sabotage ranges all the way from "passive resistance" at one extreme to violent destruction of property at the other. It does not include the destruction of machinery in every instance. In the case of "passive resistance" for example, as shown on the government owned railways of Austria, the workers simply obeyed the LAWS OF THE NATION governing traffic to the letter. They took no risks, they observed signals, they did exactly what the law told them to do. As a consequence, the railways were congested with rolling stock and traffic was practically impossible outside of 24 hours. No destruction of property occurred. That was "legal sabotage" and far from being "of no value," it resulted in getting the men what they wanted.

Again, we see numerous examples of violent destruction of property in craft union strikes in this and other countries. In the early days of English trade unionism, this form of sabotage was employed as a regular system and proved effective under conditions then prevailing. (See Charles

Reade's "Put Yourself in His Place.") In the present state of the workers' superstitious reverence for property (which they do not understand their masters have taken from them) this form of sabotage may be of doubtful value, and often reacts upon the workers with disastrous effect.

Then, once more, we have that form of sabotage now being employed by the workers on the French railways, in which a studied plan is being carried out to "ball up" the service and put it in such a state of demoralization that the employers, public and private, will have to reinstate the workers discharged during the recent general strike. This "pearled sabotage" has proven more effective and terrifying even than the general strike itself; and unlike the latter, it is one-sided, costing the workers nothing and causing enormous losses to the capitalist enemy.

Here then we come to the real point on this question of sabotage: it is a WAR MEASURE, made necessary by the nature of the class struggle.

In the case of individual or craft violence, such for example as the blowing up of a bridge manned by scab labor, or the destruction of a machine in a factory, the understanding or recognition of the class war may be wholly lacking. In that case, the act may be condemned not only by the capitalist, but by the working class as well.

But in the case of "pearled sabotage," above described, the war measure is apparent. Here the workers deliberately set about to harass their employers by a systematic and well-disciplined plan of campaign. They proceed upon the ever-new principle that "everything is fair in war" and that the weapon they have chosen will bring their masters to terms. . . .

Sabotage, resulting in impairing the traffic or property of a railway system is always "immoral" from a capitalist's standpoint because opposed to his interests. On the other hand, discharging and blacklisting 3,000 railway employees for their activity in a strike is "immoral" from the workers' standpoint; and sabotage becomes a "moral weapon" to remedy that condition. The social democrat who balks at sabotage on the ground that it is an "immoral weapon" in the class war, views that war from the standpoint of the capitalists. Sabotage as a weapon of warfare against the employers is no more "immoral" than taking the first of May as a holiday without asking the bosses for it. Both are manifestations of class instinct and power on the part of the workers. With

the possible exception, of course, of a purely individual act of revenge or reprisal which may produce more harm than good. . . .

"Sabotage," though a new word, is as old as the labor movement. It is now assuming new and complex forms in line with the development of that movement. Viewed as a war measure, sabotage has great possibilities as a means of defense and aggression. It is useless to try to argue it out of existence. We need not "advocate" it; we need only to explain it. The organized workers will do the acting.

5

This article by Frank Bohn, a Socialist Labor Party member and publicist who joined the I.W.W. in 1908, appeared in Solidarity *(May 18, 1912).*

SOME DEFINITIONS:
DIRECT ACTION—SABOTAGE

By FRANK BOHN

Direct Action:—Of all the terms made use of in our discussion during the last six months, this has been the most abused. By direct action is meant any action taken by workers directly at the point of production with a view to bettering their conditions. The organization of any labor union whatever is direct action. Sending the shop committee to demand of the boss a change of shop rules is direct action. To oppose direct action is to oppose labor unionism as a whole with all its activities. In this sense, the term has been used by those who made use of it down to the time of the late controversy. It was the misuse of this expression by the comrades who oppose class-labor unionism which has caused so much uneasiness in the Socialist Party. When we come to the question as to what direct action shall be taken and when and how—that is for the organization on the job to determine. For the Socialist Party to try to lay down rules for the conduct of unions or one union in this matter would be as ridiculous as for the Socialist Party to seek to determine what the workers shall eat for breakfast. It is the business of the Socialist Party to organize and conduct political education activity. This does not imply, however, that in a lecture dealing with unionism conducted by the Socialist Party, these matters shall not be discussed. On the contrary, it is of the highest importance that the Socialist Party shall keep its membership informed through its press and its lecture courses of the latest developments in the field of labor.

Sabotage:—Sabotage means "strike and stay in the shop." Striking workers thus are enabled to draw pay and keep out scabs while fighting capitalists. Sabotage does not necessarily mean destruction of machinery or other property, although that method has always been indulged in and will continue to be used as long as there is a class struggle. More often it is used to advantage in a quieter way. Excessive limitation of output is sabotage. So is any obstruction of the regular conduct of the industry. Ancient Hebrews in Egypt practiced sabotage when they spoiled the bricks. Slaves in the South practiced it regularly by putting stones and dirt in their bags of cotton to make them weigh heavier. An old cotton mill weaver in Massachusetts once told me that when baseball was first played, the boys in his mill stuck a bobbin in the running gear of the water wheel and so tied up the shop on Saturday afternoon that they could go and see the ball game. . . . When the workers face a specific situation, they will very likely continue to do as their interests and intelligence dictate.

6

This short story by Bert Willard appeared in the International Socialist Review (*August 1912*), *three months after the Socialist Party convention at Indianapolis adopted an amendment to the Socialist Party constitution that "any member of the party who opposes political action or advocates crime, sabotage, or other methods of violence as a weapon of the working class to aid in its emancipation, shall be expelled from membership in the party."*

FARMER JONES
ON
PARTY PROBLEMS

By BERT WILLARD

"I see by the papers that the Comrades at Indianapolis have placed the official taboo on Sabotage; hereinafter, same is not to be given kindly mention in consecrated circles on penalty of excommunication," said Farmer John, as he laid the Daily upon the kitchen table, and spat in the general direction of the wood box.

"Well, I declare," exclaimed Mary Jane. "There ain't no tellin' what them Comrades will be doin' next. Like as not we'll be electin' a President. But what on earth is that Sabotage?"

"I ain't a knowin' just exactly what it is, Mary Jane, tho' I'll admit I've been tryin' mighty hard to find out."

"Land sakes, is it that bad? Somethin' that's agin' the law and the gospels and common decency?"

"I couldn't exactly say. As near as I can make out from readin' the party papers, it all depends on whether you're for it, or whether you're agin' it."

"Is that so?"

"Yes. If you're for it, it ain't half bad; and if you're agin' it, it's simply horrible."

"Well, now that sounds plumb reediculous to me, and me bein' a Comrade, too. I reckon some of them high-brow Comrades fixed it that way so's they could have something to argy about. But are we for it, or are we agin' it?"

"I ain't a'sayin' nothin', replied John. "If we violate the party creed, we will have to take the consequences; and I've been payin' dues too long to be courtin' excommunication. I was just thinkin' tho', that it's a mighty long way between theory and practice; and when you're theorisin' you may think one thing is right and proper, but you'd think entirely different when you came to practicin'.

"For instance: Fifteen, twenty years ago a lot of us one-gallus squirrel turners from Missoury, Arkansaw, Texas, and 'joinin' ranges, was settlin' up the Cheyenne country of Oklahoma. Settlers had been slow about comin' into that country, owin' to the fact that the report had been circulated that them parts was the national habitat and rendezvous of the coyote, prairie dog, rattlesnake, horse thief, cut-throat, etcetra and soforth, and not what might be called a salubrious climate for nesters with wimmen and kids.

"Howsumever, the cowmen were soon looseherding their cattle over them prairies and when us nesters arrived on the scene, we found that the cattlemen had apportioned the range among themselves, and had it all fenced. All gover'ment land, too, and strictly agin' the law to fence gover'ment land; but shucks, what's the law between friends?

"The cattlemen naturally resented the presence of us settlers on their domains—nesters have a

FRANK P. WALSH, Chairman U. S. Industrial Relations Commission, Writes On,
"My Impressions of the Witnesses and Their Testimony"

Solidarity, July 31, 1915.

way of plowin' the ground and ruinin' the grass, you know. The cowmen would tell us we couldn't raise nothin' in them parts; no use tryin'. We'd have droughts and floods and hailstorms and hot winds and frosts and sand storms and grasshoppers and cyclones and chinch bugs; besides nothin' wouldn't grow, and it was no healthy place for nesters nohow. Which same wasn't exactly what you might call encouragin'.

"Notwithstandin' all these calamities, natural and imported, us nesters would stay, and we'd live—somehow; mostly on cornbread, sow-bellie and bean soup. We'd go barefooted through cactus, prickly-pear, and rattlesnakes; and we'd wear our old overalls as long as they would hang together. In some bachelor establishments I knowed of, a ragged shirt and a red bandaner was full dress.

"But we lived—somehow. Come fall, we would have little patches of corn, all cut and shocked as pretty as you please. Then some bright night we would be sleepin' peacefully, pleasantly dreamin' we were floatin' gently on a sea of bean soup, in which huge slabs of sow-bellie was disportin' themselves gaily, when we'd hear the rustle of cattle in the corn, and would wake up all standin'. We'd take to corn field just as we stood, and it would be 'Whoop!' 'Hi-ye-ii!' 'Git out a here you durned critters!' until broad daylight. On examinin' the fence we would find that the wires had been cut in a dozen different places.

"Well, we'd repair the fence and mozey off down to the store and post office, where we'd meet Sid Smith just drivin' in, and we'd orate as follows:

" 'Mornin', Sid.'

" 'Mornin', John.'

" 'Fairish day.'

" 'Yep, needin' rain.'

" 'How's things over your way?'

" 'O, so so. How's everything with you?'

" 'O, I ain't complainin' none. Whatcha been doin' this morning'?'

" 'Fixin' fence.'

" 'Fence down?'

" 'Yep. Sumpin' tore it down last night.'

"Other nesters would come in with the same story, and it would be whispered around that about half a dozen of Wilkin's cowboys had been seen hangin' around on the creek, at just about dusk the even' before.

"Well, everything would be quiet for about a week. We wouldn't be gittin' no rest, sleepin' with one ear open, until we'd hear the cattle in the corn again. We'd chase 'em out, then we'd get the old shotgun and as soon as one of them steers got back inside the fence we'd kerbang! and Mr. Steer would tear out of that corn field like all possessed. It wouldn't take more than four or five shots until that bunch of cattle would up-tail and across country. We'd go back to bed then, cause we knowed *them* steers wouldn't be back *that* night.

"We wouldn't much more than get in bed when we would hear boom! boom! over at one of the neighbors. In a few minutes it would be boom! boom! in another direction. We would then go to sleep, peaceful and quiet like, and wouldn't wake until the sun was an hour high. Looking out over the prairie, we would see five or six steers lyin' all stretched out as tho' they wasn't carin' for nothin' or nobody.

"We just couldn't stop to fix the fence that morning, but would mozey down to the store the first thing, to get the news; and, as usual, would arrive just as Sid Smith was drivin' in. After some and sundry discoursin' on the past, present, and possible future condition of the weather, I'd remark, casual like:

" 'Thought we heard some shootin' over your way last night, Sid.'

" 'So,' Sid'd say. 'Wife 'lowed as how she heard some shootin' over your way last night, too. And do you know, when I got out this mornin' I noticed five or six steers layin' around over there, as tho' somepin' was a-ailin' of 'em.'

"Well, the neighbors would keep comin' in until there wouldn't be whittlin' material to go 'round, when old Wilkins'd ride up, lookin' as pleasant as a grizzly bear, and we'd say.

" 'Mornin', Mr. Wilkins.'

" 'Mornin',' he'd growl.

" 'Fairish day,' we'd say, real caam like.

"Wilkins'd grunt.

" 'Needin' rain,' we'd remark next, tryin' to be agreeable.

"Wilkins'd grunt again.

" 'What's them over there?' he'd growl, pointin' at them steers.

" 'Mr. Wilkins,' we'd say, 'we reckons them's steers. They's been layin' there for sometime. We ain't never been over to em.'

" 'Umph!' he'd growl, beginning to shake. 'Six of 'em there! And five here! And eight yonder! And my riders tell me there's more of 'em over there!'

" 'Yes, six, Mr. Wilkins,' we'd say, 'it shore 'peers

like it was gettin' mighty onhealthy for range steers in these parts.'

"Wilkins'd look like he was about ready to explode.

"'Yes, sir, Mr. Wilkins,' we'd continue, 'we notices the coyotes are gittin' that fat they're too trifflin' lazy to get out of a feller's way!'

"Wilkins'd shore enough explode at that, and he'd ride off in a 'lope, bellerin' sumpin' that sounded like 'Damn!' with all the trimmings.

"Us nesters would start home then, feelin' so good we'd be whislin' 'Beautiful Land,' to beat the band. In four or five days the news would be circulatin' in the air that old Wilkins had sold out slick and clean, and was going to Old Mexico.

"Now, I ain't a-sayin' that us nesters was practisin' Sabotage—that depends on whither you're for it, or whither you're agin it, I reckon—and if we'd been settin' around in easy chairs, blowin' smoke-wreaths at the chandelier, and theorisin', I reckon we'd agreed that killin' them steers was wrong, and showed disrespect for capitalist property laws. But us farmers didn't theorise none. We didn't think about it; besides we didn't have time. We was too busy tryin' to make a living. All that we thought of was: them steers were destroying our corn, there seemed but one way of stopping 'em, we took that way *and saved our crops!*

"And we didn't call it Sabotage, nor 'other methods of violence,' nor destruction of property—*we called it Justice!*

"Now the moral of this here yarn is this: It's a mighty long way between theory and practice; and when you're theorisin' on a full stomach, you hain't the least idea what you'd do if you was practicin' on an empty one.

"But as I said 'afore, I ain't a sayin' nothin'. I've been payin' dues too long to be courtin' excommunication. Then we names the ante and you will have to put up if you want to set in the game. However, there are some things I don't understand, and one of them is, 'Why should workingmen be penalized for participatin' in the class conflict?'

"The road to the co-operative commonwealth ain't mapped, and we will have to blaze our own trail. Some will think we ought to go this way, some will say we should turn that way, others will declare the correct route lies straight ahead; at times, a few will think we are off the road entirely, but we will find the way through. For we'll get there, Mary Jane, you can bet your boots on that; and once there, law-zee! what a time we will have tellin' of the adventures we had a-comin'!"

7

This unsigned poem was printed in the New Orleans I.W.W. paper The Lumberjack *(July 10, 1913). This paper, edited by Covington Hall, was published by the I.W.W. National Industrial Union of Forest and Lumber Workers, Southern Division.*

SAW MILL "ACCIDENTS"

BY THE WOODEN SHOE KID

What's the trouble with that saw?
The carriage is out of line;
And don't it beat you maw
How the hands kill time?

The engine is running hot,
That pump needs packing again;
I heard the boss say "I've got
A hell of a bunch of men."

The fireman can't keep steam,
The carriage has jumped the track;
I wonder what does it mean,
Machinery acting like that?

Lordy! Hain't this awful bad,
That shipping clerk is a sight!
He sent the timber to Bagdad,
Which should have gone to Cavite.

The old mill is running in debt,
I think the boss is getting wise;
He came to me and said, "Jet,
What's the matter with them guys?"

I says, "Old cuss, you know full well,
That through your hellish greed;
You have given these men hell,
And kept them ever in need.

"They are awake at last,
Have donned their wooden shoes,
If you don't come clean, fast,
You'll get a case of blues."

Now slaves these words are true—
This weapon you always own—

If we our duty each will do,
Each will win a home.—Amen.

8

This poem signed by Joe Hill was first printed in Solidarity (June 27, 1914), under the title, "The Rebel's Toast." It later appeared, unsigned, in several pre-World War I editions of the I.W.W. songbook.

THE REBEL'S TOAST

By J. HILL

If Freedom's road seems rough and hard,
    And strewn with rocks and thorns,
Then put your wooden shoes on, pard,
    And you won't hurt your corns.
To organize and teach, no doubt,
    Is very good—that's true,
But still we can't succeed without
    The Good Old Wooden Shoe.

Now He Understands The Game

Solidarity, November 11, 1916.

9

This song by Ralph Chaplin appeared in Solidarity (*February 21, 1914*), *and in the seventh edition of the I.W.W. songbook.*

HEY! POLLY

By Ralph Chaplin

(*Tune: "Yankee Doodle"*)

The politician prowls around,
    For worker's votes entreating;
He claims to know the slickest way
    To give the boss a beating.

Chorus

Polly, we can't use you, dear,
    To lead us into clover;
This fight is ours and as for you,
    Clean out or get run over.

He claims to be the bosses' foe,
    On worker's friendship doting.
He says, "Don't fight while on the job,
    But do it all by voting.

Elect ME to the office, boys,
    Let all your rage pass o'er you;
Don't bother with your countless wrongs,
    I'll do your fighting for you."

He says that sabotage won't do,
    (It isn't to his liking)
And that without *his* mighty aid
    There is no use in striking.

He says that he can lead us all
    To some fair El Dorado,
But he's of such a yellow hue
    He'd cast a golden shadow!

He begs and coaxes, threatens, yells,
    For shallow glory thirsting.
In fact he's just a bag of wind
    That's swollen up to bursting.

The smiling bosses think he'd like
    To boodle from their manger;
And as he never mentions *Strike,*
    They know there is no danger.

And all the while he spouts and spiels,
    He's musing undetected,
On what a lovely snap he'll have
    When once he is elected.

10

The words and the music of this song, which is sometimes called "Tie 'Em Up," were written by George G. Allen and appeared in Solidarity (*October 14, 1916*). *Nothing is known about the author. It is one of the few I.W.W. songs for which the author wrote both the words and the music.*

THE ONE BIG STRIKE

Words and Tune by G. G. Allen

Now we have no fight with members of the old
    A. F. of L.
But we ask you use your reason with the facts we
    have to tell.
Your craft is but protection for a form of property,
And your skill that is your property you're losing,
    don't you see.
Improvements on machinery take tool and trade
    away,
And you'll be among the common slaves upon
    some fateful day.
Now the things of which we're telling you we are
    mighty sure about;
O, what's the use to strike the way you can't win
    out?

Chorus

Tie 'em up, tie 'em up; that's the way to win;
Don't notify the bosses 'till hostilities begin.
Don't let them use their gun-men, scabs and all
    their like,
What you need is One Big Union and the One Big
    Strike.

Why do you make agreements that divide you
    when you fight
And let the bosses bluff you with a contract's
    "sacred right,"
Why stay at work when other crafts are battling
    with the foe,
That your interests are identical it's time that you
    did know.

The day that you begin to see the classes waging
war
You will join the biggest tie-up that was ever
known before.
With the General Strike in progress and all
workers stand as one
There will be a revolution—not a wheel shall run.

Chorus

Tie 'em up, tie 'em up; that's the way to win;
Don't notify the bosses 'till hostilities begin.
Don't let them use their gun-men, scabs and all
their like,
What you need is One Big Union and the One Big
Strike.

11

*This song by Ralph Chaplin appeared in the
eighth edition of the I.W.W. songbook. In his
autobiography, he wrote: "My 'Sab Cat' symbolized the 'slow down' as a means of 'striking on
the job.' The whole matter of sabotage was to be
thrashed out thoroughly at our trial. . . . The
prosecution used the historic meaning of the word
to prove that we drove spikes into logs, copper
tacks into fruit trees, and practiced all manner of
arson, dynamiting, and wanton destruction. . . .
We had been guilty of using both the 'wooden
shoe' and the 'black cat' to symbolize our strategy
of 'striking on the job.' The 'sabotage' advocated
in my cartoons and stickerettes was summed up
in the widely circulated jingle:*

> *'The hours are long, the pay is small
> So take your time and buck 'em all.' "*

*A series of cartoons by Chaplin appeared in
Solidarity and the Industrial Worker in 1915–16,
showing a clean-cut, virile young Wobbly led by a
black cat into the harvest fields, toward the rising
sun of industrial unionism, and into the mines and
lumbercamps. Some of Chaplin's captions on the
cartoons read: "Kitty! Kitty! Kitty! Come to Your
Minnesota Milk! It's Your Fight! Get on the Job!
Mee-oo-ow!" As labor folklorist Archie Green has
written: "The black cat is an old symbol for malignant and sinister purposes, foul deeds, bad luck,
and witchcraft with countless superstitious connections. Wobblies extended the black cat figure
visually to striking on the job, direct action, and
sabotage" ("John Neuhouse: Wobbly Folklorist,"
Journal of American Folklore, Vol. 73, No. 289).*

THAT SABO-TABBY KITTEN

By Ralph H. Chaplin

(Tune: Dixie Land)

You rotten rats go and hide your faces,
I'm right here, so hunt your places,
    Hurry, now! wonder how? M E O W—
      SABOTAGE!
The tiger wild in his jungle sittin'
Never fights like this here kitten.
    Hurry, now! wonder how? M E O W—
      SABOTAGE!

Chorus:

O, the rats all hate and fear me; meow! M E O W!
The softest paw can be a CLAW!
They seldom venture near me.
    Hurrah! they saw your Sabo-tabby kitten!

The boss has cream for his lordly dinner,
Feed him milk and make him thinner!
    Hurry now! wonder how? M E O W—
      SABOTAGE!
If you are down and the boss is gloating,
Trust in me instead of voting.
    Hurry now! wonder how? M E O W—
      SABOTAGE!

On every wheel that turns I'm riding,
No one knows, though, where I'm hiding.
    Hurry now! wonder how? M E O W—
      SABOTAGE!
The fight is tough and you can't see through it?
Shut your traps and a cat will do it.
    Hurry now! wonder how? M E O W—
      SABOTAGE!

Lawyers have no bunk to fill me,
Cops and soldiers cannot kill me.
    Hurry now! wonder how? M E O W—
      SABOTAGE!
Step on things that the bone-heads bow to,
Come with me and I'll show you how to.
    Hurry now! wonder how? M E O W—
      SABOTAGE!

This world should have but free men in it,
Let me show you how to win it,
    Hurry now! wonder how? M E O W—
      SABOTAGE!

DON'T WEAR SABOTS; IT HURTS THE SNAKE

Solidarity, April 7, 1917.

Perch will I on the System's coffin,
On the hearse they take it off in,
    Hurry now! wonder how? M E O W—
      SABOTAGE!

12

Folklorist Archie Green analyzed these verses in
the Journal of American Folklore (*Vol. 73, No.*
289). *He wrote: "Parasites and plutes were known*
to all the Wobblies as the enemy—the master class.
The sab-cat was the symbol of sabotage. . . .
The kitten in the wheat was the black cat's off-
spring—the rock in the sheaf to break the thresh-
ing machine gears, the match on the phosphorus
in the bundle to fire the stack. The kitten was not
turned loose often—some Wobblies contend not
at all—and the song may have been sung as much
to appeal for cream for kitty as to incite action."
Green cites I.W.W. member and song collector
John Neuhouse as claiming that the "Kitten in the
Wheat" was sung to the tune, "The Girl I Left
Behind Me." These verses appeared in Solidarity
(*June 23, 1917*), *and were cited in the* Literary
Digest (*April 19, 1919*) *as an example of I.W.W.*
use of sabotage symbols.

    I.W.W. songwriter Richard Brazier has pointed
out the similarity between the third stanza of
"The Kitten in the Wheat" and the lines of the
British ballad, "Shall Trelawney Die," in an inter-
view with Archie Green (New York, December
1960):

> *"And have you picked the where and when*
> *And shall Trelawney die?*
> *There's fifty thousand Cornish men*
> *Shall know the reason why."*

THE KITTEN IN THE WHEAT

By SHORTY

A sab-cat and a wobbly band,
    A rebel song or two;
And then we'll show the Parasites
    Just what the cat can do.

And have you fixed the where and when
    That we must slave and die?
Here's fifty thousand harvest men
    Shall know the reason why!

The sab-cat purred and twitched her tail
    As happy as could be;

They'd better not throw "wobs" in jail
    And leave the kitten free.

From early spring till late in fall
    We toil that men may eat.
And "all for one, and one for all."
    Sing wobblies in the wheat.

The sab-cat purred and twitched her tail
    And winked the other way;
Our boys shall never rot in jail,
    Or else the Plutes will PAY.

You shall not keep them in the pen
    Or send them forth to die,
Or fifty thousand union men
    Shall know the reason why!

13

According to Peter Stone (letter to J. L. K., Feb-
ruary 3, 1964): "Red Doran was a West Coast
soapboxer who had quite a following in Seattle
in 1916–18. By trade he was an electrician, but he
would rather soapbox or give 'chart talks' than
work at the trade. After his release from Leaven-
worth, he became a spieler for 'Painless Parker'
(commercial dentist) in San Francisco during the
early 1920's." Doran was also the author of the
undated I.W.W. leaflets, Big Business and Direct
Action (*Lumber Workers Industrial Union No.*
500) *and* Law and the I.W.W. (*Chicago, I.W.W.*
Publishing Bureau).

    This selection from Doran's testimony during
the Chicago trial was taken from The Case of the
U.S.A. vs. William D. Haywood et al. (*Chicago,*
1918).

TESTIMONY OF
J. T. (RED) DORAN

Q.—Did you ever discuss the question of sabotage
at any of your meetings?

A.—Why, I have explained what sabotage was,
yes, sir.

Q.—Well, tell us briefly what you have said on
that subject.

A.—Well, I explained that sabotage did not
mean destruction of property. Sabotage meant
the withdrawal of efficiency, industrial efficiency,
and told the workers that they practiced sabotage

in the interest of their bosses, and illustrated the thing this way:

I said, for instance, down here in California, there is a little colony, what they call Little Landers Colony. It was located at the base of a hill, and at the top of this hill there was an extensive water supply, but in order to conserve that water it was necessary to build a dam. Now the privilege of building the dam was under the competitive system and the dam was known as the Ottay dam. Men went down on that job and it was a slave job right. They kept them on the jump all the time. Naturally, under the competition condition, contractors have to cheat on materials. They have to get the contracts, they have got to live, they cheat on materials, they squeeze and pinch here and there as the circumstances permit, so no one questions the fact but what a concrete dam could be built so solidly that nothing could take it out. I illustrate, by the Chinese wall as it stands to-day. We could duplicate that; we have the materials, but it is not done, and the reason it is not done is because of this competitive program, and the conditions under which it is operated, but it is the slaves themselves who actually practice the sabotage. Here is a fellow wheeling cement. At the instruction of his foreman he cheats a little on the cement; his gravel is not clean cut and clear. The sand is of a poor or inferior grade and the concrete, when it is poured in there is not what it should be. The consequence is that after a time, as in the case of this Ottay dam, the dam bursts— a storm came along, an unusual storm, that is granted—a storm came along and it burst this dam and the water flowed down off this mountain and drowned out all of these settlers in the low land at the base of the hill, their little one acre farms were ruined; their stock was gone; their homes scattered to the desert in every direction.

Now I explained that the workers had practiced sabotage in the interest of the bosses' profits, but that the I.W.W. said, "Go on that job and put so much cement in there, put so much clean stone in there, put so much stuff in there that they can have all the storms that it is possible to brew in southern California and that dam will still stand and there will be no loss of life or property."

On the other hand, I spoke of an incident that occurred in Jersey; I was doing some electrical work in a building one day, one of these little bungalows out in the suburbs, and a fellow was spending some time on the door sill, a carpenter, and he was making a pretty close fit of things,

as is necessary if you want protection against the weather in that country, and the boss came along, the real estate man came along and he said, "Holy smoke, man, you are putting in an awful lot of time on that doorsill; you have got to get a wiggle on." This carpenter turned to him, and he said, "Why, man alive, I am only trying to make a good job out of this thing; I am putting in a door sill here as it should be put in; I want to make a house fit to live in." The real estate man said, "Fit to live in! What are you talking about, I am not building this house to live in, I am building it to sell."

And so the same way with my work as an electrical worker. I get a job in competition with other workers, and speed, efficiency,—speed-efficiency, profit-efficiency was the gauge.

I went in to do my work. I had to eat; I had to shoot her in just as I was told to shoot her in. Of course, there were rules and regulations supposedly governing the installation, but nevertheless, I had to pinch and squeeze everywhere, and the consequence was, as a result of speed work and conditions, I had to do the best I could to get done. The idea was to get done. Electrical fires are reported all over the United States; millions of dollars worth of property destroyed because some man has practiced sabotage in the interest of the masters. We I.W.W.'s say, we electrical workers can do a good job; you muckers can do a good job. Do it. Practice sabotage in the interest of the safety and security of society. It was along those lines that I spoke of sabotage.

I spoke too of the bosses' sabotage, or, rather the commission merchants' sabotage. I told of an instance down here in Ohio, we were building a line across the country one time, and I was boarding with a farmer who put a lot of us up, we were building the line through there and he boarded us, took us as boarders temporarily, and he had a lot of sheep-nose apples, and I noticed—of course, I don't know much about those kind of things,—I noticed he had them covered over with screening, chicken screening, and I asked what that was for, and he said that was to keep the hogs from killing themselves, and the cattle from killing themselves with these fine apples. I said, "Why, goodness, man, these kind of apples, they are fine; why don't you ship them into town, it is not very far into Cleveland, why don't you ship them into town?" "Why," he said, "ship them into town, I couldn't get the price of the barrels for the apples."

I continue then, and explain that I was in New York shortly afterwards and saw children on the street passing these fruit stands wishing and desiring apples apparently from their attitude, and here was an abundance of apples going to waste, because the farmer, after having done all of the hard work necessary to raising them, could not get over the sabotage practiced by the middleman and those who operate this produce game, could not get over that. Impeding production in the interest of profits, simply meant a dead loss to him. I have seen the same thing in California, —fruits of all kinds going to waste; I have seen field after field of spuds, where farmers would not even take the trouble of taking them up. One case down here in Castorville, sitting at the depot one day, and across from the track was a fine patch of spuds, I did not know who this fellow was alongside of me. I said, "That is a fine looking patch of spuds." He said, "It is a fine patch of spuds, and the spuds are fine too. They are these Salina potatoes, the kind of potatoes that have made the S. P. famous, according to their advertising," but he says "they will never be picked, they will never be gathered." I said, "They won't, what are you talking about?" "Well," he said, "They won't." I didn't believe him. I questioned him a little further, and found that he owned the potatoes. I said, "Do you mean to tell me, man, that fine field of spuds is not to be gathered?" He said, "That is exactly what I mean." He said, "If I gather those spuds and pay 7 cents," I think he said, "for a sack, and put them on the car, they offer me 56 or 58 cents for them." He says, "I cannot pick them for that and I cannot sack them for that; they are going to waste." I was waiting for a train. I got into Oakland. The thing kind of shocked me and I said to my wife when I got home, I said, "Have you bought any spuds lately?" She said, "Yes." I said, "Where did you get them?" She said, "I got them down to the market." I said, "In what quantity?" She said, "I got a sack." "What did they cost?" "$2.25." Oakland was 80 miles on a railroad away from this town; that is also on his railroad. I explain along those lines that sabotage was practiced by the workers in the interest of the masters, and sabotage did not mean violence, did not mean destruction of property; that it was silly to talk of destruction of property when we had to recreate it, if it was a social requisite, and so on.

Q.—Did you ever advocate driving spikes into logs?

A.—No, sir.

Q.—Cutting logs short?

A.—No, sir, although—

Q.—Is that sabotage?

A.—That mere fact of cutting a log short would not be destruction of property. Cutting the log short now, that is an idea that prevails, yet it is not true—

Mr. Nebeker: This is not responsive, if the Court please. The witness should not be permitted to make an argument on every question asked. I object to it.

Mr. Christensen: Q.—Why isn't cutting logs short, sabotage?

A.—Because the only thing they succeed in doing by cutting logs short is in disorganizing the orders that the companies have. They do not waste any material which is just like the hog. All of the log is used. It is simply, if they have orders for certain sized material, it may tend to disorganize their order system; that is all, but there is no loss, no unusual loss attendant.

Q.—Did you ever say anything on the subject of fouling a gear or a line?

A.—No. You mean—well, I heard this witness here say something about fouling a line.

Q.—Well, did you ever—

A.—Say anything like that?

Q.—Make any comment about a line?

A.—Absolutely nothing of that kind.

Q.—Is that sabotage?

A.—Certainly not.

Q.—What is it?

A.—That is murder.

14

The following note (about 1920) by Miss Agnes Inglis (1870–1952) was included in her "Sabotage" folder in the I.W.W. files in the Labadie Collection. The daughter of a wealthy Michigan family, Miss Inglis for many years devoted her time to the Labadie Collection of Labor and Radical Materials donated to the University of Michigan Library in 1911 by an anarchist printer, Joseph Labadie. On Miss Inglis' death in 1952, her long-time friend, the writer John Nicholas Beffel, wrote in the Industrial Worker *(April 25, 1952): "Her connection with the library was rather informal but effective. She kept her own hours, worked quietly, intensively. . . . She accepted no wages . . . always, she lived simply and economically. Her one stipulation, which was readily granted, was that she be allowed enough money to acquire occasional new acquisitions for the Labadie Collection, and to cover express charges on gifts, and that she have ample use of the University Library's facilities for binding newspapers, periodicals, and pamphlets and any necessary rebinding of books. . . . Long before Joe Labadie died in 1933, he had the satisfaction of knowing that a tireless friend was carrying on where he had left off and that the scope and value of his gift to posterity was widening and growing because of her ceaseless effort. . . . She managed to acquire a great many rare and valuable historical items without purchase, getting them as gifts through diplomatically worded letters to individuals and institutions throughout the United States and abroad."*

A personal friend of many radicals throughout the country, Miss Inglis kept close touch with social movements in the Detroit–Ann Arbor area. Her correspondence and notebooks in the Labadie Collection are filled with accounts of meetings she attended, social causes to which she contributed, and friendships she made through her contacts with radical organizations.

NOTE ON SABOTAGE:
THE CASE OF JOHN MAHONEY

By Agnes Inglis

It was at the time they were "ruthlessly wrecking the 14 stories of the luxurious Hotel Pontchartrain" that I met one of I.W.W. boys on the street. His name was John Mahoney. As I met him his face impressed me. He looked very thoughtful and sad. He said to me "What do you think I am working at now?" I said I didn't know. He said "I'm working at a job wrecking the Hotel Pontchartrain. Just think of it! Here the workers build that beautiful building and they haven't even homes to live in themselves. And now they are being told to pull it down in order to build a big bank-building. It's a beautiful building. I call that "Sabotage!" says John Mahoney. . . .

I never forgot John Mahoney. He was an I.W.W. The Board of Commerce men would have said, "The awful I.W.W.! *They* believe in sabotage." But here was an I.W.W. He was a nice thoughtful, earnest man and an ardent I.W.W. He dreamed of a world in which workers had homes fit to live in! But workers do not have homes fit to live in. They build such things as the Hotel Pontchartrain and then are told to tear it down and then they build the First National Bank on the same spot of ground. And workers dream of a new society and are accused of practicing "sabotage."

Sabotage. . . . I never hear the word without thinking of John Mahoney. I've never thought of that word since without his tired and sad face flashing before me as he said "I call that 'sabotage!'"—And back of him I see the workers' homes. . . .

He built the road,
With others of his class he built the road.
Now o'er it, many a weary mile, he packs his load,
Chasing a job, spurred on by hunger's goad.
He walks and walks and walks and walks,
And wonders why in Hell he built the road.

The Industrial Worker (April 23, 1910).

Chapter 3

Riding the Rails: I.W.W. Itinerants

Songs to fan the flames of discontent were sung by Wobblies on picket lines, in free speech demonstrations, in I.W.W. halls, around hobo jungle fires—wherever Wobbly rebels gathered to agitate for a new world built "from the ashes of the old."

Early in 1914 when Carleton Parker, a University of California sociologist who pioneered in psychological studies of casual labor, reported on the acute conditions under which California migrants lived, he wrote that about half of the 800 men whom he interviewed "knew in a rough way the—for them curiously attractive—philosophy of the I.W.W. and could also sing some of its songs."[1]

"Where a group of hoboes sit around a fire under a railroad bridge, many of them can sing I.W.W. songs without the book."[2]

"The book" that Parker referred to was the little red songbook started by the Spokane branch of the I.W.W. about 1909. It contained the provocative subtitle, "Songs of the Workers, On the Road, In the Jungles, and In the Shops—Songs to Fan the Flames of Discontent." Over thirty known editions from 1909 to 1968 have included more than 175 songs.[3]

Folklorist John Greenway has called the little red songbook, "the first great collection of labor songs ever assembled for utilitarian purposes. . . . Historically, it is of first importance as a record of a conscious effort to carry economic and social discontent to the singing stage. . . . In the field of folksong scholarship, the I.W.W. songbook is significant for its preservation of original com-

positions which potentially are folk material."[4]

The Spokane local of the I.W.W. was situated at the crossroads of the Northwest. Its members included lumberjacks, construction workers, harvesters, ice cutters, and railroad section hands—seasonal workers who circulated the message of One Big Union.

J. H. Walsh, a Socialist Party member who had been active in Alaska, was one of the spark plugs of the local. Described as a "go-getting type, full of pep and energy and ideas,"[5] he led the "Overalls Brigade" from Portland to the 1908 Chicago convention. Walsh introduced the idea of recruiting members by preaching revolutionary industrial unionism from a soapbox. To rival Salvation Army bands in attracting crowds for Wobbly street-corner meetings, he organized a red-uniformed I.W.W. band which for a short time traveled through the Northwest. Parodying Salvation Army gospel hymns and popular songs, the band developed its own repertoire of Wobbly verses sung to well-known gospel and popular melodies. Several of these were printed on pocket-sized colored cards which were sold to the crowd for a nickel a piece. Four of the songs, "Hallelujah, I'm a Bum," "Where the Silvery Colorado Wends Its Way," "When the Roll Is Called Up Yonder," and "Where Is My Wandering Boy Tonight?" were printed in a ten-cent leaflet.

Authorship of the popular "Hallelujah, I'm a Bum" was claimed by a Spokane local member, Harry ("Haywire Mac") McClintock, a former tramp entertainer, who said he composed it to the tune of a gospel hymn he sang as a boy soprano in his church choir in Knoxville, Tennessee.[6] At least one of the other three songs in the leaflet was written by English-born Richard Brazier, a prolific parodist, who had drifted down to Spokane from a construction job in British Columbia. Brazier submitted twenty other songs to a local union song committee set up by Walsh, who decided that there was enough talent among the membership to expand the song leaflets into a Wobbly songbook.[7]

The first edition, published about 1909, contained twenty-five songs including "The Marseillaise," "The Red Flag," the Bum song, sixteen parodies by Brazier, and several others. Two of the songs, "Workingmen Unite" and "The Banner of Labor," had been sung, and perhaps composed, by members of the Industrial Union Band as the "Overalls Brigade" called itself, on the way to the 1908 convention in Chicago.[8] The contents of the little red book dramatized the ideas of the Preamble, which was printed in each copy, and reflected the spirit, humor, and experiences of the Western migrants. In general, the songs vindicated the hobo status of the segment of industrial life that Haywood called "labor at the bottom," the floating fraternity of seasonal workers.

In 1908 the nation had come through a financial panic; unemployment in all trades was close to 36 percent.[9] Low wages and periodic unemployment forced millions to drift from one industrial center to another looking for work.

Moving across country, the itinerant workers harvested crops, sawed trees, cut ice, built roads, laid railroad ties. In the Midwest, they followed the ripening crops from Kansas to the Dakotas. On the West Coast, they gathered the fruit, hops, and grain, canned the fruit and vegetables of California, Washington, and Oregon, and found whatever out-of-season employment possible. Most of them "beat their way" by freight car from one place to another, and railroad companies estimated that there were half a million hoboes riding the rails, walking the tracks, or waiting at railroad junctions to catch onto a train, at any one time. Carleton Parker noted, "This group might be called a fraction of the migratory millions actually in transit."[10]

Riding the "rattlers" (freight cars) was dangerous.[11] From 1901 to 1905, almost 24,000 trespassers were killed on the railroads and over 25,000

were injured.[12] Railroad police, whose job it was to keep hoboes off the trains, frequently pursued, beat, and terrorized the trespassers and the "shacks" (brakemen) threw them off trains. The migrant was often arrested as a "vag" (vagrant) and given the brutal third degree or "sixty days" in the county jail. Sometimes the town police, or "clowns" as the migrants called them, ordered the vagrants to "leave town by the next train," rather than clutter up the county jails at the taxpayers' expense. Caught between the town "clowns" and the railroad "bulls," the migrant had little respect for law and the administration of justice. These experiences, as Nels Anderson wrote, "sometimes put fear into his heart but do not reform him."[13]

Although the I.W.W. was as active in other parts of the country as it was in the West, the image of the "typical" Wobbly became that of a migratory or seasonal worker without close family ties. In Carleton Parker's 1914 study of California migrants, close to 80 percent were under age forty, and 55 percent had left school before age fifteen. Nearly 70 percent gave their occupation as "floating laborers" and 37 percent expressed radical views on politics.[14]

Parker concluded that the I.W.W. can be profitably viewed only as a psychological byproduct of the neglected childhood of industrial America.[15] He characterized the American I.W.W. as "a lonely hobo worker, usually malnourished and in need of medical care [who was] as far from a scheming syndicalist, after the French model, as the imagination could conceive."[16] His mind was "stamped by the lowest, most miserable labor conditions and outlook which American industrialism produces."[17]

Rexford Tugwell in his article, "Casual of the Woods," also pictured the migrant as "a rather pathetic figure . . . wracked with strange diseases and tortured by unrealized dreams that haunt his soul."[18]

Yet I.W.W. publicity made the distinction that although the migrant's situation was degrading, he himself was not degraded. An article in *Solidarity*, November 21, 1914, stated:

The nomadic worker of the West embodies the very spirit of the I.W.W. His cheerful cynicism, his frank and outspoken contempt for most of the conventions of bourgeois society, including the more stringent conventions which masquerade under the name of morality, make him an admirable exemplar of the iconoclastic doctrine of revolutionary unionism. . . . His anomalous position, half industrial slave, half vagabond adventurer, leaves him infinitely less servile than his fellow worker in the East. Unlike the factory slave of the Atlantic Seaboard and the Central States, he is most emphatically not "afraid of his job."

His mobility is amazing. Buoyantly confident of his ability to "get by" somehow, he promptly shakes the dust of a locality from his feet whenever the board is bad, or the boss is too exacting, or the work unduly tiresome, departing for the next job even if it be 500 miles away. Cost of transportation does not daunt him. "Freight trains run every day" and his ingenuity is a match for the vigilance of trainmen and special police. No wife or family encumber him. . . . Nowhere else can a section of the working class be found so admirably fitted to serve as the scouts and advance guards of the labor army. Rather they may become the guerillas of the revolution—the francs-tireurs of the class struggle.[19]

The I.W.W. migrant was called a hobo, as distinguished from a tramp or a bum. As Dr. Ben Reitman explained it, "The hobo works and wanders, the tramp dreams and wanders, and the bum drinks and wanders."[20] The word hobo may have originated from the term "hoe boy," a seasonal farm worker. It was just one of the colorful words developed by the migrants to describe the members of the different seasonal occupations. "Snipes" and "jerries" laid railroad sections; "splinter bellies" did rough carpentry work; "pearl-divers" washed dishes; "sewer hogs" dug ditches; "skinners" drove mules; "muckers" shoveled dirt, rock, and gravel from mines or excavations; "timber wolves" or "timber beasts" felled trees; "gandy dancers" tamped ties on the railroads and frequently worked with "banjos" (short-handled shovels), "muck sticks" (long-handled shovels), or "anchors" (tamping picks).[21]

But probably the I.W.W. migrant was most frequently called a "bindle stiff" or "bundle stiff" who was said to be "packing his balloon," that is, carrying his blanket in a roll. In I.W.W. and hobo speech, the words "stiff" and "working stiff" were commonly applied to all casual or migratory workers, and especially to I.W.W. members.

Between jobs, "bindle stiffs" congregated in hobo "jungles" (hobo camps) or on the "main stem," or "skid row" of a town or city. A hobo jungle was usually near a railroad junction point, close enough to a town for those hoboes who needed to "bum lumps" (ask for handouts), yet far enough away from the attention of town police. A good place for a jungle included shade trees, room to stretch a number of blanket rolls on the ground, water for cooking, and wood to keep the fire going.

The jungle was a social institution with its own rules, regulations, mores, and division of labor. It was a catalyst of hobo culture and traditions. Harry Kemp, the hobo poet, wrote about such a camp in 1911:

It is often a marvel of cooperation. Discarded tin cans and battered boilers are made over into cooking utensils and dishes. Each member contributes to the common larder what he has begged for the day. There is usually in camp someone whose occupational vocation is that of cook, and who takes upon himself, as his share of the work, the cooking of meals. Stews are in great favor in trampdom and especially do they like strong, scalding coffee. Usually the procuring of food in such a camp is reduced to a system such as would interest economists and sociologists. One tramp goes to the butcher shop for meat, one goes to the bakers for bread, and so forth. And when one gang breaks up, its members are always very careful to leave everything in good order for the next comers. They will even leave the coffee grounds in the pot for the next fellow so that he can make "seconds" if he needs to. These things are part of tramp etiquet, as is also the obligation each new arrival is under to bring, as he comes, some wood for the fire.[22]

Jungle crimes included lighting a fire at night that might attract railroad or town police, "hijacking" (robbing) other men while they slept, leaving pots dirty after using them, neglecting to rustle wood for the fire, and damaging or stealing any jungle equipment. A guilty hobo would be thrown out of camp forcibly.

The men gathered around the fire made a good audience for news and rumors about road and job conditions: police, employment "sharks," and town officials. No attempt was made to pry into one another's background or personal relations;

a man's past was his own affair. Usually, the men in a jungle welcomed all who arrived, regardless of race or nationality. At times, however, in permanent I.W.W. jungles, the Wobblies excluded anyone not carrying a red I.W.W. membership card.

A gallon of wine or a jug of cheap whiskey frequently led to impromptu entertainments. Often, long epic poems were composed and recited on the spot. Some became hobo "classics" which many committed to memory. Often humorous, these songs and poems highlighted the adventures and perils of hobo life. Frequently, they protested against the social order, such as these verses from "The Sheep and the Goats" by Bill Quirke, one of the most popular of hobo writers:

Say, mate, have you ever seen the mills
    Where the kids at the loom spit blood?
Have you been in the mines when the fire damp
    blew,
Have you shipped as a hand with a freighter's
    crew,
    Or worked in a levee flood?

Have you rotted wet in a grading camp
    Or scorched in a desert line?
Or done your night stint with your lamp,
Watching the timbers drip with damp
    And hearing the oil rig whine?

Have you had your pay held back for tools
    That you never saw or could use?
Have you gone like a fool with the other fools
To the bosses' saloon where the strong arm rules
    And cashed your time for booze?

I do no kicking at God or Fate—
    I keep my shoes for the road—
The long gray road, and I love it, mate—
Hay-foot, straw-foot—that's my gait,
    And I carry no other man's load.

I don't mind working to earn my bread
    And I'd just as soon keep straight.
But according to what the preacher said,
    I'm a ram and I've missed the gate.
But I'm joggin along and joggin ahead,
    And perhaps I'll find it, mate.[23]

Although they could pick up information in the jungle or on the main stem about jobs and job con-

ditions, for the most part, hoboes obtained work through employment agencies, which brought together the men with the jobs and the men looking for work. Usually, the agencies were in the "flop house" districts of cities which the migrants frequented between jobs. The employment agent's "office" was more than likely an almost bare store front with a table and one or two chairs for furniture. Outside, a large blackboard announced a list of needed labor. The agent, called the "shark" or "mancatcher," usually kept no books, except one small enough to fit into his pocket. Nels Anderson wrote about such agents in 1922: "Their records are not merely inadequate; they are a joke."[24]

Working on commission, the labor agents charged either the worker, the employer—or both, and raised their fees to either party according to the demand for workers or the demand for jobs. Wobblies protested against the high costs of buying jobs, charges for jobs that sometimes did not exist, and the practice of fee-splitting between the "shark" and a foreman who would fire members of a work crew after their first pay check, and replace them with another group of "suckers" who had bought the same jobs and shipped out to the camp.

Wobblies joked that the employment sharks had discovered perpetual motion—one work crew on the job, one crew going to the job, and one crew leaving it.[25]

Another type of employment agency was the boarding company which would contract with employers of seasonal labor to provide crews of men throughout the needed employment period. Boarding companies made their profits from the high prices they charged workers for room and board. Scanty food, often of the poorest quality, and bad sleeping quarters with no bathing facilities, led one Wobbly to write that he was "housed worse than a beast and treated like a dog."[26]

Frequently, after the migratory worker had accumulated a certain sum of money, known as a "stake," he quit the job if it offered unpleasant conditions and drifted off to the road or to the city. Carleton Parker's investigation in 1914 revealed that road tradition often fixed the amount of the stake, and indirectly, therefore, the period of employment. With his money, the hobo would retreat to a jungle, and, "adding his daily quarter or half dollar to the 'mulligan fund,' live on until the stake is gone. If he tends to live further on the charity of the new comers he is styled a 'jungle buzzard' and cast forth."[27]

Off the job, the city life of the hobo was graphically described in these verses from "The Boe's Lament" by an unknown writer:

O! Lord, you know I'm "down and out,"
Forever forced to roam about,
From town to town, from state to state
Not knowing what may be my fate.

And frequently I have no bed
On which to rest my weary head;
And when at times I have the price,
I find it full of bugs and lice.

You know the stem is often bad
Of course that always makes one mad,
For it means that one must carry
"The banner" in the night so airy.

Now Lord, this is no idle joke
For I am "down and out" and "broke."
I have not got the gall to beg,
And not the nerve to be a "yegg."

Unless one has the ready cash
For "coffee an neckbones," or "hash,"
For "liver," "stew," or just "pigs feet,"
He surely has no chance to eat.

Now Lord, I've often times been told
That Heaven's streets are paved with gold.
To me that does not seem quite fair,
When millions here are in despair.

Behold your creatures here below—
These multitudes who have no show,
From their cradles to their graves
Their doom is that they must be slaves.[28]

The stem, which this writer hinted was "so often bad," provided very little in the way of recreation for the hobo besides the bars and the brothels. The I.W.W. hall was one of the few places that he could find companionship, a place to rest and make a meal, pick up some books and pamphlets, and exchange ideas. Carleton Parker called I.W.W. halls "a social substitute for the saloon."[29] The Wobbly headquarters usually included a kitchen, where a large pot of mulligan simmered on the stove and an enamel coffee pot was kept full. Radical literature was available for all to read. Often there was a piano, put to use by a Wobbly who picked out popular tunes and led some singing of Wobbly favorites. At Saturday night smokers, the men improvised propaganda skits in the style of current vaudeville shows.

In the jungles, on the jobs, and while lounging around the I.W.W. hall, the I.W.W. hobo frequently read avidly. Jack London was a favorite novelist and his book, *The Iron Heel*, was popular. Works on sociology, economics, politics, and history were also widely read. I.W.W. lists of recommended reading, printed in *The Industrial Worker* and *Solidarity*, suggested books by well-known socialists, anarchists, and other left-wing writers.

Besides reading books on the problems of labor, Wobblies learned about theories of changing the social order from the I.W.W. soapboxers. Between jobs, hoboes gathered in certain city areas, such as "Bughouse Square" in Chicago, Pershing Square in Los Angeles, and Union Square in New York City, to listen to lectures on biology, eugenics, psychology, sociology, politics, and economics.

Big Jim Thompson was among the most famous of many well-known Wobbly orators and certain to gather a crowd. One of his better-known, and often repeated stories, compared a young worker in the capitalist system to an automobile. "How about your children?" he would ask, and then continue:

When they get to be wonderful young men and women with their eyes brightly shining like the headlights on a new car, and with their veins and arteries like the wiring on a new car, and their hearts beating without a murmur like the smooth running of new engines, then the capitalists say to the proud parents, "We want to use your children to produce wealth for us and our children!" . . . The parents ask, "What are our children going to get for the use of their bodies during the precious years of their lives?"

Answer, "Gas and oil." A mere living wage. The endless chain that starts and ends with work. Every increase in the productivity of labor, every invention, every victory of science and triumph of genius in the line of industrial progress only goes to increase the wealth of a parasite class. This is wage slavery, the foundation of capitalism.[30]

Other soapboxers frequently prefaced their speeches by some crowd-attracting technique.

The "Blanket Stiff"

He built the ROAD—
With others of his CLASS, he built the road,
Now' o'er it, many a weary mile, he packs his load,
Chasing a JOB. spurred on by HUNGERS goad.
He walks and walks, and wonders why
In H——L, he built the road.

Industrial Worker, April 23, 1910.

Jack Phelan, called the silver-tongued boy orator of Wobblies, would mount the box and start yelling, "I've been robbed! I've been robbed!" When enough of a sympathetic crowd gathered to help him, he would start, "I've been robbed by the capitalist system!"[31]

Another soapboxer, an outdoor lecturer in the Spokane area, had been a circuit preacher in the South. Dressed as an old Southern colonel in a longtailed black coat and a soft-brimmed black hat, he would drawl softly:

> This is my text tonight, Fellow Workers. It's about the three stars. They're not the stars of Bethlehem. They're better than the stars of Bethlehem. The stars of Bethlehem lead only to Heaven which nobody knows about. These are the three I.W.W. stars of education, organization, and emancipation. They lead to porkchops which everybody wants.[32]

Hobo songs and poems seldom talked about love or beauty, yet curiously enough, Dick Brazier, author of so many of the verses in the little red songbook, told labor folklorist Archie Green:

> . . . the West was a wide open country, the open spaces really existed. There was plenty of room to move around in, and there were scenes of great grandeur and beauty, and there were journeys to be made that took you to all kinds of interesting sections of the country. That's the feeling we all had. I think that's one of the reasons we kept on moving as much as we did. In addition to searching for the job, we were also searching for something to satisfy our emotional desire for grandeur and beauty. After all, we have a concept of beauty too, although we were only migratory workers.[33]

1

For over sixty years, the song, "Hallelujah I'm a Bum" has been a popular American folksong. It was sung by soldiers during the Spanish-American War, by marchers in Coxey's Army, by Northwest loggers, construction workers, and harvest stiffs who attended the 1908 I.W.W. convention, and by the unemployed from coast to coast during the depression of the 1930's. In 1927 Carl Sandburg included it in his collection of folksongs, The American Songbag, as a popular hobo song whose author was unknown. By the late 1920's when over a dozen music publishers had issued

sheet music of the song, Harry ("Haywire Mac") McClintock, who recorded the song in 1926, charged that they were infringing on his copyright.

John Greenway, in his book American Folksongs of Protest *(Philadelphia, 1953) has a detailed account of McClintock's claim to the authorship of the song. Mac claimed that about 1897 he put new words to the hymn tune "Hallelujah, Thine the Glory," sometimes called "Revive Us Again," a song which he had learned while a boy choir singer in a church in his hometown of Nashville, Tennessee. He called it originally, "Hallelujah On the Bum" and, as he was bumming around the country, added new verses to the song. Greenway quotes McClintock, "The jungle stiffs liked the song and so did the saloon audiences, most of whom had hit the road at one time or another, and the rollicking, devil-may-care lilt of the thing appealed to them." He sang the song to soldiers at an army training camp in Tennessee during the Spanish-American War, and in their travels they helped popularize the verses around the country.*

"Hallelujah On the Bum" was printed in the I.W.W. Industrial Union Bulletin *(April 4, 1908). It was one of the four songs printed on colored cardboard folders which were sold for ten cents by the organization before the start of the first I.W.W. songbook about 1909. The I.W.W.* One Big Union Monthly *(March 1938) included an article, "Birth of a Song Hit," on the background of "Hallelujah, I'm a Bum."*

HALLELUJAH ON THE BUM

(Tune: "Revive Us Again")

O, why don't you work
Like other men do?
How in hell can I work
When there's no work to do?

Chorus:

Hallelujah, I'm a bum,
Hallelujah, bum again,
Hallelujah, give us a handout—
To revive us again.

O, why don't you save
All the money you earn?
If I did not eat
I'd have money to burn.

Chorus:

O, I like my boss—
He's a good friend of mine;
That's why I am starving
Out in the bread-line.

Chorus:

I can't buy a job,
For I ain't got the dough,
So I ride in a box-car,
For I'm a hobo.

Chorus:

Whenever I get
All the money I earn,
The boss will be broke,
And to work he must turn.

Chorus:

Hallelujah, I'm a bum,
Hallelujah, bum again,
Hallelujah, give us a handout—
To revive us again.

2

This song, composed to the tune of "Meet Me in St. Louis, Louie," was printed in the third edition of the I.W.W. songbook. Its author, English-born Richard Brazier, emigrated to Canada in 1903 at the age of twenty. He worked on farms, on railroad construction gangs, and in a blacksmith shop. He came to Spokane in 1907, joined the I.W.W., and contributed about sixteen songs to the first edition of the I.W.W. songbook. In an interview with folklorist Archie Green, Brazier told how I.W.W. organizer J. H. Walsh started the idea of the little red songbooks: "[Walsh suggested] let's form a song committee; let the membership get together and elect their representatives to a song committee. Decide whether they want a different format, and have a real songbook out of it or go along with the cardboard song cards business." When asked how he went about composing a song, Brazier answered: "At that time there was a lot of popular songs on the market. This was the era of the sentimental ballad, mostly, and a few humorous songs. Well, I . . . attended a lot of vaudeville shows . . . every saloon had a little vaudeville show of its own with these . . . sing and dance girls. . . . And I'd go down there and listen to a lot of singing, and if I heard a song that had a tune that I liked, I'd memorize the tune, then I would work on picking words to fit the tune. . . . The melody was all important."

Brazier became secretary of the joint locals in Spokane, and in 1916, he was elected to the executive board of the I.W.W. He settled in New York City following his release from Leavenworth Penitentiary in 1923, where he had served five years of his sentence along with other I.W.W. prisoners charged with violating the espionage law. He has continued contributing poems and songs to the Industrial Worker.

MEET ME IN THE JUNGLES, LOUIE

By RICHARD BRAZIER

Louie was out of a job,
Louie was dead on the hog;
He looked all around,
But no job could be found.
So he had to go home and sit down.
A note on the table he spied,
He read it just once, and he cried.
It read: "Louie, dear, get to hell out of here
Your board bill is now overdue."

Chorus:

Meet me in the jungles, Louie,
    Meet me over there.
Don't tell me the slaves are eating,
    Anywhere else but there;
We will each one be a booster,
    To catch a big, fat rooster;
So meet me in the jungles, Louie,
    Meet me over there.

Louie went out of his shack,
He swore he would never come back;
He said, "I will wait, and take the first freight,
My friends in the jungles to see;
For me there is waiting out there,
Of a mulligan stew a big share.
So away I will go and be a hobo,
For the song in the jungles I hear."

Chorus:

Meet me in the jungles, Louie,
    Meet me over there.
Don't tell me the slaves are eating,
    Anywhere else but there;

We will each one be a booster,
　　To catch the scissor Bill's rooster;
So meet me in the jungles, Louie,
　　Meet me over there.

3

These verses by Richard Brazier appeared in the
third edition of the I.W.W. songbook.

THE SUCKERS SADLY GATHER

By RICHARD BRAZIER

(*Tune: "Where the Silvery Colorado Wends Its*
Way")

Oh! The suckers sadly gather around the Red
　　Cross office door,
And at the job sign longingly they gaze;
They think it's time they shipped out to a job once
　　more,
For they haven't bought a job for several days.
So inside they go and they put down their dough—
　　"We have come to buy a job from you," they
　　say.
The employment shark says, "Right; I will ship
　　you out tonight,
Where the silvery Colorado wends its way."

Chorus

Now those suckers by the score
Are hiking back once more,
　　For they didn't get no job out there, they say;
So to town they're hiking back
O'er that bum old railroad track,
　　Where the silvery Colorado wends its way.

The Hoboes quietly gather 'round a distant water
　　tank,
　　While the Bulls are safely resting home in bed,
And they sadly sit and ponder on the days when
　　they ate pie,
　　And occasionally some moldy punk instead.
But now they're living high when a chicken coop
　　is nigh,
　　For the ranchers send them chicken every day,
So to the jungles they skidoo to dine on chicken
　　stew
　　Where the silvery Colorado wends its way.

Chorus

There's a Bo 'neath every tree,
And they are happy as can be,
　　For the chewings 'round that place are good,
　　they say.
For they have chicken galore
And they know where there is more,
　　Where the silvery Colorado wends its way.

4

This was one of the four songs printed on a folded
colored card which I.W.W. members sold for ten
cents in the Northwest area around 1907–08. It
was sung to the tune of "Where Is My Wandering
Boy Tonight?" and was printed in the third edition
of the I.W.W. songbook. Its author is unknown.

MY WANDERING BOY°

(*Tune: "Where Is My Wandering Boy Tonight?"*)

Where is my wandering boy tonight,
The boy of his mother's pride?
He's counting the ties with his bed on his back,
Or else he is bumming a ride.

Chorus:

Oh, where is my boy tonight?
Oh, where is my boy tonight?
He's on the head end of an overland train—
That's where your boy is tonight.

His heart may be pure as the morning dew,
But his clothes are a sight to see.
He's pulled for a vag, his excuse won't do.
"Thirty days," says the judge, you see.

Oh, where is my boy tonight?
Oh, where is my boy tonight?
The chilly wind blows, to the lock-up he goes,
That's where your boy is tonight.

"I was looking for work, Oh Judge," he said.
Says the judge, "I have heard that before."
So to join the chain gang far off—he is led
To hammer the rocks some more.

Oh, where is my boy tonight?
Oh, where is my boy tonight?
To strike many blows for his country he goes,
That's where your boy is tonight.

Don't search for your wandering boy tonight,
Let him play the old game if he will—
A worker, or bum, he'll ne'er be right,
So long's he's a wage slave still.

Oh, where is my boy tonight?
His money is "out of sight."
Wherever he "blows," up against it he goes.
Here's luck!—to your boy tonight.

5

This unsigned song was included in the third edi-
tion of the I.W.W. songbook. A later edition of
the songbook cites the tune as "Give Us This Day
Our Daily Bread."

OUT IN THE BREAD-LINE

Out in the bread-line, the fool and the knave
Out in the bread-line, the sucker and slave,
Coffee and doughnuts now take all our cash,
We're on the bum and we're glad to get hash.

Chorus:

Out in the bread-line, rain or the sunshine
We're up against it today,
Out in the bread-line, watching the job-sign,
We're on the bum, boys, today.

The employment office now ships east and west,
Jobs are quite scarce—they are none of the best;
The grub it is rocky—a discount we pay,
We are dead broke, and we'll have to eat hay.

Chorus:

We are the big bums, the hoboes and "vags,"
O, we look hungry, our clothes are all rags,
While a fat grafter, sky pilot or fake,
Laughs at our troubles and gives us the shake.

Chorus:

O, yes, we're the suckers, there's no doubt of that,
We live like dogs, and the boss he gets fat,
God help his picture taken once we get wise,
He'll be the bum and we'll be the swell guys.

6

This biblical parody appeared in the Industrial
Worker *(July 2, 1910).*

THE FLIGHT INTO CALIFORNIA

By W. METCALF

Chapter 12

(1) And it came to pass in the city which is called Dunsmuir, which is near the Mount which is called Shasta.

(2) As we tarried in the wilderness which is called the jungles.

(3) We came upon a man lying by the roadside who had been set upon by thieves

(4) And robbed of many shekels by the employment thieves in the city which is called Portland, in the land of Oregon.

(5) Wherefore we gave him gump mulligan and bread and much good advice

(6) That he might return from whence he came and join the I.W.W. and cast out devils.

(7) That man may not be robbed of man for a job's namesake.

(8) As we journeyed on our way taking neither wallet nor staff, but only overalls and labor power, that we might serve the master for the lousy dollar

(9) We came unto the place which is called Cottonwood, a Sabbath day's journey from Red Bluffs.

(10) There by the River we beheld many man servants.

(11) And we went unto their camp, saying:

(12) Repent ye, for the rule of craft unions neareth an end. And as we spoke unto them they marveled, saying:

(13) Who are these men? that they cast out Gomperite devils in the name of Industrial Unionism?

(14) And they were sore afraid, lest the master behold them listening to the Gospel of I.W.W.-ism.

(15) And seeing their plight, we went our way rejoicing.

(16) And it came to pass as we went our way, casting out Patriotic and Political Devils, that we came unto the City which is called Sacto, where were multitudes of people.

(17) And we spake unto them, saying:

(18) Man gets but little here below, and if ye would that ye have more,

(19) Strike not at the ballot box

(20) Lest ye strike it with a great axe and cast it forth into outer darkness, where there shall be weeping and wailing and gnashing of political freaks' teeth.

(21) But organize into the Union which is called of man I.W.W. for your own sake.

Chapter 13

(1) Wherefore we took ourselves apart from the multitude and came unto the city which is called Stockton.

(2) Where dwelleth one called Bill which is surnamed Scissor, and seeing him sore afflicted with patriotic leprosy we administered unto him much Industrial Unionism.

(3) Saying unto him, Go thou into the harvest and work for a dollar,

(4) And when the harvest is ripe and thy lord needeth thee sorely

(5) Strike for two dollars, saying unto thy lord:

(6) Behold, thy fruit goeth unto the devil, pay us two dollars or great shall be the destruction thereof.

(7) As we journeyed forth we passed by a Roman soldier which is called of men State Bull.

(8) Casting out Blanket Stiffs for his job's sake. And all these things that the words of Industrial Unionism might be fulfilled—that man owneth not his job, and he is a wage slave, anyhow.

7

This article appeared in Solidarity (*June 3, 1911*).

A VOICE FROM THE JUNGLES

By TYLER WILLIAMS

(*Special to Solidarity*)

Sheridan, Wyoming, May 24

I was at Crawford, Nebraska, last week doing a little eight-hour talk; also looking for a master. Things were quiet, and there was a featherweight "Bill Sunday" in town so I thought I would go over and hear him spout. People said he was fine.

AN IDENTITY OF INTEREST

Industrial Worker, July 16, 1910.

Brother Farmer

Brother Farm Hand

After the head sky pilot had delivered his message on the "prodigal son" and a pretty girl sang "Where Is My Wandering Boy?" (I wanted to tell her that there was a bunch of them down in the jungles but I kept quiet), the head spouter announced that those prodigal sons and daughters who wanted to return to the father could manifest their desire by coming up and shaking his delicate hand. While he continued his call from the platform he also told the good Christians to go out and speak to their friends personally. Well, a parson struck me and here is where the fun begins. He shook my hand and I said "Howda-do." He didn't say whether he was well or not but asked me whether I would not like to go up and take a stand for God? I asked him how he knew I hadn't already. Then he said "Oh, have you?" and I told him that I had not. He asked if I didn't want to, and I said "No." Of course, he inquired why and I answered that my body was giving me more trouble just then than my soul was. Then he said "Seek ye first the kingdom of heaven and all these things will be added." The dialog continued about as follows:

Hobo—That is good news for a hungry man. If you will guarantee me three square meals, a bed and a good job, I will go.
Parson—It is no trouble to find work; but as to a good job, you will have to prove yourself. I work. I never have any trouble finding employment.
Hobo—Your hand feels like it has been some time since you have hurt yourself. And as to proving myself, I will have to have a chance first. Could you tell me where I would find a job?
Parson—Why yes. There is a bureau for that purpose here.
Hobo—I have been there. There are a dozen jobs on the board and one inside. The rest have been taken if they ever existed. The shark wants $2.00 for the job he has—a farm job at $25.00. I can see where the farmer and the shark will win and I would lose. The bureau did not know whether I would have to sleep in the barn or not, and presumed I would have to work more than eight hours. Now, would you advise me to take that job?
I knew these guys were pretty liberal with their advise.
Parson—Well— er— yes; under the existing circumstances I would.
Hobo—I see that you are about as much concerned about my business as you are about my soul. What you would like to have me do is give my heart to God and my life to the boss.
Parson—Ah, my boy, you are making a grave mistake. The good book says: "God is not mocked," and "Vengeance is Mine, saith the Lord."
Hobo—He is worse than I am. I don't want any revenge. All I want is the goods. If I wanted revenge I would burn up half the box cars and bridges along the pike.
Parson—I hate to hear you talk that way.
Hobo—It does me good.

Just then the brother up front says "Let us pray." My friend looked relieved and I felt grieved.

8

Titled "You Had Better Stay Away," this unsigned song appeared in the Industrial Worker *(March 21, 1912). It was subsequently collected by George Milburn, printed in his* The Hobo's Hornbook *(New York, 1930), and cited without source as an I.W.W. song. It also appeared in an undated booklet,* Hobo Ballads *(Cincinnati: Hobo College Press Committee) in the files of the Labadie Collection.*

EVERYWHERE YOU GO

Things are dull in San Francisco,
    On the hog in New Orleans,
Rawther punk in cultured Boston,
    Famed for codfish, God and beans.

On the fritz in Kansas City,
    Out in Denver things are jarred;
Hear 'em beefing in Chicago
    That the times are getting hard.

Same old hooey in St. Looie;
    And all the more in Baltimore;
Coin don't rattle in Seattle
    Like it did in days of yore.

Jobs are scant around Atlanta,
    All through Texas it is still
And there's very little stirring
    In the town of Looieville.

There's a howl from Cincinnati,
    New York City, Brooklyn, too;
In Milwaukee's foamy limits
    There is little work to do.

In the face of all such rumors,
It seems not far wrong to say
That no matter where you're going,
You had better stay away.

9

George Milburn in The Hobo's Hornbook (*New York, 1930*) *cites these unsigned verses as an I.W.W. song. Titled "Society's Bums," the poem appeared in the* Industrial Worker (*July 25, 1955*), *signed by "Denver Din" Crowley. It was also included in an undated booklet,* Hobo Ballads, *titled "The Bum on the Rods and the Bum on the Plush." Its original source is not known.*

THE TWO BUMS

The bum on the rods is hunted down
    As the enemy of mankind,
The other is driven around to his club
    Is feted, wined and dined.

And they who curse the bum on the rods
    As the essence of all that's bad,
Will greet the other with a winning smile,
    And extend the hand so glad.

The bum on the rods is a social flea
    Who gets an occasional bite,
The bum on the plush is a social leech,
    Blood-sucking day and night.

The bum on the rods is a load so light
    That his weight we scarcely feel,
But it takes the labor of dozens of men
    To furnish the other a meal.

As long as you sanction the bum on the plush
    The other will always be there,
But rid yourself of the bum on the plush
    And the other will disappear.

Then make an intelligent, organized kick,
    Get rid of the weights that crush.
Don't worry about the bum on the rods,
    Get rid of the bum on the plush!

10

In The Hobo's Hornbook, *George Milburn wrote that Jim Seymour, a frequenter of "Bughouse*

Square" (*Newberry Square*) *in Chicago, was one of the hobo's favorite poets. Seymour's poem, "The Dishwasher," which first appeared in the I.W.W. press in the* Industrial Worker (*May 1, 1913*) *has been frequently reprinted in I.W.W. publications at the request of readers.*

THE DISHWASHER
By Jim Seymour

Alone in the kitchen, in grease-laden steam,
I pause for a moment, a moment to dream,
For even a dishwasher thinks of a day
Wherein will be leisure for rest and for play;
And now that I pause o'er the transom there floats
A stream of the Traumerei's soul-stirring notes,
Engulft in a blending of sorrow and glee
I wonder that music can reach even me.

For now I am thinking, my brain has been stirred,
The voice of a master the lowly has heard,
The heart-breaking sob of the sad violin
Arouses the thoughts of the sweet "might have
        been";
Had men been born equal the use of the brain
Would shield them from poverty, free them from
        pain,
Nor would I have sunk in the black social mire
Because of poor judgment in choosing a sire.

But now I am only a slave of the mill
That plies and remodels me just as it will,
That makes me a dullard in brain-burning heat
That looks at rich viands, not daring to eat;
That lives with its red, blistered hands ever stuck
Down deep in the foul indescribable muck
Where dishes are plunged, seventeen at a time,
And washt!—in a tubful of sickening slime!

But on with the clatter, no more must I shirk,
The world is to me but a nightmare of work;
For me not the music and laughter and song,
No toiler is welcomed amid the gay throng;
For me not the smiles of the ladies who dine,
No warm, clinging kisses begotten of wine;
For me but the venting of low, sweated groans
That twelve hours a night have installed in my
        bones.

The music has ceased, but the havoc it wrought
Within the poor brain it awakened to thought
Shall cease not at all, but continue to spread

United Press International, Inc., photo.

Demonstration of unemployed, Union Square, New York City, 1913.

Till all of my fellows are thinking or dead.
The havoc it wrought? 'Twill be havoc to those
Whose joys would be nil were it not for my woes.
Keep on with your gorging, your laughter and jest,
But never forget that the last laugh is best.

You leeches who live on the fat of the land,
You overfed parasites, look at my hand;
You laugh at it now, it is blistered and coarse,
But such are the hands quite familiar with force;
And such are the hands that have furnished your
    drink,
The hands of the slaves who are learning to think,
And hands that have fed you can crush you as well
And cast your damned carcasses clear into hell!

Go on with the arrogance born of your gold,
As now are your hearts will your bodies be cold;
Go on with your airs, you creators of hates,
Eat well, while the dishwasher spits on the plates;
But while at your feast let the orchestra play
The life-giving strains of the dear Marseillaise
That red revolution be placed on the throne
Till those who produce have come into their own.

But scorn me tonight, on the morn you shall learn
That those whom you loathe can despise you in
    turn,
The dishwasher vows that his fellows shall know
That only their ignorance keeps them below.
Your music was potent, your music hath charms,
It hardened the muscles that strengthen my arms,
It painted a vision of freedom, of life—
Tomorrow I strive for an ending of strife.

11

*Ralph Chaplin sent the manuscript of this poem to
Miss Agnes Inglis, who included it in a file of his
poems and cartoons in the Labadie Collection.
On the manuscript Chaplin wrote that it was composed after a group of homeless men, led by Frank
Tannenbaum, had been thrown out of the Church
of St. Alphonsus in New York City in March 1914.
Tannenbaum, a bus boy, who had come to the
United States in 1905 from Austria, asked a Father
Schneider if his group of 250 unemployed homeless men could find shelter in the church. The police arrived and evicted the men. Tannenbaum
was charged with vagrancy and sentenced to
Blackwell's Island. On his release from prison a
year later, he took an undergraduate degree at*

*Columbia University and, later, a Ph.D. at Brook-
ings Institute. A member of the History Department at Columbia University, he has written books
on Latin American economic history as well as on
criminology and prison reform.*

THE PRIEST

By Ralph Chaplin

The night we came from out the drifting snow,
The winds were bitter and the streets were drear;
Who mocked us when we had no place to go?

We gaunt eyed men had watched the blizzard
    grow—
The ghastliest and wildest of the year—
The night we came from out the drifting snow.

But how could God's anointed ever know
How driving Hunger hovers ever near!
Who mocked us when we had no place to go?

We knew your piety for empty show,
But still your pillared church was warm with
    cheer
The night we came from out the blinding snow.

Some day an earth uprooting storm may blow
Your mighty temples full of screaming fear!
Who mocked us when we had no place to go?

Then you'll remember how you scoffed at woes
And met a plea for shelter with a sneer!
The night we came from out the drifting snow
Who mocked us when we had no place to go?

12

*Charles Ashleigh came to the United States from
England as a youth in 1910 and returned there in
the early 1920's after a decade spent as an I.W.W.
member, organizer, writer, and "class war prisoner." His semi-autobiographical novel, The Rambling Kid (London, 1930) describes some of his
teen-age experiences bumming around the country as a hobo and a Wobbly. After a prison term
in Leavenworth, Ashleigh was deported as an
enemy alien to England. His poems have appeared in The Masses, The Liberator, Century
Magazine, and the Little Review, and several
were included in Genevieve Taggard's anthology,
Maydays (New York, 1925). Mr. Ashleigh left the*

I.W.W. for the Communist Party and describes himself, currently, as "a worker in the cause of British-Soviet friendship" (letter to J. L. K., March 24, 1964). He is a contributor to the British Daily Worker.

THE FLOATER

By CHARLES ASHLEIGH

"For East is East and West is West, and never the twain shall meet." So sang a poet, referring to the great and almost unbridgeable gulf which divides the western peoples from those of the Orient. Judging from the mass of confusion and misconception apparent in the references made by a number of our eastern would-be sympathizers of a certain type, the migratory worker of the Pacific states is as little understood by the easterner as is the inscrutable Oriental by the son of the Occident. This was very vividly suggested to me recently by a friend of mine—a western hobo agitator, strong of body and clear of mind, who has contributed much to the development of class consciousness among the floaters of the coast. "That crowd back East thinks we western stiffs are all bums because we beat the trains," said he. "They haven't the savvy to distinguish the difference between the Bowery bum and the casual laborer of the West. Hence all this stuff about the 'bummery,' etc." This gave me furiously to think; and with much force was brought home to me the wide difference existing between the living and working conditions of the proletariat of the East and that of the West, and particularly of the Pacific coast.

In the East the first and most obvious feature which strikes the western observer is the permanence of industry. It is true that there are periodical crises which necessitate the laying off of hands, but the industries are territorially *stationary*. There are huge and complex aggregations of machinery, necessitating numerous minutely distinct functions for the processes of production, which are performed by whole populations of industrial wage earners who reside for their whole lifetime, or at any rate for periods extending into years, in the same district. In the steel industry, in the textile industry, and others of like magnitude, it is nothing out of the ordinary for several generations of workers to have lived always in the same spot and to have worked always at the same process—allowing for changes implied by the improve-ment of machinery—and to have sold their labor-power to the same boss.

In the eastern industries women and children are employed. It is common for a whole family to be working in the same mill, plant or factory. This makes for family life; a debased and deteriorated family life, it is true, lacking in all the pleasant and restful features usually associated with that term, but, nevertheless, marriage, the procreation of children and some amount of stability are assured by the conditions of industry. On the other hand, the nerve-and-body-racking, monotonous nature of the work, the close and unhealthy atmosphere, and, sometimes, chemical poisoning or other vocational diseases, and the speeding-up system, all make for loss of nervous and physical vitality and the creation of bodily weaklings.

As we journey westward we mark a change. We leave the zone of great Industry and enter country in which capitalism is still, to some extent, in the preparatory stage. We come to the source of one of the great natural resources—lumber—and to that portion of the country where the railroads are still busily extending their complex network and where agriculture on a large scale is a leading factor in economic life.

All of these three principal occupations of the unskilled worker of the Pacific coast—lumber, construction work and agriculture—are periodical in their nature. A mighty wave of fertility sweeps up through the various states into British Columbia, drawing in its wake the legions of harvest workers. In California and Oregon, the ripening of fruits brings an army of labor to the scene. The construction of railroads, aqueducts and other signs of an onward-marching capitalism, employs temporarily thousands of laborers, teamsters and the like. The same is true of the lumber industry, which is also conditioned by natural processes.

The result of this is the existence on the coast of an immense army of unskilled or semi-skilled workers, of no fixed abode, who are forever engaged in an eternal chase for the elusive job; whose work takes them away from the towns to the hills or plains or forests, for varying periods. Forever over the great western country are they traveling, seeking this or that center of temporary activity, that they may dispose of their labor-power.

The Pacific coast is the country of the bindle or blanket-stiff. On the construction jobs the workers sleep in tents. In the lumber camps they are housed in bunkhouses, rude frame structures with tiers of bunks, something similar to the forecastle of a wind-jammer on a large scale. In these bunkhouses the men wash and dry their clothes, smoke and play cards, and generally divert themselves within the small limits of their time and location. The atmosphere is anything but fresh, and vermin are usually abundant, the wooden material of the bunks rendering it easy for the nimble and voracious creatures to secrete themselves. In many camps the men are engaged in a perpetual warfare against lice. The sleeping quarters for agricultural workers consist of barns, sheds or probably the open field. Bedding is rarely provided in lumber camps and never in construction camps and on harvest work. Therefore, the worker is compelled to follow literally the advice of the founder of Christianity and "take up his bed and walk." The inevitable burden of the migratory worker is a roll of blankets, slung by a cord around his shoulders. Many hotels in the coast towns, knowing the vermin-infested state of the camps, refuse to allow blankets to be brought into the premises, and they are therefore stacked up in the cheap saloons during the stay in town of their owner.

Employment agencies play an important and predatory role in the life of the floater. A large agency will take complete control of the recruiting of labor for some big job, shipping numbers of men out each day to the scene of action from their branches in various towns. Fees ranging from one to three dollars are charged the applicant for unskilled positions. It is a well-known fact, although, by reason of the underground support of the powers that be, hard to prove in specific cases, that there is often collusion between the agencies and the petty bosses by which a constant stream of men are kept coming and going, to the mutual enrichment of the agent—or "shark," as we prefer to term him—and the "straw boss." Nothing is easier for a foreman than to discharge quantities of men on trumped-up charges after a brief period of work and thus provide more fees for his agent friends in town.

A prominent feature of every coast town of any size is the "slave market," or "stiff town," composed of a varying number of streets or blocks, according to the size of the town and its strategic position as a recruiting center for labor. As you walk down the street, you notice that the loungers are all "stiffs." Sun-tanned, brawny men, most of them in early manhood or in the prime of life, dressed in blue overalls or khaki pants and blue cotton shirts, in the lumber country in mackinaws and high, spiked-soled boots, are standing in knots around the doors of the employment sharks, watching the requirements chalked up on the blackboards displayed outside. In some of the larger agencies the office will seat a couple of hundred men, who wait patiently for the employe who appears at intervals and shouts out the news of some particular job for which men are needed. Then comes a rush! The slave market is in full swing! Numbers of disconsolate ones may also be observed who have not the price of a job and who are waiting in the hope of obtaining that much-desired thing—a free shipment. There may be a dozen such offices in two or three blocks. This is also the quarter of cheap restaurants, where a meal—of adulterated, worthless food—may be bought for ten or fifteen cents. Fifteen or twenty-cent lodging houses are also plentiful, most of them crawling with vermin, and there is an abundance of barrel houses, where the slave gets an opportunity of drowning his miseries in oblivion by "blowing in" his "stake" on rot-gut whiskey or chemical beer. Above all this wave the flaunting banners of the military, marine and naval recruiting offices, offering a desperate refuge for the jobless, homeless, starving worker; vultures hovering over the swamp of poverty, ready to sweep down upon some despairing victim, probably some confiding lad lured to this country by booster-fed visions of the "Golden West." The ostensible recruiting officers are the gaily uniformed, upright-standing men standing invitingly outside their offices; the real recruiting officers are the vampires of hunger and unemployment.

The wholesale firing of men by foremen, the arduous nature of the work, and the temporary nature of the employment, keep the worker constantly in motion. He does not usually have enough to pay his fare, if he is to exist at all in the town whilst waiting for the next job. Therefore, the only alternative is to beat the trains. This is also the only method of following the harvests over the wide stretches of country, where to pay a fare would be impossible usually and ruinous always. Hoboing is, therefore, the universal method of traveling among the migratory workers of the Pacific coast.

The railroad tracks are alive, at certain periods of the year, with men tramping the ties, under the burning sun, with heavy bundles of blankets upon their backs. The worker cannot usually travel as fast as the professional "tramp," who beats the fast passengers. His unwieldy pack makes it difficult for him to negotiate anything but a freight, although some of them achieve wonders of agility in the "making" of a "blind" or even the "rods," when hampered by their bedding. On the outskirts of practically every town may be seen the "jungles," or camp, where the meal, purchased—or, if needs be, begged—in the town, is cooked. A supply of cooking utensils is nearly always to be found in the "jungles." Primitive utensils, it is true, formed with much ingenuity out of preserve, oil or lard cans. Besides the large stew can, there is always the "boiling up" can, in which shirts and underclothes are sterilized—an inevitable feature of the incessant campaign against the plague of body lice.

The meal over, if it be winter, a huge fire is built up and, with the approach of dusk, blankets are spread, and these soldiers of western industry, out of whose sinews and brain the enormous wealth of the West is distilled, settle down for a night of fitful slumber, broken by the cold, the necessity of attending to the fire, and the arrival of newcomers. In the morning the long walk down the track is resumed or a train is boarded with caution and concealment. There are constant wrangles with the brakemen, who frequently demand a money contribution in return for the permission to ride, with the alternative of jumping off (oh, Solidarity, thy name is null among the railroaders of the West!), and the unceasing, gnawing fear of arrest for vagrancy or of a beating up by the railroad police in the yards of the town of destination. It would be hard to estimate the number of workers who in one year are sentenced to varying terms of imprisonment, usually accompanied by hard labor, for the crime of trespassing on the property of the railroad companies. Yet no other method of traveling is possible for them. The risk of imprisonment, or of rough physical handling by the yard police is an integral part of their lives. Can we wonder that among them is fast growing a spirit of passionate rebellion? To make strong men, who work out in the open air and who preserve a certain spirit of rude independence, slink for fear of the armed bullies of the city or railroad police, and to be stigmatized as bums and ne'er-do-wells by canting, ignorant magistrates, is a certain method of fostering and stimulating that revolt which is already smoldering in the consciousness of the workers of the Pacific states.

And, for all this labor and suffering, what reward? The average wage of the worker in the lumber camps is $2.75 or $3 per day of ten hours. From this, five dollars weekly is deducted for board, often of the rottenest kind. A hospital fee of one dollar per month is also compulsorily charged by the company for medical attention of a very indifferent nature and for a hospital which, in many cases, is non-existent. The truck system flourishes in camps of all kinds, the distance from the nearest town obliging the worker to purchase from the camp store, where he is charged exorbitant rates for his goods.

It must be remembered also that this work is by no means permanent, and that the savings of one job must be applied to tide the worker over until the next. Construction workers receive an average of $2.25 per day, from which 75 cents is daily deducted for board, or $5.25 per week. Here the hospital graft also prevails. If a worker remain only two days in a camp, the dollar is extorted. The work is from sun-up to sun-down. Somewhat larger wages are paid for agricultural work during the harvest rush, but the work is at breakneck speed and for extremely long hours, and lasts only for a short term.

The effects of the life lived by the slaves of the domain ruled by the Southern Pacific railroad and the lumber trust are, in many ways, disastrous. The striking feature of the Pacific country is that it is a man's country. Conditions render it impossible for the worker to marry. Long terms in isolated camps produce the same phenomena of sex perversion as exist in the army, navy and the monastery. The worker is doomed to celibacy with all its physical and moral damaging results. The brothel in the town, between jobs, is the only resort.

Yet the arduous physical toil in the open air does not have the same deteriorating effect as does the mechanical, confined work of the eastern slave. The constant matching of wits and the daring needed for the long trips across country have developed a species of rough self-reliance in the wandering proletarian of the West. In health and in physical courage he is undoubtedly the superior of his eastern brother. The phenomenal spread of the propaganda of the I.W.W. among the migratory workers indicates that this great mass, so long inarticulate, are at last beginning to realize their economic oppression and to voice their needs. The size of the local membership is an uncertain gauge in that territory of ever-moving fluid labor. Certain is it that around nearly every "jungle" fire and during the evening hours on many a job in the great westland, the I.W.W. red songbook is in evidence, and the rude rebel chants are lustily sung and discontent expressed more and more definitely and impatiently.

The free speech fights of San Diego, Fresno, Aberdeen and Spokane, the occasional strike outbursts in the lumber country, the great railroad construction strike in British Columbia and the recent tragedy of Wheatland are all indications that the "blanket stiff" is awakening. It was indeed an unpleasant surprise to the masters of the bread in the booster-ridden West when the much-despised tramp worker actually began to assert himself. The proud aristocrats of labor had also long stood aloof from them, considering them worthless of organizing efforts. And, then, sud-

denly, lo and behold, the scorned floater evolved his own movement, far more revolutionary and scientific than his skilled brother had ever dreamed of! From the lumber camps, from the construction camps, from the harvest fields, water tanks, jails and hobo campfires came the cry, ever more insistent, of the creator of western wealth. And, marvel of marvels, summit of sublime audacity, the cry of the flouted wanderer was not merely for better grub, shorter hours and simple improvements, but, including these things and going beyond them, he demanded, simply and uncompromisingly, the whole earth—the Product of his Toil!

More power to you, western brother! Go to it! And may you continue the good work and agitate and organize until you have builded up for yourself a mighty force that shall bring you your reward, the ownership of industries, and transform the vaunted, slave-driving mockery of the "Golden West" into a workers' land that shall really deserve the name.

WHICH PAPER DO YOU SUPPORT?

Industrial Worker, July 23, 1910.

13

This poem, signed J.H.B. the Rambler, appeared in the Industrial Worker *(November 1916).*

THE MIGRATORY I. W. W.
By J. H. B. THE RAMBLER

He's one of the fellows that doesn't fit in,
  You have met him without a doubt,
He's lost to his friends, his kith and his kin,
  As he tramps the world about.

At night he wanders beneath the stars
  With the mien of an ancient seer,
And often he's humming a few sweet bars,
  Of a Rebel song soft and clear.

Yes, he's one of the breed that never fits,
  And never a dollar can glean,
He's one that a scornful world requites,
  As simply a might-have-been.

But deep in the heart of his hungry soul,
  Tho' the smug world casts him out,
There burns like the flames of a glowing coal,
  The fires of love devout.

Of a world in which all may live,
  And prosperity be for all,
Where no slave shall bow to a parasite's greed,
  Or answer a master's call.

14

T-Bone Slim, whose real name was Matt Valentine Huhta, was one of the most famous and popular of I.W.W. writers. Captain of the Hudson River barge "Casey," he was drowned in 1942 while on duty for the New York Trap Rock Corporation. He was a member of the Barge Captain's Local No. 933-4 A.F.L., as well as of the I.W.W. His obituary account in the Industrial Worker *(October 24, 1942) comments: "While there have been few working-class writers in our time better known than T-Bone Slim, little was known about the man himself, even to those with whom he worked or who crossed his trail and stopped for a chat with him in his frequent tours of observation about the country. . . . Having lived almost a full life of anonymity, Fellow Worker Huhta died that*
way and was buried that way. We have an idea that's the way he wanted it to be." The nickname "Slim," which Huhta took as part of his pen name, was a common "moniker" for hobos. Several Wobbly poems and articles refer to Christ as "Jerusalem Slim."

"The Mysteries of a Hobo's Life" appeared in the seventeenth edition of the I.W.W. songbook.

THE MYSTERIES OF A HOBO'S LIFE *
By T-BONE SLIM
(Air: "The Girl I Left Behind Me")

I took a job on an extra gang,
  Way up in the mountain,
I paid my fee and the shark shipped me
  And the ties I soon was counting.

The boss put me driving spikes
  And the sweat was enough to blind me.
He didn't seem to like my pace,
  So I left the job behind me.

I grabbed a hold of an old freight train
  And around the country traveled,
The mysteries of a hobo's life
  To me were soon unraveled.

I traveled east and I traveled west
  And the "shacks" could never find me.
Next morning I was miles away
  From the job I left behind me.

I ran across a bunch of "stiffs"
  Who were known as Industrial Workers.
They taught me how to be a man—
  And how to fight the shirkers.

I kicked right in and joined the bunch
  And now in the ranks you'll find me,
Hurrah for the cause—To hell with the boss!
  And the job I left behind me.

15

"The Popular Wobbly," which first appeared in the I.W.W. magazine One Big Union Monthly *(April 1920), continues to be one of the best known of T-Bone Slim's poems, as well as one of the most popular I.W.W. songs. It was printed in*

the seventeenth edition of the I.W.W. songbook. The song has recently been adapted by members of the Student Nonviolent Coordinating Committee in a collection of civil rights sit-in songs, We Shall Overcome, edited by Guy and Candy Carawan (New York, 1963).

"THE POPULAR WOBBLY" *

By T-Bone Slim

(Air: "They Go Wild, Simply Wild Over Me")

I'm as mild manner'd man as can be
And I've never done them harm that I can see,
Still on me they put a ban and they threw me in
    the can,
They go wild, simply wild over me.

They accuse me of ras—cal—i—ty
But I can't see why they always pick on me,
I'm as gentle as a lamb, but they take me for a
    ram:
They go wild, simply wild over me.

Oh the "bull" he went wild over me.
And he held his gun where everyone could see,
He was breathing rather hard when he saw my
    union card—
He went wild, simply wild over me.

Then the judge, he went wild over me,
And I plainly saw we never could agree,
So I let the man obey what his conscience had to
    say,
He went wild, simply wild over me.

Oh the jailer, he went wild over me,
And he locked me up and threw away the key—
It seems to be the rage so they keep me in a cage,
They go wild, simply wild over me.

They go wild, simply wild over me.
I'm referring to the bedbug and the flea—
They disturb my slumber deep and I murmur in
    my sleep,
They go wild, simply wild over me.

Will the roses grow wild over me
When I'm gone into the land that is to be?
When my soul and body part in the stillness of my
    heart,
Will the roses grow wild over me?

16

Nothing is known about the author of "The Outcast's Prayer," which appeared in the Industrial Worker (July 23, 1921), although in style and content it is very similar to "The Lumberjack's Prayer" by T-Bone Slim (Chapter IX).

THE OUTCAST'S PRAYER

O Lord, we come to thee this day and seek thine assistance. We ask Thee to rectify some of the great evils that exist in this old world that Thou hast created, and to remove the causes of misery, starvation, privation, degeneration and poverty in the land of the free and the home of the brave. For the life of a workingman is burdened with many troubles and a large roll of blankets.

And we ask Thee to aid him, that he may connect with three meals a day and not have to eat yesterday's breakfast for supper the day after tomorrow. Give him Thy protection, O Lord, that he may not fall foul of Judge "Humpty-Dumpty," who dreams in gloating glee of the victims he has sent to the louse-infested cells of an unsanitary prison. Deliver us from the greed and graft that exist in this nation and from the parasites who neither toil nor spin, but bedeck their persons with finery until they glitter in the gloaming like a rotten dog salmon afloat in the moonlight.

O Lord, help us; for we have criminals, paupers and hordes of industrial cannibals, whom we call business men, who draw their salaries and convictions from the same source. Verily, our institutions are badly mixed; for we have thieves and theologians, Christians and confidence men. Also prisons and politicians, scabs and scallawags, traces of virtue and tons of vice. We have trusts and tramps, money and misery, Hoover and hunger, salvation and soup, and hypocrites who expect to pave their way into heaven by begging old pants, coats and hats and selling them to the poor, thereby helping to spread disease and vermin.

Rid us, we pray Thee, of the employment sharks that are licensed by our government to charge workingmen for a job and have contractors fire them the next day. Men are sent to jail for not having the means of support, and to the chain gang for not having the price of a job. Deliver us from a country where man is damned for the dollar and the dollar is deemed the man; where the press is paid for suppressing the truth and gets rich by telling lies.

Protect us, O Lord, and deliver us for the Grocer's Association holds us up while poverty holds us down. Deliver us from those who make canned beef out of sick cows, mules and horses, and corpses out of those who eat it; and may the price of hamburger, beef stew, waffles and "holey" doughnuts come down and our wages come up to meet them, and may we be permitted to fill up on these luxuries three times a day; for to be without them causes great pain in our gastric regions.

And, O Lord, we do not understand why poodle dogs have private baths and are attended by maids and valets, are shampooed, manicured and kissed, fed on choice steaks and drink cream, while thousands of little children live out of garbage cans. Christ never said: "Suffer little poodle dogs to come unto me."

O Lord, we ask Thee to have mercy on the blanket stiffs, such as railroaders, loggers, muckers and skinners; and may they be permitted to make at least seven dollars and six-bits before they get fired; and may their mulligan be of better class and contain no more old shoes, gum boots and scrap iron; and contain no insects that might discommode and may their blankets rest lightly on their blistered backs. May the farmer plant his spuds more closely to the railroad track, and his chickens roam close to the jungles, and we will be ever grateful to Thee!

AMEN!

JESUS REPLIES

I've heard your prayer, O Scissor-bill,
It sounds like hokum and goulash and swill
You say that you pray and work like a mule
You're not a worker but Henry Ford's tool.
You thank me for working 12 hours a day,
Why blame it on me—I never made you that way.
You scoff at the rebel and lynch him 'till dead
But I was an outcast and they called me a "Red."
You call me Christ Jesus with intelligence dim
But I was a Rebel called Jerusalem Slim.
And my brothers: the outcast, the rebel and the
    tramp,
And not the religious, the scab or the scamp
And of all creatures both filthy and drab,
The lowest of all is the thing called *scab*.
So pray thou no longer for power or pelf—
I cannot help him who won't help himself!

17

Many I.W.W. members, bumming their way from one job to another, were familiar with these signs of the road. An article "They Also Believe in Signs" appeared in the School Arts Magazine *(May 1923). It said: "Possibly you have discovered that if your family is not averse to giving food to a hungry wayfarer, you are frequently visited by such men, while your next door neighbor may never be visited. Why is it? Jeff Davis, 'King of the Hobos' (and International President of the 'Hoboes' Society') has compiled the set of symbols seen [below] on the page. While the average person may not notice the signs, they are written on his fence, gatepost, or even his doorstep. To the knights of the road they stand out as blazing letters. Water-tanks, railway bridges, stations, and roadside fences bear the glad tidings and the wise wanderer always heeds them. If you have an influx of these visitors, look at your gate or fence post. You may discover one of your modern hieroglyphics and decide that the ancient Egyptians were not so old-fashioned after all."*

MODERN HIEROGLYPHICS

18

This anecdote, typical of those told around a jungle fire, appeared in the Industrial Pioneer *(April 1924) and was reprinted in the* Industrial Worker *(October 25, 1961). It was also collected by folklorist B. A. Botkin from I.W.W. soapboxer Arthur Boose in Portland, Oregon, and included in Botkin's* Treasury of American Anecdotes *(New York, 1957).*

Arthur Boose (1878–1959), known affectionately as "Old War Horse Boose," was a well-known Wobbly organizer and soapboxer. A bachelor whose hobby was painting mountain landscapes, Boose joined the I.W.W. in 1909 after attending lectures on economics at the Milwaukee Free Thinkers Hall. During the next nine years he organized Minnesota miners, Oklahoma oil workers, and Northwest lumberjacks into the I.W.W. He was jailed for five years in Leavenworth Penitentiary following the 1918 federal trial in Chicago of I.W.W. defendants.

Boose spent his last years in Portland, Oregon, selling I.W.W. newspapers, pamphlets, and songbooks. An essay about his life, "The Last of the Wobblies," appears in Stewart Holbrook's book, Little Annie Oakley and Other Rugged People *(New York, 1948).*

HOW HE MADE IT NON-UNION

On one occasion a non-union man entered a butcher shop to purchase a calf's head. As the butcher was about to wrap it up for him the customer noticed the union shop card.

"Say, is that a union calf's head?" he asked.

"Yes, Sir," answered the butcher.

"Well, I am not a union man and I don't want union meat," said the customer.

"I can make it non-union," said the meat man, picking it up and retiring to the back room. He returned in a few minutes and laid the head on the counter with the remark, "It's all right now."

"What did you do to make it non-union?" asked the prospective buyer.

"I simply took the brains out of it."

19

Ralph Winstead (1894–1957) was the ablest of the I.W.W. short story writers. Born in Spokane, Washington, the son of a prospector, Winstead worked at odd jobs throughout his youth to supplement his father's erratic earnings. At nineteen, he homesteaded by himself on the Queen Charlotte Islands and, later, worked in mining and logging camps and on construction jobs. About 1918, he was secretary of a coal miner's local union in the Northwest, and shortly after became an active member of the I.W.W. Lumber Workers' Union No. 120. He wrote his first stories at a logging camp outside Seattle.

Winstead worked on the editorial staff of the Industrial Worker, *edited the* One Big Union Monthly *for several months in 1921, and soon after became the editor of a trade magazine,* The American Contractor. *He was employed by the N.R.A., the W.P.A., and the LaFollette Committee. In 1949 he came to Detroit to investigate the shooting of U.A.W. President Walter P. Reuther.*

Winstead wrote a series of Tightline Johnson stories in 1920–23, which appeared in I.W.W. publications. In loggers' language, the expression "to tightline" has two meanings, "to hoist" and "to harass." Winstead invented the character of the Wobbly, Tightline Johnson, and wrote about Johnson's experiences as a migrant and smelterman, coal miner, and lumberjack. "Tightline Johnson Goes to Heaven" appeared in the I.W.W. magazine Industrial Pioneer *(July 1923), signed with Winstead's pseudonym.*

TIGHTLINE JOHNSON GOES TO HEAVEN

By William Akers

Floppin' is done by the best people. It is an institution highly developed by the human race and is frequently indulged in by tired business men, cow-eyed stenographers and loggers with stag pants. It is the one thing that every man, woman and child enjoys more of than anything else that they get.

Where does a stiff find any more high-class sensations than comes to him just after rollin' in to a fine well-thrown together bunk, piled high with fluffy blankets, clean sheets, one of those double-ribbed, triple-plated, pressure-packed twenty-layers-rolled-into-one sort of mattresses,—all landed together on top of a fast feedin' set of springs in a bugless paradise?

Echo answers—"Where?"

Herb Hoover has come out strong for standardization. Me and him are unanimous on this proposition. Of course, Herb has devoted a lot of attention to fields that never interested me. His idea for instance to make only seventeen kinds of bricks bloom where a hundred and ninety cluttered up the roadside before, never aroused any undue enthusiasm in my hyphenated Scotch-Irish-Scandinavian-American heart. Somehow I always felt safer with a little heavy confetti laying round handy.

But the principle is sound. Reduce the varieties. And right here is where Herbie finds Tightline Johnson ready to do a Horatius at the Bridge with him any old time.

There is too many varieties of beds, bunks and flops. My idea is this: let's start right in and reduce the species down to about ten kinds, but all of these ten kinds to be built according to the best and most scientific plans and specifications.

I would allow skid-way to take care of any sappy notions as to outward appearance and the like. If anybody is goin' to die happier because they have a bunk all faked up like a Louie Quince, help 'em along, says I.

And this pet idea of mine has sound practical points to it that would interest any profound capitalist in the market for elbow grease, providin' these said employers had not been in the lumber business so long that the knot on top of their spinal columns had degenerated into punky butt stock.

I speak from practical experience. How is a good and willing slave goin' to give his master his undivided attention when a lumpy flop and last year's crop of fill-or-busters join hands to divert him from his proper rest?

I am with Herbie right down to the ground of his Native Oregon. I don't believe in anything extreme. Far be it from me to hint that a gold decorated bedstead, equipped with the finest auxiliary box spring mattress, supplemented with Belfast linen sheets, brocaded Astrachan blankets and a hand worked and embroidered Irish lace coverlet, should be installed for every logger that ever threw a spiked hoof on top of a bit of round stuff.

No Sir! I ain't one of these Kerenskies that want nothing less than a Czar's bed to sleep in. Not that I am sayin' anything against 'em, mind. I remember one time when I had the flop of a life time in just such a bunk.

*   *   *

It was down in the heart of the steel country during the early days of the renaissance of the Ku-Klux-Klan. Normalcy and the American Defense Society had the country by the throat. To be a foreigner was as popular them days as the corner bootlegger is during a general strike of the I.W.W.

When lots of these ignorant Europeans were asked the original question—"If you don't like this country why don't you go back where you came from?" it was surprising to find so few who could dig up a real convincing answer. The more they thought it over the more determined they got to follow the Goulds and the Astors over to Europe. So they were pullin' out by the thousands every day.

Me—I came rollin' into this vacation ground from Cleveland in the dead of winter. I was hooked up inside of a coal gondola on the Panhandle. Me and a couple of chunks of cast iron had been makin' impressions on each other and on the shack all afternoon.

This shack was one of these temperamental cusses. Must have had an unhappy home life, he was that restless and nervous. He chased me off of that string about ten times into the snow rollin' down from the chill breezes of Lake Erie.

The further south we got the colder the wind became. The exercise kept my blood flowin' freely but my ideas of the human race was becoming more and more pessimistic. I thought to myself that Schopenhauer could have written a real masterpiece if he had taken that trip.

After dark it became easier for me and harder for the shack and he got real nervous. When we pulled up to a water tank at Ambridge, about fifteen miles out of the Pitt itself, he went and brought up reinforcements. Two gunmen of the American Bridge Company rallied to save the system and they run me out of that car and up along the bank of the Ohio River like Three Finger Jack on the trail of a lost soul with a ten dollar bill.

I was always inclined to lean towards the idea that efficiency among the lower classes was enhanced by periods of unemployment, and the way these two gun men extended themselves sure cinched the argument. Here was two specimens of a class as low down as can be found and they were sure overworkin' themselves for no other reason at all so far as I could see.

After headin' upstream for a ways I decides to sprint off to my left up the side hill. The leg that I busted in the log jam at the Mary's, out in Idaho,

was in no shape for a marathon and I realized that I had to look for cover pretty pronto.

I must of run about a mile up that hill when I came to a brush hedge, stretched out along a road. I gallops along when I hear a flivver poppin' in my rear. I hears a hail and glancing back I spies the lizzie pickin' up my gladhanders. So havin' a firm idea that I was unable to compete with modern machinery by hand I finds me a nice crotch in the hedge and highclimbed it and boosted myself over.

I gave the once over to about four big back yards, each surrounded by a prickly hedge which I was just gettin' the proper hang of the way to bounce over, when they played out on me and I could see nothin' but a road on the other side of the last one. Alexander and me felt just alike regardin' new worlds to conquer.

There was only one thing to do and that was to look for a flop real handy.

*   *   *

In my mind back yards is always connected with some kind of houses, barns and the like. I soon located the back building in this shebang. It was a brick garage and had a door on it like the Union Trust Company's safe.

The house was one of these big nifty summer dumps where the hand-outs are pretty certain if a guy can get by the gardener or the lawn-mower pusher. I thinks to myself that nothing can look more lonesome than a summer cottage in the winter time and pinches my ear to see if I was bit. Sure enough, I found it frosted even after my hurdle race. Here was a hell of a fix.

There flashed into my mind the picture of a man I had seen when I was a little kid. He had both legs off at the hip and was out advertisin' artificial limbs. Both his had been froze off.

I decided that I would have a hard time seein' America first if I lost my legs all on account of two Steel Trust sluggers. I looks over this dump loomin' up alongside in the snow light.

There was a big balustraded porch on one whole side of it constructed in a pleasin' architectural style. French windows looked out on to the upper porch. Now it stuck in my mind, from seein' a few movies, that French windows are duck soup to the heroic burglar that is out to swipe back the jewels which rightfully belong to the daughter of the old man. So I qualifies for a degree in porch climbin' and ten years in the big house and tries my luck.

Sure enough, by just nickin' a piece of glass out of one corner of those panels I could reach thru and open the thing up. I stepped in, after pushing open the shutters. I lighted a match and the first thing that I seen was a big cut-glass fruit dish sittin' on the sideboard. I grabbed this like Damon receivin' Pythias and dashed out to the porch and filled it up with snow. I took it in and closed up the shutters and lit up one of the candle sticks.

At one side of the room was a bed the like of which would set an Oregon balloonist to pinchin' himself. But I paid scant attention to it then.

I flipped off my clothes and shoes and rubbed that snow into my skin for fair. A bath before retiring is wonderful for the complexion I was once told and I have been run out for repeatin' it in every loggin' camp from the Hammond outfit up to Ocean Falls. A snow bath and a rub down on a great towel that felt like a spring cushion sure set me up in business.

I climbed into a pair of pink pajamas, took a couple of wraps about myself with a plutocratic bath-robe and, armed with the candle stick set out to explore the house.

Me bein' the son of an old-time prospector and havin' done a little mushin' and pannin' myself, the ideas of hospitality in vogue amongst us sourdoughs has always struck me as bein' fair and square. Many is the time some snowshoe pushin' traveler has moved into my cabin when I was out and helped himself to the grub, livin' strictly up to the code by whittlin' shavin's and washin' the dishes before mushin' on next mornin'. And the same had been done by myself.

So here, thinks I, is an opportunity to introduce some fine healthy customs into an effete society. I finds a pantry stocked with can openers, tinned asparagus tips, oysters, corn, tomatoes, crackers and a big hunk of imported French cheese with little blue sections scattered thru it. It sure all tasted good to me.

I carried the cans down cellar and cleaned up the pantry—then I took my candle and went back to my bedroom.

"Call me early, James!" says I to myself as I blew out the candle and jumped into bed.

Boys, I am here to tell you that that was some bunk. It was so comfortable that I went to sleep quicker than Old Shuteye, the Burns stool pigeon, who was supposed to be the miners' checkweighman down at the Indiana Number 3.

And I had one of the finest dreams that was ever produced by a Welch rabbit.

∘   ∘   ∘

I was floatin' up thru a pinkish sort of sky with a feelin' of easy gracefulness like that displayed by the choir leader of United Presbyterian Church.

I flitted hither and thither and I thinks to myself—"This system of ramblin' around sure is keen. Wonder why I never thought of it before."

By and by I came to a landin'. It looked just like a chunk out of the West Kootenais—anywheres away up in the hills above timber line. A lot of rocky bluffs and a little level piece with thick mountain grass springin' up.

I strolled along but my hat blew off and I had to chase it and push it down solidly. I wondered if it would leave a red crease across my forehead.

Suddenly I was in a field of mountain blossoms and ahead of me was a big gate like they have in Garfield Park in Chicago—all built up out of flowers and trailing vines and hedges.

I started to walk thru when a funny old guy, with a beard like a Jewish rabbi, bounced out and wiggled his beard at me.

"Who are you?" he asked sadly, like an employment clerk during hard times.

"Tightline Johnson," said I.

"Look him up in the book," he sang over his shoulder to a couple of skinny lookin' angels who were sittin' on tall stools and were draped over a slant topped desk.

I stood and gawped about me. It was a funny lookin' dump. Little paths run every which way between small grass plots. They were made out of black sand just like I had shoveled up on the Stikine in British Columbia when I was muckin' the stuff into placer cradles for the Guggenheims.

A little cupid came bouncin' over with a card from an index file in his hand. Old Whiskers looked at it and shook his head.

"Mr. Tightline Johnson," he said, "you have a very bad record. It doesn't seem possible that we can let you into the Kingdom of Heaven. Very black. Very black. You have done so many things that you should not have done. You have neglected so many things that should have been done."

"Break it gently," says I. "When did they cut the wages?"

"In Heaven," he said, "there are no wages. But your case is very doubtful. I can not let you in on my own authority. You must come before the judgment throne."

"That's all right," says I. "Lead me up to the squeeze. I never liked to talk to straw bosses anyway."

The fat cupid bounced out with another card in his hand and gave it to me. I looks at it and says to the old fellow who was leadin' me along:

"Say, old timer, was you ever in Butte?"

"That sinful place! Never!"

"Well, don't get peeved. I was just wonderin' where you picked up this rustlin' card idea. I thought that system had been knocked in the head everywhere's except around the copper kings' sweat boxes. Even Gary himself is strong for the idea that each man has a sacred right to work and look for a place if he wants to. Come alive! Your outfit must be way behind the times."

"Hush!" says he, "we approach the presence!"

The old fellow took me before a grandstand bigger than the Stadium of the University of Washington that I once busted fog on. There was thousands of dim white figures sittin' in this grandstand lookin' on. Out in front on a nifty little stage was a big fellow with whiskers and wings and a long flowin' robe.

My conductor left me standin' on one side and went up and whispered in the big fellow's ear. About half a hundred court room hangers-on was sittin' and standin' around and they all give me the once-over with the same kind of expressions that I saw on the faces of a gang of reformers who came thru the Kansas City Can when I was being kept in cold storage there so as not to interfere with the benificent work of the High-jacks. It sure was a wet lookin' outfit. I punches the nearest one in the ribs and asks, "Who is the main push up there anyway?"

"You are now in the presence of the most high God!" says he.

So I looked again.

"Tightline Johnson!" God booms out. "You are here! Advance to the foot of my throne. I would speak with thee."

So I mopes up.

∘   ∘   ∘

"Johnson," he said, in his deep full tones that reminded me of Harry Feinberg singin' love songs in the Tacoma County jail,—"Johnson, I gave to you many gifts. They have been abused. I granted you many instincts. They have been perverted, twisted, crushed, or are still dormant in your breast.

"To you I granted the great instinct of sex.—The record of your life shows much of loose living, of neglect of those love-hungry women who may have longed for consolation and affection. You have produced no children. That instinct which I gave to you, which would have uplifted you into the glory of life and love, you have allowed to drag you into the mire, to torture your nights and to pollute your days.

"I gave you gregariousness so that you might live together with your fellows, leaning upon them and lending them aid in time of social need. I gave you gregariousness so that mankind could live in harmony and peace together,—the common needs of this instinct binding the whole world in chains of interdependence and human love. You have separated yourself from the run of human beings. Along the highways and by-ways of the world you have chosen to live. Far from your kind I have seen you in the hills and mountains,—away from all the average humanity I have seen you with a few of your outcast tribe building camp fires along the sides of city dumps and railroad tracks. I have seen you rambling carelessly with defiant head erect from logging camp to logging camp refusing to settle down in company with your fellows, refusing to hearken to the promptings of sexual and gregarious urges.

"You were sent forth with a soul stored with a measure of self pride in order that you might never demean yourself before your fellow creatures, in order that in every task, in every trial you would always stand forth at the peak of your accomplishment—in the height of your ability and shining glory. Yet I have seen you walk thru the filthy places of the cities clad in rags. I have seen you turn your back on offered positions which would elevate you to posts where you would in a full measure be able to gratify the urges of my great gifts. Rather than ride upon soft cushions you have hung at the peril of your very life upon the rods and the blinds of passenger trains or violated the laws of your fellow men by riding in cars constructed to carry freight.

"Acquisitiveness was given you in order that those things which were deemed worthy might appeal to you and cause you to exert yourself in order to acquire them. This great blessing of mine would have caused you to save the product of your toil, to have labored mightily and with all the cunning of hand and brain in order to gain from the storehouse of nature the wealth that lies there for your kind. What have you cared to acquire? Nothing but hard hands and calloused feet. The joys of accumulation which are known even to the tiny ant and the happy skipping squirrel are passed by untasted by you. You have scorned my gifts!

"That great instinct of workmanship which distinguishes man from most of the beasts has been restrained by you with a throttling hand. You have cast slurs at the joy of creative effort, the pleasant upsurge of pure feeling at a task well done. You have scorned the speedy workman, have abjured the creative instincts and have defied the very well springs of my life-giving and precious offerings! Think you that there is room for you here, Tightline Johnson? No! A thousand times NO!!"

A great silence fell on the assembly.

Thinks I to myself, "Kangarooed again, by God!"

There was a commotion at the entrance to the judgment hall. A tall slender figure clad all in white with hair the soft color of gold and eyes that looked like those of a married man with a family who has just got the sack because he had the guts to carry a red card.

Said he: "Father! Would you cast this fellow worker out, without giving him a chance to speak? Let us ask him why he has done these things. The ways of humans seem strange to us from here, yet I who have been amongst them, am full of compassion for those that err. Pray—let him whose hands and feet are calloused speak, that we may know what is in his heart."

"Johnson!" said God to me. "Have you anything to say for yourself?"

"I've got a mouthful," says I.

° ° °

"When I was just a kid about three times the size of that cherub over there I went to work in a lead smelter. Over in the Coeur d'Alenes. They set me on the feed floor dumpin' charge cars into the furnace. An old Swede was workin' alongside who had been leaded twice. One of his hands was fixed so he could only use the fingers for a hook, from the other one he had the use of three. His feet were lumpy. His knees knocked. The lead had him right. Every move was a squeak. He was done.

"The only thing that Swede ever thought about was gettin' a few dollars to get out of that lead poisonin'. And he worked—like a fool.

"At every pay day the company men would coax him into the bar and have one drink before he left. 'Come on, you old Scandahoovian grave cheater!—Have one on me,' they would say. 'Hell, there is many a wallop in the old boy yet—Hey?'

"For Andy Anderson was a man that knew charges. The smell of the smoke told him more than a chemist would ever find out and the company wanted to keep him, even tho it was killin' him by inches. Other men would not stay with the job, so if they could just keep Andy broke—just get him drunk—the trick was turned.

"Two pay days passed me on the job—interested in the work, tryin' to learn, just achin' to find out the why and how of things. But none of my money went over the bar. I did not spend it with the tin-horns or the chippies that the company brought in to keep us flat. No! I wanted to save my money in that hell hole—so that I could get out and learn something about what makes the wheels go around. I was crazy about machinery. I wanted to study and to have the know. And I was just a kid then, fellow worker.

"Do you think the Idaho Smelters gave a damn about that? What were they thinkin' about me anyway? They seemed to have track of Andy. How about the Kid—Johnson? They had their eye on me all right.

"This outfit run the company store. They sold the tobacco, the clothes, and shoes and operated the saloon. They handed over the booze, they operated the pool tables and over the hill they had the string of crib houses where the girls were brought in about pay day.

"They run the boardin' house—they run everything.

"They had their eyes on me all right. I wasn't spendin' all the money I made. Towards that money I was tighter than alum. You see I had instincts all right and I was tryin'—By God—*I was tryin'*.

"And what did those psalm readin' directors and flunkies of directors do? When they found that I had some money ahead of the game they laid me off for two weeks. Yes, fellow worker—gave me the sack for fourteen days so that I would have to spend my money either in camp with the company or on the road lookin' for another job, and jobs was hard them days.

"Was you ever turned loose in a smelter camp with nothin' to do for fourteen days but wait till your lay off was over? Did you ever get up in a smelly dirty bunkhouse out of a tier of bunks three high, along a wall where twenty-one men slept—seven men lengthwise and three deep? Did you ever listen thru a long night to men with the lead eatin' into their lungs and hear 'em spit out on the floor—a chunk of lung each crack? Would it drive you to drink or wouldn't it, now—I ask you straight?

"Well, it didn't drive me! I was young and I was determined that I would save money and get out to where I could learn something else than to mix a charge car by the smell of the smoke. I didn't want to have my fingers curl up in me! I didn't want to have dagger pains in every joint of my body till they reached my heart and stopped the works!

"And neither did Andy. I went back on the floor with Andy when my time was up and I still had money ahead. I still was holdin' out on the company—and they knew it.

"Two weeks after I went back to work we was paid off again. I had nothin' comin' for they took it out for my board. Andy was decoyed and tanked up again. Oh! Yes! I saw the whole thing—and I couldn't help it. But next night when Andy and I came on the Graveyard shift together I turned double trick, for the old man was down and out. Sweatin' and puffin' I pushed the buggies for both of us.

"At three o'clock in the mornin' I knocked off to throw in a gulp of black coffee and a couple of bites of sinker from my lump. When I came back on the feed floor Andy was gone. And I knew that Andy had taken his last big smell of the smoke. Leanin' over into the charge I could see an outline of his bones down below in the colored flames.

"I ran like mad to the furnace boss. But he said he dassent blow out the furnace. So at the last the company got back even the lead that had been eatin' into Andy's bones and playin' tag thru Andy's veins.

"I could never face a feed floor again. I was done.

*   *   *

"Before I got another job I was flat broke. Could I write home and tell my mother that I was already a bum beatin' my way on freight cars to every place where I heard of a job? I ask you, fellow worker, could you do that?

"When after many months I did get some money —after I did find a place in the damnable profit makin' machinery of business and sent for her— she was dead!

"Died of a broken heart, they said, while I was grabbin' armfuls of box cars lookin' for a job— at anything, for anything—except chargin' a lead furnace.

"Did that ever happen to you? Was you ever in a fix like that? Better think it over, fellow worker —seems like somethin' was wrong. Some said— hard luck. But I cut my eye teeth on that hard luck —I seen it from every side. It is worse than that.

"I had an instinct of solidarity! I had a feelin' swell up inside me at a job well done. And it was these feelin's that made a rebel out of me. I want to show my solidarity to my fellow workers at every chance by puttin' my shoulder to the wheel and helpin' them to make things better so that no other kid will have to go thru the mill that me and millions more like me has bucked up against. I got enough workmanship in me to know that a system that is slung together in such a haywire manner has had some damn poor mechanics on the job.

"I am Tightline Johnson and any bull of the woods will tell you that Tightline may be a hard-boiled wobbly but he wears no chinwhiskers as a fog buster and can handle a yarder with any man that walks on two legs. Just ask 'em and see. And what I can do with a yarder in the way of nursin' it along and makin' the parts run easy and smooth, me and the rest of us wobs has been tryin' to do with the system of production and distribution of the things we make.

"Because I am a rebel against the slave-drivin' system that takes all that a man produces and gives him no chance in life unless he lines up and fights—because I have shown my fellow workers how and why to line up—they have made an out-cast and an outlaw out of me. Every gunman's hand is against me. Every scab and fink hates me and all that are like me.

"They have kept me on the bum. They have driven me from camp to camp—blacklisting my name from Ketchikan to Eureka, Calif. They have thrown me into jails—hunted for me with ropes in their hands—hired an army of stoolpigeons and spies to sneak out the secrets of my organization when we have no secrets to hide. They have sent hundreds of my best friends and the whitest men that were ever born—have sent them into prison because they have ideals.

"I ask you is a man who is living such a life and fighting such a battle in a position to take on a wife? Can one whose very freedom is in jeopardy every day and every hour bring peace and happiness into a love life? Is it treating a girl fair to call up in her the tender feelings of love only to tear her heart to bits with fear and perhaps leave her weepin' with the little ones when they send you to the big house?

"I never walked a dirty street by choice. I never went into a brothel by preference.

"I have trembled at the thought of a sweet woman's arms clasped about me in love. I have stood with my throat choked with a string of burning lumps—outside of some bourgeois's home, and watched a while the antics of the clean children playin' on the lawn.

"You sit up there and tell me I am not wanted! You sit up there and say that I am a waster of my natural gifts! How would you act and what would you do? Just answer me that!"

And do you know the old geezer broke down and cried like a baby.——

* * *

And when I woke up it was mornin'

Chapter 4

Soapbox Militants: Free Speech Campaigns 1908-1916

"Foot loose rebels . . . come at once to defend the Bill of Rights." Such a call went out in the fall of 1909 from I.W.W. organizers in Missoula, Montana, a small, attractive university town midway between lumber and mining areas in the western part of the state.

The Missoula free speech fight was one of about thirty such struggles conducted by the I.W.W. from 1907 to 1916. Wobblies campaigned for the right to agitate on city streets, not to defend a constitutional principle or to attract publicity, but to publicize extortionist practices of labor agents and to recruit members in the "slave market" sections of cities where migrants gathered between jobs. Their soapbox speeches sounded seditious, unpatriotic, immoral, and threatening to business and commercial circles, and municipal authorities were quick to pass ordinances prohibiting I.W.W. speech-making on the streets.

Such was the case in Missoula when the city council aimed to squelch I.W.W. activities by making street speaking illegal. In answer, hundreds of Wobblies arrived by boxcar to assert their rights to free speech on soapboxes and street corners throughout the town. Soon the crowded jails clogged municipal machinery, and high costs of supporting extra police and extra prisoners led harassed town officials to rescind the ordinance and release the Wobblies. A pattern had developed, as historian Paul Brissenden points out, of "sullen nonresistance on the part of the Wobblies, and of wholesale jailings by authorities."[1]

Across the country the boldness and intransigence of the rebels exasperated town officials, aroused wrath and frequent violence from respectable town burghers, and frequently turned the free speech campaigns into bitter, bloody fights. To the Wobblies, however, the free speech campaigns were a unique direct action technique, a means of educating workers to the class struggle, and a practical necessity in countering community opposition to organizing the One Big Union.

The Missoula victory was a prelude to the I.W.W.'s major free speech fight in Spokane the following year. Spokane was in the center of the "Inland Empire" of eastern Washington and western Idaho, a region rich in agriculture, mining, and lumber. The most pressing grievance of the thousands of migratory workers who shipped out of Spokane was the way they were fleeced by employment sharks.

Beginning in 1908, I.W.W. organizers mounted soapboxes directly in front of Spokane employment agencies and urged workers, "Don't buy jobs." They crusaded for a boycott of agencies and demanded that employers hire directly through the union hall.

In turn, the employment firms organized themselves into the Associated Agencies of Spokane which pressured the city council to ban all street meetings after January 1, 1909. For a time the I.W.W. obeyed the ordinance which was applied to other organizations as well. When the ruling was amended to exempt religious groups such as the Salvation Army, the Wobblies decided to fight back.

On October 28, after I.W.W. organizer Jim Thompson was arrested for soapboxing, the *Industrial Worker* sent out a call, "Wanted—Men to Fill the Jails of Spokane." A follow-up letter was sent to all I.W.W. locals: "November 2nd. Free Speech Day. All lovers of free speech are asked to be in readiness to be in Spokane on that date. . . . It is of course needless to add that the meetings will be orderly and no irregularities of any kind will be tolerated."[2]

A five-month campaign defying the street ban began November 2, 1909. On that day, thousands of Wobblies marched from the I.W.W. hall on Front Avenue to court mass arrest.

Speaker after speaker mounted soapboxes to say "Fellow Workers," before being pulled down by the police, arrested, charged with disorderly conduct, and lodged for thirty days in jail. Frank Little, an I.W.W. organizer who had also been in Missoula, was sentenced to thirty days at the rock pile for reading the Declaration of Independence from a platform. Not all the I.W.W. members were able speakers. Many suffered from stage fright. A story is told about the Wobbly who stood on the soapbox, started, "Fellow Workers," and then in panic yelled, "Where are the cops!"[3]

By the second day, at least 150 Wobblies were in prison. By the end of the month, over 600 were herded in crowded cells on rations of bread and water. When they protested, the police closed all ventilation in the jail and turned on the steam heat. Bill Haywood later told a 1914 Senate Investigating Committee that several died from first being put into the "hot box" and then, while in a weakened conditioned, third-degreed in ice-cold cells.[4]

When the jail became full, an abandoned, unheated schoolhouse was used as a prison. The *Spokane Press* reported:

Members of the I.W.W. who are confined in the Franklin School as prisoners were marched to the central police station yesterday for their bath. Word of their coming spread, and crowds of people lined Front Avenue, intent on getting a view of the men. On their return, the crowd had increased and citizens bombarded the prisoners with a shower of sandwiches wrapped in paper, oranges, apples, and sacks of tobacco.[5]

The chief of police arrived to confiscate the food, and the men returned to their prison rations of half a loaf of bread a day and no smokes.

Police brutality and treatment of the prisoners aroused protest from the community and throughout the state. All goods coming from Spokane were boycotted by the Coeur d'Alene district of the Western Federation of Miners. The Socialist Party of Washington issued a report condemning police brutality. The A.F.L. Spokane Central Labor Council unanimously voted to demand a repeal of the street ban ordinance.

One after another, eight editors of the Spokane *Industrial Worker* got out an issue and were arrested. The *Industrial Worker* was moved to Seattle after police confiscated all the copies of the December 10 issue in which I.W.W. organizer Elizabeth Gurley Flynn, who had tried to delay her arrest by chaining herself to a lamp post, reported that the sheriff used the women's section of the jail as a brothel, with the police procuring customers and the sheriff pocketing the profits.

Early in March 1910 the struggle concluded when the mayor and law-enforcement officials, tired of using tax money to pay over $1000 a week to maintain extra police and prisoners, agreed to negotiate with an I.W.W. committee. They recognized the organization's right to rent a hall, publish a newspaper, and organize through street meetings. The free speech prisoners were released. The licenses of nineteen of the most notorious employment agencies were subsequently revoked and later investigations into the practices of employment agencies led to regulatory legislation.

Between 1909 and 1913, there were at least twenty major I.W.W. free speech fights throughout the country. All of them involved the right of the organization to recruit members at street meetings. The most important of these was in Fresno, California, where Frank Little, a veteran of the Missoula and Spokane free speech struggles, had organized a new local of unskilled fruit workers in the San Joaquin Valley.

According to the December 31, 1910, issue of the *Oakland World*, trouble started in Fresno when a contractor who found difficulty getting enough low-paid workers to construct a dam outside the city, complained to the Fresno chief of police that his labor shortage was due to I.W.W. agitators. Alarmed by the presence of Wobblies in the community, the *Fresno Herald and Democrat* wrote: "For men to come here with the express purpose of creating trouble, a whipping post and a cat-o'-nine tails well seasoned by being soaked in salt water is none too harsh a treatment for peace breakers."[6]

In May 1910, Frank Little reported to the *Industrial Worker* that police were breaking up I.W.W. meetings and arresting members on charges of vagrancy. Three months later when Little was arrested and put in jail on a twenty-five-day sentence of bread and water, he telegraphed the national office in Chicago to send help for a free speech campaign.

"Foot loose rebels" from all parts of the country arrived to test the ban on street speaking and fill the jails. Over 150 Wobblies rode the rails from Portland to the Oregon–California state line, and then to avoid arrest by railroad police, left the train to walk the rest of the way to Fresno through a snowstorm in the Siskiyou Mountains. The St. Louis *Globe Democrat* reported that an army of 100 unemployed men had left that city to march on Fresno and expected their forces to number about 1000 when they reached California. The *Denver Post* wrote in February that plans had been made in Colorado to recruit 5000 men to start for Fresno in the spring.

As the San Francisco *Call* of March 2, 1911, stated about the Fresno struggle:

> It is one of those strange situations which crop up suddenly and are hard to understand. Some thousands of men, whose business it is to work with their hands, tramping and stealing rides, suffering hardships and facing dangers—to get into jail. And to get into that one particular jail in a town of which they have never heard before, in which they have no direct interest.[7]

The Fresno jail was filled with singing, shouting rebels. At one point, to protest their bread and water diet, the Wobblies staged a soapbox demonstration through the bars of their cells, addressing an audience that had congregated outside the prison. They took turns lecturing about the class struggle and leading the singing of Wobbly songs. When they refused to stop, the jailor sent for fire department trucks and ordered the fire hoses turned full force on the prisoners. The men used their mattresses as shields, and quiet was only restored when the icy water reached knee-high in the cells.

The threat of the arrival of thousands more free speech volunteers terrified the city officials into rescinding the ban on street speaking in March 1911. The prisoners were released in small groups every few hours. They made their ways to Wobbly headquarters, collected their belongings, and went to look for jobs outside the city. Few stayed around to exercise their rights to speak on the streets. They left Fresno singing a new verse to "Hallelujah, I'm a Bum":

> Springtime has come and I'm just out of jail
> Without any money, without any bail.[8]

A few months after the Fresno prisoners were released, employers in San Diego presented a petition to their city council to prohibit street meetings and speeches in the business district of that city. In January 1912, following a period of hysteria over the dynamiting of the anti-union Los Angeles *Times* and the courtroom confession of the McNamara brothers, the San Diego council banned street speaking in the midtown district.

On the day the ordinance became effective, over 2000 members of a newly formed Free Speech League composed of anarchists, socialists, I.W.W. members, single taxers, and some A.F.L. union members paraded through the San Diego business district to defy the ban. Within the week, several hundred were in jail, charged with having violated the ruling. The March 4, 1912, issue of the *San Diego Tribune* called for the shooting or hanging of all men in the jails which, they claimed, "would end the trouble in an hour."[9] Fire department hoses were used to disperse a street meeting held in front of the prison on March 10 to protest the inhuman treatment of the jailed free speech volunteers. Arrests continued as new arrivals to the city—some 5000 in the next few months—took up the cudgels to intensify defiance.

Besides the intimidation of the prisoners inside the jails, local businessmen organized vigilante committees which terrorized community leaders sympathetic to the free speech campaign. In collusion with the police, the vigilantes would seize prisoners released from jail in the evening, load them into cars, drive out of town, and after beating and clubbing them, warn them not to return to San Diego. The editor of the *San Diego Herald* who opposed these actions was also kidnapped at night by vigilantes and beaten outside the city limits. *Solidarity* published the sworn affidavits of some of these victims. I.W.W. member John Stone testified that on March 22, 1912, after being arrested and detained at the police station for ten hours, he was released at midnight, and forced into a waiting automobile:

We were taken out of the city, about twenty miles, where the machine stopped. Then one of the escorts said to me, "Look at me, who are you?" At the same time, a man in the rear struck me with a blackjack several times on the head and shoulders; the other man then struck me on the mouth with his fist. The men in the rear then sprang around and kicked me in the stomach. I then started to run away; and heard a bullet go past me. I stopped at about a hundred feet and turned around. . . . Joseph Marko, whom they started to beat up . . . stood in the light coming from the second machine. I saw him knocked to the ground several times, and he gave several loud screams. He shortly after came up to where we were and we . . . hid in a little gully close by until the machine went by us. After which we returned and camped for the night under a large tree close to where we had been assaulted. In the morning, I examined Joe Marko's condition and found that the back of his head had been split open and a large amount of blood had flowed to such an extent as to cover his coat, vest, and shirt with blood.[10]

Anarchist Emma Goldman, who came to San Diego to lecture during this time, reported:

The Vigilantes raided the I.W.W. headquarters, broke up the furniture, and arrested a large number of men found there. They were taken to Sorrento to a place where a flag pole had been erected. There the I.W.W.'s were forced to kneel, kiss the flag, and sing the national anthem. As the incentive to quicker action, one of the vigilantes would slap them on the back which was a signal for a general beating. After these proceedings, the men were loaded into automobiles and set to San Onofre, near the county line, placed in a cattle-pen with armed guards over them, and kept without food or drink for eighteen hours. The following morning they were taken out in groups of five and compelled to run the gauntlet. As they passed between the double line of vigilantes, they were belabored with clubs and blackjacks. Then the flag-kissing episode was repeated, after which they were told to "hike" up the track and never come back. They reached Los Angeles after a tramp of several days, sore, hungry, penniless, and in a deplorable physical state.[11]

Miss Goldman's anarchist companion, Dr. Ben Reitman, was tarred and feathered by San Diego vigilantes who stuffed filth in his ears and nose, tore off his clothes and burned the letters I.W.W. into his back with a lighted cigarette.

In response to demands from several California organizations to investigate the charges of vigilante activity, Governor Hiram Johnson sent businessman Colonel Harris Weinstock to San Diego. City officials refused to cooperate with the investigation. Nevertheless, based on hearings held in April, Weinstock reported: "Local commercial bodies have encouraged and applauded the acts of these so-called vigilantes."[12] Testimony revealed "needless brutality on the part of police officers." Many I.W.W. members and sympathizers "had been taken out of the city . . . and there subjected to an inhuman beating by a body of men part of whom were police officers, part constables, and part private citizens."[13]

Weinstock called attention to the "passive resistance" of the protesters and the lack of violence or drunkenness among the I.W.W. members. Governor Johnson issued a statement supporting Weinstock's report and sent the California district attorney to San Diego to enforce the law. No prosecutions of the vigilantes were made.

Gradually, the free speech prisoners were released from jail. A smallpox epidemic hit the city prison in June, and some of the men were given short sentences in the county jail. Others were released on parole. Throughout the summer of 1912 there was a drop in violence directed at the I.W.W. members, and by September 1912 the I.W.W. held its first undisturbed rally since the beginning of the San Diego campaign. It was a meeting to protest the imprisonment of I.W.W. leaders Joe Ettor and Arturo Giovannitti jailed in Lawrence, Massachusetts, during an I.W.W. strike of textile workers 3000 miles away.

A decade of free speech fights came to a dramatic climax in the tragedy of November 5, 1916, in Everett, Washington, where the I.W.W. had been agitating along with striking sawmill workers of the Shingle Weavers Union. When the I.W.W. organizers opened a hall in Everett, a port city on Puget Sound, the city's sheriff and local police responded with savage opposition. I.W.W. soapboxers were arrested, beaten, and deported from town, many with broken limbs and internal injuries.

On October 30, forty-one Wobblies, mostly young loggers and lumberjacks, arrived by boat from Seattle I.W.W. headquarters, intending to lend support for the free speech crusade. Sheriff McRae and his deputies rounded them up at the Everett docks, drove them to a park on the outskirts of town, and forced them to run the gauntlet between rows of deputies who beat them with spiked bats. Everett citizens were shocked at the amount of dried blood found on the grass the following morning. A public protest rally addressed by Wobbly organizer Jim Thompson attracted 2000 sympathetic townspeople who felt that Sheriff McRae had gone too far.

On November 5, 1916, a delegation of 250 singing Wobblies left Seattle for Everett on a regular passenger boat, the "Verona." An additional group of I.W.W. members, plus other passengers, boarded a second boat, the "Calista," which also sailed regularly between the two cities. As the "Verona" approached the Everett docks with the Wobbly passengers singing "Hold the Fort," shooting broke out from Pier Two, where Sheriff McRae and some 200 armed vigilantes had been tipped off to the boat's arrival by Pinkerton agents in Seattle. Shooting continued for about ten minutes. At least five I.W.W. members were killed and thirty-one were wounded; it was said that additional bodies were later found washed up on a nearby beach. The toll for the Everett vigilantes: nineteen wounded and two dead.

The "Verona," sailing back to Seattle, warned the second ship to return. At the Seattle docks, nearly all the Wobblies on both boats were arrested. Seventy-four were charged with the murders of the Everett vigilantes and secretly removed at night from Seattle to the Everett county jail.

The two-month trial which began in March 1917 focused on the inflammatory propaganda of the I.W.W. as well as on Tom Tracy, the first of the defendants, who was charged with firing the first shot from the "Verona." The I.W.W. defense lawyer demanded a reenactment on the Everett docks of the November 5 tragedy. This demonstrated that it was impossible to identify any passenger from the shore and, furthermore, that the Everett vigilantes, milling around the piers, were likely to have been in each other's line of fire. The court acquitted Tracy and released the seventy-three other defendants.

The Tracy trial was won in the courts but lost in the press. Wobbly propaganda, submitted as evidence by the prosecution, produced community shivers, newspaper headlines, and still another public picture of I.W.W. members as furtive bomb-throwing anarchists. The news of the trial swept the fear of internal violence onto the doorsteps of many American communities and presented an image of a domestic enemy attacking American values of industrial peace and property. A decade of vigorous, uncompromising I.W.W. free speech activity ended as America entered the war to battle kaiserism in Europe and radicalism in its own backyard.

1

John Panzner (1883–   ), a retired automobile worker, wrote these memoirs for the Writer's Group Journal *(September 1959), issued by the West Side U.A.W. Retired Workers' Center in Detroit. Panzner, a sheet-metal worker who joined the I.W.W. in San Francisco in 1905, was a national organizer for the I.W.W., active in recruiting Northwest lumberjacks, and a strike leader of the Minnesota miners in the Mesabi Range in 1916. Following his 1923 release from Leavenworth Penitentiary, where he served a five-year sentence with other I.W.W. defendants convicted of violating the Federal Espionage Law, Panzner returned to his birthplace, Detroit. He joined the U.A.W. in 1933, was secretary-treasurer of the Hupp Local, and retired in 1952 from the Chevrolet plant and U.A.W. Local 235.*

THE SPOKANE FREE SPEECH FIGHT — 1909

By JOHN PANZNER

Before telling you the story of the Spokane free speech fight, I must say a few words about the situation in the west at that time. West of the Mississippi River, there were about two million migratory workers, sometimes called hobos. They harvested the wheat, corn, hay and picked the fruit and even planted most of the crops. They built railroads, dams, powerhouses. They did the logging in the woods.

The employers were ruthless. The conditions on the job were bad. You had to bring your own blankets, sleep in tents or bunk houses and many of them were full of lice and bed bugs. Cockroaches were in the cook houses and kitchens. Most of the men did not stay long on the job, and when the jobs were finished, thousands were laid off. So you see there always was a big unemployed army, floating from job to job or looking for a job, or waiting for a new job to open up. They had no families. Most of them did not belong to any church. They did not stay long enough in any town so that they could register and vote. They were considered outcasts in the community. Only when labor was badly needed were they welcomed.

The AFL trade unions were strong in the big cities like San Francisco, but no attempts were made to organize these nomads. The only exceptions were the small mining camps where the Western Federation of Miners were well organized. They had higher wages, better living conditions, and more freedom or civil rights because they had been organized long enough and had the power. So the IWW tried to organize these migratory workers into industrial unions instead of trade unions. Because they had low wages, we had to charge low dues. The human material was good, but the odds were against us. When you slept and ate on the company property, you had no civil rights.

In Spokane, Washington, we had a hall and four local unions. There was a street full of employment offices where the employment shark would sell you a job for a dollar. The lumberjacks, construction workers and agricultural workers would come to town and spend their money in the red light districts, saloons, restaurants and lodging houses. When they got broke or nearly broke, they would try to get another job.

It was hard and dangerous to go on company property to get new members. The easiest way to get new members was by holding street meetings. Some time in 1908, the city government stopped all street meetings. The case was taken to court by the local unions, but the judge pigeon-holed the case, so in the fall of 1909, the local unions planned to win free speech by direct action.

The plan was to call for volunteers to speak on the streets in violation of the city ordinance. If we were arrested, we would go to jail until all of the jails were full. A joint meeting of the four locals was held and a committee of ten was selected from the floor of the meeting. These ten went into the office of the secretary and picked a committee of five to be the fighting committee.

They in turn each picked one alternate to take their place in case of arrest. The alternates were to appoint other alternates. All names were to be kept secret. Every five or ten volunteers would go on the streets and speak. When they were arrested, they would go before the judge, plead guilty and go to prison.

It was about in November of 1909, that Walter T. Nef and I jumped a freight train in Portland, Oregon, and we got there in time for the meeting. I was put on the fighting committee.

It must have been the month of November, 1909 when Nef and I arrived in Spokane, because the struggle went on all winter. At one time, we had the city jail, the county jail, the Franklin School House full, and a United States' fort had eighty-five prisoners in it. The rank and file who spoke on the streets got thirty days for violation of the city ordinance, the leaders got six months in the county jail under the state conspiracy law.

We made no effort to keep out of jail. Our aim was to fill the jails, so when the judge would ask us if we were on the committee, we would gladly admit it. The police closed our hall and confiscated our weekly newspaper, the *Industrial Worker*.

While awaiting for our trial in the city jail, the state prisoners were put in one row of cells on one side of the cell block, and the city prisoners, who were convicted for speaking on the streets, were across the hallway on the other side of the cell block. They were starting to serve their thirty day sentences, but they refused to go out and work on the rock pile, so they were put on "bread and water" and kept locked in their cells.

We, who were the leaders awaiting trial were being fed "steak and fried potatoes" and other such foods, so we the leaders went on a "hunger strike." It took a lot of will power, but when they brought our food, we threw it out through the bars on the floor of the hallway. There were steaks, potatoes, bread, coffee and tin plates and cups all over the floor.

After eight days of the hunger strike, the outside committee sent word that we must stop the hunger strike because some of us were getting sick. A few die-hards held out for thirteen days.

As soon as we were tried under the state conspiracy law, we were given six months each and sent to the county jail. One of the characters in the free speech fight was a young man who came there as a reporter for a Seattle weekly paper, the official organ of the United Wage Workers

Party of the state of Washington. This was a splinter group that had left the Socialist Party. His name was William Z. Foster. He joined the IWW, spoke on the street and was sentenced to thirty days in jail. He served his term in the Franklin School House on bread and water. A German society offered the IWW the use of the German Turner Hall and defied the police to close up the hall.

Our committee sent to Chicago to the general headquarters for an out-state speaker for a meeting in the Turner Hall. They sent a beautiful Irish girl. Her name was Elizabeth Gurly Flynn. She had just married a guy by the name of Jones, the head of the Dill Pickle Club in Chicago.

Private invitations were sent out for the meeting in the Turner Hall, thus making it a private meeting and not public. They did not raid the meeting, but arrested our speaker after the meeting. The Women's Club of Spokane was aroused. They raised $5,000 for bail and got her out. Her case never came to trial. Public opinion began to turn. The newspapers claimed that one of our members was clubbed to death in his cell by the police. The powerful German Society and the Women's Club were on our side.

After we had been in the county jail about four months, the city government made an offer which was a big victory for us. We were to be allowed four street corners for meetings. All the police department asked was that we give them notice when and where the meetings were to be held.

The mayor released all of the city prisoners at once, but we were in the county jail and had to wait a few days until the governor's pardon arrived. Everything seem peaceful in Spokane after the free speech fight was over, but when I got back to Portland, Oregon, the headlines in the papers said that the Chief of Police Sullivan had been slain by someone with a shotgun on the porch of his home.

The papers tried to blame the IWW, but to our surprise, Judge Mann who had sentenced us, defended the IWW and said he knew they did not do it, that the chief had many enemies. The murder was never solved. Thus ends the story of one of the many free speech fights in the United States.

2

This account of the march on Fresno, California, made by I.W.W. members from the Pacific Northwest who were determined to take part in the Fresno free speech campaign, was printed in Solidarity (April 8, 1911). Nothing is known about its author, E. M. Clyde.

THE MARCH ON FRESNO

Graphic Account of the Free Speech Invasion From the North

Solidarity:

Acting under instructions of a committee composed of the following members of the "Fresno Relief Brigade"—Fred Meyer of L. U. 178, Tom Pearson of 434, C. F. Miller of 432, E. M. Clyde of 432, C. W. Mison a non-member, I herewith submit a report covering the most essential features of the celebrated "march on Fresno."

On the evening of Feb. 13, 1911, 47 men left Seattle bound for Fresno to assist the fellow workers who were contesting for the right to speak upon the street of that city. We were joined by others along the way, so on leaving Portland on the 15th we numbered 112, two having left us here to go by boat. About 20 of this number were members of the Socialist Party, and a very few were members of no organization.

We came from Seattle to Portland in different groups and some encountered considerable difficulty in getting over the road so we concluded that in the future we would remain in one body.

We organized ourselves and elected an executive committee with supervisory powers, a secretary-treasurer to receive and disburse all money, a committee on trains whose duty was to learn the most suitable trains to ride, running time, etc. Their usefulness suddenly ceased at Ashland, Ore., however.

We had our cook with assistants; we had a well organized police system with Joe Risik of L. U. 92 as chief, but the most important department of all was no doubt our hospital corps which we organized at Hornbrook, Calif. S. Mortimer of L. U. 380 made a most efficient Chief Medical Director, as he has spent many years in hospital service, and the success of the trip was due in a great measure to the able manner in which he cared for the sick and disabled. He at all times carried a medicine chest supplied with the ordinary remedial agents such as bandages, liniments, caustics, antiseptics, sterilizers, etc. The doctor was the busiest man of the entire party and the attention given the sick was equal or even superior to that received in many hospitals. The hospital also included 10 men who brought up the rear to see that no one should be left unaided should they become exhausted.

At Ashland, Oregon, Feb. 17th, the S. P. railroad refusing to permit us to ride further, we began our memorable march which ended at Chico, Calif., March 7th.

The distance covered on foot was 244 miles. On passing over the Siskiyou mountains we reached an elevation of 4,000 feet and broke a trail through 3 feet of snow over the State road into Hornbrook. On this trip one of our party (the operator) had his feet so badly frozen that it became necessary to send him to the hospital.

Getting over this hill we encountered no more snow until we reached Weed. At Steinman in the Siskiyous and at Weed we were compelled to spend the night by campfires on the side hill where the ground was covered with snow. Sleep, or even rest, was impossible.

At Sisson the elevation is 3,554 feet, and the snow was deeper than at any other place. Here we were picked up by the May Roberts Theatrical Co., and our fares were paid into Dunsmuir, 14 miles, where we attended the show in a body and were supplied with coffee and sandwiches at the expense of Miss Roberts. She had our pictures taken with her troupe and the R. R. and city police in the group. Later when we met her in Redding she donated $15 to our "jungle" fund.

The police force of the Southern Pacific railroad consists of 120 men which they had scattered along in the towns through which we passed, but as we made them no trouble many of them became quite friendly with us, but they always found that the more questions they asked the less they knew about us.

On March 5 we arrived in Chico where we received the first official notice that the fight had been won. On the 7th we disbanded, as our presence was no longer needed in Fresno.

Yes, we made slow progress during the trip. The pace was set by the rear guard who were determined that no one should be deserted along the way. Some of our number could easily have made 40 or 50 miles a day while it was difficult for others to make 20 and 25 miles.

We held meetings in all the towns along the way and gained the sympathy and assistance of the citizens, who donated money, clothing and food.

We laid great stress upon the eight hour day and made it a feature of the trip. Red Bluff, Calif., was the only town along the line to show a spirit of hostility. At Redding our hostess was Mrs. Clineschmidt, of the Temple Hotel, who fed all of us while there (5 meals) and furnished many with beds for the two nights.

I will not dwell upon the suffering, hardship

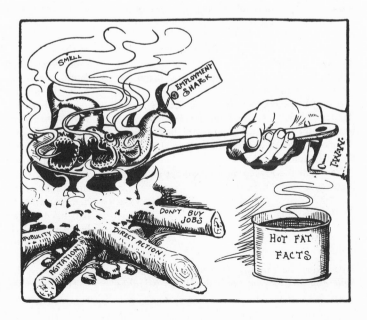

Industrial Worker, April 2, 1910.

and exposure endured, but will simply say that but few of our number were prepared for a trip of this kind. Some were lightly dressed, others nearly barefooted.

Many feet were blistered and bleeding. Over the hills we were hungry, tired and sleepy. Once over the hills it was constantly raining, through which we traveled the last 100 miles.

At no time did we allow strangers to come among us, although they tried to break in on different occasions.

At the time of disbanding we had 96 at the meeting, which was nothing short of marvelous when it is considered that they were brought together on a day's notice and many of them had no previous experience in organizations. This was 16 short of our number on leaving Portland, but a number of those who left us went ahead and reached Fresno.

It has often been asked, "Why did you not split up into small parties so you could ride the trains?" We had before us the fact that many small parties previously trying to make Fresno never reached there. Should we have split up we would not have received the support and assistance of the citizens, the police would have continually arrested and driven us out of the towns. The result would have been that but few would have reached Fresno.

True, there was some friction and dissension among us, but at no time was it permitted to obscure the real purpose of the trip, and each of the 96 expressed regret that we should not continue on into Fresno.

It is impossible for me at this time to give a financial statement, as I have not the books, but approximately $250 was collected and disbursed besides food and clothing.

It may be asked, "Would you undertake a similar trip in the future?" I believe this entire 96 would respond to a call of necessity, but we hope that no such call will be made for trivial or insufficient reasons.

Now that the Fresno fight is won let us all get busy on the eight hour day.

E. M. CLYDE

Seattle, Washington.

3

This article on the 1911 Aberdeen free speech fight appeared in the One Big Union Monthly

(March 1919). In his ninety years "Stumpy" Payne (1869–1963) had been a carpenter, farm hand, farmer, railroad man, and owner of a small stump ranch, as well as I.W.W. organizer and a former editor of the Industrial Worker. *He was the only I.W.W. member who attended both the 1905 founding convention and the I.W.W. convention of 1955. In July 1955 Payne served a six-month term as editor of the* Industrial Worker. *He was eighty-five.*

In a tribute to Payne which appeared in the Industrial Worker *(October 23, 1963) editor Carl Keller wrote: "He was a serious rebel with an amount of dignity and urbanity that was rare. He remained a dedicated Wobbly to the end of his days."*

THE MAINSPRING OF ACTION

By C. E. PAYNE

In the fall of 1911 occurred the Aberdeen, Washington, Free Speech fight. Altho shorter than many of the contests of this character that took place thruout the West shortly before and after that time, it was, while it lasted, one of the most bitterly contested struggles in which the organization took part. Also, it was by all odds the most clean-cut victory that was won by the organization in struggles of this character.

One phase of the fight that has not to my knowledge been touched upon was the psychology of the men who took part in it at the time the final and winning attack was made to regain the use of the streets for purposes of agitation. I had an exceptional opportunity to observe this state of mind, which for a better term may perhaps be properly called a religious fervor.

I had been for some time the secretary for the Free Speech Committee, and had been in the town for about six weeks before the evening of January 10, 1912, when the grand rush was made to use the streets for "free speech." As I had the correspondence of the Committee in hand at the time, I was ordered not to take any part in the demonstration for that night. However, some one had been making it his business to find out my business, and this, together with my interest in the proceedings, made a change in the program, and this change gave me the opportunity to observe this psychological phenomenon.

The demonstration was timed for 6:00 P.M.,

when it was figured the members of the Citizens' Club would be at supper, and it was thought this would give some of the men a chance to make a few minutes' talk before they could be arrested. Fifteen men had been selected to make the first attack. The manner of selecting them was by refusing to permit any one to speak unless he plainly stated that he would speak anyhow, permit or none. The Committee had decided that fifteen should be the number, but seventeen was the number that actually took part in the "speaking."

Wishing to be able to make a first-hand report of what took place on the streets, I went among the crowd, which in a few minutes after six o'clock had grown to some 3,000 persons, all eager to see the demonstration. These were gathered around the principal street corner, but there was no one in the center of the street. By common consent this was left entirely to the participants in the battle.

The first speaker would have been able to hold a crowd with a speech of half an hour or more had he been allowed the time, but he was arrested and hustled off to jail within less than two minutes after he had shouted "Fellow Workers." No sooner had he been taken thru the crowd toward the jail by two members of the Citizens' Club, than another man stepped out from the crowd and began, "Fellow Workers!" This man's voice had the twang of the Down East Yankee, and his bearing was that of a descendant of the Pilgrims of the Mayflower.

Following him came a short, swarthy German, evidently from the Schwartzwald. "Mein Fellow Vorkers! Schust you listen by me vhile I tells you sometings!" But what that "something" was he could not tell before he was seized and hustled in the wake of the other two. After the German came a large, raw-boned Irishman with the brogue of the ould sod thick on his tongue. "Fellow Worrkers! Oi'm not much of a spaker, but Oi don't suppose Oi'll be allowed to talk long, anyhow." That was all the speech he was allowed to make before he too was led away.

Next in line was an Italian who shouted the regular greeting of "Fellow Workers," spoke a few rapid fire words and was taken towards the jail. From another part of the crowd a five-foot man with the unmistakable rolling gait of a sailor sprang to center of the cleared street, shouted "Fellow Workers," and had time enough to make perhaps the longest "speech" of the evening. "I have been run out of this town five times by the Citizens' Club, and every time I have found my way back. This proves conclusively that the world is round." But when he had gone thus far with his remarks he was seized and half carried toward the jail. Behind the sailor came a lumber jack, no talker, but a power in the woods where men hold their place by strength and nerve. "Fellow Workers! There is one of the Citizens' Club fellows over there. He is going to arrest some one." The man pointed out at once made a run for the lumber worker, and he too was taken to jail.

Thus came one after another, made the common salutation of "Fellow Workers," started to talk and generally managed to say but a few words, when he too was hustled to the jail. The entire demonstration was over in less than half an hour and the crowd began to disperse. It was while leaving the scene of the demonstration that I was approached from behind by two men who came one on either side of me, and with the remark, "Oh, say! The chief wants to see you," they led me to the jail.

My arrest was the last one of the night. After being searched and questioned by the police, I was put in the "tank" with the rest of the "free speech fighters." My reception was the heartiest demonstration of welcome I have ever received. Their joy seemed to be combined with an appreciation of the joke on me, but it was none the less hearty.

After the greetings had been made, and things became comparatively quiet, I was able to look about me and see at close range the manner of men they were. Outwardly, they were of the careless, happy-go-lucky sort to whom dolce far niente appeared to be a more appropriate motto than any other that could be selected. Not one had any ties of kindred, job or financial interest in the town. Most of them had never been in the place before. Perhaps a majority never would have been there had not some member of the I.W.W. flashed the word over the country that he and others were denied the rights they claimed. Many of them would never be there again.

Here they were, eighteen men in the vigor of life, most of whom came long distances thru snow and hostile towns by beating their way, penniless and hungry, into a place where a jail sentence was the gentlest treatment that could be expected, and where many had already been driven into the swamps and beaten nearly to death by members of the Citizens' Club for the same offense that they had committed so joyously tonight. All had walked the three miles from Hoquiam in a rain to take part in the demonstration that all confidently felt would mean that they would be sent to jail until midnight, and then be driven into the swamps with clubs and guns, and that perhaps some of them would be killed, as had nearly been the case with others before them. Yet here they were, laughing in boyish glee at tragic things that to them were jokes.

One man said, "This is cold after the orange groves of California." The man he spoke to replied, "It is not as cold as the Canadian railways." One man remarked, "The snow in the Rockies is a fright," to which another replied, "It don't be worse than the Siskyouss."

A ponderous German recited the Marxian battle cry. Two men compared notes on their arrests, and laughed gleefully at some joke on a policeman. One boy who had taken a "vacation" from college to attend the Free Speech fight had composed a "yell," and this was frequently shouted with all their power. "Who are we? I.W.W., don't you see! First in war, first in peace, first in the hands of the Aberdeen police. Rah! Rah!! Rah!!! I.W.W." As the city council had been called into extra session to consider the situation, and their meeting hall was just above the tank where we were locked in, there was always extra emphasis put on the "I.W.W." for their benefit.

But what was the motive behind the actions of these men? Clearly, they would take no part in the social, political or economic life of the town, after the fight was over. No place in the country could treat them worse than Aberdeen was trying to treat them. Why were they here? Is the call of Brotherhood in the human race greater than any fear or discomfort, despite the efforts of the masters of life for six thousand years to root out that call of Brotherhood from our minds? Is there a joy in martyrdom that the human race must sense at times to make its life complete? Must humanity ever depend on the most despised of its members for its most spiritual gifts? Is it among the working class that we may see the fulfillment of the prediction that there shall be no Greek or Barbarian, no Scythian or Parthian, no circumcision or uncircumcision, but all one? These things have I often pondered as the result of the twenty-two hours in the Aberdeen jail.

4

These unsigned verses were printed in the Industrial Worker (*May 1, 1912*).

WE'RE BOUND FOR SAN DIEGO

(*Tune: "The Wearing of the Green"*)

In that town called San Diego when the workers try to talk
The cops will smash them with a say and tell 'em "take a walk."
They throw them in a bull pen, and they feed them rotten beans,
And they call that "law and order" in that city, so it seems.

Chorus

We're bound for San Diego, you better join us now.
If they don't quit, you bet your life there'll be an awful row.
We're coming by the hundreds, will be joined by hundreds more,
So join at once and let them see the workers are all sore.

They're clubbing fellow working men who dare their thoughts express;
And if old Otis has his way, there's sure to be a mess.
So swell this army, working men, and show them what we'll do
When all the sons of toil unite in *One Big Union* true.

We have put the town of Aberdeen with others on our map;
And the brass bound thugs of all of them were handy with the "sap";
But the I.W.W.'s are boys who have no fears
And we'll whip old San Diego if it takes us twenty years.

5

This remarkable speech by I.W.W. member Jack Whyte, immediately after being sentenced to jail during the 1912 San Diego free speech fight, first appeared in Solidarity (*August 24, 1912*). *It was subsequently reprinted several times and quoted*

by J. G. Brooks in American Syndicalism, The
I.W.W. (New York, 1913).

On release from jail, six months later, Whyte
went to Akron, Ohio, where he helped organize
rubber workers during an I.W.W. strike in 1913.
A speaking tour was announced in Solidarity
(June 23, 1913). The article said, "He has a pleas-
ing personality; is young, virile, and full of the
fire of rebellion. While not lacking in enthusiasm,
his speeches are replete with sanity and construction. He makes the workers see the meaning of
industrial organization and its necessity."

"HIS HONOR" GETS HIS

The following is a stenographic report of Jack Whyte's
speech before Judge Sloan, of the superior court of
San Diego County, California, on being asked why
sentence should not be passed. He was fined six
months and is now at San Diego County jail on a bread
and water diet. He is a member of Local 13, I.W.W.,
and was arrested on a conspiracy charge in the recent
San Diego Free Speech Fight.

There are only a few words that I care to say and
this court will not mistake them for a legal argument, for I am not acquainted with the phraseol-
ogy of the bar nor the language common to the
court room.

There are two points which I want to touch
upon—the indictment itself and the misstatement
of the prosecuting attorney. The indictment reads,
"The People of the State of California against
J. W. Wright and Others." It's a hideous lie. The
people in this court room know that it is a lie;
the court itself knows that it is a lie, and I know
that it is a lie. If the people of the state are to
blame for this persecution, then the people are
to blame for the murder of Michael Hoy and the
assassination of Joseph Mikolasek. They are to
blame and responsible for every bruise, every
insult and injury inflicted upon the members of
the working class by the vigilantes of this city.
The people deny it and have so emphatically denied it that Governor Johnson sent Harris Weinstock down here to make an investigation and
clear the reputation of the people of the state of
California from the odor that you would attach
to it. You cowards throw the blame upon the people, but I know who is to blame and I name them
—it is Spreckles and his partners in business and
this court is the lackey and lickspittle of that class,

defending the property of that class against the
advancing horde of starving American workers.

The prosecuting attorney, in his plea to the
jury, accused me of saying on a public platform
at a public meeting, "To hell with the courts, we
know what justice is." He told a great truth when
he lied, for if he had searched the innermost re-
cesses of my mind he could have found that
thought, never expressed by me before, but which
I express now, "To hell with your courts, I know
what justice is," for I have sat in your court room
day after day and have seen members of my class
pass before this, the so-called bar of justice. I
have seen you, Judge Sloane, and others of your
kind, send them to prison because they dared to
infringe upon the sacred rights of property. You
have become blind and deaf to the rights of man to
pursue life and happiness, and you have crushed
those rights so that the sacred right of property
shall be preserved. Then you tell me to respect the
law. I do not. I did violate the law, as I will violate every one of your laws and still come before
you and say, "To hell with the courts," because I
believe that my right to life is far more sacred
than the sacred right of property that you and
your kind so ably defend.

I do not tell you this in the expectation of getting justice, but to show my contempt for the
whole machinery of law and justice as represented
by this and every other court. The prosecutor
lied, but I will accept his lie as a truth and say
again so that you, Judge Sloane, may not be mis-
taken as to my attitude, "To hell with your courts,
I know what justice is."

6

When he wrote this poem which appeared in the
International Socialist Review (February 1917),
Charles Ashleigh was publicity agent for the
I.W.W. Everett Defense Committee. He gave the
oration at the memorial service for the men killed
on board the "Verona."

The song, "Hold the Fort," sung by Wobblies
on the "Verona," has a long history which is traced
by Joe Glazer and Edith Fowke in Songs of Work
and Freedom (Chicago, 1960). The title of the
song comes from a Civil War incident when Union
troops, trapped in a fort near Atlanta, Georgia,
were signaled by flags from mountain to mountain, "General Sherman says hold fast. We are
coming." A popular evangelist, Philip Bliss, used

IS IT ABOUT TO STRIKE?

Industrial Worker, October 1, 1910.

the anecdote as the theme for a gospel hymn he composed in 1870, and another evangelist, Ira Sankey, introduced it to England during a lecture tour a few years later. Late in the nineteenth century, members of the British Transport and General Workers Union wrote a parody of the hymn which they sang during strikes and demonstrations. In this country, members of the Knights of Labor also composed a parody:

> Storm the fort, ye Knights of Labor,
> Battle for your cause;
> Equal rights for every neighbor,
> Down with tyrant laws!

The Wobblies popularized the parody of the hymn written by the British Transport Workers Union, and "Hold the Fort" has since become a well-known union song in this country, included in many labor union songbooks.

EVERETT, NOVEMBER FIFTH°

By CHARLES ASHLEIGH

(". . . And then the Fellow Worker died, singing 'Hold the Fort.' . . ."—From the report of a witness.)

> Song on his lips, he came;
> Song on his lips, he went;—
> This be the token we bear of him,—
> Soldier of Discontent!

Out of the dark they came; out of the night
Of poverty and injury and woe,—
With flaming hope, their vision thrilled to light,—
Song on their lips, and every heart aglow;

They came, that none should trample Labor's right
To speak, and voice her centuries of pain.

Bare hands against the master's armored might!—
A dream to match the tolls of sordid gain!

And then the decks went red; and the grey sea
Was written crimsonly with ebbing life.
The barricade spewed shots and mockery
And curses, and the drunken lust of strife.

Yet, the mad chorus from that devil's host,—
Yea, all the tumult of that butcher throng,—
Compound of bullets, booze and coward boast,—
Could not out-shriek one dying worker's song!

Song on his lips, he came;
Song on his lips, he went;—
This be the token we bear of him,—
Soldier of Discontent!

7

Walker C. Smith, the author of this article which
appeared in the International Socialist Review
(*December 1916*), *was described in the Seattle*
Post Intelligencer (*November 14, 1919*): "*Walker*
C. Smith has been identified with the I.W.W. since
it first began spreading its propaganda in Seattle
and has functioned in all capacities from paper
boy, office clerk, stump speaker, writer and edi-
tor, to acting head of the organization in the
Northwest. A common figure on Washington
Street in the days when soap box oratory was at
its height, he openly led the movement until re-
cent years when war placed the organization in
a belligerent position. . . . Smith was associate
editor of the Industrial Worker, *official organ of*
the I.W.W. for several years, and later became
editor of that publication, holding the position
when the Pigott Printing Concern from which the
paper was being published was wrecked and fur-
ther publication of the paper stopped."
Smith was the author of The Everett Massacre:
A History of the Class Struggle in the Lumber
Industry (*Chicago, 1918*) *and several I.W.W. pam-*
phlets, including Sabotage: Its History, Philosophy, and Function (*Spokane, 1913*) *and* War
and the Workers (*Cleveland, n.d.*).

THE VOYAGE OF THE VERONA

By WALKER C. SMITH

Five workers and two vigilantes dead, thirty-one
workers and nineteen vigilantes wounded, from
four to seven workers missing and probably
drowned, two hundred ninety-four men and three
women of the working class in jail—this is the
tribute to the class struggle in Everett, Wash., on
Sunday, November 5. Other contributions made
almost daily during the past six months have indicated the character of the Everett authorities,
but the protagonists of the open shop and the
antagonists of free speech did not stand forth in
all their hideous nakedness until the tragic trip
of the steamer Verona. Not until then was Darkest Russia robbed of its claim to "Bloody Sunday."

Early Sunday morning on November 5 the
steamer Verona started for Everett from Seattle
with 260 members of the Industrial Workers of
the World as a part of its passenger list. On the
steamer Calista, which followed, were 38 more
I.W.W. men, for whom no room could be found
on the crowded Verona. Songs of the One Big
Union rang out over the waters of Puget Sound,
giving evidence that no thought of violence was
present.

It was in answer to a call for volunteers to enter
Everett to establish free speech and the right to
organize that the band of crusaders were making the trip. They thought their large numbers
would prevent any attempt to stop the street meeting that had been advertised for that afternoon
at Hewitt and Wetmore avenues in handbills previously distributed in Everett. Their mission was
an open and peaceable one.

The Seattle police, knowing that I.W.W. men
had been jailed, beaten and deported from Everett, singly and in crowds, during the past six
months, without committing a single act of personal violence in retaliation, made no attempt to
detain the men, but merely telephoned to the
Everett authorities that a large number had left
for that city. Two Pinkerton detectives were on
board the Verona, according to the police and to
members of the I.W.W. The capitalist press of
Seattle and Everett claim that all the I.W.W. men
were armed "to the teeth." On behalf of the
I.W.W. some have made the counter claim that
the men were absolutely unarmed, as was the
case in all former "invasions." Deputy Prosecuting
Attorney Helsell, King County, who is assisting
the prosecutor of Snohomish County, has stated
in an interview that the number of armed workers was between eighteen and twenty-five. This
would mean that less than ten per cent of the men
were armed even were the higher figure a correct one.

Following the receipt of the telephone message from Seattle, Sheriff Donald McRae cleared the Municipal dock—owned by the city of Everett—of all citizens and employes, and after the erection of a temporary barricade of heavy timbers, the several hundred gunmen, scabs, militiamen, ex-policemen and other open shop supporters who had been deputized to do vigilante duty, were stationed at points commanding any incoming boats. These semi-legalized outlaws were provided with high power rifles, side arms and many rounds of ammunition. It has been reported that a machine gun was in readiness for service on the dock. Scabs located on the Everett Improvement dock, lying to the south of the Municipal dock, also had a part to play. The scene was set, and the tragedy of the Verona was about to be staged.

As the Seattle boat swung up to the wharf shortly before 2 o'clock the I.W.W. men were merrily singing the English Transport Workers' strike song, "Hold the Fort":

> We meet today in Freedom's cause,
>   And raise our voices high,
> We'll join our hands in union strong,
>   To battle or to die.

Chorus

> Hold the fort for we are coming,
>   Union men be strong.
> Side by side we battle onward,
>   Victory will come.

> Look, my comrades, see the union
>   Banners waving high.
> Reinforcements now appearing,
>   Victory is nigh.

> See our numbers still increasing;
>   Hear the bugle blow,
> By our union we shall triumph
>   Over every foe.

> Fierce and long the battle rages,
>   But we will not fear.
> Help will come when'er it's needed,
>   Cheer, my comrades, cheer!

When the singers, together with the other passengers, crowded to the rail so they might land the more quickly, Sheriff McRae called out to them:

"Who is your leader?"

Immediate and unmistakable was the answer from every I.W.W.:

"We are all leaders!"

Angrily drawing his gun from its holster and flourishing it in a threatening manner, McRae cried:

"You can't land here."

"Like hell we can't!" came the reply from the men as they stepped toward the partly thrown off gang plank.

A volley of shots sent them staggering backward and many fell to the deck. The waving of McRae's revolver evidently was the prearranged signal for the carnage to commence.

The few armed men on board, according to many of the eye-witnesses, then drew revolvers and returned the fire, causing consternation in the ranks of the cowardly murderers barricaded on the dock. Until the contents of their revolvers were exhausted the workers stood firm. They had no ammunition in reserve. The unarmed men sought cover but were subjected to a veritable hail of steel jacketed soft-nosed bullets from the high power rifles of the vigilantes. The sudden rush to the off-shore side of the boat caused it to list to about thirty degrees. Bullets from the dock to the south and from the scab tugboats moored there apparently got in their destructive work, for a number of men were seen to fall overboard and the water was reddened with their blood. No bodies were recovered when the harbor was dragged the next day. On the tugboat Edison, the scab cook, a mulatto, fired shot after shot with careful and deadly aim at the men on the off-shore side of the boat, according to the Pacific Coast Longshoreman, the official I.L.A. paper. This man had not even a deputy badge to give a semblance of legality to his murders. That the gunmen on the two docks and on the scab boats were partly the victims of their own cross fire is quite likely.

After ten minutes of steady firing, during which hundreds of rounds of ammunition were expended, the further murder of unarmed men was prevented by the action of Engineer Ernest Skelgren, who backed the boat away from the dock with no pilot at the wheel. The vigilantes kept up their gunfire as long as the boat was within reach.

On a hilltop overlooking the scene thousands

Industrial Worker, December 8, 1910.

of Everett citizens witnessed the whole affair. The consensus of their opinion is that the vigilante mob started the affair and are wholly responsible.

Many angry citizens made demonstrations against the vigilantes as they left the dock with automobiles containing the corpse of gunman Lieut. C. O. Curtis, who had fallen early in the fight, and twenty wounded vigilantes, among whom were Jeff Beard, Chief Deputy Sheriff and former Sheriff of Snohomish county, who later died in the hospital, and Sheriff McRae with three bullet wounds in his legs. The recovery of some of the gunmen is still in doubt.

Mrs. Edith Frenette, who was later arrested in Seattle together with Mrs. Joyce Peters and Mrs. Lorna Mahler, is held on the allegation that she tried to throw red pepper in the eyes of the sheriff and then drew a revolver to shoot him as he was being removed from the dock. Mrs. Frenette was out on $1,000 bail on an unlawful assembly charge made by the Everett authorities.

An Everett correspondent, writing to the Seattle Union Record, official A. F. of L. organ, makes the following statement of the temper of the people:

"*Your correspondent was on the street at the time of the battle and at the dock ten minutes afterward. He mingled with the street crowds for hours afterwards. The temper of the people is dangerous. Nothing but curses and execrations for the Commercial Club was heard. Men and women who are ordinarily law abiding, who in normal times mind their own business pretty well, pay their taxes, send their children to church and school, pay their bills, in every way comport themselves as normal citizens, were heard using the most vitriolic language concerning the Commercial Club, loudly sympathizing with the I.W.W.'s. And therein lies the great harm that was done, more menacing to the city than the presence of any number of I.W.W.'s, viz., the transformation of decent, honest citizens into beings mad for vengeance and praying for something dire to happen. I heard gray-haired women, mothers and wives, gentle, kindly, I know, in their home circles, openly hoping that the I.W.W.'s would come back and 'clean up.'"*

Terrorism and chaos reigned in Everett following the tragedy. Over six hundred deputies patrolled the streets. A citizen who slipped into the prohibited area claims that he overheard a group of panic stricken citizen-deputies say: "We must stick together on this story about the first shot from the boat."

Certain officials called for the state militia and, without investigating, Governor Lister ordered mobilization and soon some of the naval militiamen were on the scene. Some militiamen, knowing that the call practically amounted to strike duty *refused to go to the armory.*

The Verona, with its cargo of dead and wounded, steamed toward Seattle, meeting the Calista four miles out from Everett. Captain Wyman stopped the Calista and cried out through his megaphone, "For God's sake don't land. They'll kill you. We have dead and wounded on board now."

In Seattle large bodies of police—with drawn revolvers—lined the dock awaiting the return of the two steamers. At 4:40 P.M. the Verona reached the dock and the first words of the I.W.W. men were, "Get the wounded fellows out and we'll be all right." The four dead members, their still bodies covered with blankets, were first removed from the boat and taken to the morgue. Police and hospital ambulances were soon filled with the thirty-two wounded men, who were taken to the city hospital. The uninjured men were then lined up and slowly marched to the city jail. The thirty-eight men taken from the Calista were placed in the county jail.

A competent physician is authority for the statement that Felix Baran, the I.W.W. man who died in the city hospital, would have had more than an even chance of recovery had he been given proper surgical attention upon his arrival in the hospital.

Up to this writing no inquest has been held over the five dead fellow workers.

The Seattle I.W.W. has been denied the bodies and unless relatives come forward to claim them the men will be buried as paupers. A request that the I.W.W. be allowed to hold a public funeral for the four men met with a denial. It was claimed that the display of these men to the general public would tend to incite a riot and disorder. The even hand of capitalist justice is shown by the fact that at the same time this ruling was made the funeral of gunman C. O. Curtis took place in Seattle with Prosecuting Attorney Alfred H. Lundin as one of the pallbearers. This funeral was held with military honors, Lieut. Curtis having been in the officers' reserve corps of the National Guard of Washington, and formerly of the Adjutant General's staff.

A hastily gathered coroner's jury in Everett viewed the bodies of gunmen C. O. Curtis and Jeff F. Beard, and retiring long enough to put their instructions in writing had laid these deaths at the door of the I.W.W.—"a riotous mob on the steamer Verona." The Seattle Central Labor Council on November 8 characterized the inquest as a farce and appropriated $100 for a complete investigation. They also demanded that a fair and exhaustive inquest be held, with full examination of all available witnesses.

The men in jail were held incommunicado for several days and were not allowed even the prison bill of fare—being given only bread and coffee. Mayor H. C. Gill, being aware of the fact that the public generally were sympathizing with the men, directed that they be placed upon the regular prison diet, and that they be allowed to see relatives and friends. He also saw personally to the comfort of the prisoners by providing them with 300 warm blankets and an assortment of tobacco. In an interview which appeared in a Seattle paper the mayor made the following statement:

"In final analysis it will be found that these cowards in Everett who, without right or justification, shot into the crowd on the boat, were murderers and not the I.W.W.'s.

"The men who met the I.W.W.'s at the boat were a bunch of cowards. They outnumbered the I.W.W.'s five to one, and in spite of this they stood there on the dock and fired into the boat, I.W.W.'s, innocent passengers and all.

"McRae and his deputies had no legal right to tell the I.W.W.'s or any one else that they could not land there. When the sheriff put his hand on the butt of his gun and told them they could not land, he fired the first shot, in the eyes of the law, and the I.W.W.'s can claim that they shot in self-defense."

Speaking of the men in jail, Gill said:

"These men haven't been charged with anything. Personally I have no sympathy with the I.W.W.'s. The way I have handled them here in the past ought to be proof enough of that, but I don't believe I should have these men tortured just because I have them in jail.

"If I were one of the party of forty I.W.W.'s who was almost beaten to death by 300 citizens of Everett without being able to defend myself, I probably would have armed myself if I intended to visit Everett again."

The mayor charged that Everett officials were inconsistent in their handling of this situation. He said that they permit candidates for office to violate the city ordinances by speaking on the streets and yet run the I.W.W.'s out of town if they endeavor to mount a soap box.

"Why hasn't a Benson supporter just as much right to speak in the streets as a McBride or a Hughes supporter?" said Mayor Gill.

Passenger Oscar Carlson was at the very front of the Verona when the firing commenced. He now lies in the city hospital with a number of serious bullet wounds. His affidavit has been taken. In an interview he speaks of the I.W.W. attitude on the voyage to Everett as follows:

"I never expected to have any shooting. All I heard was 'They may not let us land.' I didn't hear any threat of violence—it seemed funny. I was not acquainted and knew but two by sight only."

Although in a weakened condition, Carlson stated that he saw no guns and continued the interview long enough to say, "I tell you as it comes to me now, it seems one shot came from the dock first, then three or four from the other side, then all sides at once."

Ernest Nordstrom, another passenger, practically substantiates all of Carlson's statement.

As was to be expected, the entire capitalist press united in their opposition to the I.W.W.'s in this fight. Their tactics have embraced everything from outright lies to the petty trick of placing the words "Jew," "Irish," etc., after the names of I.W.W. men in their newspaper references in order to create the idea that the whole affair is the work of "ignorant foreigners." To combat these capitalist forces there are in the immediate vicinity three official organs of the A. F. of L., the Industrial Worker, the Northwest Worker of Everett and the Socialist World of Seattle. These are weekly papers, but the publicity they have already given the case is swinging public opinion to the side of the workers.

To arrive at an understanding of the tragedy of the Verona some knowledge of the events that preceded it is necessary.

Everett has been in a more or less lawless condition ever since the open shop lumber men imported thugs and scabs to break the shingle weavers' strike of six months ago. Union men were beaten and one picket was shot in the leg. Demands for organization brought the I.W.W. on the scene. Headquarters were opened and street meetings started to inform the Everett workers of conditions in the mills and in the northwest lumber industry generally. Obeying orders from the Commercial Club, the I.W.W. hall was closed by the police. Speakers were arrested and deported. Members of the I.W.W. from Seattle, some of them striking longshoremen, aided the shingle weavers in the maintaining of their picket line. Deportation entirely without legal process continued for some time. On September 9 Sheriff Mc-Rae and a bunch of vigilantes fired a volley of shots at the launch Wonder and arrested the captain, together with twenty I.W.W. men who were on board. Meanwhile the police were raiding the I.W.W. hall and all of those arrested were taken to jail, where they were severely beaten. Jury trials were denied and finally the prisoners were turned over to the vigilante mob, who clubbed them and illegally deported them. These tactics continued for some time, and increased in their intensity to such an extent that the citizens of Everett, some ten or fifteen thousand in number, gathered in a protest meeting on September 20. There were speakers representing all factions of the labor revolutionary movement, as well as citizens who had come to tell of the beatings they had received at the hands of the vigilantes.

Then, on October 30, occurred an outrage greater than all the preceding ones—an outrage exceeded only by the wanton murder of the I.W.W. men on the steamer Verona. Forty-one I.W.W. men, entirely unarmed and accused of no crime, were taken from a boat on which they were passengers, and at the point of guns, were searched and abused by a mob of deputized drunks. They were then thrown into automobiles and with armed guards, who outnumbered them five to one, were taken to a lonely country spot, where they were forced to run the gauntlet of the vigilantes who rained blows upon their unprotected heads and bodies with saps, clubs, pickhandles and other weapons. In this mob of 200 fiends were lawyers, doctors, business men, members of the chamber of commerce, "patriotic" militiamen, ignorant university students, deputies and Sheriff McRae. As a result of a peaceable attempt to assert a constitutional right, forty-one members of the I.W.W. were sent to Seattle hospitals, with injuries ranging from dangerously severe bruises to broken shoulders.

The answer of the I.W.W. to this damnable act of violence and to the four months of terrorism that had preceded it was a call issued through the *Industrial Worker* for two thousand men to enter Everett, there to gain by sheer force of numbers that right of free speech and peaceable assemblage supposed to have been guaranteed them by the constitution of the United States. Then came the tragedy on the steamer Verona.

The prosecution made its first legal move on Friday, November 10, when forty-one men were singled out, heavily handcuffed and secretly transported to Everett. They are charged with first degree murder. The other men are held on the technical charge of unlawful assembly, pending the filing of more serious charges.

The defense of the men will be undertaken by lawyer Fred H. Moore, assisted by Judge Hilton, Arthur Leseuer, Col. C. E. S. Wood and local Seattle attorneys, according to present advices.

The prosecution is backed by the Chamber of Commerce, the Commercial Club, the Employers' Association, the Lumber Trust and other upholders of the open shop. These men will stick at nothing to convict the prisoners so as to cover the murders committed by their hirelings.

An immediate and generous response is the only means of preventing a frame-up and wholesale conviction of these men. They have fought their class war. Are you game to back them up financially? Let your response go at once to the

DEFENSE COMMITTEE,
Box 85, Nippon Station, Seattle, Wash.

8

This one-act skit, privately printed by the author, Walker C. Smith, is included in the I.W.W. files in the Labadie Collection. Former I.W.W. acting secretary-treasurer Peter Stone writes: "I believe it was during the Everett Trial that we put on the mock trial. Both Fred Moore and George Vanderveer, the real defense attorneys, were in the audience. The occasion was one of the regular monthly smokers that we in Seattle put on to help out on expenses. The smokers consisted of four three-round boxing bouts; a voluntary professional performer; a propaganda talk by James P. Thompson or Kate Sadler, and usually a propaganda sketch. These sketches were reasonable facsimiles of a one-act play, but more often than not they were built around scenes in the 'jungles.' The format consisted of at least one 'hoosier' to bring up the standard cliches against unions and the I.W.W. in particular, and the Wobblies answering these arguments, sometimes interspersed with a Wobbly song or two. . . . The occasion on which Walker Smith's kangaroo court was put on was just such a smoker, preceded by three boxing bouts" (letter to JLK, February 3, 1964).

THEIR COURT AND OUR CLASS

A One Act Sketch

By WALKER C. SMITH

Scene—A Courtroom, with a judge, clerk, sheriff, prosecuting attorney, prisoner, prisoner's counsel, three witnesses, jurymen, spectator and messenger boy.

Place—Everett, Wash.

Time—Early in 1917.

JUDGE (*enters Courtroom from his chambers after all others are in proper position. He takes his seat.*)

COURT CLERK—Hear ye! Hear ye! The dishonorable Court of Snohomish County is now in secession. (*Turns to jury, who rise*). Do you solemnly swear to hear no evidence in this case favorable to the accused and to render a verdict of Guilty? (*pause*) Before this dishonorable court comes now the case of the City of Everett, State of Degradation, plaintiff, versus A. WISE WOBBLY, defendant; and (*monotone*) Therefore, to wit and whereas and in the manner heretofore described and all other statements to the contrary notwithstanding, the defendant, A. WISE WOBBLY, stands arraigned and accused and is arraigned and accused before the dishonorable Bar of this Court of Injustice in that he did feloniously and with malice aforethought and otherwise with deliberation cause the death and demise of A. MUTT and B. JEFF, to wit, by dodging, twisting, turning, shifting and otherwise evading bullets intended for his person and by so doing in the manner heretofore described did cause said bullets to enter the persons of the said Mutt and Jeff thus slaying, murdering, killing, putting to death, taking the life and otherwise bringing about the decease of the aforesaid Mutt and Jeff.

PROSECUTING ATTORNEY (*stepping pompously forward*) As an amendment to this charge, your Honor, I wish ° ° °

COURT CLERK (*interrupting*) Do you solemnly swear to tell the truth, the whole truth, and nothing but the truth, so help you God?

PROSECUTING ATTORNEY (*angrily*) Certainly not! Why, I'm the prosecuting attorney in this case!

CLERK (*humbly*) My mistake. Of course you won't.

PRISONER'S COUNSEL (*addressing the Court*)—I move, your Honor, that the indictment be dismissed as vitally defective in that it lacks the constitutionally required number of "whereases," and has a misplaced comma in the third line.

JUDGE (*after due reflection*) Motion denied; exceptions granted.

PROSECUTOR—In opening this memorable case I wish to emphatically state that we have such overwhelming evidence that it will be entirely unnecessary for me to say more than a few brief words to you gentlemen of the jury—you *six* good men and true who represent the sum total of the intelligence of the universe and who have sworn to uphold the noble motto of Snohomish County "In Lumber We Trust." In the name of the fair women of this great state, I ask you gentlemen of the jury to remember that each one of you has a dear mother who used to hold you in her arms and kiss your little feet and therefore it is your manifest duty to bring in a verdict of GUILTY against this defendant who would tear down the palladium of our liberties and destroy the inalienable right of the scab to work long hours for short wages. Shall we haul down the Stars and Stripes that now float proudly o'er the county jail? Shall we admit that the Statue of Liberty is hollow and the Liberty Bell is cracked? Did our brave boys in yellow give their lives in vain during the Spanish-American war against Armour's pork and beans? I appeal to that lofty spirit of patriotism which should swell the bosom of every property owner, gentlemen of the jury,—it is unpatriotic and un-American to bring in a verdict of NOT GUILTY when a working man is on trial. Look at the hardened prisoner, gentlemen! He has callouses on his hands! I tell you he is as guilty as Hell! (*pause*) I will now call my first witness, a man who has furnished the guiding spirit to our noble Commercial Club, whose thoughts control our daily press, whose philosophy supports our entire social system, and whose ideas pervade the whole history of jurisprudence—Mr. Ananias.

CLERK—Do you solemnly swear to tell the truth, the whole truth and nothing but the truth, so help you Jesus?

(*Witness assents.*)

PROSECUTOR—Mr. Ananias, will you kindly state to this dishonorable court exactly what you do and do not know about this violent I.W.W. invasion into peaceful and law-abiding Everett?

ANANIAS—In Everett, Washington, on Sunday, November fifth, Nineteen hundred Sixteen, at 2 P.M., with about 300 others, I was on the Municipal Dock lying down behind * * *

PRISONER'S COUNSEL—Object! your honor, the witness by his own admission is in the habit of lying.

JUDGE—Objection overruled! That is why the witness is here!

PROSECUTOR—Tell the court what you saw from your reclining position on the dock.

ANANIAS—I saw the Verona steam up to the dock and there was a crowd of I.W.W.'s on board. This man (*indicating the prisoner*) was one of the leaders.

PROSECUTOR—How do you know he was a leader?

ANANIAS—Because they were ALL leaders. (*Continuing story*) Cold chills ran down my spine * * *

PRISONER'S COUNSEL—Object, your honor, the spine is not in evidence.

JUDGE—'Bjection overruled. Proof of a spine is not necessary. The witness is acting for the state. (*To witness*) Proceed.

ANANIAS—As I was saying, cold chills ran down my back when I saw this mob, armed to the teeth (*general gasp from all present and low cries of Oh! Oh!*) armed to the teeth with 250 copies of the little red song book, 6 copies of the Industrial Relations Commission Report and four chair legs. (*Looks of horror on faces of jurymen*) This man (*indicating prisoner*) had a song book in one hand and a chair leg in the other and when he finished singing the I.W.W. battle hymn "Hold the Fort!" he cried out in a loud voice, "Give me Liberty or give me Death!" There was no liberty in Everett to give him, so the deputies started to give him death. I saw him *deliberately* dodge several bullets from the Improvement dock to the South and these bullets struck and killed Mr. A. Mutt and Mr. B. Jeff. The other men also dodged, but they were not so fast and we got five of them and wounded

a lot of others. The shooting from the other dock made it kind of dangerous.

PROSECUTOR—You are of the opinion, then, that the defendant is guilty?

ANANIAS—Of course, I am. He is a member of the I.W.W.

PRISONER'S COUNSEL—I move that all this testimony be stricken out on the ground that it is incompetent, irrelevant and immaterial, and that the jury be instructed to remember that they never heard it.

JUDGE—The Court declares a recess to take the matter under advisement and to get a drink. The sheriff will see that no one favorable to the defendant be allowed to speak to the jury, and will shoot the prisoner if he attempts to talk at all.

(*Judge turns his back and takes a drink. Sheriff takes a flask from his hip and refreshes himself. Prosecutor slips each juryman a cigar. Clerk piles books on Judge's desk and Judge peruses same.*)

JUDGE (*rapping on desk*) Following the celebrated precedent set by Chinwhiskers, Justice of the Peace in Sagebrush Township, State of North Dakota, Anno Domini 1863, see Reports and Digests, North Dakota Revised Statutes, 1864 to 1865, in the case of John Farmer versus Roughneck, in which evidence was stricken on the ground that an idea was introduced; reaffirmed in the case of Scissor versus Rebel in which evidence of the respondent was thrown out because he said what he meant and meant what he said, Federal Proceedings, volume 213, year 1862: therefore I rule that the portion of the evidence regarding the killing and wounding of workers be stricken out and that the jury dismiss it from their minds under penalty of Contempt of Court.

PRISONER'S COUNSEL—Mr. Ananias, you admit that you were lying on the dock. Are you not doing the same in this court-room?

ANANIAS—(*flustered*) Y-Yes.

PRISONER'S COUNSEL—That is all!

PROSECUTOR—I will now call my next witness, the famous defective, William J. Arson.

CLERK—Do you solemnly swear not to tell the truth or anything like the truth, so help you God?

(*Witness assents.*)

PROSECUTOR—Kindy tell the court, Mr. Arson, just

what misinformation you have gathered together in regard to this Everett affair.

ARSON—I was at the City Dock when the Verona pulled in and I seen this here prisoner and he had a stick of wood in one hand and a dangerous lookin' book in the other, so help me O'Higgins. He was singin' "Onward Christian Soldiers" in an incendiary and riotous tone of voice. We started shootin' at him and so did our men on the Improvement dock. I seen him duckin' the bullets and two of the deputies was killed. Lots of shootin' was did, but we killed only five of them fellows on the boat. I reckon we had been drinkin' too much and our aims was poor. Of course the men on the boat was armed.

PROSECUTOR—You state that the men on the Verona were armed. Were they *better* armed than the deputies on the docks?

ARSON—Sure they was. We had only guns and bullets and booze on our side and the I.W.W. fellows was armed with Truth and Courage and Solidarity.

PROSECUTOR—Mr. Arson, you state that five men on the Verona were killed. When did you first learn of this fact?

ARSON—On the evenin' of November 5th in the Commercial Club we all got together to fix up our stories and a telegram come in from Seattle sayin' five was dead and twenty-five wounded on the boat. We all jumped up and down and yelled "Goody! Goody! We got five of them!" I tell you us detectives and scabs and open-shoppers was sure some happy at the good news.

PROSECUTOR—Are you sure, Mr. Arson, that this story is correct in all its details?

ARSON—Sure I am. Ain't I done rehearsed it enough times!

PROSECUTOR'S COUNSEL—Mr. Arson, you state that the defendant was singing "Onward Christian Soldiers" while the preceding witness stated under oath that he was singing "Hold the Fort." Which one of you is lying?

ARSON—Both—I mean neither. It's the same song only different. It's called the "Marseillaise," and it says: "To arms! To arms! Ye brave!" Mr. Prosecutor and Judge, your honor, I object to the insinuatin' questions of this here attorney. My hearin' ain't very good, nohow, and I don't understand music.

PRISONER'S COUNSEL—This means in plain English—

PROSECUTOR—Object!! Your honor! I object!!

JUDGE—'Bjection s'stained.

PRISONER'S COUNSEL—Mr. Arson, do you believe in Capital Punishment?

ARSON—Of course! It was good enough for my father and I reckon it's good enough for me.

PRISONER'S COUNSEL—Do you understand the nature of an oath, Mr. Arson?

ARSON—Sure! Ain't I heard Sheriff McRae talk to the I.W.W. prisoners?

PRISONER'S COUNSEL—Mr. Arson, your testimony is worthless. You have sworn to tell the truth and yet you have addressed the Judge as "Your Honor." Take the witness, Mr. Prosecutor.

PROSECUTOR—Mr. Arson, I understand that you were slightly wounded in this affair. Here is one of your photographs. For the benefit of the jury please mark the exact spot in which you were wounded. (*Hands Arson photograph.*)

ARSON—(*After looking at photograph*) I can't mark it on this here picture, this is a front view.

PROSECUTOR—(*Disgusted*). That is all, Mr. Arson. (*Addresses Court*). Together with the testimony thus far given on behalf of the Lumber Trust, gentlemen of the jury, I call to your attention the fact that the men who founded this glorious country came here to worship God in their own way and to *force* others to do the same and this proves the guilt of the accused. In the sainted name of Anthony Comstock, I ask you to vote Guilty! Think of the ragged and starving soldiers at Valley Forge who were forced to steal in order to repeal the tax on tea; then consider that this prisoner and his 73 associates have had free board and steam heat in the cozy cells of our magnificent jail at the expense of the poor and struggling taxpayers of this beautiful community. This prisoner has failed to appreciate all the efforts Society has made in his behalf. We have given him municipal ownership of the city dock and of the jail and still he persists in asking for more wages and shorter hours. Why, he even wants to get *all* the wealth he produces! Where would that leave *you*, gentlemen of the jury? You would have to work for an *honest* living! Actually work! Can you doubt that the prisoner is guilty, gentlemen of the jury?

PRISONER (*Leaping to his feet*)—Justice! Justice! I demand Justice!

JUDGE (*sternly*)—Silence! The prisoner forgets that he is in a court room.

PRISONER'S COUNSEL—I regret this outburst on the part of my client. By nature he is a quiet man. This explosiveness—this inflammatory utterance —comes from the fact that there has been too much saltpetre in his mush.

JUDGE—I accept your explanation and will not sentence the prisoner to jail.

PRISONER'S COUNSEL—As the Persecutor has presented so weak a case I will bring forward but one witness before calling my client to the stand. Mr. Everett True.

CLERK — Do you solemnly swear to tell the truth the whole truth and nothing but the truth, God help your soul—I mean so help you God?

(*Witness assents.*)

PRISONER'S COUNSEL—Kindly tell the Court just what you know of this affair in Everett.

TRUE—I am a citizen of Everett. At the time of this outrage I was on a hill overlooking the dock. The deputies opened fire upon the unarmed men without warning. Shots came from two different docks and from a tugboat. Men fell to the deck and others sought cover. I think the deputies who were shot are the victims of their own cross-fire. I am not a member of the I.W.W. nor of the Commercial Club. I favor a federal investigation of the entire affair.

PRISONER'S COUNSEL—That is all, Mr. True. Cross-examine the witness, Mr. Persecutor.

PROSECUTOR—Mr. True, are you sure that you saw what you described and what was your age on your last birthday? Answer yes or no!

TRUE (*indignantly*)—I—

PROSECUTOR—Answer yes or no, sir!

TRUE (*spluttering with partly suppressed rage*)— I—I—

JUDGE—(*sternly*). You must answer the question yes or no!

TRUE (*appealing to Judge*)—How can I—

JUDGE—Ten days for aggravated contempt of court. Commit the witness.

(*Sheriff drags struggling witness from the stand.*)

PRISONER'S COUNSEL—I object, your honor! I object!

JUDGE—Objection overruled!—Do you wish to stand in contempt yourself?

I.W.W. Spectator (*coming forward*). Give me twenty days, you old fraud. I have twice as much contempt for you as True has!

(*Commotion in court room. Sheriff throws interrupter out of room.*)

PRISONER'S COUNSEL—At this point I wish to introduce as evidence an interview with Hi Gill, Mayor of Seattle, as published in that notorious labor-hating sheet—The *Seattle Times* of Nov. 8th, (*Reads clipping*)

MAYOR GILL SAYS I.W.W. DID NOT START RIOT

Seattle Executive Places Blame for Sunday Tragedy on Citizens of Everett— Gives Prisoners Tobacco

Providing the I.W.W.'s whose attempted armed invasion of Everett last Sunday resulted in seven deaths and injuries to forty-nine persons, with every comfort possible, Mayor H. C. Gill yesterday afternoon personally directed the carrying of 300 warm blankets and an assortment of tobacco to the 250 prisoners now held in the city jail.

In this manner Gill replied to criticism in Seattle and Everett for not having stopped the I.W.W.'s from going to the Snohomish County city. He supplemented this today by assailing Sheriff Donald McRae, of Snohomish County, and the posse of special deputies who met the invading I.W.W.'s at the boat.

"In the final analysis," the mayor declared, "it will be found these cowards in Everett who, without right or justification, shot into the crowd on the boat were the murderers and not the I.W.W.'s.

Calls Them Cowards

"The men who met the I.W.W.'s at the boat were a bunch of cowards. They outnumbered the I.W.W.'s five to one, and in spite of this they stood there on the dock and fired into the boat, I.W.W.'s, innocent passengers and all.

"McRae and his deputies had no legal right to tell the I.W.W.'s or anyone else that they could not land there. When the sheriff put his hand on the butt of his gun and told them they could not land, he fired the first shot, in the eyes of the law, and the I.W.W.'s can claim that they shot in self-defense."

Mayor Gill asserted the Everett authorities have no intention of removing the I.W.W.'s now in jail here to Snohomish County.

"They are afraid to come down here and get them," he declared, "because Everett is in a state of anarchy and the authorities don't know where they're at."

Asked what he would have done at Everett Sunday when the I.W.W.'s appeared at that city, the mayor said he would have permitted them to land.

"After they had been allowed to come ashore," he said, "I would have had them watched. Then if they violated the law I would have had them thrown in jail. There would have been no trouble that way."

No Fight in Seattle

"Because Everett has been reduced to a state of anarchy by their high-handed methods of dealing with this situation it is no reason they are going to attempt to bring their fight down in Seattle, at least while I am mayor.

"If I were one of the party of forty I.W.W.'s who was almost beaten to death by 300 citizens of Everett without being able to defend myself, I probably would have armed myself if I intended to visit Everett again.

"If the Everett authorities had an ounce of sense, this tragedy would have never happened. They have handled the situation like a bunch of imbeciles, and they have been trying to unload these men onto Seattle. You don't see any disturbances here, because we don't use nickel methods."

The mayor charged that Everett officials were inconsistent in their handling of this situation. He said that they permit candidates for office to violate the city ordinances by speaking on the streets and yet run the I.W.W.'s out of town if they endeavor to mount a soap box.

(Pause)—The defendant, Mr. A Wise Wobbly will now please take the stand.

WOBBLY (*Answering clerk's rigamarole*) I affirm!

Industrial Worker, February 2, 1911.

PRISONER'S COUNSEL—Kindly state to the Court, Mr. Wobbly, your version of the outrage on Bloody Sunday.

PROSECUTOR—I object, your Honor!

JUDGE—State your objections to the Court.

PROSECUTOR—This is Snohomish county and according to *our* theory of law and order a workingman is always Guilty until he is proven innocent. Therefore the prisoner should be cross-examined before he is allowed to make his statement.

JUDGE—The point is well taken. Examine the accused, Mr. Prosecutor.

PROSECUTOR—Mr. Wobbly, by the testimony of two unimpeachable witnesses I have proven that you were singing two different songs at the same time. What have you to say on this point?

WOBBLY—I was not singing at all, Mr. Prostituting Attorney, I was merely reciting the Declaration of Independence.

PROSECUTOR—Nonsense! Nonsense! I don't believe you know the Declaration of Independence. How does it start?

WOBBLY—"The working class and the employing class have nothing in common. There can be no peace so long as hunger and want are found among the millions of working people, and the few, who make up the employing class have all the good things of life. Between these two classes a struggle must go on until the workers of the world organize as a class, take possession of the earth and the machinery of production, and abolish the wage system. We find—"

PROSECUTOR (*interrupting*)—That's enough! That's enough! You know it all right!! (*pause*) Mr. Wobbly, will you tell the Court whether or not you were armed at the time the Verona docked.

WOBBLY—I had a piece of wood in my hand.

PROSECUTOR—Describe the wood.

WOBBLY—It was only a small piece.

JUDGE (*angrily*)—You must be more explicit! What size was this wood? Was it as long as my head?

WOBBLY (*reflectively*)—Yes, a little longer than your head *but not nearly so thick!*

JUDGE (*clearing his throat*)—H'mm! Prisoner at the Bar, have you anything further to say for yourself?

WOBBLY—Yes, Judge, I think you should be thankful that I'm here.

JUDGE (*surprised*)—How do you make that out?

WOBBLY—Well—suppose all the agitators and pick-

ets and union men and socialists and anarchists and birth control advocates were to strike and quit agitating—what would you judges do for a living?

PROSECUTOR (*trying to cover the Judge's confusion*)—Mr. Wobbly, what is your nationality?

WOBBLY (*proudly*)—I.W.W.

PROSECUTOR—Then you are not a patriot? Wouldn't you fight for the country?

WOBBLY—Certainly not! I live in the city!

PROSECUTOR—I mean to ask whether you would fight for your native land?

WOBBLY—I don't own any land. The I.W.W. is fighting all the landlords for all the land and all the employers for all the machinery of production. (*makes a move toward Prosecutor*). If you own any land I'll fight you for it!

PROSECUTOR (*hastily*)—Take the defendant in rebuttal.

PRISONER'S COUNSEL—Mr. Wise Wobbly, will you please tell the Court in as few words as possible just what made you decide to go to Everett on the steamer Verona on Sunday, November fifth?

WOBBLY (*whimsically*)—I could talk better if I had a soap box.

COUNSEL (*sternly*)—Tell your story, Mr. Wobbly.

WOBBLY—I am a member of that ever-increasing rebel army which is marching against the Masters of the Bread. I believe in, and am willing to fight and to die for the principle of free speech, free press, free assemblage, and the right to organize Labor into a solid industrial body that will wage the every day battles of the workers and will manage industry when capitalism shall have been overthrown. I am an I.W.W. and proud of it! For six months the tools of the Lumber Trust in Snohomish county have beaten, robbed, deported and abused all workers who did not favor the open shop and the closed mouth. Finally a mob of citizen-deputies illegally seized 41 members of my class and after taking them to the outskirts of Everett beat them so brutally that many of them had to be sent to the hospital. Then, with many others, I decided to go to Everett to gain the right to speak and organize. I thought that a body of several hundred men, with a strong sentiment already in their favor in Everett, would be able to speak without interference because of their numbers and strength. I went on the Verona with more than 250 others and,

"MOVE ON" FOR SPEAKERS, LATER WILL INCLUDE PICKETS

Industrial Worker, May 9, 1912.

altho we were unarmed, our greeting from the "keepers of the peace" was a hail of bullets that killed five of our brave fellow workers and wounded over thirty others. Then on our return to Seattle we were arrested and I am the first of seventy-four to be tried for first degree murder. The only crime I am guilty of is loyalty to the working class! I am innocent of murder but I am guilty of solidarity!! Convict me for that if you dare!!!

PRISONER'S COUNSEL—That is all. I rest my case.

JUDGE—My instructions to the jury, gentlemen, is that you disregard all evidence favorable to the accused and remain faithful to your trust—the Lumber Trust. When rendering your verdict, bear in mind that a Court is a place where justice is dispensed—with. It is your duty to vindicate the fair name of our Commercial Club and to keep the pillars of society from crumbling, and by so doing you will be able to hire your wage slaves much more cheaply in the future. ° ° °

MESSENGER BOY—Telegram for Prosecuting Attorney!

JUDGE (continuing as Prosecutor signs for and reads telegram)—Gentlemen of the jury, as I see before me your six countenances distinguished by that supreme sagacity which is the proud birthright of every freeman born or naturalized under the starry flag of this great republic, I know that you will not disregard my instructions. I instruct you to bring a verdict of——

PROSECUTOR—(In trembling voice)—Judge, your honor, read this telegram!

JUDGE (reading telegram aloud)—"The I.W.W. strongly organized in the lumber camps and mills, and in allied industries, will inaugurate an immediate general strike in case a verdict of Guilty is rendered in the Everett trial."

JUDGE (turning to jury)—As I was saying, gentlemen, it is your duty to bring in a verdict of— NOT GUILTY!

FOREMAN OF JURY—(Rises and receiving nods of assent from members of jury, addresses the court)—The final evidence in this case is so conclusive that we are forced to render a verdict of Not Guilty!

(Sheriff removes handcuffs and chains from prisoner.)

PRISONER'S COUNSEL—I move for the dismissal of the seventy-three cases pending and demand the immediate discharge of all prisoners from custody.

JUDGE—Motion granted! Prisoners discharged!! Court dismissed!! Oh Lord, give me a drink, quick!!

WOBBLY (holding chains and handcuffs aloft)— See what Solidarity of Labor has done!!! . . . (Drops chains and handcuffs to floor with a crash as curtain falls.)

(Finis)

9

This account of the prison experiences of seventy-four I.W.W. defendants following the "Tragedy of the Verona" was one of a series of retrospective articles published in the Industrial Worker *during 1945–46. This article appeared in the* Industrial Worker *(October 30, 1946).*

JAILS DIDN'T MAKE THEM WEAKEN

By JACK LEONARD

One of the 74 Everett Victims Tells How With Battleship and Solidarity They Improved the Jail

It has been suggested to me many times, that I write my personal experiences and reactions while confined in the Snohomish county and King county jails after our arrests on the first degree murder charges November 5, 1916.

The history of the events leading up to and including November 5, 1916, has been written much better than I could hope to do. The things we did to amuse ourselves; the humorous situations that arose, the bewilderment of the jailers at a group of prisoners who insisted upon and received, finally, respect from them; the lifting of authority as far as the prisoners' welfare was concerned, or the administration of all matters within the tanks and cells was concerned—these things have just been mentioned as something incidental to the trial itself.

The 74 represented a remarkable cross section of the working class, more remarkable because it was so representative. There was an Irishman from Ireland, another of Irish extraction but born in U.S.A., an English Jew, a Russian Jew and an American Jew. (All by birth, none as far as I know professing.) There were at least two from Australia. The age of the 74 ranged from a 16 year old boy to men approaching 60. There were migratory workers and resident workers; and some of them had worked at so many different jobs and at such a variety of crafts, that I honestly believe that given the tools and materials, they could have built a city complete with all utilities. In education so far as I have any knowledge none had gone to college. (Perhaps that is why Anna Louise Strong said that we reminded her of college students.)

There were as many kinds of personalities and temperaments as there were individuals. This then is the group I was to spend months with, before and during the trial of Thomas Tracy.

As was customary in those days, we migrants seldom had occasion to use the names by which our births were or were not registered, and mine had been changed from John L. Miller to J. Leonard Miller to Jack Leonard. The last seemed to stick, like burrs to a water spaniel.

As we were being booked at the Seattle city jail I got my first chuckle as the booking sergeant said: "The Leonard family is damn well represented here tonight," especially as I knew the man's name he was registering was really Leonard and since Leonard had become my moniker that was what I was going to give.

Shortly after this I was shoved into what is known as a tank with so many men that there was not enough floor space for us all to lie down. We soon managed this by having the first row lie down, the second row would lay head and shoulders on the hips of the first row, the third row heads and shoulders on the hips of the second row and so on.

The Battleship

This went on with a bread and coffee diet for a few days until we were sufficiently organized to "Build a Battleship." I do not know how the expression "Build a Battleship" originated, but to those who have not participated or witnessed such a demonstration by a bunch of determined *Wobblies*, I'll say but emphatically, you have missed something.

The building was not too suitable as it was built of concrete. The jail was several floors above the street and was divided into several tanks, so that it was hard to work in perfect concert with all groups. First we sang a few songs to warm up. Then in our tank we all huddled in the center and locked arms, and at the count of three we would all jump up from the floor and of course our combined weight would fall upon the floor at the same time. Being one of the "constructors" I cannot say for sure, but I have been told, that the building actually rocked as tho it were in an earthquake. The jailers first threatened to turn the fire hose upon us. We invited them to do so as we intended to keep on until we furnished them with a hole in the floor for the water to run out. They changed from an attitude of command to one of pleading. They told us of our dying fellow workers in the hospital below. We told them that those men would be cheered rather than depressed by our action. The jailers called the Chief of Police and the Chief of Police called the Mayor of Seattle. The Mayor agreed that we should have better food and tobacco be distributed, and things arranged so that we could at least lie down and be furnished with blankets.

Not many days afterwards we were charged by an information filed by the prosecutor of Snohomish County with first degree murder, that is 41 of us. Later 33 more were so charged.

Three Fingers

We 74 were supposed to be the "leaders." Hell, we had already informed them at the dock in Everett on November 5, that we were all leaders, so in order to get 74, just as many as the Snohomish County jail would hold, they placed some one in a padded cell—no I am not kidding—and he chose us by sticking three fingers thru a hole for yes and two fingers for no. Some picker, two at least were not members at all; some had just lined up. I had been a member less than four months and mostly by accident. Some of ability were chosen. The rest were known because of their activities for the organization.

Now as I mentioned before we were of all temperaments and as the information was read to the first 40, one fainted. Some were sarcastic enough to tell the prosecutor that they thought the charge might be something serious, some jeered, some were indignant, but before the prosecutor could leave we were all singing the "*Red Flag*" or "*Solidarity Forever.*"

A couple of nights later we were taken to Everett by interurban which then ran from Seattle to Everett. The Mayor of Seattle asked if sufficient protection had been provided for us at Everett. I did not hear the reply. But Seattle police rode in the car with us part of the way.

When we arrived in Everett we were placed in the upper tank which had 40 bunks, so one of our number had to sleep in the corridor between the cells. These cells were small, so small that there were two bunks, one over the other hung on hinges and chains to each wall, with an aisle just wide enough for a man to squeeze thru. The sanitary facilities consisted of a bucket for each four men within the cells, one toilet in the corridor, a slop sink where we washed our faces and a shower bath.

Everett's New Jail

For some time we were all but one locked in the cell at night with no access to the toilet. The food was even by jail standard terrible. We were some time getting organized, but from the first we had a jail committee which was elected every week. This committee saw that the portion of the jail which we used was kept clean and dished out what food was given to us. They were the only ones who would speak to the jailers. No one could serve on this committee the second time until each had served upon it once. Needless to say the jailers, who had been used to, and had encouraged the old kangaroo court system, were puzzled. How could they play favorites, or get stool pigeons or otherwise play one prisoner against the other, or who could they pick for the fall guy?

Now when we entered this jail it was so new that it shone. It was supposed to be escape proof. Hardened steel floor and ceiling, hardened steel bars, about four inches wide and ⅝ of an inch thick. It had a locking system which was worked by levers from outside the corridors, but inside the building. We could see that the jailers were proud of their jail.

Our breakfast in the morning was mouldy half cooked mush. One morning it was so bad that it looked as if some one had defecated into it. The committee served it into the pie pans provided for us to eat from, and then called a meeting to see what was to be done with it. We voted upon it and, as agreed, one man after another took his pan and threw the contents thru the bars at the end of the corridors and frescoed the walls and carpeted the stairs with it. Oh, their beautiful jail.

For supper we had stew or beans. If there was ever any meat in the stew, no one to my knowl-

NO. 380.   PRICE 5C.   CHICAGO, ILL, SATURDAY, APRIL 21, 1917.   S

FIVE OF THEM DEAD; NOW TO HAVE THE REST TRIED FOR MURDER!

EVERETT COMMERCIAL CLUB

EVERETT TRIALS LIFT THE LID TO H

Unthinkable Brutality of Commercial Club Brought to Light by the Defense

Solidarity, April 21, 1917.

edge ever discovered it. It consisted of carrots, turnips and spuds on two occasions. We did the same thing with the stew as we did with the mush. Then one night they served us with sour beans, that is beans that had been cooked and had spoiled. We did not discover this until most of them had been eaten up. During the night we were all seized with cramps and diarrhea. That night all of the buckets and the toilet were in constant use. All thru the next day, the jailer received such a thorough and constant cussing that they left us locked in our cells until the next morning, thereby laying keel for another "Batttle-ship."

Taking Some Liberty

Some one found that there was about ¾ of an inch slack in the locking mechanism. Now here is a lesson in organized or concerted action. Each four men in each of five cells on the two sides of the corridor all threw their weight against this slack, gaining a little each time, until nine of the ten doors upstairs were forced open far enough for us to get into the corridor. Then we took blankets, rolled them into a rope, and sprung the angle irons on one side of the door until they were never able to lock them while I was there.

Down stairs where the 33 others were kept, they had a bath tub. There was only a cold water tap to the tub. The water was heated by first filling the tub and then turning on the steam thru the pipe that ran down into the filled tub.

They were not able to get as many doors opened in the lower tank at first as we did in the upper tank, but those that got into the lower corridor somehow unscrewed this pipe and pried the doors to the locking system open. These doors were just above the cell doors. Then they unscrewed the bolts on the horizontal locking levers and by prying, twisting and bending, pulled the levers out of their place and onto the floor. This allowed those still in the cells to open the cell doors and come into the corridor.

You are probably asking what were the jailers doing all this time? Well the first thing that they did was to grab all the guns and run into the street. We were all locked into the corridors, but they were not sure whether we intended to stay there or not, and were not going to be present to say good-bye if we decided to leave. They didn't come back until they called the sheriff.

Time for Beef

Meanwhile some one discovered a barrel of corn beef out in the passage way, and tore a strip from a blanket and bent a nail into a hook. The hook was tied to the strip of blanket and thrown so it would catch on the rim of the barrel. The barrel was upset and the corn beef was drawn into the cell and part of it sent via the blanket strip and bent nail to the upper tank. Our sink had a steam pipe to heat water also, so when the sheriff and deputies came into their jail, we were steam cooking corned beef in the sink. The sheriff felt very badly about the damage to his brand new jail. So did the taxpayers. It cost over $800 to repair it.

This was the act by which we notified the sheriff who was actually in control. It was explained to him that if better food and treatment were not immediately forthcoming, he could expect not only a re-occurrence of what had just been done, but a more thorough job next time.

As one of the Irish put it: "We'll tear your damned jail down brick by brick and camp by bonfire till ye build another, then tear it down too until ye learn how to feed and treat us." That night we had our first meal that was fit to eat. Next morning we were served with corn flakes with white instead of blue milk and bacon, and coffee that we could drink without holding our nose.

Who Runs This Jail?

They allowed us to have a phonograph after this and I was elected to take it to the lower tank when some one wanted music, and play the records for them. I also played the records in the upper tank. One day I was called to play the phonograph in the lower tank. I called the jailer. He let me take the phonograph and records down the stairs, but said that I would not be allowed to go in. I called for the committee for that week in the lower tank and told them what the jailer said. This forced things right out in the open. The jailer was asked, but not gently, "Who in the hell do you think is running this jail? Now you open that door and let him come in with that phonograph, or send down to Sumner Iron Works for some more boilermakers. If he don't come in you are going to need them." The door was opened and I went in and stayed until everybody had heard all the records they wished to hear. After that it was understood by the jailers that they could either be as decent as their jobs permitted or call the boilermakers.

There were two round steel posts running from the floor of the lower tank thru the ceiling of the lower tank and the floor and up to the ceiling of the upper tank. We used to sing and march in step around these posts. I don't think the jailers or sheriff ever realized what that was doing to their steel jail. I wonder if they knew that soldiers marching across a bridge are always told to break step.

Page Ripley

As I have been reading what I have just written I find a couple of errors. We were not 74 to start with. One of our number who had been wounded on the boat Verona did not join us until he was brought from the hospital. Another found that he was named in the information. He went first to the chief of police in Seattle, and then to the sheriff of King County. Each telephoned to the Snohomish county authorities, and got the old run around. This man accused of first-degree murder had to pay his own fare to Everett to be arrested by the ones who accused him! Page Mr. Ripley.

During all of this time we were not neglecting our education. This was just after the tenth convention of the I.W.W. and changes in the constitution were to be voted upon. The old constitution and the proposed changes were discussed article by article and section by section as it stood, and as it would be after the changes were made. We called meetings with a new chairman each time. This taught parliamentary procedure to all of us. We exchanged our experiences in the class struggle, in free speech fights, in the harvest fields and on the jobs generally. We read and studied the organization literature when it became available. We sang our songs and the popular songs of the day, especially the verse from "Don McRae":

"Oh Don McRae you've had your day;
Make way for freedom's host
For labor's sun is rising soon
Will shine from coast to coast,
And when at last, the working class
Shall make the masters yield
May your portion of the victory be
A grave in Potter's Field."

We played games together and pranks upon each other. Oh, yes we were human beings. There were differences of opinion and a little quarreling, no one of course was allowed to strike another. These were all of a personal nature, but, let any issue arise between any one of us and the jailers, then we were at once united and all personal differences forgotten.

An amusing thought comes to me here. One of us whenever he quarreled, and he quarreled frequently, used to put the name of the one he quarreled with in a note book. He was going to fight with each as soon as we were released. I hope he kept that book as my name was in it. What a laugh we could have together, and how glad he would be to meet those same guys now!

Back to Seattle

The trial was set for March 5, 1917. As all the judges in Snohomish county had shown prejudice, the defense had obtained a change of venue to King county. In February I was transferred to the King county jail at Seattle. I was to be a witness in the trial. There were twenty-five in all who came as witnesses to Seattle. A week or so after we left Everett the jailers must have thought that because the number of prisoners left there was smaller, the spirit had changed. An argument came up between the Wobblies and the jailers. The jailers brought in the fire hose and wet down the jail. The Wobs mopped up the water with Snohomish county mattresses. Even if the jailers won, they lost.

Before we left Everett, we were taken before the judge to plead. Some of those who could raise beards, spent weeks trimming their beards so that the shape would match the one grown by the judge who was to hear us plead. These of course pushed their way into the front row where the resemblance could not be missed. The judge missed the sarcasm and seemed to be flattered that his whiskers were a source of derision.

I am not trying to keep this article in chronological order as I am writing entirely from memory and without notes, so if I should remember something which I think should be inserted, but happened previously to something already mentioned, I can do so without rewriting the whole article.

No Kangaroo

When we arrived at the King county jail in Seattle, we were scattered through several tanks. The first thing done by the other prisoners was to call the Kangaroo court to order. Believing in the freedom of speech and assembly even by prisoners in jail, we listened to the whole proceedings. When they had finished they were told firmly and with emphasis, that we as members of the I.W.W. would neither be governed by its rules nor be a party to it. We explained to them that we had a committee system and that so far as the I.W.W. members were concerned we intended to continue it. Seeing our determined stand the kangaroo court waived any claim of authority so far as we were concerned. As in all kangaroo courts, the kangaroo judge and sheriff were inflicting fines and manual jobs on all incoming prisoners. These fines were supposed to be equally distributed among the prisoners, but generally the larger portions were kept by the judge and the sheriff. It was not long until the other prisoners saw the difference between governing themselves and being dictated to by a clique.

In Seattle some of the various religious bodies would visit the jail. All through Sunday morning we would have to listen to wheezy portable organs, and off key voices of men and women in the last stages of galloping decrepitude. Then they would tell us about sin, and its terrible results and consequences. In fact they knew so much about sin, that we were sure they were experts in all its branches.

Memorial services held at Mt. Pleasant Cemetery for the Everett victims May 1, 1917.

After the noisy ones left, the mental healers came in. Their theme was that everything we heard, saw, felt, smelt or tasted was myth. The jail and its inhabitants as far as I could gather were just conditions of the mind along with everything else. I wonder if any of them have ever been on the wrong end of a policeman's club. Hungry as jail grub kept us, this did not improve our appetite, so we began to hold services of our own. Mostly the same tunes, but oh the difference in words! There was as much difference in the manner of singing, as there was in the words. Our singing taught defiance, not obedience to our masters.

Well the religionists and the jailers protested. We were asked if we would not give to them the same rights we demanded for ourselves. The obvious reply was that we didn't lock them up and make them listen to us. I am not sure what the reason was but soon after this most of us were placed in one tank, where we could set up our committee system again.

Making Trials Cost

We had all demanded separate trials, and under the laws of the state of Washington we were entitled to separate trials. The state chose for its first victim Thomas H. Tracy, who had been Secretary of the Everett Local of the I.W.W. The outcome is history. One of the 74, a little less noble than Judas tried to help send his fellow workers to prison. His appearance and entrance was like the hero in a ten cent melodrama. When asked if he had seen any one armed on the Verona, he pointed his finger at arm's length and pointed not to Tracy but to another of the 74 and said, "There is the man." After examination of scores of prosecution witnesses and their cross examination by the defense, no one was sure who had killed the deputy we were accused of killing. Those of us who discussed it in jail were convinced that he had stopped a bullet fired by his own side.

The defense witnesses who were held in jail found out that the longer the trial lasted, the more it would cost Snohomish county. So we agreed that when we were under cross examination by the prosecution to make our answers delay the proceedings as much as possible. The prosecution helped us unintentionally by trying to discredit us as persons. They had no hope of destroying the force of our testimony. Once a witness was asked during cross examination where he had come from, when he came to Seattle. He mentioned Yakima where he had stayed one day, Spokane, several towns in Montana, North Dakota, South Dakota, Iowa and Nebraska. It all contributed to the delay. Then he was asked how he came into Omaha. "Rode in." "On what?" "On a train." "What kind of a train?" "Railroad train." "What kind of railroad train?" "Steam train." "Was it a passenger train or a freight train?" Here the defense lawyer got in an objection which was sustained. The prosecutor had learned so much geography that he must have forgotten what he wanted the jury to find out in the first place, so he excused the witness.

No Fugitives

While the trial was going on some of the prisoners in Everett were taken for a walk for exercise. On one of these occasions the deputy who was escorting them started to walk away from them. He was called back and told by the prisoners to return them to the jail as they did not know the way.

In Seattle when any of the I.W.W. prisoner witnesses were taken out of the jail for glasses, dentistry or other treatment, the deputies escorting them more than once left them in various offices in which they were being fitted or treated, knowing that none would try to escape. Why should we? Hadn't we been chosen as witnesses? We hardly thought of ourselves as individuals and gauged our actions by the value they would be to the defense, the organization and the working class. We did not feel this as those who profess religious conviction by some sort of sudden revelation, but by the association with one another and the realization that the group and the thing that the group stood for were far more important than the individual.

Acquittal

The trial finally came to an end on May 5, 1917, with the acquittal of Thomas H. Tracy. The Lumber Barons and shingle manufacturers of the Pacific Northwest had had their Roman Holiday. They had also had a belly full of murder trials. Snohomish county was broke. The I.W.W. was stronger in membership and strength on the job. It had built up a prestige with which to carry on the lumber strike of 1917.

All names except those of the writer or Thomas H. Tracy have been omitted, not with any intention to slight them. Most of them need no mention for they for years at least were useful and active in the Class Struggle.

This is a story of a group. I have not forgotten the fellow worker who would rather be returned back to a prison from which he had escaped than be used by the prosecution; nor have I forgotten the lump in my throat when we tried to sing "Solidarity" for him in token of goodbye.

*Tomorrow I expect to take a trip to the planet
Mars and, if so, will immediately commence to
organize the Mars canal workers into the I.W.W.
and we will sing the good old songs so loud that
the learned star-gazers on earth will once for all
get positive proof that the planet Mars really is
inhabited. . . . I have nothing to say for myself
only that I have always tried to make this earth a
little better for the great producing class, and I
can pass off into the great unknown with the pleasure of knowing that I never in my life double-
crossed a man, woman or child.*

JOE HILL to editor Ben Williams
Solidarity (October 9, 1915).

Chapter 5

Joe Hill: Wobbly Bard

On November 19, 1915, Joe Hill, a thirty-three
year old Wobbly writer, was killed by a five-man
firing squad in the prison yard of the Utah State
Penitentiary. Circumstantial evidence supported
the allegation that he had shot and killed a Salt
Lake City grocer on January 10, 1914. His guilt
is still a matter of dispute.

Before he was finally executed, the Joe Hill
case had involved President Wilson, the acting
secretary of state, the Swedish ambassador to the
United States, Samuel Gompers, the daughter of
the president of the Mormon Church, and thousands of persons around the world who staged
protest demonstrations and sent letters appealing
for his release.

Hill had been a member of the I.W.W. for
probably only three years before he was arrested
for murder in Salt Lake City. He, more than any
other one writer, had made the I.W.W. a singing
movement. He was the author of dozens of Wobbly songs which were printed on song cards and
published in the *Industrial Worker, Solidarity,*
and in the little red songbook. They had tough,
humorous, skeptical words which raked American
morality over the coals.

Joe Hill's songs swept across the country; they
were sung in jails, jungles, picket lines, demonstrations. I.W.W. sailors carried them to other
countries. Wobblies knew their words as well as
they knew the first sentence to the I.W.W. Preamble.

Yet, little is known about Joe Hill before he

joined the I.W.W. about 1910, since he drifted
from job to job like most single migrants. He
chose to be reticent about the facts of his life, and
when a friend wrote to him in prison asking for
some biographical data, Hill scoffingly replied
that he was a "citizen of the world," and his birthplace was "the planet, Earth." [1]

In fact, Joe Hill was a Swede, born Joel Em-
manuel Haaglund, who came to the United States
about 1901 at the age of nineteen. It was claimed
that he learned English at the YMCA in his hometown and as a seaman on freighters running between Sweden and England. By 1910, he was an
I.W.W. member, active around the port of San
Pedro, California, and in the next three years took
part in the San Pedro dock workers' strike, the
San Diego free speech campaign, and an abortive
revolution in Tia Juana, which aimed to make
Lower California into a commune.

The date of Hill's arrival in Utah is unknown.
It is estimated that he was there about a month
before grocer Morrison's murder. His supporters
claimed that he was "framed" by the Copper Trust
and the Mormon Church because he helped organize workers at the United Construction Company at Bingham, Utah, who won a strike in 1913.
He may have come in answer to the call from
Utah's I.W.W. Local 69 to stage a free speech
fight. He was unemployed at the time of his arrest
and rooming with his friend, Otto Applequist, at
the home of some Wobblies, the Eselius brothers,
in Murray, a suburb of Salt Lake City.

On Saturday night, January 10, 1914, at about 10 P.M., J. B. Morrison was closing his grocery, helped by his sons, Alving and Merlin. Two men, masked with red bandannas, broke into the store, rushed toward Morrison with their revolvers drawn, and fired. One of them shouted, "We've got you now."[2] Fourteen-year-old Merlin later testified that he ran to the rear of the store while his older brother reached for their father's revolver, lying on a shelf near the icebox, and fired once before being shot down by the bandits who then rushed from the store. Alving died immediately; his father died later that night without regaining consciousness. Witnesses testified that as one of the men ran out the door he clutched his chest and said, "Oh, God, I'm shot."[3] Spots of blood were found in the alley at the rear of the building, although no blood was found in the store.

Morrison had spent a number of years as a policeman on the Salt Lake City force, and had told a newspaper reporter that he was afraid of reprisal from two men whom he had arrested. He was quoted in a news story as saying, "I have lived to regret that I ever was a member of the force."[4] He had been threatened twice before by bandits. In 1903 he had frustrated an attempted robbery by shooting at his assailants. Four months before his death, his store was broken into again by two armed men. At the trial Merlin testified that his father had loaded his gun "just before the men came in."[5]

About two hours after the Morrison shooting, Hill arrived at the office of Dr. F. N. McHugh, about five miles from Morrison's store. He was bleeding heavily from a bullet wound in his left lung. As McHugh helped Hill remove his blood-soaked coat, a shoulder holster containing an automatic pistol fell from his clothes. Hill explained that he had been shot in a quarrel over a woman. He asked the doctor to keep the incident quiet since he wished to protect the woman's reputation. Noting that the bullet had passed through Hill's body, McHugh treated the wound. A colleague drove Hill to the Eselius home.

McHugh reported Hill's visit to the police and agreed to cooperate in apprehending him. Three days later, he visited Hill at the Eselius home to treat the wound and drugged him in the process. A drowsy Hill was aroused soon after by four policemen, who broke into his room with drawn revolvers. One fired a shot which grazed Hill's

shoulder and went through his right hand. Although he was in critical condition from his lung and hand wounds, Hill was put into a solitary cell at the county jail rather than into the prison hospital. He was charged with the murder of John and Alving Morrison and imprisoned for five months awaiting trial.

Long before the trial, the Salt Lake City press and police had found Hill guilty. The San Pedro chief of police forwarded information about Hill's alien status and I.W.W. membership. It made good copy. The newspapers published Hill's "crime record" on January 24 and kept up a barrage of articles vilifying the man and the organization. His lawyers later claimed, "The main thing the state has against Hill is that he is an I.W.W. and *therefore sure to be guilty*. Hill tried to keep the I.W.W. out of it . . . but the papers fastened it upon him."[6]

Confusion and contradiction marked the testimony of witnesses during the trial which started June 10, 1914. None of the witnesses, including Merlin Morrison, identified Hill as one of the men who entered the grocery store. Although the bullet which had wounded Hill had passed through his body, leaving a jagged hole in the back of his coat, no slug was found during a search of the store. The bullet holes in Hill's coat were four inches lower than those in his body and his lawyers claimed that Hill's hands were over his head when he had been shot by the assailant. Dr. McHugh had seen only the handle of Hill's automatic pistol, and Hill claimed that he had tossed the gun away after leaving the doctor's office. Since the gun could not be found, it was never proven that Hill had fired the fatal shots.

Hill repeatedly refused to testify or give more information about his movements the night of January 10. He declined to give the names of the persons involved in the quarrel which he maintained to his death was the reason for his wound. He would say nothing about his roommate, Otto Applequist, suspected as the second gunman, who disappeared from Salt Lake City the night of the murder and was never found.

In a dramatic outburst during the courtroom trial Hill publicly fired his lawyers, two attorneys who had volunteered to defend him without charge. Hill claimed that they were not cross-examining the state's witnesses nor objecting to leading questions from the district attorney. Against Hill's wishes, the judge brought the lawyers back into the case as "friends of the court." Hill tried again to discharge his lawyers and attempted to conduct his own defense. Toward the end of the trial, the I.W.W. hired O. N. Hilton of Denver, Colorado, a prominent labor lawyer who had defended members of the Western Federation of Miners.

Ten days after the trial began, despite irregularities and unanswered questions, Hill was declared guilty and sentenced to be executed. Hill and the I.W.W. maintained that he had not had a fair trial.

At a time when defense funds were needed for many I.W.W. prisoners around the country, Hill was singled out for special help. An appeal for funds in the April 18, 1914, issue of *Solidarity* stated that Hill was "one of the best-known men in the movement, beloved by all who knew him," and went on to say:

Now there is not one in this organization that can say he does not know this man. For wherever rebels meet, the name of JOE HILL is known. Though we do not know him personally, what one among us can say he is not on speaking terms with "Scissor Bill," "Mr. Block" or who has not heard the "White Slave" or listened to a rendering of the famous "Casey Jones" song and many others in the little red songbook?[7]

Early in 1915, a special Joe Hill edition of the I.W.W. songbook was sold to raise money for his defense.

Characteristically, Hill's twenty-two months in prison were spent serving the "Organization." Along with a voluminous correspondence, he continued producing articles, poems, and songs which filtered through the union's channels and which

Industrial Worker, April 24, 1913.

CONSTITUTIONAL GUARANTEE:—LIFE? LIBERTY? AND THE PURSUIT OF—A JOB!

were used to raise money on his behalf. In letters to other Wobblies, he expressed concern about the costs of carrying his defense to higher courts. To his lawyer, O. N. Hilton, he wrote: "I'm afraid we'll have to let it go as is . . . because I cannot expect my friends to starve themselves in order to save my life."[8] To Haywood he wrote: "I can see where money can be used to a great advantage at present by the Organization and there is no use to be sentimental about it, Bill; we cannot afford to let the whole organization go bankrupt just on account of one individual."[9] Similar letters were sent to Ed Rowan, secretary of Salt Lake's Local 69, and Elizabeth Gurley Flynn.

As Hill's appeal made its way through the Utah courts, efforts to save him snowballed into national and international proportions. When the Utah Supreme Court turned down his appeal in July 1915, over 10,000 letters were received in the state capitol protesting the decision. Fearing an influx of Wobbly agitators, officials doubled the guards at Hill's prison and ordered machine guns placed at the entrance. Since some of the letters contained threats, the homes of Governor Spry and other state officials were put under heavy guard. Ironically, the only act of violence during this time was the shooting of an unarmed Wobbly soapbox speaker by a Salt Lake City police captain.

When the Board of Pardons met on September 18 to consider the case, Hill again refused to tell how he had been shot. Nevertheless, he insisted on having a new trial. The Board of Pardons refused to change the date of execution set for thirteen days later by the Utah Supreme Court. This touched off a series of demonstrations and intercessions which destined the Joe Hill case to be a cause célèbre in United States' history.

Thousands of letters, resolutions, and petitions from all parts of the world were received at the state capitol asking Governor Spry to pardon Hill or commute his sentence. A committee of California women and Virginia Snow Stephen, the daughter of the president of the Mormon Church, appealed to the Swedish minister to the United States to intervene and to ask for a reprieve since Hill was still a Swedish citizen. Because of the large amount of mail the State Department had been receiving and the international implications of the case, the United States' acting secretary of state also urged the governor to grant a reprieve. Convinced that Hill had not had a fair trial,

the Swedish minister contacted President Wilson the day before the scheduled execution. Wilson telegraphed Governor Spry asking for a postponement of the execution until the Swedish minister had had a chance to present his view of the case. After a meeting with the Board of Pardons, Spry replied to Wilson: "We have found no reason whatever why clemency should be extended."[10] He agreed to a stay of execution until the next Board of Pardons' meeting, sixteen days later.

On October 18, despite a direct plea for clemency from the Swedish minister, the Utah Board of Pardons denied a commutation of sentence to life imprisonment. Two days later, Hill was re-sentenced to die in a month and a day.

Hundreds of groups in the United States and abroad organized protest meetings, passed resolutions, and mailed petitions to Utah officials, President Wilson, and the press. Elizabeth Gurley Flynn and Mrs. J. Sergeant Cramm, wife of a member of the New York Public Service Commission, had a short interview with President Wilson, who promised to intercede again. A.F.L. President Samuel Gompers sent the Utah governor and Board of Pardons a resolution passed by the thirty-fifth annual A.F.L. convention in San Francisco, urging them to stop the execution and grant a new trial. Gompers telegraphed President Wilson to help save Hill's life, since there was so much doubt concerning the case.

For the second time, President Wilson wired Governor Spry asking for a thorough reconsideration of Hill's sentence. Utah officials and the state press resented this meddling, which, they claimed, was "unworthy, based on misconception and, if successful, would destroy the usefulness of the state's courts. . . ."[11] Spry replied firmly to Wilson: "A further postponement at this time would be an unwarranted interference with the course of justice."[12]

This time, all efforts on Hill's behalf failed. On his last day, Hill wired Bill Haywood: "Goodbye, Bill. I die like a true blue rebel. Don't waste any time in mourning. Organize."[13] A second telegram to Haywood read: "It is only a hundred miles from here to Wyoming. Could you arrange to have my body hauled to the state line to be buried? I don't want to be found dead in Utah."[14]

Haywood replied: "Goodbye, Joe. You will live long in hearts of the working class. Your songs will be sung wherever workers toil, urging them to organize."[15]

On the afternoon before the execution, Hill was interviewed by a reporter from the Salt Lake City *Tribune*. During the interview, Hill scribbled "My Last Will," a poem which he gave, together with his silk neck scarf, to Ed Rowan, who visited him that evening. His last letter was to Elizabeth Gurley Flynn.

In Utah a condemned man had his choice—to be hung or to be shot by a firing squad. Hill chose to be shot. Legend has it that he shouted the order, "Fire," to his executioners. The next morning, a *New York Times* editorial wondered whether Hill's death "left an opening for people to make a hero of him" and might make "Hillstrom dead more dangerous to social stability than when he was alive."[16]

Joe Hill was given a martyr's funeral. Following funeral services in Salt Lake City, his body was shipped to Chicago. There, an estimated 30,000 sympathizers attended the funeral and marched through the streets to the cemetery. His ashes were put into small envelopes and scattered to the winds "in every state of the union and every country of the world" on May Day 1916.

Immediately after Hill's execution, Governor Spry vowed in a press conference to rid Utah of the "lawless element," stop street speaking, and "use the militia . . . if necessary to clear the state. . . ."[17] Virginia Snow Stephen was fired from the faculty at the University of Utah for her support of Hill, and lawyer O. N. Hilton, who gave the funeral address in Chicago, was disbarred in Utah.

There are too few facts known to separate adequately the legend of Joe Hill from the man. Chaplin wrote that Hill neither smoked, drank, nor was a ladies' man; he was noted for his generosity and frequently "gave away his last rice."[18] On the other hand, Mac McClintock, who only met Hill two or three times, claimed he remembered him as a "real life Raffles" in a conservative blue suit and black tie, who, if he was a criminal, "robbed from the robbers."[19] But no one, recalled Mac, ever saw Hill get into a fight.

Hill's songs and writings articulated the simple Marxism of the I.W.W. Preamble and the Wobbly philosophy of "direct action." His article, "The People," complained sardonically of the attitudes of national politicians. He criticized the "ruling class" for their selfishness and lack of morality in human relations. He shared with other Wobblies

the sentiment that "war certainly shows up the capitalist system in its right light. Millions of men are employed at making ships and others are hired to sink them. Scientific management, eh wot?"[20] On the struggle for existence, he remarked:

> Self-preservation is, or should be, the first law of nature. The animals when in a natural stage are showing us the way. When they are hungry they will always try to get something to eat or else they will die in the attempt. That's natural; to starve to death is unnatural.[21]

Yet he was perceptive enough to understand that "as a rule, a fellow don't bother his head much about unions and theories of the class struggle when his belly is flapping up against his spine."[22]

Within the I.W.W. his songs were recognized for their inspiration and recruiting value because he articulated the frustrations, hostilities, and humor of the homeless and the dispossessed. As one member of the organization put it:

> How did Joe Hill come to write such songs as that? How did he know how the workers on the Fraser River felt? How did he know how it felt to have your pay envelope short of the price of two loaves of bread so you went out on the streets with the workers from the textile mills of Lawrence. . . . Wherever Joe Hill was he somehow felt like the workers and he wrote for them a song. . . . How astonishing! People from all parts of the world, all speaking different dialects and all singing the same song.[23]

A lyrical description of Hill's songs was voiced by Ralph Chaplin who wrote:

> [they are] as coarse as homespun and as fine as silk; full of lilting laughter and keen-edged satire; full of fine rage and finer tenderness; simple, forceful and sublime songs; songs of and for the worker, written in the only language that he can understand and set to the music of Joe Hill's own heart.[24]

Hill was eulogized by I.W.W. writers Ralph Chaplin, Covington Hall, Cash Stevens, Henry George Weiss, T-Bone Slim, and many others. His songs continued to be sung all over the world. "The Preacher and the Slave" and "Casey Jones" became American folk songs, and "pie in the sky," a slogan for a generation in the 1930's. Hill, the man, became a legend compared to Paul Bunyan, John Henry, Johnny Appleseed, and other folk

AS IT WAS   AS IT IS

One Big Union Monthly, November 1919.

heroes—preserved by novelists, playwrights, poets, and researchers. His story has inspired more writing than any other labor hero.

In 1947, Wallace Stegner wrote that Joe Hill's biography in Dos Passos's 1919 and Earl Robinson's ballad "I Dreamed I Saw Joe Hill Last Night,"

. . . have built Joe Hill into a folk hero, almost the number one labor martyr and legend. . . . People have made him into a Galahad, a hero, and a martyr, and they have done so because he gave them the opportunity, he offered the leads. He had what none of the other dozens of eligible martyrs had—imagination, a flair. His curtain line was magnificent: "Don't waste any time in mourning. Organize!" He died for a cause, for a principle, for a woman's honor, for the things that fire the imagination, and the world-wide scattering of his ashes was a fitting finale. That symbolic act fertilized both the movement his songs served and the legend of labor's songster.[25]

Most recently, writer Barry Nichols has called Joe Hill "the Twentieth Century's first egg-head, heman folk hero."[26]

Wobblies, socialists, communists, A.F.L.–C.I.O. members transcend sectarian differences to sing Joe Hill's songs and share his lore. The man and the martyr have combined into a continuing legend of "the man who never died."

1

"The Preacher and the Slave," sometimes called "Pie in the Sky" or "Long-Haired Preachers," is considered Joe Hill's masterpiece. It was printed in the third edition of the I.W.W. songbook and sung to the hymn tune, "Sweet Bye and Bye." Twelve years after Hill's death, Carl Sandburg included it in his collection, The American Songbag *(New York, 1927). The song quickly became a part of American folk tradition. Henry F. May in his book,* The End of American Innocence *(New York, 1961), wrote: "Here, if anywhere, was*

a clear breach with timidity, moralism, and the whole manner and content of the standard American culture. 'Long-haired preachers' try to tell us what's right and wrong, but turn out to offer only 'pie in the sky.'"

THE PREACHER AND THE SLAVE*

By Joe Hill

(*Tune: "Sweet Bye and Bye"*)

Long-haired preachers come out every night,
Try to tell you what's wrong and what's right;
But when asked how 'bout something to eat
They will answer with voices so sweet:

Chorus:

You will eat, bye and bye,
In that glorious land above the sky;
Work and pray, live on hay,
You'll get pie in the sky when you die.

The starvation army they play,
They sing and they clap and they pray.
Till they get all your coin on the drum,
Then they tell you when you are on the bum:

Chorus:

You will eat, bye and bye,
In that glorious land above the sky;
Work and pray, live on hay,
You'll get pie in the sky when you die.

Holy Rollers and jumpers come out,
They holler, they jump and they shout.
Give your money to Jesus they say,
He will cure all diseases today.

If you fight hard for children and wife—
Try to get something good in this life—
You're a sinner and bad man, they tell,
When you die you will sure go to hell.

Workingmen of all countries unite,
Side by side we for freedom will fight:
When the world and its wealth we have gained
To the grafters we'll sing this refrain:

Last Chorus:

You will eat, bye and bye,
When you've learned how to cook and to fry;

Chop some wood, 'twill do you good,
And you'll eat in the sweet bye and bye.

2

"Casey Jones—The Union Scab" is said to have been written by Joe Hill in 1911 during a strike of shop workers on the Southern Pacific Railroad in San Pedro, California, when engineers and some other skilled craft workers continued to operate the trains. Hill's parody is set to the popular "Casey Jones" song about the brave engineer who stuck to the wheel of his train. Barrie Stavis, in the introduction to The Man Who Never Died *(New York, 1954), wrote: "Joe Hill's song writing career was launched. The song helped to hold the strikers together. It was sung by the men on the picket line and by those who were clubbed and thrown into jail. It was printed on colored cards, about the size of a playing card, and sold, the proceeds going to the strike fund. Overnight the song became famous. Migratory laborers carried it on their lips as they moved across the nation; sailors carried it across the ocean."*

Two articles by folklorists Duncan Emrich and William Alderson on Joe Hill's "Casey Jones" appear in the California Folklore Quarterly *(Winter 1942, p. 293 and pp. 373–76).*

The song was printed in the fourth edition of the I.W.W. songbook.

CASEY JONES—
THE UNION SCAB*

By Joe Hill

(*Tune: "Casey Jones"*)

The Workers on the S.P. line to strike sent out a
    call;
But Casey Jones, the engineer, he wouldn't strike
    at all;
His boiler it was leaking, and its drivers on the
    bum,
And his engine and its bearings, they were all out
    of plumb.

Chorus:

Casey Jones kept his junk pile running;
Casey Jones was working double time;
Casey Jones got a wooden medal,
For being good and faithful on the S.P. line.

The Workers said to Casey: "Won't you help us
   win this strike?"
But Casey said: "Let me alone, you'd better take
   a hike."
Then some one put a bunch of railroad ties across
   the track,
And Casey hit the bottom with an awful crack.

Chorus:

Casey Jones hit the river bottom;
Casey Jones broke his blessed spine,
Casey Jones was an Angeleno,
He took a trip to heaven on the S.P. line.

When Casey Jones got up to heaven to the Pearly
   Gate,
He said: "I'm Casey Jones, the guy that pulled the
   S.P. freight."
"You're just the man," said Peter; "our musicians
   went on strike;
You can get a job a-scabbing any time you like."

Chorus:

Casey Jones got up to heaven;
Casey Jones was doing mighty fine;
Casey Jones went scabbing on the angels,
Just like he did to workers on the S.P. line.

The angels got together, and they said it wasn't fair,
For Casey Jones to go around a-scabbing every-
   where.
The Angels Union No. 23, they sure were there,
And they promptly fired Casey down the Golden
   Stair.

Chorus:

Casey Jones went to Hell a-flying.
"Casey Jones," the Devil said, "Oh, fine;
Casey Jones, get busy shoveling sulpher—
That's what you get for scabbing on the S.P. line."

3

*"Coffee An'" was printed in the fourth edition of
the I.W.W. songbook.*

COFFEE AN'

Composed by J. H. of the I.W.W.

(*Tune: "Count Your Blessings"*)

An employment shark the other day I went to see,
And he said, "Come in and buy a job from me,

Just a couple of dollars for the office fee,
But the job is steady and the fare is free."

Chorus:

Count your pennies, count them one by one,
And you'll plainly see how you are done,
Count your pennies, take them in your hand,
Sneak into a Jap's, and get your coffee an'.

I shipped out and worked and worked and slept in
   lousy bunks,
And the grub it stunk as bad as forty-'leven
   skunks,
When I slaved a week the boss he said one day,
"You're too tired, you are fired, go and get your
   pay."

Chorus.

When the clerk commenced to count, Oh, holy
   gee!
Road and school and poll tax and the hospital fee,
Then I fainted and I nearly lost my sense
When the clerk he said, "You owe me fifty cents."

Chorus.

When I got back to town with blisters on my feet,
There I heard a fellow speaking on the street,
And he said, "It is the workers' own mistake,
If they stick together they get all they make."

Chorus.

And he said, "Come in and join our union grand.
Who will be a member of this fighting band?"
"Write me out a card," says I, "By gee!
The Industrial Workers is the dope for me."

Chorus:

Count your workers, count them one by one,
Join our union and we'll show you how it's done.
Stand together, workers, hand in hand.
Then we'll never have to live on coffee an'.

4

The Industrial Worker (*April 11, 1912*) *included
a news story on a strike of construction workers
on the Canadian Northern Railroad which reported, ". . . the main thing that caused the walk-
out was the foul conditions of the camps in which
the men were herded." Four weeks later an article in the* Industrial Worker (*May 9, 1912*) *stated,*

"The strikers on the Canadian Northern are singing songs as they carry on the strike. The songs are said to be the work of Fellow Worker J. Hill. Lack of space prevents the publication of more than one of them."

WHERE THE FRASER RIVER FLOWS°

(Tune: "Where the Shannon River Flows")

Fellow workers, pay attention to what I'm gonna
    mention,
    For it is the fixed intention of the Workers of
        of the World,
And I hope you'll all be ready, true-hearted, brave
    and steady,
    To rally round the standard when the Red Flag
        is unfurled.

Chorus:

Where the Fraser River flows,
Each fellow worker knows,
They have bullied and oppressed us,
But still our Union grows.
And we're going to find a way, boys;
For shorter hours and better pay, boys;
And we're going to win the day, boys;
Where the Fraser River flows.

For these gunny-sack contractors have all been
    dirty actors,
    And they're not our benefactors, each fellow
        worker knows.
So we've got to stick together in fine or dirty
    weather,
    And we will show no white feather, where the
        Fraser River flows.

Now the boss the law is stretching, bulls and
    pimps he's fetching,
    And they are a fine collection, as Jesus only
        knows.
But why their mothers reared them, and why the
    devil spared them,
    Are questions we can't answer, where the
        Fraser River flows.

5

"Mr. Block," published in the Industrial Worker *(January 23, 1913), was the first of a group of*

eight new Joe Hill songs printed in that paper during the following four months.

Sociologist Carleton Parker, investigating the 1913 hop-pickers' strike on the Durst Brothers' ranch in Wheatland, California, wrote in his report on the Wheatland Riot that the sheriff and his deputies fired into a group of 2000 strikers who were singing "Mr. Block" (The Casual Laborer and Other Essays, New York, 1920). The song was inspired by Ernest Riebe's popular series of "Mr. Block" cartoons which appeared in Solidarity, Industrial Worker, and other I.W.W. publications.

MR. BLOCK°

By JOE HILL

(Tune: "It Looks to Me Like a Big Time Tonight")

Please give me your attention, I'll introduce to you
A man that is a credit to "Our Red, White and
    Blue";
His head is made of lumber, and solid as a rock;
He is a common worker and his name is Mr. Block.
And Block thinks he may
Be President some day.

Chorus:

Oh, Mr. Block you were born by mistake,
*   You take the cake,*
*   You make me ache.*
Tie a rock on your block and then jump in the lake,
Kindly do that for liberty's sake.

Yes, Mr. Block is lucky; he found a job, by gee!
The shark got seven dollars, for job and fare and
    fee.
They shipped him to the desert and dumped him
    with his truck,
But when he tried to find his job he sure was out
    of luck.
He shouted, "That's too raw,
I'll fix them with the law."

Block hiked back to the city, but wasn't doing well.
He said, "I'll join the union—the great A. F. of L."
He got a job next morning, got fired in the night,
He said, "I'll see Sam Gompers and he'll fix that
    foreman right."
Sam Gompers said, "You see,
You've got our sympathy."

Election Day he shouted, "A Socialist for Mayor!"
The "comrade" got elected, he happy was for fair,
But after the election he got an awful shock,
A great big Socialist Bull did rap him on the block.
And Comrade Block did sob,
"I helped him to his job."

Poor Block, he died one evening, I'm very glad to state;
He climbed the golden ladder up to the pearly gate.
He said, "Oh, Mr. Peter, one word I'd like to tell,
I'd like to meet the Asterbilts and John D. Rocke-fell."
Old Pete said, "Is that so?
You'll meet them down below."

6

"Scissorbill," one of Joe Hill's most popular songs, was printed in the Industrial Worker (*February 16, 1913*).

SCISSOR BILL°

By JOE HILL

(*Tune: "Steamboat Bill"*)

You may ramble round the country anywhere you will,
You'll always run across the same old Scissor Bill.
He's found upon the desert, he is upon the hill,
He's found in every mining camp and lumber mill.
He looks just like a human, he can eat and walk,
But you will find he isn't, when he starts to talk.
He'll say, "This is my country," with an honest face,
While all the cops they chase him out of every place.

Chorus:

Scissor Bill, he is a little dippy,
Scissor Bill, he has a funny face.
Scissor Bill should drown in Mississippi,
He is the missing link that Darwin tried to trace.

And Scissor Bill, he couldn't live without the booze,
He sits around all day and spits tobacco juice.
He takes a deck of cards and tries to beat the Chink!

Yes, Bill would be a smart guy if he could only think.
And Scissor Bill he says: "This country must be freed
From Niggers, Japs and Dutchmen and the gol durn Swede."
He says that every cop would be a native son
If it wasn't for the Irishman, the son-of-a-gun.

Chorus:

Scissor Bill, the "foreigners" is cussin';
Scissor Bill, he says "I hate a Coon";
Scissor Bill is down on everybody
The hottentots, the bushmen and the man in the moon.

Don't try to talk your union dope to Scissor Bill,
He says he never organized and never will.
He'll always be satisfied until he's dead,
With coffee and a doughnut and a lousy old bed.
And Bill, he says he gets rewarded thousand fold,
When he gets up to Heaven on the streets of gold.
But I don't care who knows it, and right here I'll tell.
If Scissor Bill is going to Heaven, I'll go to Hell.

Chorus:

Scissor Bill, wouldn't join the union,
Scissor Bill, he says, "Not me, by Heck!"
Scissor Bill gets his reward in Heaven,
Oh! sure. He'll get it, but he'll get it in the neck.

7

Joe Hill's article, "The People," appeared in the Industrial Worker (*March 6, 1913*).

THE PEOPLE

By J. HILL

"The People's flag is deepest red." Who are the people?

"God knows" Taft stands for "the people." If you don't believe it just read the "Los Angeles Crimes" and you will find out that, next to General Debility Otis, Taft is the greatest man in the country. Yes, Fatty stands for the people all right —when he is standing, but he is sitting down most of the time.

And "Teddy da Roos," who used to peddle the Bull Moose, is also very strong for "the people."

Some time ago he wasn't so strong and then it was that he invented a policeman's riot club filled with spikes. It would crush the skull of a wage slave with one blow. Yes, "Teddy da Roos," he is strong for "the people."

And Woodhead Wilson, he is for "the people" too. This is what he said in one of his speeches: "Why shouldn't the children of the workingclass be taught to do the work their parents are now doing?" Of course, he meant to say "Why shouldn't the children of the rich be taught to rob the class their parents are now robbing?" And he is going to give "the people" free silver, he says, but if a working stiff wants any silver he has to peel off his coat and hop to the stormy end of a No. 2.

When the Red Flag was flying in Lower California there were not any of "the people" in the ranks of the rebels. Common working stiffs and cow-punchers were in the majority, with a little sprinkling of "outlaws," whatever that is.

"The people" used to come down there on Sunday in their stinkwagons to take a look at "The wild men with their Red Flag" for two-bits a look. But if the Mexican or the Indian regiment happened to be a little overjoyed from drinking "mescal" and took a notion to have a bit of sociable target practice, or to try to make buttonholes for one another without taking their clothes off, then "the people" would almost break their legs to get to their stinkwagons and make a bee-line for the "Land of the Graft and the Home of the Slave."

Well, it is about time that every rebel wakes up to the fact that "the people" and the workingclass have nothing in common. Let us sing after this *"The Workers' flag is deepest red"* and to hell with "the people."

8

Set to the Stephen Foster tune, "My Old Kentucky Home," this song first appeared in the Industrial Worker (*March 6, 1913*).

WE WILL SING ONE SONG°
By Joe Hill

We will sing one song of the meek and humble
    slave,
    The horny-handed son of the soil,
He's toiling hard from the cradle to the grave,
    But his master reaps the profits of his toil.
Then we'll sing one song of the greedy master
    class,
    They're vagrants in broadcloth, indeed,
They live by robbing the ever-toiling mass,
    Human blood they spill to satisfy their greed.

One Big Union Monthly, November 1919.

Mr. Highbrow: "These wars are terrible. Here they have shot a hole in this 2,000-year old painting."
Mrs. Highbrow: "Oh! Horrors! How thoughtless of that commander not to order some peasants to stand in front of it during the battle."

Chorus:

Organize! O, toilers, come organize your might;
Then we'll sing one song of the Workers' Common-
wealth
Full of beauty, full of love and health.

We will sing one song of the politician sly,
    He's talking of changing the laws;
Election day all the drinks and smokes he'll buy,
    While he's living from the sweat of your brows.
Then we'll sing one song of the girl below the line,
    She's scorned and despised everywhere,
While in their mansions the "keepers" wine and
    dine
    From the profits that immoral traffic bear.

We will sing one song of the preacher, fat and
    sleek,
    He tells you of homes in the sky.
He says "Be generous, be lowly and be meek
    If you don't you'll sure get roasted when you
    die."
Then we'll sing one song of the poor and ragged
    tramp,
    He carries his home on his back;
Too old to work, he's not wanted round the camp,
    So he wanders without aim along the track.

We will sing one song of the children in the mills,
    They're taken from the playgrounds and
    schools.
In tender years made to go the pace that kills,
    In the sweatshops, 'mong the looms and spools.
Then we'll sing one song of the One Big Union
    Grand.
    The hope of the toiler and the slave,
It's coming fast; it is sweeping sea and land,
    To the terror of the grafter and the knave.

9

This song first appeared in the Industrial Worker
(March 6, 1913).

WHAT WE WANT

By J. HILL

(*Tune: "Rainbow"*)

We want all the workers in the world to organize
Into a great big union grand
And when we all united stand
The world for workers we'll demand

If the working class could only see and realize
What mighty power labor has
Then the exploiting master class
It would soon fade away.

Chorus

Come all ye toilers that work for wages,
    Come from every land,
    Join the fighting band,
    In one union grand,
Then for the workers we'll make upon this earth a
    paradise
When the slaves get wise and organize.

We want the sailor and the tailor and the lumber-
    jacks,
And all the cooks and laundry girls,
We want the guy that dives for pearls,
The pretty maid that's making curls,
And the baker and staker and the chimneysweep,
We want the man that's slinging hash,
The child that works for little cash
In one union grand.

Chorus

We want the tinner and the skinner and the
    chamber-maid,
We want the man that spikes on soles,
We want the man that's digging holes,
We want the man that's climbing poles,
And the trucker and the mucker and the hired
    man,
And all the factory girls and clerks,
Yes, we want every one that works,
In one union grand.

10

Joe Hill set these verses to the popular Civil War
song, "Tramp, Tramp, Tramp, the Boys Are March-
ing." It was published in the Industrial Worker
(May 22, 1913), and included fourteen years later
in Sandburg's The American Songbag.

THE TRAMP*

By JOE HILL

(*Tune: "Tramp, Tramp, Tramp, the Boys Are*
Marching")

If you all will shut your trap,
I will tell you 'bout a chap,

Sheet music of Joe Hill's song, "Don't Take My Papa Away from Me."

That was broke and up against it, too, for fair;
He was not the kind that shirk,
He was looking hard for work,
But he heard the same old story everywhere.

Chorus:

Tramp, tramp, tramp keep on a-tramping,
Nothing doing here for you;
If I catch you 'round again,
You will wear the ball and chain,
Keep on tramping, that's the best thing you can do.

He walked up and down the street,
'Till the shoes fell off his feet.
In a house he spied a lady cooking stew,
And he said "How do you do,
May I chop some wood for you?"
What the lady told him made him feel so blue.

(Chorus)

'Cross the road a sign he read,
"Work for Jesus," so it said,
And he said, "Here is my chance, I'll surely try,"
And he kneeled upon the floor,
'Till his knees got rather sore,
But at eating time he heard the preacher cry—

(Chorus)

Down the street he met a cop,
And the copper made him stop,
And he asked him, "When did you blow into town?
Come with me up to the judge,"
But the judge he said, "Oh, fudge,
Bums that have no money needn't come around."

(Chorus)

Finally came that happy day,
When his life did pass away,
He was sure he'd go to heaven when he died.
When he reached the Pearly Gate,
Santa Peter, mean old skate,
Slammed the gate right in his face and loudly
    cried:

(Chorus)

In despair he went to Hell,
With the Devil, for to dwell,
For the reason he'd no other place to go.
And he said, "I'm full of sin,
So for Christ's sake let me in!"
But the Devil said, "Oh beat it, you're a 'bo."

(Chorus.)

11

Joe Hill set these verses to the gospel hymn tune,
"There Is Power in the Blood." The song was
printed in the fifth edition of the I.W.W. song-
book.

THERE IS POWER IN A UNION°

By JOE HILL

(*Tune: "There Is Power in the Blood"*)

Would you have freedom from wage slavery,
    Then join in the grand Industrial band;
Would you from mis'ry and hunger be free,
    Then come! Do your share, like a man.

Chorus:

> *There is pow'r, there is pow'r*
> *In a band of workingmen,*
> *When they stand hand in hand,*
> *That's a pow'r, that's a pow'r*
> *That must rule in every land—*
> *One Industrial Union Grand.*

Would you have mansions of gold in the sky,
    And live in a shack, way in the back?
Would you have wings up in heaven to fly?
    And starve here with rags on your back?

If you've had "nuff" of "the blood of the lamb"
    Then join in the grand Industrial band;
If, for a change, you would have eggs and ham,
    Then come! Do your share, like a man.

If you like sluggers to beat off your head,
    Then don't organize, all unions despise,
If you want nothing before you are dead,
    Shake hands with your boss and look wise.

Come all ye workers, from every land,
    Come join in the grand Industrial band,
Then we our share of this earth shall demand.
    Come on! Do your share, like a man.

12

These verses appeared in the Industrial Worker
(*May 29, 1913*).

STUNG RIGHT°

By JOE HILL

(*Air: "Sunlight, Sunlight"*)

When I was hiking 'round the town to find a job
　　one day,
I saw a sign that thousand men were wanted right
　　away,
To take a trip around the world in Uncle Sammy's
　　fleet,
I signed my name a dozen times upon a great big
　　sheet.

Chorus

Stung right, stung right, S-T-U-N-G,
Stung right, stung right, E. Z. Mark, that's me;
When my term is over, and again I'm free,
There will be no more trips around the world for
*　　me.*

The man he said, "The U.S. fleet, that is no place
　　for slaves,
The only thing you have to do is stand and watch
　　the waves."
But in the morning, five o'clock, they woke me
　　from my snooze,
To scrub the deck and polish brass and shine the
　　captain's shoes.

One day a dude in uniform to me commenced to
　　shout,
I simply plugged him in the jaw and knocked him
　　down and out;
They slammed me right in irons then and said,
　　"You are a case,"
On bread and water then I lived for twenty-seven
　　days.

One day the captain said, "Today I'll show you
　　something nice,
All hands line up, we'll go ashore and have some
　　exercise."
He made us run for seven miles as fast as we
　　could run,
And with a packing on our back that weighed a
　　half a ton.

Some time ago when Uncle Sam he had a war with
　　Spain,
And many of the boys in blue were in the battle
　　slain,

Not all were killed by bullets, though; no, not by
　　any means,
The biggest part that died were killed by Armour's
　　Pork and Beans.

13

*"Nearer My Job to Thee" was printed in the sixth
edition of the I.W.W. songbook and set to the
tune, "Nearer My God to Thee."*

NEARER MY JOB TO THEE

Words by J. H. of the I.W.W.

Nearer my job to thee,
Nearer with glee,
Three plunks for the office fee,
But my fare is free.
My train is running fast,
I've got a job at last,
Nearer my job to thee
Nearer to thee.

Arrived where my job should be,
Nothing in sight I see,
Nothing but sand, by gee,
Job went up a tree.
No place to eat or sleep,
Snakes in the sage brush creep.
Nero a saint would be,
Shark, compared to thee.

Nearer to town! each day
(Hiked all the way),
Nearer that agency,
Where I paid my fee,
And when that shark I see
You'll bet your boots that he
Nearer his god shall be.
Leave that to me.

14

This article by Joe Hill was published in the International Socialist Review (*December 1914*).

HOW TO MAKE WORK FOR
THE UNEMPLOYED

By JOE HILL

Much has been written lately about various new
ways and tactics of carrying on the class struggle
to emancipate the workers from wage slavery.

Some writers propose to "organize with the unemployed"; that is, to feed and house them in order to keep them from taking the jobs away from the employed workers. Others again want to organize a Gunmen Defense Fund to purchase machine guns and high powered rifles for all union men, miners especially, that they may protect themselves from the murderous onslaughts of the private armies of the master class. Very well; these tactics MAY be perfectly good, but the question arises: Who is going to pay for all this?

Estimating the unemployed army to be about five millions in number and the board bill of one individual to be five dollars a week, we find that the total board bill of the whole unemployed army would be twenty-five million dollars per week.

The price of a machine gun is about $600 and a modern high-power rifle costs from $20 to $30. By doing a little figuring we find that fifty million dollars would not be sufficient to buy arms for the *miners*, let alone the rest of the organized workers. Every workingman and woman knows that, after all the bills are paid on pay day, there is not much left to feed the unemployed army or to buy war supplies with.

What the working class needs today is an inexpensive method by which to fight the powerful capitalist class and they have just such a weapon in their own hands.

This weapon is *without expense* to the *working class* and if intelligently and systematically used, it *will* not only *reduce* the *profits* of the *exploiters*, but also *create more work for the wage earners.* If thoroughly understood and used more extensively it may entirely eliminate the unemployed army, the army used by the employing class to keep the workers in submission and slavery.

In order to illustrate the efficacy of this new method of warfare, I will cite a little incident. Some time ago the writer was working in a big lumber yard on the west coast. On the coast nearly all the work around the water fronts and lumber yards is temporary.

When a boat comes in a large number of men are hired and when the boat is unloaded these men are "laid off." Consequently it is to the interest of the workers "to make the job last" as long as possible.

The writer and three others got orders to load up five box cars with shingles. When we commenced the work we found, to our surprise, that every shingle bundle had been cut open. That is,

the little strip of sheet iron that holds the shingles tightly together in a bundle, had been cut with a knife or a pair of shears, on every bundle in the pile—about three thousand bundles in all.

When the boss came around we notified him about the accident and, after exhausting his supply of profanity, he ordered us to get the shingle press and re-bundle the whole batch. It took the four of us ten whole days to put that shingle pile into shape again. And our wages for that time, at the rate of 32c per hour, amounted to $134.00. By adding the loss on account of delay in shipment, the "holding money" for the five box cars, etc., we found that the company's profit for that day had been reduced about $300.

So there you are. In less than half an hour's time somebody had created ten days' work for four men who would have been otherwise unemployed, and at the same time cut a big chunk off the boss's profit. No lives were lost, no property was destroyed, there were no law suits, nothing that would drain the resources of the organized workers. But there WERE results. That's all.

This same method of fighting can be used in a thousand different ways by the skilled mechanic or machine hand as well as by the common laborer. This weapon is always at the finger tips of the worker, employed or unemployed.

If every worker would devote ten or fifteen minutes every day to the interests of himself and his class, after devoting eight hours or more to the interests of his employer, it would not be long before the unemployed army would be a thing of the past and the profit of the bosses would melt away so fast that they would not be able to afford to hire professional man-killers to murder the workers and their families in a case of strike.

The best way to strike, however, is to "strike on the job." First present your demands to the boss. If he should refuse to grant them, don't walk out and give the scabs a chance to take your places. No, just go back to work as though nothing had happened and try the new method of warfare.

When things begin to happen be careful not to "fix the blame" on any certain individual unless that individual is an "undesirable" from a working class point of view.

The boss will soon find that the cheapest way out of it is to grant your demands. This is not mere theory; it has been successfully tried more than once to the writer's personal knowledge.

Striking on the job is a science and should be

taught as such. It is extremely interesting on account of its many possibilities. It develops mental
keenness and inventive genius in the working
class and is the only known antidote for the infamous "Taylor System."

The aim of the "Taylor System" seems to be to
work one-half the workers to death and starve the
other half to death. The strike on the job will give
every worker a chance to make an honest living.
It will enable us to take the child slaves out of
the mill and sweat-shop and give their unemployed fathers a chance to work. It will stop the
butchering of the workers in time of peace as
well as in time of war.

If you imagine "Making Work for the Unemployed" is unfair, just remember Ludlow and
Calumet and don't forget Sacramento where the
men who were unable to get work had their brains
beaten out by the Hessians of the law and were
knocked down and drenched to the skin with
streams of ice-cold water manipulated by the city
fire department, where the unemployed were
driven out of the city and in the rain only to
meet the pitchforks of the farmers. And what for?
For the horrible crime of asking the governor of
California—for A JOB!

This is the way the capitalist class uses the
working class when they can no longer exploit
them—in the name of Law and Order. Remember
this when you MAKE WORK FOR THE UN-
EMPLOYED!

15

*Joe Hill composed the words and the music to this
song, which appeared in the ninth edition of the
I.W.W. songbook.*

WORKERS OF THE WORLD,
AWAKEN!°

By Joe Hill

Workers of the world, awaken!
Break your chains, demand your rights.
All the wealth you make is taken
By exploiting parasites.
Shall you kneel in deep submission
From your cradles to your graves?
Is the height of your ambition
To be good and willing slaves?

Refrain:

*Arise, ye prisoners of starvation!
Fight for your own emancipation;
Arise, ye slaves of every nation
In One Union Grand.
Our little ones for bread are crying,
And millions are from hunger dying;
The means the end is justifying,
'Tis the final stand.*

If the workers take a notion,
They can stop all speeding trains;
Every ship upon the ocean
They can tie with mighty chains;
Every wheel in the creation,
Every mine and every mill,
Fleets and armies of the nation
Will at their command stand still.

Join the union, fellow workers,
Men and women, side by side;
We will crush the greedy shirkers
Like a sweeping, surging tide.
For united we are standing,
But divided we will fall;
Let this be our understanding—
"All for one and one for all."

Workers of the world, awaken!
Rise in all your splendid might;
Take the wealth that you are making,
It belongs to you by right.
No one will for bread be crying,
We'll have freedom, love and health
When the grand red flag is flying
In the Workers' Commonwealth.

16

*These verses set to the popular tune "Ta-Ra-Ra
Boom De-Ay" appeared in the ninth edition of
the I.W.W. songbook. Prosecuting attorneys in
some of the federal and state trials used the song
as evidence of I.W.W. intent to commit acts of
sabotage if the workers' requests for better working conditions were not granted.*

TA-RA-RA BOOM DE-AY

By Joe Hill

I had a job once threshing wheat, worked sixteen
hours with hands and feet.

And when the moon was shining bright, they kept
me working all the night
One moonlight night, I hate to tell, I "accidentally"
slipped and fell.
My pitchfork went right in between some cog
wheels of that thresh-machine.

Chorus:

Ta-ra-ra-boom-de-ay!
It made a noise that way,
And wheels and bolts and hay,
Went flying every way.
That stingy rube said, "Well!
A thousand gone to hell."
But I did sleep that night,
I needed it all right.

Next day that stingy rube did say, "I'll bring my
eggs to town today;
You grease my wagon up, you mutt, and don't
forget to screw the nut."
I greased his wagon all right, but, I plumb forgot
to screw the nut,
And when he started on that trip, the wheel
slipped off and broke his hip.

Second Chorus:

Ta-ra-ra-boom-de-ay!
It made a noise that way.
That rube was sure a sight,
And mad enough to fight;
His whiskers and his legs
Were full of scrambled eggs:
I told him, "That's too bad—
I'm feeling very sad."

And then that farmer said, "You turk! I bet you
are an I-Won't-Work."
He paid me off right there, By Gum! So I went
home and told my chum.
Next day when threshing did commence, my
chum was Johnny on the fence;
And 'pon my word, that awkward kid, he dropped
his pitchfork, like I did.

Third Chorus:

Ta-ra-ra-boom-de-ay!
It made a noise that way,
And part of that machine
Hit Reuben on the bean.
He cried, "Oh me, oh my;
I nearly lost my eye."

My partner said, "You're right—
It's bedtime now, good night."

But still that rube was pretty wise, these things
did open up his eyes.
He said, "There must be something wrong; I think
I work my men too long."
He cut the hours and raised the pay, gave ham
and eggs for every day,
Now gets his men from union hall, and has no
"accidents" at all.

Fourth Chorus:

Ta-ra-ra-boom-de-ay!
That rube is feeling gay;
He learned his lesson quick,
Just through a simple trick.
For fixing rotten jobs
And fixing greedy slobs,
This is the only way,
Ta-ra-ra-boom-de-ay!

17

While Joe Hill was in prison, his friend Sam Mur-
ray wrote from California, asking him to compose
a song about widespread unemployment during
the 1913–14 depression in San Francisco. Hill
replied: ". . . when I make a song I always try
to picture things as they really are. Of course a
little pepper and salt is allowed in order to bring
out the facts more clearly. If you send me that
sheet music and give me some of the peculiarities
and ridiculous points about conditions in general
. . . I'll try to do the best I can." Murray sent
Hill the music to, "It's a Long Way to Tipperary,"
and Hill wrote this parody. Printed on song cards,
it was sold for a nickel to raise money for Joe
Hill's defense. On March 22, 1915, Joe Hill wrote
to Sam Murray: "Yes, that Tipperary song is
spreading like the smallpox they say. . . . The
unemployed all over the country have adopted it
as a marching song in their parades, and in New
York City they changed it to some extent so as to
fit the brand of soup dished out in N.Y. . . ."
("Last Letters of Joe Hill," Industrial Pioneer,
December 1923).

The first version printed here is taken from an
early song card included in the Joe Hill files in the
Labadie Collection. The second version appeared
in the twenty-fifth edition (1933) of the I.W.W.
songbook.

IT'S A LONG LONG WAY DOWN TO THE SOUPLINE

By JOE HILL

Bill Brown came a thousand miles to work on Frisco Fair
  All the papers said a million men were wanted there
Bill Brown hung around and asked for work three times a day,
  'Til finally he went busted flat, then he did sadly say,

Chorus

It's a long way down to the soupline.
  It's a long way to go.
It's a long way down to the soupline
  And the soup is weak I know.
Good-bye, good old pork chops.
  Farewell beefsteak rare,
It's a long, long way down to the soupline,
  But my soup is there.

II

Bill Brown saw a big fine house, he knocked upon the door,
  But they told him that they only helped the "worthy poor,"
Guess I'll have to live on sunshine in the Golden West,
  Said Billy Brown, and then he joined the chorus with the rest.

III

There's a whisper round the town among "the men of means,"
  That they would be glad to give the Fair to New Orleans,
And when all is over many sharks with faces long,
  Will line up at the ferry and then sadly hum this song.

Chorus

18

IT'S A LONG WAY DOWN TO THE SOUPLINE°

By JOE HILL

Bill Brown was just a working man like others of his kind.

He lost his job and tramped the streets when work was hard to find.
The landlord put him on the stem, the bankers kept his dough,
  And Bill heard everybody sing, no matter where he'd go:

Chorus

It's a long way down to the soupline,
  It's a long way to go.
It's a long way down to the soupline
  And the soup is thin I know.
Good-bye good old pork chops,
  Farewell beefsteak rare;
It's a long, long way down to the soupline,
  But my soup is there.

So Bill and sixteen million men responded to the call
  To force the hours of labor down and thus make jobs for all.
They picketed the industries and won the four-hour day
  And organized a General Strike so men don't have to say:

Chorus

The workers own the factories now, where jobs were once destroyed
  By big machines that filled the world with hungry unemployed.
They all own homes, they're living well, they're happy, free and strong,
  But millionaires wear overalls and sing this little song:

Chorus

19

On February 13, 1915, Joe Hill wrote to Sam Murray: ". . . have been busy working on a song named 'The Rebel Girl' (Words and Music) which I hope will help to line up the women workers in the OBU" ("Last Letters of Joe Hill"). In 1916, Bill Haywood had the song copyrighted.

THE REBEL GIRL°

(Words and Music by Joe Hill)

There are women of many descriptions
In this queer world, as every one knows,

Some are living in beautiful mansions,
And are wearing the finest of clothes.
There are blue-blooded queens and princesses,
Who have charms made of diamonds and pearl;
But the only and Thoroughbred Lady
Is the Rebel Girl.

Chorus

That's the Rebel Girl. That's the Rebel Girl.
To the working class she's a precious pearl.
She brings courage, pride and joy
To the Fighting Rebel Boy.
We've had girls before
But we need some more
In the Industrial Workers of the World,
For it's great to fight for freedom
With a Rebel Girl.

Yes, her hands may be harden'd from labor
And her dress may not be very fine;
But a heart in her bosom is beating
That is true to her class and her kind.
And the grafters in terror are trembling
When her spite and defiance she'll hurl.
For the only and Thoroughbred Lady
Is the Rebel Girl.

20

Joe Hill wrote "My Last Will" during an interview in his cell with a reporter from the Salt Lake City Herald Tribune on the afternoon before his execution. The reporter later wrote that he had questioned Hill, "What disposition are you going to make of your effects, your little trinkets and personal belongings . . ?" " 'I really have nothing to dispose of,' replied Hillstrom. 'As for trinkets, keepsakes and jewelry, I never believed in them nor kept them about me. But I have a will to make, and I'll scribble it. I'll send it to the world in care of Ed Rowan and my I.W.W. friends' " (Barry Stavis, The Man Who Never Died, New York, 1954).

Soon after Hill's death, "My Last Will" was published in the International Socialist Review (December 1915), and in the ninth edition of the I.W.W. songbook. Bill Haywood included it in a letter to all I.W.W. locals instructing them to scatter Hill's ashes to the winds on the following May 1.

MY LAST WILL°
By JOE HILL

My will is easy to decide,
For there is nothing to divide.
My kin don't need to fuss and moan—
"Moss does not cling to rolling stone."

My body?—Oh!—If I could choose,
I would to ashes it reduce,
And let the merry breezes blow
My dust to where some flowers grow.

Perhaps some fading flower then
Would come to life and bloom again.
This is my last and final will.
Good luck to all of you,

JOE HILL

Photograph of Joe Hill taken by International News Service on the eve of his execution.

United Press International, Inc., photo.

Sheet music of Joe Hill's "The Rebel Girl."

THE REBEL GIRL

Words & Music by
JOE HILL

Tempo di Marcia

With spirit

There are wo-men of man - y de-scrip - tions___ In this queer world as eve - ry one
Yes, her hands may be hard-en'd from la - bor___ And her dress may not be ver - y

knows___ Some are liv - ing in beau - ti - ful man - sions___ And are wear-ing the
fine___ But a heart in her bo - som is beat - ing___ That is true to her

fin - est of clothes___ There are blue blood - ed queens and prin-cess-ess___ Who have
class and her kind___ And the graft - ers in ter - or are tremb-ling___ When her

charms made of dia - monds and pearl___ But the on - ly and tho-rough-bred
spite and de - fi - ance she ll hurl___ For the on - ly and tho-rough-bred

Copyright, MCMXV, by Wᵐ D. Haywood

The Rebel Girl ⁊

Music of Joe Hill's "The Rebel Girl."

21

Eight years after Hill's death his friend Sam Murray submitted these letters to The Industrial Pioneer. *They were published in that magazine in December 1923.*

THE LAST LETTERS OF JOE HILL

I notice that the Pioneer is going to publish a sketch of the life of Joe Hill in the November issue, so thought you might be able to use some of the letters I have and which were written by him while he was under sentence of death. These letters, to a great extent, show that peculiar spirit which enabled Joe to bear up so well under the enormous strain, while all the forces of both sides of the struggle were being marshaled—one to take his life, the other to save him.

I had been with Joe in Lower California, but had seen nothing of him and heard little, as I had been spending my time in an out-of-the-way place till August, 1914, when I arrived in Frisco and received the latest news relative to his case from a fellow worker who had just left Salt Lake.

If you could get a little poem he wrote a little while before he was shot, entitled "The Bronco Buster," and inspired by a picture of "Buster" Flynn on a pony sent to him by Gurley Flynn, it will shed some light on the love Joe always had for freedom and the untamable spirit that refuses to surrender it.

SAM MURRAY, SU-410.

I

Salt Lake City, Sept. 15, 1914.
Dear Friend and Fellow Worker:
Yours of Sept. 9 at hand. Glad to hear that you are still alive and kicking and back on the firing line again.

So, you tried to imitate Knowles, the Nature Freak, and live the simple life. It might be all right for a little while, as you say, but I am afraid a fellow would get "simple" of getting too much of the simple life.

Well, I guess the wholesale butchery going on in Europe is putting the kibosh on everything, even the organization work, to some extent. As a rule a fellow don't bother his head much about unions and theories of the class struggle when his belly is flapping up against his spine. Getting the wrinkles out is then the main issue and everything else, side issues. That's human nature or animal

instinct rather, and any amount of soapboxing will not change it. The man who coined the phrase "War is hell" certainly knew what he was talking about. Well, Sam, old boy, I guess Van has told you everything about my case and I think he knows more about it than I do, because he has been around here and on the outside. I am feeling well under the circumstances and I am fortunate enough to have the ability to entertain myself and to look at everything from the bright side. So there is nothing you could do for me, Sam. I know you would if you could.

Well, with best wishes to the bunch in Frisco, I remain, Yours for the OBU.—*Joe Hill.*
P.S. Is Jack Mosby in Washington yet or did he leave?

II

Salt Lake City, Dec. 2, 1914.
Dear Friend and Fellow Worker:
Received your letter and should have answered before, but have been busy working on some musical composition and whenever I get an "inspiration" I can't quit until it's finished.

I am glad to hear that you manage to make both ends meet, in spite of the industrial deal, but there is no use being pessimistic in this glorious land of plenty. Self preservation is, or should be, the first law of nature. The animals, when in a natural state, are showing us the way. When they are hungry they will always try to get something to eat or else they will die in the attempt. That's natural; to starve to death is unnatural.

No, I have not heard that song about "Tipperary" but if you send it as you said you would I might try to dope something out about that Frisco Fair. I am not familiar with the actual conditions of Frisco at present; and when I make a song I always try to picture things as they really are. Of course a little pepper and salt is allowed in order to bring out the facts more clearly.

If you send me that sheet music and give me some of the peculiarities and ridiculous points about the conditions in general on or about the fair ground, I'll try to do the best I can. Yours for the OBU.—*Joe Hill.*

III

Salt Lake City, Feb. 13, 1915.
Friend and Fellow Worker:
Should have answered your letter before, but have been busy working on a song named "The Rebel

Girl" (Words and Music), which I hope will help to line up the women workers in the OBU, and I hope you will excuse me.

I see you made a big thing out of that "Tipperary" song. (We had secured nearly 50 dollars by selling it for 5 cents for the Joe Hill Defense.— S.M.) In fact, a whole lot more than I ever expected, I don't suppose that it would sell very well outside of Frisco, though by the way I got a letter from Swasey in NY and he told me that "Casey Jones" made quite a hit in London and "Casey Jones," he was an Angelino you know, and I never expected that he would leave Los Angeles at all.

The other day we got ten bucks from a company of soldiers stationed on the Mexican line. How is that old top? Maybe they are remembering some of the cigars in glass bottles that they smoked at the expense of the "Tierra e Libertad" bunch.

Don't know much about my case. The Sup. Court will "sit on" it sometime in the sweet bye and bye and that's all I know about it.

Give my best to the bunch.—JOE HILL.

IV

County Jail, S. L. City, Mar. 22, 1915
Sam Murray, Napa, Cal.

Friend and Fellow Worker: Yours of March 13th at hand. I note that you have gone "back to nature" again and I must confess that it is making me a little homesick when you mention that "little cabin in the hills" stuff. You can talk about your dances, picnics and blow outs, and it won't affect me, but the "little cabin" stuff always gets my goat. That's the only life I know.

Yes, that "Tipperary" song is spreading like the smallpox they say. Sec. 69 tells me that there is a steady stream of silver from 'Frisco on account of it. The unemployed all over the country have adopted it as a marching song in their parades, and in New York City they changed it to some extent, so as to fit the brand of soup dished out in N. Y. They are doing great work in N. Y. this year. The unemployed have been organized and have big meetings every night. Gurley Flynn, Geo. Swasey (the human phonograph) and other live ones are there, and Gurley F. tells me things are looking favorable for the OBU. The hearing of my case has been postponed they say, and they are trying to make me believe that it is for my benefit, but I'll tell you that it is damn hard for me

to see where the benefit comes in at; damn hard.

Well, I have about a dozen letters to answer. Yours as ever,   JOE HILL.

V

S. L. Cy., June 6, 1915.

Friend and Fellow Worker: Your welcome letter received, and am glad to note that you are still sticking to your "little cabin in the hills." I would like to get a little of that close to nature stuff myself for a couple of months in order to regain a little vitality, and a little flesh on my rotting bones. My case was argued on the 28th of May, and according to Judge Hilton, the results were satisfactory. He says he is sure of securing a reversal, and if so, there hardly will be another trial, for the simple reason that there won't be anything to try, if I can get a lawyer that will *defend* me.

With best wishes to all the rebels, Yours for the OBU,   JOE HILL.

P.S. I've just found out that the Superior Court judges are getting ready to go on their vacation until next fall, so I guess there won't be anything decided on my case for some time. But "everything comes to him who waits" they say, and that's the only consolation I got now.—JOE.

VI

Utah State Prison, Aug. 12, 1915.

Friend and Fellow Worker: Yours of August 5th at hand, and as you see I have been moved to the state prison. The appeal was denied and I was up in court the other day and sentenced to be shot on the first day of October. We were all very much surprised at the decision, because we thought that I would be granted a new trial anyway. But as Judge Hilton says "the records of the lower court are so rotten they had to be covered somehow." I guess you can draw your conclusions from that statement. I wanted to drop the case right there and then, but from reports received from all parts of the country, I think that the case will be carried to the U. S. Supreme Court. I didn't think I'd be worth any more money. You know human life is kind of cheap this year anyway— but I guess the organization thinks otherwise and majority rule goes with me.

Well, I don't know anything new and hoping that you are successful in snaring the elusive doughnut, I remain, Yours for the OBU,

JOE HILL.

VII

Utah State Prison, Sept. 9, 1915.
Sam Murray,
Frisco, California.

Friend and Fellow Worker: Yours received O. K. Glad to hear that things are picking up. I see that you are employed at making bait for the German "sharks." Well, war certainly shows up the capitalist system in the right light. Millions of men are employed at making ships and others are hired to sink them. Scientific management, eh, wot?

As far as I can see, it doesn't make much difference which side wins, but I hope that *one side will win,* because a draw would only mean another war in a year or two. All these silly priests and old maid sewing circles that are moaning about peace at this time should be locked up in the crazy house as a menace to society. The war is the finest training school for rebels in the world and for anti-militarists as well, and I hope that all the S. S. bills in the country will go over there.

Well, Sam, I don't know anything about my case. My attorneys told me to leave it all to them, and that makes it pretty soft for me to have someone else do the worrying for me.

I believe your good work on the coast is being felt at this end of the line, though.

With best wishes I am as ever yours,

JOE HILL.

VIII

(*When the following was written, Joe expected to be shot within twenty-four hours, and all of us had given up hope. However, he later received a respite of something over a month, thus being forced to go over the strain of the last day on earth again.*)

Utah State Prison, Sept. 30, 1915.
Sam Murray, 3345 17th St.,
Frisco, Calif.

Friend and Fellow Worker: Well, Sam, I received your letter, but you shouldn't feel so sentimental about it. This dying business is not quite so bad as it is cracked up to be. I have always said "a new trial or die trying," and I'll show that I meant it. I was moved to another cell last night and have an armed guard in front of my cell. I was also given a swell feed for the first time in God knows how long, and that is one of the surest signs.

Well, Sam, you and me had a little pleasure at one time that few rebels have had the privilege of having, and I guess I've had my share of the fun after all. Now, just forget me, and say goodbye to the bunch.

Yours for the OBU,

JOE HILL.

P.S. Sent a letter to Caroline.

This was the last letter I got direct from Joe Hill. But we kept up the fight; telegraphed to the unions of Sweden, the Swedish Minister at Washington, who sent President Wilson a letter; who also wired the Governor of Utah, but to no avail, and the night before the execution finally took place we received together with some of the other organizations throughout the country, his famous farewell wire: "Goodbye, Forget me. Don't mourn, Organize," which we immediately answered, but which, as near as we could learn, he never received.

22

IN MEMORIAM: JOE HILL

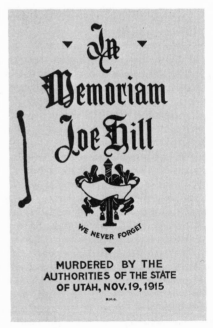

This copy of the funeral program was taken from an original program in the Joe Hill files in the Labadie Collection.

JOE HILL

"The cause I stand for, that of a fair and honest trial, is worth more than any human life—much more than mine."

JOE HILL.

West Side Auditorium, Chicago, Illinois
November 25, 1915

PROGRAM

Quartet—Workers of the World Awaken Joe Hill
Song—The Rebel Girl Joe Hill
Jennie Wosczynska
Songs—"There Is Power," "Stung Right,"
"Preacher and the Slave"
Sung by Fellow Workers
Song—John Chellman
Funeral Oration—Judge O. N. Hilton, of Denver
Song in Swedish
Address—James Larkin, of Dublin, Ireland
Address—William D. Haywood
Piano Selection—
Funeral March Rudolf von Liebich

AT GRACELAND CEMETERY

Short addresses in foreign tongues, as follows:

Swedish—W. Sodergrin
Russian—H. Martin
Hungarian—C. Rothfisher
Polish—B. Schraeger
Spanish—J. Santana
Italian—D. Mari
German—W. Penker
Yiddish—H. Rubinowitz
Lithuanian—J. Siemiaszko

Songs composed by Joe Hill

Music: Russian Mandolin Club
Rockford I.W.W. Band

23

Ralph Chaplin's description of Joe Hill's funeral appeared in the International Socialist Review *(December 1915).*

JOE HILL'S FUNERAL

By RALPH CHAPLIN

On Thanksgiving day the throngs began to gather in the great auditorium hours before exercises were to take place. By 10:30 the streets were blocked for blocks in all directions; street cars could not run and all traffic was suspended. Within the hall one could almost hear the drop of a pin at all times. The casket was placed on the flower-laden, black and red draped stage, above which was hanging a hand woven I.W.W. label (made by fellow-worker Cline in prison). So lavish had been the offerings of floral pieces from all over the city and the land, that the stage could scarcely contain them all. These were inscribed in a medley of languages. They were from English and foreign speaking locals of the I.W.W., in and out of town; from Socialist branches and local unions of the A. F. of L., from independent organizations, from anarchist groups and from dozens of individuals. Some of these wreaths and flower pieces were elaborate and costly and others were simple and plain, but all were full of the heart-deep spirit of protest and regret.

The funeral exercises were opened with the singing of Joe Hill's wonderful song, "Workers of the World, Awaken"—members of the I.W.W. leading and the audience swelling out the chorus. This was followed by Jennie Wosczynska's singing of the "Rebel Girl," written and composed by Joe Hill, after which came two beautiful tenor solos, one in Swedish by John Chellman and one in Italian by Ivan Rodems.

William D. Haywood introduced Judge Hilton with a short but powerful appeal, the keynote of which was, "Don't mourn—organize." In spite of this brave admonition, however, fellow worker Haywood's clarion voice was strangely husky as he stood beside the silent, flower-covered casket. Judge Hilton's lengthy and masterful presentation of the legal facts in the case and the part taken by the Mormon church in the perpetration of this ghastly and uncalled for murder, was listened to with absorbing interest by all present. And when the oration was concluded the thousands in the hall silently marched out to the strains of Chopin's Funeral March, played by Professor Rudolf von Liebich.

The parade formation was as follows: First, a committee to help clear the streets and to follow the prearranged line of march, then the pallbearers with the casket, followed by the flower-bearers and the band. Because of the congested condition of the street, the committee and pallbearers had some difficulty in opening a passage through the crowd to the hearse, which was waiting a short distance away. After the casket had been placed in the machine the procession started its march to the elevated station. In the main body came the English-speaking branches with almost a hundred members of Local 400 and about 75 members from Rockford, then the foreign-speaking branches, followed by a veritable throng of workingmen and women over a mile in length. Had it been possible to keep the crowd uniformly four abreast the procession would have been at least three times as long. It was found necessary to go four blocks out of the scheduled line of march in order to avoid the crush around the Auditorium building.

Slowly and impressively the vast throng moved through the west side streets. Windows flew open at its approach and were filled with peering faces. Porches and even roofs were blackened with people, and some of the more daring were lined up over signboards and on telephone and arc-light poles. The flower-bearers, with their bright colored floral pieces and wreaths tied with crimson ribbons, formed a walking garden almost a block in length. Thousands in the procession wore I.W.W. pennants on their sleeves or red ribbons worded, "Joe Hill, murdered by the authorities of the state of Utah, November the 19th, 1915," or, "Joe Hill, I.W.W. martyr to a great cause," "Don't mourn—organize. Joe Hill," and many others. The Rockford bunch was conspicuous by reason of its great crimson silk flag with the I.W.W. label on either side and the wooden shoe above the pole. Songs were sung all along the way, chiefly Joe Hill's, although some of the foreign-speaking workers sang revolutionary songs in their native tongues. As soon as a song would die down in one place, the same song or another would be taken up by other voices along the line. The procession took complete possession of the streets with the exception of a few policemen, photographers and moviemen until the elevated station at Van Buren and Halsted streets was reached. Here the pallbearers, flower-bearers, funeral, singing and speaking committees were to board a special train of five coaches, in order to be first at the cemetery and prepare for the oncoming crowd. At this place, however, the crush from behind was so great as to

almost upset all pre-arranged plans. Everyone seemed determined to board the reserve train and it took a great deal of hard work on the part of the membership to see to it that things went through according to the outlined plan that alone would insure the success of the program. The situation was explained to the crowd, which was soon pacified, and from this moment all elevated and surface lines leading to Graceland cemetery were crowded to capacity for over an hour. In some cases Joe Hill's songs were sung the entire distance.

Upon reaching the cemetery the funeral chapel was discovered to be ridiculously inadequate for the accommodation of the vast audience, and so it was decided to hold the exercises in the open air. And on the olive green slope of an evergreen-crested hill they took place. Here the casket was tenderly laid upon the earth and all the flowers and wreaths and flags were placed about it. Above —high above the casket were the evergreens and above these, a couple of tall, bare elm trees raised up into the sky their delicately etched trunks and branches. Clutched in one lofty tremulous branch, as in a hand, was one of the last summer's empty birdnests. The sky was somewhat heavy and of a pearly grey tone with tiny dove-colored clouds flitting across it hurriedly—somewhere. The air was warm and somewhat humid so that the trees were hung with a soft mist that caused the landscape to fade away into a distance that seemed fairly enchanted. Here Joe Hill's songs were sung and Fellow Workers Haywood and Jim Larkin made short but stirring addresses in English, followed by Fellow Workers W. Sodergrin in Swedish, H. Martin in Russian, C. Rothfisher in Hungarian, B. Schraeger in Polish, J. Santana in Spanish, D. Mari in Italian, Wm. Penker in German, Harry Rabinowitz in Yiddish and J. Siemiaszko in Lithuanian. A few more songs were sung and then the body was removed to the little oak beamed high-roofed chapel, and placed on a bronze stand overhung with live palms and ferns. Here those assembled were given the last opportunity to view the remains of the murdered songwriter with the pale smiling face and the bruised hands folded above the four unseen purple bullet holes in his breast.

A constant stream of people poured into and out of the semi-obscurity of the tiny room, while the great crowd gathered close around outside joined in one swelling, mighty chorus of song.

Each one of Joe Hill's songs was sung over and over again, and when the great crimson silk banner of the Rockford local appeared the song of that name was struck up and sung as it was never sung before. Three ringing cheers were then given for the Social Revolution and the I.W.W. and then more songs. The singing and cheering was something the old cemetery had never witnessed before and the guards and officials were stricken with undisguised amazement at the audacity of it all. There were a couple of dozen "harness-bulls" on the job and it was funny to see them shy away from the sunburned harvest huskies of Local 400 and the brawny Swedish fellow workers from Rockford. The "bulls" were so outclassed physically and were so insignificant looking in comparison with the I.W.W. boys that it must have been painful to see them singing and cheering unmolested in an exclusive and sedate graveyard like Graceland. But the singing continued until it was quite dark and the trees and buildings blurred into gloom with only a few lights twinkling from out the shadows—and even then it continued. Finally small groups wearing carnations and ribbons walked slowly towards the station singing or humming or talking in low voices among themselves.

As no cremating could be done on a holiday a committee of five returned to the cemetery on the next day (Friday), accompanied by numerous members of the I.W.W. and friends. It was learned that the body had been stripped to the waist in order to make photographs and to take the necessary measurements and casts for a marble bust.

A few laurel and other wreaths were saved from the floral offering, in order that they might be sent to some of the local unions of the I.W.W. in different parts of the world. The I.W.W. button was removed and also the cuff-links and necktie. These are to be preserved at headquarters and, in due time, placed in a shadow-box frame with an oil portrait of our song-writer. The casket handles were also saved and will be melted up into a plate on which can be engraved, "Don't waste time mourning for me—organize," which plate is to be used with the portrait mentioned above.

After some little delay, the casket was wheeled through an underground passage to the crematory room, where it was to be finally fed to the flames. The interior of this crematory is finished entirely in white. The walls are of white tile and even the steel doors of the furnace are enameled white.

The body was here identified for the last time and, at a word from the committeeman in charge, it was wheeled to the doors of the blast chamber, which creaked open to receive it. Within was a stone slab on a level with the doors and the casket. The whole interior was already tinted a rosy red with the fires that were soon to consume the body of our murdered song-writer. The casket was suddenly pushed out onto the center of the slab. The steel doors creaked together and the tiny room was all white once more. Only the roar of the fire-blast could be heard growing louder and louder. . . .

In order to do all that was incumbent upon it, the committee was obliged to witness a small part at flames. The interior of this cremation. A small circular hole in the far end of the furnace was reached after traversing a dark and narrow passage-way around the side of the blast room. Through this aperture the committeemen, one at a time and each with feelings all his own, viewed the flame-lashed casket containing the fine body and placid features of Joe Hill, dreamer, poet, artist, agitator, with four purple bullet holes in his young chest as punishment for the crime of being "true blue" to his class—and to himself.

The murdering of martyrs has never yet made a tyrant's place secure, and the death orgy held by that heartless bunch of Mormon murderers on the nineteenth of November, in spite of the protests of the President and many noted men and women, and in spite of the protests of tens of thousands of working people all over the land, has done more to cement together the forces that are about to overthrow the ghoulish Capitalist system than anything that has happened in decades. The state of Utah has shot our song-writer into everlasting immortality and has shot itself into everlasting shame. Thank goodness, neither Joe Hill nor the I.W.W. will ever be found dead within the boundaries of Utah!

24

Ralph Chaplin's tribute to Joe Hill was one of the most frequently reprinted poems about Hill to appear in the I.W.W. press. Other poems to Hill's memory were written by I.W.W. members Cash Stevens, Richard Brazier, C.O.G., John Nordquist, T-Bone Slim, and Covington Hall. As writer Barry Nichols stated in a recent mimeographed I.W.W. publication, Wobbly *(Berkeley, 1963): "The rich ore of Joe Hill's life and legend has been mined*

*by many writers and poets. Joe Hill is found in
books of fiction by Archie Binns; Elias Tomben-
kin; John Dos Passos; Margaret Graham; Alexander Saxton; and a number of others. He is found
in plays by Upton Sinclair; Louis Lembert; and
Arturo Giovannitti. He is found in poems by Kenneth Patchen; Kenneth Rexroth; Carl Sandburg;
Alfred Hayes; and Carlos Cortez. Writers who
deal with Joe Hill in folklore include B. A. Botkin; William Alderson; Wayland Hand; and Ray
McKinley Lawless. . . . Joe Hill appears in every
kind of book from cultural studies to regional history books to books on revolutions and national
history. . . ."*
   *This version of Chaplin's poem is from the ninth
edition of the I.W.W. songbook.*

JOE HILL*

*Murdered by the Authorities of the State of Utah,
November the 19th, 1915*

BY RALPH CHAPLIN

High head and back unbending—fearless and true,
Into the night unending; why was it you?

Heart that was quick with song, torn with their
   lead;
Life that was young and strong, shattered and
   dead.

Singer of manly songs, laughter and tears;
Singer of Labor's wrongs, joys, hopes and fears.

Though you were one of us, what could we do?
Joe, there were none of us needed like you.

We gave, however small, what Life could give;
We would have given all that you might live.

Your death you held as naught, slander and shame;
We from the very thought shrank as from flame.

Each of us held his breath, tense with despair,
You, who were close to Death, seemed not to care.

White-handed loathsome power, knowing no
   pause,
Sinking in labor's flower, murderous claws;

Boastful, with leering eyes, blood-dripping jaws . . .
Accurst be the cowardice hidden in laws!

Utah has drained your blood; white hands are wet;
We of the "surging flood" *never forget!*

Our songster! have your laws now had their fill?
Know, ye, his songs and cause ye cannot kill.

High head and back unbending—"rebel true blue,"
Into the night unending; why was it you?

25

*In an undated letter sent by I.W.W. member
George Carey to Miss Agnes Inglis about 1951,
Carey describes how he finally disposed of a
packet of Joe Hill's ashes thirty-four years after
the May 1 ceremonies in every part of the world
during which Hill's ashes were "scattered to the
winds." Carey,who had been active in the I.W.W.
since the 1909 Spokane free speech fight, sent the
empty packet to Miss Inglis. She included this
letter, and the packet, in her correspondence files
in the Labadie Collection.*

CIRCUMSTANCES RELATING TO
THE DISPOSAL OF A PORTION
OF THE ASHES OF JOE HILL

The tragedy of Joe Hill was destined to have a
profound influence on my own life. It was at a
mass meeting scheduled to raise funds for his defense, held in the city of Toledo, that I first met
the girl whom I later married. She is still with
me, the mother of my two daughters and her hair
is now as white as my own.
   It was at the first Convention of M.T.W. I.U.
#200 held in Cleveland that I first participated
in a ceremony intended to carry out his last wishes.
I was Chairman of that first convention and as I
recall the bit of ashes were brought to the gathering by F. W. Ben Klein. It was a memorable
scene, tarnished only by the fact that the meeting
was addressed by one Harold Lord Varney of
whom it is better to be charitable and say nothing.
   I little imagined then that I was destined to receive and be custodian of another portion of his
ashes for many long years. Often during those
years I should have been more than glad to have
some group of the wobblies dispose of them as
Joe had willed, but I was disappointed. My possession of them was no secret. I had found the
packet amid the ruins of the I.W.W. Hall in To-

ledo after the place had been wrecked by hoodlums after a so-called Palmer Raid. That must
have been in 1919 or thereabouts. I was Secretary
of Local Toledo at the time but there was no activity and nothing could be done at that time.
Many times down thru the ensuing years I brought
up the affair hoping that we could do as he desired but for some reason or another the I.W.W.
would have none of it. Communists and Socialists
both volunteered more than once to gain publicity
thru him but I could see none of that. An anarchist
woman pleaded with me to let her have them that
she might have them in a ring "to wear forever."
My only retort was that she was unlikely to last
forever.

It was on June 26, 1950, that I finally decided
to try and carry out Joe's last wish to the best of
my ability and to make sure that no other group
or individual would make capital out of his body.
At that time I was living in a bungalow on the
bank of Hollow Brook near Peekskill. It was just
after the bitter clash of two hideous ideologies at
that very spot. The so-called "Robeson Riots"
had taken place within earshot of my home.

On this early June morning I awoke to one of
the most beautiful June days that I have ever
known anywhere. Nature seemed to have outdone
herself that day when I awoke to the realization
that I was grown old and that I had an obligation
to carry out. The thought came to me. I was all
alone. Why not do as he requested? Here was a
spot. The grass was green, there was a yard covered with flowers and trees. Birds were singing
all over the place. No place could be more fitting.
I arose and walked out into the garden and with
no more ceremony that a murmured "Good Bye,
Joe," I carefully scattered the contents of the little
envelope over the soil. I felt at ease. My pledge

had been kept. Never now would I have to fear
that some individual or group not in sympathy
with the ideals of the I.W.W. or of Joe himself
would sanctify his mortal remains or make capital
of his final disposal.

An enclosed letter from Bill Haywood requested
the ones who disposed of them to send in a report
of such proceedings to him for the Archives of the
I.W.W. But Bill, also is gone these many years.
I am sending a copy of this to the General Headquarters of the I.W.W. altho in my opinion they
have strayed far from the ideals for which Joe Hill
gave his life. The envelope and another copy of
this letter will be given to the Labadie Collection,
General Library, Ann Arbor, Michigan. (U of M)

GEORGE CAREY

Fellow Worker:

*In compliance with the last will of Joe Hill, his
body was cremated at Graceland Cemetery, Chicago, Illinois, Nov. 20, 1915.*

It was his request, that his ashes be distributed.

*This package has been confined to your care for
the fullfilment of this last will.*

*You will kindly address a letter to Wm. D. Hay-
wood, Room 307, 164 W. Washington St., Chicago, Ill., telling the circumstances and where the
ashes were distributed.*

WE NEVER FORGET

JOE HILL MEMORIAL COMMITTEE

(*This message was printed on the empty envelope
which had contained a portion of Joe Hill's ashes.
It was sent to Miss Inglis by George Carey.*)

It is the first strike I ever saw which sang. I shall not soon forget the curious lift, the strange sudden fire of the mingled nationalities at the strike meetings when they broke into the universal language of song. And not only at the meetings did they sing, but in the soup houses and in the streets. I saw one group of women strikers who were peeling potatoes at a relief station suddenly break into the swing of the "Internationale." They have a whole book of songs fitted to familiar tunes—"The Eight Hour Song," "The Banner of Labor," "Workers, Shall the Masters Rule Us?" But the favorite of all was the "Internationale."

RAY STANNARD BAKER
in "The Revolutionary Strike,"
The American Magazine (May 1912), p. 24.

Chapter 6

Bread and Roses:
The 1912 Lawrence Textile Strike

Early in January 1912 I.W.W. activities focused on a dramatic ten-week strike of 25,000 textile workers in Lawrence, Massachusetts. It became the most widely publicized I.W.W. conflict, acquainting the nation with the plight of the unskilled, foreign-born worker as well as with the organization's philosophy of radical unionism. "Lawrence was not an ordinary strike," wrote Brissenden in 1919, "It was a social revolution *in parvo*."[1]

Lawrence in 1912 was a great textile center, outranking all others in the production of woolen and worsted goods. Its principal mills were those of the American Woolen Company, a consolidation of thirty-four factories in New England whose yearly output was valued at $45,000,000. The woolen and cotton mills employed over 40,000 persons, about half of Lawrence's population over age fourteen. Most of them were unskilled workers of many nationalities, who had come from Europe after 1900, attracted by the promises of labor contractors representing the expanding textile industry in Massachusetts.

But despite a heavy government tariff protection of the woolen industry, the wages and living standards of textile operatives had declined steadily since 1905. The introduction of the two-loom system in the woolen mills and a corresponding speed-up in the cotton industry had resulted in lay-offs, unemployment, and a drop in wages. A

report of the U. S. Commissioner of Labor, Charles P. Neil, showed that for the week ending November 25, 1911, 22,000 textile employees, including foremen, supervisors, and office workers, averaged about $8.76 for a full week's work.[2]

In addition, the cost of living was higher in Lawrence than elsewhere in New England. Rents, paid on a weekly basis, ranged from $1.00 to $6.00 a week for small tenement apartments in frame buildings which the Neil Report found "extra hazardous" in construction and potential fire-traps. Congestion was worse in Lawrence than in any other city in New England; mill families in 58 percent of the homes visited by federal investigators found it necessary to take in boarders to raise enough money for rent.[3]

Bread, molasses, and beans were the staple diet of most mill workers. "When we eat meat it seems like a holiday, especially for the children," testified one weaver before the March 1912 congressional investigation of the Lawrence strike.[4]

Of the 22,000 textile workers investigated by Labor Commissioner Neil, well over half were women and children who found it financially imperative to work in the mills. Half of all the workers in the four Lawrence mills of the American Woolen Company were girls between ages fourteen and eighteen. Dr. Elizabeth Shapleigh, a Lawrence physician, wrote: "A considerable number of the boys and girls die within the first two or three years after beginning work . . . thirty-six out of every 100 of all the men and women who work in the mill die before or by the time they are twenty-five years of age."[5] Because of malnutrition, work strain, and occupational diseases, the average mill worker's life in Lawrence was over twenty-two years shorter than that of the manufacturer, stated Dr. Shapleigh.[6]

Responding in a small way to public pressure over the working conditions of textile employees, the Massachusetts state legislature passed a law, effective January 1, 1912, which reduced the weekly hours from fifty-six to fifty-four for working women and children. Workers feared that this would mean a corresponding wage cut, and their suspicions were sharpened when the mill corporations speeded up the machines and posted notices that, following January 1, the fifty-four-hour work week would be maximum for both men and women operatives.

The I.W.W. had been organizing among the foreign born in Lawrence since 1907 and claimed over a thousand members, but it had only about 300 paid up members on its rolls. About 2500 English-speaking skilled workers were organized by craft into three local unions of the A.F.L.'s United Textile Workers, but only about 208 of these were in good standing in 1912. The small, English-speaking branch of the I.W.W. sent a letter to President Wood of the American Woolen Company asking how wages would be affected under the new law. There was no reply. Resentment grew as the textile workers realized that a reduction of two-hours pay from their marginal incomes would mean, as I.W.W. publicity pointed out, three loaves of bread less each week from their meager diet.

Polish women weavers in the Everett Cotton Mills were the first to notice a shortage of thirty-two cents in their pay envelopes on January 11. They stopped their looms and left the mill, shouting "short pay, short pay!" Other such outbursts took place throughout Lawrence. The next morning workers at the Washington and Wood mills joined the walkout. For the first time in the city's history, the bells of the Lawrence city hall rang the general riot alarm.

That afternoon a mass meeting was held at the Franco-Belgian Hall, and a telegram was sent to Joseph Ettor, an I.W.W. Executive Board member, asking that he come from New York to assist the strike. Twenty-seven-year-old Ettor had vis-

ited Lawrence in the past to preach I.W.W. unionism. He was well known in the Italian community as a veteran I.W.W. organizer who had worked in the shipyards of San Francisco, traveled through West Coast mining and lumber camps, and led the foreign-born workers of the Pressed Steel Car Company in the 1909 McKees Rocks, Pennsylvania, strike. Practical, pragmatic, and quick in decision-making, Ettor could speak English, Italian, and Polish fluently and could understand Hungarian and Yiddish.

Under his aggressive leadership, a strike committee was immediately formed of two representatives from each of the nationalities represented among the mill workers. They were to meet each morning and take complete charge of the strike. The workers' demands called for a 15 percent increase in wages on a fifty-four-hour work week, double time for overtime work, and no discrimination against any workers for their strike participation. In response to the circulation of strike leaflets throughout the town, Lawrence Mayor Scanlon ordered a company of local militia to spend the night at the armory and patrol the streets around the mills.

Mass picketing and arrests started the first week of the strike. It was the first time there had ever been mass picketing in any New England town. When crowds of workers demonstrated in front of the Atlantic and Pacific mills, they were drenched by water from fire hoses on adjoining roofs. The strikers retaliated by throwing chunks of ice. Thirty-six were arrested and most of them sentenced to a year in prison. As the judge stated, "The only way we can teach them is to deal out the severest sentences."[7] The governor ordered out the state militia and state police. One officer remarked to a writer for *Outlook Magazine:* "Our company of militia went down to Lawrence during the first days of the strike. Most of them had to leave Harvard to do it; but they rather enjoyed going down there to have a fling at those people."[8] Harry Emerson Fosdick quoted a Boston lawyer: "The strike should have been stopped in the first twenty-four hours. The militia should have been instructed to shoot. That is the way Napoleon did it."[9]

A few days after the strike began, Arturo Giovannitti, an Italian poet and orator, came to Lawrence from New York City to take charge of strike relief. He came in the interest of *Il Proletario*, the newspaper which he edited for the Italian Socialist Federation. Relief committees, a network of soup kitchens, and food distribution stations were set up by each nationality group. The Franco-Belgian station alone took care of 1200 families weekly. Volunteer doctors gave medical care. Families received from $2.00 to $5.00 each week from the funds raised throughout the country in response to the strike committee's appeal. "The problem of relief was so efficiently handled," wrote labor historian Samuel Yellin, "that during the ten-week strike there was no wavering whatsoever in the strikers' ranks."[10]

Lawrence was a new kind of strike, the first time such large numbers of unskilled, unorganized foreign-born workers had followed the radical leadership of the I.W.W. John Golden, president of the A.F.L. United Textile Workers denounced it as "revolutionary" and "anarchistic" and attempted unsuccessfully to wrest the leadership of the strike away from the I.W.W. A.F.L. President Samuel Gompers defined the strike as a "class-conscious industrial revolution . . . a passing event that is not intended to be an organization for the protection of the immediate rights or promotion of the near future interests of the workers." However, Gompers defended the lawful rights of the I.W.W. members to, "express themselves as their conscience dictates."[11]

"It was the spirit of the workers that was dangerous," wrote labor reporter Mary Heaton Vorse. "They are always marching and singing. The tired, gray crowds ebbing and flowing perpetually into the mills had waked and opened their mouths to sing."[12] And in the *American Magazine,* Ray Stannard Baker reported:

It is not short of amazing, the power of a great idea to weld men together. . . . There was in it a peculiar, intense, vital spirit, a religious spirit if you will, that I have never felt before in any strike. . . . At first everyone predicted that it would be impossible to hold these divergent people together, but aside from the skilled men, some of whom belonged to craft unions, comparatively few went back to the mills. And as a whole, the strike was conducted with little violence.[13]

Less than a week after the strike started, the police found dynamite in three different places in Lawrence: in a tenement house, in an empty lot, and in a shoemaker's shop next door to the print shop where Ettor received his mail. The press and the police were quick to assign guilt to the strikers. An editorial in the *New York Times* declared: "The strikers display a fiendish lack of humanity which ought to place them beyond the comfort of religion until they have repented."[14] The I.W.W. claimed, however, that the *Boston-American,* a Hearst paper, was off the press and on sale in Lawrence with the details of the dynamite discovery before the sticks of dynamite were actually found. Soon after, John Breen, a local undertaker and a member of the Lawrence school board, was arrested and charged with planting the explosives in a plot to discredit the workers. He was fined $500 and released on bail. President Wood of the American Woolen Company was implicated, but cleared by the court although he could not explain why he had recently made a cash payment to Breen.

One of the largest demonstrations of the strike took place on January 29 when Ettor addressed a mass meeting on the Lawrence Common, urged the strikers to be peaceful and orderly, and led them on a march through the business district. At one of the mills, a company of militiamen refused to let them pass. Ettor averted a conflict by waving the paraders up a side street. They followed, and cheered him for his good sense.

That evening, independent of the earlier demonstration, Anna LoPizzo, a woman striker, was killed when police tried to break up a picket line. The strikers said she was shot by a Lawrence police officer. Nevertheless, Ettor and Giovannitti, who were three miles away talking to a meeting of German workers, were arrested as "accessories to the murder" and charged with inciting and provoking the violence. They were refused bail and imprisoned for eight months without trial. In April, Joseph Caruso, an Italian striker, was arrested and jailed in an attempt by Lawrence police to find the man who had fired the fatal shot.

Martial law was enforced following the arrest of the two I.W.W. strike leaders. City officials declared all public meetings illegal, and Lawrence authorities called out twenty-two more militia companies to patrol the streets. A militiaman's bayonet killed a fifteen-year old Syrian boy in another clash between strikers and police.

The arrest of Ettor and Giovannitti was aimed at disrupting the strike. However, the I.W.W. sent Bill Haywood to Lawrence, and with him came I.W.W. organizers William Trautmann, Elizabeth Gurley Flynn, and, later, Carlo Tresca, an Italian

LET THE
CHILDREN COME

—HOMES OF THE
WORKERS OF
OTHER CITIES

THE LAWRENCE WAY

LAWRENCE
MASS.

THE HUNGER CITY
DIVIDENDS FOR MILL-OWNERS
STARVATION WAGES FOR WORKERS

LAW AND ORDER IN LAWRENCE

Industrial Worker, March 21, 1912.

anarchist. More than 15,000 strikers met Haywood at the railroad station and carried him down Essex Street to the Lawrence Common, where he addressed a group of 25,000 strikers. Group by group, they sang the "Internationale" for him in their various tongues. Looking down from the speaker's stand and seeing the young strikers in the crowd, Haywood roared in his foghorn voice: "Those kids should be in school instead of slaving in the mills."[15]

Throughout the strike, Haywood urged strikers to maintain an attitude of passive resistance. But this took many forms. One innovation in strike technique was an endless chain picket line of thousands of strikers who marched through the mill districts wearing white arm bands which read, "Don't be a scab." Large groups locked arms on the sidewalks and passed along the business streets. When this tactic was disrupted by the police, huge crowds of mill workers would move in and out of stores, not buying anything. As the acting head of the police later testified in Washington, "They had our shopkeepers in a state of terror; it was a question whether or not they would shut up their shops."[16]

By far the most dramatic episode of the strike

involved sending the strikers' children to sympathetic families in other cities, a measure of strike relief which had been used in Europe by French and Italian workers. About 120 children left Lawrence on February 10 and were met at the station in New York City by 5000 members of the Italian Socialist Federation and the Socialist Party singing the "Internationale" and "The Marseillaise." The youngsters were placed in homes which had been selected by a women's committee of New York sympathizers. Margaret Sanger, later famous for her work in birth control, was one of the nurses who accompanied the children on the train to New York City. She testified before a congressional committee in March: "Out of the 119 children, only four had underwear on . . . their outerwear was almost in rags . . . their coats were simply torn to shreds . . . and it was the bitterest weather we have had this winter."[17]

A few weeks later, ninety-two more children arrived in New York City and, before going to their temporary foster homes, paraded with banners down Fifth Avenue. Alarmed at the publicity this exodus was receiving, the Lawrence authorities ordered that no more children could leave the city. On February 24 when a group of

150 more children made ready to leave for Philadelphia, fifty policemen and two militia companies surrounded the Lawrence railroad station. They tore children away from their parents, threw women and children into a waiting patrol wagon, and detained thirty of them in jail. A member of the Philadelphia Women's Committee testified under oath:

> When the time came to depart, the children, arranged in a long line, two by two in an orderly procession with the parents near at hand, were about to make their way to the train when the police . . . closed in on us with their clubs, beating right and left with no thought of the children who then were in desperate danger of being trampled to death. The mothers and the children were thus hurled in a mass and bodily dragged to a military truck and even then clubbed, irrespective of the cries of the panic-stricken mothers and children. We can scarcely find words with which to describe this display of brutality.[18]

This clash between the children and the police was the turning point of the Lawrence strike. Protests from every part of the country reached Congress as newspaper and magazine articles focused national attention on the conflict. Congressman Victor Berger, a Socialist from Milwaukee, and Congressman William Wilson from Pennsylvania, who became the first secretary of labor, called for a congressional investigation of the Lawrence situation.

In early March, the House Committee on Rules heard testimony from a group of Lawrence strikers including some teenagers under sixteen years of age. "As soon as I came home I had to go to sleep, I was so tired," the congressmen were told by a fifteen-year-old girl.[19] The young workers testified that the textile companies held back a week of their wages, that they were often required to do unpaid clean-up work on Saturdays, and that in order to get decent drinking water in the mills some of them had to pay five or ten cents a week. So great was national indignation, the President's wife attended the hearings, and President Taft later ordered an investigation of industrial conditions throughout the nation.

Concerned over the public reaction to the hearings, and the possible threat to their own tariff protection, the American Woolen Company acceded to all the strikers' demands on March 12,

1912. By the end of March, the rest of the Lawrence textile companies fell in line. Wages were raised for textile workers throughout all of New England. And on March 30 the children who had been living in foster homes in New York City were brought home.

Meanwhile, in the Lawrence prison, Ettor and Giovannitti had turned their jail cells into studies. They read through the warden's library and then the books—Taine, Carlyle, Shelley, Byron, Kant—sent in by sympathizers. Ettor, interested in organization methods, requested Burke. Giovannitti had what he called his "afternoon matinees," reading an annotated edition of Shakespeare which had been sent to him by a Harvard student.

As the months dragged on without a trial, the case of Giovannitti and Ettor became a cause célèbre. "Open the jail gates or we will close the mill gates," threatened Haywood. Protest parades, demonstrations, and mass meetings in major cities throughout the country helped raise $60,000 needed for legal defense. In New York's Union Square, 25,000 persons gathered to hear Haywood appeal for funds, then march up Fifth Avenue led by Elizabeth Gurley Flynn. In Boston a great demonstration covered the Common. Massachusetts authorities indicted all the members of the Ettor-Giovannitti Defense Committee, then released them on bail.

Agitation mounted. A general strike was advocated by the I.W.W. In August, a new development in the dynamite plot made headlines. Ernest Pitman, a Lawrence contractor who had built the Wood mill of the American Woolen Company, confessed to a district attorney that the dynamite frame-up had been planned in the Boston offices of Lawrence textile corporations. Pitman committed suicide shortly after he was served papers ordering him to appear and testify before a grand jury. William Wood, who was implicated, was immediately exonerated in court.

Pitman's confession created a surge of sentiment in favor of the liberation of Ettor, Giovannitti, and Caruso. I.W.W. publicity contrasted the case of the three men who had been detained for months in prison, with the case of Breen, the dynamite planter, who had been released without jail sentence on a $500 fine. Fifteen thousand Lawrence workers walked out again on September 30 for a twenty-four-hour demonstration strike. Textile workers in neighboring cities threatened similar strikes in support of the I.W.W. leaders. Police, detectives, and the state militia were again called out. Mayor Scanlon started a "God and Country" campaign to drive the I.W.W. out of Lawrence. A parade was organized down the Lawrence main street under a banner which read:

> For God and Country!
> The stars and stripes forever!
> The red flag never!

Lawrence citizens were encouraged by the town leaders to wear little American flags in their button holes as proof of their patriotic opposition to the I.W.W.

The trial of Ettor, Giovannitti, and Caruso began in Salem, Massachusetts, at the end of September; it lasted for two months. The defendants were kept in metal cages in the courtroom while the trial was in session. Crowds of workers waited each day outside the courthouse to cheer them as they entered and left the building. In Sweden and France workers proposed a boycott of American woolen goods along with a strike against all ships bound for American ports. Numerous telegrams were sent from Italy, where Giovannitti's family lobbied actively in his behalf. Italian sympathizers demonstrated in front of the American consulate in Rome, and three Italian districts nominated Giovannitti for the Italian Chamber of Deputies. Delegations visited President Taft at his summer home in Beverly, Massachusetts, to plead for the prisoners' release.

The prosecution accused Ettor and Giovannitti of inciting the strikers to violence and murder, although witnesses proved that they were speaking to a meeting of workers several miles from the place where Anna LoPizzo was shot. Two hired detectives from a strike-breaking agency testified that Giovannitti had urged strikers to "sleep in the daytime and prowl around like wild beasts at night."[20] But the detectives admitted that the speech to which they referred was in Italian and that they had no written notes of the meeting from which to quote. Witnesses testified that Joseph Caruso was home eating supper at the time the woman striker was killed. Caruso said that he was not an I.W.W. member and had never heard Ettor or Giovannitti speak before he was imprisoned. He also said he planned to become a Wobbly as soon as he was released from jail.

Before the end of the trial, Ettor and Giovannitti asked permission to make closing statements. Joe Ettor said in part:

Does the District Attorney believe . . . that the gallows or guillotine ever settled an idea? If an idea can live, it lives because history adjudges it right. I ask only for justice. . . . The scaffold has never yet and never will destroy an idea or a movement. . . . An idea consisting of a social crime in one age becomes the very religion of humanity in the next. . . . Whatever my social views are, they are what they are. They cannot be tried in this courtroom.[21]

Giovannitti's speech, the first he had ever made publicly in English, moved even the reporters who were covering the trial. On November 26, 1912, the men were acquitted and released from jail.

Public opinion as expressed by the Eastern daily newspapers was practically unanimous in support of the acquittal of Ettor and Giovannitti. But the threat of anarchy and class war raised the fear that "a win in the Lawrence mills means a start that will only end with the downfall of the wage system." An editorial in the liberal *Survey* magazine questioned:

Are we to expect that instead of playing the game respectably . . . the laborers are to listen to subtle anarchistic philosophy which challenges the fundamental idea of law and order?[22]

Other publications around the country expressed alarm at the strange doctrines of "direct action," "syndicalism," "the general strike"—slogans of a new kind of revolution.

In the I.W.W. local in Lawrence, membership swelled to 10,000 in the year following the strike but dropped to 400 by 1914 as the depression of the preceding year cut into employment in the textile industry. In addition, textile employers initiated an espionage system in the mills to counter any further radical influence. A 50 percent speedup of the textile machines after 1912 led to additional unemployment and offset the wage increase gained by the strike settlement.

But the immediate effect of the Lawrence strike was to hearten textile workers in other Eastern areas and to prepare for the next large I.W.W. strike drama in the silk mills of Paterson within the year. The strike also made a profound impression on the public and the rest of the labor movement by dramatizing the living and working conditions of unorganized, foreign-born workers in crowded industrial areas, and communicating the spirit of their rebellion.

Following the Salem trial, literary critic Kenneth McGowan wrote in *Forum Magazine:*

Whatever its future, the I.W.W. has accomplished one tremendously big thing, a thing that sweeps away all twaddle over red flags and violence and sabotage, and that is the individual awakening of "illiterates" and "scum" to an original, personal conception of society and the realization of the dignity and rights of their part in it. They have learned more than class consciousness; they have learned consciousness of self. . . .[23]

This was a fitting interpretation of the spirit of the striking mill girls who carried picket signs which read:

WE WANT BREAD AND ROSES TOO.

1

Justus Ebert (1869–1946), the son of a former mayor of Mannheim, Germany, was in charge of publicity for the I.W.W. Lawrence Defense Committee. Ebert had worked as a newsboy, glassblower, and lapidary assistant before starting a writing and editing career at age seventeen, when a series of his articles appeared in the New York Courier. He was a Socialist Labor Party member until 1908, and assistant editor of the Daily People, *its newspaper. He resigned from the S.L.P. at that time to join the I.W.W.*

The Trial of a New Society (Cleveland, 1913), from which this selection is taken, was Ebert's first book. His other writings included the pamphlets, American Industrial Evolution from Frontier to Factory, Trade Unions in the United States, 1842–1905, *and the popular I.W.W. pamphlet,* The I.W.W. in Theory and Practice. *He was one of the editors of the I.W.W. magazine, the* Industrial Pioneer, *and the I.W.W. paper,* Solidarity.

For the last twenty years of his life, Ebert edited the journal of the Lithographers' Union. He was active in the Socialist Party, the League for Mutual Aid, and the Workers' Defense League.

Industrial Worker, August 15, 1912.

THE GENERAL STRIKE IS THE KEY THAT FITS THE LOCK TO FREEDOM

THE INDUSTRIAL DEMOCRACY ARRIVES

By Justus Ebert

On the morning of the 12th of January, 1912, the riot call was sounded on the bells of the City Hall at Lawrence, Mass. It was the first time in nineteen years that the call had been heard; and then only as a test. The call required the presence of every police officer in the city; regular, special and reserved; plain-clothes men, nightmen, in fact, all the guardians of peace and property.

The call came like a thunderbolt from a clear sky. There had been no previous indication of any need for the entire police resources of the community. Lawrence was, apparently, a peaceful and prosperous city, too active to be riotous, and too contented to be destructive. All its classes were, to all appearances, living in mutual harmony and accord. Why then this riot call? Why this hurry and scurry, this rush from all directions, this reporting at headquarters, of all its police, armed and ready for every possible affray?

The answer is one typical of the times.

Lawrence is renowned as a textile center. It outranks any other city in the nation in the production of woolen and worsted goods. In addition, its cotton industry is important. Lawrence is situated on the Merrimac River, whose immense water power has made it a favorable location for big mills.

In Lawrence, the hand loom of the early New England farm and the small mill of the last century with its tens of thousands of capital, have both been replaced by the Woolen Trust, the Whitman-Morgan combination of cotton and woolen interests, and other powerful organizations of capital, with their tens, nay, hundreds of millions of financial backing. Lawrence is, accordingly, a city dependent on corporate wealth. The mill corporations are its chief tax-payers and the chief employers of its inhabitants. Of the 85,000 population of Lawrence, over 35,000 are enrolled in the army of mill employees. They have no property rights in the mills; and are, for the most part, mere tenders of machines, without skill, and principally of foreign birth, as were the Pilgrim fathers who preceded them; and who murdered the native Indians who opposed their coming. These armies toil for the enrichment of stockholders who do not live in Lawrence and who take no part in its production of textile goods; who, in brief, are far more foreign to Lawrence, than are the most recent arrivals from abroad. Under the benign protection of Schedule K of the tariff laws of this country, they exact exceptional dividends, with more ferocity than Shylock exacted his pound of flesh. In all of which, they do not differ from the capitalist class in general, whose riches and fame are primarily due to the surplus values, that is, the wealth stolen from Labor in the form of profits, interest and rent.[1]

Let us look at these mills, therefore, a little closer; for, in looking at them, we are looking at the real Lawrence. They are the basis of its prosperity, its heart and soul! Just as the shoe and electric industries are the material basis and the heart and soul of Lynn; or the industries of any place and time are the basis of the material, legal and moral institutions—the heart and soul—of that place and time.

The principal mills in Lawrence are those of the American Woolen Company. This company is the largest single corporation in the textile industry. It is a consolidation of 34 mills, located mostly in New England. For these reasons it is known as "the Woolen Trust." The American Woolen Company does about one-ninth of the woolen and worsted manufacturing in the United States. Its 1911 output was valued at $45,000,000.

The Wood Mill of the American Woolen Co., located in Lawrence, is claimed by the company to be "the largest worsted mill in the world." It is 1,900 feet long, 300 feet wide and contains 1,300,-000 square feet of floor space. The output for 1911 is said to be valued at $9,000,000. The Washington and Ayer Mills adjoin the Wood Mill. They supply the raw material to the other mills of the company, located outside of Lawrence.

All three mills—Wood, Washington and Ayer—are situated on the South side of the Merrimac. They are modern brick structures, six stories high, almost a half-mile long altogether; and surmounted by an ornate clock-tower. A bridge at Union Street connects them with Lawrence proper. 16,500 persons, or almost one-half of the mill workers of Lawrence, are employed by the American Woolen Co. Its general offices are in Boston.

(1) For a more exhaustive study of textile evolution in New England see chapter on "New England," in Turner's "Rise of the New West," American Nation Series; "The Record of a City," by Geo. F. Kenngott; and the Citizens Committee's Report on the Lawrence Strike, Boston American, March 18, 1912.

The American Woolen Co. always pays 7 per cent on its capitalization of $70,000,000. This is said to be largely water. It is alleged in some quarters that its entire plant can be replaced at a cost ranging from $10,000,000 to $20,000,000. It is a well-known fact that its leading officers and stock-holders are connected with mill machine and construction companies that batten on its resources. William Wood, the president, owns two palatial residences. When asked in court, "How many automobiles have you?" he replied, "I don't know. I haven't any time to count them." Necessity doesn't require that he should take time to count his wealth. He has so much of it, as to render the performance superfluous.

Another noteworthy corporation on the South side of the Merrimac is the Lawrence Dye Works. This is the leading corporation in the consolidation of four mills known as the United States Worsted Co., whose properties it owns, besides its own. This $2,500,000 corporation makes a specialty of dyeing and finishing worsted goods. From 1884 to 1900 over 100 per cent was paid from its profits. Since then, the average yearly dividend has been nearly 20 per cent. The stock-holders of the Lawrence Dye Works now receive in five years that for which they formerly had to wait seven. The United States Worsted Co. itself pays 7.37 per cent annually. It manufactures fancy worsted and woolen goods in a six-story modern brick and concrete weaving mill overlooking the power dam at Lawrence.

Next in rank to the Woolen Trust mills are the Pacific Mills, located on the North side of the Merrimac, in Lawrence proper. This company manufactures cotton and worsted dress goods. Its attorney, James R. Dunbar, is also attorney for the Morgan railroad interests in New England. Men conspicuous on the boards of directors of these railroad interests are also conspicuous on the board of directors of the Pacific Mills. The Pacific Mills is erecting new mills at South Lawrence, east of the Wood Mill, whose total capacity is said to exceed that of the latter. Its employes number 6,000.

The Pacific Mills has a capital stock of $3,000,-000; and a surplus of $5,141,817. Its assets in two years—1909–1911—increased from $11,015,281 to $12,838,279, or a total of $1,822,998. This corporation paid dividends: 1907, $320; 1908, $120; 1909, $160; 1910, $120; 1911, $120; this is on nontaxable shares with a par value of $1,000. The total re-

turn to investors, in ten years, was 148 per cent. This is an average yearly return of 15 per cent. In other words, in ten years, the share-holders of the Pacific Mills not only ate their cake more abundantly than they made it, but they also have it now more abundantly than ever before. This is due to the kindness of the present system of capitalism, which takes from labor all it produces; giving in return therefrom wages, that is, enough of labor's product for labor to subsist on and reproduce more labor.[2]

After the Pacific Mills, in importance, come the Arlington Mills, owned by the Whitman interests, so-called after William Whitman, its president and principal stockholder, who is also a director in six textile corporations, closely allied to the one over which he presides. Whitman is credited on inside circles with being the father of Schedule K; also with having Morgan backing.

The Arlington Mills is capitalized at $8,000,000. Its annual output reaches the total value of $15,-000,000. Its dividends were six per cent from 1877

(2) See Special Weekly Circular, Sept. 7, 1912, Wagner, Dickerson & Co., bankers and brokers, N. Y.; Special Stock, Bank and Trust Company Circular, February, 1912, Turner, Tucker & Co., Bankers, Boston, Mass.; and articles on "The Great Textile Interests," Business Supplement, New York Sun, April 28, 1912, for statistics on dividends, capital, floor space, etc., of Lawrence Mills herein specified.

The Lumberjack, September 15, 1912.

to 1903, eight per cent from 1903 to 1912. In 1905, the Whitman Mills also declared a stock dividend of thirty-three and one-half per cent.[3]

Its mills in Lawrence employ over 5,000 operatives; and are continually expanding in size and importance. Like many other New England mills, the Arlington Mill is increasing its capacity out of its earnings. Dividends grow and so does the value of the property producing them; thanks to the productivity of Labor.

In addition to the Pacific and the Arlington Mills, there are in Lawrence proper, the Atlantic, Pemberton, Everett, Kuhnhardt, Duck and 13 other mills, whose combined capital runs well up above the Century mark. The brick buildings they own are mostly of an older type than those of the Woolen Trust, already described, and are built in close succession to one another, making them look as one. They are surmounted by belfries and smoke stacks. Fences and walls surround them. Entrance is through gates that are reached by bridges, which cross a power canal running parallel with the mills and feeding them. This canal cuts off the mills from the city, just as the moats of a medieval castle cut it off from the surrounding country.

The mills are on a private street called, very appropriately, Canal Street. A railroad runs right alongside of them and pierces them in order to get to a bridge crossing the river. All of which helps along the isolation and fortification.

All the mills on the north side of the Merrimac, thus isolated and fortified, are good dividend payers. The point is well illustrated in a story gleaned from the press and told by William D. Haywood, about Mr. Turner, Prest. of the Duck Mill, as follows: "Mr. Turner is a man of many wives and some wards. He married the last ward after he got rid of his wives. She lived in Brooklyn. They took a honeymoon. It was to Chicago. They had a palace train. Two Pullman cars were reserved for the bride's dogs. When those two carloads of dogs arrived in Chicago with their mistress, they were taken to a fashionable hotel, registered, assigned to private rooms and were fed on the choicest cuts of meat; porterhouse steak."[4]

None but the extremely wealthy, like the Woods, Turner and the textile barons of Lawrence, can indulge in such wasteful extravagancies. To even the moderately wealthy middle class, it is not given to have more automobiles than one can count; or to provide Pullman cars, fashionable hotel suites and porterhouse steaks for the dogs belonging to one's latest of many brides similarly indulged before. Such expenditures are only possible among those possessing multimillions, such as come out of the mills of Lawrence.

Contrast now the wealth, expansion and luxury of Lawrence's corporation magnates with the poverty, degradation and misery of Lawrence's wealth producers.

Despite consolidation, tariff, and perfected machinery, the wages and conditions of textile workers show a steady decline. According to the United States Census, from 1890 to 1905, textile wages had decreased 22.0 to 19.5 per cent of the value of the gross output. This is a difference of $53,686,-035; a stupendous sum to these poorly-paid workers, as will be shown further along.[5]

This decline is made possible by increasing the number of looms to the worker, while at the same time, reducing the pay, through the competition of those thus displaced. In August, 1911, a call was issued for a general organization of all the textile workers along the Merrimac River, in order to more effectively combat the tendency to reduce wages and intensify labor at one and the same time.

The appeal opens thus:

"One hundred cotton weavers are fighting against the following conditions which the Atlantic Mills are trying to impose upon them.

"Twelve looms instead of seven, at 49 cents per cut, instead of 79 cents; those are in a few words, the conditions against which the weavers are revolting.

"Seven looms producing two cuts a week at the rate of 79 cents per cut leaves a salary of $11.06 per week; 12 looms producing two cuts each per week at the rate of 49 cents per cut gives a salary of $11.76.

"Admitting that each weaver can make 24 cuts each on 12 looms, which is practically impossible, he will necessarily have to operate five looms, and produce 10 cuts more each week for the sum of 70 cents; so that it is really a theft of $7.20 per

(3) These figures and facts are furnished by a reliable Wall Street Journalist.

(4) "Speech of Wm. D. Haywood on Case of Ettor and Giovannitti, Cooper Union, N. Y.," pamphlet published by Ettor-Giovannitti Defense Committee, Lawrence, Mass. p. 7.

(5) Statement of Congressman Victor Berger, p. 8, Report of House Committee on Rules, Lawrence Strike.

week which the corporation will make on each and every weaver, and at the same time throw two employees out of five on the streets."[6]

This method of doing more work with less men at less wages than formerly, was also introduced into the Woolen Mills. Here also the employees fought the two loom system, which meant a doubling up of their toil and the cutting in half of their numbers, with the inevitable reduction of wages that the competition of the unemployed made possible. Numerous strikes were inaugurated to combat this tendency. But all of them failed, because they were partial and sporadic; fought by the craft directly involved alone, while the other crafts remained at work and scabbed on it, that is, assisted the corporations to victory.[7] This tendency was further emphasized by the speeding up, encouraged by the premium system, which added to the nervous strain, while gradually lowering wages.

Accordingly, wages in the Lawrence mills have become mere pittances. The $11.76 per week for weavers, specified above, are exceptionally good wages. The report of Commissioner of Labor, Charles P. Neil, shows that, for the week ending Nov. 25, 1911, 22,000 textile workers in Lawrence averaged $8.76 in wages. This average is for a good week only; and is inclusive of the wages paid to all grades of labor. The commissioner reports that almost one-third of the 22,000 earned less than $7, while only 17.5 per cent earned $12 and over for the select week in which the pay-roll was averaged.[8]

It is pointed out in Lawrence that over 13,000 workers are not accounted for in the commissioner's investigation. These certainly are numerous enough to be considered. It is also claimed that during the pay week preceding Jan. 12, 1912, the pay-roll for 25,000 employees amounted to $150,-000 or an average of $6 for the week. Thus the commissioner's figures are to be taken with qualifications when put forth as representing actual conditions.

The actual wages paid in some of the mills make startling reading. They recall the time in

the eighties when Henry Ward Beecher is alleged to have said: "A dollar a day is enough pay for any American laborer to live on"—a statement that aroused furious opposition. In the American Woolen Company's spinning, winding and beaming departments and dye houses, wages were $5.10, $6.05, $6.55, $7.15, and $7.55 per week in 1911. This is for a full week only; often, when work is slack, such wages as $2.30 and $2.70 a week are the rule.[9] The writer met in Lawrence weavers who informed him that they averaged $5.00 a week following the panic of 1907. And these were men with wives and families.

Custom often reveals conditions where all else may hide them. In Lawrence, it is the custom to demand weekly rents for tenements occupied by the working class. Where wages are small and employment unsteady, it is realized that monthly rents are difficult of accumulation and collection. The rents vary from $1 to $6 per week. They are higher on the average than in New York, Chicago, Philadelphia, Boston, Cleveland, Buffalo and Milwaukee. In addition, Lawrence offers none of the various social advantages of these larger cities. Boarders or lodgers were found in 58 per cent of the homes visited by Federal investigators. They are necessary to the raising of rent.[10]

Instalment houses also do a thriving business in Lawrence. "Easy Payments" is the deceptive means by which extortionate prices are made possible of payment by the workers who are already badly fleeced in the mills.

Lawrence is also the scene of much experimenting in co-operative enterprises, several of which have been successful. Where wages are low, as in Belgium and England, the economies and thrift made possible by co-operative buying and selling, becomes imperative. Especially is this true, in view of the increasing cost of living. Lawrence is by no means exempt from the latter. For instance, anthracite coal was $10.50 a ton in Lawrence during the winter of 1911–1912. The cost of living is higher in Lawrence than elsewhere.

Congestion is worse in Lawrence than in any other city in New England, Boston excepted. Frame houses and rear houses are more numerous than in the congested districts of Manchester,

(6) Appeal issued by Local 20, I.W.W., Lawrence, Mass.

(7) Report General Organizer James P. Thompson, 7th Convention I.W.W., Sept., 1912, Chicago, Ill.

(8) Report on strike of Textile Workers in Lawrence, Mass., in 1912. P. 19. Charles P. Neil, Commissioner of Labor, Washington, D. C.

(9) Report of House Committee on Rules, Lawrence Strike, 1912. pp. 139–176.

(10) P. 25. Neil Report on Lawrence Strike.

N.H., Lowell, Salem, Fall River and New Bedford, Mass. A terrible conflagration is always possible; the construction being regarded as "extra-hazardous."[11]

In addition, the rear houses are entered by alleyways and long narrow passages leading from them which make deadly flues and fire traps. These alleyways and passages are also dirty and dark, mouldy and foul-smelling. They are the playgrounds of the children who inhabit them. Juvenile offenders are numerous in Lawrence.[12] The cause is evident.

"Our valuation did not increase with our population," said Commissioner of Public Safety, C. F. Lynch, addressing the Berger Congressional investigation of the Lawrence strike; "and consequently we were faced with a serious financial problem." As a reflex of Lawrence's poverty and squalor this needs no comment.

Malnutrition and premature death are common in Lawrence. The textile industry is a "family industry." Its subdivision makes possible the employment of all of the members of the family. It also makes possible, consequently, the destruction of the textile family.

Of the 22,000 textile workers investigated by Commissioner Neil, 12,150 or 54 per cent are males, and 9,772 or 44.6 per cent are females; 11.5 per cent of all of them, being under 18 years of age. The mill workers claim that over 50 per cent of Lawrence's operatives are women and children. As there are over 13,000 to be accounted for by the commissioner, and as his figures verge very closely on the claim made, the latter may be taken for granted without discussion.

It is plain that, under the above circumstances, family life outside of the mills must suffer. Women who arise at 5:30 A.M. in order to be enabled to do housework and labor in a dusty, noisy mill until 5:30 P.M., at starvation wages, are bound to bear and rear offspring who are underfed and badly cared for. Everyone of the 119 children sent to New York in February, 1912 was found on physical examination to be suffering from malnutrition, in some form. As Wm. D. Haywood most eloquently puts it, "Those children had been starving from birth. They had been starved in their moth-

ers' wombs. And their mothers had been starving before the children were conceived."[13]

Malnutrition brings about a disease called Rachitis, or rickets. The writer has seen so many children with crooked and distorted limbs and bones in Lawrence as to be impressed with the fact. Likewise, has he observed the anemic and wizened expression, not only of infants, but also of adults. Underfeeding is common in Lawrence.

The infant death rate in Lawrence is very high. For every 1,000 births there are 172 deaths under one year of age. This is greater than 28 other cities with which Lawrence has been compared. The same is practically true of Lawrence's general death rate, which is 17.7 per 1,000 population, a rate which surpasses that of 26 other cities,[14] and is above the average for the United States.

In the matter of longevity, according to Lawrence's mortuary records, its lawyers and clergymen lead,. with an average length of life of 65.4 years. Manufacturers come next with 58.5 years; farmers follow with 57 years. Mill operatives have the shortest life span. From the mortality records of 1,010 operatives, the average length of life was found to be 39.6 years. The average longevity for spinners is three and two-fifths years less, or 36 years. On an average, the spinner's life is 29 years less than that of the lawyer's or clergyman's and 22.5 years shorter than that of the manufacturer.[15]

Says Dr. Shapleigh, a Lawrence practitioner, who made a special study of the subject: "36 out of every 100 of all the men and women who work in the mill die before, or by the time, they are 25 years of age. That means that out of the long line which enters the mill you may strike out every third person as dying before reaching maturity. Every fourth person in the line is dying from tuberculosis. And further, every second person, that is one alternating with a healthy person, will die of some form of respiratory trouble." The same authority states that "a considerable number of the boys and girls die within the first two or three years after beginning work."[16] So poorly are they nourished and developed, that they have not the stamina to withstand the strain.

(13) Cooper Union Speech on Ettor-Giovannitti case. pp. 4–5.
(14) Neil Report. p. 27.
(15) Dr. Elizabeth Shapleigh, Occupational Diseases in the Textile Industry. New York Call, Dec. 29, 1912.
(16) Ibid.

(11) Ibid. p. 24.
(12) A perusal of police court proceedings in Lawrence press will convince the reader of this fact.

Here then is the lot of the textile workers of Lawrence—steadily declining and low wages, intensified and unsteady employment, bad housing, underfeeding, no real family life, and premature death. The benefits of industrial evolution and national legislation go not to them, but to the Woods, Turners, et al., who live in wasteful extravagance upon their merciless exploitation, regardless of common decency and in defiance of the social spirit of the times.

This was the condition of affairs in Lawrence, Mass., on Jan. 12, 1912, when something extraordinary happened in the big mills there. About 9 A.M. on that date, the employes in one of the departments of the Everett Mill, swept through its long floors, wildly excited, carrying an American flag which they waved amid shouts of "Strike! Strike!! Strike!!! All out; come on; all out. Strike! Strike!!" From room to room they rushed, an enraged, indignant mass. Arming themselves with the picker sticks used in the mills, they went from loom to loom, persuading and driving away operatives; and stopping looms; tearing weaves, and smashing machines, where repeated attempts were made to run them despite their entreaties, which seldom failed of instant response. As they swept on, their numbers grew, and with them grew the contagion, the uproar and the tumult.

Out of the Everett Mill they rushed, these hundreds of peaceful workers, now aroused, passionate and tense. On the street, outside of the mill gates, they were met by excited crowds that were congregated there. All of them coalesced into one big mass, and, as such, moved over the Union Street bridge on to the Wood, Washington and Ayer Mills, where the same scenes were enacted once more. Men, women and children—Italians, Poles, Syrians—all races, all creeds, already aroused to action before the coming of the crowd outside (some of whom rushed the gates and entered), ran through the thousands of feet of floor space, shouting, "Strike! Strike!! Strike!!! All out! Strike! Strike!! Strike!!!" sweeping everything before them, and rendering operation in many departments so impossible as to cause their complete shut-down.

These thousands also poured out into the streets, and, with their fellow workers, already assembled there, choked up the highway, blocking cars and suspending traffic generally; while at the same time hooting and howling, raising speakers and leaders on their shoulders, throwing ice and snow,

and bombarding the windows in the adjoining Kuhnhardt and Duck Mills, smashing every pane of glass there—a destructive, menacing mob. Where peace had reigned before, disorder and violence now seemed rampant.[17]

The something extraordinary that had happened in Lawrence, Mass., on January 12, 1912, was an industrial revolt. The mill workers had risen. In their rising they sounded, not only a riot call, but also the keynote to the revolution of all the workers in industry—to the industrial democracy. Peaceful Lawrence, like every American city, had a submerged Lawrence, a working class Lawrence—that had erupted and, in so doing, sprung all the social layers above that held it down into the air. So the riot call was sounded. And the police tried to force the submerged down to where they formerly had been. So did the militia! So did the State! So did all the repressive agencies of modern, that is, capitalist, society. But they failed. A new force had arisen—the workers democratically and industrially organized. The workers thus united are invincible. It is Labor alone that defeats Labor.

But this is running ahead of the story; to return.

The cause of the Lawrence industrial revolt was a common thing, to wit, a wage reduction. A beneficent state law had been passed reducing hours of labor for women and children from 56 to 54 per week. When this law went into effect the mill corporations reduced wages proportionately, without any previous notice whatever. At the same time, they speeded up the machines and so got in 54 hours at 54 hours' pay, the same output that had been secured in 56 hours at 56 hours' pay.

The operatives' only notice of the reduction was the short pay in their envelopes. "Short pay! Short pay!" was the cry that had preceded the uprising. The more the workers reflected on that short pay the most resentful and unrestrainable they became. In many thousands of cases the reduction only amounted to 30 cents a week. Yet this apparently insignificant amount—the price of a good Havana cigar to a Wood or a Turner—was enough to turn Lawrence topsy-turvy and to alter the subsequent political history of the coun-

(17) In narrating events at Lawrence, the writer has drawn on the Neil Report, the Berger Congressional Investigation Report, testimony of witnesses at the Salem trial, and personal conversations with participants. His sources of information are thus both official and unofficial.

Mr. Block
He Tries To Be a Union Scab

Industrial Worker, March 6, 1913.

Left to right: Joseph Caruso, Joe Ettor, and Arturo Giovannitti.   United Press International, Inc., photo.

try; for the Lawrence strike destroyed the presidential prospects of Governor Foss and hastened the formation of the Progressive Party, with its program of industrial and social reform.

Though the wage reduction was small in amount, the textile workers of Lawrence realized from abundant experience that the wages they would receive under the 54 hours' law would not be sufficient to live on. Their position, as already shown, was near enough to absolute starvation as to leave no doubt on that point. So rather than suffer the further weekly loss of six loaves of bread, so badly needed, a great part rose en masse in spontaneous revolt. Blind, instinctive, but primal, and, therefore, fundamental and far-reaching, was the uprising of these miserable workers.

None had expected such a violent outbreak. True, according to Commissioner Neil, a far-sighted mill official in Boston, had warned against the prospect of one. But his was a lone voice, crying out in the wilderness. On January 2nd, 1912, some of the workers organized in the Industrial Workers of the World, tried to confer on the 54 hour law with the mill-owners, but were snubbed for their pains. The weaving department of the Everett Mill and the spinning department of the Arlington Mill had struck on the afternoon of January 11th. A meeting of 1,000 Italians and Poles, held in Ford's Hall on the evening of January 10, decided to walk out. Other outbursts had taken place.[18]

Notwithstanding all this, the mill corporations went right on as if nothing of importance was happening, or could happen. They were supreme and able to crush out all discontent, as before. They recked not of the terrible resentment—the general rage, long smoldering and now irrepressible—that filled the workers on beholding their robbed envelopes—and lives. And they knew not that where Labor is most suffering and most oppressed, there is it also most terrible when aroused.

Hence, the revolt was a complete surprise, that caused unprecedented alarm, and for the first time in a labor dispute in the history of Massachusetts, later on, necessitated the calling out of the militia. The Lawrence textile revolt reverberated throughout the industrial world. Large numbers in distant parts instinctively realized at once that something extraordinary had happened in New England's hotbeds of labor submission and exploi-

tation, the textile mills. The textile wage-slaves had openly and actually rebelled. Lawrence, with its exploitation and luxury for the benefit of a few capitalists on one side, and its slavery and starvation for the many workers on the other, was now enacting the world-wide drama of the class struggle—of the irrepressible conflict between the interests of capital and labor.

It was this profound fact that sounded the riot call, turned Lawrence topsy-turvy and enabled the industrial democracy to arrive.

2

On July 15, 1795, "La Marseillaise" was made the official national anthem of France. It had been written by a young French army officer, Rouget de Lisle, and dedicated to the French commander of the Army of the Rhine at a time when France had declared war on Prussia and Hungary. In 1830, it was sung by radical workers in the July Revolution against the reactionary King Charles X. Louis Philippe, Charles's successor, granted De Lisle a pension, and when he died in 1836 huge crowds of workers marched in his funeral procession.

"The Marseillaise" became popular with revolutionary movements throughout Europe and was printed in many radical songbooks. It was included in a book, Socialist Songs *(Chicago, 1901), published by the Charles Kerr Publishing Company, and printed in the first edition of the I.W.W. songbook. It was especially popular in the I.W.W. strikes in Lawrence, Massachusetts, and Paterson, New Jersey.*

THE MARSEILLAISE °

Ye sons of toil, awake to glory!
　　Hark, hark, what myriads bid you rise;
Your children, wives and grandsires hoary—
　　Behold their tears and hear their cries!
　　Behold their tears and hear their cries!
Shall hateful tyrants mischief breeding,
　　With hireling hosts, a ruffian band—
　　Affright and desolate the land,
While peace and liberty lie bleeding?

　　　　Chorus:

To arms! to arms! ye brave!
　　Th' avenging sword unsheathe!
March on, march on, all hearts resolved
　　On Victory or Death.

(18) The Neil Report. pp. 31–32.

With luxury and Pride surrounded,
  The vile, insatiate despots dare,
Their thirst for gold and power unbounded,
  To mete and vend the light and air,
  To mete and vend the light and air,
Like beasts of burden, would they load us,
  Like gods would bid their slaves adore,
  But Man to Man, and who is more?
Then shall they longer lash and goad us?

Chorus.

O, Liberty; can man resign thee?
  Once having felt thy generous flame.
Can dungeons, bolts and bars confine thee?
  Or whips, thy noble spirit tame?
  Or whips, thy noble spirit tame?
Too long the world has wept bewailing
  That Falsehood's dagger tyrants wield,
  But Freedom is our sword and shield;
And all their arts are unavailing!

Chorus.

3

A Parisian transport worker, Eugene Pottier, wrote the words to "The Internationale" in 1871, and they were set to music composed by Pierre Degeyter, a wood carver from Lille, in 1888. "The Internationale" became the anthem for radical movements throughout the world. It was the official anthem of the Soviet Union until 1944, when the U.S.S.R. adopted a new national anthem, "The Hymn of the Soviet Union." It was translated into English by Charles Kerr, head of a cooperative socialist book publishing company in Chicago, and included in a socialist songbook published in 1901. It was sung by delegates to the first I.W.W. convention in 1905, frequently reprinted in the I.W.W. press, and included in the first edition of the I.W.W. songbook.

THE INTERNATIONALE°

By Eugene Pottier

Translated by Charles H. Kerr

Arise, ye prisoners of starvation!
  Arise, ye wretched of the earth,
For justice thunders condemnation,
  A better world's in birth.
No more tradition's chains shall bind us,
  Arise, ye slaves! no more in thrall!

The earth shall rise on new foundations,
  We have been naught, we shall be all.

Refrain

'Tis the final conflict,
  Let each stand in his place,
The Industrial Union
  Shall be the human race.

We want no condescending saviors,
  To rule us from a judgment hall;
We workers ask not for their favors;
  Let us consult for all.
To make the thief disgorge his booty
  To free the spirit from its cell,
We must ourselves decide our duty,
  We must decide and do it well.

Refrain

The law oppresses us and tricks us,
  Wage systems drain our blood;
The rich are free from obligations,
  The laws the poor delude.
Too long we've languished in subjection,
  Equality has other laws;
"No rights," says she, "without their duties,
  No claims on equals without cause."

Refrain

Behold them seated in their glory,
  The kings of mine and rail and soil!
What have you read in all their story,
  But how they plundered toil?
Fruits of the people's work are buried
  In the strong coffers of a few;
In working for their restitution
  The men will only ask their due.

Refrain

Toilers from shops and fields united,
  The union we of all who work;
The earth belongs to us, the people,
  No room here for the shirk.
How many on our flesh have fattened!
  But if the noisome birds of prey
Shall vanish from the sky some morning,
  The blessed sunlight still will stay.

Refrain

Sheet music of "The Internationale."

4

Fred Beal (1895?——), author of Proletarian
Journey *(New York, 1937) from which this selection is taken, was a textile worker and textile
organizer. Convicted during the Gastonia (North
Carolina) textile strike, he jumped bail and, with
utopian expectations, fled to the Soviet Union,
where he lived for several years. Disillusioned
with his experiences, he broke with the Communist Party and returned to the United States. His
second book,* The Red Fraud *(New York, 1949),
was published by Tempo Publishers.*

STRIKE!

By FRED E. BEAL

1

I suddenly discovered that I did not want to be
a textile worker. I was fifteen. . . . Mill work was
dreary. . . .

. . . One day, at noon-time, [a] lecturer addressed the crowd in front of our mill gate. . . .
[He] urged us to organize into a union, to join
the Industrial Workers of the World, and to demand from the bosses more wages and shorter
hours. He declared with emphasis that we, the
textile workers, were *wage slaves* and that all the
mill owners were slave drivers, as bad and as
brutal as Simon Legree of *Uncle Tom's Cabin.*

This was news to me. I had always thought that
only coloured people could be slaves and that
they had been freed long ago by us Yankees who
fought in the Civil War. Yet there was something
convincing about his talk although I could not
quite understand just who were the bosses who,
according to the speaker, were enjoying the Flor-
ida sunshine while we slaved in the mills for their
profit. All the subordinate bosses I had ever known
were working in the mill, like "Slim Jim the Burglar" and Paddy Parker.

The Irish workers did not like the speaker; the
Italians did. The Irish cupped their hands to their
mouths, made strange noises every time the Ital-

Strikers held back by soldiers, Lawrence, Massachusetts, 1912.   Brown Brothers photo.

ians applauded, and yelled: "Ef ye don't loike this countr-r-ry, go back where ye come fr-r-rom!"

The speaker ignored these remarks and continued: "The working class and the employing class have nothing in common. Between these two classes a struggle must go on until the workers of the world organize as a class, take possession of the earth and the machinery of production, and abolish the wage system."

Then, rudely, as if by prearrangement, the ten-minutes-to-one bells, high up in the mill's belfry, began tolling their dismal warning to us workers that it was time for us to get back to work. *The slave bells are calling!*" yelled the I.W.W. speaker. "The master wants you back at the bench and machine. Go, slaves! But remember, these very bells will some day toll the death-knell of the slave-drivers!"

The bells tolled on defiantly.

2

That afternoon, during the rest period, we doffers talked about the I.W.W. speaker and the union he was organizing. We had good reason to talk. Things were about to happen. The State Legislature had just passed a law reducing the hours of labour from 56 to 54 per week, and there was rumour that our pay would be reduced accordingly. Our next pay day was Friday, January 12, and the grown-up workers were talking about going on strike if wages were cut. We young people thought it would be fun to strike and made plans to go skating and sleigh-riding—all but Little Eva. She and her mother were the breadwinners of the family. Her father had lost an arm at Pingree's Box Shop two weeks after they came from Canada. They sorely needed Little Eva's weekly wage of five dollars and four cents.

Old man Dwyer, the empty rovings' collector, had worked in the Pacific Mills over thirty years. There was a strike in the Pacific Mills in 1882, said Dwyer, against a wage reduction. He took part in that and lost.

"Thems that runs things gets the best of us every time," he shook his head dejectedly. "Let well enough alone." He was against going on strike. "Tain't right to be loafin'," he would say. "These dagoes, who come to this country and takes the vittels right out of our mouths by workin' for nothin' only wants more money to send home to Italy."

While the discussion was on, two Italian spin-ners came to me with a long white paper. They wanted me to be among the first to sign a petition against the threatened wage cut because, they said, I was American. The idea was to present Paddy Parker with a long list of those opposed to any reduction. I read the words at the top of the paper:

THE FOLLOWING PEOPLE WORKING IN THE SPINNING ROOM WILL GO ON STRIKE FRIDAY, JANUARY 12, IF WAGES ARE CUT—

Queenie read it over my shoulder. "Don't sign it, Lobster," she cautioned. "These wops'll get you in trouble. You'll be put on the blacklist if you sign that paper!"

But I signed it. So did Gyp and Lefty Louie.

And January 12 was only two days away.

3

On this Friday morning the atmosphere at the mill was tense with suppressed excitement. We were not sure that the company would cut our wages. We would know when the paymaster came round at eleven o'clock. The shop was full of rumours. One of these was that the big Wood Mill of eight thousand workers had already gone on strike. This almost started an immediate walk-out in our spinning room. Dwyer had it on "good authority" that we would get an increase if we stayed at work. Queenie said the priest told her not to strike.

"You goddam French-Canucks will go out if we do," snapped Gyp, "even if we have to pull you out by the tongue." Gyp was afraid his plans for skating might fall amiss.

Paddy Parker, petition in hand, called me to one side. "Young man," he said blandly, "I see your name heads this list. Did you put it there?"

"Yes, I did, because I don't think we should get a wage cut."

"You shouldn't have your name with these foreigners."

"I work with them, don't I?"

"Yes, but you want to get a better position soon, don't you? Stand by the company. I'll cross off your name."

"I'm going on strike if the others do," I said firmly.

"All right, young man, if you do, you will *never get work again in the Pacific Mills*, and I will see to it that you are blacklisted at other mills, and every other name on this list."

The threat of not being able to get work again in any of the mills made me feel miserable. Where else could I get a job? All Lawrence to me was mills, mills, mills. . . . Perhaps the best thing would be to leave Lawrence and go West, to be a cowboy like those in the movies. For the first time in my life I felt fear tugging at my heart. Hadn't I promised to help out the family? And now, if I went out on strike, I would never get another job in the mills of Lawrence and perhaps Paddy Parker could stop me from getting a job anywhere. I had to make a decision in thirty minutes before the paymaster came round.

It was my habit, in a crisis, to ask God the way out—God and Jesus Christ, because I took my Sunday-school teachings seriously. I always talked with God in private. There was no thought of irreverence in me when, sitting upon the toilet seat, I asked God about going out on strike. There just wasn't any other private place.

There was a sharp whistle. It was the call that said: "Come and get your pay!"

Just like any other Friday, the paymaster, with the usual armed guard, wheeled a truck containing hundreds of pay envelopes to the head of a long line of anxiously waiting people. There was much chattering in different languages, and much gesticulation. I stood with Gyp halfway along the line. When the great moment came, the first ones nervously opened their envelopes and found that the company had deducted two hours' pay. They looked silly, embarrassed and uncertain what to do. Milling around, they waited for someone to start something. They didn't have long to wait, for one lively young Italian had his mind thoroughly made up and swung into action without even looking into his pay envelope.

"Strike! Strike!" he yelled. To lend strength to his words, he threw his hands in the air like a cheer-leader.

"Strike! Strike! Strike!"

He yelled these words as he ran, past our line, then down the room between spinning frames. The shop was alive with cries of "Strike" after the paymaster left. A few French-Canadian spinners went back to work. A tall Syrian worker pulled a switch and the powerful speed belts that gave life to the bobbins slackened to a stop.

There were cries: "All Out!"

And then hell broke loose in the spinning room. The silent, mute frames became an object of intense hatred, something against which to vent our stored-up feelings. Gears were smashed and belts cut. The Italians had long sharp knives and with one zip the belts dangled helplessly on the pulleys. Lefty Louie and I went from frame to frame, breaking "ends," while Tony smashed windows. Queenie barricaded herself behind trucks and let loose a barrage of bobbins on Gyp, who seemed determined to get hold of her tongue. It was a madhouse, a thrilling one, nevertheless.

More cries: "Strike! All Out! Strike!"

Old man Dwyer hugged his truck of rovings and Paddy Parker was at the door when we stampeded for the street. How ineffectual he looked, standing there with the petition. It was 11:45. The company wanted to keep us in until twelve, when the bells in the belfry would again ring out the noon hour, so the gates were closed. Three workers grabbed the watchman and forced him to open up. We wanted to get out before the bells rang, and we did.

We piled out into Canal Street, singing and shouting.

It was snowing.

5

Richard Brazier's verses on shorter hours appeared in the third edition of the I.W.W. songbook.

Although the eight-hour day was not legally established in this country until 1938, with the passage of the Wage-Hour Law, agitation for a shorter work day had been carried on for over fifty years by American workers. In the I.W.W., E. S. Nelson, author of "Workingmen, Unite," spearheaded an eight-hour movement among lumber and construction workers in the Northwest. An Eight-Hour League was formed about 1912 among textile workers in Paterson, New Jersey, where no reduction had been made in the working hours of the industry since 1904. An earlier eight-hour song to the tune "The British Grenadiers" originated among the miners and was probably sung in the 1897 mine strike for a shorter work day.

THE EIGHT-HOUR SONG

By RICHARD BRAZIER

(*Tune: "Silver Threads Among the Gold"*)

Workingmen, both young and old, why will you
  wear your lives away,

For the masters making gold, while you live from
day to day?
Hungry, ragged and forsaken, millions of you
roam the earth,
All you make is from you taken, slaves you are
right from your birth.

Chorus

Arise, then, throw your chains asunder, stand up
for the eight-hour day,
Then you workers who now hunger will have work
and get more pay.

Refrain

Workers do you hear us calling, 1912, the FIRST
OF MAY?
After that date, work no longer than eight hours a
day.

The Industrial Workers ask the workers young and
old,
To organize against the shirkers, and depose those
lords of gold,
Take from them what belongs to you, all the
product of your toil,
To your class be ever true, reduce the hours you
spin and toil.

Chorus

Unite in the Industrial Union for a shorter working
day,
That the unemployed workers may get a chance to
draw some pay.

Workers who are now a-tramping, seeking for a
chance to work,
In the jungles now are camping, whilst our
masters smile and smirk
O'er the sorrows of these workers, out of work,
hungry and cold,
They call them hoboes, bums and shirkers, the
breadline is their place, they're told.

Chorus

But the call now resounding for a general eight-
hour day,
Will give the workers they are hounding a chance
for work and more pay.

6

*Frank Brechler (dates unknown) may have been
a pseudonym for another I.W.W. writer, possibly*

*Joe Hill. These verses signed by Brechler ap-
peared in the third edition of the I.W.W. songbook. An early edition of the songbook credits
"The Preacher and the Slave" to Brechler, although it was later identified as a song by Joe Hill.*

WORKERS, SHALL THE MASTERS RULE US?

By FRANK BRECHLER

(Tune: "Just Before the Battle, Mother")

Workers, shall the masters rule us?
Shall we crouch beneath their hand;
Shall they own this earth and fool us
With that two-faced gospel band?
Shall these tyrants live in plenty
While we workers have to starve?
Yes, we slaves with stomachs empty,
Is there nothing we deserve?

Think of children working daily
In the sweat shops of this land,
While there're strong men in this country
Without work, you understand.
Workers shall we change conditions
So that those things won't exist?
Show the grafters their positions;
Let them know they'll not be missed.

Workers, we must stick together;
We must join in one great band,
That's the way to fight the masters
So that they'll not rule this land.
Join the rank and don't be shirkers,
Come now, slaves, what do you say?
Join the Industrial Workers,
Let us know your name today.

7

*The following songs (nos. 7 and 8) appeared in
Solidarity (June 29, 1912) under the headline,
"Songs Sung by the Workers on the Lawrence
Picket Line," and are good examples of strike
songs created to fit the situation. "In the Good
Old Picket Line" is a parody of "In the Good Old
Summer Time." The music to the other song was
from Irving Berlin's "Everybody's Doing It."*

*"Mr. Lowe" was Arthur H. Lowe, manager of
the Lancaster Mills Corporation and one of its
large stockholders.*

FEW OF THEM ARE SCABBING IT
Lawrence, Mass., Strike Song

Few of them are scabbing it, scabbing it, scabbing
  it,
Few of them are scabbing it, scabbing it, scabbing
  it,
Few scab weavers sneaking through the line,
They're the ones Mr. Lowe will fine,
They sneak in and get their measly pay,
Let us pray, let us pray, let us pray—SAY—

Few of them are scabbing it, scabbing it, scabbing
  it,
Few of them are scabbing it, scabbing it, scabbing
  it,
Mr. Lowe says he will treat them well,
But after he's used them, he'll let them go to hell,
While the strikers cheerfully yell,
Few of them are scabbing it now.

8

IN THE GOOD OLD PICKET LINE
Lawrence, Mass., Strike Song

In the good old picket line, in the good old picket
  line,
The workers are from every place, from nearly
  every clime,
The Greeks and Poles are out so strong, and the
  Germans all the time,
But we want to see more Irish in the good old
  picket line.

In the good old picket line, in the good old picket
  line,
We'll put Mr. Lowe in overalls and swear off
  drinking wine,
Then Gurley Flynn will be the boss,
Oh Gee, won't that be fine,
The strikers will wear diamonds in the good old
  picket line.

9

*Joe Hill's song, "John Golden and the Lawrence
Strike," was a blast at the president of the A.F.L.
Textile Workers Union, who had incurred the
wrath of Wobblies by testifying against the
I.W.W. in congressional hearings on the Lawrence strike. It was printed in the fifth edition of
the I.W.W. songbook.*

JOHN GOLDEN AND THE LAWRENCE STRIKE
By JOE HILL
(*Tune: "A Little Talk With Jesus"*)

In Lawrence, when the starving masses struck for
  more to eat
And wooden-headed Wood tried the strikers
  to defeat,
To Sammy Gompers wrote and asked him what he
  thought,
And this is the answer that the mailman brought:

Chorus:

  A little talk—
  A little talk with Golden
  Makes it right, all right;
  He'll settle any strike,
  If there's coin enough in sight;
  Just take him up to dine
  And everything is fine—
  A little talk with Golden
  Makes it right, all right.

The preachers, cops and money-kings were
  working hand in hand,
The boys in blue, with stars and stripes were sent
  by Uncle Sam;
Still things were looking blue, 'cause every striker
  knew
That weaving cloth with bayonets is hard to do.

John Golden had with Mr. Wood a private inter-
  view,
He told him how to bust up the "I double double
  U."
He came out in a while and wore the Golden smile.
He said: "I've got all labor leaders skinned a mile."

John Golden pulled a bogus strike with all his
  "pinks and stools."
He thought the rest would follow like a bunch of
  crazy fools.
But to his great surprise the "foreigners" were wise
In one big solid union they were organized.

Chorus

  That's one time Golden did not
  Make it right, all right;
  In spite of all his schemes
  The strikers won the fight.

When all the workers stand
United hand in hand,
The world with all its wealth
Shall be at their command.

10

This testimony of a teenage textile worker is from the Hearings on the Strike at Lawrence, Massachusetts, *House Document No. 671, 62nd Congress, Second Session. Miss Teoli was one of a group of teenage textile workers who testified during the congressional hearings, March 2–7, 1912.*

STATEMENT OF CAMELLA TEOLI

THE CHAIRMAN. Camella, how old are you?

MISS TEOLI. Fourteen years and eight months.

THE CHAIRMAN. Fourteen years and eight months?

MISS TEOLI. Yes.

THE CHAIRMAN. How many children are there in your family?

MISS TEOLI. Five.

THE CHAIRMAN. Where do you work?

MISS TEOLI. In the woolen mill.

THE CHAIRMAN. For the American Woolen Co.?

MISS TEOLI. Yes.

THE CHAIRMAN. What sort of work do you do?

MISS TEOLI. Twisting.

THE CHAIRMAN. You do twisting?

MISS TEOLI. Yes.

THE CHAIRMAN. How much do you get a week?

MISS TEOLI. $6.55.

THE CHAIRMAN. What is the smallest pay?

MISS TEOLI. $2.64.

THE CHAIRMAN. Do you have to pay anything for water?

MISS TEOLI. Yes.

THE CHAIRMAN. How much?

MISS TEOLI. 10 cents every two weeks.

THE CHAIRMAN. Do they hold back any of your pay?

MISS TEOLI. No.

THE CHAIRMAN. Have they ever held back any?

MISS TEOLI. One week's pay.

THE CHAIRMAN. They have held back one week's pay?

MISS TEOLI. Yes.

THE CHAIRMAN. Does your father work, and where?

MISS TEOLI. My father works in the Washington.

THE CHAIRMAN. The Washington Woolen Mill?

MISS TEOLI. Yes, sir.

THE CHAIRMAN. How much pay does he get for a week's work?

MISS TEOLI. $7.70.

THE CHAIRMAN. Does he always work a full week?

MISS TEOLI. No.

THE CHAIRMAN. Well, how often does it happen that he does not work a full week?

MISS TEOLI. He works in the winter a full week, and usually he don't in the summer.

THE CHAIRMAN. In the winter he works a full week, and in the summer how much?

MISS TEOLI. Two or three days a week.

THE CHAIRMAN. What sort of work does he do?

MISS TEOLI. He is a comber.

THE CHAIRMAN. Now, did you ever get hurt in the mill?

MISS TEOLI. Yes.

THE CHAIRMAN. Can you tell the committee about that—how it happened and what it was?

MISS TEOLI. Yes.

THE CHAIRMAN. Tell us about it now, in your own way.

MISS TEOLI. Well, I used to go to school, and then a man came up to my house and asked my father why I didn't go to work, so my father says I don't know whether she is 13 or 14 years old. So, the man say you give me $4 and I will make the papers come from the old country saying you are 14. So, my father gave him the $4, and in one month came the papers that I was 14. I went to work, and about two weeks got hurt in my head.

THE CHAIRMAN. Now, how did you get hurt, and where were you hurt in the head; explain that to the committee?

MISS TEOLI. I got hurt in Washington.

THE CHAIRMAN. In the Washington Mill?

MISS TEOLI. Yes, sir.

THE CHAIRMAN. What part of your head?

MISS TEOLI. My head.

THE CHAIRMAN. Well, how were you hurt?

MISS TEOLI. The machine pulled the scalp off.

THE CHAIRMAN. The machine pulled your scalp off?

MISS TEOLI. Yes, sir.

THE CHAIRMAN. How long ago was that?

MISS TEOLI. A year ago, or about a year ago.

THE CHAIRMAN. Were you in the hospital after that?

MISS TEOLI. I was in the hospital seven months.

THE CHAIRMAN. Seven months?

MISS TEOLI. Yes.

THE CHAIRMAN. Did the company pay your bills while you were in the hospital?

MISS TEOLI. Yes, sir.

THE CHAIRMAN. The company took care of you?

MISS TEOLI. The company only paid my bills; they didn't give me anything else.

THE CHAIRMAN. They only paid your hospital bills; they did not give you any pay?

MISS TEOLI. No, sir.

THE CHAIRMAN. But paid the doctors' bills and hospital fees?

MISS TEOLI. Yes, sir.

MR. LENROOT. They did not pay your wages?

MISS TEOLI. No, sir.

THE CHAIRMAN. Did they arrest your father for having sent you to work for 14?

MISS TEOLI. Yes, sir.

THE CHAIRMAN. What did they do with him after they arrested him?

MISS TEOLI. My father told this about the man he gave $4 to, and then they put him on again.

THE CHAIRMAN. Are you still being treated by the doctors for the scalp wound?

MISS TEOLI. Yes, sir.

THE CHAIRMAN. How much longer do they tell you you will have to be treated?

MISS TEOLI. They don't know.

THE CHAIRMAN. They do not know?

MISS TEOLI. No.

THE CHAIRMAN. Are you working now?

MISS TEOLI. Yes, sir.

THE CHAIRMAN. How much are you getting?

MISS TEOLI. $6.55.

THE CHAIRMAN. Are you working in the same place where you were before you were hurt?

MISS TEOLI. No.

THE CHAIRMAN. In another mill?

MISS TEOLI. Yes.

THE CHAIRMAN. What mill?

MISS TEOLI. The Wood Mill.

THE CHAIRMAN. The what?

MISS TEOLI. The Wood Mill.

THE CHAIRMAN. Were you down at the station on Saturday, the 24th of February?

THE CHAIRMAN. I work in a town in Massachusetts, and I don't know nothing about that.

THE CHAIRMAN. You do not know anything about that?

MISS TEOLI. No, sir.

THE CHAIRMAN. How long did you go to school?

MISS TEOLI. I left when I was in the sixth grade.

THE CHAIRMAN. You left when you were in the sixth grade?

MISS TEOLI. Yes, sir.

THE CHAIRMAN. And you have been working ever since, except while you were in the hospital?

MISS TEOLI. Yes, sir.

MR. CAMPBELL. Do you know the man who came to your father and offered to get a certificate that you were 14 years of age?

MISS TEOLI. I know the man, but I have forgot him now.

MR. CAMPBELL. You know him, but you do not remember his name now?

MISS TEOLI. Yes.

MR. CAMPBELL. Do you know what he did; what his work was?

MISS TEOLI. No.

MR. CAMPBELL. Was he connected with any of the mills?

MISS TEOLI. I don't know.

MR. CAMPBELL. Is he an Italian?

MISS TEOLI. Yes, sir.

MR. CAMBELL. He knew your father well?

MISS TEOLI. Yes, sir.

MR. CAMPBELL. Was he a friend of your father?

MISS TEOLI. No.

MR. CAMPBELL. Did he ever come about your house visiting there?

MISS TEOLI. I don't know.

MR. CAMPBELL. I mean before he asked about your going to work in the mills?

MISS TEOLI. Yes, sir.

MR. CAMPBELL. He used to come to your house and was a friend of the family?

MISS TEOLI. Yes.

MR. CAMPBELL. You are sure he was not connected or employed by some of the mills?

MISS TEOLI. I don't know, I don't think so.

MR. CAMPBELL. Do they go around in Lawrence there and find little girls and boys in the schools over 14 years of age and urge them to quit school and go to work in the mills?

MISS TEOLI. I don't know.

MR. CAMPBELL. You don't know anything about that?

MISS TEOLI. No.

MR. CAMPBELL. Do you know of any little girls besides yourself, who were asked to go to work as soon as they were 14?

MISS TEOLI. No, I don't know; no.

MR. HARDWICK. Are you one of the strikers?

MISS TEOLI. Yes, sir.

Strikers' children, Lawrence, Massachusetts, 1912.   Brown Brothers photo.

MR. HARDWICK. Did you agree to the strike before it was ordered; did they ask you anything about striking before you quit?

MISS TEOLI. No.

MR. HARDWICK. But you joined them after they quit?

MISS TEOLI. Yes.

MR. HARDWICK. Why did you do that?

MISS TEOLI. Because I didn't get enough to eat at home.

MR. HARDWICK. You did not get enough to eat at home?

MISS TEOLI. No.

MR. HARDWICK. Why didn't you propose a strike yourself, then?

MISS TEOLI. I did.

MR. HARDWICK. I thought you said you did not know anything about the strike until after it started. How about that? Did you know there was going to be a strike before they did strike?

MISS TEOLI. No.

MR. HARDWICK. They did not consult with you about that?

MISS TEOLI. No.

MR. HARDWICK. You did not agree to strike?

MISS TEOLI. No.

MR. HARDWICK. You were not a party to it, to begin with?

MISS TEOLI. No.

MR. HARDWICK. Was not the reason you went into it because you were afraid to go on with your work?

MISS TEOLI. Yes.

MR. HARDWICK. You say that was the reason?

MISS TEOLI. Yes.

MR. HARDWICK. Now, did you see any of the occurrences—any of the riots during this strike?

MISS TEOLI. No.

MR. HARDWICK. You did not see any of the women beaten, or anything like that?

MISS TEOLI. No.

MR. HARDWICK. You did not see anybody hurt or beaten or killed, or anything like that?

MISS TEOLI. No.

MR. HARDWICK. Did you come down to the depot with the children who were trying to go away?

MISS TEOLI. I am only in the town in Massachusetts, and I don't come down to the city.
MR. HARDWICK. So you did not see any of that?
MISS TEOLI. No.
MR. HARDWICK. You do not know anything about those things at all?
MISS TEOLI. No.
MR. HARDWICK. You struck after the balance had struck and were afraid to go on with your work?
MISS TEOLI. Yes.
MR. LENROOT. There is a high school in Lawrence, isn't there?
MISS TEOLI. Yes, sir.
MR. LENROOT. And some of your friends—boys and girls—go to the high school?
MISS TEOLI. I don't know.
MR. LENROOT. None that you know are going to the high school?
MISS TEOLI. No.

11

Arturo Giovannitti (1882–1959) was an Italian-born writer and orator who came to Lawrence early in the strike to take charge of strike relief. A former coal miner, bookkeeper, and teacher, the twenty-eight year old Giovannitti was a leader of the Italian Socialist Federation of North America and editor of Il Proletario, *a Socialist weekly. During his nine months in the Salem, Massachusetts, jail he wrote about a dozen poems which attracted immediate attention.*

An article in Current Opinion *(January 1913) noted of Giovannitti: "He has the soul of a great poet, the fervor of a prophet and, added to these, the courage and power of initiative that mark the man of action and the organizer of great crusades. . . . This jail experience of Giovannitti's has given the world one of the greatest poems ever produced in the English language. It challenges comparison with the 'Ballad of Reading Gaol' by Wilde and is fully as vital and soul stirring as anything Whitman ever produced. 'The Walker' is more than a poem. It is a great human document."*

In Forum *(October 14, 1913), critic Kenneth McGowan wrote: "The significant thing is that here we have a new sort of poet with a new sort of song. . . . He and his song are products of something that few Americans yet understand. We do not comprehend the problem of the un-skilled just as we do not comprehend the I.W.W.*

that has come out of it. A poet has arisen to explain. . . . In 'The Walker' he has painted the prison as no man, not even Wilde, has done."

At Giovannitti's death, an obituary appeared in the New York Times *(January 1, 1960). It said: "Until the end of World War II when his health failed, he wrote and spoke extensively in the struggle to establish organized labor. At various times he was a close associate of Max Eastman, Norman Thomas, David Dubinsky, and many others. At the fiery labor rallies of the Nineteen Twenties and Thirties, Mr. Giovannitti was in great demand as a speaker. A colorful figure, with a Van Dyke beard, a Lord Byron collar and flowing tie, he addressed Italian and English-speaking audiences with an equally flowery fluency."*

"The Walker" was published in Ettor and Giovannitti Before the Jury at Salem, Massachusetts, *a pamphlet issued by the I.W.W. about 1913, and frequently reprinted in the I.W.W. and the national press. It is included in* The Collected Poems of Arturo Giovannitti, *which has recently been published (Chicago, 1962) with a foreword by Norman Thomas.*

THE WALKER

By ARTURO GIOVANNITTI

I HEAR footsteps over my head all night.
They come and they go. Again they come and they go all night.
They come one eternity in four paces and they go one eternity in four paces, and between the coming and the going there is Silence and the Night and the Infinite.
For infinite are the nine feet of a prison cell, and endless is the march of him who walks between the yellow brick wall and the red iron gate, thinking things that cannot be chained and cannot be locked, but that wander far away in the sunlit world, each in a wild pilgrimage after a destined goal.

○   ○   ○

Throughout the restless night I hear the footsteps over my head.
Who walks? I know not. It is the phantom of the jail, the sleepless brain, a man, the man, the Walker.
One-two-three-four: four paces and the wall.
One-two-three-four: four paces and the iron gate.
He has measured his space, he has measured it accurately, scrupulously, minutely, as the hang-

man measures the rope and the grave-digger the coffin—so many feet, so many inches, so many fractions of an inch for each of the four paces.

One-two-three-four. Each step sounds heavy and hollow over my head, and the echo of each step sounds hollow within my head as I count them in suspense and in dread that once, perhaps, in the endless walk, there may be five steps instead of four between the yellow brick wall and the red iron gate.

But he has measured the space so accurately, so scrupulously, so minutely that nothing breaks the grave rhythm of the slow, fantastic march.

◦ ◦ ◦

When all are asleep (and who knows but I when all sleep?) three things are still awake in the night: the Walker, my heart and the old clock which has the soul of a fiend—for never, since a coarse hand with red hair on its fingers swung for the first time the pendulum in the jail, has the old clock tick-tocked a full hour of joy.

Yet the old clock which marks everything, and records everything, and to everything tolls the death knell, the wise old clock that knows everything, does not know the number of the footsteps of the Walker, nor the throbs of my heart.

For not for the Walker, nor for my heart is there a second, a minute, an hour or anything that is in the old clock—there is nothing but the night, the sleepless night, the watchful, wistful night, and footsteps that go, and footsteps that come and the wild, tumultuous beatings that trail after them forever.

◦ ◦ ◦

All the sounds of the living beings and inanimate things, and all the voices and all the noises of the night I have heard in my wistful vigil.

I have heard the moans of him who bewails a thing that is dead and the sighs of him who tries to smother a thing that will not die;

I have heard the stifled sobs of the one who weeps with his head under the coarse blanket, and the whisperings of the one who prays with his forehead on the hard, cold stone of the floor;

I have heard him who laughs the shrill, sinister laugh of folly at the horror rampant on the yellow wall and at the red eyes of the nightmare glaring through the iron bars;

I have heard in the sudden icy silence him who coughs a dry, ringing cough, and wished madly that his throat would not rattle so and that he

Arturo Giovannitti.

Brown Brothers photo.

would not spit on the floor, for no sound was more atrocious than that of his sputum upon the floor.

I have heard him who swears fearsome oaths which I listen to in reverence and awe, for they are holier than the virgin's prayer;

And I have heard, most terrible of all, the silence of two hundred brains all possessed by one single, relentless, unforgiving, desperate thought.

All this have I heard in the watchful night,

And the murmur of the wind beyond the walls,

And the tolls of a distant bell,

And the woeful dirge of the rain,

And the remotest echoes of the sorrowful city

And the terrible beatings, wild beatings, mad beatings of the One Heart which is nearest to my heart.

All this have I heard in the still night;

But nothing is louder, harder, drearier, mightier, more awful than the footsteps I hear over my head all night.

◦ ◦ ◦

Yet fearsome and terrible are all the footsteps of men upon the earth, for they either descend or climb.

They descend from little mounds and high peaks and lofty altitudes, through wide roads and narrow paths, down noble marble stairs and creaky stairs of wood—and some go down to the cellar, and some to the grave, and some down to the pits of shame and infamy, and still some to the glory of an unfathomable abyss where there is nothing but the staring white, stony eyeballs of Destiny.

And again other footsteps climb. They climb to life and to love, to fame, to power, to vanity, to truth, to glory and to the scaffold—to everything but Freedom and the Ideal.

And they all climb the same roads and the same stairs others go down; for never, since man began to think how to overcome and over-pass man, have other roads and other stairs been found.

They descend and they climb, the fearful footsteps of men, and some limp, some drag, some speed, some trot, some run—they are quiet, slow, noisy, brisk, quick, feverish, mad, and most awful is their cadence to the ears of the one who stands still.

But of all the footsteps of men that either descend or climb, no footsteps are so fearsome and terrible as those that go straight on the dead level of a prison floor, from a yellow stone wall to a red iron gate.

*   *   *

All through the night he walks and he thinks. Is it more frightful because he walks and his footsteps sound hollow over my head, or because he thinks and speaks not his thoughts?

But does he think? Why should he think? Do I think. I only hear the footsteps and count them. Four steps and the wall. Four steps and the gate. But beyond? Beyond? Where goes he beyond the gate and the wall?

He goes not beyond. His thought breaks there on the iron gate. Perhaps it breaks like a wave of rage, perhaps like a sudden flow of hope, but it always returns to beat the wall like a billow of helplessness and despair.

He walks to and fro within the narrow whirlpit of this ever storming and furious thought. Only one thought—constant, fixed, immovable, sinister, without power and without voice.

A thought of madness, frenzy, agony and despair, a hell-brewed thought, for it is a natural thought. All things natural are things impossible while there are jails in the world—bread, work, happiness, peace, love.

But he thinks not of this. As he walks he thinks of the most superhuman, the most unattainable, the most impossible thing in the world:

He thinks of a small brass key that turns just half around and throws open the red iron gate.

*   *   *

That is all the Walker thinks, as he walks throughout the night.

And that is what two hundred minds drowned in the darkness and the silence of the night think, and that is also what I think.

Wonderful is the supreme wisdom of the jail that makes all think the same thought. Marvelous is the providence of the law that equalizes all, even in mind and sentiment. Fallen is the last barrier of privilege, the aristocracy of the intellect. The democracy of reason has leveled all the two hundred minds to the common surface of the same thought.

I, who have never killed, think like the murderer!

I, who have never stolen, reason like the thief;

I think, reason, wish, hope, doubt, wait like the hired assassin, the embezzler, the forger, the counterfeiter, the incestuous, the raper, the drunkard, the prostitute, the pimp, I, I who used to think of love and life and flowers and song and beauty and the ideal.

A little key, a little key as little as my little finger, a little key of shining brass.

All my ideas, my thoughts, my dreams are congealed in a little key of shiny brass.

All my brain, all my soul, all the suddenly surging latent powers of my deepest life are in the pocket of a white-haired man dressed in blue.

He is great, powerful, formidable, the man with the white hair, for he has in his pocket the mighty talisman which makes one man cry, and one man pray, and one laugh, and one cough, and one walk, and all keep awake and listen and think the same maddening thought.

Greater than all men is the man with the white hair and the small brass key, for no other man in the world could compel two hundred men to think for so long the same thought. Surely when the light breaks I will write a hymn unto him which shall hail him greater than Mohammed and Arbues and Torquemada and Mesmer, and all the other masters of other men's thoughts.

I shall call him Almighty, for he holds everything of all and of me in a little brass key in
his pocket.
Everything of me he holds but the branding iron
of contempt and the claymore of hatred for the
monstrous cabala that can make the apostle and
the murderer, the poet and the procurer, think
of the same gate, the same key and the same exit
on the different sunlit highways of life.

        ❖   ❖   ❖

My brother, do not walk any more.
It is wrong to walk on a grave. It is a sacrilege
to walk four steps from the headstone to the foot
and four steps from the foot to the headstone.
If you stop walking, my brother, no longer will
this be a grave, for you will give me back my
mind that is chained to your feet and the right
to think my own thoughts.
I implore you, my brother, for I am weary of the
long vigil, weary of counting your steps, and
heavy with sleep.
Stop, rest, sleep, my brother, for the dawn is well
nigh and it is not the key alone that can throw
open the gate.

12

*During the trial of Ettor and Giovannitti in Salem,
Massachusetts, Bill Haywood asked Giovannitti
to write a poem about "Sixteenth Century courts
trying to solve Twentieth Century problems." Giovannitti wrote "The Cage," which was first published in the* Atlantic *(January 1913).*

An editorial comment in the Atlantic *stated:
" 'The Cage' will call out plenty of literary criticism, plenty of expressions of social sympathy or
lack of it, but the simple point which needs emphasis is that whether the poem repels or attracts
the reader, he will find in it, if he cares to look,
more of the heart and soul of the syndicalist movement than all the papers of all the economists can
teach him. It is ever wise to listen to the serious
voices of mankind . . ."*

THE CAGE

By Arturo M. Giovannitti

Salem Jail, Sunday, October 20, 1912

I

In the middle of the great greenish room stood
the green iron cage.
All was old and cold and mournful, ancient with
the double antiquity of heart and brain in the
great greenish room.
Old and hoary was the man who sat upon the fald-
stool, upon the fireless and godless altar.
Old were the tomes that mouldered behind him
on the dusty shelves.
Old was the painting of an old man that hung
above him.
Old the man upon his left, who awoke with his
cracked voice the dead echoes of dead centuries; old the man upon his right who wielded a
wand; and old all those who spoke to him and
listened to him before and around the green
iron cage.
Old were the words they spoke, and their faces
were drawn and white and lifeless, without expression or solemnity; like the ikons of old cathe-
drals.
For of naught they knew, but of what was written
in the old yellow books. And all the joys and
pains and loves and hatreds and furies and la-
bors and strifes of man, all the fierce and divine
passions that battle and rage in the heart of
man, never entered into the great greenish room
but to sit in the green iron cage.
Senility, dullness and dissolution were all around
the green iron cage, and nothing was new and
young and alive in the great room, except the
three men who were in the cage.

II

Throbbed and thundered and clamored and
roared outside of the great greenish room the
terrible whirl of life, and most pleasant was the
hymn of its mighty polyphony to the listening
ears of the gods.
Whirred the wheels of the puissant machines, rattled and clanked the chains of the giant cranes,
crashed the falling rocks; the riveters crepitated;
and glad and sonorous was the rhythm of the
bouncing hammers upon the loud-throated
anvils.
Like the chests of wrathfully toiling Titans, heaved
and sniffed and panted the sweaty boilers, like
the hissing of dragons sibilated the white jets of
steam, and the sirens of the workshops shrieked
like angry hawks, flapping above the crags of
a dark and fathomless chasm.
The files screeched and the trains thundered, the
wires hummed, the dynamos buzzed, the fires
crackled; and like a thunderclap from the Cyclo-
pean forge roared the blasts of the mines.

Wonderful and fierce was the mighty symphony
of the world, as the terrible voices of metal and
fire and water cried out into the listening ears
of the gods the furious song of human toil.

Out of the chaos of sound, welded in the unison
of one will to sing, rose clear and nimble the
divine accord of the hymn:—

Out of the cañons of the mountains,
Out of the whirlpools of the lakes,
Out of the entrails of the earth,
Out of the yawning gorges of hell,
From the land and the sea and the sky,
From wherever comes bread and wealth
and joy,

And from the peaceful abodes of men, rose ma-
jestic and fierce, louder than the roar of the
volcano and the bellow of the typhoon, the anthem of human labor to the fatherly justice of
the Sun.

But in the great greenish room there was nothing
but the silence of dead centuries and of ears
that listen no more; and none heard the mighty
call of life that roared outside, save the three
men who were in the cage.

III

All the good smells, the wholesome smells, the
healthy smells of life and labor were outside the
great room.

The smell of rain upon the grass and of the flowers
consumed by their love for the stars.

The heavy smell of smoke that coiled out of myriads of chimneys of ships and factories and
homes.

The dry smell of sawdust and the salty smell of
the iron filings.

The odor of magazines and granaries and ware-
houses, the kingly smell of argosies and the rich
scent of market-places, so dear to the women
of the race.

The smell of new cloth and new linen, the smell of
soap and water and the smell of newly printed
paper.

The smell of grains and hay and the smell of sta-
bles, the warm smell of cattle and sheep that
Virgil loved.

The smell of milk and wine and plants and metals,

And all the good odors of the earth and of the sea
and of the sky, and the fragrance of fresh bread,
sweetest aroma of the world, and the smell of
human sweat, most holy incense to the divine

nostrils of the gods, and all the olympian per-
fumes of the heart and the brain and the passions of men, were outside of the great greenish
room.

But within the old room there was nothing but
the smell of old books and the dust of things
decayed, and the suffocated exhalation of old
graves, and the ashen odor of dissolution and
death.

Yet all the sweetness of all the wholesome odors of
the world outside were redolent in the breath
of the three men in the cage.

IV

Like crippled eagles fallen were the three men in
the cage, and like little children who look into
a well to behold the sky were the men that
looked down upon them.

No more would they rise to their lofty eyries, no
more would they soar above the snow-capped
mountains—yet, tho' their pinions were broken,
nothing could dim the fierce glow of their eyes,
which knew all the altitudes of heaven.

Strange it was to behold the men in the cage while
life clamored outside, and strange it seemed to
them that they should be there because of what
dead men had written in old books.

So of naught did they think but of the old books
and the green cage.

Thought they: All things are born, grow, decay,
and die and are forgotten.

Surely all that is in this great room will pass away.
But what will endure the longer, the folly that
was written into the old books or the madness
that was beaten into the bands of this cage?

Which of these two powers has enthralled us, the
thought of dead men who wrote the old books,
or the labor of living men who have wrought
this cage?

Long and intently they thought, but they found
no answer.

V

But one of the three men in the cage, whose soul
was tormented by the fiercest fire of hell, which
is the yearning after the Supreme Truth, spoke
and said unto his comrades:—

'Aye, brothers, all things die and pass away, yet
nothing is truly and forever dead until each
one of the living has thrown a regretless handful of soil into its grave.

'Many a book has been written since these old

books were written, and many a proverb of the sage has become the jest of the fool, yet this cage still stands as it stood for numberless ages.

'What is it then that made it of metal more enduring than the printed word?

'Which is its power to hold us here?

'Brothers, it is the things we love that enslave us.

'Brothers, it is the things we yearn for that subdue us.

'Brothers, it is not hatred for the things that are, but love for the things that are to be, that makes us slaves.

'And what man is more apt to become a thrall, brothers, and to be locked in a green iron cage, than he who yearns the most for the Supreme of the things that are to be—he who most craves for Freedom?

'And what subtle and malignant power save this love of loves could be in the metal of this cage that it is so mad to imprison us?'

So spoke one of the men to the other two, and then out of the silence of the æons spoke into his tormented soul the metallic soul of the cage.

VI

'Iron, the twin brother of fire, the first born out of the matrix of the earth, the witness everlasting to the glory of thy labor, am I, O Man!

'Not for this was I meant, O Man! Not to imprison thee, but to set thee free and sustain thee in thy strife and in thy toil.

'I was to lift the pillars of thy Temple higher than the mountains;

'I was to lower the foundations of thy house deeper than the abysmal sea;

'I was to break down and bore through all the barriers of the world to open the way to thy triumphal chariot.

'All the treasures and all the bounties of the earth was I to give as an offering into thy hands, and all its forces and powers to bring chained like crouching dogs at thy feet.

'Hadst thou not sinned against the nobility of my nature and my destiny, hadst thou not humiliated me, an almighty warrior, to become the lackey of gold, I would never have risen against thee and enthralled thee, O Man!

'While I was hoe and ploughshare and sword and axe and scythe and hammer, I was the first artificer of thy happiness; but the day I was beaten into the first lock and the first key, I became fetters and chains to thy hands and thy feet, O Man!

'My curse is thy curse, O Man! and even if thou shouldst pass out of the wicket of this cage, never shalt thou be free until thou returnest me to the joy of labor.

'O Man! bring me back into the old smithy, purify me again with the holy fire of the forge, lay me again on the mother breast of the anvil, beat me again with the old honest hammer—O Man! remould me with thy wonderful hands into an instrument of thy toil,

'*Remake of me the sword of thy justice,*
Remake of me the tripod of thy worship,
Remake of me the sickle for thy grain,
Remake of me the oven for thy bread,
And the andirons for thy peaceful hearth,
O Man!
And the trestles for the bed of thy love,
O Man!
And the frame of thy joyous lyre, O Man!'

VII

Thus spake to one of the three men, out of the silence of centuries, the metallic soul of the cage.

And he listened unto its voice, and while it was still ringing in his soul,—which was tormented with the fiercest fire of hell, which is the yearning after the Supreme Truth (Is it Death? Is it Love?), —there arose one man in the silent assembly of old men that were around the iron cage.

And that man was the most hoary of all, and most bent and worn and crushed was he under the heavy weight of the great burden he bore without pride and without joy.

He arose, and addressing himself—I know not whether to the old man that sat on the black throne, or to the old books that were mouldering behind him, or to the picture that hung above him—he said (and dreary as a wind that moans through the crosses of an old graveyard was his voice):—

'I will prove to you that these three men in the cage are criminals and murderers and that they ought to be put to death.'

Love, it was then that I heard for the first time the creak of the moth that was eating the old painting and the old books, and the worm that was gnawing the old bench, and it was then that I saw that all the old men around the great greenish room were dead.

They were dead like the old man in the old painting, save that they still read the old books he could read no more, and still spoke and heard the old words he could speak and hear no more, and still passed the judgment of the dead, which he no more could pass, upon the mighty life of the world outside that throbbed and thundered and clamored and roared the wonderful anthem of Labor to the fatherly justice of the Sun.

13

Joseph Ettor (1885–1948) was one of the I.W.W.'s most active and effective organizers. Born in Brooklyn and raised in San Francisco, he worked as a waterboy on a railroad, a saw filer in a lumber mill, a shipbuilder's assistant, and a stringer in a cigar factory before joining the I.W.W. in 1906. He helped lead strikes of Portland lumber and sawmill workers (1907), McKees Rocks, Pennsylvania, steelworkers (1909), Brooklyn shoeworkers (1910–11), New York City Western Union messenger boys (1912), and Minnesota metal miners (1916).

Professor Paul Brissenden quoted a New England wool manufacturer who said of Ettor: "This man . . . steeped in the literature of revolutionary socialism and anarchism, swayed the undisciplined mob as completely as any general ever controlled the disciplined troops . . . [and was able] to organize these thousands of heterogeneous, heretofore unsympathetic and jealous nationalities, into a militant body of class-conscious workers. His followers firmly believed . . . that success meant that they were about to enter a new era of brotherhood, in which there would be no more union of trades and no more departmental distinctions, but all workers would become the real bosses in the mills" (Paul F. Brissenden, The I.W.W.).

In 1915, Ettor was elected assistant secretary and general organizer of the I.W.W. He spent the last years of his life operating a fruit orchard near San Clemente, California.

This selection of his testimony is from Justus Ebert's Trial of a New Society.

JOSEPH ETTOR'S TESTIMONY TO THE JURY IN THE SALEM TRIAL

Gentlemen, since my views in my organization have been brought into this argument, I want to state this: that my organization has made it a prac-

tice to allow men in the past to express their views as they understood them. Now, what are my social views? I have stated some of them. I do believe —I may be wrong, but, gentlemen, only history can pass judgment upon them. All wealth is the product of labor, and all wealth being the product of labor belongs to labor and to no one else.

I know the District Attorney is weary and worried about what is going to happen to the little home or to the little savings of the working man who has saved and scraped around and managed somehow or another to put aside a few dollars. He knows full well that my social ideas have little or no relation to the working man who worked in the shoe shop or to the working man who worked on a building, or to the operative in a mill who was able to put a hundred dollars aside and then fifty dollars aside, and so on, and get a shanty in some place. He knows that my social ideas are bigger than the proposition to take away the home of the operative who has saved fifty cents here and a dollar there and seventy-five cents somewhere else.

He knows that my social views have no relation to the little property owner, but my social views have a relation so far as society is concerned. A railroad is operated by the workers. It is made possible only because there are people living in this country, and according to that argument we insist that the railroad should belong to the people of this country and not to the railroad owners, who are mere coupon clippers.

And that principle applies to the textile industry, to the shoe industry and to every industry. It does not apply to the toothbrush or to the pipe nor to the little shanty the working man is able to erect by scraping and gouging somehow or other.

I want to state further, gentlemen, that whatever my social views are, as I stated before, they are what they are. They cannot be tried in this courtroom. With all respect to you, gentlemen, and with all respect to everyone here, they cannot be tried in this courtroom. It has been tried before. Away back thousands of years the trick was tried that man's views could be brought into a courtroom or brought before the king or brought before somebody in authority and that judgment could be passed. And in those days they said, "The only way we can settle these new ideas is, first, send them to the cross;" then, "Send them to the gallows," then to the guillotine, and to the rope.

And I want to know, does Mr. Attwill believe

for a moment that, beginning with Spartacus, whose men were crucified for miles along the Appian Way, and following with Christ, who was adjudged an enemy of the Roman social order, and put on the cross—does he believe for a moment that the cross or the gallows or the guillotine, the hangman's noose, ever settled an idea? It never did.

If the idea can live it lives, because history adjudges it right. And what has been considered an idea constituting a social crime in one age, has in the next age become the very religion of humanity. The social criminals of one age have become the saints of the next.

The District Attorney talks to you about Massachusetts. Sixty years ago, gentlemen—seventy years ago—the respectable mob—not the mob in the mills, but the respectable mob, the well-dressed mob—dragged the propagandists and the agents of a new social order and a new idea through the streets of Boston, and the members of that same respectable mob now—now that the ideas of Wendell Phillips have been materialized into something, now that the ideas of Garrison and the rest have been proven of value, the offspring of that social mob rises up and says, "The traditions of Massachusetts."

Gentlemen, the traditions of Massachusetts have been made by those who made it and not those who speak of it. John Brown was hanged and the cry went up, "A social criminal"—not even that dignity to him—just a criminal. Within two years the youngest and the noblest, the strongest that this nation could offer, were marching through the fields of this country singing:

"John Brown's body lies mouldering in the grave,
But his soul goes marching on."

My ideas are what they are, gentlemen. They might be indicted and you might believe, as the District Attorney has suggested, that you can pass judgment and that you can choke them; but you can't. Ideas can't be choked.

I want to leave this matter to you with a few words. I came to the city of Lawrence feeling that I could be of some aid, that I could offer all the aid that was possible in me to secure more bread for twenty-five or thirty thousand textile workers. I did what I could. I did what I could, that is all.

If I didn't do any more it was because I couldn't do any more. I did the best I could. If you believe

and you adopt the suggestion of Mr. Attwill I should not have come to Massachusetts, not because, as he intimated with regard to my comrade, Giovannitti, I am a foreigner, but because I came from New York.

If for a moment, gentlemen, you believe that I am responsible for the death of Anna Lo Pizzo, you only can *conjure* it by the insinuations that have been offered here by Mr. Attwill. But I want to say this: Since I was a boy and I could lift my voice for the cause that I thought right, I did. I not only dared to raise my voice, but I knew full well as I went along that raising my voice for my class meant the baring of my breast against the shafts of the opposition of the monopolists and the capitalists of this country.

And as I have gone along I have raised my voice on behalf of men, women and children who work in the mines, who work in the mills and who work in the factories of this country; who daily offer their labor and their blood and even their lives in order to make possible the prosperity of this country.

I have carried the flag along. I have given cheer and hope and sung the workers on to be brave and go forward as men and women by demanding their rights. It may be possible, gentlemen, that because of the various outside things that have been introduced here, my social views, and so forth, you gentlemen believe that I am guilty of murder. If you do, of course I will pay the penalty. Don't worry about that.

I say to you, gentlemen, if you believe that I had any interest, that I had any desire, that I had any motive or knowledge in this death, then I offer no apology, I ask for no mercy, I offer no extenuations to you gentlemen. I talk to you as one man talks to twelve others. If you believe that, then I hope that you won't come back here and say in words that will mean, "Mr. Ettor may be responsible, but Mr. Ettor has done so many things that are of worth and are noble and therefore we won't let him go, but we will shut him up so that it will be impossible for him to advance his social views any more."

Gentlemen, I know not what the instructions of this Court will be on that point, but whatever your feelings may be I plead with you—I have told you my views; they are the same as my comrade, Giovannitti, the same in general. We may disagree on a word here and there, but both of us, we state plainly, will give all that there is in us that this present society may be changed, that the present rule of wage labor on one side, producing all things and receiving only a part, and idle capitalists on the other, producing nothing and receiving most, may be abolished.

We say that in the past we have given the best that was in us that the workers may rally to their own standard and that they may organize and through their solidarity, through their united efforts, they may from time to time, step to step, get close together and finally emancipate themselves through their own efforts that the mills and workshops of America may become the property of the workers of America and that the wealth produced in those workshops may be for the benefit of the workers of America.

Those have been our views. If we are set at liberty those will still be our views and those will be our actions. If you believe that we should not go out with those views, then gentlemen, I ask you only one favor, and that is this—that you will place the responsibility full on us and say to the world that Joseph J. Ettor and Arturo Giovannitti, because of their social ideas, became murderers and murdered one of their own sister strikers, and you will by your verdict say plainly that we should die for it.

As I stated before, I have carried the flag. I carry it here today, gentlemen; the flag of liberty is here. I am willing to carry it just as long as it is necessary. But if you believe and if the District Attorney has been able to insinuate and argue you into the frame of mind that I killed Anna Lo Pizzo or that I wanted anybody to kill Anna Lo Pizzo, or that I turned a finger that Anna Lo Pizzo or any other human being should be killed, then I will stand up with head erect, gentlemen, no apology to offer, no excuse to ask, I will accept your verdict and expect that you will say, "You have done what you did and now we have spoken."

I expect that if I have carried the flag along, if I have raised my voice, if I have bared my breast against the opposition, that I have done it long enough, and I want to plead with you that if I am guilty I want to pay the full price—full price; no half-way measure; the full price.

If twelve men in Essex County, chosen among the prominent citizens, among the ones who are available and can be enrolled on the list as jurors —if twelve men believe that I am guilty of murder and Comrade Giovannitti is guilty of murder, speaking for myself, I say to you that I would stand erect—and my comrade here just whispered to me, "Say it for both"—we will stand here and accept whatever your verdict may be.

I hope that whatever your views are you will decide clean cut one way or the other. If I am guilty—I tell you I am not a sentimentalist on those points; I believe in the death chair. Very well; if I am guilty I and my comrade Giovannitti will go there, with heads erect and the same song that we have lisped to our fellow workers in the field we will sing with cheer and gladness on our lips, and the flag that we have carried along and are carrying along if we have to drop it in the ditch we will drop it.

Gentlemen, I make no threat, but on the moment that we drop the flag because we have been loyal to our calls, hundreds of thousands of wage workers will pick up the flag of labor and carry it forward and cheer it on and sing its song until the flag of the working class shall wave freely and unfurled to the wind over the workshops of the world where free men and women will work and enjoy fully and without trammel the full products of their labor.

Gentlemen, those are my views, those are my feelings. If it is the last words I shall ever speak in life, I believe that I have been true. Only history can decide as to whether they are right or wrong. I consider that I could not go out and stand with head erect and have people say to me, "Joe, Mr. Attwill attacked the principle that you hold dear and you did not defend it."

If these are the last words that I shall ever speak and I shall go—if you say death—with the happy thought that on the eve of it I did willingly announce to the world that my life is dedicated to my ideals and that the ideals that I have expressed to you on the stand do not mean danger to human life or the world's happiness. I shall go out, whichever way it comes—whether it is a case of death or a case of liberty—I shall go forward with that one thought in my mind and one satisfaction in my heart, that at the last moment I did pronounce to the world my views, and that I did announce that my idea is to work for the principles that I hold dear, and if I am allowed to work for them I will, and you gentlemen will be thankful.

If not—no idea was ever choked, it can't be choked, and this idea will not be choked. On the day that I go to my death there will be more men and women who will know and ask questions.

Millions of men and women will know and they will have a right to argue that my social ideals had as much the effect of determining your verdict as the facts, and more so in this case.

Gentlemen, as I stated before, I neither offer apology nor excuse. I ask for no favors. I ask for nothing but justice in this matter. That is all, nothing else. I ask for justice. And I believe that in asking I am not asking anything against what the District Attorney has called the ideals and the traditions of Massachusetts.

Massachusetts refused to give the apostles of abolition to the rule and to the lust of the cotton kings of the South. It refused to allow their blood to act as so much balm to the cuts and to the wounds of the cotton planters of the South. And I ask you now, are twelve men in this county in Massachusetts going to offer blood now in order that the wounds, in order that the cuts and the smarts that the mill owners of Lawrence suffered because of the strike may be assuaged in balm?

Gentlemen, it is up to you, and as I stated before, I have no fear of the result. I ask for no favor. I ask only for justice, and that is all my comrade Giovannitti asks, and that is all my comrade Caruso asks.

I thank you.

14

Ettor and Giovannitti's testimonies in the Salem trial were issued as a pamphlet about 1913 by the I.W.W. An article in Current Opinion *(January 1913) stated: "Near the close of his trial [Giovannitti] made before the court the first speech he has ever made in the English language. It held all hearers spellbound. 'In twenty years of reporting,' said a veteran reporter afterward, 'I have never heard the equal of that speech.'" This excerpt from Giovannitti's statement is from the I.W.W. pamphlet,* Ettor and Giovannitti Before the Jury at Salem, Massachusetts *(Chicago, n.d.).*

ADDRESS OF THE DEFENDANT GIOVANNITTI TO THE JURY

Mr. Foreman and Gentlemen of the Jury:

It is the first time in my life that I speak publicly in your wonderful language, and it is the most solemn moment in my life. I know not if I will go to the end of my remarks. The District Attorney and the other gentlemen here who are used to

measure all human emotions with the yardstick may not understand the tumult that is going on in my soul in this moment. . . .

There has been brought only one side of this great industrial question, only the method and only the tactics. But what about, I say, the ethical part of this question? What about the human and humane part of our ideas? What about the grand condition of tomorrow as we see it, and as we foretell it now to the workers at large, here in this same cage where the felon has sat, in this same cage where the drunkard, where the prostitute, where the hired assassin has been?

What about the ethical side of that? What about the better and nobler humanity where there shall be no more slaves, where no man will ever be obliged to go on strike in order to obtain fifty cents a week more, where children will not have to starve any more, where women no more will have to go and prostitute themselves—let me say, even if there are women in this courtroom here, because the truth must out at the end— where at last there will not be any more slaves, any more masters, but just one great family of friends and brothers.

It may be, gentlemen of the jury, that you do not believe in that. It may be that we are dreamers. It may be that we are fanatics, Mr. District Attorney. We are fanatics. But yet so was Socrates a fanatic, who instead of acknowledging the philosophy of the aristocrats of Athens, preferred to drink the poison. And so was Jesus Christ a fanatic, who instead of acknowledging that Pilate, or that Tiberius was emperor of Rome, and instead of acknowledging his submission to all the rulers of the time and all the priestcraft of the time, preferred the cross between two thieves.

And so were all the philosophers and all the dreamers and all the scholars of the Middle Ages, who preferred to be burned alive by one of these very same churches concerning which you reproach me now of having said that no one of our membership should belong to them. Yes, gentlemen of the jury, you are judges. You must deal with facts. You must not deal with ideas. . . .

When I came to this country it was because I thought that really I was coming to a better and a freer land than my own. It was not exactly hunger that drove me out of my house. My father had enough money saved and he had enough energy saved to go and give an education to my brothers. He could have done the same with me and I could now be a professional man down there.

But I thought I could visit the world and I desired coming here for that purpose. I have no grudge against this country. I have no grudge against the American flag. I have no grudge against your patriotism. . . .

I ask the District Attorney, who speaks about the New England tradition, what he means by that—if he means the New England traditions of this same town where they used to burn the witches at the stake, or if he means the New England traditions of those men who refused to be any longer under the iron heel of the British aristocracy and dumped the tea into Boston Harbor and fired the first musket that was announcing to the world for the first time that a new era had been established—that from then on no more kingcraft, no more monarchy, no more kingship would be allowed; but a new people, a new theory, a new principle, a new brotherhood would arise out of the ruin and the wreckage of the past. . . .

He is not the one who is going to strangle this new Hercules of the world of industrial workers, or rather, the Industrial Workers of the World, in its cradle. It is not your verdict that will stem, it is not your verdict that will put a dam before this mighty onrush of waves that go forward. It is not the little insignificant, cheap life of Arturo Giovannitti offered in holocaust to warm the hearts of the millionaire manufacturers of this town that is going to stop Socialism from being the next dominator of the earth. No. No.

If there was any violence in Lawrence it was not Joe Ettor's fault. It was not my fault. If you must go back to the origin of all the trouble, gentlemen of the jury, you will find that the origin and reason was the wage system. It was the infamous rule of domination of one man by another man. It was the same reason that forty years ago impelled your great martyred President, Abraham Lincoln, by an illegal act, to issue the Proclamation of Emancipation—a thing which was beyond his powers as the Constitution of the United States expressed before that time.

I say it is the same principle now, the principle that made a man at that time a chattel slave, a soulless human being, a thing that could be bought and bartered and sold, and which now, having changed the term, makes the same man—but a white man—the slave of the machine.

They say you are free in this great and wonderful country. I say that politically you are, and my best compliments and congratulations for it. But I say you cannot be half free and half slave, and economically all the working class in the United States are as much slaves now as the negroes were forty and fifty years ago; because the man that owns the tool wherewith another man works, the man that owns the house where this man lives, the man that owns the factory where this man wants to go to work—that man owns and controls the bread that that man eats and therefore owns and controls his mind, his body, his heart and his soul. . . .

But I say and I repeat, that we have been working in something that is dearer to us than our lives and our liberty. We have been working in what are our ideas, our ideals, our aspirations, our hopes— you may say our religion, gentlemen of the jury. . . .

But I say, whether you want it or not, we are now the heralds of a new civilization. We have come here to proclaim a new truth. We are the apostles of a new evangel, of a new gospel, which is now at this very same moment being proclaimed and heralded from one side of the earth to the other.

Comrades of our same faith, while I am speaking in this case, are addressing a different crowd, a different forum, a different audience in other parts of the world, in every known tongue, in every civilized language, in every dialect, in Russia as in Italy, in England as in France, in China as in South Africa—everywhere this message of socialism, this message of brotherhood, this message of love, is being proclaimed in this same manner, gentlemen of the jury, and it is in the name of that that I want to speak and for nothing else.

After having heard what my comrade said and what I have said, do you believe for one single moment that we ever preached violence, that a man like me as I stand with my naked heart before you—and you know there is no lie in me at this moment, there is no deception in me at this moment—could kill a human being?

You know that I know not what I say, because it is only the onrush of what flows to my lips that I say. Gentlemen of the jury, you know that I am not a trained man in speaking to you, because it is the first time I speak in your language. Gentlemen, if you think that there has ever been a spark of malice in my heart, that I ever said others should break heads and prowl around and look for blood, if you believe that I ever could have said such a thing, not only on the 29th of January, but since the first day I began to realize that I was living and conscious of my intellectual and moral powers, then send me to the chair, because it is right and it is just. Then send my comrade to the chair because it is right and it is just. . . .

Gentlemen of the jury, I have finished. After this comes your verdict. I do not ask you to acquit us. It is not in my power to do so after my attorney has so nobly and ably pleaded for me. I say, though, that there are two ways open. If we are responsible, we are responsible in full. If what the District Attorney has said about us is true, then we ought to pay the extreme penalty, for if it is true it was a premeditated crime. If what he said is true, it means that we went to Lawrence specifically for that purpose and that for years and years we had been studying and maturing our thoughts along that line; then we expect from you a verdict of guilty.

But we do not expect you to soothe your conscience and at the same time to give a helping hand to the other side—simply to go and reason and say, "Well, something has happened there and somebody is responsible; let us balance the scales and do half and half." No, gentlemen. We are young. I am twenty-nine years old—not quite, yet; I will be so two months from now. I have a woman that loves me and that I love. I have a mother and father that are waiting for me. I have an ideal that is dearer to me than can be expressed or understood. And life has so many allurements and it is so nice and so bright and so wonderful that I feel the passion of living in my heart and I do want to live.

I don't want to pose to you as a hero. I don't want to pose as a martyr. No, life is dearer to me than it is probably to a good many others. But I say this, that there is something dearer and nobler and holier and grander, something I could never come to terms with, and that is my conscience and that is my loyalty to my class and to my comrades who have come here in this room, and to the working class of the world, who have contributed with a splendid hand penny by penny to my defense and who have all over the world seen that no injustice and no wrong was done to me.

Therefore, I say, weigh both sides and then judge. And if it be, gentlemen of the jury, that

your judgment shall be such that this gate will be opened and we shall pass out of it and go back into the sunlit world, then let me assure you what you are doing. Let me tell you that the first strike that breaks again in this Commonwealth or any other place in America where the work and the help and the intelligence of Joseph J. Ettor and Arturo Giovannitti will be needed and necessary, there we shall go again regardless of any fear and of any threat.

We shall return again to our humble efforts, obscure, humble, unknown, misunderstood—soldiers of this mighty army of the working class of the world, which out of the shadows and the darkness of the past is striving towards the destined goal which is the emancipation of human kind, which is the establishment of love and brotherhood and justice for every man and every woman in this earth.

On the other hand, if your verdict shall be the contrary, if it be that we who are so worthless as to deserve neither the infamy nor the glory of the gallows—if it be that these hearts of ours must be stilled on the same death chair and by the same current of fire that has destroyed the life of the wife murderer and the parricide, then I say, gentlemen of the jury, that tomorrow we shall pass into a greater judgment, that tomorrow we shall go from your presence into a presence where history shall give its last word to us.

Whichever way you judge, gentlemen of the jury, I thank you.

15

James Oppenheim's poem, "Bread and Roses," was inspired by one of the 1912 Lawrence strike parades in which the young mill girls carried a banner, "We want bread and roses too." Although it may have been published elsewhere earlier, it was printed in the I.W.W. newspaper Industrial Solidarity *(April 27, 1946). Oppenheim (1882–1932), a poet and novelist, was editor of the little magazine* The Seven Arts. *His poems appeared frequently in the* Industrial Pioneer *and the* One Big Union Monthly. *His poem, "Bread and Roses," was set to music by Caroline Kohlsaat. Arturo Giovannitti wrote an Italian song with the same title, "Pan e Rose," which was popular with the Italian Dressmakers Local 89 of the International Ladies' Garment Workers Union.*

BREAD AND ROSES

By JAMES OPPENHEIM

As we come marching, marching in the beauty of
the day,
A million darkened kitchens, a thousand mill lofts
gray,
Are touched with all the radiance that a sudden
sun discloses,
For the people hear us singing: "Bread and roses!
Bread and roses!"

As we come marching, marching, we battle too for
men,
For they are women's children, and we mother
them again.
Our lives shall not be sweated from birth until life
closes;
Hearts starve as well as bodies; give us bread, but
give us roses!

As we come marching, marching, unnumbered
women dead
Go crying through our singing their ancient cry for
bread.
Small art and love and beauty their drudging
spirits knew.
Yes, it is bread we fight for—but we fight for roses,
too!

As we come marching, marching, we bring the
greater days.
The rising of the women means the rising of the
race.
No more the drudge and idler—ten that toil where
one reposes,
But a sharing of life's glories: Bread and roses!
Bread and roses!

Chapter 7

Paterson: 1913

Less than a year after the Lawrence strike, Bill Haywood was describing the industrial conditions of an ideal society to an audience of striking silk workers in Paterson, New Jersey, the "Silk City" of America.

> It will be utopian. There will be a wonderful dining room where you will enjoy the best food that can be purchased; your digestion will be aided by sweet music which will be wafted to your ears by an unexcelled orchestra. There will be a gymnasium and a great swimming pool and private bathrooms of marble. One floor of this plant will be devoted to masterpieces of art and you will have a collection even superior to that displayed in the Metropolitan Museum in New York. A first-class library will occupy another floor . . . the workrooms will be superior to any ever conceived. Your work chairs will be morris chairs, so that when you become fatigued you may relax in comfort.[1]

Haywood's audience included recently arrived Italian, Jewish, and Polish immigrants who worked at unskilled or semiskilled jobs in the Paterson silk mills. Paterson, a grimy industrial city on the banks of the Passaic River, had a population of 124,000 in 1913; more than one-third of its 73,000 workers held jobs in the silk industry. The glowing picture of a future industrial society had meaning for the workers who spent ten hours a day in the silk mills, often wearing their overcoats at work in winter in the unheated buildings or suffocating in summer in workrooms where artificial humidifiers were used to provide the necessary degree of dampness for silk weaving. The dye houses were so choked with steam and acid fumes that the dyers often could not see people near them. Early deaths from tuberculosis and other respiratory diseases were frequent.

High-speed automatic looms which were simple to run had been introduced into the factories about the turn of the century. Some of these could be operated by women. Silk manufacturers moved their plants to Pennsylvania, where even lower wages were paid to the wives and daughters of coal miners, who worked to eke out a family living.

In 1911 Paterson manufacturers decided to enter the field of cheap silk production by expanding the number of looms in the plants. Where the operators had previously run just two looms, now they were required to operate three and four simultaneously. Paterson workers claimed that the new system would cause unemployment and force wages down from about $11.80 to the Pennsylvania average of $6.56 a week. "It is," wrote one writer in *Survey* magazine, "as if a vineyard were giving way to a hay farm."[2]

In addition to the four-loom system, Paterson workers protested an oppressive "docking system" for female apprentices, kickbacks in wages to foremen, abuses in measuring the yardage of the finished product, and the existence of several wage scales in the same shop. They also agitated for an eight-hour day, since there had been no reduction in the number of working hours since 1904.

The Giant and the Pigmies

(Or Gulliver Up to Date)

Solidarity, May 24, 1913.

The first mill that introduced the four-loom system in 1911 was one in which some of the workers were organized into the A.F.L. United Textile Workers. A group of protesting workers went out on strike, but returned to work when John Golden, United Textile Workers' president, proposed arbitration to settle the dispute. The four-loom system continued, however, and the strikers claimed that Golden had delayed the settlement because he really felt that the four-loom system was a technological advance in the silk industry.

Repudiation of the U.T.W. by the anti-A.F.L. strikers enabled a local of De Leon's Detroit faction of the I.W.W. to take over the strike. Several more sporadic walkouts protesting the four-loom system led to some wage increases by employers. But shortly after all the silk workers had returned

to their jobs, the mill owners refused to abide by the new wage schedules. In addition, some of the active union men were arrested and jailed for starting the strikes.

On January 27, 1913, 800 employees of the Doherty Silk Mill quit work when four members of a workers' committee were fired for trying to talk to the company's management about eliminating the four-loom system. The strike became industry-wide on February 25 when several thousand workers left their looms and held a mass meeting, addressed by I.W.W. organizers Elizabeth Gurley Flynn, Carlo Tresca, and Patrick Quinlan. Within the week, 25,000 workers were on strike, virtually all the silk workers in Paterson. Close to 300 silk mills in Paterson shut down.

"Had John Golden of the U.T.W. . . . . come to

Paterson on February 25th, undoubtedly he could have organized the workers in his union," wrote John Fitch in the June 7, 1913, issue of *Survey* magazine. "Instead came Haywood, Elizabeth Flynn, Quinlan, Tresca—empty-handed, with neither money nor credit nor with the prestige of a 2,000,000 membership, but willing to work and go to jail. They have put into the 25,000 strikers a spirit that has made them stand together with a united determination for a period that must have tried the souls of the strongest."[3]

The I.W.W. leaders who had been invited by the Paterson workers to address the February 25 meeting were well known for their work in Lawrence, Little Falls, and in a recent hotel workers' strike in New York City. Elizabeth Gurley Flynn had joined the I.W.W. in 1906 at the age of sixteen and had been active in the Missoula and Spokane free speech fights, the Joe Hill defense campaign, and the Lawrence textile strike. Carlo Tresca, who came to the United States in 1904, had been a leader of the Federation of Railroad Workers in Italy. In America he headed the Italian Socialist Federation and had helped organize miners' strikes in Pennsylvania, and textile strikes in Lawrence and Little Falls. Patrick Quinlan from Limerick, Ireland, had worked as a coal miner, steel worker, longshoreman, sailor, and union lecturer. A Socialist Party organizer, he joined the I.W.W. in 1912.

Tresca, Quinlan, and Elizabeth Flynn were arrested at the February 25 meeting. "We have no objection to our own people conducting a strike," said Paterson Police Chief Bimson, "but the day of the out-of-town agitator carrying on his profession is past."[4] After spending the night in jail, the three I.W.W. leaders were told to leave town or be responsible for their actions. They chose the latter course. Paterson's Mayor Andrew McBride declared that it was "the ancient right of cities to rid themselves of undesirables."[5]

A few days later, Bill Haywood arrived in Paterson from a rubber strike in Akron, Ohio. After a conference with Police Chief Bimson, he advised the strikers to fold their arms or put their hands in their pockets and let the manufacturers do the worrying.

"There's a red card in the home of every silk striker," said Haywood.[6] His claim, according to an article in *Outlook* magazine, was but little exaggerated. Although I.W.W. silk worker Adolph Lessig testified to the Commission on Industrial Relations that there were only 9000 paid-up I.W.W. members in Paterson, "so hard is the grip of poverty on the workers," reported writer Gregory Mason in *Outlook*, "that many have remained outside the organization that is conducting their fight simply to save the dues of thirty cents a month."[7]

The Paterson strikers, however, included not only the I.W.W. followers, but Socialists, anarchists, De Leonites, and A.F.L. members as well. Most of the ribbon weavers were English-speaking American citizens; most of the dyers were recent arrivals from Italy. The broad silk weavers were usually non-English speaking Italian and Jewish immigrants. Wives and children of workers from every part of Europe and the Middle East handled most of the unskilled jobs. The I.W.W. leaders welded these diverse groups together.

A spirit of solidarity was kept at a high pitch during the strike by mass meetings held in the strikers' halls each morning, and shop committee conferences planned for each afternoon. In addition, special meetings were scheduled for women and children.

When the Paterson school teachers spoke against the strike, the strikers' children picketed the schools. Haywood met with the youngsters. He described a future society in which adults would not continually deny their wishes. He called this place, "Kids' Town." One little boy called out from the audience, "No homework, Bill. Put that in!"[8] The children organized their own strike committee, appointed speakers, elected a treasurer, and collected money to be used for needy members. Many of them walked with their parents on the picket lines in front of the mills.

At one of the women's meetings, Carlo Tresca illustrated his talk on the need for an eight-hour day by saying that couples would have more time to spend together if there were fewer working hours. "More babies," he said jokingly. The audience of tired working wives did not cheer this suggestion. "No, Carlo," interrupted Haywood who was at the meeting, "We believe in birth control. . . . Fewer babies, well cared for." The women started to laugh and applaud.[9]

Strikers set up a finance committee and a relief board to collect and distribute funds raised by speeches and entertainments in neighboring cities and by advertisements in sympathetic journals. Two relief stations supplied food to families. A restaurant fed the single men. A grocery and a drugstore were opened and run by the workers. Arrangements were made with a sympathetic doctor and dentist to aid ailing workers at no cost. Most of the landlords in Paterson did not press for rent, and the Sons of Italy, a benevolent association, paid benefits to needy Italian workers.

Police records showed that close to 3000 pickets were arrested during the course of the strike. Arrests of strikers averaged about 100 a day throughout May and June. Most of them received a ten-day sentence in the overcrowded Paterson or Passaic County jails.

As the strike continued, the Paterson afternoon newspaper printed front-page editorials urging the formation of a vigilance committee to stop the picketing and drive out the agitators. "Los Angeles, Akron, Denver, Ottowa, and other cities kicked the I.W.W. out of town in short order," stated one editorial. "What is Paterson doing to discourage this revolutionary horde?"[10]

Another editorial about Bill Haywood, appealed, "Akron, Ohio, could not find a law to banish this dangerous revolutionist and his cohorts, but a citizens' committee of 1000 men did the trick in short order. Can Akron, Ohio, accomplish something that Paterson, N. J., cannot duplicate? The Paterson Press dislikes to believe it, but time will tell."[11]

When mass rallies within the Paterson city limits were forbidden by city officials, the strikers walked to Haledon, a neighboring town with a friendly Socialist mayor. The strikers used a silk-worker's two-story house which had a second floor porch, a convenient platform overlooking the street. Every Sunday throughout the spring, the strikers and their families gathered in Haledon to listen to long speeches. Often they were joined by delegations of students, workers, or journalists who commuted from New York City, some twenty miles away. As Elizabeth Gurley Flynn wrote about the Haledon meetings:

Our original reason for going to Haledon . . . goes deep into the psychology of a strike. Because Sunday is the day before Monday. Monday is the day that a break comes in every strike, if it is to come at all during the week. If you can bring the people safely over Monday they usually go along for the rest of the week. If on Sunday, however, you let those people stay at home, sit around the stove without any fire in it, sit down at the table where there isn't much food, see the feet of the children with shoes getting thin and the bodies of children where the clothes are getting ragged, they begin to think in terms of "myself" and lose the spirit of the mass and the realization that all are suffering as they are suffering. . . . And so our original reason for going to Haledon was to give them novelty, to give them variety, to take them en masse out of the city of Paterson some place else to a sort of picnic over Sunday that would stimulate them for the rest of the week.[12]

Haywood, who shuttled back and forth between Paterson and an I.W.W.-led strike of rubber workers in Akron, was arrested as he walked at the head of a long line of strikers going to Haledon for one of these Sunday meetings in March. He was released on that occasion, but arrests of strikers and organizers continued as the community made a concerted effort to break the strike and jail its leadership on charges of inciting to riot, unlawful assembly, and disturbing the peace. Under a New Jersey law, anything said from a strike platform amounted to "inciting a riot" or "preaching anarchy," and made the speaker liable to arrest for having committed a criminal offense. Convicted on these charges I.W.W. organizer Pat Quinlan was jailed from 1913 to 1915.

In the May 29, 1913, issue of *The Independent* magazine, a Paterson rabbi paid tribute to the I.W.W. strike leaders. He wrote:

They have held in check and directed an army of 25,000 men and women. Had they been preaching anarchism and violence, there would have been anarchism and violence. But the record of this strike is a remarkable one. Between 1200 and 1300 strikers have been arrested and jailed. Not one had a weapon.[13]

Helping the Paterson police was an army of private detectives hired by the mill owners. They were responsible for killing two workers during the strike, one on the picket line and another as he sat with his child on the steps of his house across the street from one of the dye works. Three company detectives were arrested for this crime, but were never brought to trial. Fifteen thousand workers turned out for the funeral and marched in a ten-block-long procession that was watched by half of Paterson's population. Strikers piled red carnations on top of the casket and Haywood, Gurley Flynn, and Tresca made stirring speeches at the grave.

Attempting to play on the patriotic feelings of the foreign-born workers, many who had recently become naturalized, the mill owners urged the strikers that it was their patriotic duty to return to work. They declared March 17 "Flag Day," and draped flags over every mill gate with signs calling on the strikers to return to work. The I.W.W. strike leaders pointed out that many of the flags were weatherbeaten and torn, and that the employers should at least use new flags, since flag silk was woven in Paterson. The strikers stretched a huge American flag across Main Street under which a slogan read:

We wove the flag; we dyed the flag.
We live under the flag; but we won't scab
    under the flag.[14]

Strikers pinned little flags to their lapels and carried signs on the picket lines bearing this message.

May Day, 1913, was celebrated by sending a group of strikers' children to live temporarily with sympathetic families in New York City where they would be better fed and cared for than in the strife-torn Paterson.

A special feature of the Paterson strike was a pageant presented at the old Madison Square Garden. John Reed, fresh out of Harvard, learned about Paterson from Bill Haywood, whom he met at a soiree of artists and writers in Greenwich Village. Paterson was close enough to the Village for the New Intellectuals, attracted by the direct-action anarchists, to venture out to hear the fiery speeches of Gurley Flynn, Tresca, and Big Bill.

John Reed went to Paterson on a rainy April morning. He was arrested as he stood talking to some strikers on the porch of a worker's house and thrown into a four by seven foot cell that held eight pickets who had been without food and water for twenty-four hours. His experience made picturesque copy. A New York newspaper featured the story of the Harvard boy jailed with the striking immigrants. "You gotta be careful they don't get in your spoon," the prisoners had warned Reed about dead insects in the watery soup.[15] The New York papers made more fuss about one reporter, said the Paterson police chief, than about the hundreds of workers he had jailed. Reed was released on bail after four days.

"We were frightened when we went in, but we were singing when we went out," a young girl striker had told Reed about the first day of the walk-out.[16] Emotionally involved with the Pater-son strikers, Reed dragged his friends Walter Lippmann, Hutchins Hapgood, Edmund Hunt, and Mabel Dodge to the Sunday meetings in Haledon. He conceived the idea of a gigantic pageant to publicize and raise money for the strikers' defense. Reed corralled a group of people who met frequently in the Fifth Avenue home of Mabel Dodge, a wealthy divorcee who was interested in modern art, radicalism, and Reed. He lined up financial support from Mrs. Dodge and some of her New York contacts, but it was only enough to rent Madison Square Garden for one night. Robert Edmund Jones, a nonradical Harvard friend, was drafted to stage the production. Bobby Jones also designed the poster of a crouching workman which was to appear year after year on I.W.W. publications. John Sloan painted the scenery, a great backdrop representing a tremendous silk mill with smaller mills on either side.

In three weeks, Reed trained over 1000 textile workers to reenact scenes from their strike. He led them in rehearsing songs from the little red songbook. Mrs. Dodge, swept up in the project through Reed's enthusiasm, remembered, "One of the gayest touches, I think, was teaching them to sing one of their lawless songs to 'Harvard, Old Harvard.' "[17]

On the afternoon of June 7, several thousand strikers from Paterson arrived in Hoboken by a fourteen-car train. Reaching New York City by ferries, they marched from Christopher Street up Fifth Avenue with red banners flying and an I.W.W. band playing "The Marseillaise" and the "Internationale." Margaret Sanger, a member of the pageant committee, and a police escort led the way.

That night, the letters, I.W.W., ten feet high in bright red electric lights, blazed from each side of the Madison Square tower and could be seen from miles away. Fifteen thousand persons, many who had walked from their homes, crowded the streets on every side of the block-square building. When the cheaper seats were sold out, the committee hurriedly decided to let the crowd in at a quarter apiece. The floor seats, advertised at $1.50, were sold at the last minute for whatever they could bring, and hundreds of I.W.W. members were let in free when they showed their red membership cards. The performance was delayed an hour while the thousands found their seats.

"Just let anybody say one word of disrespect to the flag and I will stop the show so quickly it will take their breath away," warned New York's sheriff Julius Harburger who had previously spoken out against the "sedition, treasonable utterance, un-American doctrines, advocating sabotage, fulmination of paranoical ebullitions, inflammatory, hysterical, unsound doctrines."[18] Sheriff Harburger took a box seat near the stage to oversee and monitor the production.

Since he arrived early, Harburger must have had time to read the program which stated, "The pageant represents a battle between the working class and the capitalist class conducted by the Industrial Workers of the World. . . . It is a conflict between two social forces."[19] The program announced that the pageant would be in six scenes, starting with the mills at six A.M. on a chill February morning.

One newspaperman described the production this way:

Fifteen thousand spectators applauded with shouts and tears the great Paterson Strike Pageant at Madison Square Garden. The big mill aglow with light in the dark hours of early winter morning, the shrieking whistles, the din of machinery—dying away to give place to the "Marseillaise" sung by surging crowd of 1,200 operatives, the fierce battle with the police, the somber funeral of the victim, the impassioned speech of the agitator, the sending away of the children, the great meeting of desperate, hollow-eyed strikers—these scenes unrolled with a poignant realism that no man who saw them will ever forget.[20]

At the enactment of Valentino Modestino's funeral, pallbearers carried a coffin down the center aisle of the Garden through the audience. Over 1000 strikers followed, singing "The Funeral March of the Workers." Sitting in a box seat, Mrs. Modestino became hysterical when the funeral procession reached the stage. The cast of strikers heaped red carnations and evergreen boughs on the bier and Haywood, Tresca, and Gurley Flynn repeated the speeches they had made at Modestino's graveside. Many in the audience wept. Mrs. Dodge remembered:

. . . for a few electric moments there was a terrible unity between all those people. They were one: the workers who had come to show their comrades what was happening across the river and the workers who had come to see it.

I have never felt such a high pulsing vibration in any gathering before or since.[21]

Almost everyone was deeply moved by the earnestness and emotion of the strikers. At the end, the audience rose to sing the "Internationale" with the cast. Reviews in the next day's newspapers spoke of the pageant as a great production and a new form of art. "Self-expression in industry and art among the masses may become a rich reality, spreading a human glow over the whole of humanity . . . from which we shall all be gainers— in real life, in justice, in art, in love," enthused Hutchins Hapgood, a liberal writer who was one of the frequenters of Mrs. Dodge's salon.[22] Newspaper editorials pointed out, however, that the pageant was produced, as one paper stated, "under the direction of a destructive organization opposed in spirit and antagonistic in action to all the forces which have upbuilded this republic."[23]

The pageant failed financially. This was a crushing blow to the Paterson strikers, who anticipated huge profits based on the overflow audience in Madison Square Garden. The expenses of a one-night performance were too high, and the audience had been too poor to make the hoped-for contributions. The hostile press accused the pageant committee of raising a large sum and "lining their pockets." Jealousies, dissensions, and suspicions marked the last days of a losing strike. Reed left for Venice with Mrs. Dodge and Bobby Jones. Bill Haywood, who had lost eighty pounds during the strike from an ulcerated stomach, was taken to Europe by a friend.

As the strike dragged on into July, the amount of funds sent by sympathizers began to dwindle. The pressures of hunger and a stepped up campaign of arresting pickets were hard to overcome. Faced with the loss of millions of dollars of business, the companies offered to deal with the strikers by shops, and on July 18, the ribbon weavers withdrew from the strike committee, announcing that they would negotiate with employers on a shop basis. Their defection broke the I.W.W. hopes of an industry-wide settlement. Split up into 300 separate shop units, the strikers were unable to win their demands and were forced to return to work under very much the same conditions they had left five months before.

Like so many other textile strikes, the 1913 Paterson strike failed. It was one more episode in the long history of textile workers' struggles against

Uncle Sam Ruled Out

low wages, long hours, speed-up, company-dominated mill towns, chronic unemployment, and instability. In the words of the concluding verse of a song written at the beginning of this century by South Carolina cotton mill workers:

> Ain't it enough to break your heart?
> Hafta work all day and at night it's dark.
> It's hard times in the mill, my love,
> Hard times in the mill.

1

This anecdote about Big Bill and the rabbi which was first printed in Solidarity *(April 19, 1913) was reprinted several times in the I.W.W. press. It is representative of similar anecdotes on the theme, "We're all leaders." On the fly leaf of his book,* New Men of Power *(New York, 1948), C. Wright Mills told the following story which he had heard from an unknown worker in Nevada in June, 1947:*

> *When the boatload of Wobblies came*
> *Up to Everett, the sheriff says*
> *Don't you come no further*
> *Who the hell's yer leader anyhow?*
> *Who's yer leader?*
> *And them Wobblies yelled right back—*
> *We don't got no leader*
> *We're all leaders*
> *And they kept right on comin'.*

WHO IS THE LEADER?

"Oh, Mr. Haywood, I am so glad to meet you. I've been wanting to meet the leader of the strike for some time."

"You've made a mistake," replied Bill, "I'm not the leader."

"What! You're not? Well, who is he?"

"There ain't any He."

"Perhaps I should have said 'they,'" persisted the prophet of the Chosen people, "Who are they?"

"This strike has no leaders," answered Bill.

"It hasn't! Well, who is in charge of it?"

"The strikers."

"But can't I meet some responsible parties elsewhere? You know I represent the other churches of the city, the Catholic Fathers and the Methodist ministers are awaiting my report. I would like to find out all I can and then maybe we could come to some agreement with the mill owners."

"The mill owners already know what the strikers want," said Bill.

"They do! Why some of the leading citizens don't know yet!"

"That's funny," smiled Bill, "I just got off a train from Akron a couple of hours ago and I know."

"Will you please tell me?"

"It's very simple," answered Bill, "They want an eight hour day, abolition of the three and four loom system in broad silks, abolition of the two loom system in ribbons, and the dyers want a minimum wage of $12 a week."

"Well, well!" mused the other stroking his rabbinical beard, "I must say it's strange we had not heard all this!"

"There's an awful lot of things you never heard of, parson," said Bill.

"Do they have a strike committee, and where do they meet?" continued the rabbi.

"Right in this hall, every morning at 8 o'clock."

"Who are they?"

"I don't know; and if I did I wouldn't tell," laughed Bill.

"How many are there?"

"One hundred and twenty-seven."

"One hundred and twenty-seven! MY GOD! What can we do with a strike committee of one hundred and twenty-seven that meets in a public hall before all the rest of the strikers?"

"I don't reckon that you can do much except the heavy looking on, parson," said Bill. "There ain't much left in the world for fellows like you to do except that, and besides this is an I.W.W. strike. In an I.W.W. strike there isn't room for anybody except the working class and the bosses; everybody else is excess baggage."

2

This article by Bill Haywood appeared in the International Socialist Review *(May 1913). In his autobiography Bill Haywood wrote: "While this strike was on, I learned something of the methods of producing silk. After the cocoons were unwound and the silk was whipped into skeins, it was dyed with the glorious colors seen in this costly fabric. All of it went through a process called 'dynamiting' where it was loaded with metals of different kinds—lead, tin, and zinc. From a fourth to a third of the weight of the silk was of these adulterants, which shortened the life and durability, though temporarily adding to the gloss and weight of the finished goods." Haywood later used this information in testifying before the Industrial Relations Commission on employer use of "sabotage" in industry. The exposé of this process caused embarrassment to the silk industry.*

THE RIP IN THE SILK INDUSTRY

By WILLIAM D. HAYWOOD

When the broad silk weavers in Henry Doherty's mill in Paterson, N. J., left their machines last February they inaugurated what has proved to be the closest approach to a general strike that has yet taken place in an American industry.

They revolted against the 3 and 4 loom system which until recently has been confined to the state of Pennsylvania. This system is restricted to the lower grades of silk, messaline and taffeta.

There are almost 300 silk mills in Paterson. Doherty was the first manufacturer to introduce this system there and later it was carried into 26 other mills. The silk workers soon realized that unless this scheme for exploiting them still further was checked, it would in time pervade the entire industry in the Jersey city.

The silk workers of Paterson are the most skilled in the United States and the employers thought that if there was anywhere in the country where this system could be successfully adopted it was in Paterson. They thought that their workers would stand for it. The workers themselves were not consulted, as the manufacturers afterward realized to their sorrow, when a general strike was called embracing the industry in all its branches and extending to all states where silk is manufactured.

At present no less than 50,000 silk workers are on strike in New Jersey, Pennsylvania, New York and Connecticut, including those in the preparatory processes, the "throwster" mills, dye houses, broad silk making in all grades, as well as in nearly all the ribbon mills.

In many respects this strike is hardly less significant than that at Lawrence. It involves nearly as many workers and the conditions are just as bad. But the Paterson revolt has attracted less public attention than did the woolen fight. This is due to several reasons.

In the first place, the manufacturers, through their control of outside newspapers, were able to bring about a general conspiracy of silence. The New York papers, for example, after the first few days in which they gave prominence to the strike, were warned through subtle sources that unless there was less publicity they would be made to suffer through loss of support and advertising. Then the Paterson strikers were fortunate in having among them several trained veterans in the labor movement, such as Adolph Lessig, Ewald Koettgen, and Louis Magnet, who had been members of the I.W.W. since 1906, and knew what to do towards putting the strike on an organized basis. For a time they were able to take care of themselves without relying much on outside help. Besides, the authorities kept their hands off for a time, after their first fright in which they threw Elizabeth Gurley Flynn, Carlo Tresca and later Patrick Quinlan and Alex Scott, the Socialist editor, into jail. These organizers got on the job instantly and have done excellent work.

The Lyons of America

Paterson is the Lyons of America. It practically has a monopoly in the making of the finer grades of silk in this country. It has 25,400 people engaged in the silk industry and in the manufacture of silk machinery and supplies. Therefore, when practically all these workers came out, the industry was tied up tight.

Fifty-six per cent of the Paterson silk workers are women and children and they have been among the most devoted and enthusiastic strikers.

As this is written, the strike has entered upon its seventh week and the demands of the workers have crystallized around a determination to have the eight-hour day. This will apply to all the workers involved, except the broad silk weavers whose principal demand, as stated, is the abolition of the grinding 3 and 4 loom system.

So greatly have wages been reduced in recent years that the weavers are now demanding the restoration of the 1894 price list which was imposed on them at the time. With the improvements in machinery that have been made, this would be a great advantage to the ribbon weavers. The dye house workers are holding out for a minimum wage of $12 a week. In other branches there is a general demand for a 25 per cent increase in wages.

Present wages, according to the manufacturers' figures, average $9.60 a week. A general call at one of the mass meetings for pay envelopes brought out hundreds which showed the average wage is much lower than this and as all wages are determined by working periods, the actual yearly wage would bring average "earnings" down to $6 or $7 a week.

Paterson manufacturers have an absolute monopoly on the finer grades of silk, like brocades, that are made on the Jacquard loom, and it would be easy for them to raise prices to meet wage increases, but because of the cut-throat competition among them, silk is cheaper, on the whole, than it was 15 years ago. This reduction in price, needless to say, has been taken out of the flesh and blood of the workers.

Untrustified Industry

The big capitalists have never tried to enter the silk trade, because it deals with a luxury. They are too busy securing their grip on the necessities of life, like food, clothing, steel, transportation, etc.

The Paterson workers, then, have not had to fight a concentrated trust, such as existed at Lawrence, but a gang of scattered employers, all jealous and fearful of each other. The strike undoubtedly would have ended much sooner had it not been for the desire of the richer manufacturers to see the smaller makers starved out and driven into bankruptcy, which already has occurred to a number of them.

The manufacturers as a whole have used as an excuse for not raising wages the plea that they cannot afford it on account of Pennsylvania's competition. But this is untrue, because the Pennsylvania mills are controlled largely by the same interests that center in Paterson.

The Pennsylvania silk mills are situated generally in mining camps and industrial centers where the wages of the men have been so reduced that women and children have been compelled to seek employment in the mills. Ninety-one per cent of the workers in the Pennsylvania silk mills are women and children.

Wages in the Pennsylvania silk mills average much less than in New Jersey and it is a peculiar fact that the men get less than the women. The men get $6.06 a week while the women are making $7.01.

There are six prominent processes in the mak-

Left to right: I.W.W. strike leaders, Adolph Lessig, Bill Haywood, and Carlo Tresca.   Brown Brothers photo.

ing of silk and they are usually done in different establishements. "Throwing" is largely done in Pennsylvania—reeling the raw silk as it comes from the cocoon, etc. The dyeing is done in separate factories.

The "Dynamiting" Process

It is at this point that the silk is "dynamited"—that is, loaded with adulterants to be later foisted on the gullible purchaser as extra fine goods. In the dye houses one pound of silk is often treated so that its weight is increased to 56 ounces! This is done by dipping the skein into a solution of which sugar, tannic acid, tin, lead, and iron are often components.

This adulteration, amounting to a direct steal, enhances the weight of the fabric but at the same time weakens the texture and destroys the life of the cloth. Silk so treated will crumble away while it stands in the wardrobe before it has been subjected to use.

One of the most alarming features of the strike to the manufacturers, was the publicity given this system of "dynamiting" or loading silk. In consequence there is a growing demand for a government stamp which will denote pure fabric similar to that which is supposed to guarantee pure food.

The work of the dyers is the most unhealthful and disagreeable in the industry and is almost the worst paid. The strike came as a welcome relief to them from day after day of filthy and monotonous toil. They work 13 hours on the night shift and 11 on the day side. They are compelled to stand in wet and soggy places, their hands are always submerged in chemicals which discolor and burn their flesh and sometimes eat off the nails of their fingers.

The Red Badge of Toil

In this connection it is worth while to relate an incident—one of the most dramatic of the strike. The Paterson bosses lost no time in injecting the "patriotic" issue, after the fashion of Lawrence, Little Falls and Akron. The red flag, they howled, stood for blood, murder and anarchy—the Star Spangled Banner must be upheld, etc., etc. Elizabeth Gurley Flynn was on the platform at a big strike meeting one day explaining the significance of the red flag when a striking dyer sprang up from the middle of the audience crying:

"I know! Here is the red flag!"

And aloft he held his right hand—stained a permanent bloody crimson, gnarled from years of toil, and corroded by the scarlet dye which it was his business to put into the fabrics worn by the dainty lady of the capitalist class as well as by the fawning prostitute.

For an instant there was silence and then the hall was rent by cries from the husky throats as all realized this humble dyer indeed knew the meaning of the red badge of his class.

Ribbon weaving is largely done by men and women. In this department the bosses have developed a speeding up system with reductions in pay, overlooking no opportunity to introduce improved machinery. Thus they increase production, at the same time they lowered the pay, until the workers are now demanding a scale which 19 years ago was imposed upon them! That is, the weavers now ask a wage that prevailed two decades ago.

The significance of this demand makes it plain that in the evolution of industry and the introduction of new machinery the workers have obtained no benefit, while the bosses have reaped ever increasing profits.

Many children are employes in the silk industry, most of them being between the ages of 14 and 16. However, there are few violations of the child labor law, not because the manufacturers care anything about either the law or the children, but because the making of high grade silk requires the careful and efficient work that only adults can give. However, the Paterson capitalists have begun to set up plants in the southern states as well as in the mining regions of Pennsylvania, installing there new style looms which can be operated by girls and children.

Meeting for Children

One of the best and most enthusiastic meetings held during the strike was that for the benefit of the children of the mills. They packed Turner Hall and listened eagerly and with appreciation as speakers outlined to them the development in the manufacture of silk from the cocoon to the completed fabric lying on the shelves of the rich department store.

The strike has been viciously fought from the very beginning. The usual combination of press, pulpit and police has labored both openly and secretly to weaken it and break it, but without avail. For seven weeks the Paterson newspapers have delivered screams of rage and fury day after day. They have not hesitated to urge any measure that might break the strike, from tar-and-feathers to murder. Day after day in big, black headlines in their front pages they have demanded that the "I.W.W. blatherskites" be driven out of town. They have constantly incited the police to violence and urged the authorities to take "drastic measures." All in vain. On the day this is written the leading organ of the manufacturers admits that the police, the administration and the courts have been helpless and it now begs the workers themselves to "drive the I.W.W. out of town," promising that if they will organize into "a decent, dignified, American union," the whole city will demand that the bosses give them the conditions for which they ask.

Little Violence

Despite this, another paper admits in its editorial columns that Paterson after all ought to be thankful. "Though 25,000 people have been on strike here for seven weeks," it says, "there has been remarkably little violence."

As was the case in Lawrence, nearly every nationality on earth is represented in the strike. The Italians and Germans are the most numerous, with thousands of Russians, Poles, Hungarians and Armenians besides. Shoulder to shoulder they have stood, with a spirit and loyalty that nothing could break or weaken. For seven long weeks they have held out and in place of food many of them have simply taken up another link in their belts and drunk a glass of water. Some relief money has come in but not enough to help any except the most needy cases.

Incidents without number could be given to show the spirit of self sacrifice and devotion among the Paterson workers. The jail has had no terrors for them, since accommodations there are hardly worse than in the "homes" they are compelled to live in. On occasions when the police have started wholesale arrests they have vied with each other in placing themselves in the hands of the "bulls." One day when the police gathered in more than 200 of them, they refused to walk to jail but demanded the patrol wagon. When the police pleaded that the patrol wagon would hold only a few at a time, they said they would wait! And the patrol wagon the police were compelled to get, making trip after trip to the jail while the arrested strikers stood in a group and laughed and sang.

The meetings we have held have been wonders.

Day after day strikers have crowded into Turner and Helvetia Halls with enthusiasm just as rampant as on the first day of the strike and on the Sundays when the Socialist city of Haledon is visited, at the invitation of Socialist Mayor William Brueckmann, for open air meetings, it has seemed as if the whole population of the northern part of New Jersey was present. To speak at such meetings is worth a whole lifetime of agitation.

3

Carlo Tresca (1879–1943), an Italian-born anarchist and writer, came to the United States in 1904 after being active in the left-wing Italian Railroad Workers' Federation. He was elected secretary of the Italian Socialist Federation of North America, took part in strikes of Pennsylvania coal miners, of textile workers in Lawrence, Little Falls, and Paterson, and of metal miners in Michigan and Minnesota. In Italy he edited the journal Il Germe, a socialist weekly. In the United States he edited L'Avvenire until it was suppressed under the federal Espionage Law, and then, for more than twenty years, edited and published Il Martello ("The Hammer"), an anti-Fascist newspaper. A leader of the Anti-Fascist Alliance, Tresca was mysteriously assassinated in New York City in 1943. His memories of Bill Haywood in the 1913 Paterson strike were posthumously printed in Il Martello (January 14, 1944).

WITH BIG BILL HAYWOOD ON THE BATTLEFIELDS OF LABOR

By CARLO TRESCA

I admired Bill greatly during those crucial weeks. I realized his influence over the masses, but wherein lay his real strength I recognized only a year later, when we were working together in the Paterson strike. At the beginning there were only Elizabeth Flynn and myself in the field. We were doing our best, but day in and day out we were confronted with the insistent question: "Where is Bill?" "When is he coming?" "Why is he not here?" It was upon the insistence of the strikers that we were compelled to invite him.

Those were days of epic struggles. We had several halls in Paterson proper: the Turnhalle, where the crowd was mostly Italian; the Helvetia Hall, with an overwhelming German attendance; we had many other halls; but our great gathering place was Haledon, New Jersey, which at that time had a socialist mayor. On Sundays, when due to the blue laws, no meetings could be held in the rest of New Jersey, we addressed between 30 and 40,000 workers from the roof of the Haledon city hall. It was into that crowd that Haywood threw himself with all the power of his unique individuality.

The number of persons involved in the strike, including strikers' families, was no less than 125,-000. All the strike relief collected for six months amounted to $72,000. The strike lasted from February to July, 1913. How could the strikers hold out? Through the spiritual power invoked in the masses by this huge, towering figure. He was not elegant. He had not much culture. He was just one of the mass. But he knew a few ideas perfectly—"class struggle," "power of solidarity," and he had an unusually clear vision of the goal of the labor movement. He was immediately convinced of the righteousness of his cause; he had a deep religious feeling regarding the I.W.W. labor movement, and his place among the workers. He was a simple man with a simple purpose, but he compressed into it all the gigantic powers of his soul. He never harangued a crowd. He "explained" things in the simplest, most beautiful, and still somehow imaginative words. It was remarkable that people like the Italians, who had a scant knowledge of English, understood his speeches. He had the unusual ability of reducing issues to their simplest realities, but these realities he knew how to present in a magically compelling way. Many speakers had talked to the workers about the necessity of holding together. Bill, however, would do this. He would lift over the crowd his huge, powerful hand. He would spread the fingers as far apart from each other as possible. He would seize one finger after the other with his other hand, saying to his audience: "Do you see that? Do you see that? Every finger by itself has no force. Now look." He would then bring the fingers together, close them into a bulky, powerful fist, lift that fist in the face of the crowd, saying: "See that? That's I.W.W." The mass would go wild. Not the least factor in his successes was his physical vigor, the unusual amount of vitality that throbbed in every one of his gestures. One certainly could not repeat Bill's demonstration with a puny fist.

I can still see him standing on that platform,— before him a sea of children's heads. The platform is crowded with children, some clinging to his huge legs, some hanging on to his coat, all of them looking up at him with adoration. All faces are lit up with ecstatic joy. Bill had no difficulty in speaking to children. He spoke to them with the very same simplicity with which he addressed adults. There was something of the child in his own make-up. He told the crowd a simple story of how he worked in his own childhood, and what he went through; he explained the meaning of the I.W.W. He held every child's heart throbbing in his big hands. The following day the picket line was crowded with children who proved to be the most faithful fighters. Subsequently Mr. Bimpton, the Paterson Chief of Police, asked me whether I could not withdraw the kids from the picket line. "For God's sake," he said, "remove those kids from the field. My men can't fight children." Later we began to place the strikers' children in the homes of workers' families in surrounding cities. This too was Big Bill's idea.

He lived like one of the people. During the six months of the strike his salary was eighteen dollars a week. He was not only what you call a leader. He actually loved to spend time with the workers, to talk with their women and children. He went to supper with the strikers nearly every night.

Few knew that this hulking figure of a notorious fighter was kindness itself. His great craving was to possess a family, to be surrounded by little tots. He hated to stay alone of the evening. He begged me to take him somewhere, anywhere. He would sleep in the houses of Italians, Syrians, Irish, Poles, Letts. People were all brothers to him. Still, how he enjoyed those little Italian families full of genuine fondness, crowded with children, with numerous other possessions that give zest to life! How he would fondle the little ones rocking them on his huge knees!

After six months in Paterson his health was completely shattered. Even Bill, with his powerful constitution, could not stand the strain. He had a trying stomach ailment which made him feel miserable. As soon as the strike was over, friends took him to Europe. It was not before a year that he completely recovered.

Bill Haywood was not only a picturesque figure. He was the type of a practical idealist who never lost sight of the realities of life, while keeping a firm hold on the ultimate goal of the movement. He will live in the memory of the working class.

4

This program of the Paterson Pageant was taken from the booklet The Pageant of the Paterson Strike, *edited by Frederick Boyd (New York, 1913).*

THE PAGEANT OF THE PATERSON STRIKE

PROGRAM
OF THE
PATERSON STRIKE PAGEANT

Scene: Paterson, N. J. *Time:* A.D. 1913.

The Pageant represents a battle between the working class and the capitalist class conducted by the Industrial Workers of the World (I.W.W.), making use of the General Strike as the chief weapon. It is a conflict between two social forces—the force of labor and the force of capital.

While the workers are clubbed and shot by detectives and policemen, the mills remain dead. While the workers are sent to jail by hundreds, the mills remain dead. While organizers are persecuted, the strike continues, and still the mills are dead. While the pulpit thunders denunciation and the press screams lies, the mills remain dead. No violence can make the mills alive—no legal process can resurrect them from the dead. Bayonets and clubs, injunctions and court orders are equally futile.

Only the return of the workers to the mills can give the dead things life. The mills remain dead throughout the enactment of the following episodes.

EPISODE ONE

1. The Mills Alive—The Workers Dead

2. The Workers Begin to Think

Six o'clock on a February morning. The mill windows all aglow. The mill whistle sounds the signal to begin work. Men and women, old and young, come to work in the bitter cold of the dawn. The sound of looms. The beginning of the great silk strike. The striking workers sing the Marseillaise, the entire audience being invited to join in the song of revolt.

EPISODE TWO

The Mills Dead—The Workers Alive

Mass picketing. Every worker alert. The police interfere with peaceful picketing and treat the strikers with great brutality. The workers are provoked to anger. Fights between police and strikers ensue. Many strikers are clubbed and arrested. Shots are fired by detectives hired by the manufacturers, and Valentino Modestino, who was not a striker or a silk mill worker, is hit by a bullet and killed as he stands on the porch of his house with one of his children in his arms.

EPISODE THREE

The Funeral of Modestino

The coffin containing the body of Modestino is followed by the strikers in funeral procession to the strains of the Dead March. The strikers passing drop red carnations and ribbons upon the coffin until it is buried beneath the crimson symbol of the workers' blood.

EPISODE FOUR

Mass Meeting at Haledon

Great mass meeting of 20,000 strikers. I.W.W. organizers speak. Songs by the strike composers are sung by the strikers. They also sing the International, the Marseillaise and the Red Flag, in which the audience is invited to join.

EPISODE FIVE

1. May Day

2. Sending Away the Children

The May Day Parade. The workers of Paterson, with bands playing, flags flying, and women and children dressed in red, celebrate the international revolutionary labor day.

The strikers give their children to the "strike mothers" from other cities. The strike mothers receive them to be cared for during the war in the silk industry. Elizabeth Gurley Flynn speaks to the strikers and the children, dwelling upon the solidarity of labor shown in this vividly human episode, and is followed by William D. Haywood.

EPISODE SIX

Strike Meeting in Turner Hall

The strikers, men and women, legislate for themselves. They pass a law for the eight-hour day. No court can declare the law thus made unconstitu-

Program cover. The Pageant of the Paterson Strikers.   Courtesy of Tamiment Institute Library.

tional. Elizabeth Gurley Flynn, Carlo Tresca and William D. Haywood make typical strike speeches.

5

The Paterson Pageant focused the attention of newspaper reporters and drama reviewers on the story of the striking Paterson textile workers. Here are two reviews of the Pageant, taken from Current Opinion *and* Survey *(June 1913).*

THE PAGEANT AS A FORM OF PROPAGANDA

In the revival of one of the earliest forms of drama, the pageant, has been found one of the most "picturesquely vivid means of teaching a lesson or winning devotion to some particular cause." So says Katharine Lord, writing on "The Pageant of the Idea" in the New York *Evening Post.* Altho this form of drama, Miss Lord points out, is supposed to be nothing but a vivid record of history, the tendency in America has been toward its use for propaganda purposes. The suffrage pageant, recently given in the Metropolitan Opera, was a symbolic pantomime rather than a pageant. The pantomime was weak, says Miss Lord, "in that it is too exclusively symbolic, and has no substructure or human action to carry the idea." On the other hand, she continues, "it is suggestive of a strong, dramatic, forceful and vivid pageant, which would have the inculcation of an idea or the advancing of a cause for its distinct purpose."

A pageant of this type was produced shortly after these words were written. So successful in depicting the cause of the striking silk workers of Paterson, N. J., was the "Pageant of the Paterson Strike," presented in Madison Square Garden on the night of June 7, by one thousand of the strikers and their leaders, that the New York *Times* found in the performance a veritable menace to existing society. It says:

"Under the direction of a destructive organization opposed in spirit and antagonistic in action to all the forces which have upbuilded this republic, a series of pictures in action were shown with the design of stimulating mad passion against law and order and promulgating a gospel of discontent. The sordid and cruel incidents of an industrial strike were depicted by many of the poor strikers themselves, but with dominating and vociferous assistance from members of the I.W.W., who have at heart no more sympathy with laborers than they have with Judges and Government officers. Their aim is not to upbuild industry but to destroy the law. ˙. . . The motive was to inspire hatred, to induce violence which may lead to the tearing down of the civil state and the institution of anarchy."

On the other hand, the New York *World* found in the strike pageant something more poetic and less menacing. Speaking editorially it said: "It was not a drama, and hardly a pageant as the word is understood. It was little more than a repetition of a single scene. But need can speak without elocutionists, and unison of thought in a great mass of highly wrought-up people may swell emotion to the point of tears. Probably few witnessed the exhibition without sympathy with the sacrifices that made it possible and satisfaction in its material success."

"It would have pleased any dramatic critic because of the sincerity with which the simple plot was carried out," says the *World,* adding further: "As viewed by a spectator unbiased either from the labor or capital standpoint, their pageant was rather in the nature of a tragedy than anything else." The New York *Tribune* partially described the strike pageant in this way:

"There was a startling touch of ultra modernity —or rather of futurism—in the Paterson strike pageant in Madison Square Garden. Certainly nothing like it had been known before in the history of labor agitation. The I.W.W. has not been highly regarded hereabouts as an organization endowed with brains or imagination. Yet the very effective appeal to public interest made by the spectacle at the Garden stamps the I.W.W. leaders as agitators of large resources and original talent. Lesser geniuses might have hired a hall and exhibited moving pictures of the Paterson strike. Saturday night's pageant transported the strike itself bodily to New York. . . .

"The first episode of the pageant, entitled 'The Mills Alive—the Workers Dead,' represented 6 o'clock one February morning. A great painted drop, two hundred feet wide, stretching across the hippodrome-like stage built for the show, represented a Paterson silk mill, the windows aglow with the artificial light in which the workers began their daily tasks. Then came the operatives, men, women and children; some mere tots, other decrepit old people, 1,200 of them, trooping sadly and reluctantly to the work the 'oppression' of the bosses had made them hate. Their mutterings of discontent were soon merged in the whir of the looms as the whistles blew and the day's work was on.

"But that day's work did not last long, for the smouldering spirit of revolt suddenly burst into the flame of the strike, and the operatives rushed pellmell out of the mills, shouting and dancing with the intoxication of freedom. The whir of the mills died down, and then rose the surging tones of the 'Marseillaise' as the strikers marched defiantly up and down before the silent mill. 'The Mills Dead—the Workers Alive'—that was the name of the second episode, best described, perhaps, in the words of the scenario of the pageant— 'Mass picketing. Every worker alert. The police interfere with peaceful picketing and treat the strikers with great brutality. The workers are provoked to anger. Fights between the police and strikers ensue. Many strikers are clubbed and arrested. Shots are fired by detectives hired by the manufacturers, and Valentine Modestino, who was not a striker or a silk-mill worker, is hit by a bullet and killed as he stands on the porch of his house with one of his children in his arms.'

"Episode three represented the funeral of Modestino, a scene that, with all the accessories of sombre realism, worked the actors themselves and their thousands of sympathizers in the audience up to a high pitch of emotion, punctuated with moans and groans and sobs. A coffin, supposed to contain Modestino's body, was borne across the stage, followed by the strikers in funeral procession to the heavy tones of the 'Dead March.' As they passed, the mourners dropped red carnations and ribbons upon the coffin, until it was buried 'beneath the crimson symbol of the workers' blood.'

"The next episode depicted a mass meeting of the strikers, with all the regulation incidents of fiery I.W.W. speeches, the singing of revolutionary songs, the waving of red flags, and the pledging of the workers never to go back to work until their boss knuckled under. Then came episode five, with its May Day parade through the streets of Paterson, and its big climax of sending away the children to be cared for in other cities, that their parents might go on and fight and starve and

struggle unhampered by their little ones. With all the details of farewell embraces and tears, and finally shouts of enthusiasm breaking through the sadness of parting, the tots were handed over to the 'strike mothers' from other cities, and taken away, while Elizabeth Gurley Flynn made a consoling speech to the weeping mothers, and roused their spirits once more to the blind determination to fight on."

Judged from the artistic standards and ideals defined by Miss Lord in her article in the *Evening Post*, the "Pageant of the Paterson Strike" seems to be truly an artistic achievement, even tho it may be, as the *Times* has pointed out, a dangerous weapon for subversive propaganda. Here is what "the pageant of the idea" must accomplish, according to Miss Lord:

"The pageant of the idea, like any other, must be judged from the viewpoint of beauty and of dramatic values; and, more than that, it must be judged by its effect upon the performers as well as its effect upon the audience. Has any other art form so complicated a criterion? At first thought it is as confusing as if the palette or the brushes, or the clay, should turn upon the critic and demand consideration, demand that the effect upon themselves individually should be placed before the effect on those who look upon the result. . . .

Considered as an art form the pageant of the idea must meet the same tests as any other form of drama. Has it continuity, has it sustained interest, has it climax? Do its pictures appeal to the eye in forms of well-ordered beauty? And is that beauty instinct with meaning that justifies its being? The pageant of the idea carries the added task of developing a graphically presented symbolism. How to represent ideas as basic facts in terms of picture and action, with idealism, and yet without undue strain upon the imagination or over-subtlety of characterization, is a problem not easy of solution, but fascinating in the extreme, and, when successfully solved, most grateful to all concerned."

PAGEANT OF THE PATERSON STRIKE

. . . The average man who went to look [at the Paterson strike pageant] and the social observer familiar with labor struggles left Madison Square Garden with a vivid new sense of the reality of the silk strike and of industrial conflict in general for that matter.

The pageant, in which a thousand strikers participated, went the "human document" one better; it gave a real acquaintance with the spirit, point of view and earnestness of those who live what a "human document" tells; it conveyed what speech and pamphlet, picture and cartoon, fiction and drama fall short of telling. The simple movements of this mass of silk workers were inarticulate eloquence. And the words of "Big Bill" Haywood, or Elizabeth Flynn or Carlo Tresca or Pat Quinlan, in their efforts to give typical strike speeches, added nothing to the effect which the workers themselves spontaneously gave. Even the speakers seemed to feel this, for what they said seemed calm in substance and delivery compared with the whole-hearted simple vigor and earnestness of the thousand.

Yet it was an earnestness that had little of the vindictive. Grimness was not the dominant note in this characterization of industrial warfare— even when the workers surrounded the coffin of Modestino, the non-silk worker who was killed on the porch of his home when the detectives fired on the strikers. There was almost a note of gayety when an Italian striker sang, to the music of one of his native folk songs, some words concerning the strike, and the refrain was taken up with much gusto by the group around him. When the strike was called, and the throng rushed from the door of the mill to the front of the stage and down the center aisle, there was dash and enthusiasm.

Perhaps the thing that struck the observer most forcibly was the sort of people the strikers seemed to be and the absence of race prejudice. A large proportion were substantial, wholesome appearing German-Americans who seemed utterly to lack the hot-headed emotionalism which most people think characterizes I.W.W. adherents. One German striker, when asked how those of his nationality got along with the Italians, said, "We're all brothers and sisters"—and it certainly seemed so, for the Italian singer was reinforced by a hearty chorus of German women.

The pageant was without staginess or apparent striving for theatrical effect. In fact, the offer of theatrical producers to help in "putting it on" was declined by those who wanted the workers' own simple action to impress the crowd. There was no complicated detail. The "episodes"—all with the same scenery, a great painted canvas mill building —showed: the workers dully going to work, entering the mill, and then rushing out a little later when the strike was called; picketing and police clubbing in front of the mill; the funeral of Modestino; the strikers giving their children for temporary keeping to "strike mothers" from other cities; and a typical strike meeting addressed by I.W.W. leaders.

The hall was decorated with great signs to enlist sympathy for the strikers and stimulate the reading of I.W.W. literature. This was sold almost by the ton. Every seat was occupied at prices ranging from ten cents to $2. This alone made it a financial help to the strikers' cause, but a large collection was taken also. That the whole occasion was most inspiriting to the strikers was very evident, surely, to any one who heard the mighty volume of .sound when the audience joined in thundering out the Marseillaise.

6

On January 31, 1914, Elizabeth Gurley Flynn analyzed the Paterson strike in a speech before the New York Civic Club Forum. The manuscript of her talk is in the Labadie Collection. Born in 1890 in New Hampshire, Gurley Flynn joined the I.W.W. in 1906 at the age of sixteen and for the next ten years was a leading organizer, soapboxer, and lecturer for the organization. She was arrested in the Missoula and Spokane free speech fights in 1908 and 1909, was a strike leader in the Lawrence and Paterson textile strikes and the 1912 strike of New York City hotel workers, and was active in the defense of Joe Hill, Ettor, and Giovannitti, and the I.W.W. prisoners arrested under the wartime Espionage Law. After leaving the I.W.W. about 1916, she helped launch the Workers' Liberty Defense League, was active in the Sacco-Vanzetti Defense Committee, and, from 1927–30, was chaiman of the International Labor Defense. In 1937, she joined the Communist Party and in 1961 became chairman of the Communist Party of the U.S.A. Her autobiography, I Speak My Own Piece (New York, 1955), contains a great deal of interesting material on the early organizing and free speech activities of the I.W.W.

THE TRUTH ABOUT THE PATERSON STRIKE

By Elizabeth Gurley Flynn

Comrades and Friends:

The reason why I undertake to give this talk at this moment, one year after the Paterson strike was called, is that the flood of criticism about the strike is unabated, becoming more vicious all the time, drifting continually from the actual facts, and involving as a matter of course the policies and strike tactics of the I.W.W. To insure future success in the city of Paterson it is necessary for the past failure to be understood, and not to be clouded over by a mass of outside criticism. It is rather difficult for me to separate myself from my feelings about the Paterson strike, to speak dispassionately. I feel that many of our critics are people who stayed at home in bed while we were doing the hard work of the strike. Many of our critics are people who never went to Paterson, or who went on a holiday; who did not study the strike as a day-by-day process. Therefore it's rather hard for me to overcome my impatience with them and speak purely theoretically.

What is a labor victory? I maintain that it is a twofold thing. Workers must gain economic advantage, but they must also gain revolutionary spirit, in order to achieve a complete victory. For workers to gain a few cents more a day, a few minutes less a day, and go back to work with the same psychology, the same attitude toward society is to have achieved a temporary gain and not a lasting victory. For workers to go back with a class-conscious spirit, with an organized and a determined attitude toward society means that even if they have made no economic gain they have the possibility of gaining in the future. In other words, a labor victory must be economic and it must be revolutionizing. Otherwise it is not complete. The difference between a strike like Lawrence and a garment workers' strike in New York is that both of them gained certain material advantages, but in Lawrence there has been born such a spirit that even when 10,000 workers were out of employment, the employers did not dare reduce the wages of a single man still in the mills. When the hours were reduced by law in New Hampshire and Connecticut in the midst of the industrial panic prevailing throughout the textile industry it was impossible for those manufacturers to reduce the wages at the same time, knowing full well that to do so would create a spontaneous war. Among the garment workers in New York there has unfortunately been developed an instrument known as the protocol, whereby this spirit is completely crushed, is completely diverted from its main object against the employers. This spirit has now to assert itself against the protocol.

So a labor victory must be twofold, but if it can only be one it is better to gain in spirit than to gain economic advantage. The I.W.W. attitude in conducting a strike, one might say, is pragmatic. We have certain general principles; their application differs as the people, the industry, the time and the place indicate. It is impossible to conduct a strike among English-speaking people in the same way that you conduct a strike among foreigners, it is impossible to conduct a strike in the steel industry in the same manner you conduct a strike among the textile workers where women and children are involved in large numbers. So we have no ironclad rules. We realize that we are dealing with human beings and not with chemicals. And we realize that our fundamental principles of solidarity and class revolt must be applied in as flexible a manner as the science of pedagogy. The teacher may have as her ultimate ideal to make the child a proficient master of English, but he begins with the alphabet. So in an I.W.W. strike many times we have to begin with the alphabet, where our own ideal would be the mastery of the whole.

The Paterson strike divides itself into two periods. From the 25th of February, when the strike started, to the 7th of June, the date of the pageant in New York City, marks the first period. The second period is from the pageant to the 29th of July, when every man and woman was back at work. But the preparation for the strike had its roots in the past, the development of a four-loom system in a union mill organized by the American Federation of Labor. This four-loom irritated the workers and precipitated many small outbreaks. At any rate they sent to Mr. John Golden, the president of the United Textile Workers of America, for relief, and his reply was substantially, "The four-loom system is in progress. You have no right to rebel against it." They sought some other channel of expressing their revolt, and a year before the historic strike the Lawrence strike occurred.

It stimulated their spirit and it focused their attention on the I.W.W. But unfortunately there came into the city a little group of Socialist Labor Party people who conducted a strike ending in disaster under what they were pleased to call the auspices of the "Detroit I.W.W." That put back the entire movement for a year.

But in the beginning of last year, 1913, there was a strike in the Doherty mill against the four-loom system. There had been agitation for three months by the Eight-Hour League of the I.W.W. for the eight-hour day, and it had stimulated a general response from the disheartened workers. So we held a series of mass meetings calling for a general strike, and that strike broke on the 25th of February, 1913. It was responded to mostly by the unorganized workers. We had three elements to deal with in the Paterson strike; the broad silk weavers and the dyers, who were unorganized and who were as you might say, almost virgin material, easily brought forth and easily stimulated to aggressive activity. But on the other hand we had the ribbon weavers, the English-speaking conservative people, who had behind them craft antecedents, individual craft unions that they had worked through for thirty years. These people responded only after three weeks, and then they formed the complicating element in the strike, continually pulling back on the mass through their influence as the English-speaking and their attitude as conservatives. The police action precipitated the strike of many workers. They came out because of the brutal persecution of the strike leaders and not because they themselves were so full of the strike feeling that they could not stay in any longer. This was the calling of the strike.

The administering of the strike was in the hands of a strike committee formed of two delegates from each shop. If the strike committee had been full-force there would have been 600 members. The majority of them were not I.W.W.; were non-union strikers. The I.W.W. arranged the meetings, conducted the agitation work. But the policies of the strike were determined by that strike committee of the strikers themselves. And with the strike committee dictating all the policies of the strike, placing the speakers in a purely advisory capacity, there was a continual danger of a break between the conservative element who were in the strike committee and the mass who were being stimulated by the speakers. The socialist element in the strike committee largely represented the ribbon weavers, this conservative element making another complication in the strike. I want if possible to make that clear before leaving it, that the preparation and declaration as well as the stimulation of the strike was all done by the I.W.W., by the militant minority among the silk workers; the administering of the strike was done democratically by the silk workers themselves. We were in the position of generals on a battle-field who had to organize their forces, who had to organize their commissary department while they were in battle but who were being financed and directed by people in the capital. Our plan of battle was very often nullified by the democratic administration of the strike committee.

The industrial outlook in Paterson presented its difficulties and its advantages. No one realized them quicker than we did. There was the difficulty of 300 mills, no trustification, no company that had the balance of power upon whom we could concentrate our attack. In Lawrence we had the American Woolen Company. Once having forced the American Woolen Company to settle, it was an easy matter to gather in the threads of the other mills. No such situation existed in Paterson. 300 manufacturers, but many of them having annexes in Pennsylvania, meant that they had a means whereby they could fill a large percentage of their orders unless we were able to strike Pennsylvania simultaneously. And those mills employed women and children, wives and children of union weavers, who didn't need actually to work for a living wage, but worked simply to add to the family income. We had the difficulty that silk is not an actual necessity. In the strike among coal miners you reached the point eventually where you had the public by the throat, and through the public you were able to bring pressure on the employers. Not so in the silk industry. Silk is a luxury. We had the condition in Paterson, however, that this was the first silk year in about thirty years. In 1913 fortunately silk was stylish. Every woman wanted a silk gown, and the more flimsy it was the more she wanted it. Silk being stylish meant that the employers were mighty anxious to take advantage of this exceptional opportunity. And the fact that there were over 300 of them gave us on the other hand the advantage that some of them were very small, they had great liabilities and not very much reserve capital. Therefore we were sort of playing a game between how much they could get done in Pennsylvania bal-

Elizabeth Gurley Flynn addressing
strikers in Paterson, 1913.

Brown Brothers photo.

anced off with how great the demand for silk was and how close they were to bankruptcy. We had no means of telling that, except by guesswork. *They* could always tell when our side was weakening.

The first period of the strike meant for us persecution and propaganda, those two things. Our work was to educate and stimulate. Education is not a conversion, it is a process. One speech to a body of workers does not overcome their prejudices of a lifetime. We had prejudices on the national issues, prejudices between crafts, prejudices between competing men and women,—all these to overcome. We had the influence of the minister on the one side, and the respect that they had for government on the other side. We had to stimulate them. Stimulation, in a strike, means to make that strike and through it the class struggle their religion; to make them forget all about the fact that it's for a few cents or a few hours, but to make them feel it is a "religious duty" for them to win that strike. Those two things constituted our work, to create in them a feeling of solidarity and a feeling of class-consciousness,—a rather old term, very threadbare among certain elements in the city of New York, but meaning a great deal in a

strike. It means, to illustrate, this: the first day of the strike a photographer came on the stage to take a picture, and all over the hall there was a quiver of excitement: "No, no, no. Don't let him take a picture." "Why not?" "Why, our faces might show in the picture. The boss might see it." "Well," I said, "doesn't he know you are here? If he doesn't know now, he will know tomorrow."

From that day, when the strikers were afraid to have their pictures taken for fear they might be spotted, to the day when a thousand of them came to New York to take part in a pageant, with a friendly rivalry among themselves as to which one would get their picture in the paper, was a long process of stimulation, a long process of creating in them class spirit, class respect, class consciousness. That was the work of the agitator. Around this propaganda our critics center their volleys: the kind of propaganda we gave the strikers, the kind of stimulation and education we gave them. Many of our critics presume that the strikers were perfect and the leaders only were human; that we didn't have to deal with their imperfections as well as with our own. And the first big criticism that has been made—(of course they all criticize: for the socialists we were too radical, for the anarchists we were too conservative, for everybody else we were impossible) is that we didn't advocate violence. Strange as it may seem, this is the criticism that has come from more sources than any other.

I contend that there was no use for violence in the Paterson strike; that only where violence is necessary should violence be used. This is not a moral or legal objection but a utilitarian one. I don't say that violence should *not* be used, but where there is no call for it, there is no reason why we should resort to it. In the Paterson strike, for the first four months there wasn't a single scab in the mills. The mills were shut down as tight as a vacuum. They were like empty junk boats along the banks of the river. Now, where any violence could be used against non-existent scabs, passes my understanding. Mass action is far more up-to-date than personal or physical violence. Mass action means that the workers withdraw their labor power, and paralyze the wealth production of the city, cut off the means of life, the breath of life of the employers. Violence may mean just weakness on the part of those workers. Violence occurs in almost every American Federation of Labor strike, because the workers are desperate, because they are losing their strike. In the street car strikes, for instance, every one of them is marked with violence, because the men in the power-house are at work, the power is going through the rails and the scabs are able to run the cars. The men and women in desperation, seeing that the work is being done, turn the cars off the track, cut the wires, throw stones, and so on. But the I.W.W. believes that it is far more up to date to call the men in the power house out on strike. Then there won't be any cars running, any scabs to throw stones at or any wires that are worth cutting. Physical violence is dramatic. It's especially dramatic when you talk about it and don't resort to it. But actual violence is an old-fashioned method of conducting a strike. And mass action, paralyzing all industry, is a new-fashioned and a much more feared method of conducting a strike. That does not mean that violence shouldn't be used in self-defense. Everybody believes in violence for self-defense. Strikers don't need to be told that. But the actual fact is that in spite of our theory that the way to win a strike is to put your hands in your pocket and refuse to work, it was only in the Paterson strike of all the strikes in 1913 that a strike leader said what Haywood said: "If the police do not let up in the use of violence against the strikers the strikers are going to arm themselves and fight back." That has, however, not been advertised as extensively as was the "hands in your pockets" theory. Nor has it been advertised by either our enemies or our friends: that in the Paterson strike police persecution did drop off considerably after the open declaration of self-defense was made by the strikers. In that contingency violence is of course a necessity and one would be stupid to say that in either Michigan or West Virginia or Colorado the miners have not a right to take their guns and defend their wives and their babies and themselves.

The statement has been made by Mrs. Sanger in the "Revolutionary Almanac" that we should have stimulated the strikers to do something that would bring the militia in, and the presence of the militia would have forced a settlement of the strike. That is not necessarily true. It was not the presence of the militia that forced a settlement of the Lawrence strike. And today there is militia in Colorado, they have been there for months. There is the militia in Michigan, they have been there for a long period. There was the militia in West Virginia, but *that* did not bring a successful

termination of the strike, because coal was being produced,—and copper was being produced,—in other parts of the world, and the market was not completely cut off from its product. The presence of the militia may play a part in stimulating the strikers or in discouraging the strikers, but it does not affect the industrial outcome of the strike, and I believe to say so is to give entirely too much significance to political or military power. I don't believe that the presence of the militia is going to affect an industrial struggle to any appreciable extent, providing the workers are economically in an advantageous position.

Before I finish with this question of violence I want to ask you men and women here if you realize that there is a certain responsibility about advocating violence. It's very easy to say, "We will give up our own lives in behalf of the workers," but it's another question to ask them to give up their lives; and men and women who go out as strike agitators should only advocate violence when they are absolutely certain that it is going to do some good other than to spill the blood of the innocent workers on the streets of the cities. I know of one man in particular who wrote an article in the "Social War" about how "the blood of the workers should dye the streets in the city of Paterson in protest" but he didn't come to Paterson to let his blood dye the streets, as the baptism of violence. In fact we never saw him in the city of Paterson from the first day of the strike to the last. This responsibility rests heavily upon every man and woman who lives with and works with and loves the people for whom the strike is being conducted.

The second criticism is "Why did we go to Haledon? Why didn't we fight out the free speech fight in Paterson?" One of the humorous features of it is that if Haledon had been a Democratic city instead of a Socialist city, that criticism would probably not have been made at all. It was not that we went to Haledon, it was that we went to a Socialist city, that irritates our critics. I want to point out to you something that you possibly never realized before, and that is that we had the "right" to speak in Paterson. There was no conventional free speech fight in Paterson. A conventional free speech fight is where you are not permitted to speak at all, where you are immediately arrested and thrown into jail and not given the right to open your mouth. That is not the kind of free speech fight that existed in Paterson.

We had the right to speak in the halls of Paterson, and we would have had that right to the last day of the strike if it had not been for the position of the hallkeepers. It was not the police that closed the halls, it was the hallkeepers, and for the reason that they could not afford to lose their licenses. And a hallkeeper is usually a saloon-keeper first and a renter of halls afterwards. If there had been any hall in Paterson where a saloon was not attached we would probably have been able to secure that hall with but very little trouble. Some of the hallkeepers in fact, if I may speak from personal experience, were very glad to get rid of us, because we were not paying any rent and we were making a lot of work around their places. We had the right to speak on Lafayette Oval. We hired a piece of land on Water Street and used it during the entire time of the strike. The only time meetings were interfered with was on Sunday, and that involved not a free speech issue but a Sunday issue, the blue law of the State of New Jersey. When you are fighting a strike with 25,000 people and you are focussing your attention on trying to keep those people lined up to win that strike, it is a mighty dangerous procedure to go off at a tangent and dissipate your energies on something that is not important, even though you may have a right to do it. We had a right to speak on Sundays, but it meant to divide our energies and possibly to spend our money in ways that did not seem absolutely advisable at the time. The free speech fight that we have in Paterson is something far more intricate than just having a policeman put his hand over your mouth and tell you you can't speak. They let you talk. Oh yes. If I had invited all of you to come to Paterson and speak they would have let you talk, and the police and the detectives would have stood off at one side and listened to you. Then you have been indicted by the grand jury for what you said, arrested and put under bonds and a long legal process started to convict you for what you said.

Therefore to call in the free speech fighters of the country would have been an absurdity, since every one of them would have been permitted to say their say and afterward would have been indicted for the language they used. There was quite a different situation from Lawrence. In Lawrence the halls were never interfered with. In Paterson we had this peculiar technicality, that while you had the right to speak they said, "We hold you responsible for what you say, we arrest you for what

you say, what you meant, what you didn't say, what we thought you ought to have said, and all the rest of it." Our original reason for going to Haledon, however, was not on account of the Sunday law only, but goes deep into the psychology of a strike. Because Sunday is the day before Monday! Monday is the day that a break comes in every strike, if it is to come at all during the week. If you can bring the people safely over Monday they usually go along for the rest of the week. If on Sunday, however, you let those people stay at home, sit around the stove without any fire in it, sit down at the table where there isn't very much food, see the feet of the children with shoes getting thin, and the bodies of the children where the clothes are getting ragged, they begin to think in terms of "myself" and lose that spirit of the mass and the realization that all are suffering as they are suffering. You have got to keep them busy every day in the week, and particularly on Sunday, in order to keep that spirit from going down to zero. I believe that's one reason why ministers have sermons on Sunday, so that people don't get a chance to think how bad their conditions are the rest of the week. Anyhow, it's a very necessary thing in a strike. And so our original reason for going to Haledon—I remember we discussed it very thoroughly—was to give them novelty, to give them variety, to take them en masse out of the city of Paterson some place else, to a sort of picnic over Sunday that would stimulate them for the rest of the week. In fact that is a necessary process in every strike, to keep the people busy all the time, to keep them active, working, fighting soldiers in the ranks. And this is the agitator's work,—to plan and suggest activity, diverse, but concentrated on the strike. That's the reason why the I.W.W. has these great mass meetings, women's meetings, children's meetings; why we have mass picketing and mass funerals. And out of all this continuous mass activity we are able to create that feeling on the part of the workers, "One for all and all for one." We are able to make them realize that an injury to one is an injury to all, we are able to bring them to the point where they will have relief and not strike benefits, to the point where they will go to jail and refuse fines, and go hundreds of them together.

This method of conducting strikes has proved so successful and so remarkable with the I.W.W. that the United Mine Workers have taken it up, and in Michigan they are holding women's meetings, children's meetings, mass picketings and mass parades, such as never characterized an American Federation of Labor strike before.

This is the agitator's work, this continual activity. And we lay awake many nights trying to think of something more we could give them to do. I remember one night in Lawrence none of us slept. The strike spirit was in danger of waning for lack of action. And I remember Bill Haywood said finally, "Let's get a picket line out in Essex street. Get every striker to put a little red ribbon on and walk up and down and show that the strike is not broken." A few days later the suggestion was carried out, and when they got out of their homes and saw this great body that they were, they had renewed strength and renewed energy which carried them along for many weeks more in the strike. That was the original object in going to Haledon.

It has been asked "Why didn't we advocate short strikes, intermittent strikes? Why didn't we practice sabotage? Why didn't we do everything we didn't do? It reminds me of the story Tom Mann told. A very pretty young lady, you know how many of them there are around New York of this type, fluttering sentimentalists, came up to him with a sweet smile and said, "Can you tell me, Mr. Mann, why the women and the miners and the railroad people and all these people don't get together in England," and he said, "Can you tell me why you didn't cut your dress on the other side instead of this side?" People are not material, you can't lay them down on the table and cut them according to a pattern. You may have the best principles, but you can't always fit the people to the best principles. And for us to have gone into Paterson for the first three months of the strike and to have advocated a short strike would have said "Aha, they got theirs, didn't they? That's what happens in every strike. They are very revolutionary until the boss gives them theirs, and then they say 'Boys, go back to work.'" In other words, we would simply have duplicated what every grafting, corrupt labor leader has done in Paterson and the United States: to tell them "Go back to work, your strike is lost." And so it was necessary for us first to gain the confidence of the people and to make them feel that we were willing to fight just as long as they were; that we were not the first ones to call quits. And why should we? We were not the ones that were making the sacrifices, we were not the ones that were paying the price. It was the strikers that were doing that.

But for us to advocate a short strike, on the other hand, would have been directly contrary to our own feelings. We felt that the strike was going to be won. And it may seem to you a very foolish piece of optimism when I say that I believed the Paterson strike was going to be won up to the Sunday before the Paterson strike was lost. We didn't tell the people to stay out on a long strike knowing in our hearts that they were losing. We couldn't have talked to them if we had felt that way. But every one of us was confident they were going to win that strike. And you all were. Throughout the United States the people were. To successfully advocate an intermittent strike or to go back to work and use sabotage was impossible for the simple reason that the people wanted a long strike, and until they themselves found out by experience that a long strike was a waste of energy it was no use for us to try to dictate to them.

People learn to do by doing. We haven't a military body in a strike, a body to which you can say "Do this" and "Do that" and "Do the other thing" and they obey unfailingly. Democracy means mistakes, lots of them, mistake after mistake. But it also means experience and that there will be no repetition of those mistakes.

Now, we can talk short strike in Paterson, we can talk intermittent strike, we can talk sabotage, because the people know we are not afraid of a long strike, that we are not cowards, that we haven't sold them out, that we went through the long strike with them and that we all learned together that the long strike was not a success. In other words, by that six months they have gained the experience that will mean it never needs to be repeated.

Sabotage was objected to by the Socialists. In fact they pursued a rather intolerant attitude. It was the Socialist organizer and the Socialist secretary who called the attention of the public to the fact that Frederic Sumner Boyd made a sabotage speech. Why "intolerant"? Because nobody ever objected to anything that the Socialists said. We tried to produce among those strikers this feeling: "Listen to anything, listen to everybody. Ministers come, priests come, lawyers, doctors, politicians, Socialists, anarchists, A. F. of L., I.W.W.,— listen to them all and then take what you think is good for yourselves and reject what is bad. If you are not able to do that then no censorship over your meetings is going to do you any good." And so the strikers had a far more tolerant attitude than had the Socialists. The strikers had the attitude: "Listen to everything." The Socialists had the attitude: "You must listen to us but you must not listen to the things we don't agree with, you must not listen to sabotage because we don't agree with sabotage." We had a discussion in the executive committee about it, and one after the other of the members of the executive committee admitted that they used sabotage, why shouldn't they talk about it? It existed in the mills, they said. Therefore there was no reason why it should not be recognized on the platform. It was not the advocacy of sabotage that hurt some of our comrades but denial of their right to dictate the policy of the Paterson strike.

What the workers had to contend with in the first period of this strike was this police persecution that arrested hundreds of strikers, fined hundreds, sentenced men to three years in state's prison for talking; persecutions that meant beating and clubbing and continual opposition every minute they were on the picket line, speakers arrested, Quinlan arrested, Scott convicted and sentenced to 15 years and $1500 fine. On the other side, what? No money. If all these critics all over the United States had only put their interest in the form of finances the Paterson strike might have been another story. We were out on strike five months. We had $60,000 and 25,000 strikers. That meant $60,000 for five months, $12,000 a month for 25,000 strikers; it meant an average of less than 50 cents a month. And yet they stayed out on strike for six months. In Ireland today there is a wonderful strike going on and they are standing it beautifully. Why? Because they have had half a million dollars since the thirty-first of August (five months) given into the relief fund, and every man that goes on the picket line has food in his stomach and some kind of decent clothes on his back.

(N. B.: Unfortunately future history shows that their pounds were not an adequate substitute for solidarity, which we had and they lacked.)

I saw men go out in Paterson without shoes, in the middle of winter and with bags on their feet. I went into a family to have a picture taken of a mother with eight children who didn't have a crust of bread, didn't have a bowl of milk for the baby in the house,—but the father was out on the picket line. Others were just as bad off. Thousands of them that we never heard of at all. This was the difficulty that the workers had to contend with in

Paterson: hunger; hunger gnawing at their vitals; hunger tearing them down; and still they had the courage to fight it out for six months.

Then came the pageant. What I say about the pageant tonight may strike you as rather strange, but I consider that the pageant marked the climax in the Paterson strike and started the decline in the Paterson strike, just for the reason that the pageant promised money for the Paterson strikers and it didn't give them a cent. Yes, it was a beautiful example of realistic art, I admit that. It was splendid propaganda for the workers in New York. I don't minimize its value but am dealing with it here solely as a factor in the strike, with what happened in Paterson before, during and after the pageant. In preparation for the pageant the workers were distracted for weeks, turning to the stage of the hall, away from the field of life. They were playing pickets on the stage. They were neglecting the picketing around the mill. And the first scabs got into the Paterson mills while the workers were training for the pageant, because the best ones, the most active, the most energetic, the best, the strongest ones of them went into the pageant and they were the ones that were the best pickets around the mills. Distraction from their real work was the first danger in Paterson. And how many times we had to counteract that and work against it!

And then came jealousy. There were only a thousand that came to New York. I wonder if you ever realized that you left 24,000 disappointed people behind? The women cried and said "Why did *she* go? Why couldn't I go?" The men told about how many times they had been in jail, and asked why couldn't they go as well as somebody else. Between jealousy, unnecessary but very human, and their desire to do something, much discord was created in the ranks.

But whatever credit is due for such a gigantic undertaking comes to the New York silk workers, not the dilettante element who figured so prominently, but who would have abandoned it at the last moment had not the silk workers advanced $600 to pull it through.

And then comes the grand finale—no money. Nothing. This thing that had been heralded as the salvation of the strike, this thing that was going to bring thousands of dollars to the strike,—$150 came to Paterson, and all kinds of explanations. I don't mean to say that I blame the people who ran the pageant. I know they were amateurs and they gave their time and their energy and their money. They did the best they could and I appreciate their effort. But that doesn't minimize the result that came in Paterson. It did not in any way placate the workers of Paterson, to tell them that people in New York had made sacrifices, in view of the long time that *they* had been making sacrifices. And so with the pageant as a climax, with the papers clamoring that tens of thousands of dollars had been made, and with the committee explaining what was very simple, that nothing *could* have been made with one performance on such a gigantic scale, there came trouble, dissatisfaction, in the Paterson strike.

Bread was the need of the hour, and bread was not forthcoming even from the most beautiful and realistic example of art that has been put on the stage in the last half century.

What was the employers' status during all this time? We saw signs of weakness every day. There was a minister's committee appointed to settle the strike. There was a businessmen's committee appointed to settle the strike. The governor's intervention, the President's intervention was sought by the manufacturers. Every element was brought to bear to settle the strike. Even the American Federation of Labor; nobody believes that they came in there uninvited and no one can believe that the armory was given to them for a meeting place unless for a purpose. What was this purpose but to settle the strike? The newspapers were clamoring that the strike could and must be settled. And we looked upon all this,—the newspapers that were owned by the mill owners, the ministers and the business men who were stimulated by the mill owners,—we looked upon all this as a

Paterson strikers marching up Fifth Ave. to Madison Square Garden, June 5, 1913.

United Press International, Inc., photo.

sign that the manufacturers were weakening. Even the socialists admitted it. In the New York *Call* of July 9 we read this: "The workers of Paterson *should* stay with them another round or two after a confession of this kind. What the press had to say about the strike looks very much like a confession of defeat." This was on the 9th of July. Every sign of weakness on the part of the manufacturers was evident.

But there came one of the most peculiar phenomena that I have ever seen in a strike; that the bosses weakened simultaneously with the workers. Both elements weakened together. The workers did not have a chance to see the weaknesses of the employers as clearly, possibly, as we who had witnessed it before, did, which gave us our abiding faith in the workers' chances of success, but the employers had every chance to see the workers weaken. The employers have a full view of your army. You have no view of their army and can only guess at their condition. So a tentative proposition came from the employers of a shop-by-shop settlement. This was the trying-out of the bait, the bait that should have been refused by the strikers without qualification. Absolute surrender, all or nothing, was the necessary slogan. By this we did not mean that 100 per cent of the manufacturers must settle, or that 99 per cent of the workers must stay out till 1 per cent won everything. The I.W.W. advice to the strikers was —an overwhelming majority of the strikers must receive the concession before a strike is won. This was clearly understood in Paterson, though misrepresented there and elsewhere. Instead, the committee swallowed the bait and said, "We will take a vote on the shop-by-shop proposition, a vote of the committee." The minute they did that, they admitted their own weakness. And the employers immediately reacted to a position of strength. There was no referendum vote proposed by this committee, they were willing to take their own vote to see what they themselves thought of it, and to settle the strike on their own decision alone.

Then it was that the I.W.W. speakers and Executive Committee had to inject themselves in contradistinction to the strike committee. And the odd part of it was that the conservatives on the committee utilized our own position against us. We had always said, "The silk workers must gain their own strike." And so they said, "We are the silk workers. You are simply outside agitators. You can't talk to this strike committee even." I re-

member one day the door was virtually slammed in my face, until the Italian and Jewish workers made such an uproar, threatening to throw the others out of a three-story building window, that the floor was granted. It was only when we threatened to go to the masses and to get this referendum vote in spite of them that they took the referendum vote. But all this came out in the local press and it all showed that the committee was conservative and the I.W.W. was radical, more correctly the I.W.W. and the masses were radical. And so this vote was taken by the strikers. It resulted in a defeat of the entire proposition. 5,000 dyers in one meeting voted it down unanimously. They said, "We never said we would settle shop by shop. We are going to stick it out together until we win together or until we lose together." But the very fact that they had been willing to discuss it made the manufacturers assume an aggressive position. And then they said, "We never said we would settle shop-by-shop. We never offered you any such proposition. We won't take you back now unless you come under the old conditions."

One of the peculiar things about this whole situation was the attitude of the socialists on that committee. I want to make myself clearly understood. I don't hold the socialist party officially responsible, only insofar as they have not repudiated these particular individuals. The socialist element in the committee represented the ribbon weavers, the most conservative, the ones who were in favor of the shop-by-shop settlement. They were led by a man named Magnet, conservative, Irish, Catholic, Socialist. His desire was to wipe the strike off the slate in order to leave the stage free for a political campaign. He had aspirations to be the mayoralty candidate, which did not however come to fruition. This man and the element that were behind him, the socialist element, were willing to sacrifice, to betray a strike in order to make an argument, the argument given out in the "Weekly Issue" a few days before election: "Industrial action has failed. Now try political action." It was very much like the man who made a prophecy that he was going to die on a certain date, and then he committed suicide. He died, all right. Industrial action failed, all right. But they forgot to say that they contributed more than any other element in the strike committee to the failure of the strike. They were the conservatives, they were the ones who wanted to get rid of the strike as quickly as possible. And through these ribbon weavers the break came.

On the 18th of July the ribbon weavers notified the strike committee, "We have drawn out of your committee. We are going to settle our strike to suit ourselves. We are going to settle it shop by shop. That's the way they have settled it in New York at Smith and Kauffmann." But a visit had been made by interested parties to the Smith and Kauffmann boys prior to their settlement, at which they were informed that the Paterson strike was practically lost: "These outside agitators don't know anything about it, because they are fooled in this matter. You had better go back to work." When they went back to work on the nine-hour day and the shop-by-shop settlement, then it was used by the same people who had told them that, as an argument to settle in the same way in Paterson. And the ribbon weavers stayed out till the very last. Oh yes. They have all the glory throughout the United States of being the last ones to return to work, but the fact is that they were the first ones that broke the strike, because they broke the solidarity, they precipitated a position that was virtually a stampede. The strike committee decided, "Well, with the ribbon weavers drawing out, what are we going to do? We might as well accept;" and the shop-by-shop proposition was put through by the strike committee without a referendum vote, stampeded by the action of the English-speaking, conservative ribbon weavers.

So that was the tragedy of the Paterson strike, the tragedy of a stampede, the tragedy of an army, a solid phalanx being cut up into 300 pieces, each shop-piece trying to settle as best for themselves. It was absolutely in violation of the I.W.W. principles and the I.W.W. advice to the strikers. No strike should ever be settled without a referendum vote, and no shop settlement should ever have been suggested in the city of Paterson, because that was the very thing that had broken the strike the year before. So this stampede came, and the weaker ones went back to work and the stronger ones were left outside, to be made the target of the enemy, blacklisted for weeks and weeks after the strike was over, many of them on the blacklist yet. It produced discord among the officers in the strike. I remember one day at Haledon, the chairman said to Tresca and myself, "If you are going to talk about the eight-hour day and about a general strike, then you had better not talk at all." And we had to go out and ask the people, "Are

we expected here today and can we say what we think, or have we got to say what the strike committee has decided?" We were unanimously welcomed. But it was too late. Just as soon as the people saw that there was a break between the agitators and the strike committee, that the ribbon weavers wanted this and others wanted that, the stampede had started and no human being could have held it back.

It was the stampede of hungry people, people who could no longer think clearly. The bosses made beautiful promises to the ribbon weavers and to everybody else, but practically every promise made before the settlement of the Paterson strike was violated, and the better conditions have only been won through the organized strikes since the big strike. Not one promise that was made by the employers previous to breakup on account of the shop-by-shop settlement was ever lived up to. Other places were stranded. New York, Hoboken, College Point were left stranded by this action. And on the 28th of July everybody was back at work, back to work in spite of the fact that the general conviction had been that we were on the eve of victory. I believe that if the strikers had been able to hold out a little longer by any means, by money if possible, which was refused to us, we could have won the Paterson strike. We could have won it because the bosses had lost their spring orders, they had lost their summer orders, they had lost their fall orders and they were in danger of losing their winter orders, one year's work; and the mills in Pennsylvania, while they could give the bosses endurance for a period, could not fill all the orders and could not keep up their business for the year round.

I say we were refused money. I wish to tell you that is the absolute truth. The New York *Call* was approached by fellow-worker Haywood, when we were desperate for money, when the kitchens were closed and the people were going out on the picket line on bread and water, and asked to publish a full page advertisement begging for money, pleading for money. They refused to accept the advertisement. They said, "We can't take your money." "Well, can you *give* us the space?" "Oh, no, we can't afford to give you the space. We couldn't take money from strikers, but we couldn't give space either." And so in the end there was no appeal, either paid for or not, but a little bit of a piece that did not amount to a candle of light, lost in the space of the newspaper. However, on the

26th of July, while the ribbon weavers and some of the broad silk weavers were still out, the *Call* had published a criticism by Mr. Jacob Panken of the Paterson strike. Lots of space for criticism, but no space to ask bread for hungry men and women. And this was true not only of the *Call*, but of the other socialist papers. So, between these two forces, we were helpless. And then we had to meet our critics. First came the socialist critic who said, "But the I.W.W. didn't do enough for the socialist party. Look at all the money we gave you. And you don't say anything about it." Dr. Korshet had a long article in the New York *Call.* Anyone may read it who likes to refresh his memory. Just this: "We gave you money and you didn't thank us." Well, I would like to know why we *should* thank them. Aren't the socialists supposed to be workingmen, members of the working class, just the same as we are? And if they do something for their own class we have got to thank them the next ten years for it. They are like the charity organization that gives the poor working woman a little charity and then expects her to write recommendations to the end of the end of the earth. We felt that there was no need to thank the socialist party for what they had done, because they had only done their duty and they had done very little in comparison with what they have done in A. F. of L. strikes, in the McNamara cases.

They make the criticism that we didn't give them any credit. How about the 5,000 votes that the I.W.W. membership gave the party in Paterson for a candidate who was a member of the A. F. of L. and who did not get a single vote from his own union? All his votes came from the I.W.W. If they wanted to invest money, the money that they invested for each vote in Paterson was well spent, on a purely business basis.

A sample of the foreign language pamphlets issued at various times by the I.W.W.

And then Mr. Panken's criticism was that we should have settled the strike shop by shop. A humorous criticism, a cynical, sarcastic criticism, when you consider that's exactly what was done, and that's exactly why we lost the Paterson strike. But a few days before the strike was over, before this collapse came, we received a little piece of paper through the delegates to the New York-Paterson Relief Committee, and on this little piece of paper it said, "The following gentlemen are willing to bring about a settlement of the Paterson strike if the strike committee will send them a letter requesting them to do it." And on this piece of paper were the names of Jacob Panken, Meyer London, Abe Cahan, Charles Edward Russell, and two others. In other words, a few days before the Paterson strike collapsed there were a committee of six socialists in New York who had such faith that the strike was going to be won, including the man who criticized us for not settling shop by shop, that they were willing to settle it for us on this condition that they incidentally take all the glory of the settlement if we asked them to do it. We didn't ask them. We said, "If there is anybody that thinks he can settle the Paterson strike and he calls himself a socialist or a friend of labor he will do it without being asked to do it in an official manner." They did not do it. They criticized.

Our position to the strikers was "If the I.W.W. conception had been followed out you would have won all together, or you would have lost all together, but you would still have had your army a continuing whole." Every general knows it is far better for an army to retreat en masse than it is to scatter and be shot to pieces. And so it is better to lose all together than to have some win at the expense of the rest, because losing all together you have the chance within a few months of recovering and going back to the battle again, your army still centralized, and winning in the second attempt.

What lessons has the Paterson strike given to the I.W.W. and to the strikers? One of the lessons it has given to me is that when the I.W.W. assumes the responsibility of a strike the I.W.W. should control the strike absolutely through a union strike committee; that there should be no outside interference, no outside non-union domination accepted or permitted, no Magnet permitted to pose as "representing the non-union element." That direct action and solidarity are the only keys to a worker's success or the workers'

success. That the spirit throughout this long weary propaganda has remained unbroken, and I will give you just three brief examples.

The 5,000 votes for the socialist party was because the workers had this in mind: "Maybe we will strike again, and the next time we strike we want all this political machinery on our side." They would not have done that if their spirit had been crushed and they had no hope for another strike. The free speech fight for Emma Goldman that was recently successfully waged in Paterson was made because the strikers have an unbroken spirit still. Many of them did not know Emma Goldman. I say this with no disrespect to her. Many of them are foreigners and did not know anything about her speeches and lectures. But they knew somebody wanted to speak there and their constitutional enemies, the police, were trying to prevent it, and so they turned out en masse and free speech was maintained in Paterson. And just around Christmas time there was an agitation for a strike, and then instead of stimulation we had to give them a sort of sedative, to keep them quiet. Why, they were so anxious to go out on strike that they had great mass meetings: "now is the time, eight-hour day, nine-hour day, anything at all; but—we want to strike again!" Every time I go to Paterson some people get around and say, "Say, Miss Flynn, when is there going to be another strike?" They have that certain feeling that the strike has been postponed, but they are going to take it up again and fight it out again. That spirit is the result of the I.W.W. agitation in Paterson.

And so, I feel that we have been vindicated in spite of our defeat. We have won further toleration for the workers. We have given them a class feeling, a trust in themselves and a distrust for everybody else. They are not giving any more faith to the ministers, even though we didn't carry any "No God, no master" banners floating through the streets of Paterson. You know, you may put a thing on a banner and it makes no impression at all; but you let a minister show himself up, let all the ministers show themselves against the workers and that makes more impression than all the "No God, no master" banners from Maine to California. That is the difference between education and sensationalism.

And they have no more use for the state. To them the statue of liberty is personified by the policeman and his club.

"Yaas," said the farmer reflectively, "all the I.W.W. fellers I've met seemed to be pretty decent lads, but them 'alleged I.W.W.'s' must be holy frights."

I.W.W. Songbook, fifteenth edition
(1919), p. 19.

Chapter 8

Organizing the Harvest Stiffs

In early August 1913, some 2800 men, women and children were camped on an unshaded hill near Marysville, California, on the hop ranch of E. B. Durst, the largest single employer of migratory labor in the state. They came in answer to Durst's newspaper advertisements for 2700 hop pickers. Many walked from nearby towns and cities. They arrived to find that Durst had deliberately advertised for twice as many pickers as he needed and that living conditions were totally inadequate even for half their number. Some of the people slept on piles of straw rented from Durst at seventy-five cents a week. Others slept in the fields. Nine outdoor toilets provided the only sanitary facilities for the entire group. Irrigation ditches became garbage disposals and the stench in the camps was nauseating. Dysentery spread.

The resulting episode, known as the Wheatland Hop Riot, has been called, "one of the most significant incidents in the long history of labor troubles in California."[1] It was the first such outburst of migratory farm labor in this century which resulted in national publicity. It affected the future of the I.W.W. in California profoundly and aroused some interest in the living and working conditions of agricultural workers in that state.

In addition to the intolerable living conditions, Durst offered ninety cents a hundred weight to the crowd of unskilled laborers he had attracted to the ranch. The going rate that season was $1.00. He held back a ten-cent "bonus" to be paid if the worker stayed through the harvest. He also required "extra clean" picking which further reduced the workers' earnings.

The men, women, and children started work at four A.M. and often picked crops in 105 degree heat during the day. They went without drinking water since no water was brought into the fields. Durst's cousin sold lunch wagon lemonade, which could be bought for five cents a glass. Because the stores in surrounding towns were forbidden to send delivery trucks into the camp, the hop pickers were forced to buy their food and supplies at a concession store on the ranch.

Only about one hundred of the workers had at any time been I.W.W. members. About thirty of them immediately formed an I.W.W. local on the ranch to protest the living and working conditions. "It is suggestive," the official investigation report later stated, "that these thirty men through a spasmodic action, and with the aid of deplorable camp conditions, dominated a heterogeneous mass of 2,800 unskilled laborers in three days."[2]

A mass meeting of the workers held three days after their arrival at the ranch, chose a committee to demand drinking water in the fields twice a day, separate toilets for men and women, better sanitary conditions, and an increase in piece-rate wages. Two of the committee, Blackie Ford and Herman Suhr, had been in the I.W.W. free speech campaigns in Fresno and San Diego. Ranchowner Durst argued with the committee members and slapped Ford across the face with his gloves.

The following day, August 3, the Wobblies

called a mass meeting on a public spot they had rented for the occasion. Blackie Ford took a sick baby from its mother's arms, and holding it before the crowd of some 2000 workers, he said, "It's for the kids that we are doing this."[3] The meeting ended with the singing of Joe Hill's parody, "Mr. Block." While the singing was going on, two carloads of deputy sheriffs drove up with the district attorney from Marysville to arrest Ford. One of the deputies fired a shot over the heads of the crowd to "sober the mob."[4] As he fired, fighting broke out. The district attorney, a deputy sheriff, and two workers were killed. Many were injured, and, as the deputies left, another posse of armed citizens hurried to the ranch.

In the following panic and hysteria, the roads around the ranch were jammed with fleeing workers. Governor Hiram Johnson dispatched five companies of the National Guard to Wheatland "to overawe any labor demonstration and protect private property."[5] Burns detectives rounded up hundreds of suspected I.W.W. members throughout California and neighboring states. Some of them were severely beaten and tortured and kept incommunicado for weeks. One I.W.W. prisoner committed suicide in prison and another went insane from police brutality. A Burns detective was later convicted of assault on an I.W.W. prisoner, fined $1000, and jailed for a year.

At a trial beginning eight months later, Ford and Suhr were charged with leading the strike which led to the shooting and convicted of second-degree murder. They were sentenced to life imprisonment and jailed for over ten years.

In his testimony before the Industrial Relations Commission in San Francisco in 1914, Austin Lewis, the Socialist lawyer who defended Ford and Suhr at the Marysville trial, drew the parallel between conditions in agriculture and those in factory work. He called the Wheatland Riot "a purely spontaneous uprising . . . a psychological protest against factory conditions of hop picking . . . and the emotional result of the nervous impact of exceedingly irritating and intolerable conditions under which those people worked at the time."[6] I.W.W. agitation about the Wheatland episode led to an investigation by the newly created Commission on Immigration and Housing in California which made subsequent annual reports on the living and working conditions of migrants. Professor Carleton H. Parker was appointed to make a report on the hop riot and investigate abuses in labor camps.

After Wheatland, the California press denounced both the I.W.W. and the exploiters of farm labor. The conservative *Sacramento Bee* on February 9, 1914, editorialized:

The I.W.W. must be suppressed. It is a criminal organization, dedicated to riot, to sabotage, to destruction of property, and to hell in general. But it will not be suppressed until first are throttled those conditions on which it feeds. Great employers like Durst who shriek the loudest against the I.W.W. are the very ones whose absolute disregard of the rights of others, and whose oppressions and inhumanities are more potent crusaders to swell the ranks of the I.W.W. than its most violent propagandists.[7]

In the year following Wheatland, forty new I.W.W. locals started in California. Five national organizers and over one hundred volunteer soapboxers agitated throughout the state. The I.W.W. blanketed California with stickers and circulars urging a boycott of the hop fields until Ford and Suhr were released, and living and working conditions improved. Members were urged to organize on the job and slow down if their demands were not met. Employers charged that the I.W.W. members burned haystacks, drove copper spikes into fruit trees, and practiced other acts of malicious sabotage during this campaign. Although much of the I.W.W. propaganda included a hunched black cat showing its claws, an emblem of sabotage, the stickers condemned such practices. I.W.W. opponents claimed that the propaganda ironically advocated the very acts advised against.

"It is no use appealing to the master's sense of justice for he has not got any, the only thing left is action on the pocketbook . . ."[8] read an I.W.W. statement of this time. By the end of 1914, the I.W.W. Hop Pickers' Defense Committee claimed that action on the pocketbook had left the hop crop 24,000 bales short. Three years later, the I.W.W. estimated that their boycott of the hop fields had cost California farmers $10,000,000 a year, while the farmers themselves charged that their total losses were between $15–20,000,000 since 1914.[9]

Ranch owners like Durst financed their own private police force of gunmen and detectives to eliminate the I.W.W. It cost them an estimated average of $10,000 each a year.[10] In addition, a Farmers' Protective League, organized to see that strikes and riots would never threaten the har-

I.W.W. Songbook, Third Edition.

vesting of a ripened crop, turned its attention to lobbying with the federal government for federal prosecution of the I.W.W.

In October 1915, the governors of California, Oregon, Washington, and Utah urged President Wilson to investigate the I.W.W. immediately. They stated:

> California, Oregon, Washington, and Utah are experiencing abnormal disorder and incendiarism. These experiences are coincident with threats made by I.W.W. leaders in their talks and publications, and are in harmony with doctrines preached in their publications. Local or state apprehension of ring leaders is impracticable, as their field of activity is interstate. . . . Through federal machinery covering the whole territory involved, the national government might get at the bottom of this movement. . . . Exigencies of the situation demand absolute secrecy.[11]

A Department of Justice agent was sent from Washington to look into these charges, but found that the I.W.W. numbered some four thousand members in California and Washington, and that it was composed "chiefly of panhandlers, without homes, mostly foreigners, the discontented and unemployed, who are not anxious to work."[12] The Farmers Protective League found this a disappointing report.

I.W.W. activity was moving out of the cities onto the farms. Hundreds of thousands of industrial workers left jobless by the 1914 financial depression hopped freights in hope of finding work in the harvest fields. Professor Paul S. Taylor described the situation this way:

> In the second decade of the twentieth century, American radicalism in the form of the I.W.W. spread rapidly among these men. It became unsafe to ride the freights unless one carried a "red card." Farmers learned the meaning of strikes for better wages and working conditions, and responded with vigilante mobs, driving agitators and workers from towns at points of guns. Class warfare broke out in the most "American" sections of rural America.[13]

Based on over a decade of experience, there developed within the I.W.W. a growing demand to build an organization with a more permanent membership. More than 300,000 Wobbly membership cards had been issued since 1905—but workers often passed through the I.W.W. and did not stay. Usually, I.W.W. branches were "mixed locals" of members from many industries which at times were dominated by the transient workers and at times by the homeguards, the more permanently employed.

In September 1914 the national I.W.W. convention passed a resolution endorsing a conference of representatives from I.W.W. agricultural workers' locals. This meeting, held in Kansas City in April 1915, organized the Agricultural Workers' Organization, with headquarters in Kansas City. The A.W.O. was called No. 400 in reference to Mrs. Astor's ballroom, to indicate that, "the new union was being formed by the elite of the working class."[14]

The A.W.O. was set up initially to improve working conditions in the 1915 harvest season. But it proved so effective that it continued as a branch of the I.W.W. for several years. It was the first union to organize and negotiate successfully higher wage scales for harvest workers. It was one of the most dramatic union efforts ever to appear on the American scene.

Practical policies met the problems of organizing the wheat industry, in which thousands of farmers over a vast region hired seasonal workers. The most novel innovation was that of the "job delegate system," a mobile set of organizers who worked on the jobs, starting at the Mexican border in the early spring and winding up in the late fall in the Canadian provinces. Each local could nominate job delegates who reported regularly to the A.W.O. general secretary. It was the job delegate system of volunteer organizers who "carried the entire office in their hip pocket"—application cards, dues books, stamps, and Wobbly literature —that enabled the organization to spread so rapidly in the wheat fields. One of the job delegates described the opening drive for A.W.O. members in 1915:

With pockets lined with supplies and literature we left Kansas City on every available freight train, some going into the fruit belts of Missouri and Arkansas, while others spread themselves over the states of Kansas and Oklahoma, and everywhere they went, with every slave they met on the job, in the jungles, or on freight trains, they talked I.W.W., distributed their literature, and pointed out the advantage of being organized into a real labor union. Day in and day out the topic of conversation was the I.W.W. and the new Agricultural Union No. 400. . . . Small town marshals became a little more respectful in their bearing toward any group who carried the little red card, and the bullying and bo-ditching shack had a wonderful change of heart after coming in contact with No. 400 boys once or twice. As for the hijacks and the bootleggers, one or two examples of "direct action" from an organized bunch of harvest workers served to show them that the good old days, at least for them, were now over, and that there was a vast difference between a helpless and unorganized harvest stiff and an organized harvest worker. But best of all, the farmer, after one or two salutary examples of solidarity, invariably gave in to the modest request of the organized workers, with the result that the wages were raised, grub was improved, and hours shortened.[15]

The Kansas City Conference decided to abandon street agitation and soapboxing in harvest towns in favor of conserving energy for on-the-job organizing. An agriculture workers' handbook stated this new policy:

Waiting in town or in the "jungles" while holding out for higher wages is a poor policy. This tends to help the organized men "on the 'bum'" while the unorganized do nothing to improve conditions. The place to take action is *on the job* and it is the only way to get results. Other tactics that are harmful are soapboxing by ignorant or inexperienced members . . . and throwing unorganized workers off freight trains. . . . We are out for 100 percent organization, but we must keep the issues of the big struggle constantly in mind and use judgment and foresight. Tactics that have proved successful are: *take out organizers' credentials* . . . line up as many of the crew as possible and then make demands if conditions are not what they should be. The slowing-down process will be found of great help where employers are obstinate.[16]

"Get on the Job!" and "Never Mind the Empty Street-corners: The Means of Life Are Not Made

Mr. Block

He Goes Harvesting

Industrial Worker, August 21, 1913.

There!" became the new slogans of the campaign.

The A.W.O. pressed for a uniform wage increase of fifty cents to raise wages to a daily rate of $3.50 in the 1915 wheat harvest. In many areas it was successful. It won its demands through sporadic strikes on the job which became a characteristic form of I.W.W. direct action. Members were instructed to bring other Wobbly crews onto the struck job to strike again if necessary, or effect a slow-down until their wage demands were granted.

Membership expanded to a peak of 70,000 in 1917 as A.W.O. organizers followed the harvest crews into lumber and mining areas to sign up off-season workers. Wherever harvest stiffs met in the Midwest, they sang Wobbly songs. Whenever farm workers had a grievance, the A.W.O. job delegates would be their spokesmen. In some areas cooperative train crews honored the little red membership card as a train ticket and allowed I.W.W. members to move freely from one harvest town to another. The Wobbly card often protected its holder from hijackers and hold-up men who were afraid of molesting an I.W.W. member for fear of incurring the wrath of the organization. Thus the A.W.O. became entrenched in the wheat fields and was regarded as the I.W.W. in the Midwest.

Using the A.W.O. as a model, the 1916 I.W.W. convention set up other industrial branches which absorbed some of the nonagricultural members of the A.W.O. In March 1917, No. 400 was rechartered as Agricultural Workers' Industrial Union No. 110, and restricted solely to organizing agricultural workers. Its members became known as the "one-ten cats." Despite its depleted membership, the A.W.O. remained the financial backbone of the I.W.W. until about 1925.

From the start of the A.W.O., I.W.W. attempts to recruit farm labor met with organized hostility in some rural communities. Vigilante committees, known as "pick-handle brigades," sprang up to take care of the "Wobbly menace." In one small community in South Dakota, for example, the newspaper advised "every member of the vigilante committee over twenty-one to supply himself with a reliable firearm and have it where he can secure it at a moment's notice."[17] As the nation entered the war, newspaper stories fanned the hysteria of local village and farm groups by repeated exposés of "I.W.W. plots" of widespread sabotage and destruction of property.

In March 1918, Thorstein Veblen drafted a memorandum to the U.S. Food Administration based on an investigation he had made of the availability of farm-labor to harvest wartime crops. He wrote:

These members of the I.W.W., together with many of the workmen who are not formally identified with that organization, set up the following schedule of terms on which they will do full work through the coming harvest season: (a) freedom from illegal restraint; (b) proper board and lodgings; (c) a ten-hour day; (d) a standard wage of $4.00 for the harvest season; and (e) tentatively, free transportation in answering any call from a considerable distance.

These are the terms insisted on as a standard requirement; and if these terms are met, the men propose a readiness to give the best work of which they are capable, without reservation. On the other hand, if these terms are not met in any essential particular, these men will not refuse to work, but quite unmistakably, they are resolved in that case to fall short of full and efficient work by at least as much as they fall short of getting these terms on which they have agreed among themselves as good and sufficient. It should be added that there is no proposed intention among these men to resort to violence of any kind in case these standard requirements are not complied with. Here, as elsewhere, the proposed and officially sanctioned tactics of the I.W.W. are exclusively the tactics of nonresistance, which does not prevent occasional or sporadic recourse to violence by members of the I.W.W. although the policy of nonresistance appears, on the whole, to be lived up to with a fair degree of consistency. The tactics habitually in use are what may be called a nonresistant sabotage, or in their own phrasing, "deliberate withdrawal of efficiency," in other words, slacking and malingering. . . .

They will, it is believed, do good and efficient work on the terms which they have agreed to among themselves. They are, it is also believed, deliberately hindered from moving about and finding work on the terms on which they seek it. The obstruction to their movement and negotiations for work comes from the commercial clubs of the country towns and the state and municipal authorities who are politically affiliated with the commercial clubs. On the whole, there appears to be virtually no antagonism between employing farmers and these members of the I.W.W., and there is a well-founded belief that what antagonism comes in evidence is chiefly of a fictitious character, being in good part due to mischief-making agitation from outside.[18]

The fear that I.W.W. strikes in mining and lumber during the war years would spread to agriculture, led to stepped-up legal and extra-legal suppression. The federal government banned strikes in those industries which were "vital to national defense"—including mining, lumber, and agriculture. In July 1917, sixty I.W.W. organizers were arrested in Ellensburg, Washington, and charged with "interfering with crop harvesting and logging in violation of Federal statutes."[19] In the same month, army officers in South Dakota announced that they knew of a state-wide plot to destroy South Dakota's crops and that Wobbly organizers were ready to set fire to the fields when a certain signal was given. Vigilante violence and a wave of arrests greeted this announcement. Headlines in the *Morning Republican* in Mitchell, South Dakota, read: "Shotguns Will Greet Any Attempts of I Won't Workers To Destroy Ripened Grain Crops."[20] The newspaper story stated, "Any of them who attempt to carry out the threat of wholesale crop destruction will be roughly handled and will be lucky if they escape with their lives."[21]

In many towns, I.W.W. members were arrested for loitering, for riding trains without having tickets, and on various other charges. Troops and vigilante groups raided I.W.W. headquarters, burned records, and smashed and destroyed furniture and other property.

In addition to mass arrests and vigilante activity, the local authorities attempted to suppress I.W.W. activities by recruiting less militant types of labor for farm work. Women and young boys were enlisted to work in the harvest fields throughout 1917 in anticipation of a labor shortage. Mexicans and Indians from the reservations were used in California. Chambers of commerce, working with the employment service set up by the U. S. Department of Labor, recruited and screened farm laborers. "County Councils for Defense," organized by county agricultural agents and farmers to handle harvest workers, were started during 1917. "Work or fight" orders were sent to men in the fields who, for one reason or another, balked at living or working conditions.

In California, where the I.W.W. had conducted a successful strike among vineyard workers near Fresno in early 1917, a roundup of I.W.W. members and leaders was launched in the fall of that year. Based on a story in the Fresno morning paper describing charges of I.W.W. sabotage on local growers, the I.W.W. hall in Fresno was raided. Over one hundred men were seized, and nineteen were arrested. Later raids and arrests were carried out in Stockton, Hanford, and elsewhere in the state. The round-up continued throughout the rest of the year. Farmers having labor trouble were directed to get help at a U. S. Department of Justice office in Fresno.

Finally, the Agricultural Workers' Industrial Union was completely disorganized when the federal government cracked down on the I.W.W. in the fall of 1917 and arrested more than one hundred Wobblies around the country on charges of violating the federal Espionage Act.

Legal suppression of the I.W.W. continued during the postwar period. Throughout the country, I.W.W. organizers and members were arrested and jailed under the terms of state syndicalism laws passed as postwar emergency measures. Postwar demobilization and unemployment created a surplus labor supply which further weakened the union organization.

However, meeting in September 1920, the "one-ten cats" resolved to launch another organizing drive in the Midwest wheat fields. They had spotty success. In Colby, Kansas, for example, Wobbly harvesters controlled the town's labor supply for a week when they collectively refused to work at the going wage rates. In some areas the harvest drive was quite successful through the mid-twenties. Elsewhere, however, mechanized harvesters were replacing mobile harvest hands. The combine, developed as a labor-saving device during the war, cut and threshed grain in a single operation. Five men did the work of 320. As Paul Taylor wrote:

As the use of the combine spread, migratory labor declined, and with it labor radicalism and the social problems caused by a great male migration disappeared from the harvest fields. When radicalism came again to the Middle West it was the farmers who agitated and organized, not the laborers.[22]

Mr. Block

He goes to the Dakota harvest

Industrial Worker, February 13, 1913.

1

These verses were printed in the third edition of the I.W.W. songbook. Little is known about Walquist except that he was the author of a popular I.W.W. pamphlet, The Eight Hour Work Day: What It Will Mean and How to Get It.

I WENT TO THE COUNTRY
By August Walquist

(Tune: "My Wife Went to the Country")

It was on a sunny morning in the middle of July,
I left in a side-car Pullman that dear old town
  called Chi.
I got the harvest fever, I was going to make a stake,
But when I worked hard for a week I found out my
  mistake.

Chorus

I went to the country, Oh! why? Oh! why?
I thought it best, you know; the result nearly
  makes me cry,
For sixteen hours daily, Oh! say; Oh! say;
John Farmer worked me very hard, so I'm going
  away.

When I left that old farmer he cussed me black
  and blue;
He says, "You gol durned hoboes, there's nothing
  will suit you,"
So back to town I'm going, and there I'm going to
  stay.
You won't catch me out on a farm; no more you'll
  hear me say:

Chorus

I went to the country, Oh! why? Oh! why?
I thought it best you know; the result nearly makes
  me cry.
For sixteen hours daily, Oh! say; Oh! say;
John Farmer worked me very hard; so I am going
  away.

Now the Industrial Workers, they have put me
  wise;
They tell me I won't need a boss if the slaves will
  organize.
They're all a bunch of fighters; they'll show you
  where they're right.
So workingmen, come join their ranks and help
  them win this fight.

Chorus

Then we'll own the country, Hurrah! Hurrah!
We'll set the working millions free from slavery;
We'll get all that we produce, you bet! you bet!
So, workingmen, come organize along with the
  rest!

2

These verses by Ed Jorda appeared in the Industrial Worker *(October 3, 1912).*

CLASS COMMUNION
By Ed Jorda

(Tune: "Yankee Doodle")

A farmer boy once worked in town,
  He thought to make a fortune;
The bosses cut his wages down
  By capitalist extortion.

Chorus

The I.W.W. waked him up
  By preaching class communion,
Said fire the bosses all corrupt
  By forming *One Big Union.*

He thought to get another job
  And so regain his losses,
But found it was the same old rob
  And by the same old bosses.

He then returned unto the farm,
  Perhaps you think it funny;
The farmer boy did all the work—
  The boss got all the money.

This farmer boy then came to see
  The need of class communion.
Went like a man and paid the fee
  And joined the *One Big Union.*

He joined in with a mighty throng;
  I know you think it funny.
He only worked just half as long
  But got just twice the money.

So they in winning full control
  Depend on class communion.
Demand the earth from pole to pole,
  All bound in *One Big Union.*

3

*Mortimer Downing (1862– ?) a former editor
of the* Industrial Worker, *was a member of the
I.W.W. Construction Workers' Industrial Union
No. 310. He was a chemist and assayer by trade.
Convicted in the 1918 federal trial of I.W.W.
members in Sacramento, California, Downing was
one of the leaders of the "silent defenders," the
group of I.W.W. prisoners who refused to testify
before the court. After his release from prison, he
took an active part in writing publicity to obtain
the release of I.W.W. members who had been
arrested in California under the state criminal syndicalism law. Downing's account of the Wheatland Hop Riot appeared in* Solidarity *(January 3,
1914).*

BLOODY WHEATLAND

By MORTIMER DOWNING

Bloody Wheatland is glorious in this, that it united
the American Federation of Labor, the Socialist
Party and the I.W.W. in one solid army of workers to fight for the right to strike.

Against the workers are lined up the attorney
general of the state of California, the Burns
Agency, the Hop Growers' Association, the ranch-
owners of California, big and little business and
the district attorney of Yuba County, Edward B.
Stanwood. For the army of Burns men, engaged
in this effort to hang some of the workers, somebody must have paid as much as $100,000. The
workers have not yet gathered $2,000 to defend
their right to strike.

Follow this little story and reason for yourself,
workers, if your very right to strike is not here
involved.

By widespread lying advertisements Durst
Brothers assembled twenty-three hundred men,
women and children to pick their hops last summer. A picnic was promised the workers.

They got:

Hovels worse than pig sties to sleep in for which
they were charged seventy-five cents per week, or
between $2,700 and $3,000 for the season.

Eight toilets were all that was provided in the
way of sanitary arrangements.

Water was prohibited in the hop fields, where
the thermometer was taken by the State Health
Inspector and found to be more than 120 degrees.
Water was not allowed because Durst Brothers

had farmed out the lemonade privilege to their
cousin, Jim Durst, who offered the thirsting pickers acetic acid and water at five cents a glass.

Durst Brothers had a store on the camp, and
would not permit other dealers to bring anything
into the camp.

Wages averaged scarcely over $1 per day.

Rebellion occurred against these conditions.
Men have been tortured, women harassed, imprisoned and threats of death have been the portion of those who protested.

When the protest was brewing, mark this: Ralph
Durst asked the workers to assemble and form
their demands. He appointed a meeting place with
the workers. They took him at his word. Peaceably and orderly they decided upon their demands. Durst filled their camp with spies. Durst
went through the town of Wheatland and the surrounding country gathering every rifle, shot gun
and pistol. Was he conspiring against the workers?
The attorney general and the other law officers
say he was only taking natural precautions.

When the committee which Ralph Durst had
personally invited to come to him with the demands of the workers arrived, Durst struck the
chairman, Dick Ford, in the face. He then ordered
Dick Ford off his ground. Dick Ford had already
paid $2.75 as rental for his shack. Durst claims
this discharge of Ford broke the strike.

This was on Bloody Sunday, August 3, 1913,
about two o'clock in the afternoon.

Ford begged his fellow committeemen to say
nothing about Durst's striking him.

At 5:30 that Sunday afternoon the workers were
assembled in meeting on ground rented from
Durst. Dick Ford, speaking as the chairman of
the meeting reached down and took from a mother
an infant, saying, "It is not so much for ourselves
we are fighting as that this little baby may never
see the conditions which now exist on this ranch."
He put the baby back into its mother's arms as he
saw eleven armed men, in two automobiles, tearing down toward the meeting place. The workers
then began a song. Into this meeting, where the
grandsire, the husband, the youth and the babies
were gathered in an effort to gain something like
living conditions these armed men charged. Sheriff George Voss has sworn, "When I arrived that
meeting was orderly and peaceful." The crowd
opened to let him and his followers enter. Then
one of his deputies, Lee Anderson, struck Dick
Ford with a club, knocking him from his stand.

Anderson also fired a shot. Another deputy, Henry Dakin, fired a shot gun. Remember, this crowd was a dense mass of men, women and children, some of them babies at the breast. Panic struck the mass. Dakin began to volley with his automatic shot gun. There was a surge around the speaker's stand. Voss went down. From his tent charged an unidentified Puerto Rican. He thrust himself into the mass, clubbed some of the officers, got a gun, cleared a space for himself and fell dead before a load of buckshot from Henry Dakin's gun.

Thirty seconds or so the firing lasted. When the smoke cleared, Dakin and Durst and others of these bullies had fled like jack rabbits. Four men lay dead upon the ground. Among them, District Attorney Edward T. Manwell, a deputy named Eugene Reardon, the Puerto Rican and an uniden-

tified English lad. About a score were wounded, among them women.

Charges of murder, indiscriminative, have been placed for the killing of Manwell and Reardon. This Puerto Rican and the English boy sleep in their bloody graves and the law takes no account —they were only workers.

Such are the facts of Wheatland's bloody Sunday. Now comes the district attorney of Yuba County, the attorney general of the state of California and all the legal machinery and cry that these workers, assembled in meeting with their women and children, had entered into a conspiracy to murder Manwell and Reardon. They say had no strike occurred there would have been no killing. They say had Dick Ford, when assaulted and discharged by Durst, "quietly left the ranch, the strike would have been broken." What matters

John Farmer's First Lesson

Solidarity, September 2, 1916.

to these the horrors of thirst, the indecent and immodest conditions? The workers are guilty. They struck and it became necessary to disperse them. Therefore, although they, the workers were unarmed and hampered with their women and children, because a set of drunken deputies, who even had whisky in their pockets on the field, fired upon them, the workers must pay a dole to the gallows.

To vindicate and establish this theory an army of Burns men have been turned loose. They took one Swedish lad, Alfred Nelson, carried him around the country through six jails, finally beat him brutally in a public hotel in the city of Martinez. One of these Burns thugs is now under a sentence of a year in jail and $1,000 fine for this act.

These same Burns men arrested Herman D. Suhr in Prescott, Arizona. He was confined like a beast in the refrigerator of a box fruit car. These Burns men poked him with clubs and bars to keep him awake. He was taken to Los Angeles and tortured in that jail. Thence they carried him to Fresno for further torture. Thence to San Francisco, thence to Oakland. Here for four days three shifts of Burns men tortured him by keeping him awake. In order that no marks should show on his person, they rolled long spills of paper and thrust the sharp points into his eyes and ears and nose every time his tired head dropped. He was placed in a three-foot latticed cell so that these animals could easily torture him without danger from his fists. He went crazy, signed a "confession," and the judges of Yuba and Sutter counties and the district attorneys thereof have tried to make it impossible for him to even swear out a warrant for his torturers.

Mrs. Suhr's wifehood was questioned when she first visited her husband.

Edward B. Stanwood, the present district attorney of Yuba County, has had more than a score of men arrested. He has kept them for months in jails at widely separated points. Burns men have been permitted to enter their cells and use every effort to frighten them into confessions. Men say they have been brought before Stanwood, himself, and when they told the truth about their actions these Burns men have called them "God damned liars." Stanwood has sat by. Again and again Stanwood has refused to take any action concerning Durst's gathering of arms, concerning the actions of the Burns men. He has refused to put charges against these men until compelled to do so by writs of habeas corpus.

Here were a band of men, all of them armed, many of them drunken, who charged a peaceful meeting endangering the lives of women and children. Stanwood says it was because of a conspiracy among the workers that anybody was killed. None of the workers had arms. All the deputies had pistols and rifles.

In the city of Marysville, where the trials will take place the newspapers constantly allude to the men in jail as fiends. The judge is the life-long friend of the dead Manwell, every juror possible knew the sheriff and the other deputies. They publicly allow them to be called fiends. The acts of the Burns men are excused as necessary. To cinch the whole thing the courts have refused a change of venue. The whole community fears that this case should be tried by a jury not involved directly in the facts.

Under the same law the next strike can be broken in the same way. Let a drunken Burns man or a deputy or strike breaker fire upon strikers, kill some of them and the same method will be used. If only these two workers had been killed the six men now held would be charged with murder. It is only handy and incidental to the movement of the bosses that two of their own were involved, whose deaths enrage their friends. The case is plain, workers. Unite to free these six men or it will be your turn next.

4

These unsigned verses about the Wheatland Hop Riot appeared in Solidarity (*August 1, 1914*).

OVERALLS AND SNUFF
(*Tune: "Wearing of the Green"*)

One day as I was walking along the railroad track,
I met a man in Wheatland with his blankets on his
    back,
He was an old-time hop picker, I'd seen his face
    before,
I knew he was a wobbly, by the button that he
    wore.
By the button that he wore, by the button that he
    wore
I knew he was a wobbly, by the button that he
    wore.

He took his blankets off his back and sat down on
    the rail

We Are Coming Home, John Farmer---We Are Coming Back to Stay

Solidarity, September 30, 1916.

And told us some sad stories 'bout the workers
    down in jail.
He said the way they treat them there, he never
    saw the like,
For they're putting men in prison just for going out
    on strike.
Just for going out on strike, just for going out on
    strike,
They're putting men in prison, just for going out on
    strike.

They have sentenced Ford and Suhr, and they've
    got them in the pen,
If they catch a wobbly in their burg, they vag him
    there and then.
There is one thing I can tell you, and it makes the
    bosses sore,

As fast as they can pinch us, we can always get
    some more.
We can always get some more, we can always get
    some more,
As fast as they can pinch us, we can always get
    some more.

Oh, Horst and Durst are mad as hell, they don't
    know what to do.
And the rest of those hop barons are all feeling
    mighty blue.
Oh, we've tied up all their hop fields, and the scabs
    refuse to come,
And we're going to keep on striking till we put
    them on the bum.
Till we put them on the bum, till we put them on
    the bum,

We're going to keep on striking till we put them
   on the bum.

Now we've got to stick together, boys, and strive
   with all our might,
We must free Ford and Suhr, boys, we've got to
   win this fight.
From these scissorbill hop barons we are taking no
   more bluff,
We'll pick no more damned hops for them, for
   overalls and snuff.
For our overalls and snuff, for our overalls and
   snuff
We'll pick no more damned hops for them, for
   overalls and snuff.

5

*Richard Brazier's song, "When You Wear That
Button," was printed in the fourteenth edition of
the I.W.W. songbook. Brazier, who was a delegate
to the founding conference of the I.W.W. Agricultural Workers' Organization, wrote these verses
during the 1915 harvest drive.*

WHEN YOU WEAR THAT BUTTON

By RICHARD BRAZIER

(Tune: "When You Wore a Tulip")

I met him in Dakota when the harvesting was o'er,
A "Wob" he was, I saw by the button that he wore.
He was talking to a bunch of slaves in the jungles
   near the tracks;
He said "You guys whose homes are on your backs;
Why don't you stick together with the "Wobblies"
   in one band
And fight to change conditions for the workers in
   this land."

Chorus

*When you wear that button, the "Wobblies" red
   button
And carry their red, red card,
No need to hike, boys, along these old pikes, boys,
Every "Wobbly" will be your pard.
The boss will be leery, the "stiffs" will be cheery
When we hit John Farmer hard,
They'll all be affrighted, when we stand united
And carry that red, red card.*

The stiffs all seemed delighted, when they heard
   him talk that way.
They said, "We need more pay, and a shorter
   working day."
The "Wobbly" said, "You'll get these things
   without the slightest doubt
If you'll organize to knock the bosses out.
If you'll join the One Big Union, and wear their
   badge of liberty
You'll strike that blow all slaves must strike if they
   would be free."

6

*Pat Brennan (1878–1916) also wrote the fre-
quently reprinted poem "Down in the Mines"
(Chapter X). "Harvest War Song" was one of the
most popular of the I.W.W. agricultural workers'
songs. The line, "We are Coming Home, John
Farmer," was used as the caption for several
I.W.W. cartoons. The "Harvest War Song" was
submitted by the prosecution in federal and state
trials of I.W.W. members, as evidence of the Wobblies' intent to destroy the crops if their demands
were not met. It was printed in the seventeenth
edition of the little red songbook. An earlier
shorter version appeared in Solidarity (April 3,
1915).*

HARVEST WAR SONG°

By PAT BRENNAN

(Tune: "Tipperary")

We are coming home, John Farmer; We are
   coming back to stay.
For nigh on fifty years or more, we've gathered up
   your hay.
We have slept out in your hayfields, we have heard
   your morning shout;
We've heard you wondering where in hell's them
   pesky go-abouts?

Chorus:

It's a long way, now understand me; it's a long way
   to town;
It's a long way across the prairie, and to hell with
   Farmer John.
Here goes for better wages, and the hours must
   come down;
For we're out for a winter's stake this summer, and
   we want no scabs around.

You've paid the going wages, that's what kept us
on the bum.
You say you've done your duty, you chin-
whiskered son of a gun.
We have sent your kids to college, but still you
rave and shout.
And call us tramps and hoboes, and pesky go-
abouts.

But now the long wintry breezes are a-shaking our
poor frames,
And the long drawn days of hunger try to drive us
boes insane.
It is driving us to action—we are organized today;
Us pesky tramps and hoboes are coming back to
stay.

7

*Elmer Rumbaugh, whom Ralph Chaplin credited
with authoring the song "Paint 'Er Red," was the
author of these verses that appeared in* Solidarity
(*June 2, 1917*).

PESKY KRITTERS
By ELMER RUMBAUGH
(*Tune: "Arrah Wannah"*)

To the North Dakota harvest came the wobbly
band,
Singing songs of revolution and One Big Union
grand,
Old Farmer John sat and cussed 'em—called 'em
pesky tramps
Just because they would not work by the light
of carbide lamps.

Chorus:

We want more coin; that's why we join
The One Big Union Grand—
The pork chops for to land.
And Farmer John may cuss and rare
And loudly rave and tear his hair;
But one thing understand:
For shorter hours and better wages
We all united stand.

Now fellow workers all together—Let us organize
Into One Big Fighting Union! When will you
get wise?
Can't you see the bosses rob you of your daily
bread?

They half starve you, pay bum wages, with a
haystack for your bed.

8

*Joe Foley wrote these verses to the tune, "Down
in Bom Bom Bay." They were printed in* Solidarity (*June 9, 1917*).

DOWN IN HARVEST LAND
By JOE FOLEY

If you're tired of coffee an'
Beef stew, hash and liver an'
Come, be a man
Join the union grand;
Come organize with us in harvest land—
Down in harvest land.

Chorus

Down in harvest land
United we will stand,
With the A.W.O.
We're out for the dough
Out for to make old Farmer John come through
Down in harvest land,
The one big union grand
If Farmer John don't please us
His machine will visit Jesus,
Down in harvest land.

If you're sick of bumming lumps,
Bread lines and religious dumps;
When you're broke
You're a joke
They tell you Jesus is your only hope,
Down in harvest land.

When the winter comes around
You are driven out of town
You've got to go,
In the hail and snow
Cause you wouldn't line up with us, Bo,
Down in harvest land.

9

*These verses by George G. Allen, who wrote the
popular "One Big Industrial Union," were taken
from the file of I.W.W. songs and poems in the
Labadie Collection. The source is not known.*

ALONG THE INDUSTRIAL ROAD
TO FREEDOM

By G. G. ALLEN

(*Tune: "Along the Rocky Road to Dublin"*)

One day a western passenger train in the northern
belt of wheat
In the burning summer heat, just stopped in time
to meet
A little band of "400" men who were standing by
to wait,
For a faster train upon the main and surer than a
freight.
Oh scenery, Bo! Oh scenery, Bo! Think while I
relate:

Chorus

Along the Industrial Road to Freedom,
They were rolling along, singing a song
Though they fight the shacks they need 'em,
On the transportation lines.
And when the crew came round to collect
They never seemed to care
To try to put the dead head off
Who wouldn't pay his fare.
For a little direct action
It sure never fails at showing the rails
The spirit of that solidarity that has for its call
An injury to one concerns us all,
Along the Industrial Road to Freedom.

Now For the Eastern Invasion!

Solidarity, October 14, 1916.

By and by, a hard boiled guy, who was hungry for
a lunch,
Confided to the bunch that he'd follow up a hunch;
He led the way to the front of the train and all sat
down in seats,
In the dining car where the good things are and
ordered all the eats.
Oh jungle, 'Bo! Oh, jungle, Bo! Think of all the
sweets.

10

E. F. Doree who wrote this article for the International Socialist Review *(June 1915) was a leader
in the Agricultural Workers' Organization and
was later sentenced to Leavenworth Penitentiary
after the I.W.W. Chicago trial.*

GATHERING THE GRAIN

By E. F. DOREE

The great, rich wheat belt runs from Northern
Texas, through the states of Oklahoma, Kansas,
Nebraska, South and North Dakotas, into Canada,
and not a few will point with pride to the fact that
last year WE (?) had the largest wheat crop in
the history of this country. But few are the people
who know the conditions under which they work
who gather in these gigantic crops. It is the object
of this article to bring out some of these vital facts.

About the middle of June the real harvest com-
mences in Northern Oklahoma and Southern Kansas. This section is known as the "headed wheat
country," that is to say, just the heads of grain are
cut off and the straw is left standing in the fields,
while in the "bundle country" the grain is cut close
to the ground and bound into sheaves or bundles.

In the headed grain country the average wage
paid is $2.50 and board per day, but in the very
end of the season $3 is sometimes paid, the in-
crease due to the drift northward of the harvest
workers, who leave the farmers without sufficient
help. This is not a chronic condition, as there are
usually from two to five men to every job.

The board is average, although fresh meat is
very scarce, salt meat being more popular with the
farmer because it is cheaper. Most of the men
sleep in barns, but it is not uncommon to have
workers entering the sacred portals of the house.
Bedding of some kind is furnished, although it is
often nothing more than a buggy robe.

The exceedingly long work day is the worst feature of the harvesting so far as the worker is concerned. The men are expected to be in the fields
at half past five or six o'clock in the morning until
seven or half past seven o'clock at night, with
from an hour to an hour and a half for dinner. It
is a common slang expression of the workers that
they have an "eight-hour work day"—eight in the
morning and eight in the afternoon.

Most of the foreign-born farmers serve a light
lunch in the fields about nine o'clock in the morning and four o'clock in the afternoon, but the
American farmers who do are indeed rare.

In this section the workers are sometimes paid
so much per hundred bushels, and the more they
thresh the more they get. On this basis they generally make more than "goin' wages,"* but they
work themselves almost to death doing it. No
worker, no matter how strong, can stand the pace
long; the extremely hot weather in Kansas proves
unendurable. Twenty-five men died from the heat
in one day last year in a single county in Kansas.

The workers threshing "by the hundred" must
pay their board while the machine is idle, due to
breakdown, rain, etc.

About the time that the headed grain is reaped
the bundle grain in Central and Northern Kansas
and Southern Nebraska is ready for the floating
army of harvesters.

Here the wages range from $2 to $2.50 and
board per day. They have never gone over the
$2.50 mark. Small wages are paid and accepted
because thousands of workers are then drifting up
from the headed wheat country and because of
the general influx of men from all over the United
States, who come to make their "winter's stake."
This is about the poorest section of the entire harvest season for the worker. The following little
story is told of the farmers of Central Nebraska:

"What the farmers raise they sell. What they
can't sell they feed to the cattle. What the cattle
won't eat they feed to the hogs. What the hogs
won't eat they eat themselves, and what they can't
eat they feed to the hired hands."

In Nebraska proper the farms are smaller, as a
rule, than elsewhere in the harvest country and
grow more diversified crops. Almost every farmer
has one or more "hired men," and for that reason
does not need so many extra men in the harvest,

---

* "Goin' wages" is an expression used by the farmer in
answer to the question, "What do you pay?" It really
means the smallest wages paid in the country.

YOU CAN NEVER TELL; STRANGE THINGS HAPPEN IN THE LAND OF JOHN FARMER

Industrial Pioneer, July 1924.

but in spite of this, the whole floating army marches up to get stung annually. Most of the "Army From Nowhere" cannot get jobs and have a pretty hungry time waiting for the harvest farther north to be ready.

The farmers in South Dakota do not believe in "burning daylight," so they start the worker to his task a little before daybreak and keep him at it till a little after dark. If the farmer in South Dakota had the power of Joshua, he would inaugurate the twenty-four-hour workday.

The wages here range from $2.25 to $2.50 and board per day, while in isolated districts better wages are sometimes paid. A small part of the workers are permitted to spend the night in the houses, but most of them sleep in the barns. Sometimes they have only the canopy of the heavens for a blanket.

As soon as the harvest strikes North Dakota wages rise to $2.75 or $3.50 and board per day, the length of the workday being determined by the amount of daylight.

The improved wages are due to the fact that thousands of harvesters begin leaving the country because of the cold weather, and the fact that the farmers insist on the workers furnishing their own bedding. At the extreme end of the season wages often go up to as high as $4.00 and board, per day.

The board in North Dakota is the best in the harvest country, which is not saying much.

In North and South Dakota no worker is sure of drawing his wages, even after earning them. Some farmers do not figure on paying their "help" at all and work the same game year after year. The new threshing machine outfits are the worst on this score, as the bosses very seldom own the machines themselves and, at the end of the season, often leave the country without paying either worker or machine owner.

This, however, is not the only method used by the farmers to beat the tenderfoot. In some cases the worker is told that he can make more money by taking a steady job at about $35.00 a month and staying three or four months, the farmer always assuring him that the work will last. The average tenderfoot eagerly grabs this proposition, only to find that thirty days later, or as soon as the heavy work is done, the farmer "can no longer use him." There have been many instances where the worker has kicked at the procedure and been paid off by the farmer with a pickhandle.

The best paying occupation in the harvest country is "the harvesting of the harvester," which is heavily indulged in by train crews, railroad "bulls," gamblers and hold-up men.

Gamblers are in evidence everywhere. No one has to gamble, yet it is almost needless to say that the card sharks make a good haul. Quite different is it, though, with the hold-up man, for before him the worker has to dig up and no argument goes. This "stick-up" game is not a small one, and hundreds of workers lose their "stake" annually at the point of a gun.

As is the rule with a migratory army, the harvesters move almost entirely by "freight," and here is where the train crews get theirs. With them it is simply a matter of "shell up a dollar or hit the dirt." Quite often union cards are recognized and no dollar charged, and the worker is permitted to ride unmolested.

It is safe to say that nine workers out of every ten leave the harvest fields as poor as when they entered them. Few, indeed, are those who clear $50.00 or more in the entire season.

These are, briefly, the conditions that have existed for many years, up to and including 1914, but the 1915 harvest is likely to be more interesting if the present indications materialize.

The last six months has seen the birth of two new organizations that will operate during the coming summer. The National Farm Labor Exchange, a subsidiary movement to the "jobless man to the manless job" movement, and the Agricultural Workers' Organization of the Industrial Workers of the World.

The ostensible purpose of the National Farm Labor Exchange is to handle the men necessary for the harvest systematically, but its real purpose is to flood the country with unnecessary men, thus making it possible to reduce the wages, which the farmer really believes are too high. If the Exchange can have its way, there will be thousands of men brought into the harvest belt from the east, and particularly from the southeast. It is needless to say that these workers will be offered at least twice as much in wages as they will actually draw.

News has come in to the effect that the farmers are already organizing their "vigilance committees," which are composed of farmers, businessmen, small town bums, college students and Y. M. C. A. scabs. The duty of the vigilance committee is to stop free speech, eliminate union agitation, and to drive out of the country all workers who demand more than "goin' wages."

Foreign language pamphlets issued by the I.W.W.

Arrayed against the organized farmers is the Agricultural Workers' Organization, which is made up of members of the I.W.W. who work in the harvest fields. It is the object of this organization to systematically organize the workers into One Big Union, making it possible to secure the much needed shorter workday and more wages, as well as to mutually protect the men from the wiles of those who harvest the harvester.

The Agricultural Workers' Organization expects to place a large number of delegates and organizers in the fields, all of whom will work directly under a field secretary. It is hoped this will accomplish what has never been done before, the systematization of organization and the strike during the harvest, as well as the work of general agitation.

Both of these organizations intend to function so that the workers in the fields will have to choose quickly between the two. If the farmers win the men to their cause, smaller wages will be paid and the general working conditions will become poorer; if the workers swing into the I.W.W. and stand together, then more wages will be paid for fewer hours of labor. Both sides can't win. Moral: Join the I.W.W. and fight for better conditions.

Mr. Worker, don't do this year what you did last, harvest the wheat in the summer and starve in breadlines in the winter.

Let us close with a few "Don'ts."

Don't scab.

Don't accept piece work.

Don't work by the month during harvest.

Don't travel a long distance to take in the harvest; it is not worth it.

Don't believe everything that you read in the papers, because it is usually only the Durham.

Don't fail to join the I.W.W. and help win this battle.

11

This poem may have been written by T-Bone Slim. In some editions of the I.W.W. songbook it is signed "T-Bone and H," in others, "T. D. and H." It first appeared in the seventeenth edition of the I.W.W. songbook.

HARVEST LAND
By T-D AND H.
(Air: "Beulah Land")

The harvest drive is on again,
John Farmer needs a lot of men;
To work beneath the Kansas heat
And shock and stack and thresh his wheat.

Chorus

Oh Farmer John—Poor Farmer John,
Our faith in you is over-drawn.
—Old Fossil of the Feudal Age,
Your only creed is Going Wage—
"Bull Durum" will not buy our Brawn—
You're out of luck—poor Farmer John.

You advertise, in Omaha,
"Come leave the Valley of the Kaw."
Nebraska Calls "Don't be mis-led.
We'll furnish you a feather bed!"

Then South Dakota lets a roar,
"We need ten thousand men—or more;
Our grain is turning—prices drop!
For God's Sake save our bumper crop."

In North Dakota—(I'll be darn)
The "wise guy" sleeps in "hoosiers" barn
—Then hoosier breaks into his snore
And yells, "It's quarter after four."

Chorus

Oh Harvest Land—Sweet Burning Sand!
—As on the sun-kissed field I stand
I look away across the plain
And wonder if it's going to rain—
I vow, by all the Brands of Cain,
That I will not be here again.

12

Signed "E. H. H.," this short story appeared in the Industrial Pioneer (October 1921). The "Palouse," a French-Canadian word, refers to the grassy hill lands north of the Snake River.

AN ILL WIND IN THE PALOUSE
By E. H. H.

The Palouse Harvest being in its full twelve hour swing, "Rhode Island Red" and I, "Plymouth Rock Whitey," decided to give the struggling farmers a lift and help them "gather in the sheaves."

Now, for some reason or other, Red was not as enthusiastic over the harvest work as he should be.

He claimed that even if he harvested all the wheat in the country, chances were he would be in the soup line in the winter time.

Whatever becomes of the wheat, he says, is a deep mystery to him, except that he knows Wall Street stores a lot of it up where the stiffs can't get at it.

Anyhow, we landed in the town of Colfax with Red growling over conditions, bum grub and high prices of the local restaurants. After eating some of their "coffee and at two bits a throw," we sauntered out on the main street to look for a farmer who wanted a couple of enterprising harvesters.

We were approached by a long, thin individual with close set eyes of the codfish order. He was wearing a disguise of spinach on his chin and inquired in a high pitched voice, "Were ye boys looking fer work?" To which I says: "Yes, we certainly are that!" Red busts in then and asks him how much he pays and how many hours he works.

This seemed to be a leading question, altogether irrelevant and immaterial to the farmer's point of view. He looks Red over and says, "Guess you boys ain't looking for work, be you?" With that parting shot he walks away and leaves us standing there like a couple of lost dogs.

Now Red has no diplomacy whatever so I told him to keep his remarks to himself, and the next time I would do the talking.

Then we removed ourselves to another corner as our chin-whiskered friend was pointing at us from across the street and waving his hands in the air. He seemed to be delivering an oration to some of his fellow farmers.

Red says they ain't really honest to God farmers in this section but are illegal descendants of horse thieves and train robbers and we would be better off if we got the hell out of the Palouse district and into the United States again.

But his brain storm was cut short by another "son of the soil" planting himself in front of us and asking in an oily tone of voice, "Gentlemen, are your services open to negotiations? I need a couple of scientific side hill shockers and thought that you probably would consider a proposition of taking on a little labor."

I was about to accept his offer of work but Red "horns in" again about the hours and wages and our friend left us with the remark that he thought we were gentlemen when he first sized us up but now he knew different.

He even went as far as to remark that he thought

we might be connected up with that infamous organization known as the I.W.W. and ought to be in the county jail and that we better be a lookin' out or he would get a bunch together with a rope and a bucket of tar and a few flags and show us if we could fool around with a real 102 per cent American and his wheat crop. By Heck! Consarn ye!

I then took Red up an alley and had a short talk with him about keeping out of these arguments and letting me get a word in now and then.

Red agreed to keep quiet next time, but I had very little confidence in Red's being able to hang onto himself so I steered him into a pool hall and went out on the street by myself.

While walking down the street a bright idea permeated into my "ivory dome" as Red calls it.

You are all aware that when a farmer buys a horse he sizes its muscles up and inquires about the price of it. He don't ask the horse how many hours he will work a day. That, I surmised, was probably the reason the farmer gets hostile when you ask him how many hours you are supposed to work per day. It is contrary to his purchasing habits.

Putting myself on the same basis as the farm horse I accordingly went into an alley and took off my shirt, rolled back my undersleeves and wrapped a couple of old gunny sacks around each arm.

When I put the shirt on over that rig I had a regular set of arms on that would make the world's champion strong man turn green with envy. "Now watch me captivate the old farmer," thought I as I burst into view again on the main stem.

A half dozen farmers were lolling and milling around on the opposite corner admiring each other's twelve cylinder cars and spitting tobacco juice on the sidewalk.

But they forgot all about the late war and the price Wall Street was going to give them for their wheat when they laid eyes on my muscular arms.

A wild scramble ensued in my direction. One farmer tripped his fellow farmer up and "blood flew freely." They surrounded me like a bunch of wild Indians with loud howls for me, Plymouth Rock Whitey, 100% to go to work! It kind of reminded me of the old times of work or fight in 1919.

But who was it said that "the best laid plans of mice and men will sometimes land you in the pen"? The sons of Colfax got hold of my shirt in

The Harvest Worker Finds A Place In The Sun

The Rebel Worker, September 1, 1919.

commenced. At any rate Red has a distinct taste for poultry which, so he says, was highly exacerbated by the sight of fat pullets and the absence of any such from the festive board. Being able to see at night he informs me is one of the first requirements for a poultry dinner.

'Tis an ill wind that never stirs a chicken feather.

13

Folklorist Archie Green collected the song, "The Big Combine" from Glenn Ohrlin, a working cowboy and traditional musician now living in Mountain View, Arkansas. Ohrlin told Green that he had learned the song in an Oregon bar and that it was written about 1919 by Jock Coleman, a Scotch cowboy and harvest hand around Pendleton, Oregon, who was known as the "Poet Lariat" of that region.

The I.W.W. was frequently mislabeled the Independent Workers of the World, and "The Big Combine" might have been an I.W.W. song. "The Big Combine," sung by Glenn Ohrlin, is included on a recent LP record, "The Hell-Bound Train," issued by The University of Illinois Campus Folksong Club. In the notes to that recording, Professor Green states, "To my knowledge, 'The Big Combine' has never been collected or published as a folksong. Hence, Glenn's version is significant as: (1) a traditional document of a by-gone agricultural practice; (2) an addition to the corpus of Wobbly songs collected from a nontrade union oriented singer; (3) a new branch in the already abundant 'Casey Jones' family tree."

"The Big Combine" is set to the tune "Casey Jones." In this song, as in Joe Hill's parody, the train engineer is portrayed as anti-union.

THE BIG COMBINE

Well, come all you rounders that want to hear
The story of a bunch of stiffs a-harvesting here,
The greatest bunch of boys ever come down the
line,
Is the harvesting crew on the big combine.

There's traveling men from Sweden in this grand
old crew,
Canada and Oregon and Scotland, too.
I've listened to their twaddle for a month or more,
I never saw a bunch of stiffs like this before.

their wild excitement, and tore it off, exposing my gunny sack camouflage.

Now just to show you the inconsistency of mankind, these Palousers got angry. In fact they got violent and if I had not been a good sprinter I fear I would have never lived to tell about this. I left, going strong and decided then and there that a pleasant position circulating among the best people would be preferable to a life of unconventional freedom amongst toilers of the soil.

As for Red, he stuck to his cruder and more common methods of selling himself and eventually found a master. That the results of the bargain were mutually satisfactory cannot be stated unreservedly. However, Red gained some accomplishments that in due season will probably come in handy.

For instance he is now quite as able to see in the dark as in the day. He claims that he owes the accomplishment to his labor in the Palouse country, as they seemed to have no clear conception down there as to just when day stopped and night

Oh, you ought to see this bunch of harvest
    pippins,
You ought to see, they're really something fine,
You ought to see this bunch of harvest pippins,
The bunch of harvest pippins on the big
    combine.

Well, there's Oscar just from Sweden, he's as stout
    as a mule,
He can jig and dance and peddle the bull,
He's an Independent Worker of the World as well,
Says he loves the independence but the work is
    hell.

Well, he hates millionaires and he wants to see
Them blow up all the grafters in the land of
    liberty,
Says he's going to leave this world of politics and
    strife
And stay down in the jungle with his stew can all
    his life.

Oh, Casey Jones, he knew Oscar Nelson,
Casey Jones, he knew Oscar fine,
Oh, Casey Jones, he knew Oscar Nelson,
He kicked him off the boxcars on the SP line.

Well, the next one I'm to mention, well, the next in
    line
Is the lad a-punching horses on the big combine,

He's the lad that tells the horses what to do,
But the things he tells the horses I can't tell you.

It's Limp and Dude and Dolly, you get out of the
    grain,
And get over there, Buster, you're over the chain,
Oh, Pete and Pat and Polly, you get in and pull,
And get over there, Barney, you durned old fool.

You ought to see, you ought to see our skinner,
You ought to see, he's really something fine,
You ought to see, you ought to see our skinner,
You ought to see the skinner on the big combine.

Well, I'm the head puncher, you can bet that's me,
I do more work than all the other three,
A-working my hands and my legs and my feet,
Picking up the barley and the golden wheat.

I got to pull the lever and turn on the wheel,
I got to watch the sickle and the draper and the
    reel,.
And if I hit a badger hill and pull up a rock,
Well, they say he's done it, the durn fool Jock.

I'm that lad, I'm the head puncher,
I'm that lad, though it isn't in my line,
I'm that lad, I'm the head puncher,
I'm the head puncher on the big combine.

. . . one who has seen the glow of the great Wobbly dream light the faces of the lumberjacks has seen the unforgettable, the imperishable . . . they plan a new order they will never know . . . they can dream and dreaming, be happy.

REXFORD G. TUGWELL
"The Casual of the Woods,"
Survey (July 3, 1920), p. 472.

Chapter 9

Lumberjacks: North and South

"Before the strike of two years ago," an I.W.W. lumberjack told writer Floyd Dell in 1919, "a lumberjack wasn't a man. He was a lousy animal. Everywhere he went he carried his lousy blanket on his back and everywhere he went he wore his 'tin pants' and his 'corks'—shoes with spikes in the soles to give him a footing on a slippery log. And when he went in town, he saw signs in store windows 'no corks allowed in here.' And the only thing he could do in town was get drunk and be robbed of six-months' wages and go back with his filthy blanket on his back to slave ten hours a day for six months more."[1]

Faced with the intractable attitudes of the lumber operators toward unionism, living a remote group life when working, and "on the rods" between jobs, the concept of the One Big Union made sense to the lumberjack. Often the I.W.W. hall in the lumber region trading town or city was his only home. "He has one tie to bind him to his fellow man," wrote Rexford Tugwell, "the red card of the Wobbly."[2]

The I.W.W. started organizing in the lumber industry in February 1907 in a strike of 2000 sawmill workers in Portland. It was the organization's first major West coast activity, and it launched the reputation of the I.W.W. throughout the Northwest when a small wage increase was won in the industry.

The South was the second largest lumber producing area, and when some Wobblies who had worked in the Northwest made their way to the Gulf states, they helped catalyze the resentments and rebellion of the southern sawmill and lumber-camp workers. Unlike the lumberjack of the Northwest, the southern lumberworker was usually a "homeguard" or "sodbuster"—a local farmer who worked seasonally in a sawmill or lumber camp to eke out a living. About half the labor force were Negroes who, like the white farmers, lived in company-owned housing in lumber camps or mill villages. In many places where the semimonthly payday was ignored, workers in need of money borrowed it from their employers at usurious rates of interest. When they were paid, it was frequently in scrip, redeemable only at high-priced company stores.

In 1910 the Brotherhood of Timber Workers was organized as an independent union in Louisiana. The Southern Lumber Operators' Association, which was started in 1907 to combat lumber unionism, met to "declare war" on the organization. It opposed the Brotherhood with a seven-month lockout, blacklisting 7000 of the most active union members. For its part, the Brotherhood demanded $2.00 a day wages, a ten-hour work day, bimonthly payment in lawful United States currency, freedom to trade in independent stores, reduced rents and commissary prices, and the right to meet together on union business.

The Brotherhood was one of the first southern unions to admit Negro members. In May 1912 Bill Haywood was invited to address the union's convention in Alexandria, Louisiana. Haywood was surprised to find no Negroes at the meeting, and when he was told that it was illegal to hold interracial meetings in Louisiana, he replied:

> You work in the same mills together. Sometimes a black man and a white man chop down the same tree together. You are meeting in convention now to discuss the conditions under which you labor. This can't be done intelligently by passing resolutions here and then sending them to another room for the black men to act upon. Why not be sensible about this and call the Negroes into the Convention? If it is against the law, this is one time when the law should be broken.[3]

The Negroes were invited into the convention sessions which voted three to one to affiliate with the I.W.W. National Industrial Union of Forest and Lumber Workers. Negro as well as white delegates were elected to attend the 1912 I.W.W. convention.

The Brotherhood had a short, tragic existence. Company lockouts were intensified following the official I.W.W. affiliation, as lumber companies decided to "fight the question to a finish."[4]

At Grabow, Louisiana, a company town which was enclosed like a stockade behind a high wooden fence, company guards shot and killed three strikers who were taking part in a union meeting on a public road near the town. The coroner's jury charged officers of the company with murder, but the grand jury indicted fifty-eight union men and no company officials. The union members were lodged for three months in the prison known as the "Black Hole of Calcasieu" in Lake Charles, Louisiana, before the start of a dramatic four weeks' trial. The jury took only one hour to acquit the I.W.W. members after state's witnesses testified that company officers had distributed guns to the guards and encouraged them to get drunk before the union meeting. The testimony also revealed that the councils of the Brotherhood were honeycombed with company detectives, including one who had stolen the union's records and membership lists.

Following the Lake Charles trial, a prolonged strike at Merryville, Louisiana, protested company blacklisting of the trial's defense witnesses. A campaign of terrorism from a vigilante brigade, known as the Good Citizens' League, coupled with continuing discrimination against union members, wrecked the union, and by 1913 its blacklisted

leaders and active members moved west to agitate for industrial unionism in the oil fields of Oklahoma.

In the Northwest, living conditions in lumber camps were notoriously bad and constituted a major grievance for lumberjacks. Going from job to job, the men were forced to carry rolled up blankets on their backs, since the companies provided no bedding. As late as September 1917, an article in the *New Republic* described typical housing for lumberjacks this way:

> Forty loggers occupied a bunk house that should not have accommodated more than a dozen—the men sleeping two in a bunk with two more in a bunk on top; a stove at either end, sending the steam rising from lines of clothes strung the length of the room; beds made in many cases by dumping hay into a wooden bunk; food that was unsavory; the crudest kind of provisions for cleanliness and sanitation.[5]

A month after it was organized in February 1912, the I.W.W. Forest and Lumber Workers' Industrial Union struck all the sawmills of Aberdeen, Hoquiam, and Raymond, Washington, against the ten-hour day and low wages. Several thousand loggers in western Washington walked out in sympathy. Many strikers were jailed on trumped up charges; others were dragged from their beds at night, marched into the swamps, and beaten. At Hoquiam, a vigilante committee loaded 150 strikers into boxcars for deportation, but the railroad workers refused to move them. In nearby Raymond, 100 Greek and Finnish workers were shipped out of town. The strike lasted five weeks and was partly successful. A citizens' committee recommended a slight increase in wages, exclusion of I.W.W. members, and a preference for American-born workers. Membership in the I.W.W. lumber locals dropped off; only a few scattered branches remained, and the National Union of Forest and Lumber Workers fell apart.

Spurred by success in the drive to organize harvest workers, the I.W.W. made plans in 1917 to renew efforts in the lumber camps. Lumber Workers' Industrial Union No. 500 was formed at the I.W.W. 1917 convention, and a strike was planned for the Spokane short-log region.

The demands of the I.W.W. lumberjacks in 1917 indicate major grievances. They called for an eight-hour day, no Sunday or holiday work, higher wages, satisfactory food served in porce-

Industrial Worker, October 27, 1909.

lain dishes with no overcrowding at the dinner tables, and sanitary kitchens.

They also pressed for sleeping quarters with a maximum of twelve people in each bunkhouse, single spring beds and shower baths, adequate lighting in the bunkhouses, free hospital service, and semimonthly pay by bank check. They called for the end of child labor in the sawmills and of discrimination against I.W.W. members in the camps.

The I.W.W. lumber strike of 1917 was the most spectacular controversy that had taken place in the industry up to that time. In many areas, close to 90 percent of the men became I.W.W. members. By August 1917, the strike which started on July 1, had paralyzed more than 80 percent of the lumber industry in western Washington, threatening the manufacture of airplanes for the war and the supply of lumber for cantonments and for crating shipments.

Newspaper articles in the Northwest charged that the I.W.W. lumber strike was financed with German gold and organized by the Wobblies to oppose the war effort. The governor of Washington proposed a state-wide vigilante committee; police frisked men on streets and on trains for red cards or other signs of I.W.W. membership. I.W.W. members were detained in stockades built in many communities in northern Washington, and I.W.W. halls were raided and wrecked throughout the Northwest. Local lawyers refused to de-

fend Wobblies who were imprisoned, and, in Congress, some of the senators from Utah, Montana, and Washington urged the use of military force to drive the Wobblies out of the lumber camps.

As the strike progressed, Secretary of War Baker asked lumber employers to concede an eight-hour day. An editorial in the *American Lumberman* answered this appeal. It said:

> It is really pitiable to see the government . . . truckling to a lot of treasonable, anarchistic agitators . . . playing into the hands of our enemy and doing tremendously more harm to our allied cause than the German army is doing. . . . With a little firmness . . . this situation could be relieved.[6]

Employers refused mediation by federal or state officials and linked their stand to the national defense efforts. Members of the Lumberman's Protective Association raised a half million dollar "fighting fund" to break the strike. Any member who gave into demands for the eight-hour day would be fined $500.

Wobblies met the challenge. Alarmed at dwindling strike funds, arrests of strike leaders, and use of scab crews in the camps, Wobblies went back to work in the forests. But, instead of doing a full day's work, they would "hoosier up," that is, act like "greenhorns" who had never seen the woods before. A lumberjack described the tactics this way:

> We went out together and we came back together, that's what the lumber bosses couldn't fight. And then, of course, we learned some new tricks about striking. Ever hear of the "intermittent strike"? Well, we tried that. Our funds were getting low, so we decided to strike on the job. A bunch of us would go back to work. The bosses were glad to see us—thought we'd given up. And then—well, the rules and regulations aren't usually observed very well when you're at work. We observed 'em. It certainly did slow things up! Everything went wrong. And then, to finish, somebody would institute the eight-hour day by pulling the whistle two hours before quitting time. Naturally, everybody stopped work. The bosses had a fit and fired us. So we moved on to the next camp, and wired headquarters to send another bunch to the last place. It certainly worked. I never saw a more peaceful strike in my life than that one, and I've seen some strikes.[7]

Mr. Block

He Works in the Woods

Industrial Worker, December 26, 1912.

There was also evidence that some members, acting as individuals, drove spikes into logs to break saws, wasted materials through planned carelessness, and engaged in other acts of "conscientious withdrawal of efficiency." But attempts to prove acts of criminal sabotage on the part of the I.W.W. proved fruitless.

The Northwest lumber industry panicked at the disorganization and confusion. As Senator Borah remarked:

> . . . you cannot destroy the organization. . . . It is something you cannot get at. You cannot reach it. You do not know where it is. It is not in writing. It is not in anything else. It is a simple understanding between men, and they act upon it without any evidence of existence whatever.[8]

President Wilson sent a Mediation Commission to investigate and, if possible, settle the crisis. The commission reported that the lumber operators took advantage of the wartime hysteria to fight not only the I.W.W. but all unions. It said:

> The I.W.W. is filling a vacuum created by the operators. . . . The hold of the I.W.W. is riveted instead of weakened by unimaginative opposition on the part of the employers to the correction of real grievances. . . . The greatest difficulty in the industry is the tenacity of old habits of individualism.[9]

The commission condemned the opposition of the lumber owners to the eight-hour day, since lumber was the only major industry on the West coast in which it did not prevail.

As the unmet need for lumber for the war effort continued, the War Department detailed Colonel Brice P. Disque of the U. S. Army Signal Corps to organize a "Loyal Legion of Loggers and Lumbermen" to establish harmony between employers and employees. The "4 L's" became known as Colonel Disque's "weapon to bomb pro-Hunism out of the Northwest Woods."[10] The I.W.W. claimed that the 4 L's was a company union which included employers, and charged that "the police, the press, and cleverly manipulated mob violence all were used as a club to enforce membership."[11] Colonel Disque advised unionists to suspend union activities and organizing until the end of the war.

In March 1918 Colonel Disque took matters in hand and announced that from then on the lumber industry in the Northwest would go on an eight-hour day. The I.W.W. lumberjacks took credit for this victory. They celebrated May Day 1918 by burning their old bedding rolls so that the companies were forced to provide bedding or have no workers.

One lumberjack said after the 1917 strike:

> Now the lumberjack is a man. He has burned his lousy blankets and made the company furnish him a decent place to sleep. Why in some camps, the men even have sheets to their beds as if they were regular human beings! And when he goes to town he puts on ordinary human clothes and leaves his corks behind. And he feels like a man, for he has time after an eight-hour day to do some thinking.[12]

After the Armistice was signed the 4 L's lost its government support, although the West Coast Lumbermen's Association urged that it continue. Colonel Disque was elected president of the 4 L's and promised again to stamp out anarchy and sabotage. Although the organization existed until the 1930's, membership dropped off as both the A.F.L. and I.W.W. recruited lumber workers after the war, and the organization proved ineffective against company-wide wage cuts during the next decade.

The antiradical hysteria which had gathered momentum in the Northwest during the war was climaxed in the lumber town of Centralia, Washington, in November 1919. Centralia had a history of anti-Wobbly activity. The I.W.W. hall had been wrecked during a Red Cross parade on Memorial Day, 1918, its American flag torn from the wall, the victrola auctioned in the street, and the desk confiscated by a Centralia banker. The newsstand of a blind Wobbly sympathizer, Tom Lassiter, was demolished in June 1919 because Lassiter sold the I.W.W. *Industrial Worker*. Lassiter was kidnapped, driven out of town, dumped into a ditch, and told never to come back at the risk of his life.

When the I.W.W. opened a new hall in Centralia, the Centralia Protective Association, a local businessmen's group, issued regular bulletins warning of the I.W.W. menace. A secret committee was appointed to work out details of driving the I.W.W. from the town. Word leaked out that there was a conspiracy to raid the I.W.W. headquarters during an Armistice Day parade in November. Elmer Smith, the I.W.W. lawyer in Centralia, went to see the governor to try to get protection for the organization. The owner of the building which the I.W.W. rented appealed to the police for help. Centralia Wobblies circulated a leaflet door to door asking townspeople for aid in meeting threats against them.

On November 11 Centralians jammed the streets to celebrate Armistice Day and watch a parade of returned veterans. The postmaster and former mayor carried coils of rope. When the marching legionnaires reached the I.W.W. hall, they were halted by the commanding officer. There were conflicting statements as to what happened. Dr. Frank Bickford, a Centralia merchant who had been in the parade, testified that someone suggested a raid on the hall. He said:

I spoke up and said I would lead if enough would follow but before I could take the lead there were many ahead of me. Someone next to me put his foot against the door and forced it open, after which a shower of bullets poured through the opening about us.[13]

Dr. Herbert Bell, also a marcher, testified that he heard a shout from the ranks ahead while the marchers were standing in front of the hall. He saw the ranks in front of him break and move toward the building.

It seemed to me that it was at the same time that I heard shots. The shooting and movement of men were as nearly simultaneous as any human acts could be.[14]

The legionnaires rushed to the hall. Shots were fired from the hall, from a hotel room across the street, and from a nearby hillside where several I.W.W. members were stationed. Three legionnaires were killed, including the Legion commander who was at the head of the invaders.

As the paraders broke into the hall, five I.W.W. members hid themselves in an unused icebox in a back room where they stayed until they were arrested. Wesley Everest, a war veteran I.W.W. member, ran out of the back door chased by the legionnaires. Surrounded by a mob on the banks of the Skookumchuck River, he offered to give himself up to any police official in the crowd. As the men rushed to get him, he shot and killed one of the legionnaires.

Everest was knocked unconscious and dragged back to the jail by a strap around his neck. That night the town lights were turned off while a crowd entered the jail, seized Everest, and drove him to the outskirts of town where he was castrated, according to Ralph Chaplin who investigated the tragedy, and lynched. His body was hung to a railroad trestle above the Chehalis River, and as word spread through the town, automobile parties drove out during the night to see the hanging corpse by automobile lights. His body was taken to the jailhouse the following day where it was laid in the corridor to be viewed by the eleven other I.W.W. prisoners. Four of the Wobblies, under guard, were forced to bury it in an unknown grave in a potter's field so that no pictures would be taken of the body.

Centralia was in a state of hysteria and panic. The American Legion controlled the town, organized armed posses to hunt for Wobblies, and threatened to remove the chief of police for not showing more interest in jailing the Wobblies they rounded up. Arrests of suspected I.W.W. members numbered over 1000. "The city commissioners were deprived of their police power," wrote a University of Washington professor who had come to investigate the case. "This power has been assumed by the American Legion."[15]

The Lewis County Bar Association warned its members that they would be disbarred for defending an I.W.W. member. "Even to sympathize with the perpetrators of the tragedy is proof evident that the sympathizer is a traitor to his country," the Centralia *Chronicle* editorialized.[16] In nearby Elma, the newspaper declared: "Hanging is none too good for them."[17] The Montesano *Vidette* called I.W.W. members "copperheads and reptiles" and reported that a movement had been started to make punishment for I.W.W. membership life imprisonment or death.[18] Washington's governor authorized the suppression of all seditious literature and wrote to police chiefs and sheriffs encouraging them to arrest all radicals in their towns. Local officers of the Department of Justice closed down the newspaper offices of the A.F.L. Seattle *Union Record* and arrested its editorial board for having called on its readers to hear both sides of the story before judging the case.

Seven of the I.W.W. prisoners were declared guilty of second-degree murder in the trial which took place in Montesano, Washington. Two of the prisoners, including the I.W.W. lawyer Smith, were acquitted, and a third was declared insane. Ignoring the jury's recommendation of leniency for the defendants, the judge sentenced them to maximum jail terms of twenty-five to forty years in Walla Walla Penitentiary. Several years after the trial, six of the jury members gave affidavits to lawyer Elmer Smith, who worked on the case until his death in the early 1930's. They stated that they would have voted to acquit all the defendants if they had known the full story of the legionnaires' raid on the I.W.W. hall. One juror wrote:

> I cannot get it out of my mind these many years; maybe I go back to Sweden . . . no one will say "there goes Pete Johnson; he helped send innocent men to prison." [19]

One of the I.W.W. prisoners died in Walla Walla of tuberculosis. Following the work of amnesty and church groups, five of the prisoners were paroled in 1933. One who insisted on a full pardon rather than a parole, was finally released in 1940 when the court commuted his sentence to the eighteen years which he had served. The Centralia American Legion built a monument to the Legion captain, Walter Grimms, killed in front of the I.W.W. hall on Armistice Day, and the story of ex-soldier Wesley Everest has been preserved in prose and poetry by Wobbly writers and sympathizers.

The Centralia tragedy climaxed the career of the I.W.W. lumberworkers' organization in the Northwest. Wobbly lumberjacks threw their efforts into fighting the "gyppo," or piecework, system, which employers initiated after the 1917 strike, and kept up their agitation to secure employer-provided bedding in camps where bindle stiffs were still forced to carry their own blanket rolls. Numerically, however, the union never recovered from the postwar, antiradical campaign.

I.W.W. efforts in the lumber industry were marked by tough campaigning and tragic climaxes against employers determined to destroy union efforts in lumber camps and sawmills. The tactics developed by the Wobblies to meet the rigors of the industry, their reaction to the patriotic appeals used against them, the victory of the 1917 strike, and the tragedies of Grabow and Centralia created a rich Wobbly literature flavored with humor and pathos.

1

This unsigned article, an early account of living and working conditions in lumber camps, appeared in the Industrial Worker *(July 2, 1910).*

WHO SAID A LOGGER LIVES?

The question has often been asked: "What constitutes living?" If it is the mere fact that we have life in our bodies and are plodding along in search of a job with our blankets on our back, then we are all living.

If "living" means to have all the good things of life, all the comforts of a home, and a life guarantee that such comforts shall continue as long as we are willing to do our share of the work, then we are not living, but simply saving funeral expenses.

It is estimated that there are 50,000 loggers along the Pacific coast, and it is a conservative statement to make that not one percent of them can say that their home consists of anything better than a dirty bunk furnished by the boss and a roll of blankets that they are compelled to tote about from pillar to post, many times only to make room for another toiler who has left $2 for the job in the tender care of a fat Employment Hog, who will divvy up with the foreman or superintendent. This is incentive enough to soon discharge him, so that a new recruit can be divorced from his $2, and so this endless chain of men tramping to and from the employment shark and the job.

Do They Drink?

Sure they drink. That is, the most of them do. Saloon keepers have waxed fat from the scanty earnings of the lumberjack. The saloonman knows when every pay day is in every camp in his neighborhood. He also knows that the lumberjack will bring his blankets into the saloon for safe keeping until he has a look about the burg and buys another job. The saloon is the only home he has, and there are to be generally found his friends from other camps, who are, of course, always glad to see him. Then the check has to be cashed, which is considered a favor, and the lumberjack reciprocates by buying a drink "for the house," which means all hands, if the gang is not too large. The saloonman is also glad to meet the new arrival with the check, and he too does the honors by "setting them up." Sometimes the checks do not admit of a large "blow-in," as the two-by-four (time check) was administered before a "stake" was made. In parts of Montana this employment ticket graft is "worked to a frazzle." There are camps that are known to have three crews of men. One crew coming to the camps with the "tickets for a job"; another with a two-by-four going away, and the other crew at work in the woods producing 20 times more for the boss than the wages could buy back at night. When men are plentiful and the labor market is well stocked, then the employment shark reaps the harvest. If men are scarce and times are good (which means lots of hard slavery) the boss generally tries to "hang onto" his crew after he has selected a good, sound, husky bunch. He can't afford to monkey with the "divvy on the employment ticket" then, as there is much more money to be made in keeping a full crew.

Checks for 5 Cents

Pay checks have been issued to first-class lumberjacks in Montana by no smaller a corporation than Jim Hill's railway, for amounts ranging from 5 cents and up; scores of them for amounts less than $1. The reader will doubt this statement and immediately say that it would be almost impossible to figure a man's time down so fine. Not so. This check may represent all the cash a worker will receive after working four or five days and perhaps longer. The employment fees in these particular cases are deducted from the wages earned, as in hard times the men have not the money to put up

to the "HOG" in advance. Then there is the dollar for the doctor and hospital. (There is generally no hospital and the doctor could not pare a corn.) Poll tax must be paid, which is generally about $4, if it has not been paid at some other camp, and if the worker loses his receipt, he pays again. Spring mattresses are on sale generally, and as they are fixtures to the bunk, they have to be paid for. The next fellow buys them over again. Boots, rubbers, socks, tobacco, etc., are for sale by the benevolent company at double their town value, and, of course, the woodsmen must have clothes and tobacco. It is now easy to understand how a man could be paid off with a nickle, 15 cents, 31 cents, etc. After all the grafts are worked and deducted from the wages due, the bank check represents the balance due.

Every employer of labor in the camps does not work the graft for all it is worth, but the employment shark graft is quite general, as is also the doctor.

The Food

The food is generally of the coarsest kind. Although not the fault of the cook, as many of the camp cooks are of the best in the land. Good but-

Industrial Worker, December 26, 1912.

THE REASON

ter is a rare article in a logging camp. Some of it is as white as wax, and as rotten as a putrid carcass, if smell goes for anything. This brand of "Ole," as the men call it, is very cheap, but strong. Strength is what the boss wants.

A lumberjack in Montana put some butter on the railroad track (so the story goes) and the train was derailed.

The "main squirt," or superintendent, occasionally visits the camp and eats with HIS MEN. He pronounces the food fine, especially the butter, and shows how tough he is by plastering it good and thick on the bread. He generally takes to the timber or the automobile immediately after supper.

Environment

The environment in which the lumberjack as logger lives is anything but a pleasant one. It consists of working long hours, eating poor food, sleeping in overcrowded bunk-houses, which are alive with vermin (lice and fleas), being robbed by Employment Hogs, packing the blankets, and having to leave them in the saloon in town, where many call home. From the toil of these men a few have made millions and live in the palatial mansions in the cities. The streets are named after them, and they are generally the leading citizens. They have their automobiles and their yachts, and to say the least, they revel in luxury. When the logger has produced more logs than can be sold or consumed, he is immediately laid off until a demand is created. The boss calls this "CURTAILING PRODUCTION," and the lumberjack calls it H—L. If a machine can be procured that will get out twice as many logs as men and donkey engines, with the same sized crew, in it goes. The "flying machine" does this very thing and it was only this year that thousands of men were laid off for a month at a stretch on Hoquiam Harbor to satisfy the great productivity of the "flying machine." The boss got rich, as the "flying machine" drew no wages, and did not need feeding when standing idle. The workers got poor, because the boss did not want them to work. They had by long hours of labor, together with some working man's invention, worked themselves out on the street.

The boss logger is organized to control the price of logs and lumber. Whether times be good or times be hard he has a cinch on the situation.

The slave logger is not organized to control that which he has to sell to the boss—HIS LABOR POWER.

No effort has been made to shorten the hours of labor. No organized effort has been made to rid themselves of the "EMPLOYMENT HOG." Thousands of loggers are buffeted about on the sea of capitalism with their blankets on their back, having no other purpose in life than to be "looking for jobs," and thus satisfying the greedy man or a few parasites who have by hook or crook gotten control of one of the natural resources of the earth, which was provided by Nature for the common use of mankind.

If we are agreed that the forests were intended for mankind and not for the enrichment of a few gluttons, then it is up to the loggers and all workers employed in the lumbering industry to wake up and organize right, so that they may at least live.

Let us begin by getting an eight-hour work day and tying a can to the employment shark. It is up to the workers to do the curtailing by doing less work each day. There is only one union that is really worthy of the name of a "labor organization" in America. It is founded on the truth—THE CLASS STRUGGLE. The irrepressible conflict between the toilers and the parasites; between those who own the tools and do not use them, and those who use them and do not own them. Between master and slave. Join your union today and take an interest in the work of getting all together. It's your duty. Do it. If there is not a local of your industry in your nearest town, then start one. If you don't know how to start one just ask the "INDUSTRIAL WORKER," or the first I.W.W. secretary you can locate.   A LOGGER

2

Covington Hall (1871–ca. 1951), who often wrote under the pen name Covington Ami or Covami, was one of the most prolific of the I.W.W. writers. He was born in Mississippi, the son of a Presbyterian minister and a wealthy southern belle. For more than fifty years, he was active as a writer, speaker, and publicity agent in farmer-labor struggles. He began as a follower of William Jennings Bryan, took an active part in many strenuous political campaigns, and for several years was one of the Farmers' Non-Partisan League's publicity chiefs.

Covington Hall edited The Lumberjack *(Alexandria, Louisiana), published by the National Industrial Union of Forest and Lumber Workers,*

Southern District. The Lumberjack *was later published in Portland, Oregon, as the* Voice of the
People. *Hall also edited* Rebellion, *a little monthly
magazine of radical essays and poetry. "Us the
Hoboes and the Dreamers," which Covington said
was written during the strike of the Brotherhood
of Timber Workers in Louisiana, Arkansas, and
Texas in 1911–12, appeared in* Rebellion (June
1916). *It was one of his most popular and frequently reprinted poems.*

US THE HOBOES AND DREAMERS

By COVINGTON HALL

*Written when we Lumberjacks, Sodbusters, Ho-
boes and Dreamers were fighting the Lumber
Barons of Louisiana and Texas, with our backs to
the wall, back in 1910–14.*

We shall laugh to scorn your power that now holds
  the South in awe,
We shall trample on your customs and shall spit
  upon your law;
We shall come up from our shanties to your
  burdened banquet hall,—
We shall turn your wine to wormwood, your honey
  into gall.

We shall go where wail the children, where, from
  your Race-killing mills,
Flows a bloody stream of profits to your curst,
  insatiate tills;
We shall tear them from your drivers, in our
  shamed and angered pride,
In the fierce and frenzied fury of a fatherhood
  denied.

We shall set our sisters on you, those you trapt into
  your hells
Where the mother instinct's stifled and no earthly
  beauty dwells;
We shall call them from the living death, the death
  of life you gave,
To sing our class's triumph o'er your cruel system's
  grave.

We shall hunt around the fences where your
  oxmen sweat and gape,
Till they stampede down your stockades in their
  panic to escape;
We shall steal up thru the darkness, we shall prowl
  the wood and town,

Till they waken to their power and arise and ride
  you down.

We shall send the message to them, on a whisper
  down the night,
And shall cheer as warrior women drive your
  helots to the fight;
We shall use your guile against you, all the
  cunning you have taught,
All the wisdom of the serpent to attain the ending
  sought.

We shall come as comes the cyclone,—in the
  stillness we shall form—
From the calm your terror fashioned we shall hurl
  on you the storm;
We shall strike when least expected, when you
  deem Toil's route complete,
And crush you and your gunmen 'neath our
  brogan-shodded feet.

We shall laugh to scorn your power that now holds
  the South in awe,
We shall trample on your customs, we shall spit
  upon your law;
We shall outrage all your temples, we shall
  blaspheme all your gods,—
We shall turn your Slavepen over as the plowman
  turns the clods!

3

*In 1912, Bill Haywood toured several of the lum-
ber camps in Louisiana, Arkansas, and Texas as
part of a trip south which included speaking at
the 1912 convention of the Brotherhood of Timber
Workers in Alexandria, Louisiana. This account
of his observations appeared in the* International
Socialist Review (*August 1912*).

TIMBER WORKERS AND
TIMBER WOLVES

By WILLIAM D. HAYWOOD

A. L. Emerson, President of the Brotherhood of
Timber Workers, is in jail at Lake Charles, La.
He was arrested following the shooting at Grabow, La., where three union men and one company hireling were killed outright and nearly two
score of men were more or less seriously wounded.
  The shooting is the outcome of the bitter war

I.W.W. Hall in Everett, Washington, 1916.

waged against the members of the Brotherhood of Timber Workers by the Lumber Trust for the last eighteen months. The scene of the tragedy that occurred on Sunday, July seventh, is a typical Southern lumber camp. The mill at this place is operated by the Galloway Lumber Company. In common with all others, it is surrounded by the miserable houses where the workers find habitation, the commissary store of the Company being the largest place of business in the town. A strike has been on at this place since the middle of last May. The single demand on the part of the union men was for a bi-weekly pay day. Heretofore the pay days have been at long intervals—usually a month apart.

During the intervening weeks, when the men were in need of money to meet the necessities of life, they could secure advances on their pay but not in real money. They were compelled to accept *Company Scrip* payable only in *merchandise* and exchangeable only at the company commissary. If accepted elsewhere it is uniformly discounted from 10 to 25 per cent on the dollar.

In the commissary stores where the cash prices are always from 20 to 50 per cent higher than at the independent stores, the company has established another means of graft by making two prices—the coupon or scrip price being much higher than that exacted for real cash.

The conditions at Grabow can be used as an illustration of nearly all of the other lumber camps of the South.

The commissary store is not the only iniquity imposed upon the Timber Workers. For miserable shacks they are compelled to pay exorbitant rents; sewerage there is none; there is no pretense at sanitation; the outhouses are open vaults. For these accommodations families pay from $5 to $20 a month. In one camp worn-out box cars are rented by R. A. Long, the Kansas City philanthropist, for $4 a month. Insurance fees are arbitrarily collected from every worker, for which he receives practically nothing in return, but whether his time be long or short—one day or a month—with the company, the fee is deducted. The same is true of the doctor fee and the hospital fee, which, in all places, is an imaginary institution. The nearest thing to a hospital that the writer saw was an uncompleted foundation at De Ridder, the place visited a few days prior to the Grabow tragedy. The gunmen and deputy sheriffs are an expensive innovation in the manufacture of lumber. These miserable tools are to be found everywhere and are used to browbeat and coerce the workers.

The lumber crews are hired without regard to color or nationality. In building up the Brotherhood of Timber Workers the officials of that organization have followed the lines laid down by the bosses and have brought into the ranks such persons as the bosses have employed. With wisdom and forethought they have refused to allow a discordant note to cause dissension in their ranks. This spirit of class consciousness aroused the ire of the lumber company to such an extent that no member of the Brotherhood of Timber Workers or the Industrial Workers of the World is given employment.

The spirit of the organization was plainly shown in its recent convention held at Alexandria where an effort was made on the part of the authorities to prevent a joint convention of white and black members. The Democratic officials of the county threatened to have an injunction issued or some other process of law invoked to prevent the body from coming together. As there is no law in Louisiana that prohibits the mixing of the races on the job, the B. of T. W. could not understand why they should not confer and council with each other in convention about their daily work, it being the purpose of the organization to improve the conditions under which its members labor.

After the Alexandria Convention adjourned, the first effort of the Timber Workers was to establish the semimonthly pay day at Grabow. The demand was made of the company that pay day should come every two weeks. The demand was flatly refused and the strike followed and has continued since. The Galloway Lumber Company, the concern affected, tried to operate their mill in the meantime with non-union men who had been induced to fill some of the places of the striking timber workers. It was for the purpose of bringing these men into the organization that President Emerson, accompanied by a hundred or more members and sympathizers from De Ridder, went to Grabow.

While Emerson was addressing the crowd that had assembled a shot was fired from the direction of the lumber company's office, which struck a young man standing by his side. This shot seemed to be the signal for a fusilade, coming not only from the office but from barricades of lumber and from the houses occupied by company thugs, one of whom stepped to the door and fired a shot

Arlington, Washington, branch of the Lumberworkers' Industrial Union No. 500, December 1917.

which lodged in the abdomen of Bud Hickman, a farmer, who with his wife in his buggy, was trying to get away from the conflict.

Roy Martin and Gates Hall, two union men, were killed outright and A. W. Vincent, a company man, was also killed.

That the company was prepared and looking for an opportunity to make just such a murderous assault is evidenced by the fact that the office had been converted into an arsenal.

The first news received at New Orleans, which later reports seem to verify, was that managers, superintendents and gun-men from other lumber companies were ambushed in the Galloway Lumber Company office and that a wholesale slaughter of union men had been deliberately planned. That the murder of Emerson was intended is clearly shown by the fact that the man standing closest to him was the first shot down. Emerson was the desired victim. He had long been a target for the lumber barons' hatred and venom.

Emerson is in jail, being held without bail at the time of this writing to await the action of the Grand Jury, that is to convene on the 15th of August. He is charged with murder on two counts. It will be proven in the course of time that his only crime is that of trying to lessen the burden and lengthen the lives of his fellow workers.

Before the campaign of organization now inaugurated by the Industrial Workers of the World is closed the lumber barons of Dixieland will have learned that it is impossible to fell trees with rifles and saw lumber with six shooters.

It should be mentioned here that of the nine men arrested four are non-union men, two of them, John and Paul Galloway, being owners of the Lumber Company. All are charged with murder. This, perhaps, indicates that the Trust has not entirely corralled the officialdom of Louisiana. It is certain that they are in bad repute with the business element in nearly all of the towns as their commissaries have been the means of controlling nearly the entire earnings of their employees, who are compelled to trade with the companies or lose the only means they have of making a living.

To maintain their absolute control of the camps the lumber companies, with the aid of their thugs, patrolled the towns; in some places inclosures were built around the mills and shacks. Notices were posted warning away union men, peddlers and Socialists.

Only a few days ago, H. G. Creel, one of the

Rip-Saw editors on a lecture tour, was roughly handled at Oakdale and De Ridder, La. He was compelled to leave the first-named place, being threatened and intimidated by gun-men.

The small merchant realizes that if the workers are allowed to trade where they choose some of their money would pass over their counters and they know if wages are increased there would be a corresponding increase in their day's receipts. This will account for the fact that the small businessman and farmer have given their sympathy and a measure of support to the growing union of timber workers.

Arthur L. Emerson and Jay Smith, both southern born, are the men around whom interest centers. They are the men who organized the Brotherhood of Timber Workers. Emerson had made two trips to the West—one to the Lumber District to the Southwest and the other to the Northwest. It was during the time that he worked with the lumberjacks of the Pacific Coast that he learned the need of organization. This thought was especially developed when he came in contact with the Lumber Workers' Union of St. Regis and other points in the Bitter Root Range of Mountains. Being a practical lumberjack and sawmill hand and mill-wright himself, he saw at once the discrepancy in wages between the Pacific Coast and the Gulf States and upon his return to Dixieland he immediately took up the burden of organizing the workers as the only possible means of bringing up their wages and conditions to the level of the already too-low Western scale.

His first attempt was at Fullerton, Louisiana, where, after securing employment in the mill, by energetic work, he had in a few days secured a list of eighty-five of the one hundred and twenty-five employes who signified their willingness to join an organization such as he, in his earnestness, explained to them, outlining the benefits to be derived if all would stand together in one union.

Emerson traveled from place to place securing a few days' employment in the different lumber camps, carrying his message of unionism to the slaves of the pine forests and cypress swamps of the southern states.

In this work of organization, he soon enlisted Jay Smith, his colleague in office, the present Secretary of the organization, and thousands of other stalwart men of the woods and sawmills, never hesitating at the color line or the nature of a man's work.

The framework of the Brotherhood of Timber Workers was as solid as the heart of the mighty oak that they converted into lumber. It was securely rooted. With headquarters at Alexandria, La., it branched out into the surrounding states. Its membership rapidly increased until thirty thousand of the wage slaves of the Lumber Trust were enrolled in its ranks.

Through the system of espionage which the Trust has established throughout its domain, the managers of the companies kept themselves informed of the work of the organization and its rapid growth. They realized that with this kind of an organization to contend with, their despotic methods would be at an end and they determined to destroy it root and branch.

To this end the Southern Lumber Operators' Ass'n. applied the most drastic action, closing down without notice forty-six mills. The thousands of workers who were employed in the lumber industry were thus deprived of their means of livelihood and left to shift for themselves. This arbitrary shut-down was continued for a period of nearly six months, and it is only now that the operators are endeavoring to run their mills as the demand for lumber has become so great and as the prices are higher than at any period in the history of the lumber industry the most vigorous efforts are being made to man the mills with nonunion labor.

Being unsuccessful a few of the largest companies have withdrawn from the Association; have granted the demands of the Timber Workers and are now running their mills night and day to fill accumulated orders.

The more obstreperous members of the Association are still trying to maintain their black list through the agency of their labor clearing house which has recently been established at Branch Headquarters located at Alexandria.

Their black-listing system is the most complete in operation anywhere. A man is compelled to give his name, birthplace, his color is recorded, the name and residence of his relatives, his former place of employment, the reason of his discharge or leaving his last place of work and particularly is he compelled to abjure all connection with the Brotherhood of Timber Workers or the Industrial Workers of the World. No later than the Fourth of July, celebrated as Independence Day in this country, John Henry Kirby, one of the wealthiest timber barons of the South, in a spread eagle oration, declared:

"That we do ask a man when he applies to us for work whether he is a member of the B.T.W. or I.W.W. If he is, we have nothing that he can do."

Thus a free-born American citizen, or one who has adopted this "Freeland" as his country, is denied the right to live and at the same time belong to this organization. The two having now merged, Mr. Kirby will have to refer to them as one in the future.

At the last convention of the Brotherhood of Timber Workers, attended by the writer, which was held last May, by an almost unanimous vote, application was made to the Industrial Workers of the World for a charter. The action of the convention was submitted to a referendum of the rank and file and has been sustained without a single opposing vote.

In September the Timber Workers of the South will meet in Convention representatives of timber workers from all other districts.

This meeting will be held in Chicago at about the time of the general convention of the Industrial Workers of the World. Then a National Industrial Union of Timber and Lumber Workers will be formed. This will include all of the workers employed in the United States, Canada and Mexico, in this industry, which in this country, is the third largest in importance and employs, perhaps, more men than any other.

Until the American Labor Union, which later merged with the I.W.W. began organizing the Lumber Workers, these millions of men were without a union of any kind. The organization which has now such a splendid foothold, will not limit its jurisdiction to any craft, section or division of the industry, but will include every man employed in the woods, the mills and the co-related industries.

The fight will be a long one and a bitter one. The struggle will be intense. Members and their families will suffer keen heart pangs, as the lumber barons will not loosen the stranglehold on their ill-gotten profits until they have exhausted every weapon that Capitalism has armed them with. But now that the workers of the Southland have joined hands with their fellow workers of the North, there can be but one result as the outcome of their united efforts. It can be recorded in one word—VICTORY! And the first step has been taken in the onward march toward Industrial Freedom!

Industrial Worker, August 25, 1917.

4

This unsigned poem appeared in Solidarity *(August 4, 1917) during a major I.W.W. strike in the Northwest lumber camps for better living and working conditions. A second version of the poem, collected by folklorist William Alderson, appeared in the* California Folklore Quarterly *(Vol. I, 1942).*

FIFTY THOUSAND LUMBER JACKS°

(Tune: "Portland County Jail")

Fifty thousand lumberjacks, fifty thousand packs,
Fifty thousand dirty rolls of blankets on their backs.
Fifty thousand minds made up to strike and strike like men;
For fifty years they've "packed" a bed, but never will again.

Chorus:

"Such a lot of devils,"—that's what the papers say—
"They've gone on strike for shorter hours and some increase in pay.
They left the camps, the lazy tramps, they all walked out as one;
They say they'll win the strike or put the bosses on the bum."

Fifty thousand wooden bunks full of things that crawl;
Fifty thousand restless men have left them once for all.
One by one they dared not say, "Fat, the hours are long."
If they did they'd hike—but now they're fifty thousand strong.

Fatty Rich, we know your game, know your pride is pricked.
Say—but why not be a man, and own when you are licked?
They've joined the One Big Union—gee—for goodness sake, get wise!
The more you try to buck them now, the more they organize.

Take a tip and start right in—plan some cozy rooms
Six or eight spring beds in each, with towels, sheets and brooms;

Shower baths for men who work keep them well and fit;
A laundry, too, and drying room, would help a little bit.

Get some dishes, white and clean; good pure food to eat;
See that cook has help enough to keep the table neat.
Tap the bell for eight hours' work; treat the boys like men,
And fifty thousand lumberjacks may come to work again.

Men who work should be well paid—"A man's a man for a' that."
Many a man has a home to keep same as yourself, Old Fat.
Mothers, sisters, sweethearts, wives, children, too, galore
Stand behind the men to win this bread and butter war.

5

William Alderson wrote in the California Folklore Quarterly *(Vol. I, 1942, p. 376): "In the Spring of 1942, Dr. Harold Barto of Ellensburg, Washington, gave me this I.W.W. song which he learned in the logging camps of northern Idaho in 1917. . . . It is sung to the tune of 'A Son of a Gamboleer' . . . Professor Arthur G. Brodeur has pointed out to me a general similarity in metrical pattern and even in phrase—'twenty-thousand Cornish men'—between 'Trelawny' and this song."*

FIFTY THOUSAND LUMBERJACKS

1. Fifty thousand lumberjacks
     Goin' out to work,
   Fifty thousand honest men
     That never loaf or shirk
   Fifty thousand lumberjacks
     They sweat and swear and strain,
   Get nothin' but a cussin'
     From the pushes and the brains.

2. Fifty thousand lumberjacks
     Goin' in to eat
   Fifty thousand plates of slum
     Made from tainted meat,

Fifty thousand lumberjacks
   All settin' up a yell
To kill the bellyrobbers
   An' damn their souls to hell.

3. Fifty thousand lumberjacks
     Sleepin' in pole bunks
  Fifty thousand odors
     From dirty socks to skunks,
  Fifty thousand lumberjacks
     Who snore and moan and groan
  While fifty million graybacks
     Are pickin' at their bones.

4. Fifty thousand lumberjacks
     Fifty thousand packs
  Fifty thousand dirty rolls
     Upon their dirty backs
  Fifty thousand lumberjacks
     Strike and strike like men;
  For fifty years we packed our rolls,
     But never will again.

6

Archie Sinclair, head of the I.W.W. California Defense Committee, was the author of this poem, which appeared in the Industrial Worker *(February 16, 1918).*

BINDLELESS DAYS

By Archie R. Sinclair

The loggers all say, on the First of May,
Our bindles we will shed.
From the First of May till Judgment Day,
We'll nevermore carry a bed.

      *   *   *

From that time on, at dusk or dawn,
When hiking over the road,
Morning or night, we'll travel light,
Not one will carry a load.

      *   *   *

If the boss wants to pack a bed on his back
We have nothing more to say.
But nary a jack will carry a pack
After the First of May.

      *   *   *

So here is a toast to the men of the Coast
The loggers and job delegate,

For a "Bindleless Day" on the First of May,
All the workers will agitate.

7

T-Bone Slim wrote this very popular statement which was printed on small colored cards and sold to raise money for the organization. This version was taken from such a card in the I.W.W. files in the Labadie Collection.

THE LUMBER JACK'S PRAYER

I pray dear Lord for Jesus' sake,
Give us this day a T-Bone Steak,
Hallowed be thy Holy name,
But don't forget to send the same.

Oh, hear my humble cry, Oh Lord,
And send us down some decent board,
Brown gravy and some German fried,
With sliced tomatoes on the side.

Observe me on my bended legs,
I'm asking you for Ham and Eggs,
And if thou havest custard pies,
I like, dear Lord, the largest size.

Oh, hear my cry, All Mighty Host,
I quite forgot the Quail on Toast,
—Let your kindly heart be stirred,
And stuff some oysters in that bird.

Dear Lord, we know your Holy wish,
On Friday we must have a fish,
Our flesh is weak and spirit stale,
You better make that fish a whale.

Oh, hear me Lord, remove these "Dogs,"
These sausages of powder'd logs,
Your bull beef hash and bearded Snouts.
Take them to hell or thereabouts.

With Alum bread and Pressed-Beef butts,
Dear Lord you damn near ruin'd my guts,
Your white-wash milk and Oleorine,
I wish to Christ I'd never seen.

Oh, hear me Lord, I am praying still,
But if you won't, our union will,
Put pork chops on the bill of fare,
And starve no workers anywhere.

ANSWER TO THE PRAYER

I am happy to say this prayer has been answered—by the "old man" himself. He tells me He has furnished—plenty for all—and that if I am not getting mine it's because I am not organized SUFFICIENTLY strong to force the master to loosen up.

He tells me he has no knowledge on Dogs, Pressed-Beef Butts, etc., and that they probably are products of the Devil. He further informs me the Capitalists are children of Hisn—and that He absolutely refuses to participate in any children's squabbles. He believes in letting us fight it out along the lines of Industrial Unionism.

Yours in faith,
T-BONE SLIM.

NOTE—The money derived from the sale of these, goes for the payment of putting out free literature.

PRICE 10 CENTS

8

This short story about "technological improvements" in the lumber camps appeared, unsigned, in the I.W.W. publication The Lumberjack Bulletin *(May 4, 1918).*

TALL TIMBER TALES

The newest member fell in behind Lumberjack Joe on the trail and spoke up rather resentfully:

"Well, anyhow, I'll bet you and Paul Bunyan never logged with a flying machine. Now did you?"

"Son," answered Joe over his shoulder, "men were too cheap in them days to bother much about machinery, but the cook did rig up one of them contraptions to turn flapjacks with and load them onto the men's plates. You see he had to cook for a crew of one thousand scissorbills and even with their roller skates the flunkeys couldn't get the flapjacks down to the far end of the big table until they were too cold to eat. When Paul laid eyes on the handy rig he raised the cook's wages to $18 a month."

"Eighteen a month!" exclaimed the cub member. "And what wages did the loggers get?"

"We paid them a package of Peerless each day, a bottle of whiskey every Saturday night, $10 in commissary and $5 in cash each month, and charged them for wear and tear on the tools. They had to furnish their own lanterns and it kept them broke most of the time buying oil, until Paul hit on a scheme to get them free light. It worked fine until John D. put it on the bum."

"What was the scheme?" inquired the newest member.

"The men filled their lantern globes with lightning bugs," answered Joe, "and they gave a better light than kerosene. Coal-oil Johnny sure was sore at us, and when he failed to make an injunction stick against us, he got a bunch of sentimental old women to organize a Society for the Abolition of Firefly Slavery and made us turn all the bugs loose. Then when Paul went East and got the machinery idea in his nut he came back with a jiggermaroo that dumped 800 of the crew down the skid road onto the bread line. All we needed was loaders."

"Gee!" exclaimed the cub member with his mouth hanging wide open. "What kind of a machine was it?"

"It was a 90 foot Improved McCormick Reaper and Harvester with 15 foot blades as sharp as razors. Paul hitched the old blue ox onto it and mowed down every tree in Kansas. The machine cut them close to the ground, trimmed them clean, ground up the tops into patent breakfast food, and tied up the logs in bundles of five. We made a million dollars every day and were known all over the country as great philanthropists because all the breakfast food we didn't feed to the ox and the crew we sent down to be given away to the hungry lumberjacks on the bread line."

"But I'll bet that the high lead camps have about the last word in logging machinery," remarked the newest member.

"Forget that noise," said Lumberjack Joe a trifle impatiently. "There is no such thing as a last word in machinery. There are machines to make machines to make machines. But the latest thing in machinery for the woods is the motor chain saw which will cut down a thirty inch tree in two minutes, and cut it low without waste. It would have made Paul Bunyan jump with joy to see one of them. That machine will make I.W.W. members out of the loggers who still think their skill makes them better than other workers, faster than all the speeches of the delegates. Say, son, if every wobbly were jailed tomorrow, the machine would produce a fresh crop of revolutionary industrial unionists within a year. We should worry!"

And Lumberjack Joe stopped with the bunch long enough to find out what his new duties were to be.

ALL "BINDLES" WILL BE BURNED ON MAY FIRST

MAY THE FIRST 1918

Industrial Worker, February 9, 1918.

9

*George Milburn collected this unsigned I.W.W.
poem and included it in* The Hobo's Hornbook
(*New York, 1930*). *Its source is not known.*

THE TIMBER BEAST'S LAMENT

I'm on the boat for the camp
With a sick and aching head;
I've blowed another winter's stake,
And got the jims instead.

It seems I'll never learn the truth
That's written plain as day,
It's, the only time they welcome you
Is when you make it pay.

And it's "blanket-stiff" and "jungle-hound,"
And "pitch him out the door,"
But it's "Howdy, Jack, old-timer,"
When you've got the price for more.

Oh, tonight the boat is rocky,
And I ain't got a bunk,
Not a rare of cheering likker,
Just a turkey full of junk.

All I call my life's possessions,
Is just what I carry 'round,

For I've blowed the rest on skid-roads,
Of a hundred gyppo towns.

And it's "lumberjack" and "timber-beast,"
And "Give these bums a ride,"
But it's "Have one on the house, old boy,"
If you're stepping with the tide.

And the chokers will be heavy,
Just as heavy, just as cold,
When the hooker gives the high-ball,
And we start to dig for gold.

And I'll cuss the siren skid-road,
With its blatant, drunken tune,
But then, of course, I'll up and make
Another trip next June.

10

*Signed with the initials, "J. B.," this song appeared
in the* Industrial Worker (*October 11, 1919*). *It is
almost identical with a poem, "The Wino's Nose,"
by Ed Anderson, which was included in a scrapbook compiled in 1919–20 by I.W.W. member
E. Rose and donated some years ago to the Labadie Collection. The undated clipping is headed*
California Defense Bulletin, *an I.W.W. publication issued in 1919–20.*

In his Journal of American Folklore *article,
Archie Green discussed this song. He wrote: " 'The
Dehorn Song' is no lyric masterpiece, but it reveals
facets of labor folklore. It also shows that the
Wobbly could poke fun at himself; he possessed
a strain of humor sadly lacking in other sections
of the radical movement. The song flays the drunkard but not in the saccharine tones of a temperance
tract, for behind the portrait lay the militant de-
horn squad—an instrument of social control developed by outcasts consciously dedicated to rebuild-
ing society."*

*The melody as well as the inspiration for "The
Dehorn's Nose" and "The Wino's Nose" is Jim
Connell's "The Red Flag."*

THE DE-HORN'S NOSE IS
DEEPEST RED
By J. B.

The De-Horn's nose is deepest red,
The one bright spot on an empty head.

To get his booze he begs and steals,
    Half-naked goes, and without meals.

         Chorus

O! De-Horn why don't you get wise?
    And quit the booze and organize.
A sober mind shall win the day,
    The One Big Union' shows the way.

And when the De-Horn gets a job,
    He's satisfied, the dirty slob,
A pile of straw will do for bed,
    On which to rest his weary head.

To stick around and fix the job,
    It never pierced his empty nob,
For fifty cents will get him drunk,
    And fifteen cents a lousy bunk.

But when the De-Horn gets stake-bound,
    And starts to dreaming about town,
He kicks about the rotten chuck,
    And never saw such a sticky muck.

O! Point to him with nose so red,
    With tangled feet and soggy head,
For, all this life to him will yield,
    Is just a grave in potter's field.

11

"Anise" was the pen name of Anna Louise Strong (1885—), an American journalist and writer who has written about revolutions all around the world. Miss Strong was feature editor of the Seattle Union Record *from 1916 to 1921 and reported on the Montesano (Washington) trial of the Wobblies sentenced to prison following the Centralia Armistice Day massacre in November 1919. These free-verse poems, describing the I.W.W. defendants in the trial, were in the file of I.W.W. poems in the Labadie Collection. Their source of publication is not known.*

CENTRALIA PICTURES

By ANISE

1. Eugene Barnett

"I was born," he said,
"In the hills of Carolina,
And the schooling I got

In this great free land
Of compulsory schools
Was very simple;
My MOTHER taught me
Reading and writing
And I went to school
For a three-months' term,
And a five-months' term!
Then
I was EIGHT years old
And my father went
As a STRIKE-BREAKER
To the West Virginia mines.
I remember the TENTS
Of the UNION miners,
Driven from their homes
CAMPING
Over the river.
They put me to work at once
UNDERGROUND
And when the inspectors came
I had to HIDE
In the old workings,
For the legal age in the mines
Was FOURTEEN years,
But neither the BOSS
Nor my FATHER
Cared about LAW!
I was caught
In the Papoose explosion
At the age of eleven,
And I ran away from home
At thirteen.
I followed MINING
All over the country
Joining the UNION
In Shadyside, Ohio.
I was SIXTEEN then
And had worked EIGHT years,
And in all those years
My only chance for schooling
Was a short time
After a FEVER,
When I was TOO WEAK
To WORK!

But somehow I managed to get
A good-looking wife
Who encouraged me
To improve myself!
We had a little girl that died
And a boy that lived,
He's two years now
And a BRIGHT KID;
Can't keep still!
We took a homestead
Over in Idaho
Till the government called
For MINERS,
So I came to Centralia
At the country's call
And after the Armistice
There wasn't much work!
I saw the raid on the hall
And the starting
Of the MAN-HUNT,
And I rode home
For my GUN
To get some law and order
In Centralia!
When they arrested me
I didn't tell all I knew,
For I was afraid if I did
I mightn't live to see
A court-room trial!"

2.   Ray Becker

It was through the bars
Of the county jail
That he told his story,
While the jailer waited
In a corner,
And the other boys
Were washing up
For supper:
"I'm twenty-five," he said,
"And I studied four years,
Intending to be
A SKY-PILOT!
But after I saw

The INSIDE WORKINGS
I QUIT!
Not overnight, of course,
Nor in a day,
It took some time.
For I come
From a PREACHER family!
My father has a pulpit
And one of my brothers
Has a pulpit.
But I found most people
Wouldn't PRACTICE
What you PREACH,
And I didn't see HOW
To get them to.
Besides,
To be real FRANK
I no longer believed
MOST of the stuff
And I didn't want
To preach it.
Since 1915
I've been in the WOODS
And I joined the Wobblies
In 1917.
After the raid on our hall
I was one of the occupants
Of the ICE-BOX
And I had
An Iver Johnson .38!
That was how
I come to be HERE,—
But I figure
The only practical Christians
TODAY
Are the I.W.W.'s
And the Socialists,
And the folks
That are trying to get
A NEW WORLD!
Anyway,
Christ was a TRAMP
Without a place
To 'lay his head,'
And WE are tramps,

And I guess
That fifth chapter
Of the epistle of James,
Telling the RICH FOLKS
To weep and howl
For what was COMING,
Must have been written
By a WOBBLY!"

3.   Bert Bland

All life's uncertainties
Sat lightly on him,
He was of the WOODS
And YOUNG enough
To smile at danger,
Indeed, he smiled
On all the world
With joyous greeting
As if everyone he met
Gave him PLEASURE,
"I was three years old," he said,
"When they brought me to Washington
From the Illinois farm
Where I was born.
My father, too, was born
In Illinois
In Lincoln's time,
And my mother came
From the SOUTH,—
I guess I'm about as near
An American
As they make them,
And if I ever had ancestors
From any foreign land
They got lost somewhere
In the PRAIRIES!
I was sixteen
When I became a LOGGER
And for eight years
I've followed the WOODS,
It's a great life
If you don't weaken,
But the CAMPS
Are certainly ROTTEN!

Fourteen of us slept
In a 10 by 14 bunkhouse
Over in Raymond,
With our wet clothes
STEAMING
In the middle of the shack!
The bad conditions drove me
From camp to camp,
Twenty-two different ones
In a single year,—
And only one of them all
Had a BATH!
I've been a WOBBLY
For about three years
Hoping to change conditions.
When they raided our hall
I shot from the hill
To defend it,
And then I fled to the woods!
A lynching party
Had me surrounded once
But I crawled through them
About 1 A.M.
On my hands and knees,
And lay out in the hills
For seven nights.
I was the lucky guy,—
For by the time they got me
In a train-shed,
Things had quieted some,
So I missed
The TERRORIZING
The others got
In the Centralia jail,
And the worst they handed me
Was watching OILY ABEL,
The Lumber Trust's pet lawyer
Helping the state hand
'JUSTICE'
To rebel Lumberjacks!"

4.   Britt Smith

The weight of the world
Seemed resting

On his shoulders,
He was thirty-eight
And had followed the woods
For twenty years.
He knew to the full
The lumber camps of Washington,
And he had no more
ILLUSIONS
He sawed the timbers
To build the great flume
At Electron,
Where the mountain waters
Come pouring down
To give, light and power
In Tacoma,
And to carry
The LUXURIOUS Olympian
Over the Cascades,
Softly and smoothly,
With passengers warm
And COMFORTABLE.
But he and his fellows
Had slept in a SWAMP
On cedar PLANKS,
And had no place
To WASH
After their day's labor.
He said: "I have slept
WEEKS at a time
In WET CLOTHES,
Working
All day in the rain,
Without any place,
To DRY OUT.
I have washed my clothes
By tying them
To a stake in the river,
Letting the current
Beat them partly clean.
It was often the only place
We had for washing."
It was HE
The LYNCHERS sought
That night of terror
When the lights went out

And they broke into the jail
And dragged forth Everest
To torture
And mutilation
And hanging,
Crying: "We've got Britt Smith!"
For he was secretary
Of the I.W.W.s
And lived in a little room
At the back of the hall
Which he tried to defend
In the RAID,—
It was his only HOME
He had spent his strength
And used his youth
Cutting LUMBER
For the homes of others!

Wesley Everest.
Labadie Collection photo files.

12

Wesley Everest is one of the trilogy of I.W.W. martyrs (Joe Hill, Frank Little, Wesley Everest) which has inspired tributes from Wobbly and non-Wobbly writers. John Dos Passos compared Wesley Everest to Paul Bunyan in his novel Nineteen Nineteen *(New York, 1932). Robert Cantwell re-created the situation in Centralia in his story "The Hills Around Centralia," included in the* Anthology of Proletarian Literature *(New York, 1935). Richard Brazier wrote two poems in memory of Everest, "The Ballad of Wesley Everest" and "The Hidden Grave of Wesley Everest," and several of the other Centralia defendants paid tribute to him in verse.*

This poem on Wesley Everest by Ralph Chaplin is taken from the Industrial Pioneer *(July 1921). It has been frequently reprinted in the I.W.W. press.*

WESLEY EVEREST

By Ralph Chaplin

Torn and defiant as a wind-lashed reed,
Wounded he faced you as he stood at bay;
You dared not lynch him in the light of day,
But on your dungeon stones you let him bleed;
Night came . . . and you black vigilants of
    Greed . . .
Like human wolves, seized hard upon your prey,
Tortured and killed . . . and silently slunk away
Without one qualm of horror at the deed.

Once . . . long ago . . . do you remember how
You hailed Him king for soldiers to deride—
You placed a scroll above His bleeding brow
And spat upon Him, scourged Him, crucified . . .
A rebel unto Caesar—then as now
Alone, thorn-crowned, a spear wound in his side!

13

Two more Tightline Johnson stories by Ralph Winstead find Johnson attempting to improve conditions in the lumber camps. After World War I, lumber companies started a piecework system, called "the gyppo system" by Wobblies, in an attempt to counter the effects of collective bargaining. As Fred Thompson wrote: "They brought it in with a sugar coating, letting men earn three and

four times as much as they would make at hourly rates, but wiser heads knew this was to get it going. The need to settle prices for each operation would bring individual bargaining and eventually less pay for more work. . . . Opinion among I.W.W. members differed. The general sentiment was that no Wobbly would work gyppo. . . . A few who knew their economics suggested that given these circumstances of a money-hungry majority, and the current high rates offered for piece work, the judicious thing was for the union to allow it on the proviso that the rates be set for each operation by collective bargaining and kept so high that unit costs would exceed those resulting from an hourly rate" (The I.W.W.: Its First Fifty Years).

"Chinwhiskers, Haywire, and Pitchforks" was printed in the One Big Union Monthly *(January 1921). "Johnson, the Gypo" is from the* Industrial Pioneer *(September 1921).*

CHIN-WHISKERS, HAY-WIRE, AND PITCHFORKS

By Ralph Winstead

I was moping down the skid road, sort of upending the fact that pretty soon I would have to buy a master or give the grub question the go-by. Them kind of thoughts are never frolicsome, but of themselves is not liable to superinduce these here railroad blues. I have sort of got used to havin' the bottom of the sack just a few jingles down, and you know we are never very much concerned over what we have grown accustomed to, like the feller says of his wife.

But this here moribund condition of mine had justification for bein'. The very night before, I had got stood against a wall by Keefe and his Red Squad while they vacuum-cleaned me, looking for the red card. It is true, they didn't get anything on me because when I hit these malevolent sections I leave the little due book up where the chambermaid can see if I am paid up or not. The job, I maintains, is the place to carry the card at.

I turned the corner goin' down towards Archie's slave market when who should I bump into but Pearlie MacCann. Now, Pearlie is just the right sort of antidote for any dark-brown morning that comes along. He just radiates joy. In fact, just to think about that fellow worker is to raise up a glow that is more intoxicating than a shot and a half of Dehorn.

You don't know Pearlie MacCann? Say! Pearlie is the most all-there he-man that ever hit the sticks. He savvies how to get out the round stuff, too, but better than that he knows all the methods for gettin' conditions improved in some of the insect laboratories that are to be found even yet on parts of the Coast.

As a scizzorbill evangelist he sure gets the goods. Why, he went single-handed into the cook shack up at hostile Clallan Bay and pulled out the camp, cook house crew and all, till the Super came thru with the grub that the cook wanted, and then decided that it was better to put up that dry-house than to take a chance on losing his job.

MacCann shipped into the outfit as a pearl-diver, and that is how he got the name of Pearlie. This was early in 1918, too, when to be a Wob was about as tough as it is now, only more so.

When Pearlie saw me he grinned a welcome like a shark. "Hello, there, Tightline!" he said warmly as he hooked me with that grip of his. "Where have you been all these days since old Paulson reclaimed the bunk space we was usin'?"

I give him a list of my late ambulations and he returned with his. Then he sprung a job on me.

"Say, Tightline, you still nosin' 'round the grease pots?"

I nodded.

"Why don't you take a rest from this fog bustin' and do a little real work? Come on and load for me for a few months or so."

I was startled. "What do you mean,—months? Have you got a pull with old Weyerhauser lately? The longest I ever saw you keep one master was six weeks."

"Well, anyway, you could come out and give a fellow a start," he said. "You see, I got a recommend from Archie as bein' an A-One hooker if I ain't crossed, and one of these gunny-sack parasites decided to hire me and let me pick my own loader. There's a donkey puncher already on the job, or I would put you next to the graft. But as I always said, a man is a chump that will scald himself in good summer weather alongside a yard hog. Come on out and load for me."

I knew right then that I was goin' to go to work, but for appearances' sake I stalled a bit. "What kind of a show you got?" I asks.

"Fine!" says Pearlie. "Couldn't be better. There's two settin's where the logs is four deep and not a stump in the ground!"

"Thasso?" says I. "And I suppose the riggin' is all ginney line with whistle wire for a haul back.

I'm your man. If you run me out on a work-house job I'll make you buy an organization stamp for every drop of sweat that leaks out of me. Say! Where is this young heaven?"

"Well, to tell the truth, I haven't exactly given the lay-out the once-over quite, but the proud owner was tellin' me that the hooker he had was loadin' three cars, and that the men was all kickin' on account of hard work. I says to myself: "Here's where I make a reputation."

Next afternoon Pearlie and me hitches our suit-cases onto a Redmond stage and climbs in for Camp Three. The chauffeur let us off at a little trail and we started along, as directed, towards the camp. 'Twas about a mile, he told us.

I've picked up books with yards of stuff in 'em tellin' about leafy bowers, twittering birds and the like. I never could see no sense in puttin' such stuff down into books when there it is, right in front of a feller in real life, if he only goes out and looks at it. These here writin' fellers ought to write more about conditions and organization and things that are more important, and let people that are interested in nature-lovin' go out and get their nature first hand. I think the reason a lot of ink is spilled on this nature proposition is that the spillers are afraid to get off the cement for fear they might get lost, or bit, or something.

Anyhow, it was late spring, and everything had that tang to it that peps a fellow up and puts some sass into him. There is a different sort of feeling in the air than there is in the fall, say in November. November is a sort of dreary, reactionary month when everything sort of goes backwards. It ain't for nothin' that November was the month when they hung the victims of the Haymarket riots. I bet the weather had a lot to do with the Everett Massacre, with killing Joe Hill and with the Centralia Conspiracy. But here I am a-gettin' clear off.

At the end of the trail we came out into a little clearing in which was as pretty a picture of a haunted house as you ever see. An old clap-boarded farmhouse gone to seed. There was two or three pig and hen houses scattered around, but I didn't see nothin' that looked like a camp.

We piked up to the door of the fenceless and unprotected house, and met the bull-cook goin' after water. Pearlie tells him he was the new hook-tender, and the bull-cook he shows us over to the nearest pig-house, which is fixed up with three bunks.

We dumps down our suit-cases and squints

about to see the lay-out. No sign of stickers on the walls, no literature on the table, not even a capitalist rag. The shack was one to delight a fresh-air fiend, except that the dust and cobwebs might have caused a sneeze or two. The bunks were of ordinary steel, such as our bosses, prompted by a rush of emotions to their heads, installed at the time of the big Job Strike.

I ain't never been interested much in this architecture stuff, but I sure didn't have no taste for the mixture that was in that shack. It seemed to have been built in three installments, each installment put on like a patch on a pair of overalls. There was a cedar puncheon-and-shake foundation with an overcoat of fir lumber and shingles, and then to give the modern touch of orneriness there was some tin and paper stuck around to fill up the holes.

Under such conditions there is generally a flock of double-deck bunks and crummy sougans to sleep under, with the boss a-proddin' all the time to get the new men to bring their own blankets. Here, however, there was only the three half bunks, and while the sougans were not new, yet they wasn't clammy with the rubbin's from pants and shoes,—not so far.

So we surmised to ourselves that this must be the parlor where only the brains was allowed to sleep.

Pearlie pokes his thumb over at the third bunk and asks the bull-cook who sleeps there.

The bull-cook looks mysterious and says in a tone that was meant to sound like he was goin' to give the devil his due even if it went against the grain: "That's Hal Whicombe's. He is slingin' the riggin' as a rule, but is tendin' hook till you get here. He is a pretty good, steady worker." He takes a long pause to think over the next, then he springs this: "If I were you I would be careful what I said to him, 'cause he is liable to let it out."

"Huh," thinks I, "a stool pigeon!"

Pearlie and me looks at each other. Then Pearlie turns to the bull-cook. "How long has this Whicombe been here?" he asks casual like.

"Well, let's see, I been here eighteen months now and he come about a month after I started. Yeah,—he's been here seventeen months."

Pearlie stops monkeyin' with his clothes and sits down on the bed. The bull-cook remembers his water bucket and goes out. Pearlie goes to the door to see if he is really gone, and then comes back and says to me: "There is something phoney here. This bull-cook spills some slave ideas and then brands this riggin' slinger as a stool, after advertisin' that he himself is a bill from backwater. Here he says he's been on the job for eighteen months and then tells us strangers that this stool come since he did. Something dungy some place."

"All I got to say, Pearlie, is that if this guy is a stool, you and me will sure lead him a cheerful life between us, on the job and off. Anyway, we better wait till we run into him before we lay plans to put the skids under him. It may be a grudge this bull-cook has or somethin'."

So Pearlie and I kept on unpackin'. Neither of us unloaded any of the books and literature we had. We wanted to size up this said stool first.

I mopes around the camp to find the drinkin' water and Pearlie goes over to the cook shack. After gettin' a drink I takes a squint at a couple of shacks that were built about like the one we had camped in, and finds only one with bunks in. There was four bunks. I was puzzled. What kind of a phoney outfit was this, anyway? I wouldn't have put it beyond Pearlie to go out to a seven-man loggin' camp, but I couldn't savvy no such camp bein' run. I made up my mind that there was another camp some place around—perhaps up on the railroad track.

I goes back to the shack and pulls out a book I had brought along from Andy's Library, and lays down to read. By and by Pearlie blows in. He gives a grunt and lays down, too. His grunt wasn't a sociable one, so I let him alone.

We could hear the donkey whistling signals as the men logged, away off towards the timber. By and by they blow for quits and in half an hour or so the third roomer in our flat showed up.

He says "Hello," and wants to know if one of us is the new hooker. Pearlie says, "Yes."

This third party is very chatty and twaddles along about the weather and the water and the soap and nothin' at all while he is gettin' off his boots and socks and puttin' on his change.

Then he grabs a rag from the wall that does for a towel and goes out to the wash-bench by the creek. By and by he comes back as confidin' as ever and starts to talk about the work. He gets a lot of slave ideas off his chest in one way and another, about how many they yarded on this day and how much they would have got on that day if they hadn't had bad luck with the haul back, etc., etc. Finally I asks him how many there was in the crew. He starts countin' 'em up by name and finally gets about thirty-five. Then he starts tellin' about them: "This feller isn't much good," and "That feller is a jim dandy," and, "This other guy is a piker."

Finally Pearlie asks him what kind of a guy this here bull-cook is. Pearlie casts no remarks about the bull-cook, just a plain question, but the riggin' slinger seems glad of a chance to get something off his chest. "Wah," he says, "That guy ain't to be trusted. Say there ain't hardly any of the boys here that like him. O' course, those that are his kind like him all right, but I ain't got no use for that bunch."

"How's that?" asks Pearlie. "What's the trouble with him?"

"Ah! He's liable to tell everything you let him find out about you."

I nearly fainted. Here was two stools whose chief occupation seemed to be stoolin' on each other. I was commencin' to get real curious to see what the rest of this famous crew was like. The chow bell rang and we went over to the cookshack and climbed up the dilapidated steps, entered the squee-geed doorway and found ourselves in the table room. The bull-cook had graduated into the flunky now and was standin' ready to show us the place we should sit in. The Super was there and they put Pearlie alongside of him while I got a seat down at the other end.

I'll say this for the grub, I've eat worse, but also can say that I've had a lot better. There was eight men at the table. I was wonderin' where the rest of the crew was at. It wasn't Saturday, so that they'd all be gone to town. This here strangeness was gettin' on my nerves. Nothin' was run the way it ought to be. Instead of thirty or two hundred men shovelin' in the chuck, here was eight. Then here was all this loose talk about stools the first thing a fellow hits camp, and nobody seemed to have a good idea what there was to stool about. Then because of the rummy actions that had already come to notice, every other move on the part of the crew seemed rumdum.

There was a woman cook that we could hear talkin' in the kitchen. The pie was dished up in a saucer and one piece was supposed to satisfy. The crew was all talkin' loud at the table, which sure ain't no proper way for a crew to act. Everything made me think that I had gone to some country where loggin' was unknown.

Pearlie didn't show up after supper, so I supposed that he was still listenin' to the Super. I moped over to the other bunk-house and was stared at for a while by the inmates. I never felt quite so ornery. These freaks were sure the strangest bunch of loggers I ever seen. I got up and left when I couldn't get no talk or sense out of them and walked up to the spring for a drink. There I met the fourth character just comin' back.

He says right away like a real human, "Well, what do you think of this lay-out?" I told him that I didn't hardly know yet and was so pleased at his slow grin that I could have hugged him.

"Did you bring any papers?" he says, just as tho out of a dream, to me.

"Well, I got a P. I.," I come back.

"Huh," he scoffs, "I see too much of the P. I. to suit me."

"All right, fellow worker," I says, "come over to the bunk-house and see if there is anything I can give you that will suit."

"Have you got any stamps?" he asks.

"Do you want some?" I counters.

"Yeah," he says thotfully, "I think I'm behind. I'll go over and get my book. I'll be right over to your shack."

I went into my old valise and dug up my supplies. Then I spread the latest working class papers out on the bed and the stranger soon appeared with his little old red card.

He was an old-time dirt-mover and so I transferred him into 120. While I was busy with his card he looks over the papers and literature and picks out all the late copies. He sticks the papers in his pocket and sits down for a talk.

Before he had a chance to commence I asks him what was the matter with this outfit. I says, "Here is supposed to be a loggin' camp. Loggin' camps generally have a few loggers around and there is nobody here. Then, the first thing we hit camp there is two fellows accuse each other of bein' stools and I commence to believe both of 'em. Everything has a phoney air and rumdum look. What is the answer? Is it the Dehorn or moonshine, or what? Is it real or just company manners? If I don't find out what's the matter with this layout I am goin' to be as batty as the rest."

The dirt-mover laughs. "Didn't you ever see a bunch of stump ranchers before?" he inquires.

"Sure I seen stump ranchers!"

"Well, these is the real homespun short-horn variety."

"I seen all kinds of stump ranchers," say I. "But what is the idea of brandin' each other as stools?"

"That's all over the cook. You see, this cook hasn't lived here quite as long as the rest of the old hens in the neighborhood, and then she gets the job of mixin' the mulligan and gets all the rest of the old dames sore. Then there is church jealousies tangled up in it, too. Maybe she don't dip in the same duckin' pond as the rest. Anyway, there is two factions in camp. One faction favors the cook and the other faction's against the cook. They have a string of talk that would make you weep. It runs like this: 'Sally come over to the house the other day and says so and so. My old woman got right back at her and tells her so and so.' This is repeated every day by the bushel, yard or scraper full."

"And the class struggle?" asks I, "where does that come in?"

"The class struggle is like the Irishman's flea—it bites, but it ain't there."

Then the oldtimer starts to askin' for information about the organization. Him and me had played different parts of the country, but I give him what late news I had and he soon gets up and goes to read the papers. "I haven't been able to jar a single idea loose in this whole camp," he says. "These hoosiers just stare at you and don't get a single point. Maybe with the three of us we can do more, but I won't be much help to you because I am on the grade and will only get to you at night. Well, so long!"

In a few minutes Pearlie come in and his eyes was ashine with excitement. "Tightline," he whoops, "we've struck a virgin field. Every whichaway you look you see a scizzorinhus. I been out scoutin' around and I seen whole droves of chinwhiskered blocks as innocent of intelligence as a dehorned sailor. Just think," he rambles on, "of yellin' at a whistle punk with the whiskers of Karl Marx and cursin' at a donkey puncher that is a deacon in the church. I bet there ain't a man in camp that knows that the Czar of Russia has even had a chill."

"You're wrong again, Pearlie," says I, folding up my report sheet. "I have already sold four papers and an Ebert Pamphlet, and stamped one man up."

Then I told Pearlie about the dirt driver and what he had said about the camp. Pearlie was enthusiastic. He was already thinkin' up ways to get under the hides of stump herders. "To-morrow," says he, "I'm to be Queen of the May."

To-morrow came with the bang and the clang of the bull-cook's hammer on the old circular saw that hung outside the kitchen door. We stirred from our bunks and washed the wrinkles out of our eyes at the wash-bench. Then we filed into the cook-shack with the bang of the second bell.

It was just getting daylight and the shivers still ran over us as we gulped down the breakfast and left for the shack to get the rest of our loggin' clothes on. Still shivery, we climbed on the loggin' truck that a wheezy, dirty loggin' dinky locomotive shoved up the track from the mill to the landing where the loggin' was done.

Over the uneven track we jolted and turned around curve after curve. Nearly all the crew was piled on the truck and they were carryin' on a gabblin' about this and that. One had come by a calf during the night. Another was still grumbling because his wife was too sick to get his breakfast. Spud plantin' and plowin' was discussed in detail. They were a sodden crew, and the misty morning air was no pep instiller.

Arrived at the job we all piled off and the crew scattered to their different places while the locey went back with the empty truck. I went over and sized up the loadin' outfit and found it hay-wire, right. It was one of these single jack crotch-line rigs with hooks instead of tongs. Pearlie moped around and looked over the riggin', also hummin' a little tune to himself and takin' a squint at everybody in sight. Neither of us found any signs of efficiency goin' to waste in the arrangement of the riggin'.

The Deacon blew the whistle for startin' time and Pearlie called the riggin' crew out to where there was a stump that was in the road. First rattle would be to pull the stump. He climbed up in easy hailin' distance and directed the setting of chokers and the shiftin' of blocks necessary to jerk the big root out of the ground. When everything was set he turned to the donkey and roared: "Hoi, hoi! Hoi, hoi! Skinner, back there, the length of a hoe handle, old timer!"

The Deacon donkey-puncher started and looked hurt. "A hoe handle," says he, under his breath. "How did he know I was a-hoein' the garden last night?"

With his mind on the garden he opened up on the haul-back too far and made at least three times too much back-run. Pearlie's "Hoi!" was wasted.

"Hoi, hoi, hoi!" yelled Pearlie again in an effort to land the bull-hook in the right place. The "Whoa-Back" and the line stopped and stood still, —exactly right.

"Slack off the length of a cow barn," ordered Pearlie, who ran the slack back to the stump which was to be pulled, and hooked it in the block. The riggin' all set at last, and all clear, Pearlie again mounted his stump.

"Twist her tail now, old mischief! Prod her with the pitchfork! Hoi!"

At the signal the Deacon opened wide the throttle, the lines tightened, the spar tree shivered, the guy lines strained, and then the mighty stump heaved, flew in the air, and was in the way no more.

"Unhalter the stump, boys, and we'll plow out this corner this mornin'," said Pearlie.

All mornin' the crew was loggin' around close to the landin', and every sentence that Pearlie let loose had some reference to the farm in it. He even come over to me and wanted to know if we couldn't fork the logs up on the load easier if we had some good drinkin' water. I made a motion to hang the loadin' hook in his head, but we scared up some spring water at that.

When the locey came to take us down to dinner it was a different crew than which had come up in the mornin'. There wasn't much conversation at all, and what there was, was mostly on other things besides farmin'.

Dinner was the one meal that these stump ranchers got. They gobbled down their grub at the cook-house, and with each additional plate-full over and above what an ordinary human could eat I could see a calculatin' look,—them a-figurin' how much they was a-savin'. Why, there was one stumper opposite me that used both hands; and say! If he'd made a mistake with either hand he'd a lost an eye!

That afternoon the landin' crew took it pretty easy as the yardin' was all long haul. We was sittin' around and as Pearlie was out by the tail-block I suppose the stumpers thought they was safe from ridicule.

Anyway, they started to talkin' and of course bein' as there was only two subjects outside of the women folks that they could talk about that had any sense at all they was soon harpin' on them. Loggin' and farmin' was two subjects that was not to be rooted out till something else was substituted.

Milk and the price of milk lead to creameries and co-operatives. The foolish notions these rubes had of these outfits were comical. Yeah! They was sure that the reason that their co-op creameries had failed was because the workin' plugs didn't have brains enough to run such a business. It took

brains and money to put something like that across, says they, and if a workin' plug had brains he would be in business for himself, so the best way to get ahead was to try and get the most for what you raised and maybe pick up a good contract or somethin', so as to pile up a few dollars.

Then I took a hand. I showed them just why their co-ops always went to the wall just as soon as they were a menace to Big Biz. I showed them figures from the Pujo Money Report as to how the financiers had all the credit facilities tied up in their pocket. I pulled out a copy of the Industrial Relations Commission report and showed them the way wealth was distributed and why. Then I explained the buying and marketing of raw and finished products and the dependence on credit facilities.

"When the financiers control the credit system," I asked, "how do you expect them to give credit to some one who is goin' to cut out some of their henchmen's profits?"

"That's so," says the fireman. "There was old man Nelson that couldn't raise ten thousand dollars on his thirty thousand dollar ranch in order to pay the few notes that was outstandin' against the Polt Co-op Condenser, so she went under."

"Well," says one optimist, "there must be some way to get at these here guys,—these here trusts and things."

"Sure there is," I tells 'em. "It's as easy as fallin' off a log. You and me and anybody else that does any work is producers. We don't get robbed when we go to the store to buy anything. We get robbed because we don't get what we produce. The farmer don't sell his milk for what it is worth, and the middleman gets the profits. It is as a producer that he is robbed, and not because he has to pay fifteen dollars for a pair of shoes. The man who is bein' robbed in that shoe transaction is the man that works at the machine and makes those shoes, and the man that robs him is the owner of the machine and the middlemen, too. All we got to do is to get all the producers together and get them organized, each according to what he produces, and put the financiers out of business."

Wrinkles was a-commencin' to break out in places, so I let somebody else take the lead. The loadin' donkey puncher took a whirl at the problem.

"We're producin' logs right here now. You mean to say that we are not gettin' robbed because we have to pay twenty cents a pound for beans down at the company store, but because we only get paid around seven dollars a thousand for the logs we send down the track, which the mill sells for forty to twenty dollars a thousand? Then, who is the robber in this bean proposition? I buy these beans at the store, so don't he rob me when he sells them at such a price?"

"Naw," says the bright fireman, who had sure got an earful. "The guy that gets robbed in this here bean proposition is the guy that grows the beans. He's just like the guy that made the shoes. If we got what we produced in logs we could easy enough pay for the beans and the farmer could sure buy more lumber if he got all that his beans was worth. Couldn't he?"

"Yeah!—that sounds fine," says the second loader, "but how are you goin' to do all this gettin'?"

For half a minute I listened to the silence and then I told them about the One Big Union, the Industrial Workers of the World. I explained it to 'em as I had learned it. All about how industry was to be managed, not for profits but for efficient production and use.

I showed them what advantages the organization had brought to each of 'em in immediate gains right now. The eight-hour day, the better grub, and everything which had been put up by the boss because in the other camps the Wobs had fought and made the bosses come thru with a lot more than that. This boss was just taggin' along after the rest, and all the workers on this job was gettin' some of the benefits of what had been fought for by the Wobblies in other places. I talked about the One Big Union idea for fightin' the capitalists. I talked about the One Big Union idea for production for use.

When at last we got up from the chinnin' bee to load the last car there was a lot of stump ranchers that had heard things to make 'em think. They chewed the rag amongst themselves and popped a lot of questions at one time an' another, and generally showed some more life than they had before.

From then on Pearlie cut out his barn-yard vocabulary. He took a hand in the game, and, anyway, he is a lot better at explainin' things than I am. He tells it so it sounds real and not like it was bein' read from a book.

The fireman was the first to line up. I got to sellin' literature to the rest of 'em and they read it, too. Conversation commenced to perk up and I listened in to a lot of hot discussions between

some of these stumpers on subjects that took in economics, psychology, and a lot of other things that never would have been dreamed of by these home guards a short time before this literature had got to 'em.

It's funny that way. Here Pearlie and me could have said all the things in the books in our own way and nobody would have listened to us. But if you get down on print paper with the facts where a fellow can see them, lookin' at the words is a lot like lookin' at the things themselves. If you only hear somebody say it, why, that don't carry no weight. Most anybody can make a noise.

One by one the stumpers commenced to line up, and from all the pamphlets that was bought I bet that a lot of ranchers growed weeds that spring. Then came a little test of job action which showed that our efforts had not been wasted. The mill store sent up a case of rotten butter that they had got stung with. Now, anybody knows that fightin' for good butter ain't the social revolution, but anybody also knows that hittin' a punchin' bag ain't knockin' Dempsey out, neither. Both of these stunts is good practice for the event aimed at, and if enough pep is showed up in the practice, why, this practice is sure goin' to help in the big event.

Anyway, this butter was shoved under our noses right noticeable, and Pearlie gets real hostile. Grub has always been more or less grub to me since the little jolt I had in the can, where a fancy taste is not exactly encouraged, so I didn't pay much attention, but I noticed that at dinner there was a considerable murmur about the comparative strength of this butter and skunks and like things. After the meal was over some of the boys come to me and asked what was customary in a case of this here kind and I sort of suggested callin' a meetin'.

The meetin' was called, too, and it was unanimous opinion that this butter was out of place on a weak, wobbly table. It had ought to be standin' on its own.

A committee was nominated and elected to inform the boss of our sentiments in this matter and, of course, Pearlie and me makes the committee along with one more. The Super was kinda cool, but he couldn't deny that the butter was too powerful, and yet he was thinkin' about the same thing as we was: If these loggers get what they want in the butter question, maybe they will be demandin' something else before long that is liable to hurt when it comes to fork over.

"Well," he says, "I will see that the butter is taken back, but I want to state this: I ain't goin' to have nobody dictatin' to me how this camp is goin' to be run. I would have sent the butter back anyway without you tellin' me about it. It seems to me that there is a lot of agitation against the government goin' on here that ought to be stopped, and if it goes any further something will be liable to happen."

This government bunk has been throwed up by every grafter I ever run across, and it seems to me that the parasites must have mighty little confidence in the staying power of Uncle Sam, the way they are always fearful of these U. S. bein' overthrowed and destroyed. Anyway, I told the Super I didn't get the connection between bad butter and the U. S. government, although after readin' about all the war industries' scandals and the shippin' board frauds I seemed to smell somethin' similar in nature.

At this he gets sore and walks away and we goes back and reports to the men that better butter is for those that demand it.

I could see that my time was in for this camp, so I got out the old defense collection book and made the rounds that night. I got a donation from everybody in the camp, includin' the cook, whose factional squabble had, by the way, sort of died down. Three days later the Super told me that one of my loads had landed in the ditch an' that he wanted some one who could load cars to ride and not to roll, and for me to get my time. I told him that he was gettin' his pay for makin' out and handin' people their time, and that I would be on the job any time that he had a slip for me.

So he came back with the slip all right and I kissed this outfit good-bye. Pearlie, he stuck around a while to get a couple of other prospects that we was workin' for.

I blowed into Seattle and went out to a real camp. No more of these hay-wire, chin-whiskered outfits for mine. I'm thru.

14

JOHNSON THE GYPO

By Ralph Winstead

This here Gypo proposition reminds me of the old woman who had a peppy daughter. She used to moan and plead with the girl to change her state of mind and be a good girl. This old woman was faced with a condition of things, not a state of mind and the only way for to deal with conditions is by the use of tactics, not by using a line of appeals to be good.

Now there is one time honored tactic that has been used by old dames on their daughters since and before the human race had thumbs. This line of action was to turn the refractory young female over a bony knee and administer to the well being of her ideas by hand.

That ain't the only tactics to fit this particular problem by a whole lot but at least it has some advantages over appealing to 'em to be good. They got inside urges as to what they want and need and all the appeals in the world don't cut much ice in the face of a human urge. Tactics is what counts.

Now it's the same way with the Gypo proposition. These here bushel maniacs just naturally got the same sort of nature as John D. Rockefeller and a lot of other humans includin' all of us. They wants to get rich quick and are goin' to listen to that interior urge to gather in the mazuma when the gatherin' is good in spite of any appeals to be good saintly wobs and travel the narrow path.

But mostly we have been playin' the part of the noble mother and been pleadin' with these here almost human Gypo birds to be good, and spurn the pitfalls of their evil ways. What we got to do is use a few tactics on 'em. Maybe spankin' would be justifiable but maybe it wouldn't get the goods as quick as a way that me and a bunch of other wobs tried up at Grinnon one time.

Of course, as I say, tactics is the thing to use and when tactics is decided on in a whole industry it takes a lot of organized action and workin' together that is a lot harder than just goin' around spoutin' about the humpbacked species that has ruined the organization and is now keepin' us on the bum. In order to put any real tactics across we got to have a real plan worked out and have got to put the thing over by co-ordinated action and not by sanctimonious prayers to stay away from the sinful contract and keep pure and undefiled.

One time I blowed into Seattle with a short stake and was prepared to stick around town for a week or two. There was a good bunch in town and we lit out to take a little relaxation. Snowball Smith and me was roomin' together and was takin' on the said relaxation mostly in company. About the first stunt we done was to go out to Alki point and gather an eyeful along the beach. Of course this was before the short skirts made the beaches unnecessary for purposes of sight seein' but even aside from this sight satisfaction we was both longin' for a salt water swim, and got it.

It was the next afternoon after this excursion amongst the darin' dressers that I was walkin' down the slave market when I noticed on old man Moore's board a sign that caught the eye: "Wanted eight men to take contract bucking and falling. Details inside."

There it was, straight Gypo stuff. Chance to make a co-operative fortune right in my hand. Me —well, I looked around real quick to see if there was a humpbacked Swede in sight and not seein' any I high balled right up to the room and got hold of Snowball.

Now Snowball is one of these here plugs that is never restin' with his trigger on safety. They ain't no neutral gear in his make-up. Snowball is always ready to go and further more after the goin' is a long ways from the start and gets rough, why, he ain't the bird to crawfish neither. Maybe he ain't exactly what you call an executive genius that can lay out and get others to carry through a big campaign but he don't need to ponder over no proposition for three weeks to see if it'll hold water. Snowball makes up his mind quick and stays with it.

So when I suggests to him that we become the original humpies and go scabbin' on ourselves just for a little fun and tactical experience, why, Snowball don't bat an eye but hustles his lid and we streaks for Moore's. Nobody had beat us to it so we got all the details.

Eight men was wanted to sign a contract to fall and buck a full section of timber up at Grinnon which as you know is a sort of steeple jack outfit up in the Olympics off of Hoods Canal. The ground was level we was told and the timber was good. The rate was 60c per thousand and we had a bunk house all to ourselves.

The company furnished the tools but we had to do the saw filing. We was to eat in the company boarding house and they would deduct the board bill at the pay off. We could draw only fifty percent of what our log scalein' called for till the job was finished. Everything in regular Gypo style.

Snowball did most of the talkin'. He made rapid estimates with greedy eyes at how much we could clean up in the summer. I almost got in earnest on the finance end of it myself. It sure sounded good the way he mentioned the thousands of dollars.

Moore agreed to hold the job till we got six more fellows to go in with us and so we set out

to round up six good wobs that was willin' to mar their perfectly good reputations in order to put the Gypo game in bad at Grinnon. We had a hard time. Some of our best known wobs sneered at the idea and told us we was just lookin' for an excuse. But we kept travellin' in spite of little set backs and raised a crew.

The eight of us signed on and got our John Hancocks on a big contract that was goin' to make or break somebody. Then we separated and rustled our clothes and spent the night listenin' to advice not to go and tryin' to explain why we was goin' to the bunch, but they wouldn't pretend to believe us. Fainthearted wobs never went Gypoin' yet is my claim. The pressure was awful, but we stuck it out. A fellow's friends and fellow workers can always be depended on to state the right and wrong of things. Right and wrong I always claims is matters of gettin' results.

Next mornin' we grabbed the boat for the first lap of the trip and after changin' into busses and back onto boats a few times we made the landin' at Grinnon. We was met by the time keeper with a speeder and made the trip up over the steepest known loggin' track in the country and that is sayin' a heap.

We didn't see where the nice level ground mentioned in the sacred contract was comin' in but we sure enjoyed the scenery which is sure pleasant in this section.

Mountains and valleys with clear tumblin' rivers and misty clouds hangin' half way up can sure wipe out the memory of a lot of squalid misery found in more civilized sections. Somehow they make a fellow feel that life is big and not exactly centered about himself.

And this feelin' is most necessary to get real action these days. Most of us like to stick our chests out about two inches further than is necessary for deep breathin' and seem to forget that there are others in the world that might be just as wise as—the big center of things—me. There are a lot of us that have to learn to think and act according to the biggest benefit to the greatest number instead of in the way that our own ideas points.

We made the camp alright and found a bunk house fixed up for us that was pretty fair. The boss give us the icy eye as if he was only in on this Gypo proposition by compulsion but the manager was all smiles and explained to us over and over that he had only left his office work in town to come up and see that we got a good start.

Of course we was grateful. We even told him

so. The grub was good too but the flunkies set it down before us with a bang and the cook looked cross-eyed at the whole bunch of us. Sure a guy must have to suffer a lot from just wantin' to make a few lousy dollars via the Gypo route in some places. I even commenced to be scared somebody that knew me would write it up for the Worker and demand that I turn in my card. Such would have sure ruined me for life but then I been ruined more than once anyhow.

Well, we went out and looked over the ground. It was level, too. A fine bunch of trees in a level valley that just seemed to happened along by accident in the steep canyons. Then we organized ourselves. Snowball was elected to do the filing and the Bull buckin' and the rest of us scattered out in the trees.

I started in with the fallin' gang not knowing anything about this end of the loggin' game and we dropped the first tree fine except that the blamed thing hooked up and it took us most of the day to get it down where we could look at it.

Then we done better. The manager came around and found all of us sweatin' and puffin' so he went off to town satisfied that he had solved the problem of bustin' up these here pesky wobs by makin' 'em take an interest in the work. Yeah, we done better. In the afternoon me and my pardner dropped three fine big trees, every one of 'em with high grade timber in 'em—number one flooring stock, but the blame sticks dropped on stumps and was busted all to hell. It was sure tough but I cheerfully took the blame as I didn't know much about the fallin' game anyway.

When I looked over the rest of the crew's work I commenced to think that I had picked the biggest bunch of green horns that could be found in the whole organization. Not one of 'em seemed to know as much about fallin' or buckin' as I used to.

The newly elected bull bucker came around to me and he pulled his face into a sorrowful twist and explained that we wasn't makin' more than three or four dollars a day and was a dullin' a lot of saws.

The Centralia Prisoners.   Labadie Collection photo files.

This of course was awful news as it meant that maybe we wouldn't make that young fortune we was a lookin' for here. I promised to speed up and we did manage by workin' a little overtime to drop another fir, but it was punky.

The funny part of the whole thing was that we didn't seem to improve as the days went by. Some of the gang got lazy and wouldn't drop as many trees as they should and then they would blame Snowball for bein' a bum sawfiler but I couldn't see anything wrong with his filin'.

The boss dropped around and looked over the work we had done and I saw him goin' away with his hat off and him a scratchin' his head. He appeared to be plum puzzled by our progress. In the meantime I got friendly with the blacksmith's helper and he told me that the boss once carried a card in the early days and that there was a good bunch of wobs that had been sent down the road to make room for us damn scabs.

You bet I got *real friendly* with that helper. He made it a point to see that he wasn't handlin' any hot irons when I happened around. Well, we stuck to this job for a month. Things went from bad to worse. I commenced to lose faith in the co-operative movement when it comes to gettin' work done. We didn't seem to have the right spirit for work no matter which way we tried to bring it out. Still I learned a lot about fallin' trees but the fallin' pardner didn't seem to think so. He said that I couldn't hit even the ground more than once out of three times without him. Well, I thought if he was so wise I would try my hand at buckin'. So we made the switch.

I went on with a big Finn that agreed to show me how to buck. But I soon wished that I hadn't done it. Buckin' is even harder work to my notion than fallin', besides I was no good at it and didn't seem able to learn much. About every time that I got a real good log about half bucked out, why, somethin' was sure to happen to the wedges and the blame log would split. I must of spoiled a lot of 'em that way but I learned how to buck 'em off square at last but the bunch decided to let me buck on the split ones about this time so I didn't get any real practice at that.

In other ways, however, things went fine. For instance the cook finally seemed to get over his grouch and was real friendly. He came out and looked over our job and even got jolly about it. Then we sort of decided to take it easy anyway. About this time, why, we got a good bunch of pa-

pers and magazines up and it got so it was harder and harder to tear ourselves away from the literary field. We enjoyed discussions on a lot of highbrow topics and sometimes when the job got irksome we took a hike up on some of the hills and looked around.

Maybe I am a little off on the subject but I sure admire the scenery in the Olympics. The more I saw of it the more I admired it. Finally it got so that it appealed to me more than even the buckin' did though I admit that that was sure fascinatin'. It certainly was wonderful to get away up on the mountain side and look down on the riggin' crew a sweatin' and strainin' like little ants down in the valley while the donkeys would shoot steam like these little peanut roasters on the pop corn stands in town.

Oh, it was a great life. I could see where there was all sorts of temptation to be a gypo. I commenced to think that I would like to do this regularly.

The good grub and the pleasant companionship sure didn't make none of us feel bad either. Snowball said that he wore a full inch off of some of the saws just to keep himself busy about the shack while we was out on the job but I think he was exaggeratin'. I never did think that he always told the whole truth about some things especially about how hard he worked but I will say that he changed the looks of some of them saws alright.

All good things come to an end at last, however, and one day the scaler come up to scale up our cut and see where we was at. He come out on the job unexpected but as it happened three of us was workin'.

He started to work scalin' the logs and seemed to grow real excited. He didn't stop, however, to make any remark to us but kept on all day. Well, he stayed with the job and so did we. When he got finished he come over to tell us about it. He was so mad he was almost happy.

"Well, you birds have sure got away with somethin' this time," he tells us in our bunk house the night he finished. "You have been here thirty days and have eat up four hundred dollars' worth of grub. You have knocked down and mutilated a million feet of timber, whether from pure cussedness or because you are damned fools, I don't know and no one can prove. But I sure have a bright suspicion because none of you look like plum idiots to me."

"The foreman wrote into town advisin' the manager to abrogate the contract a couple of weeks ago but then the manager had an idea he was still opposed to the contract system. Now I know what he was opposed to, allright."

We all asked him what was wrong. We wanted to know if he was goin' to get us fired from our good job. In fact we made him feel that we sure enjoyed the stay up there but that didn't seem to help him any. He went away madder than ever. I heard later that he had three shares of stock in the company.

The manager came up and told us that our contract was not worth a damn and that the quicker we got out of camp the better he would be pleased. He said that if we wanted to collect the money for the trees that we had put down we could bring suit and see what we got.

We pulled out and blew into Seattle but so far none of us has taken up the matter of our legal rights to pay for our work. And on the other hand I saw the boards down at Moore's chalked up heavy for buckers and fallers workin' by the day at Grinnon right away after we hit town.

Tactics, I claims, will get the goods where dealin' out the sneers and peddlin' the holy solidarity stuff only makes a man feel ashamed and unnatural but don't stop him from wantin' to obey that inner urge. In fact some of the looks I got up in Grinnon made me think that maybe I was a superior bein' and not in the crude and unsophisticated circle of common workin' stiffs.

Providin' that I hadn't already known better I feel sure that that idea would have got stuck in me somehow or other. It's funny that way. Everybody is always ready to believe that he or she (especially she) is different from the rest of the people. You know the line of bunk I mean and how if you shoot it out just right, how it always gets results.

Well, Gypos don't want to get no chance to think that they are different from you and me. Just use a few organized tactics and the humps on some of the loggers' backs will look like a camel's that has been through a famine worse than a term in the Spokane City jail in a free speech fight.

Suppose we just get together and put across a few tactical manoeuvers on these birds and see that they don't obstruct the progress of the organization any more. That is my idea.

15

This unsigned article appeared in the Four L Bulletin *(October 1922), the monthly publication of the Loyal Legion of Loggers and Lumbermen. The organization was set up by the government with lumber company support during the World War I period to counteract the influence of the I.W.W. in the Northwest woods.*

WHY I AM A MEMBER OF THE I.W.W.

A PERSONAL RECORD BY ONE OF THEM

What is it turns men to organizations like the I.W.W.?

We asked a logger, prominent in the councils of the local I.W.W., to tell our readers in his own words the reasons for his association with the organization; to review his own life with the idea of noting those things which led him to become an enemy of society as it is and an advocate of drastic change.

This I.W.W. is a sincere, earnest individual; his natural tastes are literary and studious. The point of view which he expresses here is important for all of us to study, for his convictions, based on that point of view, are those of thousands of other lumberjacks. Behind the point of view is a cause, or a series of them, which would seem to be far reaching. This author says the cause is essentially American—the result of rapid development of industry on a large scale.

EDITOR

I think my answer to this question will interest your readers, as I come from a part of Europe which furnishes a very large percentage of the loggers in the northwest.

As to my past I might say that life has offered me a very varied bill of fare. From my seventh to my fourteenth year I generally put in from seven to eight months a year at the "point of production." We kids in the sugar beet fields of southern Sweden began our day at 6 A.M. and were kept busy until 8 P.M., with three rests a day, totaling altogether two hours, making a twelve-hour day. You can easily imagine how much time we had for play or study and how physically fit we were for either.

So my childhood was lost and I was an old man at 14, when I struck a job in a grocery store, and at the age of 23 I found myself manager for quite a large business enterprise in my native country—a co-operative association composed of several thousand members. The co-operative movement is to some extent related to socialism, its ideology is socialistic, and the reason I took such an interest in it was entirely due to my previous study and participation in the socialistic movement.

At the age of 25 I emigrated to the United States. To me it was not a question of journeying to some place where I hoped to gain fortune and fame. It was merely the satisfying of a desire for adventure and for knowledge of the world, a desire long suppressed for reasons of entirely personal nature. My first job in this country was in a packing plant at South St. Paul, Minn. There I received a splendid illustration of Upton Sinclair's book, "The Jungle," perhaps the most read book in Sweden at the time of my departure. It was a ten-hour day with lots of overtime at regular pay, 16½ cents per hour. Never do I see a sign advertising a certain brand of ham and bacon without thinking of the terrible high premium in sweat and blood, in misery and starvation, in ignorance and degeneration, the workers in those establishments have to pay before these products reach your table.

I turned down offers to again enter the commercial field back in Minnesota in order to be able to study another class of men, the man of the "wild west," as well as the wild west itself, and early in March, 1910, I headed for this coast.

I'll never forget my first experience in camp. It was a railroad camp up in the Rockies. I was tired after the hike with my bundle on my back, and attempted to sit down on a bed, the only furniture I could see that would furnish me a rest. Before I could accomplish the deed I was told in a very sharp voice in my mother tongue not to do so. I moved a little and tried another bed, when another Swede gave a similar command. After a third experiment which ended in a similar way, I got kind of peeved and began to lecture my countrymen a little as to civilized manners, when one of the boys explained: "We only warn you so as not to get lousy."

Suffice it to say that I made no more attempts to rest in that camp, but took a freight train that very evening and stayed two nights and one day in a box car before I, nearly froze to death, was dumped off at Hillyard, Wash., penniless, with no one I knew, and unable to speak a word in English.

Shortly after this incident I found myself in a logging camp in Idaho, across from the city of Coeur d'Alene. It was double beds two stories high, sleep on straw, work eleven to twelve hours per day, but the board was fairly good. I stayed there for several months, mostly because I wanted to stay away from my countrymen in order to learn the language. From there I went to British Columbia. Put in one year in a logging camp in the Frazer Valley and then one year and a half in a railroad camp on the Kettle Valley railroad. It was here I aligned myself with the I.W.W., and may I state that there was no delegate in that camp, and, to the best of my knowledge, not one member. I went over a hundred miles into Vancouver, B. C., to get that "little red card."

The Reasons

Why did I do it?

The reasons were many. While young I had associated myself with the prohibitionists, joining the Independent Order of Good Templars. I soon came to the conclusion that the liquor traffic itself is but a natural outgrowth of our existing social system, and that I could not abolish it without a fundamental change in society itself.

When working on the Kettle Valley road I observed quite a few interesting facts in this connection. Of over three thousand workers employed for a couple of years I doubt if there were two dozen men who left that job with sufficient funds to carry them for two months. The general routine was to work for a month, draw your check, go down to a little town named Hope (the most hopeless city I've seen) composed of two very large saloons, a couple of dirty rooming houses, a couple of stores and half a dozen houses of prostitution, and to spend, in a day or two, your every nickel in either the saloons or the brothels, usually in both. I saw one Christmas how in one camp of about 150 men, they carried in over 450 bottles of whisky, and not one book or newspaper, and all had a "glorious time."

The Workers' Welcome

Have you ever thought of how we, the workers in the woods, mines, construction camps or agricultural fields, are really approached and "entertained" when we visit our present centers of "civilization" and "culture"? What is the first thing we meet? The cheap lodging house, the dark and dirty restaurant, the saloon or the blind pig, the prostitutes operating in all the hotels, the moving picture and cheap vaudeville shows with their still cheaper, sensational programs, the freaks of all descriptions who operate on the street corners, from the ones selling "corn removers" and shoestrings to the various religious fanatics and freaks. Did you ever see a sign in the working class district pointing the way to the public library? I have not. Did you ever meet a sign in any one of the rooming houses where we are forced to live, advertising a concert or a real play of any of our great writers, such as Ibsen, Shaw, Suderman, Gorky, Tolstoy, Shakespeare or others? Never.

I mention this because I, like all others, have certain desires I want to satisfy. We want a break in the monotony of camp life. That's why we go to the cities. We want to see and partake in all those manifestations of civilized society, we want amusements, comfort, leisure. We also want a clean and healthy environment composed of both sexes, we want a home, family, children. We want to see ourselves and our ideals in life perpetuated in our own offspring. And may I say that I hold this to be a blessing for humanity. Whoever does not strive and fight for the good things of life is, in my opinion, dangerous to society. But due to our perverse social system we are prevented from satisfying our desires and the majority of our class accepts whatever is offered as substitute.

Can you condemn them? I cannot. I don't believe in condemnation; I do believe in correcting what is wrong. So I found that I could not accomplish much by abolishing liquor—and in fact, could not abolish this damnable traffic—without a fundamental change in society itself, as the liquor traffic is simply part and parcel of our present social order. It is maintained for the sake of profit and it is necessary for the sake of profit, at least until such time as something equally suitable is ready to take its place.

What the I.W.W. Offered

The I.W.W. seemed to me then and seems to me now the only group offering me any sensible program under which I could operate with a view to gaining these good things in life, and such changes in society as I desired. The I.W.W. declared that our real ruler is our boss. He decides our wages and thereby our standard of living, our pleasure or our misery, our education as well as the education of our children, our health and our comfort

in life; in fact, he almost decides if we shall be allowed to live. The I.W.W. also told me that by uniting with my fellow-workers in the industry and all industries combined into One Big Union of all the workers, we could successfully combat our masters' One Big Union and gain the good things in life. We did not need to live in misery, we did not need to be ignorant for lack of time and access to study. And furthermore, we would become trained and organized for our final task, the control and management of industries. And as this program met my demands I naturally joined the I.W.W.

Some particular influences caused me to devote my whole life to the organization, and I am sure that perhaps thousands of others have been similarly influenced and simply forced to align themselves with the movement.

I knew a young fellow-worker in Seattle, by name Gust Johnson. He was only a little more than 20 years of age, a very quiet and very studious fellow. He surely had the courage of his convictions and he practiced what he preached to the limit of his ability. He was refined in manners, exceedingly clean, neat and orderly. He had been in the United States for about two years, when the Everett free-speech fight took place. He went on board the Verona to go with the bunch to Everett on the fifth of November, 1916, to assist in enforcing the constitutional right of free speech and free assemblage. In the shooting that followed Gust Johnson was the first one who fell with a bullet through his heart. Gust Johnson, who would hesitate even to kill a fly, Gust Johnson, to whom violence and disorder were an abhorrence.

For the Defense of Friends

I did what every one of you would have done for a true friend on whom such a cruel outrage had been committed. I threw myself into the harness and faithfully worked for the defense of the seventy-two victims, unjustly arrested, until the day of their release, and until the memory of Gust Johnson and the other four victims of the Everett tragedy stood shining bright before their relatives and their class.

During this defense work I got acquainted with another countryman of mine who toured the country in behalf of the I.W.W. His name is Ragnar Johanson. Ragnar has all the advantages in life which I lack. He is well educated, well built, handsome, a gifted orator and accomplished writer. Now, there is no intelligent human being who thinks that any question can be solved by violence. So Ragnar's theme has always been: "Violence signifies weakness; reason, strength." In hundreds of lectures I have heard this man urge his fellow-workers to educate themselves, to study and organize, but never have I heard him utter one word about using brutal force or violence to accomplish their ends. On the contrary he has always argued against all such teachings as being harmful and detrimental to the workers as a class or as individuals. Where is Ragnar Johnson now? He is serving ten years in the Leavenworth, Kan., federal prison, together with about seventy other fellow-workers who are my personal acquaintances or friends.

And lastly, although I am a foreigner, it is only because I am in America that I am an I.W.W. For, contrary to the belief of many, the I.W.W. is an outgrowth of advanced economic developments in America, and the Italian, the Russian or the Swede that you may find in the organization here would not have been "wobblies" had they remained in their native countries.

The economic law which says "that commodities shall be produced by that method which allows for the least expenditure of human labor" is the real ruler of society. This law cannot be abrogated by any combinations, trusts, monopolies, parties or organizations of any kind. To explain thoroughly this law would force me to a lengthy discussion of economics which space forbids. At present time production on large scale affords the greatest conformity to this law, hence the success of the trusts and the great industrial combinations. United States, with its immensely large natural resources and its shortage of labor power in years gone by has offered the best opportunity for the development of machine production on a large scale, while at the same time the aforesaid shortage of labor power has served as a spur to progress in this direction. The result is that no country in the world is so far advanced, industrially, as the U. S., particularly in leading industries, such as agriculture, mining, lumbering and manufacturing of machinery and means of locomotion.

The saving of labor power appears through a thorough-going specialization of the work, through elimination of competition by means of amalgamations into large trusts whereby unnecessary labor in management in advertising, in salesmanship, and in distribution are avoided, and at the same time over-production with its loss of values in perishable goods, etc., is limited to a minimum. The trust is the bosses' One Big Union whereby they not only control the price on labor power, but also safeguard themselves against waste of labor power.

The I.W.W. is the result of the trust, the bosses' One Big Union. As the trust becomes universal, succeeds in organizing the industries internationally, so will the I.W.W. expand. As the trust is the logical outcome of technical progress in our mode of production, is a means by which commodities can be produced with a smaller expenditure of human labor than under a competitive system, so is the I.W.W. outcome of the same forces whose object is to counteract the power of the trust and ultimately take full control of the trusts and the means of production for the benefit of mankind as a whole. Neither of them can be talked, written or legislated away. Let's make an effort to understand them and the underlying causes for their existence, and much suffering and much hatred will be avoided.

Yours for industrial freedom.

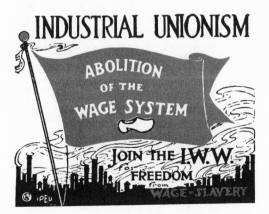

I rustled the High Ore
I rustled the Bell
I rustled the Badger
I rustled like hell,
I rustled the Tramway,
I rustled the View
And I finally found work
At the Ella-ma-loo (Elm Orlu).

"Rustler's Song" by Ralph Workman,
Western Folklore (January 1950), p. 25.

Chapter 10

Down in the Mines

The early struggles of the Western miners imprinted a militant heritage on the Industrial Workers of the World. Strikes in the gold, silver, copper, and lead camps of the West made revolutionary unionists of the miners as vigilante committees, state militia, and armed mine guards wrecked their homes and halls, locked them in bull pens, and dominated mining towns. Arrests, beatings, individual killings, machine gunning of union meetings imbued the Western miner with a fierce independence characteristic of the reckless and lawless frontier life.

In 1897 the Western Federation of Miners withdrew from the American Federation of Labor, claiming that the A.F.L. had betrayed the miners' cause. Disillusioned about legal protection from local courts, state legislatures, and the federal government, mine union leaders like Bill Haywood and Vincent St. John became convinced that political action was useless and that direct economic action was the only way to effect a change. As a result, the Western Federation of Miners attempted to broaden its support, first, through spearheading the organization of the Western Labor Union, then the American Labor Union, and finally, the I.W.W.—radical industrial unions that, hopefully, would be able to counter the mine owners' force with the force of united labor groups.

A strike in Goldfield, Nevada, a goldmining town of some 15,000–20,000 persons, was the first practical test of W.F.M.–I.W.W. cooperation. It failed. The Goldfield strike came in the midst of the 1907 depression, immediately after the Idaho trials of W.F.M. President Charles Moyer, I.W.W. leader Bill Haywood, and a blacklisted miner, George Pettibone. It came at a time when the I.W.W. organization was split over the issue of direct vs political action.

The Goldfield strike was marked by violence, the activities of a hostile citizens' committee, and martial law. It was complicated by a jurisdictional dispute between the W.F.M. and an A.F.L. carpenters' union, as well as by a sympathetic strike of miscellaneous town workers organized into an I.W.W. local.

Goldfield became an armed camp. A restaurant owner was killed. The town's businessmen locked out I.W.W. members. President Theodore Roosevelt sent in federal troops at the mine owners' request and, on the day the troops arrived, the mine companies cut wages and announced an open shop policy. A commission which investigated the Goldfield situation reported:

> The action of the mine operators warrants the belief that they had determined upon a reduction of wages and the refusal of employment to members of the Western Federation of Miners, but that they feared to take this action unless they had the protection of Federal troops and they accordingly laid a plan to secure such troops and then put their program into effect.[1]

The loss of the strike in Goldfield gave further impetus to the Western Federation of Miners to withdraw from the I.W.W. Growing increasingly more conservative, the officers of the W.F.M. charged that the "propaganda of the spouting hoodlums" had been one of the reasons for the failure of the strike. On the other hand, Vincent St. John and other I.W.W. organizers claimed that the I.W.W. was abused because the union did win important concessions from the mine companies in Goldfield: higher wages, an eight-hour day, and job control. St. John later looked back on the Goldfield strike as a golden age of I.W.W. effectiveness. He recalled:

No committees were ever sent to any employers. The unions adopted wage scales and regulated hours. The secretary posted the same on a bulletin board outside of the union hall, and it was the LAW. The employers were forced to come and see the union committees.[2]

Butte, Montana, was another setting for the growing hostility between the W.F.M. and the I.W.W. Butte miners had been organized since 1878 in the largest and strongest metal miners' organization in the West. For a long time they claimed that Butte was "the strongest union town on earth," where no employment was possible for a man who did not hold a union card. Oral tradition has it that even the two Butte chimney sweeps had their own union and that a local of miscellaneous workers once debated whether to boycott the Butte cemetery in order to help the grave-digger win better working conditions.[3]

Butte miners helped organize the Western Federation of Miners in 1893 and received the Federation's first charter. For the next fifteen years they benefited from a divided enemy, as the "copper bosses," in their wars with one another, encouraged the unions and wooed union leaders.

Dissension started in Butte Miners Union Local No. 1 about 1908, following the withdrawal of the W.F.M. from the I.W.W. Radicals among the Butte miners railed against the position taken by W.F.M. national officers, and factionalism broke out in the open in 1911 when the W.F.M., after fourteen years as an independent union, rejoined the A.F.L.

In 1912 several hundred Finnish Socialist miners were fired by the Butte mining companies. Company officials fumed against proposals, introduced by the Socialists elected to the town's city council, to tax mine tonnage for the city's benefit. In an attempt to rid Butte of radicals—for a time the mayor of the town was a Socialist—the Anaconda Copper Company initiated a "rustling card" system.

A miner applied at the company's central employment department, gave his personal and job history, and a list of references. He waited for several weeks while his references were checked out. If he was cleared, he was given a "rustling card" which gave him access to "rustle the Hill," that is, to apply directly for work at any of the Anaconda mines and mines of other companies which required the rustling card as a minimum job qualification. When a miner was hired, his card was sent back to the central employment department. If he quit work, he had to reapply at the rustling card office and go through the same procedure. The card could be withheld if the company regarded him "undesirable" for any reason. Only the small Elm Orlu mine, known among miners as the "Ella-ma-loo," did not require a rustling card. The company's president held that it was "un-American."[4]

The reason for the rustling card was given by an Anaconda Company official in a speech before the Chamber of Commerce in Missoula, Montana, on August 29, 1917. He said:

It became apparent to the officials of the Anaconda Company that in view of the increasing number of such characters [I.W.W.'s and radicals] in Butte, many of whom were working in the mines, that in order to do any part of its duty to the community and to itself it must first establish some system of knowing its employees. This was the main reason for the adoption of the rustling card system.[5]

The discharge of the Finnish Socialist miners and the adoption of the rustling card system became immediate issues. A committee of Butte Miners Union Local No. 1 recommended no opposition to the rustling card. But the radicals in the union vehemently attacked the rustling card system and were backed up by a referendum vote taken in the local. The issue was carried to the 1912 convention of the W.F.M. Tom Campbell, the leader of the Butte radicals, ran for the office of national union president against the incumbent, Charles Moyer. Campbell lost, 8318 to 3744. The W.F.M. convention rejected his charges that the conservative W.F.M. officials had taken no action in the firing of the Finns and refused to fight the rustling card system.

In turn, the W.F.M. convention expelled Campbell from the Federation for "conduct unbecoming a member of the Western Federation of Miners . . . by disseminating the lie that the Western Federation of Miners was floundering on the rocks of destruction and was impotent to protect its membership."[6]

Dissension in the next few years split the Butte local. Three miners' unions vied for membership: the older Butte Miners Union (W.F.M.), a radical independent group led by miner "Muckie" MacDonald, and a small I.W.W. local. Factionalism culminated in rioting, gunfire, and death when the hall of the Butte Miners Union was dynamited by twenty-six blasts during a visit of W.F.M. President Charles Moyer to the town.

The Butte mayor, a Socialist, charged Moyer's followers with firing the first shot from the union hall. The editor of the W.F.M. national magazine reported that he had reliable information that the dynamiting had been done by agents from a private detective company in the mine owners' employ. Professor Paul Brissenden wrote in 1920:

> It is not likely that the responsibility for this disaster will ever be definitely fixed. The mine operators place the blame on the shoulders of the agitators and malcontents in the union. The members of the radical unions in the Butte district generally explained it as an act of the mine operators perpetrated in order to discredit the union and if possible disrupt it and so bring about an open shop camp.[7]

The dynamiting of the Miners' Hall ended over two decades of Butte's role as a closed-shop, union town. The mining companies declared martial law. Troops crushed the new organization of radicals, known among miners as "Muckie MacDonald's Union," and ended job control by the W.F.M. and A.F.L. craft unions as well. MacDonald and Joe Bradley, the officers of the radical group, were sentenced to three to five years for their alleged part in the bombing. The Anaconda Copper Company, by far the largest producer in the town, declared Butte "open shop."

Two years later in 1916, the seventy-mile-long Mesabi Iron Range in northern Minnesota was the setting for a major I.W.W. metal mine strike. Some 7000 to 8000 immigrant miners—Finns, Swedes, and Slavs—who had been brought to the Range in 1907 to scab on striking W.F.M. members, now demanded better wages, shorter hours, and an end to a system of graft practiced by company foremen who elicited "kick-backs" for placing miners on more productive veins of ore.

An unorganized walkout started at the Aurora Mine on June 3 against the Oliver Company, a subsidiary of United States Steel Corporation. The I.W.W. national office responded to a call for help from the miners and sent I.W.W. organizers Elizabeth Gurley Flynn, Carlo Tresca, Sam Scarlett, Joe Ettor, and others to the Range. By the middle of June, the entire Range was out on strike.

When the first clash of the strike resulted in the death of a miner, the governor of Minnesota sent an investigator to the Range. He was told by the secretary of the I.W.W. miner's local: "We don't want to fight the flag, we don't want to fight anybody, what we want is more pork chops."[8]

A second clash between strikers and deputies resulted in the death of two deputies and led to the arrest of a group of miners as well as the I.W.W. strike leaders. No trial was held. Instead, local legal authorities attempted to make a deal with Judge O. N. Hilton who had been called in by the I.W.W. as defense attorney. Five of the I.W.W. organizers would be released if the other Wobbly prisoners pleaded guilty of manslaughter. Authorities persuaded three Montenegrin miners who spoke little English to plead guilty and sentenced them to prison for terms of one to seven years. Bill Haywood, who had become I.W.W. secretary-treasurer in 1914, charged that the I.W.W. organizers should never have consented to such an arrangement and terminated their connection with the I.W.W. at that time for "breaking solidarity."

Throughout September the strikes spread to the Cayuna and Vermilion ranges, until a 10 percent wage increase was won and an eight-hour day promised for the following May 1. At the same time, several thousand miles away in Pennsylvania, the I.W.W. agitated for shorter hours and higher pay for anthracite coal miners who had organized about a dozen I.W.W. locals in the region. The strike, which had made some headway in the Lackawanna area, was broken, however, by the activities of the Pennsylvania State Constabulary. Mounted troopers raided a union meeting of 250 miners at Old Forge in June and arrested and jailed all those present. Four months later the prisoners were released because no evidence against them could be found.

Somebody Has Got to Get Out of The Way!

Solidarity, August 19, 1916.

In the Southwest, Wobblies stepped up their organizing campaign in Arizona's four metal mining districts in the fall of 1916. By 1917 their agitation won support from some members of the International Union of Mine, Mill, and Smelter Workers (formerly the W.F.M.) and several A.F.L. unions who joined them in a general walkout in June and July 1917. Following the declaration of war in 1917, wages in the copper camps fell far below the wartime price increase in copper. The copper companies met the unions' demands for wage increases with a consistent refusal to adjust or arbitrate grievances.

The Arizona strike was denounced as "pro-German," as the companies stockpiled arms and ammunition, organized vigilante committees, hired additional guards and gunmen, and publicly declared their intention of removing labor agitators from the area. The Bisbee, Arizona, sheriff wired the state's governor that most of the strikers were foreigners, that the strike appeared to be a pro-German plot, and that bloodshed was expected imminently.

On July 6, 1917, a Loyalty League was organized in Globe, Arizona. It resolved

that terrorism in this community must and shall cease; that all public assemblies of the I.W.W. as well as all other meetings where treasonable, incendiary, or threatening speeches are made shall be oppressed; that we hold the I.W.W. to be a public enemy of the United States; that we absolutely oppose any mediation between the I.W.W. and the mine owners of this district; that after settlement . . . [we are] opposed to employment of any I.W.W. in this district; that all citizens deputized be retained as such.[9]

Within a few days the Loyalty League circulated application blanks to all citizens in Globe and Miami. They announced: "Every refusal will be noted. . . . We will take an inventory of the citizenship of the district. . . . The names of I.W.W. members and sympathizers are wanted."[10] The Loyalty League boycotted those who would not sign.

Four days later, sixty-seven I.W.W. members were rounded up in Jerome, Arizona, forced into cattle cars, and shipped to Needles, California. Two days later the Bisbee Loyalty League surpassed this performance. An organized posse of over 1000 citizens, wearing white handkerchiefs around their arms to identify each other, were deputized by the sheriff. They took over the telegraph office of the town so that no news of the raid would leak out. Rounding up 1200 I.W.W. members, townspeople, and sympathizers, they drove them to a ball park at the edge of town, where a "kangaroo court" asked them to choose between returning to work, arrest, or deportation. Close to 1200 were loaded in groups of fifty into a twenty-seven car cattle train. Guarded by 200 deputies, the train ended up in Hermanas, New Mexico, where the prisoners were kept for thirty-six hours without food before being sent by federal authorities to Columbus, New Mexico. Here they were put into a stockade under army guard and kept until the middle of September, when the camp was disbanded because the federal government refused to continue supplying food.

Most of the deportees returned to Bisbee. Some were arrested; others were allowed to stay unmolested. A year later, a federal grand jury indicted twenty-one leaders of the Bisbee Loyalty League. None was convicted.

The President's Mediation Commission sent in to settle the strike and investigate the deportations, found that of the 1200 deportees, 381 were A.F.L. members; 426 were Wobblies; and 360 belonged to no labor organization. It also found that 662 were either native-born or naturalized citizens, 62 had been soldiers or sailors, 472 were registered under the Selective Service Act, 205 owned Liberty Bonds, and 520 subscribed to the Red Cross. The foreign-born deportees included 179 Slavs, 141 Britishers, 82 Serbians, and only a handful of Germans.

The copper mining strikes in Arizona were ended by the deportations and by the President's Mediation Commission which investigated the situation in October 1917. The commission reported that the strikes were neither pro-German, nor seditious, but "appeared to be nothing more than the normal results of the increased cost of living, the speeding up processes to which the mine management had been tempted by the abnormally high market price of copper."[11] Its settlement, however, excluded any miner who spoke disloyally against the government or who was a member of an organization which refused to recognize time contracts. Thus, as Perlman and Taft have written, the commission put the I.W.W. "beyond the pale."[12]

The copper companies were protected by the umbrella of the Sabotage Act of 1918, which classified the mines as "war premises" and their output as "war materials." Army troops which had been sent in during the 1917 Arizona strike were given the authority "to disperse or arrest persons unlawfully assembled at or near any 'war premise' for the purpose of intimidating, alarming, disturbing, or injuring persons lawfully employed thereon, or molesting or destroying property thereat."[13]

Federal troops stayed in Arizona until 1920 in an effort to curb the "Wobbly menace." They protected strikebreakers, dispersed street crowds, guarded mine property, broke up public meetings, and patrolled "troublesome" sections of the community. They were billeted in quarters built for them by the mine owners and were brought up-to-date on industrial conditions by reports of private company detectives.

As Perlman and Taft wrote of the I.W.W. and A.F.L. efforts in the Arizona copper camps: "Unionism of either variety failed to survive the experiences of 1917."[14]

In June 1917 fire broke out on the 2400-foot level of the Speculator Mine in Butte and killed 164 miners who were smothered or burned to death. It was one of the worst mining tragedies in history. In the words of a Butte miner:

They were caught like rats in a trap by the explosion of gas in the lower levels, the exits of which were blocked by solid concrete bulkheads with no opening in them. The holocaust was the last straw. The miners, galling under abuses and working under conditions which endangered their lives every minute underground, decided to call a halt to this condition of affairs and not return to work until assured by the operators that the conditions would be corrected and the lives of miners fully protected.[15]

Miners charged that the tragedy was caused by the mine company's disregard for safety regulations. Trapped on the lower levels, they clawed at concrete bulkheads which the company had built instead of the steel manholes required by the law. Over half of the bodies were so badly burned they were unable to be identified.

Fourteen thousand incensed Butte miners immediately struck for adequate safety provisions in all the mines, an increase in wages, and the absolute abolition of the rustling card system. Under the leadership of Tom Campbell who had run against Charles Moyer in the 1912 W.F.M. convention, an independent Metal Mine Workers Union was formed. The I.W.W. members set up the Metal Mine Workers Industrial Union No. 800, which numbered about 1200 members in 1917.

Again, martial law was declared in Butte. The press screamed "sedition," "enemy of the government," and "pro-German," and once more stereotyped the strike as I.W.W. inspired. Company owners refused to meet the unions' grievance committees. W. A. Clark of the Clark mining interests declared that he would rather flood his mines than concede to strikers' demands. The miners held a mass meeting and petitioned the government to take over the mines, "so that the miners may give prompt and practical evidence of their patriotism."[16] They also lodged a formal protest against the rustling card system with Secretary of Labor Wilson, which led to a later investigation of labor conditions in Butte.

In July the Anaconda Company agreed to an increase in wages, but refused to give up the rustling card system, although holding out the inducement of a "temporary card" which could be used until a miner's record was fully checked. The strikers refused this offer.

In the early morning of August 1, 1917, a group of gunmen broke into the boardinghouse room of I.W.W. organizer Frank Little. He had been an I.W.W. member since 1906 and was one of the

Twisting His Tail For Him!

LIES SLANDER ROT

$1,000,000 DIVIDENDS

STEEL TRUST

I.W.W.

Solidarity, August 26, 1916.

leaders of the Missoula, Spokane, and Fresno free speech fights. A member of the I.W.W. Executive Board, Little had come to Butte from the Mesabi Range. In August 1916 he had been arrested at Iron River, Michigan, taken out of jail, beaten, threatened with lynching, and left unconscious in a ditch with a rope around his neck.

George Tompkins, a Butte miner, told what happened to Little in Butte:

At 3 o'clock in the morning of August 1st, six masked, heavily armed men broke down the door of Little's room and dragged him from his room in his night clothes, placed him in an auto, and took him to a railroad trestle at the edge of the town, and there hanged him. To his dead body was pinned a card which read, "First and Last Warning—3-7-77," followed by the first letters of the names of prominent members of the strikers, which indicated that the perpetrators of the crime intended more violence on other members of the strikers.[17]

The numbers 3-7-77 was the sign used by the old-time vigilantes in Adder Gulch, Montana, to threaten road agents with death. They signified the dimensions of a grave.

Little's funeral was one of the largest the state had ever seen. The five-mile route to the cemetery was lined with thousands of miners. The *Butte Miner* of August 6, 1917, wrote:

Funeral paraders in silent protest. . . . 2,514 in procession in demonstration against lynching. . . . Remains of Frank H. Little, I.W.W. Board Member, are borne down principal streets of Butte on the shoulders of red-sashed pallbearers marching through solid lanes of many thousand spectators. . . . Brief services at cemetery.[18]

A band played the funeral march from Beethoven's *Eroica Symphony.*

Gradually, the strikers drifted back to work, accepted small wage increases, and the modified rustling card system. The strike ended in December 1917.

But the federal troops which had been called in the year before, stayed on in Butte until 1921. The head of the Butte "Council of Defense" warned:

> The minute the military here stop detaining men for seditious acts we have got to take it into our own hands and have a mob and we don't want to start that. I can get a mob up here in twenty-four hours and hang half a dozen men.[19]

Mine owner W. A. Clark stated, "I don't believe in lynching or violence of that kind unless it is absolutely necessary."[20] While the troops remained at Butte, the Chamber of Commerce reported, "Every businessman . . . feels perfectly safe."[21]

Historian William Preston, the author of a recent study on suppression of radicals during the World War I period, described what followed the end of the 1917 strike:

> Anaconda seemed intent on a show down. Its detective informers were high in the ranks of the Butte I.W.W. In violently incendiary speeches, these company provocateurs encouraged their cohorts to adopt a position that the government would define as seditious and disloyal. In other words, the copper company was having its paid agents help organize a wartime strike against itself as a ruse for the indictment and elimination of the local radical menace.[22]

Professor Preston's footnote to this information stated, "The special agent of the Bureau of Investigation and United States Attorney Wheeler discovered and reported the existence of these company provocateurs."[23]

When the Butte I.W.W. local did strike on September 13, 1918, army troops, swelled by private detectives, local police, and mine officials, raided the I.W.W. hall, the hall of the independent radical Metal Mine Workers' Union, and the offices

and printing plant of the radical newspaper, the *Butte Bulletin.* They confiscated literature and records, arrested and jailed forty miners, and put the union halls and newspaper office under military guard. In the next few days the army arrested seventy-four additional miners without warrants, charged them with sedition, and held them for investigation by the Department of Justice. All but one were later released for lack of evidence on which charges against them could be made.

The Butte I.W.W. strike culminated in April 1920 with the incident called the "Murder of Anaconda Hill," in which mine guards armed with rifles and machine guns, fired on pickets marching in front of the Neversweat Mine. Fourteen strikers were wounded and one man was killed. The Butte *Daily Bulletin* issued an extra edition a short time after the shooting. The newspaper had the following headline set in 96 point type. This, it charged, was the order mine company officials had given to the guards:

SHOOT THE SONS OF BITCHES

The newspaper edition, as well as the Butte I.W.W. strike, was suppressed.

1

In 1913 and 1914, Ralph Chaplin wrote a series of poems, signed "by a Paint Creek Miner," which he sent to the International Socialist Review. *In his autobiography, Chaplin wrote: "At the time we had moved to Westmoreland [W. Va.], the daily papers were carrying stories about the strike in Kanawha County, but they were far from being of headline importance. Even at meetings of the Socialist local, little attention was then given to that strike. It had started in 1911 as a spontaneous unorganized protest against an accumulation of grievances. The officials of the miners' union [U.M.W.] ignored it. After months of neglect and inattention it was discovered that the smoldering discontent was assuming ominous proportions. That was just about the time I became associate editor of the Labor Star [Huntington (W. Va.) Socialist and Labor Star]. At this stage the mine-owners were preparing to reinforce their private guards with state militia and with professional gunmen recruited through the Baldwin-Felts agency. From that time on reports of the slugging and manhandling of miners began to trickle through. Then came stories of skirmishes and shooting on both sides . . .*

The Real Murderers Are Outside!

PREPARE TO OPEN THE JAIL DOORS
BY CLOSING THE MILLS AND MINES

on Range, the latest district
the strike, was taken on their
tiative, without any solicita-
m the strikers in the other
or from the I. W. W.
strike is spreading, and will
to spre---   -ause the con-
districts of

"In spite of a budding desire to be objective and 'constructive,' my passion was aroused by the brutalities of the strike . . . The inadequacy of strike relief and of publicity seemed to me inexcusable. The horrible conditions in Kanawha County were not arousing indignation beyond the borders of the state. One or two of my 'Paint Creek Miner' sonnets had been reprinted in the Review and the Masses. Beyond that, to my knowledge, no word was reaching the outside world. In the strike zone, however, one of my sonnets, a vitriolic thing titled 'Mine Guard,' created a sensation. Someone with a rare sense of recognition tacked it on Captain Fred Lester's door . . . At that time Lester was decidedly unpopular with the miners. He had just been promoted from the state guard to a captaincy in the Baldwin-Felts outfit.

"This incident which transformed the situation from a strike into a small scale civil war was the 'Bull Moose Special.' We were tipped off in Huntington that an armored train was being rigged up at the Chesapeake and Ohio yards for use against the miners . . . We spread a warning to the hills and waited anxiously for newspaper headlines announcing new atrocities. We didn't have to wait long. It was at Holly Grove. In the dead of night, with all lights extinguished, the armored train drew up over the sleeping tent colony and opened fire with rifles and machine guns. Wooden shacks were splintered and tents riddled with bullets. One woman was reported to have both legs broken by the rain of lead. A miner holding an infant in his arms, and running from his tent to shelter in a dugout, fell, seriously wounded. The baby, by some miracle was unhurt, but it was reported that three bullet holes had tattered the edge of her calico dress. Men, women, and children ran hastily through the night, seeking the cold shelter of the woods . . ."

Chaplin described a trip he and Elmer Rumbaugh made to collect information for an article, immediately after the Holly Grove incident. He wrote: "In every town we passed, miners were gathered in little anxious groups. Feeling was running high. I heard miners saying on every side, 'Just wait until the leaves come out!' This remark puzzled me until the desperate implications became apparent. The leafless hillsides made the miners targets for enemy fire and exposed their movements when they were seeking points of vantage from which to take pot shots at guards and militiamen. . . . At two roadway junctions we could plainly see the yellow wigwams of the militiamen, with stacked rifles glistening beside them. Several times we caught glimpses of machine guns overlooking the frail tent colonies of the miners."

"When we were on our way back home hell broke loose in the entire Kanawha Valley. We were caught in the midst of it. Armed miners from all parts of the state were on the march with the avowed purpose of destroying the hated 'Death Train.' . . . There were hundreds of incidents . . . We passed through a district where, in a single engagement, sixteen men had been killed or, as the strikers put it, 'four men and twelve gun thugs.' . . . We were exposed to intermittent fire for three full days before we finally caught a freight back to Charleston. I arrived in Westmoreland once more, dog-tired and black with cinders, I sat down at the kitchen table and scribbled stanzas of 'When the Leaves Come Out.' It had been tormenting me all the way home. It has tormented me, in a different way, many times since then, because I have found it tucked away in too many miners' homes."

"The Kanawha Striker," "Mine Guard," and "When the Leaves Come Out," which were printed in the International Socialist Review (1914), were collected in a privately printed edition of Chaplin's early poems, When The Leaves Come Out (Chicago, 1917). Ralph Chaplin sent the manuscripts to Miss Inglis who included them in the file on Ralph Chaplin in the Labadie Collection.

THE KANAWHA STRIKER

By Ralph Chaplin

Good God! Must I now meekly bend my head
And cringe back to that gloom I know so well?
Forget the wrongs my tongue may never tell,
Forget the plea they silenced with their lead,
Forget the hillside strewn with murdered dead
Where once they drove me—mocked me when I
   fell
All black and bloody by their holes of hell,
While all my loved ones wept uncomforted?
Is this the land my fathers fought to own—
Here where they curse me—beaten and alone?
But God, it's cold! My children sob and cry!
Shall I go back into the mines and wait,
And lash the conflagration of my hate—
Or shall I stand and fight them till I die?

2

WHEN THE LEAVES COME OUT

By A Paint Creek Miner

The hills are very bare and cold and lonely;
  I wonder what the future months will bring?
The strike is on—our strength would win, if only—
  O, Buddy, how I'm longing for the spring!

They've got us down—their martial lines enfold us;
  They've thrown us out to feel the winter's sting,
And yet, by God, those curs could never hold us,
  Nor could the dogs of hell do such a thing!

It isn't just to see the hills beside me,
  Grow fresh and green with every growing thing.
I only want the leaves to come and hide me,
  To cover up my vengeful wandering.

I will not watch the floating clouds that hover
  Above the birds that warble on the wing;
I want to use this GUN from under cover—
  O, Buddy, how I'm longing for the spring!

You see them there below, the damned scab-
    herders!
  Those puppets on the greedy Owners' String;
We'll make them pay for all their dirty murders—
  We'll show them how a starving hate can sting!

They riddled us with volley after volley;
  We heard their speeding bullets zip and ring,
But soon we'll make them suffer for their folly—
  O, Buddy, how I'm longing for the spring!

3

THE MINE GUARD

By A Paint Creek Miner

You cur! How can you stand so calm and still
  And careless while your brothers strive and
    bleed?
  What hellish, cruel, crime-polluted creed
Has taught you thus to do your master's will,
Whose guilty gold has damned your soul until
  You lick his boots and fawn to do his deed—
  To pander to his lust of boundless greed,
And guard him while his cohorts crush and kill?

Your brutish crimes are like a rotten flood—
  The beating, raping, murdering you've done—
  You sycophantic coward with a gun:
The worms would scorn your carcass in the mud;
  A bitch would blush to hail you as a son—
You loathsome outcast, red with fresh-spilled
    blood!

4

*Pat Brennan, author of the popular "Harvest War
Song," composed these verses which appeared in*
Voice of the People (*September 17, 1914*).

DOWN IN THE MINES

By Pat Brennen

We delve in the Mines, down below, down below.
Yes, we delve in the Mines down below;
We give to the World all the wealth that we mine,
Yet we're slaves to the mines down below;
We're stripped to the waist like a savage of old,
Down in the regions where cold is unknown.
Our Masters have made us, for ages untold,
Their Slaves in the mines down below, down
    below,
Their Slaves in the mines down below.

With shovel and pick we work till we're sick,
Down in the mines down below, down below;
Down in the mines, down below.
With hammer and drill we drive and we fill
Our lungs with the gases, the gases that kill;
We're sent to the "Flats," all rigid and still,
Us Slaves from the mines down below, down
    below,
Us Slaves from the mines down below.

But let's stand together for once at the top,
Then you bet your sweet life the murders will
    stop—
And don't go to work till you've had your own
    way,
Down in the mines down below, down below,
Down in the mines, down below.

5

This unsigned song appeared in Solidarity (*August 5, 1916*) *during the strike of the iron ore miners on the Mesabi Range in Minnesota.*

The Certain Means Of Rescue

Solidarity, September 16, 1916.

THE IRON ORE MINERS

(Written in Jail)

(Tune: "It's a Long Way to Tipperary")

The Miners of the Iron Range
Know there was something wrong
They banded all together, yes,
In One Big Union strong.
The Steel Trust got the shivers,
And the Mine Guards had some fits,
The Miners didn't give a damn,
But closed down all the pits.

Chorus—

It's a long way to monthly pay day,
It's a long way to go
It's a long way to monthly pay day,
For the Miners need the dough,
Goodbye Steel Trust profits,
The Morgans they feel blue.
It's a long way to monthly pay day
For the miners want two.

They worked like hell on contract, yes,
And got paid by the day,
Whenever they got fired, yes,
The bosses held their pay.
But now they want a guarantee
Of just three bones a day,
And when they quit their lousy jobs
They must receive their pay.

Chorus—

It's the wrong way to work, by contract
It's the wrong way to go.
It's the wrong way to work by contract
For the Miners need the dough.
Goodbye bosses' handouts,—
Farewell Hibbing Square.
It's the wrong way to work by contract
You will find no Miners there.

John Allar died of Mine Guards' guns
The Steel Trust had engaged.
At Gilbert, wives and children
Of the Miners were outraged
No Mine Guards were arrested,
Yet the law is claimed to be
The mightiest conception
Of a big democracy.

Chorus—

It's the wrong way to treat the Miners,
It's the wrong way to go.
It's the wrong way to best the Miners,
As the Steel Trust soon will know.
God help those dirty Mine Guards,
The Miners won't forget.
It's the wrong way to treat the Miners,
And the guards will know that yet.

The Governor got his orders for
To try and break the strike.
He sent his henchmen on the Range,
Just what the Steel Trust liked.
The Miners were arrested, yes,
And thrown into the jail,
But yet they had no legal rights
When they presented bail.

It is this way in Minnesota
Is it this way you go?
It is this way in Minnesota,
Where justice has no show.
Wake up all Wage Workers,
In One Big Union strong.
If we all act unified together,
We can right all things that's wrong.

Chorus—

It's a short way to next election,
It's a short way to go.
For the Governor's in deep reflection
As to Labor's vote, you know.
Goodbye, Dear Old State House,
Farewell, Bernquist there.
It's a short way to next election
And you'll find no Bernquist there.

Get busy, was the order to
The lackeys of the Trust,
Jail all the Organizers
And the Strike will surely bust.
Trump up a charge, a strong one,
That will kill all sympathy,
So murder was the frame-up,
And one of first degree.

Chorus—

It is this way in Minnesota
Is it this way you go?
It is this way in Minnesota,

Where justice has no show.
Wake up all Wage Workers,
In One Big Union strong.
If we all act unified together,
We can right all things that's wrong.

6

*The following five songs were included in an un-
dated, paperbound collection of twenty-five poems
and songs, titled* New Songs for Butte Mining
Camp. *Acquired by I.W.W. member John Neuhouse and now in the library of folklorist Archie
Green, this booklet has been microfilmed by the
Stanford University Library. A copy of the micro-
film is in the Labadie Collection.*

*Page Stegner, in an unpublished study, "Protest
Songs from the Butte Mines," wrote: "It may
safely be said that few if any of the songs in this
book have ever been reprinted, and there is considerable doubt whether they were widely known
in Butte even at the time they were written. Apparently, they never entered oral tradition, the
principal scholars in the field have not noted their
existence, and they are not remembered by anyone yet interviewed who lived and worked in
Butte. In any scholarly definition they cannot be
considered folksongs, yet this does not eliminate
their importance to the folklorist or the labor historian. Their real value lies in the insights they
give into the actual causes of the strikes and labor
problems from the viewpoint of the miner and
labor organizer. Furthermore, they are representative not only of the causes of labor agitation, but
also of what the labor organizers thought would
be the most stirring issues among Butte workmen
and most useful for organizing the labor class.
They are social documents of this class in the
Butte mining area."*

*Tom Campbell, who is mentioned in these
poems, was the Butte miners' leader who ran
against Charles Moyer for the presidency of the
Western Federation of Miners in 1912, charging
that W.F.M. officials had done nothing to oppose
the newly instituted "rustling card" system in
Butte nor the discharge of a large number of
Finnish Socialist miners. Campbell was expelled
from the W.F.M. for these charges. In 1917 he was
elected president of a new union, the Metal Mine
Workers, formed after the June 1917 Speculator*
Mine fire of the North Butte Mining Company.

*"Con" Kelly was Cornelius Kelly, vice-president
of the Anaconda Copper Company, the largest
ore producer in Butte. Kelly is reported to have
said that he would see the grass grow on the muck
heaps in Butte before meeting the demands for
better working conditions presented to the company by the I.W.W. This remark is preserved in
Scottie's song, "Cornelius Kelly."*

*Page Stegner noted: "Perhaps one of the most
important contributions of the song book to labor
history and the labor historian is the way in which
several of the songs reflect the difficulties labor
organizers had in breaking down ethnic barriers
and getting workers to cooperate with other racial
groups. Scottie's song, 'Workers Unite,' is one of
the best examples of this problem."*

*Both Scottie and Joe Kennedy were remem-
bered by a retired electrician, Tiger Thompson,
a Wobbly who worked in the mines of Butte in
1917 and 1918, who was interviewed by Stegner
in Portola Valley, California.*

THE MINER

By "SCOTTIE"

(*Tune: "Standard on the Braes O May"*)

The miners in the mines of Butte
Are in rebellion fairly,
The gathering clouds of discontent
Are spreading fast and surely.
The miner's life is full of strife,
In stopes and drifts and raises,—
Don't judge him hard, give him his due,
He needs our loudest praises.

Down in these holes each shift he goes
And works mid dangers many,
And gets the "miner's con" to boot,
The worst disease of any;
In hot-boxes he drills his rounds,
Midst floods of perspiration,
And clogs his lungs with copper dust,—
A hellish occupation.

The merry breezes never blow
Down in these awful places
The sun's rays are one-candle power
That shines on pallid faces;

The only birds that warble there
Are "buzzies" and "jack hammers,"
Their song is death in every note,
For human life they clamour.

Conditions such as these, my friends,
Have made the miners rebels,
The under-current is gaining strength,
The mighty system trembles;
The revolution's coming fast,
Old institutions vanish,
The tyrant-rule from off the earth
For evermore 'twill banish.

7

THE CAMPBELLS ARE COMING

By "Scottie"

(*Tune: "The Campbells Are Coming"*)

The Campbells are coming, Hooray! Hooray!
The "Campbell's real union" is here to stay
The buttons are blazing, the bosses are raving
The Campbells are coming, Hooray! Hooray!

The Englishman, Scotchman and Irishman, too,
American, Dutchman, Finlander and Jew,

Drawing It Tighter All the Time.

Solidarity, July 7, 1917.

Are all turning Campbells, good luck to the day,
The Campbells are coming, Hooray! Hooray!

The rustling card system, it sure has to go,
Six dollars we ask and more safety below,
And after awhile six hours in the day
The Campbells are coming, Hooray! Hooray!

The prostitute-press is bucking us hard,
And the A. F. of L. is just quite as bad,
But we'll show them all we're made of right clay,
The Campbells have come and they're going to
    stay.

The Campbells are coming, Hooray! Hooray!
The "real Campbell's union" is here to stay,
The buttons are blazing, the bosses are raving,
The Campbells are coming, Hooray! Hooray!

Solidarity, July 14, 1917.

8

CORNELIUS KELLY

Of all the men in old Butte City,
That needs contempt or even pity,
There's one that rules on the Sixth Floor
That's got them all skinned, by the score.
This old gent's name is Cornelius Kelly,
Was meant to crawl upon his belly,
But listen, boys, he's good and true
The Company's interests to pull thru,
But when it comes to working men,
He'd rather see them in the pen,
Or burning in eternal hell,—
His nostrils would enjoy the smell.

"The grass would grow," so says this plute,
"In Anaconda and in Butte,
Before I meet the men's demands,
As this is final as it stands."
All right, old boy, the time will tell,
You cannot stop the ocean's swell;
It's we who dig the copper ore,
While you lie in your bed and snore;
It's we who fold our arms and stand
Until we get our just demand.
Five months ago we told you so—
(The grass is coming very slow).

9

THE COPPER STRIKE OF '17

By Joe Kennedy

On the twelfth of June we called a strike
Which filled the miners with delight,
In union strong we did unite,
On the rustling card to make a fight.

The Bisbee miners fell in line,
And believe me, Miami was not far behind;
In Globe they surely were on time,
To join their striking brothers.

The companies were money mad,
This strike made dividends look sad;
The men to Con these words did say,
"They'll be twice as short before next May."

The local press it came out bold
And said it must be German gold,

Although we did not have a dime
The morn we hit the firing line.

Although we're classed as an outlaw band,
We've surely made a noble stand,
Our fight is just for liberty
And make Butte safe for democracy.

Six hundred gunmen came to town
And tried to keep the strikers down,
In spite of all we're full of vim,
Our password is, "we're bound to win!"

The old war-horse is in the game
I know all rebels heard his name,
For thirty years and more, I'm told,
His fellow-workers never sold.

The A.C.M. they tried their skill,
When Fellow-Worker Little's blood did spill,
The day will come when union men
Will have a voice in Butte again.

Fellow-Worker Campbell, true and bold,
His comrades would not sell for gold;
He said to Con, "Why, I'll get mine
By standing on the firing line."

Now respect to all true union men,
Who have courage to fight until the end;
To copper barons we will say,
"The rustling card has gone to stay."

10

WORKERS UNITE

By "Scottie"

Ye sons that come from Erin's shore,
Just list to what I've got in store,
Of Celtic race and blood you came,
Of fighting blood and noble strain.

Your blood on every battle field,
You've shed for master class to wield,
The Iron Hand in name of state,
To bring you to an awful fate.

But, Irishmen, you're not to blame,
In other lands it's just the same,
The workers of the world are slaves,
The parasites are heartless knaves.

If you'd be free, you've got to stand,
With working men from every land;
Race prejudice you've got to banish
From out your minds and not be clannish.

Our interests are just the same
From County Cork to State of Maine,
The master rules with iron hand,
From Australia to Baffin's Land.

So Workers of the World unite
Beneath one banner for the right,
In Labor's ranks there is a place
For every man of every race.

Now, Erin's sons, again I say,
Don't be a slacker in the fray;
The world for workers be your cry,
Resound aloud from earth to sky.

Frank Little.
Labadie Collection photo files.

11

*Like Bill Haywood, Frank Little had only one
good eye. He boasted of being half Indian. He
was one of the most courageous and dynamic of
the I.W.W. organizers. Chairman of the I.W.W.
General Executive Board, Little had been active
in the I.W.W. since 1906. He had helped lead the
Missoula, Spokane, and Fresno free speech fights,
and had organized lumberjacks, metal miners, oil
workers, and harvest stiffs into the One Big Union.
With one leg in a plaster cast from an accident he
had while organizing in Oklahoma, Frank Little
arrived in Butte, Montana, shortly after the Speculator Mine fire, when infuriated Butte miners refused to go back to work until their demands were
met for improved safety conditions and an end to
long-standing grievances. Following a speech at
the ball park in Butte on July 31, 1917, Little went
to his room at the Finn Hotel. That night, six
masked and armed men broke into his room, beat
him, and dragged him by a rope behind their
automobile to a Milwaukee Railroad trestle on the
outskirts of Butte. There he was hung. On his
coat was pinned a card: "First and last warning!
3-7-77. D-D-C-S-S-W." It was said that the numbers referred to the measurements of a grave and
that the initials corresponded to the first letters of
the names of other strike leaders in Butte, thereby
warning them of similar treatment if their strike
activities were not stopped. No attempt was made
to find Little's assailants.*

*The poem, "To Frank Little," by Viola Gilbert
Snell appeared in* Solidarity *(August 25, 1917).
"When the Cock Crows" by Arturo Giovannitti
appeared in* Solidarity *(September 22, 1917).*

TO FRANK LITTLE

By Viola Gilbert Snell

The plains you loved lie parching in the sun,
The streets you tramped are sweltering in the heat,
The fertile fields are arid with the drouth,
The forests thick with smoldering fires and smoke.

    Traitor and demagogue,
    Wanton breeder of discontent—
    That is what they call you—
    Those cowards, who condemn sabotage
    But hide themselves
    Not only behind masks and cloaks

But behind all the armored positions
Of property and prejudice and the law.

    Staunch friend and comrade,
    Soldier of solidarity —
    Like some bitter magic
    The tale of your tragic death
    Has spread throughout the land,
    And from a thousand minds
    Has torn the last shreds of doubt
    Concerning Might and Right.

    Young and virile and strong—
    Like grim sentinels they stand
    Awaiting each opportunity
    To break another
    Of slavery's chains.
    For WHATEVER stroke is needed.
    They are preparing.
    So shall you be avenged.

Within our hearts is smoldering a heat
Fiercer than that which parches fields and plains;
Your memory, like a torch, shall light the flames
Of Revolution. We shall not forget.

12

WHEN THE COCK CROWS

*To the Memory of Frank Little
Hanged at Midnight*

By Arturo Giovannitti

I

Six MEN drove up to his house at midnight, and
    woke the poor woman who kept it,
And asked her: "Where is the man who spoke
    against war and insulted the army?"
And the old woman took fear of the men and the
    hour, and showed them the room where he slept,
And when they made sure it was he whom they
    wanted, they dragged him out of his bed with
    blows, tho' he was willing to walk,
And they fastened his hands on his back, and they
    drove him across the black night,
And there was no moon and no star and not any
    visible thing, and even the faces of the men
    were eaten with the leprosy of the dark, for they
    were masked with black shame,
And nothing showed in the gloom save the glow of
    his eyes and the flame of his soul that scorched
    the face of Death.

II

NO ONE gave witness of what they did to him, after they took him away, until a dog barked at his corpse.

But I know, for I have seen masked men with the rope, and the eyeless things that howl against the sun, and I have ridden beside the hangman at midnight.

They kicked him, they cursed him, they pushed him, they spat on his cheeks and his brow,

They stabbed his ears with foul oaths, they smeared his clean face with the pus of their ulcerous words,

And nobody saw or heard them. But I call you to witness, John Brown, I call you to witness, you Molly Maguires,

And you, Albert Parsons, George Engle, Adolph Fischer, August Spies,

And you, Leo Frank, kinsman of Jesus, and you, Joe Hill, twice my germane in the rage of the song and the fray,

And all of you, sun-dark brothers, and all of you harriers of torpid faiths, hasteners of the great day, propitiators of the holy deed,

I call you all to the bar of the dawn to give witness if this is not what they do in America when they wake up men at midnight to hang them until they're dead.

III

UNDER a railroad trestle, under the heart-rib of progress, they circled his neck with the noose, but never a word he spoke.

Never a word he uttered, and they grew weak from his silence,

For the terror of death is strongest upon the men with the rope,

When he who must hang breathes neither a prayer nor a curse,

Nor speaks any word, nor looks around, nor does anything save to chew his bit of tobacco and yawn with unsated sleep.

They grew afraid of the hidden moon and the stars, they grew afraid of the wind that held its breath, and of the living things that never stirred in their sleep,

And they gurgled a bargain to him from under their masks.

I know what they promised to him, for I have heard thrice the bargains that hounds yelp to the trapped lion:

They asked him to promise that he would turn back from his road, that he would eat carrion as they, that he would lap the leash for the sake of the offals, as they—and thus he would save his life.

But not one lone word he answered—he only chewed his bit of tobacco in silent contempt.

IV

NOW BLACK as their faces became whatever had been white inside of the six men, even to their mothers' milk,

And they inflicted on him the final shame, and ordered that he should kiss the flag.

They always make bounden men kiss the flag in America where men never kiss men, not even when they march forth to die.

But tho' to him all flags are holy that men fight for and death hallows,

He did not kiss it—I swear it by the one that shall wrap my body.

He did not kiss it, and they trampled upon him in their frenzy that had no retreat save the rope,

And to him who was ready to die for a light he would never see shine, they said, "You are a coward."

To him who would not barter a meaningless word for his life, they said, "You are a traitor."

And they drew the noose round his neck, and they pulled him up to the trestle, and they watched him until he was dead,

Six masked men whose faces were eaten with the cancer of the dark,

One for each steeple of thy temple, O Labor.

V

NOW HE IS dead, but now that he is dead is the door of your dungeon faster, O money changers and scribes, and priests and masters of slaves?

Are men now readier to die for you without asking the wherefore of the slaughter?

Shall now the pent-up spirit no longer connive with the sun against your midnight?

And are we now all reconciled to your rule, and are you safer and we humbler, and is the night eternal and the day forever blotted out of the skies,

And all blind yesterdays risen, and all tomorrows entombed,

Because of six faceless men and ten feet of rope and one corpse dangling unseen in the blackness under a railroad trestle?

No, I say, No. It swings like a terrible pendulum
    that shall soon ring out a mad tocsin
    and call the red cock to the crowing.
No, I say, No, for someone will bear witness of
    this to the dawn,
Someone will stand straight and fearless tomorrow
    between the armed hosts of your slaves, and
    shout to them the challenge of that silence you
    could not break.

VI

"BROTHERS—he will shout to them—"are you, then,
    the God-born reduced to a mute of dogs
That you will rush to the hunt of your kin at the
    blowing of a horn?
Brothers, have then the centuries that created new
    suns in the heavens, gouged out the eyes of your
    soul,
That you should wallow in your blood like swine,
That you should squirm like rats in a carrion,
That you, who astonished the eagles, should beat
    blindly about the night of murder like bats?
Are you, Brothers, who were meant to scale the
    stars, to crouch forever before a footstool,
And listen forever to one word of shame and
    subjection,
And leave the plough in the furrow, the trowel on
    the wall, the hammer on the anvil and the heart
    of the race on the knees of screaming women,
    and the future of the race in the hands of bab-
    bling children,
And yoke on your shoulders the halter of hatred
    and fury,
And dash head-down against the bastions of folly,
Because a colored cloth waves in the air, because
    a drum beats in the street,
Because six men have promised you a piece of
    ribbon on your coat, a carved tablet on a wall
    and your name in a list bordered with black?
Shall you, then, be forever the stewards of death,
    when life waits for you like a bride?
Ah no, Brothers, not for this did our mothers
    shriek with pain and delight when we tore their
    flanks with our first cry;
Not for this were we given command of the beasts,
Not with blood but with sweat were we bidden to
    achieve our salvation.
Behold: I announce now to you a great tidings of
    joy,
For if your hands that are gathered in sheaves for
    the sickle of war unite as a bouquet of flowers
    between the warm breasts of peace,

Freedom will come without any blows save the
    hammers on the chains of your wrists, and the
    picks on the walls of your jails!
Arise, and against every hand jeweled with the
    rubies of murder,
Against every mouth that sneers at the tears of
    mercy,
Against every foul smell of the earth,
Against every hand that a footstool raised over
    your head,
Against every word that was written before this
    was said,
Against every happiness that never knew sorrow,
And every glory that never knew love and sweat,
Against silence and death, and fear,
Arise with a mighty roar!
Arise and declare your war:
For the wind of the dawn is blowing,
For the eyes of the East are glowing,
For the lark is up and the cock is crowing,
And the day of judgment is here!"

VII

THUS shall he speak to the great parliament of the
    dawn, the witness of this murderous midnight,
And even if none listens to him, I shall be there
    and acclaim,
And even if they tear him to shreds, I shall be
    there to confess him before your guns and your
    gallows, O Monsters!
And even tho' you smite me with your bludgeon
    upon my head,
And curse me and call me foul names, and spit on
    my face and on my bare hands,
I swear that when the cock crows I shall not deny
    him.
And even if the power of your lie be so strong that
    my own mother curse me as a traitor with her
    hands clutched over her old breasts,
And my daughters with the almighty names, turn
    their faces from me and call me coward,
And the One whose love for me is a battleflag in
    the storm, scream for the shame of me and
    adjure my name,
I swear that when the cock crows I shall not deny
    him.
And if you chain me and drag me before the Beast
    that guards the seals of your power, and the
    caitiff that conspires against the daylight de-
    mand my death,
And your hangman throw a black cowl over my
    head and tie a noose around my neck,

And the black ghoul that pastures on the graves of
the saints dig its snout into my soul and howl the
terrors of the everlasting beyond in my ears,
Even then, when the cock crows, I swear I shall
not deny him.
And if you spring the trap under my feet and hurl
me into the gloom, and in the revelation of that
instant eternal a voice shriek madly to me
That the rope is forever unbreakable,
That the dawn is never to blaze,
That the night is forever invincible,
Even then, even then, O Monsters, I shall not
deny him.

13

This unsigned poem appeared in the One Big Union Monthly (*August 1919*). *It is the only piece of
writing found thus far to commemorate the events
of July 12, 1917, in Bisbee, Arizona, when an
armed vigilante committee raided the homes of
striking miners, loaded over 1160 of them into cattle cars, and deported them to the town in the
desert where they were retained until September, following the end of their strike.*

BISBEE

FOR THE SECOND ANNIVERSARY

By Card No. 512210

We are waiting, brother, waiting
Tho the night be dark and long
And we know 'tis in the making
Wondrous day of vanished wrongs.

They have herded us like cattle
Torn us from our homes and wives.
Yes, we've heard their rifles rattle
And have feared for our lives.

We have seen the workers, thousands,
Marched like bandits, down the street
Corporation gunmen round them
Yes, we've heard their tramping feet.

It was in the morning early
Of that fatal July 12th
And the year nineteen seventeen
This took place of which I tell.

Servants of the damned bourgeois
With white bands upon their arms

Drove and dragged us out with curses
Threats, to kill on every hand.

Question, protest all were useless
To those hounds of hell let loose.
Nothing but an armed resistance
Would avail with these brutes.

There they held us, long lines weary waiting
'Neath the blazing desert sun.
Some with eyes bloodshot and bleary
Wished for water, but had none.

Yes, some brave wives brought us water
Loving hearts and hands were theirs.
But the gunmen, cursing often,
Poured it out upon the sands.

Down the streets in squads of fifty
We were marched, and some were chained,
Down to where the shining rails
Stretched across the sandy plains.

Then in haste with kicks and curses
We were herded into cars
And it seemed our lungs were bursting
With the odor of the Yards.

Floors were inches deep in refuse
Left there from the Western herds.
Good enough for miners. Damn them.
May they soon be food for birds.

No farewells were then allowed us
Wives and babes were left behind,
Tho I saw their arms around us
As I closed my eyes and wept.

After what seemed weeks of torture
We were at our journey's end.
Left to starve upon the border
Almost on Carranza's land.

Then they rant of law and order,
Love of God, and fellow man,
Rave of freedom o'er the border
Being sent from promised lands.

Comes the day, ah! we'll remember
Sure as death relentless, too,
Grim-lipped toilers, their accusers,
Let them call on God, not on you.

14

This "Tightline Johnson" story by Ralph Winstead finds the Wobbly Johnson in a coal mining camp. It appeared in the Industrial Pioneer (*January 1922*).

LIGHT EXERCISE AND CHANGE

By RALPH WINSTEAD

Education accordin' to my idea is a matter of grabbin' onto and arrangin' in the mind all sorts of new ideas and experiences. When a fellow just grabs onto ideas and never has any experiences, why, about all he is good for is to spread ideas. When it comes to action the idea guy is handin' out the absent treatment.

Coal minin' is not generally listed as one of the essentials to a finished education, but it is sure a form of experience that is liable to change one's ideas. My first mingling with the black diamonds happened after I had put in about seven months on the shelf with a busted leg. The Doc, in his last once over, had told me that all I needed was light exercise and change, and so I started out to find the change, intendin', of course, to take my exercise as lightly as possible.

After ramblin' around for a few crispy fall days and nights I landed without malice or forethought in a coal camp out of Tacoma some considerable ways. The two strings of whitewashed miners' shacks strung along a narrow canyon with the railroad, wagon road, promenade and kids' playground occupyin' the fifty feet of space between the rows of workingmen's places completed the residence section.

The mine buildings mostly lay up on the side hill and looked like the dingiest collection of hangman's scaffolds that ever happened. There is some things that all the doctorin' and fussin' in the world ain't goin' to make restful to sore eyes, and a coal mine is one of 'em. Everything, from the bunker chutes up to the hoist house, is usually covered with the dust of dirty years and the buildings are, as the British remittance man says of his squaw wife, "Built for use and not for display."

When I first ventured on the scene the night shift was just gatherin' toward the biggest scaffold of the whole bunch, so I wandered over that way myself. The big tower supported two bull wheels that ran in opposite directions, guiding cables which were pulling a trip of loaded coal cars up on one track while the other cable was sending down the empties on the other track.

The hole in the ground, into which these cables ran from the bull wheel, went straight in for about fifty feet and then seemed to jump off. Electric lights made the inside bright as day so that the well of inky blackness beyond the lights showed up strong. The cables roared and the ground shook to the rapid explosion of the steam hoist. This, I surmised, was a place for a cool head and a steady hand.

While I was watchin', a coal smeared lad about of a size to be studyin' fractions moseyed out to the jumpin' off place. The roar of the cables increased, then was drowned in a growin' mightier noise. The lad crouched as for a spring. The mighty roar achieved a climax. A hurtling black shape come pushing over the brink. The boy leaped in the air and landed square on the end of the moving mass.

He stooped, grasped the couplin' that fastened the hoistin' cable to the end of the car and, jerkin' it loose, threw clevis and gear clear of the track. He leaped to the ground and gave scarcely a glance at the swift movin' train of loaded one ton cars which went chargin' through a muddle of switches out onto a trestle, where another and smaller boy took them in charge.

I was all excited by these maneuvers. I felt just like the time when the high climber accidentally cut his life rope with the axe and climbed down hangin' onto the bark of the spare tree with his hands. Nobody else seemed to be much excited and the kid that had gone through the performance least of all. He hustled some empties into the tunnel, hooked 'em up and fastened the cable on and soon another trip was hurryin' up from the guts of the earth while the empties were goin' down.

On all sides there was a bunch of little shavers scurryin' around amongst the cars spraggin', oilin', shovin' and pushin'. There was a whole raft of 'em. Kids and coal minin' seem to work together. I grew a lot of respect for coal miners in a few minutes. "If the kids were set at this sort of a job," thinks I, "what was expected of the men?" I turned and sized up the group that was hangin' round.

I saw right away where I was goin' to horn in on some light exercise, for each one of these grimy slow movin' plugs was exercisin' some sort of a light. Some wore 'em on their caps like a posie on a summer bonnet, while another sort was carried in the hand like a little lantern.

I felt a big desire to have a shining light hung on me, so I approached one of the nearest light bearers and probed him as to how to get a job in the outfit.

Did you ever notice the hostility of some slaves toward the strangers that are rustlin' a job from their masters? Well, this strange-cow-in-the-pasture attitude was noticeable for its absence here. I got all the information wanted cheerfully, and then went over and tackled the shifter, who looked just like the rest of the gang except that he carried two lights and a little more dry black mud.

He seemed almost human. Instead of askin' about my lurid past or family connections, he seemed interested in the jobs to be filled and my ability to fill 'em. He went into the lamp house to see how the gang was lined up and came out with the haulage boss, who sized me up and said a few words about trips and number seven motor while I looked wise. I hooked a job ridin' trip and was told to report the next day for afternoon shift.

After enterin' my name and number in the office I went down to look for the boardin' house. This affair was in one of the bigger white-washed shacks and the boardin' boss was a big fat woman with a cockney accent and a warm and generous smile.

Accommodations was not exactly luxurious. I got a little single cot in a room with two other fellows. I was informed that the union had a big bath house by the mine so that all washin' up would be done there.

While I was sittin' in the main room on one of the luxurious kitchen chairs, the missus came in for a chat. She asked me about my clothes and finances as if she was an old pal. Finding that I was goin' to work on the haulage crew she told me right off that I would need a miner's cap and some shoe grease. Then she wrote out a slip that made my face good at the company store and I went up to this institution and got the goods.

The company store is a sort of clearing house. The bookkeeper is the postmaster, the timekeeper and paymaster all rolled into one by hand. He was a busy plug. A miner would put in so much time in the mine and would be given credit on the books for so much. His store bill, union dues and doctor's fees were deducted from his credit balance and what was over he could get in cash every two weeks or so.

What struck me most was the spirit of friendliness that everyone showed. There was little of the backbitin' and hate that is found in so many small towns and camps. A tolerant spirit was floatin' around in the air and one seemed to grab onto it right away. Yet it was a rough and critical tolerance and not of the smooth, oily sort that one finds among the so-called cultured people.

I mentioned the fact to the boardin' missus. She told me that there was jealousies and hates all right, but the general ideas of the miners discouraged 'em. She rattled off a few phrases like solidarity and direct action and the like, tryin' to describe the past battles and conditions and I sat up and took notice. The boardin' missus was no slouch to my mind. She explained how conditions were fought for.

Durin' the evenin' I had a good time listenin' to the rag chewin' that was carried on in the sittin' room and out on the porch. Some of the boys had good ideas and I sat there as pleased as a bald headed man in the front row.

Next afternoon at three o'clock I reached the pit mouth and after gettin' my lamp and brass check number I hung around with the rest of the bunch and watched the top cager go through his gymnastics with the gallopin' cars. One of the miners came over and told me in a friendly way that I should be sure not to take any matches down with me, as that would raise hell if I did. I searched every pocket and got rid of all that I had. Later on I found that this gentle-voiced old Finn was chairman of the safety committee.

They rolled out the man cars. They was queer lookin' rigs, just big open topless boxes on wheels with boards for seats, nailed crossways and slanting up in the air at an angle like the cow guards on a railroad crossing. When the car was runnin' down the slope the seats was about horizontal.

As one car went down with a load of night shift men the other car came up from the bottom with a load of the day shift. The plugs comin' off sure didn't impress one with bein' specimens of manly beauty. Smeared with coal dust and mud, with their clothes sticky and black with scrapins from chute and wall they was sure a hard lookin' bunch.

Finally I got into the car with a big Italian that had taken me under his wing. We moved out slowly to the jump off and then picked up speed goin' down the steep slope.

Everything was dark except for the light in our caps and these made the timbers that capped the

COPPER TRUST TO THE PRESS: "IT'S ALL RIGHT, PAL; JUST TELL THEM HE WAS A TRAITOR."

Solidarity, August 11, 1917.

slope and the posts and walls on the sides, quite plain. Half way down we passed the other car comin' up. All that we could see was a blur of lights as they whizzed by.

In order to make me feel good Tony alongside told about mines where the cable had broken while they were pullin' the men out. He told about the runaways with such happy satisfaction that I figured that he was kiddin' me. Later I found that he was only happy because it was the truth. You know a fellow always gets a sort of kick out of doin' dangerous things cheerfully. The coal owners sure used short sightedness when they plastered the pit buildings full of safety first posters with the old bunk that it never pays to take a chance. If the miners really acted on that idea there would be a lot of perfectly good machinery and coal burnin' stoves bein' lugged up to the pawn shop, right away. Coal would be an interestin' specimen.

At last we rolled out on the bottom of the eighteen hundred foot slope and we scrambled out on one side of the car while a gang of fierce eyed, muddy and sweaty miners piled in on the other side. There was no confusion however as the first men down were the first ones up and there was strict enforcement of the rule. The car climbed up and disappeared and I looked around me at this electric lighted gallery so deep under ground. The first thing that took my eyes was some petrified clam shells on the hangin' wall just as natural as if they were ready to furnish the makins of a Coney Island chowder. Many a thing had happened in this highly important world of ours since they had played their last squirt in the sunshine on the beach.

We checked in, to a man with a book, and a big pencil, who kept track of the trip loads comin' down and goin' up. As I was walking on past groups of miners waitin' their turn to go up, a little hard lookin' Scot jumped out at me with a pad and pencil.

"Hi Laddie—sign this paper!" he commanded.

"What is it?" I asked thinkin' maybe it was a contribution list for indignant Armenians or somethin' like it.

"It's the union check off, Laddie," he said seriously, "and you'll have to sign it if you work wi' us." So I signed up and was a miners' union man, except for the sacred oath with the right hand on the left breast in front of the Imperial Lizard.

Then I came to a little Italian who was the haulage boss on my shift. He was an excitable high ball artist but was ashamed of it and tried to cover it up with a forced good nature. He kept his mind fixed on the tonnage at all times. Otherwise he seemed a hell of a fine fellow. He had a hard case of producers' mental cramp.

This boss took me over to a squat fat Austrian who was tinkerin' with a low, wicked lookin' motor, that looked like an armored car more than anything else. They told me to sit down and wait till the rest of the trips had pulled in to the different veins and chutes to load up and then we would start.

The night shift trooped by to their places in the interior and trip by trip the crowd of men on the bottom lessened. When the watch said four o'clock the trips commenced to roll out of the bottom with their ten and fifteen cars into the dark narrowness of the miles of tunneled gangways each foot of which had its danger to the trip rider and haulage man.

At last we too hooked onto a string of cars and went rolling into the mysterious inside. The big blue sparks from the trolley snapped and flamed while faster and faster the trip moved into the darkness with Johnny the boss, and myself draped over the end of the last car.

In places the roof was low and timbers had to be dodged or they would brush a plug off like he was a fly. Then the trolley hung low and there was a constant danger of touchin' it and gettin' electrocuted about half way.

A thousand dangers was on every hand. The little light on my cap was all that enabled me to see the overhead things that was ready to cave in my dome at any time I grew careless.

Johnny explained that I would get to know these dangers and would safeguard myself without thinkin' about it. "It's like a guy walkin'," he said. "He's takin' a chance every minute dat he might fall down and bust his neck but he gets so used to it dat he protects himself widout any worryin' at all. Besides dis is nuttin'. You'd ought to see what de miners is up against, up de pitch."

We turned off of one tunnel into another and passed yawning black gangways to right and left but kept on goin'. These miles of track down here that took so many hours and days of workin' together to build, these thousands of timbers each set of which took plannin' and figurin' of whole gangs workin' for one impersonal end, the dozens of miles of galleries, gangways, chutes, counter air courses, and escapeways, all of these played up by the flickin' light of my head lamp and emphasized by the pitchy blackness that was only relieved by the station lamps shinin' so far away, these things sure made a guy feel like he was only a small part of somethin' and not the whole cheese.

Mines I decided was no place for individual freedom. The more I saw of my job that day the more I figured that this was correct. We loaded trip after trip of cars full to overflowing, from the chutes. The miners up the pitch depended on us to use our heads at all times so that they would not be cut off in the black damp and gas that was sure to gather when the air courses were diverted.

Every thing you did had to be done just so, on account of the peculiar desire that a lot of the rest of us have, to remain all in one piece that can move around some. And that is what coal mining amounts to. It is a wild struggle to get the wages that can be had by diggin' coal, diggin' the coal and stayin' in such a shape so that the wife will recognize you when you come home. This complication naturally needs unionism and real helpful understanding of the local problems.

Unionism is my long suit and you can bet I was interested in the one that I had just joined. A lot of us has heard about the United Mine Workers and the funny thing is that the news is mostly in two classes, that is the sort of news that we can rely on. One sort of material is like the facts of the Ludlow Massacre and the West Virginia battles of the last twenty years.

Then there is the other sort. The facts that Mitchell, one time official of the Mine Workers, died with an estate of hundreds of thousands of dollars, and the way that the officials often have of letting the rank and file carry on the battles of the organization when they get in a tight place while they sit back and issue public interviews discouraging the members.

Naturally I was interested in the whys and wherefores of such an organization and you can bet I was on hand to take in anything that had a bearin' on the subject.

At the very next union meeting I got my first earful. After bein' solemnly swore in I took a seat and looked at the maze of faces that looked out from the seats arranged, like the Russian bond holders, with the backs to the wall.

There was a safety committee report to listen to and I heard myself bein' issued instructions from the body assembled not to leave any ties or rails layin' alongside the track in the gangways and was impressed with the need to handle things with an eye to the welfare of my fellow workers. These fellows was lookin' after the bosses' business in order to keep out of the little plot of holyground up on the hill.

Then they discussed methods of pullin' pillars and seemed to take exception to the technique of one of the bosses in this respect. The said boss was called in and made his statement in regards to the matter and was issued instructions to pull his pillars in the way that provided some chance of escape in at least nine out of ten times if you're lucky.

I commenced to wonder what was the need of the confounded Super that had held down the office chair anyway. With a management committee and the office force organized I had a notion that this mine would run some considerable more coal per shift under a workers' society.

Still it seemed we was just startin'. The Pit committee made a report and it was announced that the Grand Kleagle up in the office had been forced to change his mind about the amount of time supposed to be put in at cleanin' the slope. Full pay was given for three quarters of a shift for all in this class. Other little matters of discussion had been talked over with The Most Noble One and been settled, it was reported.

I commenced to think I had landed right down in a camp where the wobblies' dream had come true. But after a while I changed my mind some. The Royal dignitaries from the district office took the floor under good and welfare and proceeded to solemnly warn us about the nefarious influences that was at work to bust up our glorious solidarity. Them infernal wobblies in one of the sister locals had kicked over the traces through utter ignorance and had voted out a lot of real funds from the local treasury for the benefit of some of those criminals that the wobs called class war prisoners. It was very painful to relate, we was told, but the special session of the executive board had passed a motion that no funds should be spent from local treasuries for purposes of this kind. That in the future any such expenditure would have to be made by means of a special assessment levied per capita on the members of the local.

It was a grand speech. It overflowed with respect for a few individuals that had been taken in by the insidious propaganda of these violent reds, but no member of this great union was goin' to stand by and see the great American flag insulted by this ignorant gang of scabs and dual unionists if the district officers and loyal members could help it. There was about an hour of this first by one indignant pie card and then another.

As soon as the oratorical debauch was over somebody with a sweet talking voice in the body made a motion that we go back to new business. It was slid across the floor without a squeak. Then something banged. Somebody in the back of the hall got the floor and said "Mr. Prayzident! I moof dat we donate wan hunderd dollars to the Northwest Districk Defense Committee." Somebody shouted a second. Then there was a lot of racket. It was evident that the well oiled machinery had slipped a cog.

But the riders of the tricky office chairs was not to be felled so easy. Long practice had made 'em sticky. When quiet was restored there was a point of order made. The motion was out of order because the executive board had already ruled that no such action could be taken. The chairman, the honorable president, declared the motion out of order.

Then came the intended motion to endorse the action of the executive board. The fattest and most oratorical of the Royal dignitaries secured the floor. We listened for three quarters of an hour to his bunk. We heard about the history of the I.W.W. from the day that the first of these degenerates ever got together right down the descent they had made till the present day. Then somebody else got the floor. He said that he had different ideas about the I.W.W. He said the I.W.W. had some of the finest principles in the world but they was the worst managed organization under the sun. He was a grand friend of the I.W.W., he was. He managed to throw more slams and venom than any enemy I ever heard. And so it was. Even I commenced to wonder if the I.W.W. had been foolin' me all these years. And then the motion was put to a vote on a call of the previous question. It was put fast too.

Amongst the members of the local there was seven for the motion and eight against. Ninety-five not votin'. Motion lost and meetin' adjourned.

Now my idea is that most mines is just like this one. Just as most loggin' camps and crews is a lot alike. If the minority has the pep and guts to put things across on the boss by gettin' their fellow workers to act then the conditions is liable to improve and the boss is liable to receive a set back in his pocketbook. But if not—not.

I found by lookin' round that here was enough plugs with real workin' class ideas on hand to swing the union meetings any way they wanted to providin' they was organized to do it. That is where you run into pitch. They wasn't organized.

They never laid plans on how to get the real stuff across in meetings. The militant workers went up to buck the fine machine of the officials with no system at all. It was like a Siwash tryin' to compete with an express train. There wasn't a chance.

Now I ain't no steady miner because I like the looks of the tall timber best but what I seen of this camp showed me that the only way to clean out the bunch of parasites that is betrayin' the miners' cause, is to build up a nifty little workers' machine in every local.

A little honest study over the best ways and means to get action in the coal camps will show this to be a fact. We got to organize the thinking workers that are already there into small groups that hold special meetings. We got to line up the boys that understand. These special meetings on the side should work out plans for action. They can easy enough spread literature to the rest of the miners and arrange for educational meetings.

These here miners got the stuff in 'em. We need to use the same tactics that the officials are usin', and learn that the only way to compete with a smooth runnin' machine is to use a better one.

With every wobbly member that is workin' in the coal mines organized into a job committee bent on developin' the miners' union into a real fightin' force instead of Johnny Lewis' plaything there would soon be a fighting spirit among the miners that would make the world sit up and take notice. The wobs could do it too along with the other boys that savvy if they would just form their own little group and tell the reactionaries to slide down some other cellar door.

Maybe this sounds like a lot of free advice. Maybe at this minute I—Tightline Johnson—ought to be jugglin' the black diamonds myself and formin' one of these little committees. Maybe so, maybe so but the reasons that I ain't is another story, as a feller's wife generally calls his excuses.

. . . if every person who represented law and order and the nation beat you up, railroaded you to jail, and the good Christian people cheered and told them to go to it, how in hell do you expect a man to be patriotic? This war is a businessman's war and we don't see why we should go out and get shot in order to save the lovely state of affairs which we now enjoy.

An I.W.W. member to Carleton H. Parker,
The Casual Laborer and Other Essays
(New York: Harcourt, Brace, and Howe, 1920), p. 102.

Chapter 11

Behind Bars: War and Prison

"We will resent with all the power at our command," the members of the I.W.W. General Executive Board stated in 1916, "any attempt to compel us—the disinherited—to participate in a war that can only bring in its wake death and untold misery, privation, and suffering to millions of workers, and only serve to further rivet the chains of slavery on our necks, and render still more secure the power of the few to control the destinies of the many."[1]

As early as 1914, the I.W.W. had declared itself officially opposed to World War I in a resolution which read: "We as members of the industrial army will refuse to fight for any purpose except the realization of industrial freedom."[2] Wobbly soapboxers lambasted the European conflict as an object lesson in capitalist folly in which workers were being sent into senseless slaughter to help line the pockets of the owners of industry.

"Don't Be a Soldier. Be a Man," read an I.W.W. stickerette issued about 1916. "Join the I.W.W. and fight on the job for yourself and your class."

Since the founding of the I.W.W. in 1905, Wobblies had opposed war not only on the basis of anticapitalism, but on the grounds of antinationalism and antimilitarism as well. "In the broad sense," said Wobbly soapboxer J. P. Thompson, "there is no such thing as a foreigner. We are all native-born members of this planet and for members of it to be divided into groups or units and taught that each nation is better than others leads to clashes and world war. We ought to have in

the place of national patriotism, the idea that one people is better than another, a broader concept —that of international solidarity."[3]

Instead of "yelping at the boss," Wobblies took the position in the pre-World War I period that the only cure for militarism was industrial anticapitalism and that they must organize industrially before they had the power to stop war. I.W.W. strikes continued. The organization's leaders maintained that these were not attempts to sabotage the war effort but efforts to improve conditions for the workers in industries such as lumber, agriculture, and mining. A President's Mediation Commission, investigating the strikes in Arizona, supported this view. In 1917 Arizona mine owners reported an increase of more than $23,000,000 over the output value of the preceding year, and, although the Wobbly-led strikes were denounced by many companies as pro-German and seditious, the commission reported that they "appeared to be nothing more than the normal results of the increased cost of living, the speeding up processes to which the mine management had been tempted by the abnormally high market price of copper."[4]

Although there were hundreds of A.F.L.-led strikes during this period, the I.W.W. strikes were outside the realm of mediation since the organization refused to recognize contracts. Frightened at the prospects of labor shortages at a time when there was a heightened demand for their products, employers vented their fury against the dissenters who, they claimed, were threatening both national security and the capitalist system.

Commenting on the 1917 lumber strike, the *Chicago Tribune* declared: "This outrageous outburst in the West is . . . nothing less than rebellion."[5] The *Cleveland News* editorialized: "While this country is at war, the only room it can afford I.W.W.'s is behind the walls of penitentiaries."[6] Newspaper columns carried stories of I.W.W. plots of destruction and sabotage which were never proved in court. News stories accused Wobblies of planning to arm themselves and take possession of industries, poisoning the nation's supply of beef, and plotting to burn crops and cities. The Fargo, North Dakota, *Forum* declared: "Its members live by the stiletto, firebrand, and bomb."[7] The *New York Tribune* suggested that I.W.W. and German agents could account for a series of mysterious fires and explosions in munitions factories around the country.[8] A Cleveland paper declared that "German influences are behind the labor troubles at Butte,"[9] and Theodore Roosevelt addressed a Saratoga, New York, audience in July 1918 on the "frank homicidal march of the I.W.W."[10] In Tulsa, Oklahoma, the *Daily World* ran an editorial headed, "Get Out the Hemp," which said, in part:

A knowledge of how to tie a knot that will stick might come in handy in a few days. . . . The first step in the whipping of Germany is to strangle the I.W.W.'s. Kill them, just as you would kill any other kind of a snake. Don't scotch 'em; kill 'em dead. It is no time to waste money on trials and continuances and things like that. All that is necessary is the evidence and a firing squad.[11]

The charges that I.W.W. members were German agents and that their strikes were supported by German gold were never verified by the slightest evidence. The source of some of these stories became apparent when Robert Breure, a New York writer, interviewed lumber operators in Washington on a trip he took with the President's Mediation Commission which was investigating wartime strikes.

The lumber operators admitted that their public relations men manipulated public opinion about the Wobblies. A lumber company owner told Breure:

. . . in war—and a strike is war—anything is fair. We have fought the I.W.W. as we would have fought any attempt of the A.F.L. to control the workers in our camps. And of course, we have taken advantage of the general prejudice against them as an unpatriotic organization to beat their strike.[12]

In the middle of 1917 Bill Haywood publicly declared that German money had nothing whatever to do with the strikes of the Wobblies:

It's true that we think there is only one fight in the world, and that is between capital and labor. It's true that we are not interested in nationalities. We will fight for German workers or French workers or Norwegian workers just as hard as we will fight for American workers. But do you think we want to see the Prussian military system prevail? How would we stand to gain anything from that?[13]

Although the I.W.W. remained openly antimilitary, it never officially opposed the draft after America entered the war. In July 1917 I.W.W. General Executive Board members, usually scattered throughout the country, met for an emergency meeting at Chicago headquarters. At the national office letters had been received daily from I.W.W. members anxious to know the organization's policy about conscription. The Wobbly leaders knew they would be damned by their members if they recommended registering for the draft and damned by the public if they officially opposed the draft. The sessions were deadlocked for three days. Ralph Chaplin, the editor of *Solidarity*, was called into the meeting. In his autobiography, *Wobbly*, he reported the following exchange:

"If we oppose the draft, they'll run us out of business," Richard Brazier had said.
"They'll run us out of business anyway," insisted Frank Little. "Better to go out in a blaze of glory than to give in. Either we're for this capitalist slaughterfest or we're against it. I'm ready to face a firing squad rather than compromise."[14]

But compromise the Executive Board did. Chaplin was instructed to write a signed editorial for *Solidarity* which advised I.W.W. members to register for the draft as "I.W.W. opposed to war." The morning after the meeting broke up, Frank Little came up to Chaplin's office on his way to Butte, Montana, where he was to be killed a few months later. "You're wrong about registering for the draft," he told Chaplin, "It would be better to go down slugging."[15]

Many I.W.W. members served in the war or worked in war-related jobs. On the other hand, some members agitated against the draft, refused to register, or left the country for Mexico. But only in two areas was there any significant antiwar demonstration. In Rockford, Illinois, about 100 Wobblies, Socialists, and pacifists protested in front of the city hall. On the Mesabi Iron Range in Minnesota a large number of Finnish miners who shared their native country's traditional fear of America's ally Russia, refused to be conscripted. As an organization, however, the I.W.W. staged no antiwar strikes and threw its efforts into leading on-the-job activities.

In the spring of 1917, responding to pressures from bankers, businessmen, mineowners, lumber operators, and farmers, the War Department authorized local army officers to "sternly repress acts committed with seditious intent."[16] Army officers were permitted to arrest Wobblies who committed violence "or similar acts . . . in pursuance of pre-arranged plans contemplating violence."[17] Army officers were available to help county sheriffs and district attorneys round up any industrial non-conformists in order to protect communities from the alleged threats of Wobbly violence.

Little effort, however, went into protecting Wobblies from community hysteria. Throughout the summer of 1917, army troops raided I.W.W. halls, disrupted meetings, dispersed outdoor gatherings, jailed Wobblies, guarded industrial property, and patrolled "troublesome sections" of various towns and cities.

On September 5, 1917, numerous federal investigation agents simultaneously raided Wobbly headquarters, halls, and members' homes around the country, collecting tons of membership records, books, Wobbly literature, official and personal correspondence, minutes of meetings, buttons, badges, stickers and membership cards. Richard Brazier calls this haul, "The Big Pinch."[18] The federal government had enough exhibits to bring the Wobblies to court on the charges that the I.W.W. was "a vicious, treasonable, and criminal conspiracy which opposed by force the execution of the laws of the United States and obstructed the prosecution of the war."[19]

Around the country 184 members of the organization were arrested by federal agents and charged with interfering with the war effort, encouraging resistance to the Selective Service Act, conspiring to cause insubordination and disloyalty in the armed forces, and injuring citizens selling munitions to the government. The prisoners were tried in three separate groups in Chicago, Sacramento, and Wichita, Kansas.

In Chicago the trial of about 100 Wobblies opened on April 1, 1918, in the courtroom of Judge Kenesaw Mountain Landis. The men had spent seven months in Chicago's Cook County Jail waiting trial.

Landis, a frail, aged man, wore a business suit instead of conventional judicial robes. He permitted the defendants to take off their coats in the hot courtroom, move around, read newspapers, and doze on the hard benches during the long hours of testimony.

Landis often left the judge's bench to come down and sit on the steps of the jury box. He asked people not to rise as he entered or left the courtroom. John Reed, who was covering the trial, wrote: "It takes some human understanding for a Judge to fly in the face of judicial ritual as much as that."[20] Less flatteringly, Reed wrote of Landis:

> Small on the huge bench sits a wasted man with untidy white hair, an emaciated face in which two burning eyes are set like jewels, parchment skin split by a crack for a mouth; the face of Andrew Jackson three years dead.[21]

The government based its case on I.W.W. theories about capitalism, internationalism, militarism, the class struggle, direct action, and conscription. Some of the exhibits used to support its case dated back to the founding of the I.W.W. in 1905. Statements made in pamphlets, letters, songs, stories, and poems were used by federal prosecutors to prove the conspiratorial nature of the organization. In turn, I.W.W. members were guilty of the charges against them because they had joined an unlawful confederacy.

Sixty-one defendants testified during the five-month trial which lasted throughout the summer months of 1918. James P. Thompson led off as the first witness, soapboxing to the audience in the courtroom about I.W.W. principles. "Red" Doran lectured for five hours on political economy and used a blackboard to illustrate the points of his testimony. When he finished, he smiled at the jury members and said: "It is customary for I.W.W. speakers to take up a collection, but under

WILL HE CONTINUE, OR WILL HE BUCK?

G STRIKE IN BUTTE, MONTANA

Solidarity, June 16, 1917.

these circumstances, I think we will dispense with it."[22] The audience in the courtroom, Judge Landis, and the jury members roared with laughter.

I.W.W. attorney George Vanderveer tried to base his defense on the right of labor to strike during wartime and attempted to submit sworn statements on working conditions in the sweatshops of the Chicago Loop within eyeshot of the courtroom. Landis ruled him out of order stating that the I.W.W., not American industry, was on trial.

To testify in behalf of the I.W.W. defendants, Vanderveer introduced forest rangers who said Wobblies had helped them fight forest fires, farmers who praised the reliability of their Wobbly workers, public officials from several cities who spoke of the peaceful nature of I.W.W. activities in their areas, and Philadelphia longshoremen who reported that Wobblies had handled war supplies for the Army quartermaster general. Of the 100 Chicago defendants, only one had refused to register for the draft.

The defense completed its case during the last week in August. The prosecution gave its closing arguments, and Judge Landis instructed the jury. A little more than an hour later, the jury returned to the courtroom. The members had reached a verdict of "guilty" as charged by the indictment. In the lobby of the courthouse, a band started playing "Hail Columbia," and waiting crowds outside the building cheered.

On August 30 the sentences were pronounced. Fifteen Wobblies received 20 years, 35 ten years, 33 five years, and 12 one year and a day. Those that were left got nominal sentences. In addition, the defendants were fined a total of $2,300,000.

In the courtroom, I.W.W. General Executive Board member Ben Fletcher, the only Negro defendant, remarked to Bill Haywood: "The Judge has been using very ungrammatical language. His sentences are much too long."[23]

While police held back jeering crowds, the hand-cuffed prisoners were marched down Austin Avenue to the LaSalle Street Depot, where a special train waited to take them to Leavenworth Penitentiary.

In California, arrests of Wobblies by federal agents netted fifty-three prisoners who were thrown into a common prison cell, twenty-one feet square, in Sacramento. One cotton blanket was given to each prisoner. Since there was not room for all to lie down to sleep at night, the Wob-

blies took turns sleeping and sharing blankets. When Fred Esmond, a leader of the I.W.W. defense efforts in California, notified the attorney general of the deplorable prison conditions, he was arrested and held incommunicado for eight months.

Mail for the Wobbly prisoners was censored. The I.W.W. defense office in San Francisco was raided seven times in six months and all the files and records were confiscated.

The Sacramento trial started in December 1918. Five of the prisoners had died in jail while awaiting trial. The defendants, who had suffered mentally and physically during their agonizing months in prison, were convinced that they would not get a fair trial. Forty-three of them decided on a policy of "no defense" as a protest against their treatment.

Mortimer Downing, spokesman for the "silent defenders," explained:

> We decided upon the silent defense because we despair of justice for the working man being achieved through the courts. The Mooney case, the Frank Little incident, the Bisbee cases, the Chicago trials, these have convinced us of the uselessness of legal defense. We are tried in a prejudiced community . . . this "silence strike" is to preserve the self respect of ourselves as members of organized labor.[24]

After a six-weeks' trial, all forty-six defendants were found guilty. The silent defenders, however, were given heavier sentences. Fred Esmond, weak from ten months of jail, cried out after the sentences had been passed:

> I am not asking for mercy, I'll take neither mercy nor pity from you or any representative of this government. . . . I want to go on record for myself and this organization as saying that we, the outcasts, have been framed up, clubbed, beaten, slugged, martyred, and murdered. Is it any wonder that I do not consider myself bound by your procedure when this court and its proceedings are a disgrace to the United States? You have done more than any I.W.W. could possibly do to drag your stars and stripes through the mire.[25]

In Kansas, thirty-four Wobblies were kept in county jails for over two years awaiting trial. They had been arrested by the federal government in November 1917 on charges of interfering with the

Espionage Act and the Lever Act, which provided further for the national security and for controlling the distribution of food products and fuel. Most of the Kansas prisoners had been active in organizing Oil Field Workers' Industrial Union No. 450 in Kansas and Oklahoma. Caroline Lowe, their lawyer, said they were arrested on John Doe warrants "at the suggestion of agents of the Carter Oil Company, the Sinclair Oil Company, Gypsey Oil Company and other oil companies doing business in this part of the country."[26]

The Kansas prisoners suffered the worst possible jail conditions. In one of the county jails, ten of them were kept in a pie-cut revolving drum without windows. For punishment they were thrown into a pitch-dark vault in the subbasement of the jail, where they were refused food and bedding. A deputy jailor told how the guards maintained discipline: "We go in and knock the guts out of those fellows."[27] Most of the prisoners became ill; some died of TB; several became insane. Reporter Winthrop Lane, who did a series of articles on the Kansas county jails for *Survey*, wrote:

For a year and a half these men had been idle in body and brain. They spent their days in crawling from cell to bull pen and from bull pen to cell—seeing always the same ghastly faces in the glimmer of the electric light, hearing always the same voices, and smelling always the same smells. Their muscles, once strong, grew flabby and their minds, once alert, grew dead.[28]

Their indictment, while not citing specific instances where they had interfered with either national security or the production of food and fuel, mentioned "The Harvest War Song" and "Ta Ra Ra Boom De Ay" from the little red songbook as examples of Wobbly intent to commit sabotage. In December 1919, after two years of torment, the defendants were brought to trial and found guilty. They were sentenced to terms ranging from one to nine years in Leavenworth Penitentiary.

The imprisonment of Wobblies round the country had a profound effect on the organization. In May 1918 Bill Haywood asked attorney George Vanderveer to go through the little red songbook and take out anything that in his opinion might be construed as advocating sabotage, violence, or crime. Eighteen songs were deleted from the 1918 edition, including Joe Hill's "Ta-Ra-Ra Boom De-Ay," and John Kendrick's controversial poem, "Christians at War," which few people

knew was a parody of an earlier poem said to have been written by William Lloyd Garrison. A postwar edition of Justus Ebert's pamphlet, *The I.W.W. in Theory and Practice* stated: "The war has caused the I.W.W. rejection of doctrines which it may have preached but never practiced."[29]

Although some of the I.W.W. songs and poems were temporarily removed from publication, the bulk of Wobbly literature was enriched by the writings of the "class-war prisoners." For most Wobblies a jail sentence was a badge of distinction, and the I.W.W. press called the list of Wobbly prisoners, "The Honor Roll." While in Chicago's Cook County Jail, Wobblies had issued a penciled prison newspaper, "The Can Opener." They held weekly meetings at which members would make speeches, recite original poems, or tell stories. Many Wobblies took correspondence courses, book review discussions were scheduled, and, as one class-war prisoner remembered, "We always tried to find an interesting person to cell with, so the talk would be good."[30]

The hundreds of prison poems, songs, and essays written during this period reflected the Wobblies' idealism and high spirits. Some of the poems were first published in the Leavenworth *New Era*, the prison newspaper; others were printed in I.W.W. defense bulletins or in national magazines such as *Outlook*, *Survey*, *The Liberator*, *New Masses*, and *Nation*.

The number of Wobbly prisoners sentenced in the federal trials was swelled by the prisoners convicted in trials held under the criminal syndicalism laws passed by twenty-one states and two territories from 1917 to 1920. These were aimed at destroying the I.W.W. Most of the state laws followed the wording of the Idaho law, passed in 1917, which defined criminal syndicalism as "the doctrine which advocates crime, sabotage, violence, or other unlawful methods of terrorism as a means of accomplishing industrial or political reform."[31] The Idaho law further stated: "The advocacy of such a doctrine, whether by word of mouth or writing, is a felony."[32] Most of the laws stipulated a penalty of prison terms ranging from one to ten years, a fine of $1000 to $5000, or both. South Dakota imposed a maximum penalty of twenty-five years of prison, a fine of $10,000, or both. State supreme courts uniformly upheld the constitutionality of the criminal syndicalism laws.[33]

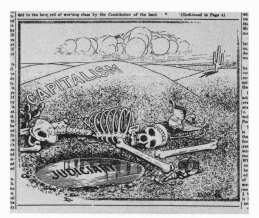

Defense News Bulletin, November 2, 1918.

From 1919 to 1924 in California alone, over 500 Wobblies were indicted. Of this number 164 were convicted and 128 sentenced to prison terms of one to fourteen years. In his inaugural address, California's newly elected governor, William D. Stephens, devoted some words to the I.W.W. which reflected anti-I.W.W. sentiment in that state. He said:

These Huns of industry seek the destruction of every honest impulse and of every fair and just rule which men out of their age-long experience have created for their material benefit. These terrorists do not represent labor, but are the bitter enemies of all honest workers. During the war they did all in their power to aid the enemy. They must be suppressed with a determined hand and I would recommend the enactment of such stringent legislation as will aid and assist officers of the law in more effectively dealing with this law-defying element.[34]

California's criminal syndicalism bill passed the state senate without a single opposing vote.

In most of the California criminal syndicalism trials, the prosecution used the same two witnesses who claimed they were former Wobblies and testified to the organization's advocating and committing acts of crime and sabotage. These professional witnesses later admitted that they had been paid to make such statements. Defense witnesses who testified that they were I.W.W. members were arrested as they left the courtroom and, in turn, brought to trial under the criminal syndicalism law. In 1923 Judge Charles Busick issued

a statewide injunction which enjoined the acts listed as crimes in the criminal syndicalism law. The Busick injunction eliminated jury trials, costly for the state, and speeded up the process of sentencing prisoners arrested under the law, since now a judge could sentence any Wobbly without a jury trial.

Wobbly prisoners kept active and alert throughout their jail terms. They maintained their organizational identity within the prison, elected committees, planned education programs, and circulated books and literature. They asserted their rights within the jails as they had done on their jobs. Direct action techniques were used, as far as possible, to obtain better jail conditions. In San Quentin, one fellow worker refused to work until he obtained a cot which he had been demanding for over a month. When he was thrown into solitary confinement, thirteen other Wobblies insisted on going along to keep him company. After four days of their protest, jailors found a bed not only for the striking Wobbly but for thirty-nine other bedless prisoners as well.

In another San Quentin strike, the Wobbly prisoners stopped work after one of their group had been beaten by a prison guard. In Los Angeles Wobblies demonstrated against being beaten by police when they refused to stop singing rebel songs in the jail. Their protests attracted the attention of the American Civil Liberties Union, which investigated their charge and found notorious prison abuses. The subsequent publicity eventually led to some prison reforms.

Throughout the nation I.W.W. members and sympathizers raised hundreds of thousands of dollars to pay for legal defense, publicity about the trials, and relief for the prisoners and their families. Some mortgaged their homes. Maintaining an active defense effort for the prisoners became a major problem since the Post Office Department intercepted, delayed, and confiscated I.W.W. defense mail.

Many Wobblies, however, were opposed to legal defense, which they held was political action, detracting from organizational efforts. James Rowan, a popular leader of the lumber workers, took such a stand. In the August 31, 1918, issue of the *Defense News Bulletin* he wrote: "When we begin to depend on courts and lawyers instead of our own activities on the job, then we become decadent as an organization, and must soon go the way of all the unfit."[35]

FELLOW WORKERS:

Remember!

WE ARE IN HERE FOR YOU; YOU ARE OUT THERE FOR US

Solidarity, August 4, 1917.

Tensions within the organization increased when Bill Haywood and eight other I.W.W. defendants skipped bail in 1921 and sailed for Russia under false passports. Haywood, suffering from failing eyesight and severe diabetes, had been persuaded by Communist Party leaders to escape to Russia and help Lenin fight world capitalism. He knew that return to prison was certain to shorten his life, and he was assured by party officials that his bond money would be repaid. In Russia, Haywood was warmly greeted and appointed an administrator of the Kuznetz Basin Colony. A few years later, he returned to Moscow, disillusioned and ill. He died in May 1928 and his ashes were divided for burial between the Kremlin Wall and Chicago's Waldheim Cemetery, near the graves of the Haymarket martyrs.

The Communist Party failed to repay the bond losses and the I.W.W. started a voluntary assessment to raise the $80,000 forfeited by the non-returnees.

Haywood's flight to Russia came at a time when the I.W.W. had already grown critical of the highly centralized organization of the Third International, although the news of the Russian Revolution had at first been greeted enthusiastically by the organization. On receiving a long communication from Moscow about the goals of international communism, Haywood had told Ralph Chaplin right after the Russian Revolution, "Ralph, here is what we have been dreaming about; here is the I.W.W. all feathered out."[36] But in 1921, the report of the I.W.W. delegate George Williams, who attended the Congress of the Red Trade Union International in Moscow, attacked communist efforts to dominate workers in other countries. Developments in the Soviet Union in 1920 and 1921 made the I.W.W. realize that, as Fred Thompson wrote, "No matter how 'left' the Communists might be, they were still politicians, primarily concerned with getting and holding the power to rule."[37] For the I.W.W., the philosophy and activities of the Third International were "un-Marxian."

Government suppression of the I.W.W. was a prelude to a wider attack on all radicals. On January 2, 1920, simultaneous raids were made on radicals in over thirty cities. Approximately 2500 socialists and communists were arrested, 3000 deportation warrants were served, and over 500 persons were ordered deported. Several hundred were arrested for violating various state criminal syndicalism and criminal anarchy laws.

In November 1921 a Joint Amnesty Committee was formed to coordinate activities for the release of political prisoners. It was endorsed by many labor and religious organizations. Several delegations visited President Harding. A congressional petition, signed by fifty congressmen, declared that many political prisoners "were sentenced to terms of imprisonment more severe than those inflicted for similar offenses by any other country engaged in the war."[38] It went on to state:

They are still in prison, although every other country in Europe has released prisoners of the same class. We believe that this great Republic of ours ought to be equally humane. In the interest of an era of good feeling for which you, Mr. President, are so earnestly working, we express the hope that you will proclaim a general amnesty for political prisoners whose only offense was written or spoken opinions and not any overt act against the government.[39]

A children's crusade of prisoners' children presented Harding with a petition containing thousands of signatures demanding the release of their fathers.

By July 1922, responding to the growing pressure for release of political prisoners, President Harding let it be known that he would be sympathetic to individual pleas for clemency. But at Leavenworth Penitentiary this news was greeted with scorn. Fifty-two of the seventy-one Leavenworth I.W.W. prisoners wrote an open letter to Harding. They refused to sign individual appeals and demanded that all or none of them be pardoned. They wrote:

We are not criminals and are not in prison because we committed crimes or conspired to commit crimes. From the beginning justice has been denied us and the truth of our case withheld from the consideration of the public. . . . We know that we are now in prison solely for exercising the constitutional right of free speech at a time when discretion might have been the better part of altruism. If it is a crime to exercise the right for which our fathers laid down their lives, then we have no apology to offer. Free speech has always been the one thing we have prized above all others. In this regard we are unchanged. . . . Our "conspiracy" to oppose the war consisted in pointing out the economic causes of all wars and in showing that unemployment, reaction, and misery invariably follow in their wake.[40]

Antagonisms arose between prisoners willing to take individual pardons (called the "clemency hounds") and prisoners who refused to compromise. Feelings ran so deep that delegates to the 1922 I.W.W. convention resolved to expel all members appealing for individual clemency and to circulate the names of all those who "broke solidarity" to I.W.W. halls around the country. When individual prisoners like Ralph Chaplin and Charles Ashleigh were induced by government agents to appeal individually for release, they were made a target by articulate Wobblies still in prison. As James Rowan wrote from Leavenworth: "The principle involved is vital, and the outcome may determine whether the I.W.W. is to remain a clean-cut, virile, militant organization . . . or become a crooked, yellow, opportunistic, fakeration dickering with the bosses and selling out the workers for the benefit of a few job-holding politicians."[41]

The amnesty campaign gained momentum in all parts of the country. "Wherever we seek to suppress these radicals, a civil liberties union promptly gets busy," said detective William Burns.[42] I.W.W. activity was channeled through I.W.W. defense committees and such direct action techniques as boycotts of prison-made goods and intermittent strikes, especially on the Pacific coast and in the Northwest. A nationwide strike called by the I.W.W. in 1923 to demand the release of class-war prisoners was primarily effective in the San Pedro, California, area where 3000 Wobblies protested that state's criminal syndicalism law, the continued jailing of political prisoners, and the hated "fink hall," an anti-union employment bureau in that town.

A free speech fight in San Pedro, the last major I.W.W. effort of this kind, developed from the protest strike. Upton Sinclair was arrested for reading the Declaration of Independence, and hundreds of Wobblies and other liberal sympathizers were jailed in specially built stockades. A year later, San Pedro vigilantes raided the I.W.W. hall during an evening social, beat up the men and women, and dumped several young children into a cauldron of steaming coffee. Five Wobblies were taken out to the desert and tarred and feathered.

In the Northwest the May 1, 1923, protest strike was memorable for the work of I.W.W. "dehorn squads." As Fred Thompson described it:

Knowing that alcohol and strikes don't mix well,

that "you can't fight booze and the boss at the same time," the dehorn squads told the smilo joints to close up for the duration of the strike. Those that didn't were closed by Carrie Nation direct action or the threat of it.[43]

In several areas, members of the Wobbly squads were jailed by police who, as Thompson pointed out, were tolerating and perhaps profiting from the bootleggers' establishments.

But although the cumulated pressures on President Harding brought about the release of all political prisoners in federal jails by the end of 1923, and although I.W.W. postwar organizing efforts lead to a steady increase in membership, the organization had been severely crippled by the problems, tensions, antagonisms, and factionalism of the preceding seven years. Without a doubt, the intensified public and government attack on all radicals during the war and postwar period had severely affected the I.W.W. As Bill Haywood characteristically admitted in 1919, the I.W.W. had been shaken, "as a bull dog shakes an empty sack."[44]

1

"Comrades," by Lawrence Tully, was printed in Solidarity (*October 10, 1914*).

COMRADES
By Lawrence Tully

I went into the Reichstag
   My comrades there to see.
They sat in all their pomp and power
   And broad humanity.

   It was Comrade this and Comrade that
   And "Comrade, you are first."
   And "Comrade, let me help you,
   Ere with eloquence you burst."

And then a man rose up in front
   And "Comrades," says, says he,
"We're gathered here this blessed day,
   To consider our army."

"Our Comrades, 'cross the Channel,
   They're arming to the teeth,
We must grab them by their hairy throats,
   We must shake them off their feet."

It was Comrade this and Comrade that
And "Comrade, let me shake,"
And "Comrade, you're a poltroon
When the Fatherland's at stake."

I walked the streets of Paris
And I hadn't walked so far,
Ere the thought was born within me:
The nation's going to war.

Beneath a spluttering torch-light,
For the day was turning dark,
A Red was loudly shouting,
And I stopped to hear him bark.

It was Comrade this and Comrade that,
"But our German comrades! God!
We must bayonet them and burn them
We must plant them neath the sod."

For, Comrades, you're my brother,
No matter what your 'ality,
But you're a hissing, crawling serpent,
When it comes to boundary.

I stood upon the battle field
And watched the spitting flow
Of life-blood from the Saxon
And his stalwart Teuton foe.

And Comrade this and Comrade that
Had drenched themselves again;
They had done their masters' bidding,
And were numbered 'mongst the slain.

Now many words could type this sheet
Of what I saw cross the sea,
But what's the use of wording
When it comes to you and me.

For Comrade this and Comrade that
It sounded very fine.
The bomb has burst beneath you,
You are swallowed in a mine.
And the cant that turned to cannon,
And the handclasp that was mailed
Will record unto ages
The philosophy that failed.

2

"Blasphemy," by Covington Hall, who frequently used the pen names "Covington Ami" or "Covami" is included in the I.W.W. file of songs and poems in the Labadie Collection.

BLASPHEMY

By COVINGTON AMI

"You shall not kill. You shall love your neighbor
    as yourself.
You shall not spend your days in piling pelf on
    pelf.
You cannot serve both God and Mammon, for you
    must
In one or yet the other put your heart and trust.

"Call no man master. To the truth be ever true.
The light within you, keep it burning, clear and
    pure!
He who denies the truth the truth to be,
Unpardonable in the Father's sight is he.

"As brothers work and live. All things in common
    hold.
Remember this: Love's spirit is not bought nor
    sold:
He who is without sin let him first cast the stone:
Not by your words but by your works shall you be
    known."

And this was "blasphemy," so they who heard him
    said,
And forth to Pilate they, the "rebel Wobblie," led;
And he was hanged. The charges? Oh, the same:
    "Intent
To dethrone God and overthrow the government."

3

The unsigned poem "Onward Christian Soldiers" was printed in Voice of the People *(December 4, 1913), the publication edited by Covington Hall. Exactly two years later on December 4, 1915, two poems were printed side by side in* Solidarity. *One of them was attributed to William Lloyd Garrison (1805–79), the abolitionist. The other was signed "John F. Kendrick." Titled "Christians at War," Kendrick's poem was first included in the thirteenth edition of the Wobbly's songbook. The harsh language and supposedly antireligious sentiment of "Christians at War" caused a furor, and the poem was used as evidence in several federal and state trials as proof of the Wobblies' anti-Christian, anti-American position. Little is known about John Kendrick. It is claimed that he was a Chicago newspaperman.*

ONWARD CHRISTIAN SOLDIERS

Onward, Christian Soldiers,
　　March into the War,
Slay your Christian Brothers,
　　As you've done before.
Plutocratic masters,
　　Bid you face the foe,
Men who never harmed you,
　　Men you do not know.

Raise the Christian War-whoop,
　　You who love the Lord,
Hearken to your masters,
　　Buckle on the sword;
Bombshells, bullets, grapeshot,
　　Shower on the foe,
Heed your Christian Chaplain,
　　Into battle go.

Heed not dying groans from
　　Those whom you have slain,
Heed not pleas for mercy,
　　Nor the shrieks of pain.
Plunge the sword and dagger
　　Through your brothers' heart,
Never shirk your duty,
　　Always do your part.

Onward Christian Soldiers
　　Into brutal war,
Break the hearts of mothers
　　As you've done before;
Close your eyes to horrors
　　Of the bloody field,
Forward into battle,
　　Slay with sword and shield.

Thus you prove your love for
　　Him who lived for all,
And without respect to
　　Persons great or small,
Said to his Disciples
　　If my name you'd seek,
Love you one another,
　　Turn the other cheek.

Onward Christian Soldiers
　　To plunder Mexico;
Onward Christian Soldiers,
　　Into battle go;

Onward Christian Soldiers,
　　Shoot your brothers through,
While your chaplain's praying,
　　They do the same to you.

4

ONWARD CHRISTIAN SOLDIERS

By WILLIAM LLOYD GARRISON

The Anglo Saxon Christians, with gattling gun and
　　sword
In serried ranks are pushing on the gospel of the
　　Lord;
On Afric's soil they press the foe in war's terrific
　　scenes
And merrily the hunt goes on throughout the
　　Philippines.

What though the Boers are Christians; the
　　Filipinos, too!
It is a Christian act to shoot a fellow creature
　　through.
The bombs with dynamite surcharged their
　　deadly missiles fling,
And gaily on their fatal work the dum-dum bullets
　　sing.

The mahdis and the sirdars along the great
　　Soudan
Are learning at the cannon's mouth the brother-
　　hood of man;
The holy spirit guides aloft the shrieking shot and
　　shell,
And Christian people shout with joy at thousands
　　blown to hell!

The pulpits bless the victor arms and praise the
　　bloody work,
As after an Armenian raid rejoiced the pious Turk;
The Christian press applauds the use of bayonet
　　and knife,
For how can social order last without the
　　strenuous life?

The outworn, threadbare precept, to lift the poor
　　and weak,
The fallacy that this great earth is for the saintly
　　meek;
Have both gone out of fashion: the world is for
　　the strong;
That might be Lord of right is now the Christian
　　song.

Then onward, Christian soldier, through the fields
    of crimson gore,
Behold the trade advantages beyond the open
    door!
The profits on our ledgers outweigh the heathen
    loss;
Set thou the glorious stars and stripes above the
    ancient cross.

5

CHRISTIANS AT WAR*

By John F. Kendrick

(*Tune: "Onward, Christian Soldiers"*)

Onward, Christian soldiers! Duty's way is plain;
Slay your Christian neighbors, or by them be slain.
Pulpiteers are spouting effervescent swill,
God above is calling you to rob and rape and kill,
All your acts are sanctified by the Lamb on high;
If you love the Holy Ghost, go murder, pray and
    die.

Onward, Christian soldiers, rip and tear and smite!
Let the gentle Jesus bless your dynamite.
Splinter skulls with shrapnel, fertilize the sod;
Folks who do not speak your tongue deserve the
    curse of God.
Smash the doors of every home, pretty maidens
    seize;
Use your might and sacred right to treat them as
    you please.

Onward, Christian soldiers! Eat and drink your
    fill;
Rob with bloody fingers, Christ O.K.'s the bill.
Steal the farmer's savings, take their grain and
    meat;
Even though the children starve, the Saviour's
    bums must eat.
Burn the peasants' cottages, orphans leave bereft;
In Jehovah's holy name, wreak ruin right and left.

Onward, Christian soldiers! Drench the land with
    gore;
Mercy is a weakness all the gods abhor.
Bayonet the babies, jab the mothers, too;
Hoist the cross of Calvary to hallow all you do.
File your bullets' noses flat, poison every well;
God decrees your enemies must all go plumb to
    hell.

Onward, Christian soldiers! Blighting all you meet,
Trampling human freedom under pious feet.
Praise the Lord whose dollar-sign dupes his
    favored race!
Make the foreign trash respect your bullion brand
    of grace.
Trust in mock salvation, serve as pirates' tools;
History will say of you: "That pack of G— d—
    fools."

6

*Ralph Chaplin's poem "The Red Feast," signed "a
Paint Creek Miner," was printed in the* International Socialist Review *(October, 1914). This re-
written version was included for the first time in
the twenty-first edition of the I.W.W. songbook.*

THE RED FEAST*

By Ralph Chaplin

Go fight, you fools! Tear up the earth with strife
    And give unto a war that is not yours;
Serve unto death the men you served in life
    So that their wide dominions may not yield.

Stand by the flag—the lie that still allures;
    Lay down your lives for land you do not own,
And spill each other's guts upon the field;
    Your gory tithe of mangled flesh and bone.

But whether in the fray to fall or kill
    You must not pause to question why nor where.
You see the tiny crosses on that hill?
    It took all those to make one millionaire.

It was for him the seas of blood were shed
    That fields were razed and cities lit the sky;
That he might come to chortle o'er the dead;
    The condor thing for whom the millions die!

The bugle screams, the cannons cease to roar,
    "Enough! enough! God give us peace again."
The rats, the maggots and the Lords of War
    Are fat to bursting from their meal of men.

So stagger back, you stupid dupes who've "won,"
    Back to your stricken towns to toil anew,
For there your dismal tasks are still undone
    And grim Starvation gropes again for you.

What matters now your flag, your race, the skill
    Of scattered legions—what has been the gain?
Once more beneath the lash you must distil
    Your lives to glut a glory wrought of pain.

In peace they starve you to your loathsome toil,
    In war they drive you to the teeth of Death;
And when your life-blood soaks into their soil
    They give you lies to choke your dying breath.

So will they smite your blind eyes till you see,
    And lash your naked backs until you know
That wasted blood can never set you free
    From fettered thraldom to the Common Foe.

Then you will find that "nation" is a name
    And boundaries are things that don't exist;
That Labor's bondage, world-wide, is the same,
    And ONE the enemy it must resist.

7

Signed with the initials "O.E.B.," "My Country" was printed in Solidarity (*July 29, 1916*).

MY COUNTRY

By O. E. B.

I have a country
I love my country
I love it with a love that is lasting
And that must be returned.
If love of one's country
Makes a patriot
Then I am a good patriot.

My country is boundless
It has no limit
No king, no potentate—
Only a race of human beings.

There need be no hunger, nor cold,
No want in my country.
There is room for all the
Children of the world there;
And they can dwell in peace,
And plenty, and happiness,
And joy forever
In my country.

I do not dwell in my country,
But I can live in the hopes it holds

For the future,
When many shall sojourn therein.

I can be a patriotic subject
Of my country
Without robbing or slaying
One of my brothers.
I need not wrest from others
Land, or riches of any sort,
That I may pour them into the coffers
Of a group, or of an individual.

I can be a true patriot
And love all the people of the earth
As I love my own family.
My country demands of her patriots
That they be charitable to all mankind.

I can work and fight
For my country,
And die, if need be,
But I cannot dwell there alone.
Humanity is the population
Of my country.

Industrial Democracy
Is my country.

8

Contrasting the antimilitary position of the I.W.W. with the prowar position of the A.F.L., the antiwar tract "The Deadly Parallel" was printed on the front page of Solidarity (*March 24, 1917*). *Although plans had been made to distribute it as a leaflet once the U.S. entered the war on April 6, 1917, Bill Haywood told* Solidarity *editor Ralph Chaplin to cancel an order to have additional copies printed. "The Deadly Parallel" was read into the record by the prosecution at the Chicago trial as evidence that the I.W.W. opposed the war. To these charges, Bill Haywood answered, "The Deadly Parallel was never circulated from headquarters after war was declared." As Professor Philip Taft wrote in his article, "The Federal Trials of the I.W.W.," in the Winter 1962 issue of* Labor History: "*It is noteworthy that only members of the I.W.W. were prosecuted on conspiracy charges, although the I.W.W. never took an official position on the war. In contrast, the Socialist Party, which held a special convention in St. Louis to define its attitude and issued a militant anti-war declaration, was never prosecuted*

Penciled Program of an I.W.W. entertainment in Cook County Jail, Chicago.

Labadie Collection file of cartoons and pictures.

for conspiracy, although many individual Socialists, including Eugene Victor Debs, were jailed for encouraging opposition to or interfering with the war effort."

THE DEADLY PARALLEL

A DECLARATION

By the Industrial Workers of the World.

We, the Industrial Workers of the World, in convention assembled, hereby reaffirm our adherence to the principles of Industrial Unionism, and rededicate ourselves to the unflinching prosecution of the struggle for the abolition of wage slavery, and the realization of our ideals in Industrial Democracy.

With the European war for conquest and exploitation raging and destroying the lives, class consciousness, and unity of the workers, and the ever growing agitation for military preparedness clouding the main issues, and delaying the realization of our ultimate aim with patriotic, and therefore, capitalistic aspirations, we openly declare ourselves determined opponents of all nationalistic sectionalism or patriotism, and the militarism preached and supported by our one enemy, the Capitalist Class. We condemn all wars, and, for the prevention of such, we proclaim the anti-militarist propaganda in time of peace, thus promoting class solidarity among the workers of the entire world, and, in time of war, the general strike in all industries.

We extend assurances of both moral and material support to all the workers who suffer at the hands of the Capitalist Class for their adhesion to the principles, and call on all workers to unite themselves with us, that the reign of the exploiters may cease and this earth be made fair through the establishment of the Industrial Democracy.

PLEDGE GIVEN

To Nation by American Federation of Labor.

We, the officers of the national and international trades unions of America in national conference assembled, in the capital of our nation, hereby pledge ourselves in peace or in war, in stress or in storm, to stand unreservedly by the standards of liberty and the safety and preservation of the institutions and ideals of our republic.

In this solemn hour of our nation's life, it is our earnest hope that our republic may be safeguarded in its unswerving desire for peace; that our people may be spared the horrors and the burdens of war; that they may have the opportunity to cultivate and develop the arts of peace, human brotherhood and a higher civilization.

But, despite all our endeavors and hopes, should our country be drawn into the maelstrom of the European conflict, we, with these ideals of liberty and justice herein declared, as the indispensable basis for national policies, offer our services to our country in every field of activity to defend, safeguard and preserve the republic of the United States of America against its enemies, whosoever they may be, and we call upon our fellow workers and fellow citizens in the holy name of labor, justice, freedom and humanity to devotedly and patriotically give like service.

9

The unsigned poem "I Love My Flag" was printed in the Industrial Worker *(April 14, 1917).*

I LOVE MY FLAG

I love my flag, I do, I do,
Which floats upon the breeze
I also love my arms and legs,
And neck, and nose, and knees.
One little shell might spoil them all
Or give them such a twist,
They would be of no use to me;
    I guess I won't enlist.

I love my country, yes, I do,
I hope her folks do well.
Without our arms, and legs and things,
I think we'd look like hell.
Young men with faces half shot off
Are unfit to be kissed,
I've read in books it spoils their looks;
    I guess I won't enlist.

10

The unsigned "Yellow Legs and Pugs" was printed in Solidarity *(May 5, 1917).*

YELLOW LEGS AND PUGS

If soldiers all were pugilists there would not be a war,

For pugilists would want to know what they were
fighting for.

FOR INSTANCE

If Tommy Atkins had been told to beat up
Herman Schmitz

And Herman had been told to blow the other into
bits,

And if they had been pugilists they would have
answered "No!

We will not fight unless we get a section of the
dough.

We will not risk our arms and legs and shed our
ruddy gore

While you who fatten on the fight make millions
by the score.

Although it is a noble stunt to redden hill and dale,

We will not fight unless we get a portion of the
kale."

And thus the world-wide warfare would be ended
in a minute,

For bankers would not start a war if there were
nothing in it.

11

*This sworn testimony of the secretary of the
I.W.W. local in Tulsa, Oklahoma, is an account
of how I.W.W. members in that city were beaten,
tarred, and feathered by a vigilante mob. It was
printed in the* Liberator *(April 1918).*

TULSA, NOVEMBER 9, 1917

"On the night of November 5, 1917, while sitting
in the hall at No. 6 W. Brady Street, Tulsa, Okla.
(the room leased and occupied by the Industrial
Workers of the World, and used as a union meeting room), at about 8:45 P.M., five men entered
the hall, to whom I at first paid no attention, as I
was busy putting a monthly stamp in a member's
union card book. After I had finished with the
member, I walked back to where these five men
had congregated at the baggage-room at the back
of the hall, and spoke to them, asking if there was
anything I could do for them.

"One who appeared to be the leader, answered
'No, we're just looking the place over.' Two of
them went into the baggage-room flashing an
electric flashlight around the room. The other
three walked toward the front end of the hall. I
stayed at the baggage-room door, and one of the
men came out and followed the other three up to

the front end of the hall. The one who stayed in
the baggage-room asked me if I was 'afraid he
would steal something.' I told him we were paying rent for the hall, and I did not think anyone
had a right to search this place without a warrant.
He replied that he did not give a damn if we were
paying rent for four places, they would search
them whenever they felt like it. Presently he came
out and walked toward the front end of the hall,
and I followed a few steps behind him.

"In the meantime the other men, who proved to
be officers, appeared to be asking some of our
members questions. Shortly after, the patrol-
wagon came and all the members in the hall—10
men were ordered into the wagon. I turned out
the light in the back end of the hall, closed the
desk, put the key in the door and told the 'officer'
to turn out the one light. We stepped out, and I
locked the door, and at the request of the 'leader
of the officers,' handed him the keys. He told me
to get in the wagon, I being the 11th man taken
from the hall, and we were taken to the police
station.

November 6th, after staying that night in jail, I
put up $100.00 cash bond so that I could attend to
the outside business, and the trial was set for 5
o'clock P.M., November 6th. Our lawyer, Chas.
Richardson, asked for a continuance and it was
granted. Trial on a charge of vagrancy was set for
November 7th at 5 P.M. by Police Court Judge
Evans. After some argument by both sides the
cases were continued until the next night, November 8th, and the case against Gunnard Johnson,
one of our men, was called. After four and a half
hours' session the case was again adjourned until
November 9th at 5 P.M., when we agreed to let the
decision in Johnson's case stand for all of us. . . .

"Johnson said he had come into town Saturday,
November 3d, to get his money from the Sinclair
Oil & Gas Co. and could not get it until Monday,
the 5th, and was shipping out Tuesday, the 6th,
and that he had $7.08 when arrested. He was rep-
rimanded by the judge for not having a Liberty
Bond, and as near as anyone could judge from the
closing remarks of Judge Evans, he was found
guilty and fined $100 for not having a Liberty
Bond.

"Our lawyer made a motion to appeal the case
and the bonds were then fixed at $200 each. I was
immediately arrested, *as were also five spectators
in the open court-room*, for being I.W.W.'s. One
arrested was not a member of ours, but a property-

owner and citizen. I was searched and $30.87 taken from me, as also was the receipt for the $100 bond, and we then were all placed back in the cells.

"In about forty minutes, as near as we could judge about 11 P.M., the turnkey came and called 'Get ready to go out you I.W.W. men.' We dressed as rapidly as possible, were taken out of the cells, and the officer gave us back our posessions, Ingersoll watches, pocketknives and money, with the exception of $3 in silver of mine which they kept, giving me back $27.87. I handed the receipt for the $100 bond I had put up to the desk sergeant and he told me he did not know anything about it, and handed the receipt back to me, which I put in my trousers' pocket with the 87 cents. Twenty-seven dollars in bills was in my coat pocket. We were immediately ordered into automobiles waiting in the alley. Then we proceeded one block north to 1st Street, west one-half block to Boulder Street, north across the Frisco tracks and stopped.

"Then the masked mob came up and ordered everybody to throw up their hands. Just here I wish to state I never thought any man could reach so high as those policemen did. We were then bound, some with hands in front, some with hands behind, and others bound with arms hanging down their sides, the rope being wrapped around the body. Then the police were ordered to 'beat it,' which they did, running, and we started for the place of execution.

"When we arrived there, a company of gowned and masked gunmen were there to meet us standing at 'present arms.' We were ordered out of the autos, told to get in line in front of these gunmen and another bunch of men with automatics and pistols, lined up between us. Our hands were still held up, and those who were bound, in front. Then a masked man walked down the line and slashed the ropes that bound us, and we were ordered to strip to the waist, which we did, threw our clothes in front of us, in individual piles— coats, vests, hats, shirts and undershirts. The boys not having had time to distribute their possessions that were given back to them at the police stations, everything was in the coats, everything we owned in the world.

"Then the whipping began, A double piece of new rope, ⅝ or ¾ hemp, being used. A man, 'the chief' of detectives, stopped the whipping of each man when he thought the victim had had enough. After each one was whipped another man applied

the tar with a large brush, from the head to the seat. Then a brute smeared feathers over and rubbed them in.

"After they had satisfied themselves that our bodies were well abused, our clothing was thrown into a pile, gasoline poured on it and a match applied. By the light of our earthly possessions, we were ordered to leave, Tulsa, and leave running and never come back. The night was dark, the road very rough, and as I was one of the last two that was whipped, tarred and feathered, and in the rear when ordered to run, I decided to be shot rather than stumble over the rough road. After going forty or fifty feet I stopped and went into the weeds. I told the man with me to get in the weeds also, as the shots were coming very close over us and ordered him to lie down flat. We expected to be killed, but after 150 or 200 shots were fired they got in their autos.

"After the last one had left, we went through a barbed-wire fence, across a field, called to the boys, collected them, counted up, and had all the 16 safe, though sore and nasty with tar. After wandering around the hills for some time—ages it seemed to me—we struck the railroad track. One man, Jack Sneed, remembered then that he knew a farmer in that vicinity, and he and J. F. Ryan volunteered to find the house. I built a fire to keep us from freezing.

"We stood around the fire expecting to be shot, as we did not know but what some tool of the commercial club had followed us. After a long time Sneed returned and called to us, and we went with him to a cabin and found an I.W.W. friend in the shack and 5 gallons of coal oil or kerosene, with which we cleaned the filthy stuff off of each other, and our troubles were over, as friends sent clothing and money to us that day, it being about 3 or 3:30 A.M. when we reached the cabin.

"The men abused, whipped and tarred were Tom McCaffery, John Myers, John Boyle, Charles Walsh, W. H. Walton, L. R. Mitchell, Jos. French, J. R. Hill, Gunnard Johnson, Robt. McDonald, John Fitzsimmons, Jos. Fischer, Gordon Dimikson, J. F. Ryan, E. M. Boyd, Jack Sneed (not an I.W.W.).

"This is a copy of my sworn statement and every word is truth."

∘   ∘   ∘

"It was very evident that the police force knew what was going to happen when they took us from

jail, as there were extra gowns and masks provided *which were put on by the Chief of Police
and one detective named Blaine, and the number
of blows we received were regulated by the Chief
of Police himself, who was easily recognizable
by six of us at least.*"

<h2 style="text-align:center">12</h2>

*The material seized in the September 5, 1917,
raids on I.W.W. halls, headquarters, and homes
throughout the country was presented to the
grand jury of the United States District Court of
Illinois. On September 28 members and leaders
of the I.W.W. were arrested and indicted on five
counts. From that time until the Chicago trial
opened on April 1, 1918, many of the prisoners
were confined in Chicago's Cook County Jail.
This report on I.W.W. prison activities at the Chicago jail was written by Bill Haywood. It was
printed in the* Liberator *(May 1918).*

ON THE INSIDE
By WILLIAM D. HAYWOOD

Clang! clang! a bell rang out, big iron doors slid
back, the auto patrol wheeled up to the rear entrance of the Cook County Jail; and here we are.

We are in the wing of the "old jail," a room
about 60 by 60 with a double row of cells four
tiers high; our cells face the alley to the west.
Cells are six by eight, about eight feet high with
ceiling slightly sloping to the rear.

This cell is parlor, bedroom, dining room and
lavatory all in one. Decorations black and white—
that is, the interior is painted solid black on two
walls, black half way on the other two walls. The
ceiling is mottled white. Wash bowl, toilet, water-
pipe, small bench, a narrow iron bunk, flat springs,
corn husk mattress, sheet and pillow case of rough
material, blanket, tin cups and spoons, constitute
the fittings of our temporary homes where we
spend twenty hours out of every twenty-four, in-
voluntary parasites, doing no more service to society than the swell guys who loll around clubs or
attend the functions at fashionable resorts.

The reveille of this detention camp is the sharp
voice of the "runner," "Cups out! Cups out!"

It is the beginning of a new day. The light
streams through the grated door and falls in a
checkered pattern across the cell floor.

Bill Haywood.
United Press International, Inc., photo.

One stretches his body on the narrow cot and
awakens to the fact that he is still in jail, accept-
ing the situation philosophically, wondering, some
of us perhaps, what manner of independence and
freedom it was that our forefathers fought for in
this country.

A prison cell is the heritage we gain for the
blood and lives our forefathers gave; they fought
for religious freedom and left us with minds free
from superstitious cant and dogma; they waged
war for political justice; they carried on the struggle against chattel-slavery—these were the titanic
battles that were fought, bringing us to the thresh-
old of the greatest of all wars—the class war—in
which we are enlisted as workers, against all kinds
of exploiters.

*Abolish the wage system, is our battle cry. With
an idea that is imperishable, Organization and
Education as our weapons, we are invulnerable.*

With thoughts of this kind imprisonment becomes a period of improvement. It may be remarked that members of the Industrial Workers
of the World have had many opportunities to take
advantage of these enforced vacations.

Many thousands of members of the I.W.W. have in the past few years wakened in cells similar to this, to the reveille of "Cups out! Cups out!" until the jails have become recognized as a temporary home—a detention camp of the Master Class—where we are confined or interned as it were, not as criminals, but as victims—prisoners of the class war. Over 400 members of the I.W.W. are in jail in different parts of this country at present.

So we roll out, wash and dress to snatches of I.W.W. songs from other cells, make the beds, sweep out and are ready for "breakfast." The cell doors are unlocked by the guard at 9:30; we have the range of the narrow corridor until 11:30; dinner at 12 M.; out again at 1:30 until 3:30. In the Wing of the "old" jail these hours are spent in diverse ways. Here there are none but members of the I.W.W. Every day there is a physical culture class—breathing and exercise—to help keep the boys in good health in spite of the dismal damp and cold of the jail. The afternoons are devoted to discussion, gossip and song. Business meetings are held at regular intervals and a big entertainment is held each Sunday with recitations, dramatic sketches and songs. There are 48 men confined in this part of the jail.

In the "big tank," or main portion of the "old jail," there are about 58 members incarcerated. These men are locked up and must exercise with about five hundred criminals of all walks of crime.

It is on this side that all executions take place. There are three black holes on the corner wall into which the beams of the gallows are adjusted. When the gallows are not in use an old piano takes their place and this grewsome spot is sanctified each Sunday by sermons and religious hymns. It was in this corner that the martyrs of the eight hour movement of '87 danced upon the air, and that Parsons, over thirty years ago, delivered his unforgettable prophecy: "The day will come when our silence will be more eloquent than the voices you strangle today."

Of course it is impossible for the I.W.W. men on this side of the jail to hold business meetings and entertainments as they do in the "wing," but, nevertheless, the spirit of all is characterized by the cheery buoyancy and unbreakable determination of the One Big Union.

The class-war prisoners have a prison library that is remarkable in many respects. It contains many of the finest works on Sociology, Economics, History and poetry that are obtainable, as well as novels by the best modern novelists. A new book is always welcomed with great enthusiasm. These books were nearly all donated by members or sympathizers on the outside. One is safe in saying that more books have been read in this gloomy old institution since the I.W.W. boys have been held there than were ever read in the place before.

The prison fare, never too plentiful, has, on account of war conservation, almost reached the point of starvation. Only one piece of coarse prison bread is now served with each "meal." In the morning the menu consists of a dry piece of "punk" and a cupful of a libelous decoction of "coffee," at noon, stew, fish or sausage—usually of a quality that is fairly nauseating. For supper, "coffee" and dry bread again with an occasional cupful of suspicious "soup."

Aside from the poor food and ventilation, overcrowding is the chief cause of discomfort and illness. Three, and sometimes four, men are locked up twenty hours out of every twenty-four in a cell about as large as the average bathroom in a city dwelling. Sunlight seldom filters through the grimy, gray, and iron-barred window panes—nothing but the sickly glare of electric lights, day and night.

In spite of the brave efforts the men are making against this unwholesome environment, the poor food, foul air and the prison chill have made awful inroads upon their health. One young Russian fellow-worker, Jancharick, who entered the jail in rugged health, was taken out to a hospital—spitting blood—and just in time to die. Nigra, an Italian miner who was terribly beaten up in the Springfield, Ill., jail, before being brought to Chicago, is in a hospital suffering the tortures of hell because of lack of proper treatment for his wounds while in the Cook County jail. Miller, a textile worker and member of the General Executive Board, was forced to undergo an operation because of an ulcerous growth, probably caused by the foul air and rotten food. Kimball, an Arizona miner and one of those deported from Bisbee last July, has been released on bail after a great deal of effort. He is now a physical wreck—"spitting up his lungs" as his fellow workers say; a mere shadow of his former self. MacDonald, Ashleigh and Lossieff are each either on the sick bed or near it, and many other fellow-workers have lost vitality that can never be regained.

Then there is the case of Henry Meyers. His incarceration cost him his reason. Day by day he

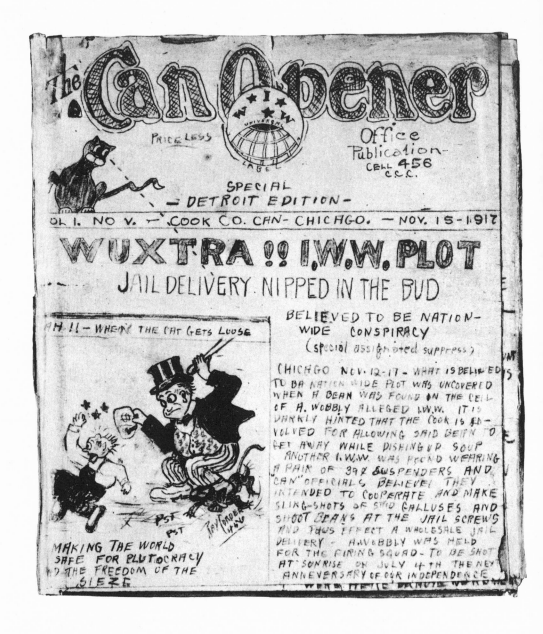

Cover of the Can Opener, *a penciled newspaper put out by I.W.W. prisoners in Cook County Jail, Chicago.*

Labadie Collection file.

became more secretive and morose. With furtive glance he sulked about among the hundreds of prisoners in the "bull pen." One of them had told him that he would be hung. Beneath the weight of worry and fear his sensitive artist mind gave way. Like a frightened animal he ran wild around the galleries until captured by the guards. He is now in the madhouse at Kankakee—his reason has fled.

It was he who painted the well known picture of Joe Hill. He made the death masks of our martyred members who were murdered on the "Verona," that fateful Sunday morning in November, 1916. It was his deft fingers that shaped the clay that forms the face of fearless Frank Little that hangs upon the wall of the Chicago Recruiting Union.

This young fellow worker I do not believe ever committed a crime. He united his strength with others to improve conditions of all. Now his mind has lapsed; he is dead to the life he knew; his strong body is as useless as a burned-out cinder. This is but another indictment of the frightful system under which we are living. And this is only one of the stories that could be written of this frightful place. Be it recorded now that we are pledged to a new method of living—a new society, where injustice will not be known, where jails and prisons such as this will be things of the past, and where a human being will enjoy a friendly communal interest from the cradle to the grave.

The 106 class-war prisoners in the Cook County jail are of many different nationalities and from nearly all industries. They are strong, rugged, open-air types, taken right off the job and thrown into prison. They have undergone and are undergoing hardships and suffering, but in spite of all they manage to make the gloomy walls ring with rebel songs. They have been in jail, some of them for eight and nine months, most of them for six months, but their spirits are as dauntless as ever. During the long winter months they have been walking round and round the narrow corridors in the very shadow of the gallows. Always round and round, like angle worms in the bottom of a tin can, go the prisoners in the Cook County jail. But the members of the I.W.W. keep hope and courage alive in spite of all.

Such a group of men one is proud to be associated with—workers, clean hearted, clear eyed; all fighting for the principles so plainly set forth in the Preamble of the Industrial Workers of the World, which proclaims the only kind of democracy worth going to jail to advocate—and this Preamble, the chief count in the indictment against us—is still nailed to the masthead!

13

"We Shall Eat—Bye and Bye" appeared in the Industrial Worker (*April 27, 1918*).

WE SHALL EAT—BYE AND BYE

MENU—COOK COOK JAIL

Breakfast
(EVERY DAY)

Limited to—
Coffee Royal—(Shoe soles and H_2O—
Ratio: 2 to 3,000.)
Bread—Two slices ("War" bread. Reference:
Gen. Sherman.)

Dinner
A la carte. (Service from la wagon.)

SUNDAY
Equine pickled in sodium chloride.
Cabbage leaves—Boiled en dishwater.

MONDAY
Piece de Calcarecus Resistance—Jail Stew.
(Prepared from No. 3 stock. Beyond criticism.)

TUESDAY
"Meatless day"—Chef blind in left eye—Never sees
that "M."
(Reward offered anyone finding anything edible
on Tuesday.)

WEDNESDAY
The Riddle of the Universe—Hash.
(Spuds fermenta and other things.)

THURSDAY
"Dog days"—Dachhund pups.

FRIDAY
Modern miracle—See holy writ—Jailer emulates
Christ!—Feed 1,000 prisoners with five fishes—
(the same five.)

SATURDAY
What was left from Monday—Third stage
decomposa.

Supper

(Sunday, Tuesday, Thursday and Saturday.)
The same thing as breakfast.
(Monday, Wednesday and Friday.)
"Soup"—Boiled relics of the past with a fragrance
of "Bubbly Creek."
(See "Story of the Stockyards.")

NOTICE:—The management is not responsible
for the "overcoats" left in the spuds.

Any guest that can discover a carrot or a cabbage leaf that has been deprived of its original
real estate please report to the manager.

Anyone desiring a second serving of dinner is
reminded that the head waiter, Guard Goldberg,
is deputy food administrator. His duty is to guard
potatoes—not prisoners.

14

*At the Sacramento Trial of the I.W.W. defend-
ants which opened on December 13, 1918, forty-
three of the forty-six prisoners decided upon a
policy of no defense. They refused to be represented by legal council and refused to defend
themselves.*

*The forty-three silent defenders received prison
terms of from one to ten years; their appeals were
rejected. However, the tactic of the "silent defense" gave the Wobblies nationwide publicity
and the support of many liberals and organizations. The I.W.W. General Defense Committee
immediately began a campaign for their release,
as well as the release of all the "class-war prisoners." Finally, in December 1923, President Coolidge commuted the sentences to the terms already served by the persons convicted under the
wartime Espionage laws at the Chicago, Kansas
City, and Sacramento trials.*

*Anna Louise Strong's poem "Somebody Must"
was printed in the I.W.W. publication* New Solidarity *(December 28, 1918). It is the only song
or poem found thus far which commemorates the
Sacramento prisoners' "silent defense."*

SOMEBODY MUST

By ANISE

Down in Sacramento
Forty-nine wobblies
Are ON TRIAL

And they have REFUSED
LAWYERS
And REFUSED
To TESTIFY
And refused to recognize
The COURT
In ANY WAY.
Only one spokesman,
Elected by the rest,
Will STAND FORTH
And read their statement.
"This is OUR PROTEST," he says,
"Against the COURTS
Of California.
We have seen what
They did to MOONEY:
We have seen the death
Of five fellow-workers
Confined in this jail;
We have seen how officers
Act towards us:
And so we ANNOUNCE
To the world
That a trial
Of WORKING MEN
In California
Is only a LEGAL
LYNCHING."
Well, of course we know
What those men will get
For being so NERVY,
And slapping the LAW
In the face.
But I remember
The "passive resisters"
Of England,
And I remember how
Roger Baldwin
REFUSED to give BAIL
And buy a month's freedom,
Saying: "I do not believe
In the system of BAIL
Which allows a man
With MONEY
To be at large,
While the poor man
ROTS in jail."
And I thought: "I wouldn't like
To be in their place,
But SOMEBODY has to do it.
While all the rest of us
Are passing resolutions

And organizing
And voting,
And all of it counts;
There comes at last a time
When SOMEBODY
Has to get up and say,
Looking the judge in the face:
'This is a crooked game,
And I WON'T PLAY IT
Until the RULES are changed
And the cards UNSTACKED!' "

15

Harrison George (1889–1961), who wrote the song, "Remember," which was printed in the four-teenth edition of the I.W.W. songbook, was a spokesman for the left-wing at the time of the Rus-sian Revolution. He later joined the Communist Party. An I.W.W. organizer of metal miners dur-ing the 1916 Mesabi Range strike, he was one of the I.W.W. defendants at the Chicago trial and served a prison term in Leavenworth. George served as editor of the Peoples' World, *a Com-munist Party publication, from its founding in 1937 until shortly after World War II. He left the paper and broke with the Communist Party at that time. "Remember" was written while George was in the Cook County Jail awaiting trial.*

REMEMBER

By HARRISON GEORGE

Cook County Jail, Oct. 18, 1917.

(*Tune: "Hold the Fort"*)

We speak to you from jail today
    Two hundred union men,
We're here because the bosses' laws
    Bring slavery again.

Chorus

In Chicago's darkened dungeons
    For the O. B. U.
Remember you're outside for us
    While we're in here for you.

We're here from mine and mill and rail
    We're here from off the sea,
From coast to coast we make the boast
    Of Solidarity.

We laugh and sing, we have no fear
    Our hearts are always light,
We know that every Wobblie true
    Will carry on the fight.

We make a pledge—no tyrant might
    Can make us bend a knee,
Come on you worker, organize
    And fight for Liberty.

16

Manuel Rey, who wrote "Thoughts of a Dead-Living Soul," was one of the Chicago defendants sentenced to Leavenworth. His poem appeared in the One Big Union Monthly (*August 1919*).

THOUGHTS OF A DEAD-LIVING SOUL

By MANUEL REY

20-year Class-war Prisoner No. 13,111, Leavenworth, Kansas.

I am spending the numberless days
Of my sweet and youthful life
In a felon's lonesome cell
For so many and lonely years.
Who knows how long it will be?

Twenty long years of prison life
Is indeed a cruel and bitter fate,
When one is all around encased
By stony walls and iron bars
Far away from the outside world.

I am spending the sweetest days of my life
Far, far away from Mother and Friends
All alone, without having the right
To the beautiful things of life
That bountiful Mother Earth
Gave to each one and all of us
When born to this mysterious world.

And so I am to spend the best of my life
In a prison cell so dark and cold.
And I know how cruel is its sting
On the mind and the tortured heart
To pass away these countless days
As a dead and yet a living soul,
Missing the scent of beautiful flowers
And the songs of the birds of fields and woods.

And yet I am one of those
Who have produced so many
Of the most precious things of life!

I am spending the numberless days
Of my sweet and youthful life
For the cause and the noblest thoughts
Of the future human race.
Oh! I ask who has the right
To make our life a living grave?
And to deprive us of freedom's might
And our birth-share of equal right
To all the broad heart of life?
Nobody, that I know.

For are we not a part
Of the human race!
So why should any of us be closed
In prison dungeons for his noblest thoughts?
Nobody that I know would put us here
Except the plutes and exploiters of humankind.

I am spending the numberless days
In a determined, yet cheerless way.
For I think that everyone
Is happy and enjoys the flow of blood
Of which his heart is full,
That all enjoy the beautiful thoughts
That human mind can possibly possess
In this mysterious life.

With these beautiful thoughts in an iron cage
I am spending the numberless days
To tell you that here suffers a man
In body, but not in mind.
For his powerful will
And high and noble thoughts
Conquer all the evils
Of even prison life.

I am spending the numberless days
In this stony and lonesome cell
With my mind and thoughts
Flying all over the endless world
To find the beautiful things of life.
And that is why I don't care
What the world may think of me,
A felon in a stony cell.
Neither what they might want
To make of my body and my life.
For my beautiful thoughts

My great ideas and unconquered will
Shall in the future
Conquer them all.

17

*Ralph Chaplin sent Miss Agnes Inglis the manu-
scripts of his prison poems. Most of them were
written, in pencil, in a small black covered auto-
graph book which is now in the Ralph Chaplin
file in the Labadie Collection. In his autobiography, Chaplin wrote: "One sleepless night I lay
looking at the dirty whitewashed wall back of my
bunk. On it had been scribbled the names, initials, and monikers of previous occupants of the
cell. I had been thinking of Edith and Vonnie
[Chaplin's wife and son], of the Haymarket martyrs, of Joe Hill and Frank Little, and of Lind-
strom, a convicted murderer who was shortly to
be hanged. While listening to the sounds of the
indifferent world that came in through the bars
from the darkness outside, the rhythm of a poem
started to beat inside my skull. I found room on
the wall to write down the stanzas as they came
to me. It was my first prison poem, 'Mourn Not
the Dead.'"*

*"Mourn Not the Dead" was written in Cook
County Jail. "To My Little Son" and "Prison Noc-
turne" were written at Leavenworth and first published in the prison paper, the New Era, while
Chaplin was a prisoner in the penitentiary. All
three poems made their rounds of the radical press
and were used by the I.W.W. in defense publicity.*

PRISON NOCTURNE

By RALPH CHAPLIN

Outside the storm is swishing to and fro;
    The wet wind hums its colorless refrain;
Against the walls and dripping bars, the rain
Beats with a rhythm like a song of woe;
Dimmed by the lightning's ever-fitful glow
The purple arc-lamps blur each streaming pane;
The thunder rumbles at the distant plain,
The cells are hushed and silent, row on row.

Fall, fruitful drops, upon the parching earth,
    Fall, and revive the living sap of spring;
    Blossom the fields with wonder once again!

And, in all hearts, awaken to new birth
   Those visions and endeavors that will bring
A fresh, sweet morning to the world of men!

18

MOURN NOT THE DEAD

By Ralph Chaplin

Mourn not the dead that in the cool earth lie—
   Dust unto dust—
The calm, sweet earth that mothers all who die
   As all men must;

Mourn not your captive comrades who must
      dwell—
   Too strong to strive—
Within each steel-bound coffin of a cell,
   Buried alive;

But rather mourn the apathetic throng—
   The cowed and the meek—
Who see the world's great anguish and its wrong
   And dare not speak!

19

TO MY LITTLE SON

By Ralph Chaplin

I cannot lose the thought of you
   It haunts me like a little song,
It blends with all I see or do
   Each day, the whole day long.

The train, the lights, the engine's throb,
   And that one stinging memory:
Your brave smile broken with a sob,
   Your face pressed close to me.

An Injury to One Is an Injury to All

California Defense Bulletin, January 13, 1919.

HERE IS AN I.W.W. "SERVICE FLAG" FOR THE 47 IN
SACRAMENTO WHO ARE ABOUT TO SERVE FOR YOU.

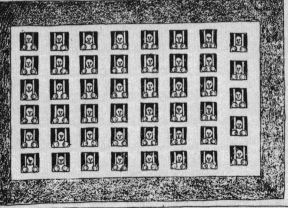

HAVE YOU A LITTLE
WOBBLY SERVICE FLAG
IN YOUR LOCAL?

HERE IS A "GOLD STAR"
SERVICE FLAG FOR JOE
HILL OR FRANK LITTLE.

HANG ONE OUTSIDE OF YOUR WINDOW.

Their Message Is: Don't Mourn, But Organize

Lips trembling far too much to speak;
    The arms that would not come undone;
The kiss so salty on your cheek;
    The long, long trip begun.

I could not miss you more it seemed,
    But now I don't know what to say.
It's harder than I ever dreamed
    With you so far away.

20

Signed "Card No. 41894, Los Angeles County Jail," this poem was printed in One Big Union Monthly *(July 1920).*

WHAT I READ IN THE PAPER
By CARD No. 41894

Los Angeles County Jail (San Quentin-bound),
April 30, 1920

I read in the paper today
All about Bluebeard Watson
And his twenty-five wives
And how he killed four of them
And that the Los Angeles teachers
Are all "for" Hoover,
Who will bring down
The price of sugar
So "they" say—
The mysterious "they"—
And then I read
How a bank robber
Attempted suicide
In the county jail
And that agents of
The Department of "Justice"
Were going to catch
All the "Reds"
That they had not caught
In previous raids
On May first.
And I saw
(By the same paper)
That Jack Dempsey
Is in trim
For his picture was there
Four times,
And I wondered how
He is coming out with
That charge about evading

The draft
And why he was not in
Leavenworth or in
The County Jail with me.
And there was a whole
Lot more in the paper
About bankers, and workers,
And work, and economizing,
For the latter.
And all about Baseball
And Golf and other sports
And sugar hoarding and
Potatoes. And
A good many divorces
And all about the
Conference at
San Remo, where
All the world's troubles were
Settled. And all about
Mexico. And more
Divorces. And pictures
of wives, and society "belles"
And Hoover's platform
And a great deal more
Sugar thirty-one cents
A pound.
Switchmen on strike
Trying to keep up
With prices set
By profiteers
And miners put in jail
For striking,
And switchmen, too.
For interfering with
Production and Distribution
Of the Necessities of Life.
But in Louisville
(Kentucky) the profiteers
Went free
Because the Lever act
Could not be applied
To THEM.
But there was nothing
(In the same paper)
About any arrest
Of any profiteers,
Exploiters of Labor
(Same family)
Who are the cause
Of all the chaos,
Strikes and suffering.
And there was nothing

At all in favor
About the One Big Union,
For all the workers,
Which will cure
Their ills.
But it is true
There is a scarcity
Of newsprint paper
And space is scarce,
And the workers are
Too tired anyhow
To read it.

21

*Pierce Wetter's article, "The Men I Left at Leaven-
worth," appeared in* Survey *(October 1922) and
reflects the growing interest of the national magazines in the issue of amnesty for prisoners convicted under the wartime Espionage Law.*

THE MEN I LEFT AT LEAVENWORTH

By Pierce C. Wetter

The other day I was riding in a street car in New
York behind two well dressed men deep in their
daily papers. Their comments on some of the dis-
patches about the railroad strike reminded me
more of James Whitcomb Riley's refrain: "The
goblins'll get yer if yer don't look out" than anything I had heard for a long time.

"I tell you, those I.W.W. fellows . . ." one of
them rumbled.

"It doesn't say it's proved yet they were around
. . ." the other suggested timidly.

"Huh! Doesn't need to!" the first shook his head
ominously. "Nowadays a man takes his life in his
hand wherever he goes. I believe in giving that
kind of vermin a wide berth. I never saw one of
them and I never want to!"

The next instant there was some sort of mix-up
with a truck on the track and we all got a violent
jolt. The speaker, who had risen in his seat to get
off at the next corner, became rather badly tangled with some passengers across the aisle. I
helped to disentangle them and he was at once
all smiles and amiability—"Almost like one of our
college football rushes," he grinned, in the easy
fellowship an earlier generation is apt to accord
its successors on the same campus.

I should have liked to watch his face when I
told him that I am a sincerely convinced, indelible

I.W.W.; that I had just been released from Leavenworth prison on expiration of a five-year sentence under the 1918 Chicago indictment; and
that I am now working with all the strength and
ability I possess in the interest of my fifty-two
fellow-workers, fellow-prisoners, still in Leavenworth, some with twenty-year sentences.

But "We're late for that appointment," his companion reminded him, and I missed my chance.

He will doubtless go on indefinitely repeating
his "bogey-man" stuff about people whom he admits he has never seen and knows nothing of except by hearsay. I wonder how many people who
read this have done exactly the same thing? And
how long they are going to keep on doing it?

That is why, when I.W.W.'s are on trial, whether
in courts or in newspapers, practically "everything
goes." But in all such movements, persecution
only serves as propaganda, and weeds out the
worthless material—those who "can't stand the
gaff" and go back on their principles—and shows
the grain of the men who cannot be bribed or
bought, who have the courage to stand by their
convictions at whatever cost.

There are fifty-two such men in Leavenworth
today. Over two-thirds of them are American-
born. They have been there since 1918, and most
of them have ten- or twenty-year sentences. I
know these men; and I want everyone else to
know them. They are of the stuff that makes history, the sort of stuff that went to the making of
our country in the beginning, and that is needed
just as much right now, perhaps more, to keep
our country true to its big ideals.

I am not going to try to give fifty-two full biog-
raphies (though I wish I could, for every one of
them is a story in itself—an almost unbelievable
story!) but just a suggestion or a characteristic
here and there of a few of the men. They are all
very human, the same hopes and desires, the same
flesh and blood we are all made of—fathers, husbands, brothers—it means as much to every one
of them to stay there in prison year on year under
those hideously monotonous, unsanitary, galling
conditions, as it would to any of you who read
these words. Try for one moment to realize what
these things mean. Try *honestly*. And then try to
understand what it means in terms of *character* for
these men to stay there rather than to compromise.

Not long ago the Rev. Richard W. Hogue, known
doubtless to many *Graphic* readers as the inter-

California Defense Bulletin, January 20, 1919.

national secretary of the Church League for Industrial Democracy, made a visit to Leavenworth, and James P. Thompson was one of the men with whom he talked.

"How can we, how can any decent, self-respecting man," Thompson said to him, "buy his release at the cost of his manhood, by promising to refrain ever after from expressing his convictions and standing by his principles? It would be degrading and dishonest for us to accept 'parole' on the terms on which it has been offered us. We will go out of here as *men,* when we do go, not as 'criminals' purchasing 'liberty' with the barter of our convictions and our consciences. When we leave this place it will be with our heads up. . . ."

Thompson has been called the "rough-necked Isaiah of the American proletariat." Over six feet tall, with clear-cut features, deep-set eyes and level brows, he is not altogether unlike the common conception of ancient prophets, especially when he thunders—"The very people who are abusing the I.W.W. today, would, if they had lived in the days of our forefathers, have been licking the boots of King George. They would have said of the boys fighting barefooted in the snow at Valley Forge, 'Look at them! They haven't shoes to their feet, and they are talking about liberty!' The people who are knocking the I.W.W. are the same type as those who dragged William Lloyd Garrison through the streets of Boston with a rope round his neck; who killed Lovejoy and threw his printing press into the Mississippi River." He is fond of quoting Woodrow Wilson's *The New Freedom* where it is developed in detail how the industrial interests of America control the whole machinery of government: of quoting Supreme Court Justice Brandeis as saying that "America has a hereditary aristocracy of wealth which is foreign to American ideals and menacing the nation as a democracy," and ex-President Taft: "We must keep law and justice a little closer together in order to justify the law," and Judge Cullen:

"There is danger, real danger, that the people will see with one sweeping glance how we lawyers in the pay of predatory wealth corrupt law at its fountainhead; that the furies may then break loose and all hell will ride on their wings."

After some three years on the Leavenworth "rock pile," during which time he studied mechanics in all his spare hours, especially with reference to motors, Thompson now has charge of the prison garage, and also teaches in the prison night school.

Practically all these fifty-two men have taken up some definite study or course of reading and are fitting themselves for various kinds of work and social service. They have in a sense, insofar as such a place will permit, dominated their surroundings and made their own world. Several have enrolled in the University of Wisconsin extension courses in electricity, medicine, and so on, many of them teach in the prison school, many are writers—Ralph Chaplin's poems, for instance, are too well known perhaps to need much comment here.

Then there is Mortimer Downing, nearly sixty years old, a newspaper man, well educated, widely travelled, with friends among people of influence all over the world. Not long ago he was offered a post in the prison printing-plant, a position for which he is eminently well fitted, and one not requiring hard or very monotonous labor. But he refused it and remained as "runner" for the "rock-pile gang" (a tedious post, involving exposure and considerable exertion, the "rock pile" being the official Gehenna of the prison) because in this way he could keep in closer touch with this group of fifty-two (all I.W.W.'s, as he is) and continue to be of service to them individually. A practical example of the fine sense of fellowship and solidarity that characterizes all I.W.W.'s worthy the name.

G. J. Bourg is a construction worker, imperturbable, indomitable. One of his chief distinctions with us is the grit with which he used to keep doggedly on with his organizing—harvest fields, lumber camps, everywhere—no matter how many times he was "beaten up" by "Vigilantes" and "Citizens' Committees." He would crawl into camp and stay long enough to get "fit," and out he would go again. He does not seem to know what fear means. George O'Connell is another construction worker—white haired, slow of speech, gentle-

Amnesty leaflet issued by the I.W.W. General Defense Committee about 1922.

Labadie Collection file.

voiced, his infrequent smile is a reward in itself; he is another hard student and has made himself proficient in electricity. And Alexander Cournos, who was assistant "weather man" out in South Dakota—short, slender, keen-eyed, wiry—would rather calculate than eat or sleep.

Sam Scarlett (whose very name conjures visions of the time of Robin Hood) claims he is a "citizen of industry" and has no other nationality.

"Where is your home?" he was asked by the prosecution during the Chicago trial.

"Cook County Jail."

"Before that?"

"County Jail, Cleveland, Ohio."

"And before that?"

"City Jail, Akron, Ohio."

"Are you a citizen?"

"No."

"That's enough."

BIG BUSINESS (to Labor, generously): "My good fellow, you'll be well paid for your patriotic action in 'tending this glorious plant; you shall have all the fruit above the ground—I'll take ONLY the roots!"

Industrial Pioneer, June 1925.

Scarlett was a champion soccer football player for some years and is also a skilled machinist and electrician and one of our best speakers and organizers. Robert Connellan, a man of almost sixty, is a chemist, a graduate of the University of California, and a musician (playing in the prison orchestra). We know him best as never too tired to explain something to some of us younger fellows, to explain carefully, in detail, no matter how tedious the matter may be. He is one of the famous "Silent Defense" men who survived those awful days in the vile Sacramento jail—an ordeal intended to break their spirit but which instead shattered their health but confirmed them in their principles.

One Saturday afternoon there was a movie show at the penitentiary, and for no reason whatever we I.W.W.'s were singled out (and particularly the long-sentence men, contrary to the custom in all prisons) to shovel coal while the rest went to the show. Of course we refused, and equally of course we were all put in The Hole. We missed the show, but we made a stand against the policy of domineering injustice that officials had inaugurated against us. For the first three years we were in prison, we were kept steadily on the "rock pile"—a deputy warden, since transferred, told us he had orders "from Washington" "not to give us any easy time" but to "break our spirit," and he was going to give us "good reason to know that *he* was running that prison."

Two of our men—Caesar Tabib and Edward Quigley—are suffering from tuberculosis aggravated if not contracted in the Sacramento jail where they spent a year before they were brought to trial. Because of their physical condition, these two men were prevailed on by the rest of us to make application for release, for "clemency," but their application was coldly refused by the Department of Justice. Apparently they are not yet near enough to death to make it "safe" to release them.

Another of our number, William Weyh, was kept on the "rock pile" last December until the exposure resulted in severe illness, hemorrhages—twelve in a single day. He was so emaciated as to be scarcely recognizable. It was at this point that a prison official said to him: "I don't believe you have another ten hours to live if you stay in this place. Drop your I.W.W. affiliations, and you can go out of here as soon as you please." Weyh's answer was: "No. I'll die first." We had

been urging him to make application for release and he at last consented, and the authorities agreed, apparently preferring that he should die outside the walls. He stipulated, however, in writing, that "I have not wavered in my adherence to the I.W.W. and its principles."

There is not space here to go further down the list of these fifty-two men; they all have the same splendid spirit, the same high courage, the same sense of the crucial human value of solidarity.

Again and again I am asked by those who depend only upon newspapers for their information, *why* we refuse to ask for "clemency"; and last July, when a petition for general amnesty (that is, for unconditional release for all charged with the same "offence") signed by some three hundred thousand names from all over the country, was presented to President Harding by a delegation of representative men and women, the President expressed "surprise" about this refusal on our part, and of course at the same time went through with that same ancient formula—"No one advocating the overthrow of the government by violence will be pardoned." This phrase is continually used by officials, apparently in lieu of any *reason* they can give for our continued imprisonment.

The truth of the matter is, not one of these fifty-two men was ever even indicted on the preposterous charges brought against them in the press during war-time hysteria, such as the receipt of German gold, and being spies. They are in prison now *solely for expression of opinion,* and none of those opinions have anything to do with the overthrow of any government in any way—they are merely opinions *against war.* Note also that these men are confined under the Espionage Act only, though it is now no longer in force. In lieu of any legal reason for their continued incarceration, Attorney General Daugherty even felt obliged to resort to giving out false information in reply to inquiries made on this subject by the Federal Council of Churches (see March 11, 1922, issue Information Service Research Department, Commission on Church and Social Service, F.C.C.C.A., room 604, 105 East 22 Street, New York).

Now, to revert to the President's "surprise" that we are unwilling to crawl out, I don't for a moment doubt his genuineness. It is entirely likely that it really is very difficult for him to understand such a thing. Let me quote from the Open Letter since prepared by these fifty-two men and sent a month ago not only to the President, but also to all Cabinet officials, Congressmen, the Governors of the forty-eight states, and to a number of editors and others throughout the country. (I shall be very glad to send a copy to any one who will write me in care of the *Survey*.)

We are not criminals and are not in prison because we committed any crimes or conspired to commit them. From the beginning, justice has been denied us and the truth of our case withheld from the consideration of the public. . . . In the press, the I.W.W. is like the Mexican in the movie show; he is always the villain. . . . We are in prison now solely for exercising our constitutional right of free speech. . . . If it is a crime to exercise the right for which our fathers laid down their lives, we have no apology to make. . . . To make application for pardon would make hypocrites of us all. . . . We refuse to recant, and continue to refuse to beg for a pardon which in common justice should have been accorded to us long ago. . . . We are but a small group, insignificant in the universal scheme of things, but the ideas we are standing for are not insignificant. They are big and vital and dynamic and concern every man, woman and child in America. It matters little what happens to us, but if the American people lose the right of free speech, the loss to the whole world will be irreparable. . . . We believed before we were convicted and we believe now that the present economic order is wasteful, planless, chaotic and criminal. . . . We seek to replace it with a well-ordered and scientifically managed system—in which machinery will be the only slave . . . a civilization worthy of the intelligence of humanity. . . . Persecution is not new to us. Some day the truth of the incredible atrocities perpetrated upon our workers in this "Land of the Free" will become known to the world. Our imprisonment is only a single episode in the long history of brutality, . . . onslaughts of cruelty to be compared only with the burning of witches—exile and torture and deliberate murder have for years been our invariable lot. But ideals cannot be altered by force; human convictions cannot be caged with iron bars; human progress cannot be damned with a prison wall. . . .

Captain Sidney Lanier, of the U. S. Military Intelligence Corps, with the facts of this case weighing heavily on his conscience, made a direct appeal to President Wilson: "I am of the opinion," he declared, "that these men were convicted contrary to the law and the evidence, solely because they were leaders in an organization against which public sentiment was aroused, and the verdict rendered was in obedience to public hysteria." His opinion is borne out by the fact that war-profiteers, German agents, and others convicted of direct assistance to Germany during the war have long since been released, and of the 946 convictions under the so-called Espionage Act (of persons not I.W.W.'s), all but five are now free.

Solidarity—the basic, ineradicable, human faith that an injury to one *is* an injury to all—is the spirit, the very essence of our organization. Compromise of any sort, for any purpose, is cheap enough; to compromise the principle of solidarity is essentially disloyal not only to the rest of the group, but to the whole vital cause for which we stand. "We were not convicted as individuals, but as a group. We were convicted of a 'conspiracy' of which we are all equally innocent or all equally guilty."

These men in prison are bearing the brunt of intolerance and repression bred of the war and of the forces that bred the war. They are standing by their ideals at the cost, literally, of their lives in the full knowledge that for them individually there is everything to lose and nothing to gain, that no advantage can possibly accrue to them personally.

You who read these words: do none of you *care* whether justice is done? Do none of you care *enough* to make it your serious, personal concern to get the facts, *all* the facts, the *whole truth*, about this matter? And then add your influence to the forces already at work for the release of these men.

22

Vera Moller's poem "Our Defense" and the song "We Made Good Wobs Out There" were frequently reprinted in the I.W.W. press. "Our Defense" was printed in the Industrial Worker *(August 1923); "We Made Good Wobs Out There" was included in the twenty-third edition of the I.W.W. songbook.*

E. S. Rose, an I.W.W. leader in Detroit, included a newspaper clipping of "Our Defense" in a scrapbook of Wobbly songs and poems which he presented to the Labadie Collection. Unfor-

I.W.W. headquarters in New York City after raid on November 15, 1919.
Labadie Collection photo files.

*tunately, he did not cite the sources for the items
he selected. On the clipping of the poem "Our
Defense" in the E. S. Rose scrapbook is the following anecdote which is printed after the verses:*
    *"Ex. from the Chicago trial. 'Well, they grabbed
us. And the deputy says, 'Are you a member of
the I.W.W.? I says, 'Yes,' so he asked me for my
card, and I gave it to him, and he tore it up. He
tore up the other cards that the fellow members
along with me had. So this fellow member says,
'There is no use tearing that card up. We can get
duplicates.' 'Well,' the deputy says, 'We can tear
the duplicates too.' And this fellow worker says, he
says, 'Yes, but you can't tear it out of my heart.'"*

OUR DEFENSE

By Vera Moller

In the end the loss or triumph of the case shall not
    be hung,
    On the golden ease and smoothness of a hired
        lawyer's tongue
Nor ably or how bungling every man shall plead
    his cause,
    It's something beyond the courtroom that
        makes judge and jury pause.
For they sense the mighty forces in the mutterings
    of unrest
    And the songs of hope and freedom rising in
        the Workers' breast
And wherever men are willing for their beliefs to
    do and dare,
    There's a cause that stands behind them and
        they feel its power there.
Over treachery and cunning, thru all darkness and
    suspense,
    'Tis the cause itself shall triumph and in that is
        our defense.

23

WE MADE GOOD WOBS OUT THERE

By Vera Moller

(Tune: "Auld Lang Syne")

Though we be shut out from the world,
Here worn and battle scarred,
Our names shall live where men walk free
On many a small red card.

So let us take fresh hope my friend,
We cannot feel despair,
Whate'er may be our lot in here,
We made good Wobs out there.

When we were out we did our bit
To hasten Freedom's dawn,
They can't take back the seed we spread,
The truths we passed along.

'Tis joy to know we struck a blow
To break the master's sway,
And those we lined up take the work
And carry on today.

Though we be shut out from the world
And days are long and hard,
They can't erase the names we wrote
In many a small red card.

So let us take fresh hope my friend
Above our prison fare,
Whate'er may be our lot in here,
We made good Wobs out there.

Labor
produces
all wealth

all wealth
must go
to Labor

We are emerging from a period in which the American worker has been peculiarly unresponsive to proposed radical changes. We think we are through that period. The development of the machine, automation, is rapidly changing the workers' way of life. It will change their thinking, too. The up-to-the-minute I.W.W. is here waiting for them. We doubt if any person out shopping for a good labor organization to join up with has ever turned down the I.W.W. because he really believed it to be out of date. Some have thought it too far advanced to be practical in the present day. Many have been afraid to join because "it's too radical." But out-of-date? It doesn't sound possible.

CARL KELLER
Industrial Worker, August 14, 1963.

An I.W.W. Miscellany: 1924-1964

The ordeal of the antiradical campaigns of the war and postwar years culminated in a serious schism in the I.W.W. organization in 1924. Tensions had arisen over the issue of individual amnesty for political prisoners, the rivalry between the strong lumber workers Industrial Union No. 120 and the agricultural workers Industrial Union No. 110, and the attempt of the Communist Party to infiltrate the I.W.W.

From Leavenworth Penitentiary, James Rowan, a popular leader of the lumberjacks, organized a rump faction known as the E.P.'s from its writing of an "Emergency Program" which attacked the centralized program at I.W.W. Chicago headquarters and advocated a loose federation of highly autonomous I.W.W. locals. With his large following, Rowan had been nicknamed the "Jesus of Nazareth of the Lumberjacks of the Northwest." When he got a court injunction to restrain I.W.W. headquarters' officials, primarily two A.W.O. leaders Doyle and Fisher, from continuing to hold the property and funds of the I.W.W., John MacRae, a Wobbly prisoner at San Quentin, penned the following irreverent lines:

TO FAN THE FLAMES OF COURT RESPECT

James Rowan Forever

I must save the proletariat from the tactics of the stools,

The officials, Doyle and Fisher, they have broken all the rules,
And the forty-thousand wobblies are a bunch of —— —— fools,
But the Injunction makes us strong.

Chorus

Second Jesus Jimmy Rowan
Second Jesus Jimmy Rowan
Second Jesus Jimmy Rowan
And Injunctions make him strong.

It will cost them all the money; but I do not care for that,
I would rather pay a lawyer than to go and buy a gat,
And I must protect one-twenty from the bunch of one-ten cats;
So Injunctions make me strong.

To me the whole of labor ought to burn a special joss;
But for me this wobbly union would have been a total loss;
And I'm pretty sure His Honor will appoint me as their boss;
While Injunctions make me strong.[1]

Rowan organized his followers into what labor historian Robert L. Tyler called "something resembling a Puritan reform sect," and on his release from prison started issuing a newspaper, *The*

Industrial Unionist, which lasted about a year. The Emergency Program faction, which now considered itself the "real I.W.W.," held its own sixteenth convention in Utah in 1925 and rewrote the constitution to provide complete autonomy for I.W.W. local industrial unions and an end to the per capita tax to national I.W.W. headquarters. It also passed a resolution against owning any property. Membership in the E.P. faction, never very high, dwindled until the group died out in the early 1930's. The Chicago I.W.W. continued as the spokesman for the Midwestern and Eastern locals, numerically depleted in membership strength.

Rivalry with the American Communist Party, organized in 1919, also resulted in a membership decline as the gulf between the I.W.W. and the C.P. widened in the 1920's. In 1920 Moscow wooed the Wobblies to join the Communist International, praising the "long and heroic service of the I.W.W. in the class war." Writing for the Comintern, Gregory Zinoviev urged the I.W.W. not to wait until the "new society is built within the shell of the old." The new society, he wrote, must overthrow the existing state and, in turn, organize a dictatorship of the proletariat.[2]

The Russian Bolshevik coup attracted some I.W.W. leaders and activists such as Bill Haywood, Elizabeth Gurley Flynn, Harrison George, George Hardy, and Charles Ashleigh. The majority of Wobblies, however, rejected the proposal to affiliate with the Comintern and became increasingly critical of the Soviet system. The distinction between the I.W.W. and the Soviet Union's philosophies of communism was pointed out by historian Paul F. Brissenden who wrote: "On the whole, the I.W.W.'s have been Bolshevik and anti-syndicalist in their concepts of industrial unionism and the structure of a new society, and syndicalist and anti-Bolshevik in their rejection of political action. . . . The I.W.W. believes in the gradual acquisition of control of industry by economic action 'on the job' and has no clear idea of how the final overthrow of capitalism is to be accomplished; the communists accept industrial unionism but insist that it is necessary to overthrow the capitalist state and organize a dictatorship of the proletariat in order to build up the new society."[3] In the struggle for the leadership of the American left wing, the I.W.W., according to Brissenden, "rapidly lost ground to the communists," who attempted to assume leadership of some of the more militant strikes and campaigns.[4]

In many respects the I.W.W. became a victim of changing American industrial technology following World War I, changes which it had intellectually anticipated and against which it continued to rebel. In the Pacific Northwest the automobile brought the logging camp closer to civilization. Migrations of Southerners to the area, and a general influx of population from other parts of the country reduced the need for single, transient lumber workers as more and more "homeguards" were hired by the logging industry.

In agriculture the expanding use of farm machinery also cut down the use of transient migrant laborers. The "auto tramp" replaced the "bindle stiff," as whole families traveled by jalopy from one harvest to another. Thus, in addition to the losses suffered from ruthless employer suppression and doctrinaire organizational factionalism, the I.W.W. was confronted with fundamental changes in the work force, which contained fewer and fewer of the kinds of workers who had responded to its past appeals. Despite these problems, however, the I.W.W. carried on its organizing activities for the next several decades, losing ground in the 1930's to the expanding industrial unions of the C.I.O.

The most important I.W.W.-led strike after 1917 took place in the Colorado coal fields, where for four months in 1927 and 1928 10,000 miners battled against conditions imposed by the company union, the Rockefeller Industrial Representation Plan, installed in the mines and mills of the Colorado Fuel and Iron Company following the Ludlow Massacre in Colorado in 1914. When the I.W.W. called a two-day protest strike in the summer of 1927 against the execution of Sacco and Vanzetti, two anarchists sentenced to death for a Massachusetts hold-up murder, half of Colorado's 12,000 miners stopped work. Their protest led to a strike which started on October 18, 1927, against company domination and lack of outlet for miners' grievances. On the first day of the strike, I.W.W. leader Paul Seidler, in charge of strike publicity, instructed strikers:

> You are not to abuse anyone. You are not to strike anyone. Tell them they are hurting themselves as well as the rest of us. There will be no rough stuff on the job. The sheriff's orders to his men are they must not shoot or abuse anyone. If anyone is going to be killed, let it be one of our men first.[5]

Despite Seidler's nonviolent policy statements,

opposition to the I.W.W.-led strike spread throughout Colorado. Military law superseded civil law in areas which the authorities declared were in a state of insurrection and riot. At Walsenburg the town's mayor led a band of citizens in demolishing the I.W.W. hall. At the Columbine Mine of the Rocky Mountain Fuel Company, state police and mine guards fired on an unarmed picket line, killing six workers and wounding twenty-three others. National Guard infantrymen and cavalry troops kidnapped and beat strike leaders, suspended union meetings, raided strikers' homes and headquarters without warrants. Two more strikers and a sixteen-year old bystander were killed as strikers paraded to a hearing of the Industrial Commission in Walsenburg. The coroner's jury pronounced the shooting unprovoked and condemned state police for showing "total disregard for human life," but the policemen who fired the shots could not be found.[6]

The Colorado coal strike introduced innovations in strike technique. Striking miners used car caravans to carry their message to other communities to persuade workers to come off their jobs. I.W.W. organizer E. S. Embree and Milka Sablich, known as "flaming Milka, the rebel girl," toured the United States on a fund-raising campaign. The Junior Wobblies was started by the children of strikers. Its goal was "to form educational classes to prepare the members to take their places in the ranks of organized labor and to arrange recreational programs."[7] Initiation fees were ten cents, and dues, five cents a month.

At the end of four months, the Colorado miners won an increase of a dollar a day, checkweighmen on the tipples, union pit committees in the mines, and enforcement of all state mining laws. "For the first time in the history of the Colorado coal fields," wrote Donald J. McClurg in a recent study of the Colorado strike, "a general strike of miners had succeeded . . . (strike leadership of the I.W.W.) way in all ways exceptional."[8]

During the depression years the I.W.W. joined with various organizations of unemployed workers that sprang up across the nation and set up its own Unemployed Unions which provided housing and food for jobless Wobblies while they carried on I.W.W. agitation. A handbill of the organization suggested, in part:

The jobless have to get together, somehow, and make so much noise in the world as to attract attention. Only by making a public scandal in every city and town will you break the silence of the press and receive notice. Only the fear of a general social conflagration will make the employers of labor, private or governmental, get together and devise ways and means. As long as you are contented to rot to death in silence, you will be allowed to do so. . . . But then, when you do get a job, then is your chance to take steps that it shall not happen again. Organize industrially in such great numbers that you are able, with your organized might, to cut down the workday to the required number of hours to provide employment for the jobless. This will possibly tide us over until we are able to take complete control and put an end to unemployment forever.[9]

The I.W.W. never recovered from the 1924 split in the organization. It lost its printing press and its building which it had bought in 1925 with the aid of money from the Garland Fund. When a new I.W.W. general secretary took office in 1932, he found only $29.00 cash with which to run the activities of the organization.

A large amount of money had been expended in the preceding two years in aiding the defense of miners charged with murder in the bloody and bitter Harlan, Kentucky, coal mining strike. In May 1930, 18,000 mountaineer miners in Harlan and Bell counties quit work to protest wage cuts and widespread layoffs. "We starve while we work; we might as well strike while we starve," miners stated in a struggle widely publicized by left-wing organizations and the national press.[10] For two years Harlan County remained in a virtual stage of siege—"a concentration camp which outsiders entered at the peril of their lives."[11] A gun battle between miners and mine guards at Evarts, Kentucky, left three mine guards and a miner dead, and forty-four miners indicted for murder. "What's the use of going to law?" a Kentucky miner asked New York Times writer Louis Stark, "ain't no justice for us in Harlan courts."[12]

The I.W.W., which had been called into the Harlan strike when some of the Kentucky miners petitioned for a charter, undertook to help defend the miners indicted for the Evarts shooting. Zealous defense efforts saved all of the prisoners from the death penalty, and the last prisoner was released from jail in 1941. Despite this victory, the Harlan strike was lost, and "bloody Harlan" earned its reputation for being "the toughest place in the country to unionize."[13]

Industrial Pioneer, June 1925.

Throughout 1932 and 1933, I.W.W. agitation and organization in Detroit added impetus to the growing unrest of automobile workers suffering from layoffs, wage cuts, and the tensions of speed-up in the auto plants. Soapboxing, leafleting, a daily radio program, and weekend socials at the I.W.W. hall on Woodward Avenue provided the growth of a skeleton I.W.W. organization in some of the large auto plants, which helped spur quickie strikes against wage cuts in the Briggs, Hudson Body, and Murray Body plants. Metal finishers at the Hudson Body plant passed out I.W.W. leaflets which read, "Sit down and watch your pay go up." The sit-ins resulted in five successive wage boosts in that department.

Inspired by this victory, the I.W.W. helped organize a strike at the Murray Body plant in December 1932. The failure of this strike, which came on the eve of wholesale layoffs due to a change in body design, was a blow to the I.W.W. organizers. Fred Thompson, an organizer in that campaign, wrote:

The loss of the Murray strike was the loss of the I.W.W. campaign in Detroit. Early in it, the big hall and the radio program were dropped. . . . Through the strike, but on a reduced scale, organizing efforts continued at other plants; and after it, house to house visiting centered on the Murray recruits; yet all but a few of the newly won members dropped out and new recruits became rare. The I.W.W. in Detroit was left with most of its members the unswerving Finns and Hungarians who had constituted its backbone in 1930.[14]

Some of the I.W.W. organizers moved on to Cleveland where, during the next few years, they leafleted, organized, and soapboxed, gave impetus to a strike of charwomen, whose picket lines stretched several blocks around the office buildings which they cleaned at night, and gained membership in several foundries and metal shops.

The I.W.W. achieved a longer record of collective bargaining in these Cleveland shops than anywhere else in its history. Shops organized in 1934, such as American Stove Company, were still in the I.W.W. in 1950, when the Cleveland local left the organization over the issue of signing Taft-Hartley affidavits.

Elsewhere in the early 1930's I.W.W. construction workers struck at Nevada's Hoover Dam, Cle Elum Dam in Washington, the Mississippi Bridge near New Orleans, the Los Angeles Aqueduct, and the New York water tunnel. A branch of the I.W.W. Marine Transport Workers Union was started in Stettin, Germany, in 1929 and during the early 1930's helped get supplies to the anti-Hitler underground. Likewise, the M.T.W. kept up protest for the four-watch system and the restoration of the old Shipping Board manning and wage scale. A harvest drive through the wheat belt met with vicious opposition in several of the grain-growing states, where authorities and farmers raided the workers' camps, beat I.W.W. members, deported many, and jailed hundreds. In the Yakima Valley in Washington, a strike of I.W.W. "fruit glommers" against wages of seventy-five cents for a ten-hour day led to the jailing of hundreds in specially built stockades.

During World War II, I.W.W. activity, carried on in Western mining camps and along the waterfront, led *Business Week* to comment on January 6, 1945: "The I.W.W. shows signs of life. In the metal shops of Cleveland, the vanadium mines of California, the copper diggings of Butte, on the waterfront of San Diego, New Orleans, and New York, the dead past is stirring and men are carrying red cards." [15] A year after the war, the *New York Times* reported that I.W.W. membership numbered 20,000. *Time* magazine reported on the 1946 I.W.W. convention with its characteristic flippancy: "Thirty-nine men and a grandmotherly looking woman met in an office building on the northside of Chicago to pass resolutions denouncing Capitalism, Fascism, Nazism, the C.I.O., the A.F.L., and war. . . . With that off their chests, the Industrial Workers of the World went home." [16]

The wartime revival of the organization was not long lasting. Although at its 1946 convention, the I.W.W. had reaffirmed its opposition to the Communist Party in a resolution which read, in part, "we look upon the Communist Party and its fledglings as a major menace to the working class . . . the interests of world peace can best be served by labor movements that clearly represent the interests of labor and not the interests of any political state," the I.W.W. was placed on Attorney-General Tom Clark's list of subversive organizations. Soon after, the Treasury Department ruled that the I.W.W. was subject to paying a corporate income tax, and the final blow came when I.W.W.

leaders refused, on principle, to sign the non-communist affidavit required by the 1947 Taft-Hartley Act and, in the process, lost the Cleveland members.

The I.W.W. picketing which probably attracted the most attention in recent years was held at the *New Republic* magazine in April 1948. When an article by Wallace Stegner in the January 6 issue suggested that Joe Hill might have been guilty, the Friends of Joe Hill Committee formed and asked that corrective information be published in the magazine. The Committee engaged in extensive research and submitted a study of the Joe Hill case to the magazine. The *New Republic* ran a synopsis of the study; the whole document was printed in the *Industrial Worker* on November 13, 1948; the picketing was covered by the *New Yorker* and the *New York Times* and the editor of the *Nation* wryly commented:

> We found the Stegner piece interesting, but we doubt whether the legendary figure of Joe Hill can or even should be discredited by the disclosure of the failings of a mere man, Joe Hillstrom, who happened to be turned to legendary use. Such figures are not disposed of so easily. We are not surprised that Wobblies, who are legendary themselves, have appeared before the *New Republic*'s door. We shan't be surprised, either, to hear that Joe Hill is among them. [17]

The Taft-Hartley Act, the subversive list, and the cold-war period took its toll of I.W.W. membership, and the I.W.W. celebrated its fiftieth anniversary unable to engage in collective bargaining anywhere. Historian Robert L. Tyler described a recent visit to the I.W.W. hall in Seattle, once a busy center for Wobbly activity and membership:

> Inside the hall near the door stand two battered roll top desks stacked high with piles of papers and newspapers. A naked light bulb hangs from the ceiling over the desks. In the rear of the hall, several elderly men in work clothes play cribbage at a heavy round table. Against the wall near the door stands a book case, the library of the Seattle I.W.W. branches. A few titles are readily discernible, Marx's *Capital*, the Bureau of Corporations' investigations and report of the lumber industry published in 1913 and 1914, Gustavus Myer's *History of the Great American Fortunes*, Darwin's

Industrial Pioneer, August 1926.

Origin of Species and, oddly enough, T. S. Eliot's *Collected Poems.* Above the book case, the Wobblies have hung three ancient photographs, portraits of the three principal Wobbly "martyrs," Joe Hill, Frank Little, and Wesley Everest. Underneath the picture of Everest someone had hand-printed his last words, spoken as the lynchers dragged him from the Centralia jail, "Tell the boys I died for my class." These three pictures give a curious ikon-like impression.[18]

Yet the I.W.W. persists to the present day; its biweekly newspaper issued from the Chicago headquarters is as lively and provocative as former I.W.W. publications. Its tiny group of members remains zealous, idealistic, and strongly class conscious, convinced that the working class needs the type of organization it has been striving these sixty years to build.

Feared yesterday, almost forgotten today, the Wobblies nevertheless left an indelible mark on the American labor movement and American society. Fighting capitalism and Soviet communism, embracing direct action and democracy, the Wobblies awakened the idealism and stirred the imaginations of millions of workers. Although the I.W.W. never numbered more than 100,000 at the peak of its membership, its doctrine of One Big Union found a response from all types of workers that was to help motivate later and more successful unions.

More than any other early American labor movement, the I.W.W. laid the groundwork for the mass organization of the unskilled and foreign born in the C.I.O. and many A.F.L. unions of the 1930's and '40's. Many of its members, trained in free speech fights and militant strikes, steeled by trials and frame-ups, helped form the industrial unions of the 1930's and provided local leadership for the strikes of that decade.

I.W.W. strike techniques—the sit-downs in Schenectady and Detroit, the chain-picketing in Lawrence, the car-caravans in Colorado—once considered revolutionary, became the practices of later A.F.L. and C.I.O. unions. Defiant and flamboyant in their speeches, the Wobblies were damned, as Haywood once said, for preaching what less radical unions practiced.

They left their mark in the civil liberties field when Wobbly free speech fights, trials, and persecutions by vigilante groups aroused liberals across the country to the need for defense organizations to protect the rights of social dissidents. Wobbly fights for better conditions in the bunkhouses and farms focused attention on the problems of migratory agricultural labor which instigated official investigations and some attempts at reform. Their agitation in jails against notorious prison abuses and use of prison contract labor led to public awareness which eventually brought about more humane prison conditions.

The legend and influence of the I.W.W. endures along with its contribution to our literature, language, and folklore. As historian Robert L. Tyler has written about the I.W.W.: "It is a story of the spurned and downtrodden who fought to win respect and dignity as something due their power, who knew that respect and dignity were not a gift but a payment demanded by strength. Though perhaps not true to all details of the record, it is this legend that survives, and makes even contemporary conservatives a little sentimental about the Wobblies, and that has enriched the tradition of the labor movement."[19]

Sentimental legend, perhaps. But the Wobblies earned a prominent place in the history of American social protest movements and left all workers a genuine heritage expressed in the concept of their 1905 Manifesto, and made meaningful by their sacrifices and battles—industrial democracy.

1

Millions of words have been written about the case of Sacco and Vanzetti, a shoemaker and a fishpeddler convicted in Massachusetts of a 1920 hold-up murder and sentenced to an execution which took place in 1927. The case has inspired editorials, novels, plays, speeches, pamphlets, articles, and poems as well as lengthy legal analyses. Convicted during the height of this country's fear of foreign-born radicals, to many Americans the men symbolized a threat to the American way of life and American religious, patriotic, and property values.

But, as Professor Robert Weeks writes in his book, Commonwealth vs. Sacco and Vanzetti *(New York, 1958): "To millions, Sacco and Vanzetti, irrespective of their being anarchists, draft dodgers, and convicted murderers, were saintly, dignified men—martyrs to social prejudice. Vanzetti in particular became a hero to a whole generation of liberal intellectuals, who memorized phrases from his unidiomatic but powerful speeches and letters."*

The following three tributes to Sacco and Van-
zetti were printed in the I.W.W. press. The first,
"Sacco and Vanzetti" by the popular poet Jim
Seymour, was printed in the Industrial Pioneer
(December 1921). The second, "A Jest," by an
unknown writer who signed herself "Lisa," was
printed in the Industrial Pioneer *(July 1924).*
The third, also from the Industrial Pioneer *(July*
1924), is an article by Matilda Robbins (Rabino-
witz), who was active in the I.W.W. Sacco-Van-
zetti Defense Committee.

SACCO AND VANZETTI

By JIM SEYMOUR

What's all this fuss they're makin' about them
      guys?
Darned if some people ain't kickin' because they
      got
What was comin' to 'em;
Sayin', be Jesus,
It's 'cause they're reds.
That's bad enough,
But that ain't all—
Not by a damn sight.
Why, man alive,
They're only a couple o' God damn dagoes!
I don't see how anybody can expect white people
To do anything for the likes o' them.
What are they good for anyway?
What's their whole damn tribe good for?
There don't any of 'em know anything
Till they get over here.
When they get over here they hear some good
      music—
Band pieces an' grand op'ra an' jazz.
Why, they can put a nickel in the piano
An' hear the very latest!
An' as fer arky—arky—
Fine building—
Why, you'd think they never even looked
At our office buildings.
An' how about that statue of McKinley in the park!
Solid cast iron, be Jesus!

An' books—oh, boy!
Didn't they ever hear about Elinor Glyn?
Or Diamond Dick?
Or Marie Corelli? . . .
Or the free poet-ry?

Why the hell don't they read
An' learn something?
Then maybe they'd ketch up with the people
Tha't got wireless telegraphs.

But the hell of it is, they ain't got no—
Wotta ya call it?—
Oh yes, no historic past.
If they ever get one o' them they'll be all right.
Then they can talk about 1776
Instead of yellin' their fool heads off
About Garrybaldeye an' Spartycuss.

But they're nothin' but God damn dagoes.
Now *me:* I'm an American, *I* am.
We're the real people, *we* are.
We ain't dagoes—not on yer tintype.
We got railroads, 'n' telephones 'n'—
*Auto*mobiles 'n'—
Office buildings 'n'—
Them places where ya look at the stars.
An' we got some of the biggest deserts in the
      world.
An' we keep 'em unirrigated in spite o' hell 'n' high
      water.
There ain't nobody gointa make *our* land so dang
      cheap
That ev'rbody can own a piece of it
An' put the price o' truck
Down t' nothin' . . .
Not us.
We ain't dagoes.

No s'r, I ain't sheddin' no tears
Over them two guys.
It serves 'em right.
It ain't so much because they're reds—
That's bad enough, God knows,
But bein' a damn ignorant foreigner is the limit.
They not only don't know nothin' about books 'n'
      music,
'N' inventin' 'n' science,
'N' makin' purty pictures 'n' such things,
But they don't even know howta talk
The American language right.

Send 'em up, say I,
Show 'em that *our* courts is American.
We don't get our law from Italy.
We don't care whether they done it or not.
To hell with 'em!
They're dagoes.

O UNITE SURGING UNEMPLOYED

ect Contract
Completion In 1938

at 50 Foot Bores; Six Companies
Contract; Total Cost To Be
er Temperature About 125

a statement given by the Six
ed of the Utah Construction Co.
atel and Kaiser, McDonald and
ea and Co., who were awarded
e Hoover (Boulder) dam for
vill be the construction of four
ter and 4,000 feet long, two on
er to divert the water around the
the work.

**VANCOUVER MEN
STARVE ON THE**

UNION OF J
IN CHICAG
WITH VIE

Jobless Workers Wl
On To Join N
Cards Ready

New York,
cisco, all cities
tance, have swu
of the I. W. W. t
ing the Six Hour
workers instead
tion, the danger
Get going, fello
industrial center
now is the time t

With the rapid spread of this leaflet among the unemployed calls are increasing
daily upon the General Office of the I. W. W. for copies. Fifty thousand copies have been
distributed free and o' s are ready for distributi Thr to

Industrial Solidarity, March 24, 1931.

2

A JEST

By LISA

Old Lady Life has strange gifts
In her rag-bag carry all.
You can hear her cackle indecently as she hands
    them around.

There is an Italian man—
His name is Bartolomeo Vanzetti.
He has a round face, and genial drooping
    mustache,
But his eyes are gaunt with love
For that Old Harridan.
Mostly he is sober, but when he smiles
A thousand sunbeams dance a jig around him.
He is a man who hates all moneyed things.
Joy comes to him through velvet, starless nights
    and yellow days;
Through those, his masters first, and now his
    friends,
He served in solitude—
Karl Marx, and young Rousseau,
And Tolstoy, Dante, and Garibaldi

And many hundred others.
Joy comes to him through teaching brother-love
And freedom to those slaves,
Whose slavery tears his heart.
He has no hate for little things
Like men and gods—
But most, most bitterly he hates
That ceaseless, grinding mill
That some call capital and others greed—
That grinding, grinding, grinding, night and day
Crushes those men he loves to nameless dust.
His life was crowded out of time for love
Of women.
But children used to crawl upon his back
To tweak his hair, and like a bear
He'd growl and shake them off
And they would scream with laughter and climb
    back.
Sometimes he was a laborer, a cook,
A dish wiper behind a dirty bench.
He fished, he was a porter, kept a store,
And times he roamed about from place to place
Just living.
A dish of ravioli and a not too good cigar
Made Plato all the sweeter
To Vanzetti.

Wouldn't you think that shameless Old Spinster
Would be generous to a man like that?
She cackled indecently and pawed through her
    rag-bag carry-all
Then she handed out a conviction of
Murder in the First Degree
For a particularly bloody business.
The Old Lady has a wry sense of humor.

3

ONE OF OURS

BY MATILDA ROBBINS

We waited. The high-ceilinged room with iron bars for walls through which could be seen the stone stairs leading to tiers of cells, was the prison reception hall. It was June outside, but here the stone floor and the cold, stale air coming up thru the grated walls chilled. Keys clanked. Doors opened and shut. Huge doors that were portions of the walls. They were opened by a guard whose sole duty seemed to be the opening and shutting of these doors. Opening and shutting of doors. He clanked his keys. They were the only living thing about him. He moved like an automaton opening and shutting doors. His face was expressionless. The guard at the table in the center of the dim, gray hall looked neither to the left nor right of him. He sat rigid, looking straight ahead of him. Into the depths he seemed to look through the grated wall.

Doors opened and shut. Keys clanked. Children came to see their fathers. Mothers their sons. Wives their husbands. A young prisoner was smiling up at his sweetheart. Looking up into her eyes ingratiatingly. His own eyes were feverish. There were deep marks around them of sleepless nights and torment.

The west wing door opened and shut. The guard shook his keys and stepped aside. Vanzetti! He came toward us with a quick, springy step, his figure taut, his wonderful smile falling upon us like a pale ray of sunlight. He shook hands with us. "I am so pleased to see you, comrades!" How soft and vibrant his voice! How his sensitive mouth quivered under his drooping mustache.

I had not seen him in three years. Not since that scorching day in July, 1921, when I saw him and his fellow victim, Sacco, in the steel cage in a Massachusetts' courtroom. He leaned intently forward, his soft gray eyes full of questioning and of sorrow, while about him was being cast a net of lies upon which the Commonwealth built up its case and found him and Sacco guilty of murder. There was a light in those gray eyes then that could not be extinguished. Four years of the dim cell in the west wing have failed to extinguish it.

We talked. It was hard for me to bring the words up out of my throat. They got mixed up with the tears welling up in it and hurt with their throbbing. Vanzetti has a soft, melodious voice, but charged with the passionate appeal of the dreamer and the social rebel. Except for his comment that his ill-ventilated cell hurts his lungs and that he cannot see the sky from the prison workshop where he makes automobile plates, he did not refer to himself again. But he repeated twice that he could not see the sky. He wanted so to see the blue sky!

How eager he was for news of the proletarian movement! How those soft eyes would light up with hope of labor's triumph; how sadden at labor's defeats!

Vanzetti has learned English during his four years of prison. He speaks it with the precision of a foreigner acquiring a new tongue. But he invests it with a charm of liquid inflection with which his own Italian tongue is so exquisitely beautiful. When he spoke to his two Italian friends who were with us, it was like music that rose up and vibrated through the prison catacomb. His smile was like a benediction. His eloquent hands play upon the hearts.

"You have many friends everywhere," I said to him, "friends who love you and will continue to work for your liberation."

I shall always remember the wonderful light of gratitude that came into his eyes as he said, "Ah, I know, I know, I feel. That is why I am still living."

Still living! This noble soul, this generous heart, this dreamer of human brotherhood and beauty still living under the shadow of the electric chair! There was the night when 20,000 volts of lightning snuffed out the life of one man! What a night of horror! He lies awake thinking of the men killed and the men that kill. Passionate apostle of freedom and of service to mankind; rebel against a world where men maim their fellow men in the name of law; where justice is in the hands of men who cannot hear, who cannot see, who cannot understand the spirit of Vanzetti.

The jailor brought a little piece of yellow paper and slipped it into Vanzetti's hand. He clutched it. Under his mustache he bit his lips. The prison clock struck four. The visit was at an end. I held his hand for a moment and quickly turned away. Doors were opening and shutting. Keys clanked. I looked back. With head high and quick step Vanzetti was walking through the grated wall of the west wing.

4

The I.W.W. Marine Transport Workers Union, started in 1913, reached its peak of influence about 1923. It had members on waterfronts and among seamen, engine crews, and stewards on boats sailing from the Atlantic and Pacific coasts and *the Gulf of Mexico. In 1919 the M.T.W. established a Latin American branch with headquarters in Buenos Aires. During the 1920's members of the union struck jointly with members of the International Longshoremen's Association in Portland and helped tie up the ports of San Pedro, Aberdeen, New York, Philadelphia, Baltimore, Mobile, and Galveston during the 1923 I.W.W. protest strike against the continued imprisonment of "class war prisoners." Conflicts with other dockworkers' and seamen's unions contributed to losses in M.T.W. membership and by the mid 1930's the union had lost its effectiveness.*

"The I.W.W. on a Full-Rigged Ship" by Harry Clayton was printed in the Industrial Pioneer *(September 1926). It is one of the few stories about the influence of I.W.W. unionism on a sailor's life.*

Industrial Worker, July 26, 1932.

THE I.W.W. ON A FULL-RIGGED SHIP

By Harry Clayton

A considerable amount of trade is still conducted in sailing vessels. These old relics of a bygone industrial era are, like other backwaters of capitalism, an opportunity for exploitation of labor to make up for technical inferiority. The fact that they can be still kept running shows that the power of exploitation is something marvelous. As I am now a slave on a "windjammer" and have not seen this particular part of the capitalist system recently exposed to the shame it deserves, I will take this opportunity to spread a little information about it, not new perhaps to the marine workers, but probably interesting to those who have never "gone to sea."

We signed on "The Star of Russia" in Tacoma, June 1st of this year and are now out at sea thirty days. During that time we have seen but one steamer, the "President Wilson," and have sighted no land except some island of the "Union Group" —these a long distance away over the waters of the South Pacific. How long the voyage will take depends entirely on the winds. A direct course to our final destination would be something like 6,000 miles, but we are apt to cover 10,000 or more because of weather conditions over which we have no control.

A Venerable Old Hulk

The "Star of Russia" is a full-rigged sailing vessel, formerly owned by the Alaska Parkers' Association. It has been sold by them to a French company in New Caledonia, a French possession, 700 miles off the north coast of Australia, where the French capitalist government maintains a penal and exile colony, and inflicts like blessings of civilization upon the native population. The French company expects to strip down our ship and use it as a barge in Noumia, New Caledonia.

Talk as you like about the famous old shell games, three card monte games, and other million to one chances to lose money which the gambling fraternity has invented, but those propositions were highly moral and fair compared with the deals handed to the workers in these days. Our case, that of the "Star of Russia," is one in point. The Alaska Parkers, a Guggenheim outfit, finds it

convenient to dispose of this relic of the past, so they sell it to the Frenchmen for many times its original cost. But they are not satisfied with this, they must make still more profits and take out of the workers' hides the cost of delivering the obsolete old hulk. So workers in Tacoma load her with timber to be delivered and sold at ports on the way for a handsome profit, and this much more than pays the few dollars the crew get for delivering the ship itself to the buyer in Noumia. They put on 1,500,000 feet of lumber in Tacoma; 250,-000 feet will be discharged at Appia, Samoa, our first stop, and the rest at Noumia.

A Senator Speaks of Ships

And what do we get out of it? If you believe some people, we ought to pay for the privilege of living such a happy life. Senator Free, of California, in speaking officially on maritime affairs, said in substance that all that is required of those who man the ships of every sea is a strong back and a weak mind, and intimated that of course that is all they should be paid for. He was speaking in opposition to a raise in wages for American seamen. He arrived at this conclusion after making a few trips as a first class passenger on a steamboat.

This wordy congressman from the worthy state of California now knows full well that any lubber, himself included, can box the compass, keep the ship on its course in very troubled water, pull the braces, square and brace the yards, "jump up aloft" (sometimes 200 feet or more) and make fast the sails, launch the lifeboats without mishap to life or limb, splice wire and rope, set up standard rigging, stand by the fore bolling when the top sail is hauled in tacking ship, go up the old wooden gallen yard and put on a head earing without using the bull wunger. The good congressman is quite sure that any lubber, himself included, will know the difference between a bunt line and a gant line, and will realize when it is necessary to rig down a royal yard. Should the elements tear the sails to shreds, the expert Congressman Free will tell you that no skill or intelligence is necessary to distinguish between the roping of a sail and the flat seam in order to use a palm and needle; most any "hairy ape" will know how to put in a reef cringle when it is torn away; the seaman with nothing but muscle headgear to recommend him will keep cool and collected in times of trying emergencies when the lives of all on board depend on his executing complicated and technical orders with precision and exactness. Nothing need be said of the courage (perhaps the congressman doesn't know what it means) needed to face snowstorms and climb aloft to make fast sails while terrific gales are raging and when cold blasts have covered the rigging with ice.

Well, Congressman Free was discussing the wages of sailors. He probably knows, but how many of the workers on land realize, how little a seaman has to look forward to when he reaches his voyage's end? Ordinary seamen receive $47.50 on Shipping Board Vessels, and "A. B.'s" get $62.50. Crews on other ships (they are in a majority) rate less wages—even as little as $20 a month on the Panamanian Line. One cannot be particular as to what flag he sails under, as economic necessity knows no national boundaries. At the highest rates a seaman can earn $750 for a 365-day year, which means that he would have to have a steady berth, a thing that almost never happens; there is a long time of waiting between trips that must be spent "on the beach" in unremunerative idleness.

But wages are not after all our major interest, or should not be. One of the most deplorable features of the whole system is the fact that the workers in all industries measure their welfare almost exclusively in dollars, in the amount of wages paid them, neglecting conditions, and especially living standards. The workers as a whole do not yet realize that since they produce all the wealth that there is, they are entitled to the very best and finest there is in life. One who makes this assertion will still meet with ridicule from workers themselves. They think it a huge joke when anybody seriously affirms that workers should ride in Pullman cars instead of box cars and in first class cabins instead of stuffy, foul-smelling fo'c'sles, or if one says that workers should have choice cuts of meat instead of hamburger steak—and in general should scorn the scraps and crumbs of the social product and demand and take the best.

On ship board they may not even get enough scraps. On this particular ship we know what actual hunger is. As I write it is just past midnight. Those on the "graveyard watch" (12 to 4 A.M.) are on duty. The night is cold, the kind of a night when men would relish a warm cup of coffee, but we are not allowed even that. The table is bare with the exception of some dry bread. We would like to have that congressman here!

When we are fed it is nothing wonderful. There was a time, when I enjoyed the hospitality of the State of Sovereign Moronity, California, that I looked upon beans as a hateful abomination. But now pork has usurped the place of beans in my hierarchy of dislikes.

Our cook hasn't washed himself since the three wise men went to visit the savior; the crew has him marked for frying if we should ever be wrecked and cast adrift on some foodless island, for he is already larded. But our cook, God rasp his greasy hide, is a genius of a sort. He can think of more ways to cook pork than the bible has contradictions. We get pork plain, parboiled, souped, fried, made into cakes, as wet hash and as dry hash, and as a spread for bread. Salt, fat pork it is, without a streak of lean, for breakfast, dinner and supper, all these many days. It's ancient, too; I'm inclined to think that we are just now eating, on this voyage, the male of that famous pair of swine that was saved from the wrath of God at the time of the flood.

We begin to think kindly of cannibalism. It is said that these South Sea Islanders had only one domestic animal, the pig. What wonder that they went to any extreme to secure a change of diet? And these supposedly ignorant savages of New Caledonia and such places live on the most aristocratic meat in the world, man meat, while we poor sailors get the flesh of that mud wallowing, filth devouring, slime hound, the hog—and eat it right to the bristly snout! It's not fair.

Of course, there is other food served to us. There is salt canned horse. Poor old Dobbin! After long years of arduous service, his well hardened muscles to be ungratefully stewed and dished out to us, his fellow slaves! This "hoss" we are eating now, I am persuaded, is the same identical one made famous so many years ago in song and story by Oliver Wendell Holmes—the "hoss" that pulled the One Hoss Shay.

Then, salt cod! Salt cod laid to rest in a hogshead when the art of salting was first invented, along about the time they built the Great Chinese Wall!

Looking forward to meal time is about as joyful as the last days of a condemned man.

On this sort of diet we are supposed to work twelve hours a day in fair weather and any number of hours in bad weather, to be called from our bunks in the wee hours of the morning to help tack ship, or to climb aloft in the dangerous, shrieking dark. It is far-fetched imagination that can find any pleasurable romance in this. Poets sing the beauty of the stars, but men who work watches of four hours on and four off find themselves too fagged to enjoy anything but the tired doze of a beast. Even the impressiveness of the mighty Pacific Ocean palls on one when we see nothing but its vast expanse of water, day after day.

This sort of life is bad for men, and surely nobody has to be convinced of it. But it was not until the I.W.W. came aboard this ship that anything was done to help much. On the last trip the whole crew was unorganized. There was a mixture of nationalities, and two men were part colored. The second mate, who is a born sucker, took every mean advantage of them and roundly abused them, calling the two mixed bloods, "Niggers," and "Black Bastards," flourishing a gun while he did all this.

Seven of that crew are still with us, but you can bet your sweet life that none of them are abused in the manner described, by mate, second mate, or skipper. As a matter of fact, the second mate now gives "orders" in a tone of apology. We made him realize right from the start that we were sticking together against those "aft" and that we would consider an injury to one an injury to all, resenting it with direct action.

This condition was brought about by the fact that soon after we came aboard, we lined up the seven old members of the crew, making it 100 per cent organized, I.W.W. We found that the old-timers on board had been working for less than the Shipping Board wage. We held a meeting, formulated demands for a uniform scale but didn't present them until the skipper came to give orders to "cast off lines." How could the master win and how could we lose with this kind of direct action tactics? He couldn't do anything else but give in. He has to submit or stand to lose many times the sum involved in the raise in wages.

It didn't take a ton of beef to convince the new members of the I.W.W. on this ship that the I.W.W. form of organization can deliver the goods. They may not all stay with the union, but the majority of them will, and they will be real social rebels. It is rebels we need.

The skipper may try some tricks on us at the end of the voyage, but we look to our solidarity to frustrate him. As I was writing the above he had the messboy in his cabin to feel him out about the crew. He asked the messboy, "Are you a W? You better keep away from them, Young Man, it's a good thing to keep clear of those W's."

But his whole crew are "W's" now.

5

Following his release from an Idaho prison where he had been sentenced under the state's criminal syndicalism law, I.W.W. organizer E. S. Embree settled in Colorado to build the skeleton of a coal miner's union in that area. Progress was slow until August 1927, when half of Colorado's 12,000 miners responded to the I.W.W. call for a protest strike against the execution of Sacco and Vanzetti. After that successful two-day demonstration, organization of the miners proceeded rapidly, and on October 18, 1927, under I.W.W. leadership, the miners started a walk-out which lasted until February of the following year. The unsigned poem "Hold Fast: the Cry of the Striking Miners" was printed in Industrial Solidarity (*January 17, 1927*).

HOLD FAST: THE CRY OF THE STRIKING MINERS

They buried us for eighteen hours in their slimy
    burrows,
They killed us by the thousands beneath their
    rotten tops,
They blew us skyward from the muzzles of the
    gassy shafts.
They paid our sweat and blood and broken bones
    With wormy beans and rancid fat.
They made us live in shacks unfit for swine and
    dogs.
They forced us to go begging crusts of bread
    From brothers poor as we, displaying stumps
    and
    Blinded eyes as our right to beg.
They kept us in their stinking camps behind
    barbed wire
    And stockades like prisoners of war, like
    convicts
    Doing time.
And scarcely had the last clod hit our coffin when
    they drove
    Our loved ones from their company shacks—
    To scrub, and wash, to beg or steal,
    Or starve or rot.
And then we met in the dark of night, in culverts,
    caves,

And deserted shafts to find a way from woe and
    want,
From slavery and misery.
Thus the Union was born.
How we struggled, how we fought and bled
    For that puny Union babe. Oh, the tears we
        wept
    And the blood we spilled and the lives we paid
    To raise that precious child!
At Braidwood, Ludlow, Panther Creek, at Mingo,
    Latimer and Virden,
    Mute tombs still speak of the price we paid
    For our Union.
We, too, had our Valley Forge, where we slept on
    frozen ground

With shivering limbs and empty guts.
We, too, left the tracks of bleeding feet in the snow
    Of many a camp.
We, too, had our Fredericksburg and our
        Appomattox
    In the war to preserve the Union.
We, too, had our Mons and Argonne fighting for
    democracy.
Now, you ask us to desert our Union—the Union
    that made us free.
You ask, and the hell we will.
Ask a starving mother to swap her child for a pot
    of beans.

Industrial Worker, June 6, 1936.

THE UPPER CRUST

"Why, you dear fellow—I suppose you're writing a
poem about Mother Nature?"
"Nuts, lady, I'm just figuring out when I'll be dead
from starvation."

6

*"Education" by Clifford B. Ellis is taken from the
I.W.W. pamphlet* Twenty-Five Years of Industrial
Unionism *(Chicago, 1930). Ellis, who later be-
came one of the editors of the* Industrial Worker,
was also author of an important I.W.W. pamphlet,
Unemployment and the Machine *(Chicago, 1934).*

*An accountant by trade, Ellis taught for a while
at the Work Peoples' College. He was a well-
known labor orator, especially in the Portland,
Oregon, area.*

EDUCATION

By Clifford B. Ellis

Editor of The Industrial Worker

THE PURPOSE OF EDUCATION

Education, in a practical and applied sense, may
be defined as that training which enables one to
understand and adapt one's self to material reality.
When we say "material" we remove the question
beyond the field of metaphysical philosophy. The
primary concern of the average human is to make
a living—to survive—and that is a purely material
problem. It deals only with the material factors
of health, education and access to the material
means of life unrestricted by man-made laws and
inhibitions. If all men and women had an equal
opportunity to make a living, education might be
reduced to a simple and uniform course of instruction; but where equal access to the means of
life is denied, the uniformity of school and college courses leading to uniform "degrees" makes
the usual education no education at all. Most of
our education today is mere mental gymnastics.
It is designed not to fit one to make a living, but

adapt one to the social order and teach respect for the class division of society into masters and wage slaves.

If education is to prepare one to perform the duties of life, as Webster says, it is apparent that it should be specialized to suit the needs of the individual. It is assumed by our educators that all members of society have certain duties in common, such as duties to the State, a common moral code and the amenities of social intercourse. If all the members of society were of approximately equal economic condition, the assumption might be accepted as a practical working proposition; but in a society divided by class lines, it is an absurdity. The most important material fact of modern social organization is completely and deliberately ignored in education; namely, that society is divided into two fairly well-defined classes consisting of those who work for wages and those who exploit the wage workers for profit and live by a species of gambling in the wealth produced by the other class.

Even technical education is divided quite unnaturally and unnecessarily into two branches along class lines. These are the mechanical arts on the one hand and the so-called professions on the other. No one can tell just where the line of division between the two branches should be drawn. No one knows just at what point a carpenter becomes an architect or a building engineer; or at what point a reporter becomes a "journalist" or when a real estate huckster becomes a "realtor." Obviously, the line of division lies outside of the technical factors involved and concerns itself with something else. Roughly, it depends on whether you are going to use the technical knowledge gained by study to do useful and practical things—to produce wealth—or whether you are going to use it in the exploitation of those who do the useful things. Or it depends on whether you are going to be a wage worker, get a "job" and draw wages; or whether you are going to exploit or direct the exploitation of wage workers; in which latter case you draw a "salary" or fees or profits and hold a "position." These distinctions have arisen with the advance of bourgeois society. In the earlier stages of capitalism and before, no such divisions existed. Benjamin Franklin never took a formal scientific course leading to a professional degree; Lincoln did not become an "L.L.B." by reading law as he lay on his stomach before the fireplace by the light of a pine-

knot; the inventors whose work revolutionized modern society such as Stephenson, Watt, Arkwright, Eli Whitney, Blanchard, Elias Howe, Samuel F. B. Morse, Robert Fulton and others were just workers; they had no degrees and were not "professors." The class lines had not yet been sharply drawn when these did their work. They were members of a revolutionary class that had just come into power and they sprang from the masses of the common people. The necessity of educating them in the mental attitude of the ruling class had not yet developed in the minds of the rising bourgeoisie.

These distinctions of class grew out of the economic division of the people into masters and wage slaves as capitalism developed from the close of the eighteenth century onward. The pioneers of capitalism were revolutionists—an oppressed class. They were not distinguished or distinguishable in their earlier origins from the masses of peasants, artisans and laborers who were victimized, robbed, "plundered, profaned and disinherited" by the feudal nobility against whom they made common revolutionary warfare.

Our early bourgeois idealists thought they were establishing a "natural" society to succeed the social organization founded upon the artificialities of special privilege, birth and aristocratic rank. They asserted with perfectly naive sincerity that "all men are created equal"; that is, equal in the opportunity to engage in trade or business and by cleverness and artfulness, to get the best end of a business dicker. It was the philosophy of glorified huckstering and its avatar was a pushcart peddler exalted to the n-th degree of success. It was quite natural in an age when vast new continents were open to adventures for exploitation and when the individual trader was free to pit his wits against every other individual trader on a fairly even basis, unhampered by the gigantic combinations and mergers of the modern world. It then seemed needful only to rid the world of the feudal laws in restraint of trade to free the world and establish a democracy of opportunity in which only the naturally inferior would fail.

But, as H. M. Hyndman says, "events move faster than minds." The rise to power of this trading and exploiting class after the revolutionary destruction of the power of the feudal aristocracy, quickly developed the same class divisions and class contradictions that had formerly characterized feudal society. The trading class, formerly

The Upper Crust

"Yeah—he's the bosses son—learning business from the bottom up."

Industrial Worker, June 13, 1936.

repressed, became the dominant class. It soon acquired class consciousness and awareness of the property distinctions that separated it by an immeasurable gulf from the wage workers who created the commodities in which it trafficked. But the ideas and ideology of its origins persisted in its educational system and education was founded upon the fallacy that bourgeois society had established its ideal—equality of opportunity. It persists in that absurd assumption today, when the integration of its capital, the concentration of wealth into fewer and fewer hands, with the spread of its dominion across the world have absorbed the formerly undeveloped resources of the earth and left the newer-born generations nothing but the opportunity to become wage slaves to

the class which owns and controls the tools of wealth production and all the natural resources of land and minerals. These newer arrivals upon the world scene constitute a distinct class in society. They are the disinherited millions, ever increasing in relative and absolute numbers, who are born without wealth and educated into a social universe in which they have neither property nor the means of acquiring property. They constitute the world proletariat—the masses who have nothing to traffic in but their labor power which they must sell to the owning and employing class for the right to live. To impose upon them an impractical bourgeois education in which the idea of growing rich by engaging in trade and business prevails, when they will never have that opportunity, and when the State itself is devoted to the business of barring them from such an opportunity and fixing their status as wage slaves eternally, is an obvious absurdity. And yet that is just what bourgeois education does.

By way of practical illustration, we have selected at random from the hundreds of classified ads in the weekly "Nation" under the heading, "Positions Wanted," the following three, which are typical of the absurd miseducation for a career in life in which the opportunities are disappearing as the class system in society develops a class crisis:

YOUNG MAN, university senior, competent to tutor in Latin, French, Greek, Music, English, desires position with family for summer. An excellent companion for adults. Drives car well. Box 2368, c/o The Nation.

VERSATILE YOUNG MAN, college graduate, would like to make a travel-tour with family, as tutor. Authority on drama, English, French, Latin. Plays piano well, drives any make of car. Charming adult conversationalist, indispensable at the bridge-table. Box 2369, c/o The Nation.

HARVARD LAW STUDENT desires job for summer; experienced chauffeur, lifeguard, swimming instructor, hotel clerk, waiter, and tutor. Anything will do. What have you? Box 2287, c/o The Nation.

An "authority on drama, English, French, Latin. Plays piano well, indispensable at the bridge table," wants a job driving a car! A "Harvard law student, chauffeur, life guard, swimming instructor, hotel clerk, waiter and tutor" wants a job at anything. "What have you?" Such is education in bourgeois society! Sterile versatility that leads to nothing and nowhere!

The purpose of education is to teach one to understand reality and to adapt one's self to it in the struggle for existence. Reality and the means of survival are one thing to a worker and quite another to an exploiter of labor; to one who has to make a living with his hands and skill and to another whose purpose in life and means of life are the deception and spoliation of those who labor. The one is a creator; the other is a beast of prey. They have nothing in common—not even a common morality. To instruct the workers in the righteousness of the methods and morality of a system that despoils them and denies them access to the means of life is to defeat the primary object of education. It is to discipline them as victims of a condition that not only does not adapt them to the realities of life, but makes them oblivious to the realities about them which work to their destruction.

Working Class Education

Workers' education is, of necessity, an education in class consciousness. It is so because the economic structure in which they are born and without adaption to which they can not survive, is owned and controlled by a distinct class—the capitalist class. If the truth is taught to the working class it must reveal to them the character of that function which they perform in the economic structure. It must show them how the economic structure works in all its parts. It must analyze the working of the pitiless machine and reduce to exact measurement the benefits which they as sellers of labor power—their inevitable lot—receive; and what the other class—the owners of the structure—receives. If it does not reveal this it fails to educate at all. It miseducates and deceives. It creates a false concept of the world and of social relationships. It prepares them for helpless exploitation and victimization. If the facts of society are taught to the worker he just inevitably becomes class conscious.

The necessity of class education is imposed upon the working class by the facts of industry. That striving toward life—the will to live—which is inherent in every living cell of life, makes it necessary to educate the workers in matters that are deleterious to their health, detrimental to their lives and restrictive of their chances of survival. The capitalist system or any system in which one class lives at the expense of and by the deliberate exploitation of another, is opposed to the chances of survival of the workers. Their lives are lived at a hazard by the imposition of adverse working and living conditions. Their meager share in the social division of the wealth produced by their labor is insufficient to sustain life. The hazard of existence is increased by their function in the economic structure as workers while that of the owning class is reduced at the expense of the workers. Life insurance and health statistics prove this to be a fact—a reality. To neglect instruction in such vital facts is to miseducate. And to fail to attribute the facts cited to their cause—a class system in society—is to lie by suppression of the truth. That is why education in class consciousness is necessary.

Class systems are not eternal. They are an incident in the history of the human family. Class division is at war with the biological forces that make for race survival. That is why every class system in society has ultimately been overthrown by revolution. That is why the growth of the economic structure, which is a thing distinct and separate from the race itself, has revealed a constant tendency to widen the scope of the ruling class and to embrace an ever widening number of the race. Modern history is a comparatively brief span of years compared to the biological ages. It is a period of some few thousand years as contrasted with the millions of years in which the race was developing from the firstlings of human kind. It emerges at its dawn from a stage of primitive communism in which the individual was supreme. It begins the building of a social economic structure. It gains security of existence by sacrificing individual liberty. But evermore throughout the comparatively brief period in which the economic structure has been in process of evolution, the biological forces have been at war with the class forms. Revolution after revolution has broadened the ruling class lines and admitted an increasing number of the race to opportunity. The slave owning patrician gave way before a more numerous class—the feudal nobility; the feudal nobility in turn was overthrown by a more numerous class—the bourgeoisie; the increasing numbers of the proletariat are challenging the bourgeoisie for control of the economic structure and the class lines have a tendency to broaden and disappear in a final classless society in which the workers will be the only class, embracing the entire human family, with ownership and control of the means of life in the hands of the collectivity. This is the final solution of social problems—industrial democracy.

Passing of Class Systems

The necessity that gave rise to classes in society has passed. The social economic structure is fairly complete. Its capacity to produce wealth has increased to a point where it is more than ample to provide sustenance for all who will work. The masses have been disciplined to use the social machinery socially without coercion. The only anarchic survivals are the ruling class and their parasitic existence. Production has been socialized. It remains only to socialize control of the economic structure and eliminate expropriation.

Workers' education comprehends this outline. Its purpose is to teach the facts of industry instead of the slave morality of the bourgeois schools. Its technical training is to develop technique for the co-ordination of the productive forces in production for use and not for the maintenance of a useless class of capitalist parasites. It is to render education a vital, living, needful thing that makes for human survival instead of suppression. It is to develop the spirit of freedom and democracy without which the race can make no progress.

The I.W.W. is engaged in this task because it is one of the necessary functions in working class progress. It is the light-bearer of modern democracy—industrial democracy. It is, like every progressive force in society, opposed by the class antagonisms of an outworn system of ruling class education in "social control." It is devoted to realism and scientific truth. It is opposed to class fictions and illusions. It is purely materialistic. Its purpose is to strip the social structure of all its traditional myths and lay its structure and its workings bare. It is to train the working class mind and hand to freedom from ruling class control and exploitation—to enable the working class to master the world and control it in the interest of mankind. It is to enable them to "build the structure of the new society within the shell of the old."

To accomplish this it carries on its work of education by the means that lie at hand—through its papers, pamphlets, lecture bureaus, and through its first established college, the Work Peoples College of Duluth. But more potent still is the education it carries on at the point of production, on the job.

7

Nothing is known about the Mrs. Mary Atterbury who wrote the satiric piece "Depression Hits Robinson Crusoe's Island." It was published in the Industrial Worker *(February 9, 1932).*

DEPRESSION HITS ROBINSON CRUSOE'S ISLAND

By Mrs. Mary Atterbury

"Friday," said Robinson Crusoe, "I'm sorry, I fear I must lay you off."

"What do you mean, Master?"

"Why, you know there's a big surplus of last year's crop. I don't need you to plant another this year. I've got enough goatskin coats to last me a lifetime. My house needs no repairs. I can gather turtle eggs myself. There's an overproduction. When I need you I will send for you. You needn't wait around here."

"That's all right, Master, I'll plant my own crop, build up my own hut and gather all the eggs and nuts I want myself. I'll get along fine."

"Where will you do all this, Friday?"

"Here on this island."

"This island belongs to me, you know. I can't allow you to do that. When you can't pay me anything I need I might as well not own it."

"Then I'll build a canoe and fish in the ocean. You don't own that."

"That's all right, provided you don't use any of my trees for your canoe, or build it on my land, or use my beach for a landing place, and do your fishing far enough away so you don't interfere with my riparian rights."

"I never thought of that, Master. I can do without a boat, though. I can swim over to that rock and fish there and gather sea-gull eggs."

"No you won't, Friday. The rock is mine. I own riparian rights."

"What shall I do, Master?"

"That's your problem, Friday. You're a free man, and you know about rugged individualism being maintained here."

"I guess I'll starve, Master. May I stay here until I do? Or shall I swim beyond your riparian rights and drown or starve there?"

"I've thought of something, Friday. I don't like to carry my garbage down to the shore each day. You may stay and do that. Then whatever is left of it, after my dog and cat have fed, you may eat. You're in luck."

"Thank you, Master. That is true charity."

"One more thing, Friday. This island is over-populated. Fifty percent of the people are unemployed. We are undergoing a severe depression, and there is no way that I can see to end it. No one but a charlatan would say that he could. So keep a lookout and let no one land here to settle. And if any ship comes don't let them land any goods of any kind. You must be protected against foreign labor. Conditions are fundamentally sound, though. And prosperity is just around the corner."

8

One of the feature columns of the Industrial Worker *for many years was a column by T-Bone Slim (Matt Valentine Huhta), which was headed, simply, "T-Bone Slim Discusses." Fred Thompson, one of the former editors of the* Industrial Worker, *described how T-Bone Slim went about putting together his columns: "He regularly kept a pad in his pocket—not a notebook, but a pad on which he wrote his inspirations in a fine script that editors gave to the printer without typing or editing. There usually was no continuity to his columns. They consisted of items as he jotted them down. . . . He was fond of unusual twists that could be given to words. He ran a feud with the Hearst front page columnist, Arthur Brisbane, and out of that feud came two of T-Bone's most favored expressions—'brisbanalities,' and 'Arthur Twistbrain.'*

"He was largely a 'loner,' hoboeing alone, rustling a job alone, and often seeking and getting the kind of job that kept him by himself, such as barge captain which he was for many seasons in the New York City port. This was not because he was unsocial—he periodically sought and enjoyed company and conversation or listening to the sound of people talking. But I think that he had a sort of built-in recording system for it, and liked to spend ten hours reviewing and digesting these sounds for every hour spent picking them up."

This example of T-Bone Slim's many columns was titled "T-Bone Slim Discusses the Big Potato" and was printed in the Industrial Worker *(July 12, 1932).*

T-BONE SLIM DISCUSSES THE BIG POTATO

Let me point out once more, in my gentle way, the depression in this country is not political and a billion politicians one or all working ain't gonna cure it; the running of a bunch of patriots ain't gonna cure it; the running of a bunch of christians ain't gonna cure it; the running of a bunch of convicts, combines or cleopatras ain't gonna cure it. These have little more effect on a trouble that is economic than has a row of brass monkeys.

To cure depression, you must join a good labor union, preferably the I.W.W.—whatever union you choose, it must be its composition—or no cure. If you do not join a labor union you thereby go on record as of being well pleased with the depression. And I hope you will continue to like it.

Life in a political arena is a precise reflex of the gigantic economic struggle as between banks and plants, going on, at this moment, in this country. Plants take a wallop at the banks and Brookhart goes spinning like a headless rooster in a cornfield. Banks haul off with an upper cut and Massachusetts goes wet. Plants land a long swing to the snout and Mooney stays in the can. Banks put in a low punch and Kresel shows signs of being an angel of high emprise. Plants rock banks' head with a terrific left to the jaw and Britt Smith, Centralia Boys, stay in Walla Walla, and so on.

Interference in this struggle by an outsider shall cause Banks and Plants to turn on the intruder.

Coolidge said we've got lots of prosperity, have some soup.

Harding before him said take the teapot, we got lots of it.

Hoover said, we've got lots of it and declared in favor of a moratorium just as Europe was about to pay its debts. We've got lots of it—last week in New York City I didn't get one single meal. What I got was as follows:

Forty-two cups of coffee (frail stuff). Sixty-two rolls of all description and some of no description at all.

Eighty-three slices of bread and sixty cubes of grease.

About one bathtubful of soup.

One mushmelon, eight bananas—all of 'em rotten.

THE UPPER CRUST

"And please don't let them sit down in my factory"

Industrial Worker, January 30, 1937.

Note: I didn't try to influence the city either one way or another—this diet is her voluntary contribution to science. It never occurs to N.Y.C. that Germans and Finns have thrived since time immemorial on full meals and that an occasional bellyful couldn't hurt a guy even if he is unemployed. Nay brother, political action is no action—it is a result.

For me to say, farmers or store keepers can remedy this depression by organizing farmer or storekeeper union is to say a falsehood—they can not. They are not numerous enough and they are not on the ground floor.

They are merely the flora in the potato patch—labor is the big baked potato. Labor is the only power in this world that can cure this depression—and cure it to stay cured. This it can do only by organizing a one big union of the workers and by declining all help from parasites or their representatives.

Industrial Worker, April 1, 1939.

THE UPPER CRUST

"He hates Jews, Catholics, Protestants, Negroes and himself."

The minute it gets any help from bosses of any shade or description the bets are all off—and the depression shall have a relapse. Labor or Oblivion!

P. S.—The fight between Banks and Plants is for to determine which shall be permitted to skin labor—a senseless, insane struggle.—Soup versus Worms: Do not think me unduly prejudiced against soup. Soup is all right in its place. I can conceive of nothing more suitable for fish to swim in—a combination of sport and nourishment, barbless breakfast you might say. And in re N.Y.C.'s soupability, let me say, I could have changed that at any time by lying a little, tell Mr. Knickerbocker that the soup-shower occurred the week before. He would have risen to the occasion promptly—but a test is a test. As in buying a pair of sox I fell one penny short of the price: Knickerbocker howled loud and long that he must not be driven to the wailing wall, he must get his full ten cents.

"Now lookit here, Knick," says I dropping the pennies into my pocket, "I'm a poor man whose family passed off by starvation.—Why not make it a gift of a pair of sox so I can cover my nakedness?" "I'll tell you what I'll do," says Knick, "I'll give you that pair of sox for nine cents."

You see, Knick stood to lose sox or gain nine cents—he chose the nine—business is business.

Soup we will have even in the workers' commonwealth, and the parasites shall eat it.

9

This song "by a Briggs striker" appeared in the Industrial Worker (*March 14, 1933*) *during the I.W.W. organizing campaign among auto workers in Detroit and an early sit-down strike of metal finishers at the Briggs Highland Park Plant.*

BALLAD OF BIG BOSS BRIGGS

By A Briggs Striker

(*Tune: "King of Borneo"*)

O, Walter Briggs came home one night
As rich as he could be;
He saw a letter on his plate
Where his meal ought to be.

"My dear wife, my darling wife,
My loving wife," said he,
"What is that upon my plate
Where my meal ought to be?"

"You big boob, you silly ass,
You lazy bum," said she,
"That is a telegram
As any fool can see."

So W. O. opened it
And this is what he read:
"Six thousand men have left the pen,
And now Production's dead."

"My dear wife, my darling wife,
My loving wife," said he,
"What can this wire really mean
That Henry's sent to me?"

"You big boob, you silly ass,
You lazy bum," said she,
"It simply means your men's on strike.
As sore as they can be."

So Big Boss Briggs, he took a plane
Up from the sunny South,
And when he saw that picket line,
He opened wide his mouth:

"Oh my, oh me, what shall I say?
These slaves want higher pay:
But I shall see Judge Conolly
And General Henry."

He cut "dead time"; with reason and rime,
He gave the big boys hell,
For Henry Ford, the Auto Lord,
His dollars and cents do tell.

Now Big Boss Briggs, O how he jigs,
He and his henchmen three:
"Heinie," Hund and Connoly
And Jacob Spolansky.

They called their dicks with riot sticks,
Police with tear guns, too;
But the men were onto their dirty tricks,
For they were nothing new.

Each paper tries to spread its lies;
But the strikers hold their line.
They organize, for they are wise—
Their union will be fine.

Then they'll grab each lousy scab,
They'll kick 'em in the pants;

And Big Boss Briggs and his stooling pigs,
O—O, how they will dance!

Now Walter Briggs comes home at night
As sore as he can be. . . .
"Those workers fight with all their might,
They'll wreck my factory."

"My dear wife, my darling wife,
I've got an awful pain—
My head aches, my belly aches—
They're driving me insane."

Etc. Etc.—. . . . . .

10

*The very popular "Boom Went the Boom" was
first published in the* Industrial Worker *(April 18,
1933). It was signed "W. O. Blee." It is the most
recent song to be added to the corpus of I.W.W.
songs in the little red songbook and was first
included in the twenty-fifth edition.*

BOOM WENT THE BOOM *

By W. O. BLEE

(*Tune: "Ta-ra-ra-Boom—dee—Ay"*)

I had a job in twenty-nine
When everything was going fine.
I knew the pace was pretty fast
But thought that it would always last.
When organizers came to town
I'd always sneer and turn them down:
I thought the boss was my best friend
And he'd stick by me to the end.

Chorus

Ta-ra-ra—BOOM—dee—ay
Ain't got a word to say,
He chisled down my pay,
Then took my job away.
Boom, went the boom one day,
It made a noise that way.
I wish I had been wise,
Next time I'll organize.

I had a little bank account,
Not very much, a small amount
Which to the savings bank I took
And all they gave me was a book.

I pinched on food, I scraped on rent,
I hardly ever spent a cent,
My little savings grew and grew,
I thought I'd be a big shot, too.

Chorus

Ta—ra—ra—BOOM—dee—ay,
It made a noise that way,
There went my hard-earned pay,
Saved for a rainy day.
I must have been a wick,
This soup-line makes me sick.
Where can that banker be?
He tore his pants with me.

Then finally it came to pass
That all I had to eat was grass.
The wolf don't bother anymore.—
He starved to death right by my door.
With soup and gas and club and gun
They tried to make the system run.
They said, "Dear friends, now don't get sore,
We'll make it like it was before."

Chorus

Ta—ra—ra—BOOM—dee—ay,
It busted up one day
These guys that stole my pay
Went flying every way.
All that I've got to say,
I hope they've gone to stay;
Each dog must have its day,—
Ta—ra—ra—BOOM—dee—ay!

11

*Louis Burcar was the pseudonym of an I.W.W.
member in Detroit who was active in the early
sit-down strikes in the auto industry. "Auto Slaves"
was printed in the* Industrial Worker (*July 18,
1933*) *during the period of intense I.W.W. organizing activity in the automobile plants in Detroit.*

AUTO SLAVES

(*Graveyard Shift—Stamping Plant*)

By Louis Burcar

With automatic movements timed to great
Machines, these metal-workers seem to reel
In some weird dance. Like marionettes they wheel
With insane music at a maddening rate.

Automatons . . . What if they learn to hate
Machines whose hungry maws demand a meal
Of metal—piece upon piece of sweat-stained steel?
They work. Monotony and madness wait . . .

For these are human beings racked with pain,
Grotesquely hued by blue-green mercury lights . .
Monotony within this noisy hell
Will breed maggots of madness in the brain—
Stop the tongue so it can never tell
Of torturing toil through these unending nights.

12

*Covington Hall's poem "The Politician Is Not My
Shepherd," which was frequently reprinted in the
I.W.W. press after it first appeared in the* Industrial Worker (*December 26, 1933*), *reflected the
skepticism of members of the organization toward
the nation's growing dependency on President
Franklin Roosevelt to solve the country's economic
problems.*

THE POLITICIAN
IS NOT MY SHEPHERD

By Covington Hall

The Politician is not my shepherd,
He turneth me over to the wolves,
Taking it on the chin,
Keeping my mouth shut,
Waiting for prosperity to come "around the corner."
Too much bull is weariness of the flesh,
Yea, I am fed up on it.
On the "New Freedom" and on "Normalcy,"
On the "Glorious Period" of the "Good Calvin,"
On "Rugged Individualism," and on "Misery Relief";
"Saving the Socialist Fatherland" put no
Fried chicken under my belt.
The "New Deals" or "Fair Deals" from the old
deck gets us no good.
Turning pigs into fertilizer puts no pork-chops on
our tables.
Plowing under cotton, no glad rags on our backs.
Paying landlords to keep workers from producing
wheat and corn, sugar and coffee, fruit and
everything.
And,
Taking all this undestroyed;
And,

Flooding the world with imaginary money,
May "Save the price structure"
But,
It is Hell on thee and thine, on me and mine.
And, me and mine, us and ours.
That's what's troubling me, oh, Fellow Workers!
And that's more than enough,
Yea, verily, I am burned out and turned sour with
    weary waiting for the Millennium—
2000 years this Christmas!
It is too long between drinks!
Besides,
Hooching oneself into freedom, peace and plenty
    ain't so hot.
The night before is all right, but . . .
The morning after!
Well! Fellow Workers, you ought to know how
    that was, is and ever will be.
There is nothing to it
As the Bible says,
"All politicians are liars."
Therefore, if ye would be "saved,"
Save yourselves.
And lastly hear this:
The only hope of "The Damned" is,
"The Damned I.W.W."
It is the One Big Union or
One wholesale starvation for us and ours,
O, Fellow Workers!

13

"Our Line's Been Changed Again," an anticommunist satire ridiculing the "United Front" or "Popular Front" of 1935–40, was published in the Industrial Worker *(November 16, 1935). Whether or not it was written by an I.W.W. member is not known. It was later credited to writer Alton Levy.*

OUR LINE'S BEEN CHANGED AGAIN

A COMMY WAR SONG

(*Tune: "Them Bones Shall Rise Again"*)

United fronts are what we love, Our line's been
    changed again.
From below and from above, Our line's been
    changed again.

Chorus:

I knows it, Browder, I knows it, Browder,
I knows it, Browder,
Our line's been changed again.

We once had unions by the score, Our line's been
    changed again.
But now these unions ain't no more, Our line's
    been changed again.

Chorus:

Bourgeois tricks we'll have to use, Our line's been
    changed again.
Our women must not wear flat shoes, Our line's
    been changed again.

Chorus:

Imperialist wars we once attacked, Our line's been
    changed again.
But since the Franco-Russian pact, Our line's been
    changed again.

Chorus:

While France is fighting you will see, Our line's
    been changed again.
The revolution must not be, Our line's been
    changed again.

Chorus:

We're now a party with finesse, Our line's been
    changed again.
With bourgeois groups we'll coalesce, Our line's
    been changed again.

Chorus:

Religion was an opiate, Our line's been changed
    again.
Since church groups with us demonstrate, Our
    line's been changed again.

Chorus:

We're simply Stalinists devout, Our line's been
    changed again.
We don't know what it's all about, Our line's been
    changed again.

Chorus:

Kaleidoscopic, what I mean, Our line's been
    changed again.
Now we're red and now we're green, Our line's
    been changed again.

Chorus:

The "New Deal" was a Fascist plan, Our line's
    been changed again.
Now Roosevelt is the people's man, Our line's
    been changed again.

Chorus:

The League of Nations we used to hate, Our line's
been changed again.
Now with it we've linked our fate, Our line's been
changed again.

Chorus:

Class against class, our slogan true, Our line's been
changed again.
The people's front, red, white, and blue, Our line's
been changed again.

Chorus:

14

The skit, "Nuthouse News," printed in the One
Big Union Monthly *(June 1938), is typical of the
skits written and presented by students at the
Work Peoples' College in Duluth, Minnesota. Formerly a Lutheran theological seminary, the Work
Peoples' College became first a school run by
Finnish Socialists, and then, about 1916, a resi-
dential college run by a board of directors which
included a majority of Finnish I.W.W. members.
During the winter, courses in Finnish and English
were offered in economics, labor history, public
speaking, mathematics, and English composition.
There was also a summer session for young people. Frequently, groups of students from the Work
Peoples' College went on tour to raise money by
presenting programs of skits such as "Nuthouse
News" at organizational meetings around the
country.*

NUTHOUSE NEWS

*A Skit Prepared by Work Peoples' College
Drama Department*

Scene: Fence with gate in it. Fence extends across
stage; gateway near middle. Arch over gateway
reads "NUT HOUSE"; sign suspended from center
of it: "No Nuts Allowed Except by Special Permission." The audience gets an eyeful of this before Hobo comes sauntering in, singing "Hallelujah, I'm a Bum."

Hobo sees butt of cigarette on walk. Picks it up
and starts re-rolling it for a smoke as Nut comes
along inside fence, slowly wheeling a wheel-bar-
row upside down. He watches Nut and laughs.

NUT: What are you laughing at?
HOBO: You.

NUT: What's so funny about me?
HOBO: You've got your wheelbarrow upside down.
NUT: What's wrong with that?
HOBO: You can't put anything in it when it's up-
side down.
NUT: That's why I keep it that way. If I turn it the
other way up, people may put something in it.
HOBO: You're not so crazy! What did they put you
in for?
NUT: I used to keep my barrow right-side-up like
you nuts.
HOBO: How come they put you in for that?
NUT: They used to fill it up that high with bricks.
HOBO: They can't put you in for that.
NUT: Well, I used to take my clothes off when at
work.
HOBO: What did you do that for?
NUT: I figured that if I had to work like a horse,
I might as well look like one, too.
HOBO: No—not so nutty after all.
NUT: Did you ever run one of these things? (*Indi-
cating barrow.*)
HOBO: Often—I'm an expert on that thing.
NUT: Which side did you keep up?
HOBO: I kept the other side up.
NUT: I'll bet that made it hard work—but if that
was the right way to run it, why didn't you keep
on running it?
HOBO: The job blew up.
NUT: An explosion?
HOBO: No—it got finished. We did all the work.
There wasn't anything more to do. We worked
ourselves out of a job.
NUT: You should have run it like I run mine. Where
are you going now?
HOBO: I'm going downtown to see if I can find
some breakfast.
NUT: I ate mine a couple of hours ago. Where are
you going to get it?
HOBO: I don't know, but I'll get it somewhere
likely.
NUT: I think you're crazy. Where are you going to
eat dinner?
HOBO: I don't know. If I can't get it in this town,
I'll get it in some other town.
NUT: I get mine at sharp noon everyday. You must
be goofy. Where are you going to sleep tonight?
HOBO: I don't know. Last night I found a pretty
good reefer.
NUT: What's a reefer?
HOBO: It's a box car with double walls, and an ice-
box in each end for keeping things frozen.

NUT: And you think that's a pretty good place to sleep? I always sleep in a nice, soft, warm, clean bed.

HOBO: Say, who are you anyway?

NUT: Last week I was Napoleon, but that was by my first marriage; when I got divorced that made me General Lee; but next week I'm going to be Washington crossing the Delaware.

HOBO: You can be Napoleon if you want to, but you insult me when you say you're George Washington. He was the father of our country. Do you mean to tell me he was crazy?

NUT: Haven't you seen a picture of him crossing the Delaware?

HOBO: Sure—every good American has.

NUT: Isn't he standing up in the boat instead of sitting down?

HOBO: Yes.

NUT: Isn't that crazy?—Say, how much of this country do you own?

HOBO: I don't own any of it.

NUT: Then you're crazy to call it your country. (*Starts to trundle away with barrow.*) Say, when you were running a wheel barrow what were you making?

HOBO: We were building a flour mill.

NUT: What are you doing with the flour mill now?

HOBO: I'm not doing anything with it. It isn't mine.

NUT: How did you lose it?

HOBO: It never was mine.

NUT: If you fellows that built it don't own it, who does?

HOBO: Why the owners own it.

NUT: Did they work to build it?

HOBO: That kind of people never work.

NUT: The folks that didn't build it own it, and the fellows who built it don't own it. I think that's crazy.

HOBO: Why that's the way with every job. When we get through making something, we never own it. It always belongs to the people who don't work.

NUT: That's why I want the guard to turn this sign around. The way it hangs now, people would think the nuts were on this side of the fence, wouldn't they?

HOBO: That's why it's there.

NUT: But it should be turned around, for the nuts are all on the other side. (*Starts to trundle barrow away, but stops.*) Say, when do you think you'll start running a wheel barrow again?

HOBO: I'll get a job soon—I hear we may go to war.

NUT: That's terrible! Who are you going to kill?

HOBO: It may be the Japs and it may be the Chinks, I'm not sure who it will be.

NUT: Where are you going to kill them, in town here?

HOBO: Hell, no—we'll go over to their country and kill them.

NUT: Ever been over there?

HOBO: No.

NUT: Ever seen the fellows you're going to kill?

HOBO: No.

NUT: Did they ever hit you, or hurt you, or do anything to you?

HOBO: No.

NUT: And when you go to kill them, maybe they'll kill you?

HOBO: Sure, we've got to take that chance.

Industrial Worker, September 9, 1939.

THE UPPER CRUST

"Just work hard for the next 20 years, son, and maybe you'll be where I am now."
"Where's that, Pop?"
"On this side of the machine."

NUT: How far away do these Japs and Chinese live?

HOBO: I guess about three or four thousand miles.

NUT: So you're going three or four thousand miles to kill some poor people you never saw, who never hit you or hurt you or did anything to you, and you may be killed doing it? That is crazy . . . Or may be they're the fellows who took your flour mill away from you?

HOBO: No—those fellows live in Minneapolis.

NUTS Quick—before the guard comes—give me a hand and we'll turn this sign around.

HOBO: Maybe we ought to.

NUT: No—we can't do it now—I see the guard coming, and he won't let us.

HOBO: Don't those guards ever get afraid of you nuts?

NUT: No—I asked him once and he said that even if there were a thousand of us nuts and only four guards, they still wouldn't be afraid of us.

HOBO: Why?

NUT: He said it was because nuts never organize.

— CURTAIN —

15

During the Spanish Civil War, the I.W.W. had an assessment for the support of the C.N.T. and maintained friendly relations with the anarchist International Workingmen's Association. Many I.W.W. members fought with C.N.T. forces. This article by a Wobbly participant in the Spanish Civil War was one of a series that ran in the One Big Union Monthly *(April 1938).*

REMINISCENCES OF SPAIN

BY RAYMOND GALSTAD

It is midafternoon. We are in a huddle reading a bulletin that has just been posted on the wall. It contains a list of the names of men who are to leave for Paris this evening. Discharges and repatriation papers are in the office ready for distribution. Some read the bulletin and dash down the corridor to the office. Those unable to run just shuffle. There's a brightness in their eyes as though they just gulped a bracing drink. Satisfied smiles stretch across their sun-parched faces. Monosyllables of joy snag in their throats. They're the lucky ones. They're going home.

I'm new here. Just arrived from the hospital a few minutes ago. My name is not up yet. I might just as well get used to it here for a while. I think a tour of inspection of my new headquarters is in order, so I take a gander at the dormitory. My nose sniffs the smell of freshly laundered sheets strongly bleached. The odors are clean and medicinal like the hospital, or maybe my memory of the hospital is playing tricks with me.

Uniformed men sprawl across the beds taking "siestas" with their eyes wide open and their lips moving in conversation that sends up a hum of French, Spanish, and English. Over in a corner a few Frenchmen are making melody with the "Waiting Song," a tune composed by a wounded British veteran of the International Brigade while he waited at Albacete for his discharge papers. The soldiers make up their own words, as soldiers will, when inspiration moves them.

I introduce myself to a group and we start rubbing our memories together, making warm conversation. The front is still the favorite bone to chew on. We mentally place our bets on the outcome of the next battle. One intelligent face says the best defense is an attack, and nodding heads approve, and that puts the favorite bone back in the cupboard of memory until we become intellectually hungry for the Front again. We just sit and regard each other silently for a while with vacant wool-gathering eyes. It's not an embarrassing silence. It's just as if we intuitively agreed to dream for a few moments. I call them to attention with a question, and they all start talking at once. I gather there are a bunch of Americans and Canadians waiting here, but they're out doing the town right now, from what I'm told. I thank them for the information and take my leave of them.

I meet another American, and we walk into the messroom together. I put the bum on him for some tobacco. He says he ain't got none. Says he's been here four days and the Commissars ain't putting out, though he hears there's a whole warehouse bulking with Luckies. He's been down on the waterfront all day trying to mooch some butts from the English sailors, but he didn't have much luck. Wishes to hell his papers were O.K.'d so he could leave for the French border tonight. Even French smokes would beat nothing.

We bump into a Canuck who's been around a lot, and knows Barcelona to a "T." We learn from him that English smokes can be had from a bootlegger uptown. The stuff is priced, though, at one

THE UPPER CRUST

"How can I respect a man who lets a union bulldoze him?"

Industrial Worker, September 16, 1939.

hundred pesetas a pound, about two dollars in American coin, according to him, and my friend's chin drops like the '29 stock market. That's a lot of money for a buck private, earning seven pesetas a day, to have on him all at one time, we agree. But I was paid off this morning, and I'm still holding forty-seven pesetas, so I suggest we hold a conference on the matter. We decide to ask three others to chip in, and go off to round up the unsuspecting donors.

It isn't hard to persuade the other three to chip in. They want to inhale some smoke as badly as we do, so we collect the necessary money, and detail the Canuck to sally forth to the tobacconist's, and make arrangements to meet him in the park across the road from the barracks.

It doesn't take him long to carry out his mission. We see him coming back with a small tinfoil package with the evening light glinting off it, like sunstarts off a mirror. He's walking a great deal more leisurely than when he left us to go after the weed. A cigarette is dangling listlessly from a corner of his lips. We run up to him and relieve him of the burden, and nervously begin to fashion cigarettes with our fingers.

We stroll back across the road to the park, and our group grows to eleven members. They're attracted by the smell of burning tobacco. The park itself comes under discussion. One young soldier remarks that it's the finest and largest park in Spain. He says he likes the zoo and the museum, and the statues, but best of all he likes the palm trees, and the lime trees, and the orange trees. They give good shade in the day-time, and he likes shade, he says. Another soldier interrupts him and says he talks too much; that he should give others a chance. The youthful one makes excuses for his monopolizing the conversation. He says the doctors told him he would lose his voice any time now as a result of a shrapnel wound in his throat, and he's determined to hear his voice as much as he can as long as he can.

The mention of his wound invites the others to start talking of their disabilities, like a bevy of old ladies discussing their operations and their miscarriages. The names of the battlefields, Belchite, Guadamalga, Bilboa, Saragossa, Cordoba, and Madrid seem like a checkerboard of blood, becoming more gloriously gory as they talk about how they lost a leg, an arm, an eye, a hand, or acquired a scar as a precious souvenir of battle. The lad whose voice will go haywire notes pointedly that we didn't get any medals, but he's glad about it,

somehow because nobody will mistake him for a Commissar with all medals and no scars. We laugh a little at that.

An American West Coast seaman feels like rehashing the story of the part he filled in the Guadamalga offensive. He says it was a tough scrap. The Loyalists went up against the German troops and they had machine guns 'til hell wouldn't have 'em. How the Loyalists took their objective, Christ only knows! The boys were dropping all around him like ripe apples in a gale. He lost his buddy; saw him fall right in front of him, but he kept going. They got within throwing distance of the fascists and let loose with hand grenades. That's what got 'em. When you get close enough to toss the grenades, the fascists either come out of their trenches and meet you face to face, or they retreat. They hate like hell to be in the dug-outs when the grenades start pouring in. They don't want to be in the trenches when you're ready to jump 'em, either. Not when you got that cold piece of steel, two feet long, sticking on the end of your rifle. That's scary stuff, and plenty hard to take. And when a guy's on top, he's got all the breaks in the world, they know that. Just one good thrust, and you know there's one fascist scab that ain't gonna win the war for Franco . . .

He keeps talking about the strategies of combat in his tangy voice and the rest of us listen to the familiar details as if they were being carried out before our eyes. With his one arm he churns the air with emphatic gestures, his fist opening and closing like the maw of a sea anemone.

Speaking of battle tactics, a Britisher has something to say about the fight at the Cordoba front. His voice is clear and his language faultless, and he isn't selling his H's short like an English Cockney. All his listeners seem enlisted for action as they lean toward him to learn that the front was very quiet for several weeks, with no excitement at all, and no signs of war about. Then the Rebels came over the top with their right arms in salute, and singing the Internationale. It looked like they were surrendering. But they went into action and dished out hell. It was a furious hand to hand battle. But they were driven back to their trenches. Three days later they came over again with women on the lead. They used the girls as shields. The Loyalists held their fire and were nearly wiped out. Only fifty men returned from the skirmish, and every one of them wounded. The English Brigade lost over four hundred that day.

The listeners agree it was a moral victory, and

take some comfort in it, even though they regret the loss of Cordoba.

The Canuck was a chauffeur in the ambulance corps. He says his job wasn't a snap, either, what with administering first aid before loading the wounded into the ambulance, and driving over the rough roads full of shell holes, unloading at the base hospital, and driving back again . . . all the while providing a swell target for fascist bombers. He says it's no fun changing tires out in the battle areas with only a revolver strapped to your belt, and the wounded moaning in the bus, and a plane swooping overhead pouring lead into the ground around your feet. He says that a revolver is about as useful as a bow and arrow against a tank in such situations, and he rolls up his sleeve to display a groove of purple scars running from his wrist to his shoulder, just to prove the point.

We pass the tobacco around again, and the six of us who have a vested interest in the weed, walk away from the group, each one of us thinking we're paying too high a price for chinning with our fellow veterans. The Canuck lets them know what we're thinking, and they smile. One says he'd swap a story any time for a cigarette.

We walk into a nearby bar and order some drinks, and sit there while the town grows dark, waxing discursive again, but not about ourselves. The Asturian miners and their courageous fight in Santander, with only dynamite and mining tools as weapons, strikes us as an admirable display of guts. We tie up the story with miners' struggles everywhere, and try to prove our theory that miners are a brave lot because they toil under dangerous conditions where death stalks close at hand, and they get used to being brave without knowing how brave they are, and their work develops in them a reckless fatalistic spirit that makes them formidable fighters in battle. We conjured up the battles of the Molly Maguires, Ludlow, Paint Creek, Cripple Creek, Mesabi Range, the Rocky Mountain Fuel Company strike in Colorado in the United States; the sit-downs of the French miners, and we feel satisfied that our theory about the miners' militancy is adequately supported by history. Time passes. The yawning hour approaches, and we vote to go back to barracks and to bed.

Shafts of morning sun pierce the barracks' windows, and pry open the eyes of sleepy veterans. Some turn their faces into the pillows or pull the covers over their heads to ignore the rude intrusion of the sunlight. Others sit up; rub their eyes; pucker their lips to prime up saliva for their dry tongues, and make wry faces. A few who piled into the sheets late last night, hold their heads and emit Ohhhs of brain-ache. Hairy legs and wrinkled nightgowns change into militarily dressed vertebrates that a woman might look at without horror.

At breakfast the Canuck and I are talking to each other again, formulating our plans for the day. A lazy walking tour of the town seems agreeable to both of us, and we gulp down the food in haste to be off. The steward hollers at us to haul in the dishes, and we're full of blundering apologies, but he doesn't stop scowling at us through his shaggy brows. I can feel his stare itching my back as I stroll with the Canuck out into the street.

We walk awhile in silence, both feeling a sense of shame for forgetting to carry our dishes to the kitchen. We feel like kids caught with jam on their fingers. Disrupting the spirit and practice of cooperation is weighing heavily upon our consciences. With no high command running things at the waiting barracks, everything is left to the soldiers' initiative and rank and file judgment; and in running counter to that judgment, however slightly, we're feeling we betrayed the wishes of our fellow-soldiers. The Canuck looks at me, and we snap out of our conscience-stricken coma. He says we'll carry the dishes back and forth tomorrow just to make it up to the steward, and we laugh, forgetting all about it.

The buzz of industry whirrs in our ears as we pass through the factory district on to Rambla Street, the main thoroughfare, where we board a street car. We're used to the idea of riding street cars without paying any fare. Very reasonable people, these transportation workers. The Canuck tells me that before the war there were more people employed counting the money taken in by the street car and bus conductors than there were actually operating the vehicles of transportation. They just decided to put the cashiers to doing useful work by abolishing the price system in the transportation industry. The fare now is to look like a fighter, a worker, or a child. In other industries where the C.N.T.–F.A.I. have control, he is telling me, a modified wage-system is still the economic vogue, and will be for some time if the workers desire greater productive capacity. If they wish to build greater industries, they must necessarily pile up surpluses. The thing that's amazing about all this, in spite of the fact that workers still

POLITICANUS
A VILE BIRD
THAT LAYS
ROTTEN
EGGS

POLITICS

GOVT. LIES
CONTROLS
DICTATORS

UNIONS

CES

Industrial Worker, January 7, 1939.

its fur with its tongue. Night-time workers in trunks, and children naked, are swimming in the water and playing on the beach. We slip behind a crag and undress, and wade into the water with our shorts. The sailors best us in the swimming. They josh us a bit for our splashing like sidepaddlers, and offer to teach us the crawl and the sidestroke. But we're hopeless amphibians, the Canuck and I. They think we're okeh, for being revolutionists, though.

The Canuck starts indoctrinating the British navy with the C.N.T. philosophy, and they don't find it so bad, this class war "business." One gob confesses he joined the navy to escape the slums. Says he was willing to die for British imperialist capitalism; do anything, just so he didn't have to live out his span of life in London's Lower East End. He sees the sense of the class struggle plainly enough. The workers have got to organize and lose their chains and their slums, too. Says when he's through with his hitch in the navy he'd like to climb into the trenches and help these Loyalists. But he'll be scrubbing decks for six more years, and the Canuck says he hopes the workers own the world by then . . .

16

Pat Read, the editor of the Industrial Worker *for several years in the 1940's, was a master at inventing new words. He coined the term "Gumpets," perhaps meaning government pets, and one of his most frequently used contractions was "Paccio" for P.A.C.-C.I.O., the Political Action Committee of the Congress of Industrial Organizations, frequently the subject of Read's barbs. This unsigned satire on the New Deal may very well have been written by him, for he was the editor of the* Industrial Worker *at the time this poem was published (March 31, 1945).*

Read, who died in November 1947, was an Irish-born radical who had been a member of the C.N.T. while in the Spanish Civil War. At his death the obituary in the Industrial Worker *said: "Gifted with a warm heart, a keen mind, and a caustic tongue, he lashed at the humbug and hokum of the labor fakir and politician, at the futile reformer, and the labor shackling 'do-gooder.' . . . He contributed much to the analysis of the labor movement. His approach was predominantly the psychology of what makes it tick—and what stops it from ticking."*

receive wages, is that they democratically decide what their wages shall be; the profit-seeking owning class is out of the picture; and the aggregation of lands and machinery are socially owned and controlled. And he is saying that if that ain't something to fight for, he'll eat his shirt; and a very unpalatable shirt it is that a soldier wears.

We step off the car and walk down to the quays. French and British gun-boats are tied up to the docks. We start talking to a few British sailors who want to know more about the war, and we invite them to come down to the beach with us for a swim.

The sand sparkles like Xmas-card snow, and the blue waves lap the shores as gently as a cat strok-

PACCIO HYMN TO THE NUDE EEL

(Tune: "Whack Fol the Diddle Doll")

We'll sing a song of peace and love
Whack fol the diddle doll the dido day,
To the Man who from Washington reigns above,
Whack fol the diddle doll the dido day,
May wars in plenty be His share
Who kept our homes from Want and Care
"Mein Gut und Roosevelt" is our prayer
Whack fol the diddle doll the dido day.

Chorus

Whack fol the diddle doll the dido day
So we say "Hip hooray!"
O come and listen while we pray
Whack fol the diddle doll the dido day.

When we were savage, fierce and wild
Whack fol the diddle doll the dido day
He came like a poppa to His child
Whack fol the diddle doll the dido day
He gently raised us from the slime
And kept our hands from stay-in crime
And—gave us conscription in his own good time
Whack fol the diddle doll the dido day.

Our fathers oft were naughty boys
Whack fol the diddle doll the dido day
Slowdowns and strikes are dangerous toys
Whack fol the diddle doll the dido day
From Detroit's Briggs to Bishop's Hill
They dug their mitts in their masters' till
But—Meester Roosevelt loves us still
Whack fol the diddle doll the dido day.

O Workingmen, forget the past
Whack fol the diddle doll the dido day
And think of the day that's coming fast
Whack fol the diddle doll the dido day
When we'll all be civilized,
Neat and clean, No—strike advised
Oh—Won't Meester Roosevelt be surprised?
Whack fol the diddle doll the dido day.

17

Matilda Robbins (Rabinowitz), who died in 1963, had been an organizer for the I.W.W. in the Little Falls, Massachusetts, textile strike and the Akron, Ohio, rubber workers' strike of 1913. Later, *a social worker in Los Angeles, she was active in the Socialist Party in California. Over the years, she contributed many poems and articles to the* Industrial Worker *and wrote a regular column, "From My Notebook." She satirized union "pie cards" (paid staff officials and officers) and business unionism in the poem "It Happened One Night," which was printed in the* Industrial Worker *(June 10, 1949).*

IT HAPPENED ONE NIGHT

By Matilda Robbins

The beer was cold, the liverwurst
Was tasty as could be;
And there were cheese and sausages
And pickles sweet and tea—
The last was odd—but there was one
Who drank tea-totally.

Now weeks of strike had ended
And gathered for a spree
Were poor but happy workers
Who struggled mightily
And won two cents an hour more—
Or maybe it was *three.*

All was friendliness and cheer
Till a simple lad began
To ask some questions impolite
Of a leading labor man
Who was busily expounding
A ten-year contract plan.

The lad was young and puzzled—
A rank-and-filer he—
"How come," he asked, "that you receive
Six times more pay than we?
I cannot see the reason for
Such strange disparity."

The leader bristled as he spoke:
"It is because we're able
To push the union enterprise
Around the conference table;
And know our wage scales and can talk
About the union label."

Another leader joined in—
Known for his verbal darts—
"And don't forget statistics, man,
And differential parts,

And escalator clauses,
And cost-of-living charts!"

"Now, listen here," a third one puffed—
A cagey little guy—
Who talked to presidents as well
As he managed the small fry,
"Take my advice and hold your tongue—
It's better not to pry."

The union brothers were impressed
By these superior men;
But still some said the lad had sense;
And some said more, but then
They didn't know what else to say—
They were peaceful union men.

"Now, fellows, let's not spoil the fun.
Forget it! Have a drink!"
A lively brother interposed
With an impish little wink—
"We'll settle this some other time—
It's later than you think."

"Hear! Hear! Good fellow!" cried the men.
Someone proposed a cheer
For wise, intrepid leaders
And all of them drank beer
And talked about another raise—
Perhaps *four cents*—next year.

18

John Forbes, the author of "Nothing Down," which appeared in the Industrial Worker (*December 26, 1955*), *was the most recent member of the I.W.W. to go to jail for his antimilitary position. Born in Missouri in 1926, he served in the Army in 1945–46. In 1947 Forbes burned his draft card and refused to register for the draft. He graduated from the University of Chicago in 1947 and worked at laboratory technician jobs in hospitals until 1954, when he was sent to Springfield, Missouri, Medical Center for Federal Prisoners on a three-year sentence for nonregistration for the draft. During this time he was a regular contributor to the Industrial Worker and wrote a series of satiric poems,* The Bunkum Times. *After his parole in 1956 he went to Puerto Rico and has worked as a social worker, laboratory technician, and administrator of a prepaid medical plan.*

NOTHING DOWN

By John Forbes

We nowadays sing of the company store
    That held men in bondage of ever more debt
And think it belonging to ages of yore—
    But the monster is with us, enslaving us yet.

Those marvelous trinkets of our jaded age,
    Appliances, autos, TVs (with big screens)
The poorest of people who slave for a wage,
    No matter how abject, find inside their means.

The trick is with credit. One pays nothing down;
    But monthly for years from his paycheck they
    grub
So that interest, insurance, on cost put a crown
    Much more than the cost—and, aye, there's the
    rub!

And the little grubs added amount to a pile
    Of mountain proportions that peace of mind
    banishes.
Defaulting must come after struggling a while—
    They're reclaimed, and the phantom of
    property vanishes.

MORALS

1

With phantom dollars people buy
And credits keep the prices high.

2

For the warehouse they produce
What common sense would mean for use.

3

*On such a system one must frown—
Buying one's chains for nothing down!*

19

Fred Thompson, a former editor of the Industrial Worker, *wrote "The Art of Making a Decent Revolution" which was printed in the* Industrial Worker (*July 29, 1957*). *Thompson, who was born in New Brunswick, took part in the Halifax shipyards strike of 1920 before coming to this country. He was a member of the One Big Union in western Canada before coming to the United States in 1922. Arrested under California's criminal syndi calism law, he was a "class-war prisoner" from 1922 to 1927. He organized for the I.W.W. in the mines in Butte in the late 1920's, in the auto plants in Detroit in the early 1930's, and in fabricating plants in Cleveland. He was on the teaching staff at the I.W.W. Work Peoples' College in Duluth. Thompson is the author of* The I.W.W., Its First Fifty Years *(Chicago, 1955). In June 1964 the U.S. Court of Appeals, Seventh District, ordered the federal judge to grant Thompson U.S. citizenship, which had been denied him because of his I.W.W. membership.*

THE ART OF MAKING A DECENT REVOLUTION

By Fred Thompson

The I.W.W. aims at some major changes in the social order. It wants to abolish the wages system. It wants to replace production for profit with production for use. It wants to substitute industrial democracy for the growing autocracy, oligarchy and bureaucracy of the world.

These objectives have been declared worthy, good and necessary by many thinking people outside the ranks of the I.W.W. The distinctive characteristic of the I.W.W. in this respect is the choice of means by which we hope to see these objectives attained.

In distinction from most of those who share these ideas, we do not count on legislation to create the good world. We count instead on what workers themselves can do for themselves.

Our Way

Our hope is that workers will build large and effective unions that are run by the rank and file; that the structure of these unions will correspond to the actual economic ties between workers, so that workers on every job will be in a position to determine more and more what happens on that job, and through a collective class-wide structure, decide what happens in industry as a whole.

It is in this way, as we see it, that the working class can reshape its world into something consistent with our better aspirations and with the technical capacities mankind has developed.

This choice of means grew some sixty years ago probably from a plain distrust of politicians. Since then there has been wide experience in welfare programs, in nationalization schemes, in the experiments of fascism, in the Soviet system, in the entire history of the last 40 or so years, to indicate that this choice of means was wise. Reflecting this experience there has been an increasing concern in the various social sciences, about the cause and effect relation between social means chosen, and results achieved. The conclusions developing there, form a major buttress for the sort of choice the I.W.W. made long ago.

The Question

This question of the relation between means chosen and results obtained, is a typically modern question. It used to be customary to assume that about the only question to ask about a proposed way of getting a result—apart from law and morals—was its adequacy—or so to speak was the hammer big enough to drive the spike? The experience of the last four decades has shown that when we are talking about social means, we have to question more than its adequacy. We have to ask: How will the choice of this way of seeking our objective reshape the situation after we have made extensive use of it?

The older notion was that any means, if it could do the job, could bring the desired result. The idea fitted the makeshift devices of individual action in a pioneer age. If a nail had to be driven and no hammer was at hand, a rock took the place of the hammer; the housewife who wanted another nail in the kitchen wall so she could hang up her frying pan, took off her shoe and drove the nail with the heel. Final outcome seemed the same regardless of means selected.

Nothing in our experience since then will refute that conclusion so long as we are talking about individual or small scale action. But today the question of means and ends relates to efforts to be made on a large social scale, and that reasoning no longer applies. If everyone drove nails with shoes, among other consequences the manufacture and sale of hammers would decline, and the shoe business would boom. And that, while the assumption is absurd, illustrates quite fully the sort of consequences that follow from the use of any means of a wide social scale, whether as a matter of national policy or as a widespread practice.

Means Outvote Purpose

With that point of view in mind, it is instructive to look back at history and note that the schemes of mankind have left as their only result the expansion of the means that have been used, regardless of purpose.

At times the purposes for which these means were selected, have been approximated. At other times the purposes have not been achieved. The only invariable result was the expansion of the means used.

For this reason we should most certainly avoid the selection of means when the growth of those means will be repugnant to us.

We can reason further that to achieve a social goal we must make that selection of means which, upon expansion, will constitute the goal. The I.W.W. program of building democratic unionism and prodding it to have steadily more to say about the industrial process, is such a rational choice of means.

It is surprising how little attention has been given to the causal relation between social means and ends. Most of the discussion of the question has been of a rather moralizing character: the question of whether a drastic means is morally justified, or what will be the psychological effect of its use upon the user. This discussion however relates to the scientific problem: what is causal relation between the means we adopt on a large scale to solve a social problem, and the results it brings us?

The question has an answer only if we keep in mind the circumstance that it relates to action on a large scale—social action. Perhaps a couple more illustrations as absurd as the shoe versus hammer one already given, will put the issue into a cartoon-like simplicity.

To Fry an Egg

When you fry an egg, it makes no significant difference in result whether you cook with gas, electricity, oil, coal or wood. The egg will fry the same. But if we should all become determined to cook with wood, it would make a vast difference. The facilities for all to cook with wood do not exist. But if we persisted in that determination, eventually the mechanics of supply and demand by way of stiff prices and extensive reforestation could make it possible. The fried eggs would go the way of all fried eggs. The net result of the decision, the permanent result, would be the extensive woodlots, the widely distributed yards for distributing firewood, the piles of wood in back yards, the accumulation of wood-stoves—in short, the expansion of the means used. There would be

a parallel reduction in other industries and other means of cooking. Those two sets of increased and decreased means constitute the assured result.

We are not likely to develop a collective determination to fry eggs on wood-stoves. Conceivably the womenfolk may develop a decided preference for heating homes and cooking with electricity. If they do, it will be necessary to re-route the gas and coal they would otherwise have burned to the additional plant facilities for generating the electricity they would then use, and to convert or replace stove and furnace manufacturing facilities. By Tuesday, Monday's heating and Sunday's cooking will all be gone—and what will be left will be the expanding facilities for doing it all over again. And one should note that this sort of change is not simply that of demand stimulating supply. The young couple setting up housekeeping buys the sort of stove that is in style for burning the sort of fuel most likely to be available—just as it brings up its children to speak the language of the community and to share the heroes and hopes and folkways of the community.

As it is with fried eggs and fuel, so is it with whatever we go after on a large scale, whether as a matter of social policy or as widespread custom. To prepare the way for considering this larger question is our excuse for meditating on fried eggs and kitchen ranges.

How History Works

In this H-bomb age, we should keep the foregoing relation in mind as we recall that two generations have forged arms to defend democracy against militarism and given their lives to that end. Further they have won. Yet the result is obviously the expansion of the means used, and that only. Democracy has not grown sturdier, nor has militarism abated. One finds it instructive in that connection to trace the history of conscription back to its "democratic" start during the French Revolution to withstand the kings of Europe. It proved such a military asset (remember Napoleon?) that Prussia adopted it. When Prussia went to war with other countries, they too adopted it. Early in this century when Britain and America found conscription repugnant, they called it Prussianism, and later adopted it to defeat Germany—twice. Now we have it even in peacetime. This is but one phase of one of the more horrendous growths of selected means in our lifetime. The purpose has not shaped the outcome. The means have.

Or, to take another example: Generations have

fought crime with bigger and actually better penitentiaries, with parole and probation systems,
with special courts for this type and that type of
offender. The result has been: the expansion of
the means, and that only.

Generations have likewise observed that somehow the machinery of democracy did not yield
them government responsive to their wishes. They
have elaborated this machinery with direct pri-
maries, referendum and recall, and sundry other
devices. The result has been: the expansion of the
means—and that only.

We could draw illustrations from almost any
phase of our social lives: advertising, the prohibition experiment, the use of autos and the resultant
bottlenecks, the growth of this industry and the
decline of that, the growth of that imperial power
and the decline of another, trust-busting, or what
have you. Nor is the experience confined to our
Western or capitalist culture. Back in 1917 the
Bolsheviki over in Russia established a dictatorship to achieve the blessings of peace and bread
and the withering away of the state. To date there
has been no observable withering of the state, but
only an expansion of the means they have used.

The General Case

To multiply illustrations however does not prove
the proposition. The general case may be argued
thus:

1. The entire social apparatus may be viewed
in many ways. One valid way is to look at it as
a series of means for doing things: companies
formed to produce goods and make profits, unions
to haggle over the pay, languages with which to
attempt communication, schools to check the orig-
inality or aboriginality of the young, families to
provide them with TV-sets, food and latch-keys,
etc., etc.

2. The selection of any such social means for
doing an additional job, results in more of the
energy available to society flowing through that
means, and thus in its expansion and elaboration.
(You may have noticed that in regard to governments and taxes lately.)

3. If the additional energy flowing through the
selected means comes from a new source, the role
of that means is absolutely increased. If, as usual,
the energy to flow through it must be diverted
from other means, then the relative increase in
role is even greater.

4. The more the selected means has grown, the
more readily available it becomes for selection

for further ends, including the solution of the
problems that have been created by its growth.
The chance of alternative means becoming selected or seeming suitable, steadily grows less.
The officeholders attached to the expanded means
will drive also for the perpetuation and expansion of their social role.

Limits to Process

That is the general case. The obvious objection is
that "it proves too much." It would require that
all social trends set up in the past should have
expanded indefinitely, and this plainly has not
been so. It is again a case that "the trees do not
grow into the sky."

In physics there is a generalization, usually
named after the physicists Braun and Chatelier,
that when any force alters an equilibrium, the reactions it sets up are of the nature and direction
to minimize the change the new disturbance tends
to make. While this generalization was drawn up
to describe strictly physical processes, social par-
allels are obvious. It appears to be a general statement true of experience as a whole. It summarizes
at any rate what would otherwise be the very
lengthy, though intriguing story of why there are
eventual limits to the expansion of selected means.

Practical Conclusions

The practical conclusions are the issue at point.
If you give government the job of solving your
problems, the assured result is not the solution of
your problems but the growth of government—
and of its take, and of its bite into your paycheck.
If you look to government to remake the social
order, the outcome is a social order in which you
work and exist for the government.

If you look to labor leadership to solve your
problems, the outcome is large union office buildings, with larger desks and larger swivel chairs,
presumably with ever larger and larger labor leaders occupying them.

If you look to the joint action of yourself and
your fellow workers to cope with your problems,
you move forward with time into situations where
steadily you and they cut a larger role in life,
where the decisions about your work are steadily
more and more made by you fellows, where the
product of your labor steadily redounds more and
more to your benefit, where the world more and
more becomes as you wish it.

We think it makes a powerful lot of difference,
what means you select, not only for here and now,

but for the generations to follow. If you agree, don't go fry an egg, but help us build Industrial Democracy.

20

"Chazzdor" is the pen name of Charles Doehrer, a young I.W.W. member in Chicago who for a time edited the Industrial Worker *and contributed a number of science fiction stories to the I.W.W. press. This satire was published in the* Industrial Worker *(July 29, 1957).*

PARABLE OF THE WATER PUMP

By CHAZZDOR

Man, there was this crazy land called Uzay—off in a void it must have been, because they tell me the folks there did nothing all day but lug water from this here well they'd dug when they was sore in need of water.

The story doesn't say what for they need this water—most folks I know can take it or leave it alone—but the tale is real clear about what made them sore.

It seems that just after they tapped this subterranean keg of cloud juice, what happens but along comes this legal eagle and slaps 'em with a writ of habeas aquas sworn out by a fat cat—a real dog—named Daddio Warbucks.

One of the folks slipped his monocle on and read from the top of the writ. "Lo," it said, "whereas you folks been poachin' water on the private property of one Daddio Warbucks, duly granted to him by the Secretary of the Give-Away under terms of the Land Grab Act, you gotta cease and desist poachin', pronto!"

The folks of Uzay didn't bother to read the fine print, but they knew the writ was water-tight because down there at the bottom it was signed by General D. D. Eisenmotors, chief caddy of all Uzay. So, the folks conga'd over to visit Daddio Warbucks and beseeched him thusly:

"Keep your pepsi, and keep your coke,
But give us water, lest we choke."

Then, while his charming daughter, Blank Eyed Annie, beat out rhythm with a wire brush, Daddio turned to the people and spake:

"I'll sell you water, don't you weep,
Two bucks a quart, and that's dirt cheap.

So, bring your buckets and bring your mugs,
Bring your large, economy sized jugs.
Ooby dooby, ooby dooby, ooby dooby do."

"Woe!" shouted the folks, "two bucks a quart! Pop, that's outrageous; has been for ages. Next you'll be tellin' us to go out and work for wages."

"Sic 'em, Daddio!" said Blank Eyed Annie, pokin' her wire brush into the face of one of the folks.

Daddio clipped the brat and spake soothingly unto the people. "Folks," he said, "you've hit on a mad, mad scheme. Work for wages, that's the ticket. In fact, I'll even hire you to lug water from my well you dug. Wild, huh?"

"Whoa," shouted the folks, "we're on to that cool game. According to the classical script you're gonna offer to pay us one buck for each two-buck quart of water we lug, so that we can only buy back half the water. No deal, Daddio, we'll thirst first!"

"Pure, unadulterated Hooverism," chided Daddio. "I got a new script, written by the Grime, Dice and Chicago Tribune school of modern economics. You see, friends, I am an enlightened Capitalist."

"Oh," said the folks.

"Sic 'em, Daddio!" said Blank Eyed Annie.

"Yes, friends, I am a modern capitalist and I will pay you two bucks for each two-buck quart of water which you lug . . ."

"Wow!" said the folks.

"Yes, two bucks for each quart, minus a few reasonable deductions, such as six per cent as a reasonable profit, six per cent as reasonable rent upon the land, six per cent to pay off the bank for the loan I used to acquire the land, six per cent for taxes, six per cent for research and six per cent for capital expansion so that we may dig more wells. Six per cent of two bucks," muttered Daddio, counting on his fingers, "is twelve cents; six twelves is 75. Seventy-five from two bucks leaves . . . a dollar twenty in round figures. So, reasonably, your wage will be a full $1.15 for each quart of water which you lug."

"Ouch!" said the folks. "We will not stand for this. We will form a union, for in union there is strength."

"Arf!" said Blank Eyed Annie.

"Sic 'em, Annie . . . oops, I mean, fine 'n dandy. Enlightened capitalists are hep to unions, friends. Who is your piecard . . . oops, I mean, your leader, so I may deal with him collectively?"

Industrial Worker, October 5, 1951.

The people muttered among themselves, and a handful of them wearing knives, pistols, clubs and deputy sheriffs' badges, went among the others, electioneering.

At length, one of the people spake, saying, "Thir, we hath elected Dave Bulk ath our thpokesman. Inthidentally, thir, can you thuggest an inexpenthive dentist? I theem to have bumped my thilly head againtht the fitht of one of Mr. Bulk's friendth."

Later, when Dave Bulk returned from his chit-chat with Daddio, the folks gathered about to hear the results. "Yea," spake Bulk, "there's good news today. It was a tough fight but, thanks to my dauntless leadership, Daddio agreed to increase your wage by thirty-five cents a quart . . ."

"Nifty," said the folks.

". . . minus a few deductions he forgot before; namely, six percent for Azure Crutch protection, six percent for Social Security—you should live so long—and six percent union dues to me."

"Yeah," spake the folks, "we might have got fringe benefits, too."

And so, like it was told to me, the folks began to work for wages, lugging water from Daddio's well they had dug. Everything went along peachy-keen until this here water tank began to fill up with more water than the folks were able to buy back. They complained about high prices, some of them were laid off, and some was getting a little thirsty. It was a crisis, and Daddio called in his advisors to seek a solution.

First came the hucksters. "What's the trouble, boys?" Daddio inquired of the chief huckster, the A.E., or Account Executive. "Why aren't we merchandising enough water to keep inventory/production ratio in balance?"

"We haven't finalized our thinking yet," saith the A.E., "but to get right down to where the rubber meets the road, Sir, we've got a great campaign we'd like to skim on the pond to see if it reaches the other side before the cookie crumbles."

"Will it sell water?" shouts Daddio. "What's your idea? Speak, man, speak. Don't stand there flippin' your food flap idly."

"Well," saith the A.E., "Cigarettes, everything's gotta have a filter to sell, these days."

"Most!" said Daddio. "We'll filter the water."

"Utmost!" spake the A.E. "Fine idea you just had, Daddio."

"Rather," said Daddio. "Now tell me what other bright ideas I've got."

"Well, Sir, it's the trend to change the package . . . strengthen the brand identification . . . big red letters on the label . . . make it distinctive, wholesome sounding, like . . . DADDIO'S OLD FASHIONED PURE WATER . . . yes, sir, that's it . . . and, umm, handy six-can pack to make 'em buy in larger quantities . . . ummm . . ."

"You're gone, man; keep it up," shouts Daddio.

"Umm . . . just speaking off the top of my head," continued the A.E., "we might try improving the flavor and appearance. But we'll have to cross-pollinate with Research on that."

"Hip! Remind me to deduct fifteen per cent from their wages for your agency fee," said Daddio as he summoned his research men.

"Ok, eggheads," spake Daddio to the bunsen burner mob, "what good use have you been makin' of these here research grants I been donating to science and progress?"

"Sir," said the PH.D. Burner, proudly, "we've discovered a cheap substitute for margarine . . . namely, surplus butter . . . which we have chopped, molded and mixed with vitamins and, when we've worked out one small problem—specifically, that it tastes like rubber cement—it will be ready for market. It's merely a matter of unlinking the third proton in the middle from the molecular . . ."

"Man," spake Daddio, "you atomize me, but what have you been doing about water? How can we produce cheaper water?"

"It's still in the research stage, sir, but we're working on a process to $water$ the water. It's just a matter of molec . . ."

"You're levitating," says Daddio. "Now, how about this problem of improving the flavor and appearance? How about that?"

"Umm . . . we might sweeten it . . . add CO_2 to give it sparkle . . . food coloring . . . a little cola flavor, perhaps . . . and some preservative so it will stay fresh longer."

"Out of this world, man, but it sounds gooey. Can they bathe in it? That's half the market."

"Umm . . . we can add a little detergent, too."

"Next," shouts Daddio. "Where are my economists?"

"Here," spake the economists, looking up from the latest issue of Dice Magazine, "and we've just worked out a new margin theory. See, it's printed right here in the margin of the editorial page."

"Readin' Dice Magazine is my favorite intellectual pursuit," said Daddio. "Read me out from it. What's it say there in the margin?"

New Year — Same old path

Industrial Worker, January 16, 1953.

"It says the government should buy some of the surplus water to pour into the Suez area to widen the canal from Syria to Algeria and solve the whole Middle Eastern crisis. Yes, and right after that it says we should start priming the pump, like in the old days, and that the people should learn to be more thrifty so they can enjoy the fruits of our high standard of living."

"Hmmm . . ." reflects Daddio. "Pump-priming, you say. Gad, that Dice Magazine never fails to come through with a sound, modern, enlightened pitch. Summon my engineers."

"Get me a pump for the well," spake Daddio to the engineers.

"Jolly," spake the engineers. "We will automate your well with a pump, sir, increasing the efficiency to double the output with half the manpower."

Then, from the rear of the throng of advisors, spake loudly and defiantly the voice of Dave Bulk. "Take it slow, pop. You can't get away with that automation stuff. As head of the union, I protest, you wizened, old plutocrat. If you put a pump on the well, there will be even more unemployment among my dues payers. We will strike, STRIKE, do

you hear me? You'll have the longest, strongest strike on your hands you ever had. We might even make it a general . . ."

"Finest, man. Greatest idea I've heard today. Nothing like a nice long strike to cut the payroll. Lunch, Bulk?"

"Lunch, Daddio. Country Club again?"

"Check, Bulk. Then, we'll bang out eighteen while we consult with D.D."

* * *

"Iron, sir?" said D. D. Eisenmotors, the chief caddy, as Daddio and Dave Bulk walked along the fairway.

"Check, D. D.," spake Daddio. "Oh, and by the way, D. D., I'm having a little trouble with my water . . . too much of it . . . folks claim the price is too high. What's the answer, D. D.?"

"Threat from the East," answered D. D. promptly. "We must arm the people."

"Bring it down to earth, D. D.," saith Daddio, glumly. "How'll that get rid of my surplus water?"

"Water pistols, Man, water pistols . . . latest weapon," spake D. D.

"The sheerest!" gurgled Daddio. "We can take another six per cent for cost of defense."

"Sixty denier!" burbled Bulk. "Defense contracts will put the people back to work, fillin' water pistols. We can call off the strike . . . take the no-strike pledge."

"Check," squeals Daddio. "Call off the strike. By the way, Bulk, how'd you like to marry my charming daughter, Blank Eyed Annie?"

"Yeah, and by the way, Bulk," grinned D. D. infectiously, "how'd you like to run on the ticket with Dickie in '60? I'm thinkin' of retirin' to devote full time to the links."

"Labor Party?" asks Bulk, bargaining slyly.

"Umm," pondered D. D. "Why not? Might unify the folks for the big effort . . . the cause!"

"Aw, fellas," spake Bulk, "you're too good to me."

* * *

Thus it was in Uzay that the folk sorely hauled water from Daddio's well they had dug. And, so it was that when Elmo Groper with his poll went out among the people—passing out free, handy six-ounce size samples of DADDIO'S OLD FASHIONED PURE WATER with added tranquilizers—asking them, "Are the folks getting a fair shake?" Ninety-nine per cent of those polled replied, "Yeah, man, we're all shook up. Do we get a refund on the bottle?"

21

Carlos Cortez, a frequent contributor to the In-
dustrial Worker, writes from Milwaukee, Wiscon-
sin: "I was born right here in Milwaukee of a Mex-
ican Wobbly father and a German Pacifist Socialist
mother. Between them they created another radi-
cal. With the exception of various jaunts, I spent
most of my life doing such things as common la-
bor, record salesman, book salesman, and various
other things. During the last war, I pulled a two-
year sentence in a federal correctional for refus-
ing to go into military service. Oh, date of birth,
August 13, 1923." His following two poems ap-
peared in the Industrial Worker (*May 2, 1960, and*
October 11, 1961).

WHERE ARE THE VOICES?

By CARLOS CORTEZ

Where are those loud voices
That rang thru the land in its towns and cities,
In its hop fields and lumber camps,
In its textile mills and steel mills,
In its wheat fields and its waterfronts,
Voices so loud that entire police forces would
    attend their rallies
To give riot-gun ovations and billy club caresses?

Where is the voice of the young Swedish hobo
    song writer
Who the mines bosses stood against a prison wall
    in Utah
And filled his body full of bullets
Like his colleague of two thousand years earlier,
    the young Jew hobo carpenter
Who the disgruntled money changers impaled on
    a cross with rusty nails
And two thousand years later are still pounding
    those nails?

Where are the voices of the young Aztec peon
Shouting Land and Liberty
Who the Hacendado and Standard Oil puppets
    silenced forever with an ambush
And the young Spanish poet
Who so infuriated that bosom buddy of the State
    Department
That his cutthroats saw to it those hands would
    write no more poetry
While across the Tyrrhennean Sea
A sad-eyed Italian suffered a similar fate?

Where are the voices of the two Italian dreamers
Who in Massachusetts were strapped to a chair by
    the sons of Cotton Mather
And barbecued with high voltage
And the anarchist editor who because he wrote too
    much
Was found by a bullet on a dark New York street
While the "finest" just shrugged their shoulders
And the passionate Jewess who fleeing one tyranny
Had found only another tyranny and came back
    broken?

Where are the voices of the half-Indian Wobbly
Who a committee of solid citizens, using tortures
    no Indian ever dreamed of
Could not get the satisfaction of hearing one cry
    of pain
Or plea for mercy from his lips
And a fellow worker of his, not quite so stoic,
Castrated and hung by his toes from a railroad
    trestle
Shouting, "Kill me, you bastards!"
And the burly miner who jumped bail to go to the
    workers' paradise
And lushed up his last years in disappointment?

Where are the voices of the stout-hearted
    Haymarket Germans
Who in Chicago had started a tide
No army of pinkertons and finkertons could hold
    back
And paid for with their lives to bring
The extra hours of leisure time
That working fools like you and me now enjoy?

Where are those voices?

Have they been buried beneath labor-manage-
    ment contracts,
Buried beneath closed-shop agreements and no-
    strike clauses,
Buried beneath banquets for pie-cards and their
    shop owner buddies
With patriotic posters showing labor shaking
    hands with management
Under the gaze of a beaming Uncle Sam,
Buried ever so deeply beneath overtime pay-
    checks?

Have the voices been drowned out by technicolor
    soundtracks,
Radio and television,

Juke boxes and squeaky musaks,
Long voluptuous high-powered automobiles
And bright new vacuum cleaners
All thru the miracle of easy-term time payments
Insipidly singing to us,
"Where else but here could you have it so good?"

Have those voices been outshouted by the voices
    of the cynic
And the tired radical
And the objective analyzer
Loudly insisting the movement is dead?

The old timers are gone, but their voices they
    never took with them,
Their lingering voices blending in with an ever-
    growing symphony,
Bursting out from the Earth's four corners
From Caribbean jungles and North African deserts
To Arizona reservations and South African slum
    towns,
From sunny Mediterranean islands and
    Catalonian alleys
To Kilimanjaro foothills and sunny Southland
    lunch counters,
Heard above the tanks and guns in Budapest
    streets
And heard above banana boughten airplanes
Roaring low over Central American rooftops,
Heard in the defiant anthems of Bantu men and
    women
Falling beneath apartheid clubs and bullets,
Laughing along with walking commuters
Who are
Hitting Jim-Crowed bus lines
Real hard in the pocketbook
And such voices can be heard by all but the very
    deaf!

From Northern Minnesota's scrub-timbered
    wastes
To Southern Arizona's dry hillsides
And from Puget Sound's bleak islands
To central Missouri's padded cells
Still echo the voices of the conscientious young
    men
Who are proud they did not pay taxes
The year atomic power was brought into this
    World.

From a sun-drenched Southwestern mesa
A proud people living a life of values so ancient

Yet so new to invading barbarians
Who seek to destroy that which they cannot
    understand
To a group of would-be mariners
Attempting to sail a ship into nuclear waters
And gaining the love of a people
Whose fishermen die fishing for contaminated sea
    food.

From missile bases in Nebraska and Wyoming
Where youths picket around the clock and suffer
    broken legs
To a grimy Southern prison cell
Where languishes a small gentle-faced man
Who dares to dream of freedom for his island;
Down the long broad highways
With a bushy-haired anarchist catholic
Spreading his own gospel of revolution
To a dingy second-floor office
On the dingy street
Of one of the dingiest metropolises
Spreading a badly needed message
And the roll call goes on.

Those are the voices of men and women
Who seek no refuge in gray-flannel-suited
    anonymity
Or khaki-colored respectability
Or chromium-plated mediocrity.
Those are the voices of the inheritors
Of a million years' struggle
From primeval quadruped to quixotic biped
And neither Roman arenas
Nor medieval floggings,
Inquisitional torture chambers,
Guillotines,
Firing squads,
Electric chairs
Nor congressional investigations
Can still those voices
For those are the voices only Freedom can silence!

22

DIGGING THE SQUARES
AT JACK LONDON SQUARE

By Carlos Cortez

Just a couple of blocks away from the Western
Pacific depot where the Weepys tracks run down
the middle of the street;

Industrial Worker, December 12, 1955.

Now Will They Quit Pulling Against Each Other?

Stands the same little old shack that has stood up for many years including those years before the Quake when it stood up straight;

This little shack no longer stands up straight with its underpinnings long shaken loose by the Quake and its bottom slowly sinking in the mud of the Oakland waterfront;

This same little shack that used to be a whaling ship whose boards were torn down to build a bunk house for the workers from the oyster beds in the Bay, then a flop house for sailors, then was changed into a saloon—an arrangement that was agreeable to both sailors, proprietor, oyster workers, and everybody;

Where the sailors used to stop off for one last fling before going out to sea;

And where they whooped it up when they came back;

And they called the place Heinolds First And Last Chance;

And because one of these sailors who between jaunts to the Klondike and between jaunts to the South Seas and between drinks would sit at his special table in the corner of the small barroom to write stories;

Heinolds First And Last Chance is now famous;

Famous because this sailor boy who sat in the corner of the barroom and wrote stories wanted to sell his stories to the big magazines and after many tries and many sailings and many drinks did sell his stories;

And that is how Heinolds First And Last Chance has never been torn down;

As the sailors first and last chance for a drink is now this Bay city's first and last chance at the tourist buck;

No longer do the old schooners dock there any more, and where the horse drawn paddy wagons used to pull up, the rubberneck buses pull up instead;

With boy scout troops whose scoutmasters make sure those tender young minds are exposed to nothing more potent than his dog stories and no longer need worry that tender young ears will be exposed to the sailors' rough language tell their young charges about the great rags to riches American dream;

Yes, Jack,

YOU who wrote THE IRON HEEL the boy scouts are looking at your old hangout;

Prim and prissy little nuns with their candid cameras reflecting on that great rags to riches American dream;

Yes, Jack,

YOU who wrote THE WAGE SLAVE, the nuns are taking snaps of your old hangout;

Well-fed rotarian types with their well-fed wives and their expensive movie cameras;

Yes, Jack,

YOU who wrote THE DREAM OF DEBS, the rotarians are taking polychrome movies of your old hangout to show to the club members back in flatsville;

The foreign exchange students looking around in vain and seeing only cocktail bars and seafood grottos asking why there is no Jack London Bookshop;

And the old rail-cat who happens to be standing nearby telling them they would have better luck buying his books back home since all they bother to print in this country now are his dog stories;

Yes, Jack,

Your old hangout is still there but as you would walk into that little old bar that you loved so well, you would find the martini and cocktail crowd a poor substitute for your old whiskey and beer bunch;

Sitting there in their pinafores and aloha shirts and even evening dresses, cameras slung around their necks and guidebooks in their pockets;

OOhing and AHing and really having a ball slumming it up with their empty chatter;

Sitting at the same tables and sitting in the same chairs and sitting at the same bar and sitting on the same barstools;

Where you and your gang of roughnecks used to come and whoop it up.

But, Jack, I want you to know that
I still love the place;
I love the place because it is like
A shrine to me;
You made it a shrine;
Because you're just one more cat that has
Shown the whole damn World
That art doesn't need
An ivory tower. . . . . !

23

"Hiroshima," by Lin Fisher, was published in the Industrial Worker *(August 23, 1961).*

HIROSHIMA

By LIN FISHER

I, a child knew nothing then
but bonfires in the streets, the smiles
tin triumph of the radio
You were older and perhaps
understood and were ashamed.
I grew to grammar school
the air-raid drills an ugly game
and there beneath my desk with me
the children of Hiroshima.
They grew with me. I read too much
Began to see and understand
The rain of bones and blood and guilt
began to fall around my skull.
The fur of terror touched my neck
Those children screamed at the terrible light.
And blind, they saw and knew in dark
the ways of man the braille of death.
Under the covers at night I heard
the beating of my blood—or heard
the engines of the planes that day
the bombers of Hiroshima
Began to see the children's hands
as blisters jeweled the gentle flesh
that groped but could not hold their lives.
Now grown, I wake at night to hear
the beating of my bomber-blood
I wonder do they listen too
the children we may someday kill
and wake with sweat to hear the planes
that brightly lift their humming death.
The radar spins across the sky
a mesh of secret hunting planes

Industrial Worker, May 23, 1960.

We've let men offer all our lives
for empty words and pride and threats
They tell us that we have the time
to hide our children underground
They will not see the final light
They will not know the way they die.
We sleep between our righteous sheets
and never wake from sheltered dreams
to hear our planes drone overhead
that carry hate and death and Hell
and senseless vengeance round the earth.
"Deterrent" politicians say
and each deters by building death.
What pride to us when we are dead
that others roast and scream and die
that cities melt and earth and flesh?
So threat by threat they train our minds
to slaughter millions for a few
(Is this a heritage for pride?)
for differences that don't exist
that man have made and can unmake
there is no difference, one and one
each man just loves, creates and dies.
And we who stood aside and saw
the yellow children's groping death
still watch and let them build again
a thousand new Hiroshimas.
Will death some night illuminate
the guilt we let each nation make
Each man a killer by default
who turns his head, afraid to say
I will not help you murder men

24

This recent statement of I.W.W. ideals was writ-
ten by J. F. McDaniels and was printed in the
Industrial Worker *(April 22, 1964). McDaniels*
writes about himself (letter to J. L. K. June 30,
1964): "Born in a sod shanty on my father's home-
stead in Dakota Territory, January 29, 1886. Of
peasant-proletarian stock. 'Graduate' of fifth grade,
Colorado Street School, Butte, Montana. Occu-
pations: peddler, clerk, lumber worker. Entered
radical world in 1934, when Upton Sinclair ran
for governor of California. Contributed to his
weekly newspaper, The Epic News. *. . . No close*
organizational affiliations now. Just a retired radi-
cal philosopher." A California resident, McDaniels
frequently contributes articles to the Industrial
Worker.

TODAY'S DREAM, TOMORROW'S REALITY

By J. F. McDaniels

We have not yet reached that point in civilization where a person who lacks religious or patriotic convictions is regarded as a good citizen. He may have equal rights before the law, but we find him not fully socially acceptable. If he has no love for his God or his country, we have none for him.

We like our people to be believers, rather than thinkers. Thinkers are not likely to be good conformists. Conformism is an integral part of our social establishment. Thinkers are disturbers of our peace of mind. Those who govern us do not like that. A contented people, a satisfied electorate; of such does the politician dream.

We who hold the radical point of view dream a little sometimes, too. We dream of dissent, discontent, disbelief, and many other matters disturbing to the tory-minded.

We let our thoughts dwell on the gross social inequalities that burden the American poor. We dream of simple social justice for the great masses of common people.

We even have grand dreams of a brotherhood of man, reaching around the world; of ending poverty and war's destruction in all the lands of Old Earth.

We think great thoughts of "Liberty, Equality, Fraternity," as the French motto so eloquently expresses it. We would gear the ideals of the noblest minds in history to the building of a civilization inclusive of all the races of mankind.

In these daydreams of ours, we would pluck the rich from their mansions, and put them to work among commoners, and tear down the slums of the poor and build them houses where they can dwell in decency and comfort.

We dream of a new day dawning when there will be an end of luxury and ostentation among the rulers of humanity.

We will harness the forces of nature to the feeding of a vast world population. We will apply the wonders of science to the welfare of people, and not to their destruction.

And so the radicals dream, as the ancient Greeks did, centuries ago. Many of their ideals are now reality, as ours will one day be. They contributed mightily to democracy.

Notes

Chapter 1

1 *Proceedings of the First Convention of the I.W.W.* (New York, 1905), pp. 1–2.
2 *Ibid.*, p. 82.
3 *Ibid.*
4 *Ibid.*, pp. 575–76.
5 Robert E. Doherty, "Thomas J. Hagerty, the Church, and Socialism," *Labor History*, 3 (Winter, 1962), p. 53.
6 *Proceedings of the First Convention of the I.W.W.* (New York, 1905), pp. 228–31.
7 *Ibid.*, p. 575.
8 "The I.W.W. Preamble," in Paul F. Brissenden, *The I.W.W.: A Study of American Syndicalism* (New York, 1920), p. 350.
9 Ralph Chaplin, "Solidarity Forever," *Solidarity*, January 9, 1915.
10 Quoted by Brissenden, p. 137.
11 Brissenden, Chapter 5.
12 Daniel De Leon, "The I.W.W. Convention," *Weekly People*, October 3, 1908, quoted by Brissenden, p. 224.
13 "The I.W.W. Preamble," in Brissenden, p. 350.
14 "The International Party" ("The Internationale"), in *Socialist Songs* (Chicago, 1901), p. 2.
15 Chaplin, "Solidarity Forever."

Chapter 2

1 United States Commission on Industrial Relations, *Industrial Relations, Final Report*, Senate Executive Doc. No. 415, 64th Congress, 1st Sess., 2 (Washington, 1916), p. 1452.
2 *Ibid.*, p. 1453.
3 Vincent St. John, *The I.W.W.: Its History, Structure, and Methods* (Chicago, n.d.), p. 17.
4 Justus Ebert, *The I.W.W. in Theory and Practice* (Chicago, n.d.), pp. 59–60.
5 *Solidarity*, December 18, 1909.
6 Andre Tridon, *The New Unionism* (New York, 1917), p. 32.
7 *World's Work*, 26 (1913), p. 417.
8 Quoted by Justus Ebert, *The Trial of a New Society* (Chicago, 1913), p. 61.
9 St. John, *The I.W.W.: Its History, Structure, and Methods*, p. 12.
10 George G. Allen, "The Big Strike," *Solidarity*, October 14, 1916.
11 *Solidarity*, September 4, 1915.
12 Waldo Browne, *What's What in the Labor Movement* (New York, 1921), quoted by Archie Green, "John Neuhouse: Wobbly Folklorist," *Journal of American Folklore*, 73 (No. 289), pp. 214–15.
13 Fred Thompson, *The I.W.W.: Its First Fifty Years* (Chicago, 1955), pp. 81–82.
14 Walker C. Smith, *Sabotage, Its History, Philosophy, and Function* (Spokane, n.d.), p. 8.
15 Elizabeth Gurley Flynn, *Sabotage: The Conscious Withdrawal of the Workers' Industrial Efficiency* (Cleveland, 1915), p. 5.
16 *Solidarity*, June 4, 1910.
17 *Ibid.*
18 *National Constitution of the Socialist Party* (Article II, Section 6) (Chicago, 1914), p. 2.
19 *Testimony of William D. Haywood Before the Industrial Relations Commission* (Chicago, n.d.), p. 35.
20 *Ibid.*, p. 23.
21 Fred Thompson, *The I.W.W.: Its First Fifty Years* (Chicago, 1955), p. 85.
22 *Solidarity*, October 3, 1914.
23 Joe Hill, "A Rebel's Toast," *Solidarity*, June 27, 1914.
24 See "Language of the Migratory Worker."
25 Robert Bruere, "The Industrial Workers of the World," *Harper's Magazine*, 137 (July 1918), p. 256.
26 Robert Bruere, "Following the Trail of the I.W.W." (New York, 1918), p. 18.
27 *Report of the President's Mediation Commission to the President of the United States—Unrest in the Lumber Industry* (Washington, 1918), p. 15.
28 National Civil Liberties Bureau, *Memorandum Regarding the Persecution of the Radical Labor Movement in the U.S.* (New York, 1919), p. 4.
29 E. F. Dowell, *A History of Criminal Syndicalism Legislation in the United States* (Baltimore, 1939), p. 36.
30 "Paint 'Er Red," *Solidarity*, November 7, 1914.

~er 3

1 Carleton H. Parker, *The Casual Laborer and Other Essays* (New York, 1920), p. 189.
2 *Ibid.*, p. 190.
3 Archie Green, "John Neuhouse: Wobbly Folklorist," *Journal of American Folklore*, 73 (No. 289), p. 201; see note 5.
4 John Greenway, *American Folksongs of Protest* (Philadelphia, 1953), p. 179.
5 Manuscript of an interview with Richard Brazier by Archie Green, New York City, December 31, 1960, in the library of Archie Green, University of Illinois.
6 Greenway, p. 199.
7 Richard Brazier interview.
8 *Industrial Union Bulletin.* October 24, 1908.
9 Parker, p. 119.
10 *Ibid.*, p. 121.
11 For a description of "riding the rods," see the introduction to George Milburn, *The Hobo's Hornbook* (New York, 1930).
12 Parker, p. 121.
13 Nels Anderson, *The Hobo: The Sociology of the Homeless Man* (Chicago, 1923), p. 110.
14 Parker, pp. 71–72.
15 *Ibid.*, p. 100.
16 *Ibid.*, p. 106.
17 *Ibid.*, p. 105.
18 Rexford G. Tugwell, "Casual of the Woods," *Survey*, 44 (July 3, 1920), p. 472.
19 *Solidarity*, November 21, 1914.
20 Anderson, *The Hobo*, p. 87.
21 See "Language of the Migratory Worker."
22 Harry Kemp, "The Lure of the Tramp," *Independent*, 70 (June 8, 1911), p. 1270.
23 Bill Quirke, "The Sheep and the Goats," in Hobo College Press Committee, *Hobo Ballads* (Cincinnati, n.d.), p. 12.
24 Anderson, p. 110.
25 Fred Thompson, *The I.W.W.: Its First Fifty Years* (Chicago, 1955), p. 47.
26 Quoted in an unpublished manuscript by William Haber, "The I.W.W.: Their Activities During the War" (University of Wisconsin, 1921), p. 28, in the library of Dean William Haber, University of Michigan.
27 Parker, pp. 78–79.
28 "The Boe's Lament," in Hobo College Press Committee, *Hobo Ballads* (Cincinnati, n.d.), p. 8.
29 Parker, p. 115.
30 James P. Thompson, "Revolutionary Class Unionism," *Twenty Five Years of Industrial Unionism* (Chicago, 1930), pp. 6–7.
31 Fred Thompson, interviewed by Joyce L. Kornbluh (Chicago, Illinois), October 16, 1963.
32 Richard Brazier interview.
33 *Ibid.*

Chapter 4

1 Paul F. Brissenden, *The I.W.W.: A Study of American Syndicalism* (New York, 1920), p. 261.
2 *Industrial Worker*, October 28, 1909.
3 Fred Thompson, *The I.W.W.: Its First Fifty Years* (Chicago, 1955), p. 49.
4 *Testimony of William D. Haywood Before the Industrial Relations Commission* (Chicago, n.d.), p. 12.
5 *Spokane Press*, November 2, 1909.
6 Quoted in the *Industrial Worker*, October 26, 1910.
7 *San Francisco Call*, March 2, 1911.
8 Hyman Weintraub, "The I.W.W. in California: 1905–1931" (unpublished master's thesis, Department of History, University of California at Los Angeles, 1947), p. 157.
9 Quoted in the *Industrial Worker*, March 21, 1912.
10 *Solidarity*, April 13, 1912.
11 Emma Goldman, *Living My Life*, 2 (New York, 1931), p. 494.
12 "Report of Commissioner Harris Weinstock," Los Angeles *Citizen*, May 24, 1912, quoted by Selig Perlman and Philip Taft, *History of Labor in the United States 1896–1932*, 4, *Labor Movements* (New York, 1935), p. 241.
13 *Ibid.*

Chapter 5

1 Joe Hill to Oscar Larson, September 30, 1915, in *Revolt*, December 1915 (in Joe Hill files in the Labadie Collection).
2 Quoted in Barry Stavis, *The Man Who Never Died* (New York, 1954), p. 29.
3 Testimony of Mrs. Vera Hanson, as cited in James O. Morris, "The Joe Hill Case" (unpublished manuscript in Labadie Collection).
4 *Deseret Evening News*, January 12, 1914, quoted in Morris, p. 7.
5 Stavis, p. 29.
6 *Voice of the People*, May 21, 1914.
7 *Solidarity*, April 18, 1914.
8 *Solidarity*, July 31, 1915, quoted by Vernon H. Jensen, "The Legend of Joe Hill," *Industrial and Labor Relations Review*, 4, (April, 1951), p. 360.
9 Stavis, p. 53.
10 *Ibid.*, p. 76.
11 *Ibid.*, p. 88.
12 *Ibid.*, p. 90.
13 *Ibid.*, p. 91.
14 *Ibid.*
15 *Ibid.*
16 *New York Times*, November 20, 1915.
17 Stavis, p. 108.
18 Ralph Chaplin, "Joe Hill: 'A Biography," *Industrial Pioneer*, 1 (November 1923), p. 24.
19 John Greenway, *American Folksongs of Protest* (Philadelphia, 1953), p. 192.
20 "Last Letters of Joe Hill," *Industrial Pioneer*, 1 (December 1923), p. 54.
21 *Ibid.*, p. 53.
22 *Ibid.*
23 Undated letter by Fred Fischer (in Joe Hill file in the Labadie Collection).
24 Ralph Chaplin, "Joe Hill: A Biography," p. 23.
25 Wallace Stegner, "I Dreamed I Saw Joe Hill Last Night," *Pacific Spectator*, 1 (Spring, 1947), p. 187.
26 Zapeta Modesto (Barry Nichols), "Joe Hill, Some Notes on an American Culture Hero," *Wobbly* (Berkeley, 1963), p. 9.

Chapter 6

1 Paul F. Brissenden, *The I.W.W.: A Study of American Syndicalism* (New York, 1920), p. 291.
2 *Report on the Strike of Textile Workers at Lawrence, Massachusetts*, 62nd Congress, 2nd Sess., Senate Doc. 870 (Washington, 1912), p. 72.
3 *Ibid.*, p. 154.
4 *Hearings on the Strike at Lawrence, Massachusetts*, 62nd Congress, 2nd Sess., House Doc. No. 671 (Washington, 1912), p. 32.
5 Dr. Elizabeth Shapleigh, "Occupational Diseases in the Textile Industry," New York *Call*, December 29, 1912.
6 *Ibid.*
7 Quoted in Bill Cahn, *Milltown* (New York, 1954), p. 140.
8 Al Priddy, "Controlling the Passions of Men in Lawrence," *Outlook*, 102 (October 19, 1912), p. 344.
9 "After the Strike in Lawrence," *Outlook*, 101 (June 15, 1912), p. 341.
10 Samuel Yellen, *American Labor Struggles* (New York, 1936), p. 183.
11 *Hearings*, 124–39.
12 Quoted in Richard O. Boyer and Herbert M. Morais, *Labor's Untold Story* (New York, 1955), p. 175.
13 Ray Stannard Baker, "The Revolutionary Strike," *American*, 74 (May 1912), pp. 30A–30B.
14 *New York Times*, January 26, 1912.
15 Fred Beal, *A Proletarian's Journey* (New York, 1937), p. 39.
16 *Hearings*, pp. 294–95.
17 *Ibid.*, p. 227.
18 *Ibid.*, p. 24.
19 *Ibid.*, p. 164.
20 Yellen, p. 203.
21 Quoted in Brissenden, p. 291.
22 "After the Battle," *Survey*, 28 (April 6, 1912), pp. 1–2.
23 Kenneth McGowan, "Giovannitti: Poet of the Wop," *Forum*, 52 (October 1914), p. 611.

Chapter 7

1 "Haywood's Battle in Paterson," *Literary Digest*, 46 (May 10, 1913), pp. 1043–44.
2 "Strike of the Jersey Silk Workers," *Survey*, 30 (April 19, 1913), p. 81.
3 John Fitch, "The I.W.W.: An Outlaw Organization," *Survey*, 30 (June 7, 1913), p. 361.
4 Quoted in New York *Tribune*, February 26, 1913.
5 *Ibid.*, February 28, 1913.
6 Quoted by Gregory Mason, "Industrial War in Paterson," *Outlook*, 104 (June 7, 1913), p. 287.
7 *Ibid.*
8 *Bill Haywood's Book* (New York, 1929), p. 269 .
9 Elizabeth Gurley Flynn, *I Speak My Own Piece* (New York, 1955), p. 152.
10 Quoted by Fitch, p. 361.
11 Excerpts from the Paterson *Press* reprinted in Industrial Relations *Final Report*, 3, pp. 2583–84.
12 Elizabeth Gurley Flynn, "The Truth About the Paterson Strike" (speech delivered to New York Civic Club Forum, January 31, 1914), p. 13 (manuscript in Labadie Collection).

13 Leo Mannheimer, "Darkest New Jersey," *Independent*, 74 (May 29, 1913), p. 1190.
14 *Solidarity*, July 19, 1913.
15 Granville Hicks, *John Reed* (New York, 1936), p. 98.
16 *Ibid.*, p. 101.
17 Mabel Dodge Luhan, *Movers and Shakers* (New York, 1936), p. 204.
18 Hicks, p. 102.
19 *The Pageant of the Paterson Strike* (New York, 1913).
20 Luhan, p. 205.
21 *Ibid.*, p. 204.
22 Hicks, p. 103.
23 *Ibid.*

Chapter 8

1 Stuart M. Jamieson, *Labor Unionism in American Agriculture*, Bureau of Labor Statistics Bull. No. 836 (Washington, 1945), p. 63.
2 Carleton H. Parker, *The Casual Laborer and Other Essays* (New York, 1920), p. 189.
3 *Ibid.*, p. 191.
4 *Ibid.*, pp. 191–92.
5 Quoted in William Preston, Jr., *Aliens and Dissenters* (Cambridge, 1963), p. 57.
6 Industrial Relations, *Final Report*, 5, p. 5000.
7 Sacramento *Bee*, February 9, 1914, quoted by Woodrow Whitten, "The Wheatland Episode," *Pacific Historical Quarterly*, 17 (1948), p. 41.
8 Quoted in Preston, p. 59.
9 *Ibid.*
10 *Ibid.*
11 *Ibid.*, p. 60.
12 *Ibid.*, p. 61.
13 Paul S. Taylor, *Migratory Farm Labor in the United States*, Bureau of Labor Statistics Bull. No. R. 530, pp. 2–3.
14 Tom Connors, "The Industrial Union in Agriculture," *Twenty-Five Years of Industrial Unionism* (Chicago, 1930), p. 38.
15 Don D. Lescohier, "With the I.W.W. in the Wheat Lands," *Harpers*, 147 (August 1923), p. 376.
16 *Agriculture—The World's Basic Industry and Its Workers* (Chicago, 1929), p. 26; Jamieson, p. 402.
17 Mitchell, South Dakota *Morning Republican*, quoted by Jamieson, p. 402.
18 Thorstein Veblen, "Using the I.W.W. to Harvest Grain," in "An Unpublished Paper on the I.W.W. by Thorstein Veblen," *Journal of Political Economy*, 40 (December 1932), pp. 372–77.
19 Jamieson, p. 402.
20 Jamieson, p. 403.
21 *Ibid.*
22 Taylor, p. 3.

Chapter 9

1 Floyd Dell, "The Invincible I.W.W.," *Liberator*, 2 (May 1919), p. 9.
2 Rexford G. Tugwell, "The Casual of the Woods," *Survey*, 44 (July 3, 1920), p. 472.

wood's Book (New York, 1929), pp. 241–42. __ted by Vernon H. Jensen, _Lumber and Labor_ (New York, 1945), p. 89.

5 C. Merz, "Tying Up Western Lumber," _New Republic_, 12 (September 29, 1917), p. 242.

6 _Ibid._, p. 244.

7 Dell, pp. 9–10.

8 _Congressional Record_, 65th Congress, 2nd Sess., 56 (1918), p. 3821.

9 _Report of the President's Mediation Commission to the President of the United States—Unrest in the Lumber Industry_ (Washington, 1918), p. 14.

10 Jensen, p. 130.

11 Ralph Winstead, "Enter a Logger: An I.W.W. Reply to the Four L's," _Survey_, 44 (July 3, 1920), p. 475.

12 Dell, p. 9.

13 American Civil Liberties Union, _The Issues in the Centralia Murder Trial_ (New York, 1920), p. 7.

14 _Ibid._

15 Teresa McMahon, "Centralia and the I.W.W.," _Survey_, 43 (November 29, 1919), p. 174.

16 Federal Council of Churches of Christ in America, _The Centralia Case: A Joint Report on the Armistice Day Tragedy at Centralia, Washington, November 1919_ (New York, 1930), p. 23.

17 _Ibid._

18 _Ibid._

19 Jensen, p. 144.

Chapter 10

1 _Labor Troubles at Goldfield, Nevada_, 60th Congress, 1st Sess., House Doc. No. 607, p. 21.

2 Vincent St. John, _The I.W.W.: Its History, Structure and Methods_ (Chicago, 1919), p. 18.

3 Works Projects Administration, _Montana: A State Guide Book_ (New York, 1939), p. 70.

4 Paul F. Brissenden, "The Butte Miners and the Rustling Card," _American Economic Review_, 10 (December 1920), p. 765.

5 _Ibid._, p. 764.

6 Vernon H. Jensen, _Heritage of Conflict_ (New York, 1950), p. 323.

7 Brissenden, "The Butte Miners and the Rustling Card," p. 757.

8 Quoted in Selig Perlman and Philip Taft, _History of Labor in the United States 1896–1932_, 4, _Labor Movements_ (New York, 1935), p. 389.

9 Quoted in Jensen, pp. 396–97.

10 _Ibid._, p. 397.

11 Robert W. Bruere, "Copper Camp Patriotism," _Nation_, 106 (February 21, 1918), p. 202.

12 Perlman and Taft, p. 400.

13 Quoted by William Preston, Jr., _Aliens and Dissenters_ (Cambridge, 1963), p. 109.

14 Perlman and Taft, p. 401.

15 George R. Tompkins, _The Truth About Butte_, p. 35, quoted by John Steuben, _Labor in Wartime_ (New York, 1940), pp. 89–90.

16 Work Projects Administration, _Montana_, p. 74.

17 Tompkins, p. 37, quoted by Steuben, pp. 90–91.

18 Work Projects Administration, _Copper Camp: Stories of the World's Greatest Mining Town, Butte, Montana_ (New York, 1943), p. 67.

19 Quoted in Preston, p. 111.

20 _Ibid._

21 _Ibid._, p. 112.

22 _Ibid._, p. 113.

23 _Ibid._, p. 309.

Chapter 11

1 I.W.W. General Executive Board Statement on War, quoted by William Preston, Jr., _Aliens and Dissenters_ (Cambridge, 1963), pp. 88–89.

2 Industrial Workers of the World, _Proceedings of the Tenth Convention 1916_ (Chicago, 1917), p. 138.

3 James P. Thompson, quoted by Walker C. Smith, _The Everett Massacre: A History of the Class Struggle in the Lumber Industry_ (Chicago, n.d.), p. 183.

4 Selig Perlman and Philip Taft, _History of Labor in the United States 1896–1932_, 4, _Labor Movements_ (New York, 1935), p. 400.

5 John S. Gambs, _The Decline of the I.W.W._ (New York, 1932), p. 47.

6 Gambs, p. 48.

7 _Ibid._

8 _Ibid._

9 _Ibid._

10 _Ibid._

11 National Civil Liberties Bureau, _The "Knights of Liberty" and the I.W.W. Prisoners at Tulsa, Oklahoma_ (New York, 1918), pp. 9–10.

12 Quoted by Gambs, p. 44.

13 "What Haywood Says of the I.W.W.," _Survey_, 38 (August 11, 1917), p. 429.

14 Ralph Chaplin, _Wobbly: The Rough and Tumble Story of an American Radical_ (Chicago, 1948), p. 209.

15 _Ibid._

16 William Preston, Jr., _Aliens and Dissenters_ (Cambridge, 1963), p. 105.

17 _Ibid._

18 Letter from Richard Brazier to the editor, December 14, 1963.

19 _The United States of America vs. William D. Haywood, et al._; Indictment on Sections 6, 19, and 37 of the Criminal Code of the United States, and Section 4 of the Espionage Act of June 15, 1917 (Chicago, n.d.).

20 Art Young and John Reed, "The Social Revolution in Court," _Liberator_, 1 (September 1918), p. 20.

21 _Ibid._

22 _Bill Haywood's Book_ (New York, 1929), p. 322.

23 _Ibid._, p. 324

24 Jean Sterling, "The Silent Defense in Sacramento," _Liberator_, 2 (February 1919), p. 15.

25 Undated, unsigned clipping belonging to Mary Gallagher, quoted in Hyman Weintraub, "The I.W.W. in California" (unpublished ms., University of California, 1947), p. 157.

26 Quoted by Philip Taft, "The Federal Trials of the I.W.W.," _Labor History_, 3 (Winter 1962), p. 79.

27 Winthrop D. Lane, "Uncle Sam, Jailor," _Survey_, 42 (September 6, 1919), p. 808.

28 *Ibid.*
29 Justus Ebert, *The I.W.W. in Theory and Practice* (Chicago, 1921), p. 61.
30 Interview with Fred Thompson, June 23, 1963.
31 E. F. Dowell, *A History of Criminal Syndicalism Legislation in the United States* (Baltimore, 1939), p. 18.
32 *Ibid.*
33 *Ibid.*, p. 20.
34 Inaugural address of California Governor William D. Stephens, quoted in Weintraub, pp. 162–63.
35 Quoted by Gambs, p. 59.
36 *Bill Haywood's Book*, p. 360.
37 Fred Thompson, *The I.W.W.: Its First Fifty Years* (Chicago, 1955), p. 137.
38 Taft, "The Federal Trials of the I.W.W.," p. 86.
39 *Ibid.*
40 *An Open Letter to President Harding from 52 Members of the I.W.W. in Leavenworth Penitentiary* (Chicago, 1922), pp. 2, 3, 11.
41 Quoted by Gambs, p. 64.
42 American Civil Liberties Union, *The Record of the Fight for Free Speech in 1923* (New York, 1924), cover page.
43 Thompson, p. 147.
44 William D. Haywood, "Break the Conspiracy," *One Big Union Monthly*, 1 (December 1919), p. 7.

Chapter 12

1 John S. Gambs, *The Decline of the I.W.W.* (New York, 1932), pp. 117–18.
2 Robert L. Tyler, "The I.W.W. in the Pacific N.W.: Rebels of the Woods," *Oregon Historical Quarterly*, 55 (March 1954), p. 40.
3 Paul F. Brissenden, "Industrial Workers of the World," *Encyclopedia of the Social Sciences*, 8, p. 16.
4 *Ibid.*
5 *Ibid.*
6 Trinidad *Chronicle-News*, October 19, 1927, quoted by Donald J. McClurg, "The Colorado Coal Strike of 1927 —Tactical Leadership of the I.W.W.," *Labor History*, 4 (Winter 1963), p. 77.
7 Gambs, p. 150.
8 Rand School of Social Science, *The American Labor Year Book 1931* (New York, 1931), p. 129.
9 McClurg, p. 89.
10 Gambs, p. 154.
11 Irving Bernstein, *The Lean Years: A History of the American Worker 1920–1933* (Boston, 1960), p. 378.
12 Selig Perlman and Philip Taft, *History of Labor in the United States 1896–1932*, 4, *Labor Movements* (New York, 1935), p. 611.
13 Bernstein, p. 366.
14 *Ibid.*, p. 377.
15 Fred Thompson, *The I.W.W.: Its First Fifty Years* (Chicago 1955), pp. 167–68.
16 *Business Week*, January 6, 1945, quoted in the *Industrial Worker*, February 27, 1945.
17 *Time*, 57 (April 1, 1946), p. 24.
18 Quoted by Zapeta Modesto (Barry Nichols), "Joe Hill, Some Notes on an American Culture Hero," *Wobbly* (Berkeley, 1963), p. 5.
19 Tyler, p. 43.

Language of the Migratory Worker

Including hobo, lumberjack, and mining terms

Alky — grain alcohol

Anchor — pick

Angel food — mission preaching

Balloon — bed roll

Banjo — short-handled shovel

Benny — overcoat

Bill — short for "scissorbill"

Bindle — roll of bedding in which a bindle stiff wraps his personal possessions

Bindle stiff — worker who carries his bedding

Biscuit-shooter — short-order cook

'Bo — abbreviated form of hobo

Boiler — cook who avoids baking and frying; a "wet" cook

Boomer — temporary worker, a wanderer, one who follows "booms" (good times)

Boom man — worker who rafts logs in the water

Bull — police

Bull bucker — strawboss of the timber-cutting crew; used in long log country only

Bull cook — chore man in any work camp

Bull of the woods — top boss in a logging camp

Bull pen — tank of a jail; sometimes a "men only" flophouse

Bumpers — riding space between freight cars

Bunyan camps — logging camps in which bedding is not provided

Buy a master — to pay a fee to an employment shark for a job

Buzzies — extension drilling machines used in mining

California blankets — newspapers used for bedding

Camp inspector — vagrant logger, a logger making one-night stops at lumber camps looking for work

Can — police station

Carrying a balloon — carrying a bed roll

Carrying the banner — avoiding the expense of a bed at night by walking the streets, sleeping on a subway, pretending to wait for a train at the depot, nursing a cup of coffee in an all-night diner, sitting in an all-night movie, etc.

Cat — worker well fitted in with some occupational subculture, such as "hep cat"; a worker who follows a specific occupation, such as "straw cat" for harvest hand; sometimes short for "sab cat," the symbol of sabotage, such as "turn the cat loose"

Catting in — using another's fire to cook on

Chinwhisker — pertaining to a farmer, such as "chinwhisker outfit"

Chokers — loop of wire rope used for yarding logs in a lumber camp

Chow — food

Chow-bell — dinner bell

Chuck — food ready to be eaten; (verb) to throw

Clam-gun — shovel designed for digging clams

Class-war prisoner — anyone jailed for his class-conscious views or acts

Coin — money

Coll — hobo deluxe dish of mashed baked potatoes, onions, and liverwurst

...onductor

...*ave Commonwealth* — the ideal of a new ...ocial order which recognizes no national, occupational, or racial distinctions and represents the united economic force and social will of all workers in the world

Corks — correct spelling, "calks," projections on shoes to prevent slipping; used as a name for shoes having calks

Crotch line — device for loading logs onto railroad cars

Crum — louse

Crum boss — janitor in a camp bunkhouse

Crummy — lousy; as a noun it means caboose

Crum up — to contaminate lodgings; since lice can be eliminated only by boiling, the delousing operation was termed "boil up"

Damper — cash register

Deck — roof or floor of a passenger train; as a verb, to pile logs on a skidway in a lumber camp

Dehorn — denatured alcohol or bootleg whiskey of inferior quality; anything that makes a worker depart from proper class-conscious behavior

Dehorn squad — Wobbly committee that would close up bars, speakeasies, and brothels during an I.W.W. strike

Dick — detective

Dingbat — the sort of tramp that could be described as "homeless, helpless, and harmless"

Dirt-hider — road grader

Ditch — to throw off a train; to dispose of something

Donkey — stationary engine; also, as a term for a silly person

Donkey-puncher — engineer on a donkey

Drag — street

Drifts — main tunnel in a mine

Dry house — miners' lockerroom or change room

Ducket — ticket

Dump — recognized place or hangout

Enlightened — informed, intelligent, educated

Fallers — loggers who fall lumber

Fanned — hit on the soles by a police club

Farmer — any stupid, incompetent person

Fellow-worker — term used by Wobblies to address each other

Fink — strike breaker; an informer; may be derived from Pinkertons, private agency detectives frequently used by employers to break strikes

Fish — county jail term for new prisoners

Fix the job — direct action on the job; quickie strikes, passive resistance, deliberate bungling aimed to win better working conditions

Flag — to halt a train

Flats — hot cakes

Flip — to board a train in motion

Flipping — train riding

Floater — hobo; wanderer

Flop — shelter; place to sleep

Flunkey — cookhouse helper

Frisk — to search

Fritz, on the — in bad shape

Fruit tramp — migratory worker in fruit-picking operations

Gaffer — foreman

Gandy dancer — section man in an extra gang on the railroad

Gay cat — new hobo

Get my time — collect pay and leave camp

Glim — match or a light

Glom — to catch onto; to grab, as to "glom a gump," to get a chicken without paying for it

Gob — worked out chambers in a mine into which waste rock is dumped

Groundhog — tunnel workers

Gump — chicken

Gump light — miner's carbide light

Gunnels — steel struts beneath a box car

Guts — bracing rods beneath a box car

Gut robber — stingy cook

Gyppo — any piece-work system; a job where the worker is paid by the volume he produces rather than by his time

Hand out — lunch handed out in a paper bag

Hangin' — overhead part of a mine tunnel

Hard tails — mules

Harness bull — uniformed policeman

Harp — nickname for the Irish

Harvest stiff — migratory agricultural worker

Hayburners — horses

Haywire — the wires used to tie bales of hay, available for temporary patching on jobs where horses were fed; thus, where equipment was held together with haywire, and therefore, anything below standard, such as in the term, "haywire outfit"

Highball — fast

Highball camp — camp where work is speeded up by foreman

Hijack — hold up, or hold-up man

Hit the ball — working at above normal pace

Hitting the grit — to jump off a moving train; to hike or walk

Hobo — migratory worker

Hog, on the — broke

Homeguard — town worker who does not move around from job to job

Hooker — hook tender, boss of the yarding crew in high lead country

Hoosier — anyone who is incompetent; farmers or villagers

Hoosier-up — to act incompetent; to withdraw efficiency consciously

Hot box — overheated journal box on railroad car; sometimes used to refer to a mine where oxidation of minerals created excessive heat

Hurry boggy — patrol wagon

Idiot stick — shovel

Jake — satisfactory

Java — coffee

Jerries — section hands

John — farmer

Jungle — meeting place, usually near a railroad division point, regularly occupied by hoboes for preparing food, "boiling up," and sleeping

Jungle buzzard — hobo who hangs around a jungle waiting to be fed

Kangaroo court — court established among prisoners to raise revenue or tobacco as a mutual-aid project; the court "tries" new arrivals on the charge of breaking into jail without the consent of the inmates; it may also resolve grievances among prisoners and maintain discipline

Kicks — shoes

Kitten — the sab-cat's offspring; verb, "to kitten," to "fix the job"

Knowledge box — schoolhouse

Layout — an outfit, a logging concern

Live one — logger with money

Lousy — bad

Lump — parcel of food acquired by begging

Lush — drunkard

Make a riffle — acquire the price of a meal or a night's lodging by begging

Makin' out — getting paid and leaving a logging camp

Mancatcher — employment agent

Mark — easy mark; person or a place easy for food or money

Miner's con — silicosis

Mission stiffs — men who made a profession of "getting saved"

Mongee — food; may have been derived from the French word "manger"

Moniker — name or nickname

Moocher — common beggar

Muck — any material to be shoveled; rock broken in mine blasting

Mucker — miner who loads cars with ore or rock; anyone who operates a manual shovel

Muck stick — long-handled shovel

Mule — corn alcohol

Mulligan — stew

Mulligan mixer — cook

Nose bag — lunch pail; lunch served in a paper bag or pail

O.B.U. — initials of One Big Union; Wobblies signed their letters, "Yours for the o.b.u."

On the hog — broke

One Big Union — i.w.w. ideal of a single world-wide organization of labor

Outfit — company; logging or mining operation

Packing the banner — same as "carrying the banner"; walking the streets

Packing the rigging — carrying Wobbly literature and organization supplies

Packing mustard — carrying hod

Panhandling — begging on the streets

Parasite — labor's class enemy

Pay-pole — log

Pearl diver — dishwasher

Peddle out — selling clothes to a used-clothes dealer

Peddler — slow freight or local train

Pie in the sky — reference to the bourgeois heaven; from Joe Hill's song, "The Preacher and the Slave"

Pinkerton — Pinkerton Agency detective

Play the woods — work in a logging camp

Plush — seats on a passenger train; also called "cushions"

Plute — short for plutocrat

Pokeout — handout

Pond monkey — man who pushes logs around in a sawmill pond

Pot latch — grand reunion; a social

Pulled out — left the job; left town

Punch — to drive horses or cattle

Push — foreman

Pusher — boss; contractor

Raises — stope which is raised above the level of a drift in a mine

Rattler — fast freight train

Rebel — in Wobbly usage, a class-conscious worker who wishes to end the capitalist system

Reuben — farmer or villager

Rods — drawrods beneath a freight train

Rolls — blanket rolls

Round — in mining, the cycle of blasting, mucking out, timbering, and drilling to the next blast

Rube — short for "Reuben"

Rummy — drunk, or one who behaves as though alcohol had reduced his capacity for reason or action

Rustling — getting busy finding food or a job

Sap — policeman's stick

Scab — person who works after a strike has been called and who takes the job of a striking union member

Scissorbill — worker who is not class conscious; a homeguard who is filled with bourgeois ethics and ideas

Set-down — invitation to come inside for a meal

Setup — company; same as "layout" or "outfit"

Sewer hogs — ditch diggers

Shacks — brakemen on train

Sharks — employment agents

Sheets — newspapers

Shorthorn — young lad

Short stake — any worker apt to quit when he has earned a small sum

Shotgun — speedy

Single jack — manual drill used with a hammer by the same worker

Skid road — district migrants frequent in towns; formerly the road over which logs were pulled

Slave — wage earner

Slave market — employment agency

Slinging the rigging — attaching wire rope to the main yarding line in a lumber camp

Sloughed — arrested

Slum — short for "slumgullion," a stew

Smilo joint — "smilo" may have been the trade name for a proprietary near beer within prohibition limits; smilo joints were speakeasies or taverns serving bootleg liquor

Snipe — section hand; cigarette butt; as a verb, to retrieve a cigarette butt

Stake — sum of money intended to last until the next job

Stakebound — having accumulated a sum of money on a temporary job and feeling free to leave it

Stamps — Wobbly dues stamps

Stem — any principal thoroughfare; the main stem is the main street in the business district; as a verb, to beg on a business street

Stew bum — brokendown hobo

Sticks — any nonurban area, including the suburbs

Stiff — any kind of hobo worker, such as "harvest stiff"; also used to mean a corpse

Stope — a working off the main tunnel in a mine

Straw boss — foreman

Stump rancher — someone who settles on logged off land and who usually continues to work, at least part time, for wages

Sugan — a quilt

Taking five — knock off work for five minutes

Ten-day miner — tramp miner

Throw — spend freely

Throw the guts — talk too freely

Tie 'em up — "fix the job"; stop production until workers' demands are met

Timber beasts — lumberjacks

Timber wolves — lumberjacks

Tin horn — petty gambler

Tin pants — logger's pants

Town clown — village constable

Traipse — travel around

Tramp — vagrant who lives by begging

Trap — mouth

Turkey — canvas bag

Ukulele — short-handled shovel

Vag — "without visible means of support"; police court charge of vagrancy

Walking delegate — union organizer who moves from job to job

Wob, Wobbly — an I.W.W. member; origin of the word is unknown

Working by the inch, working by the mile — piece work

Yap — farmer

Yarded — assembled

Yeggs — safecrackers

Yellow legs — mounted government authority, such as cavalryman, who wore yellow puttees

Selected Bibliography

Chapter 1. One Big Union

Books

Brissenden, Paul F., *The I.W.W.: A Study of American Syndicalism*. New York: Columbia University Press, 1920.

Brooks, J. G., *American Syndicalism, The I.W.W.* New York: Macmillan, 1913.

Chaplin, Ralph, *Wobbly: The Rough and Tumble Story of an American Radical*. Chicago: University of Chicago Press, 1948.

Debs, Eugene V., *Writings and Speeches of Eugene Victor Debs*. New York: Hermitage Press, 1948.

De Leon, Daniel, *Socialist Reconstruction of Society*. New York: New York Labor News Co., 1920.

Dulles, Foster Rhea, *Labor in America*. New York: T. Y. Crowell Co., 1955.

Foner, Philip S., *The Industrial Workers of the World, 1905–1917*. New York: International Publishers, 1965.

Ginger, Raymond, *The Bending Cross: A Biography of Eugene Victor Debs*. New Brunswick: Rutgers University Press, 1949.

Groat, George G., *An Introduction to the Study of Organized Labor in America*. New York: Macmillan, 1916.

Hoxie, Robert F., *Trade Unionism in the United States*. New York: Appleton, 1917.

Karson, Marc, *American Labor Unions and Politics*. Carbondale: Southern Illinois University Press, 1958.

Madison, Charles A., *Critics and Crusaders: A Century of American Protest*. New York: H. Holt and Co., 1947.

———, *American Labor Leaders*. New York: Ungar, 1962.

Perlman, Selig and Taft, Philip, *History of Labor in the United States, 1896–1932* (John R. Commons and Associates), Vol. 4, *Labor Movements*. New York: Macmillan, 1935.

Proceedings of the First I.W.W. Convention. New York: New York Labor News Company, 1905.

Rayback, Joseph G., *A History of American Labor*. New York: Macmillan, 1959.

Renshaw, Patrick, *The Wobblies*. New York: Doubleday and Co., 1967.

Saposs, David, *Left-Wing Unionism*. New York: International Publishers, 1929.

Savage, Marion D., *Industrial Unionism in America*. New York: Ronald, 1922.

Shannon, David A., *The Socialist Party of America*. New York: Macmillan, 1955.

Thompson, Fred, *The I.W.W.: Its First Fifty Years*. Chicago: Industrial Workers of the World, 1955.

Pamphlets

Craft Unionism—Why It Fails. Chicago: I.W.W., n.d.

Ebert, Justus, *The I.W.W. in Theory and Practice*. Chicago: Industrial Workers of the World, n.d.

Ettor, Joseph J., *Industrial Unionism: The Road to Freedom*. Chicago: I.W.W. Publishing Bureau, n.d.

Haywood, William D., and Bohn, Frank, *Industrial Socialism*. Chicago: Charles H. Kerr and Co., 1911.

The I.W.W.: A Statement of Its Principles, Objects and Methods. Chicago: I.W.W., n.d.

I.W.W., One Big Union: The Greatest Thing on Earth. Chicago: I.W.W. Publishing Bureau, n.d.

The I.W.W.: What It Is and What It Is Not. Chicago: I.W.W., n.d.

Marcy, Mary E., *Shop Talks on Economics*. Chicago: I.W.W., n.d.

One Big Union of All the Workers: The I.W.W. Chicago: I.W.W., n.d.

Perry, Grover H., *The Revolutionary I.W.W.* Cleveland: I.W.W. Publishing Bureau, 1916.

St. John, Vincent, *The I.W.W.—Its History, Structure, and Methods*. Cleveland: I.W.W. Publishing Bureau, n.d. (revised editions, 1917, 1919).

Trautmann, William E., *Handbook of Industrial Unionism.* No place, n.d.

———, *Industrial Unionism.* Chicago: Charles H. Kerr and Co., 1909.

———, *One Big Union: An Outline of a Possible Industrial Organization of the Working Class with Chart.* Chicago: Charles H. Kerr and Co., n.d.

Twenty-Five Years of Industrial Unionism. Chicago: I.W.W., n.d.

What Is the I.W.W.? A Candid Statement of Its Principles, Objects and Methods. Chicago: I.W.W., n.d.

Williams, Ben H., *Eleven Blind Leaders of "Practical Socialism" and "Revolutionary Tactics," from an I.W.W. Standpoint.* Newcastle, Penna.: Solidarity Literature Bureau, 1910.

Woodruff, Abner E., *The Advancing Proletariat.* Chicago: I.W.W., 1919.

———, *The Evolution of Industrial Democracy.* Chicago: I.W.W., n.d.

Articles

Bohn, William E., "Development of the Industrial Workers of the World," *Survey,* 28, May 4, 1912, pp. 220–25.

Brooks, J. G., "The Shadow of Anarchy," *Survey,* 28, April 6, 1912, pp. 80–82.

Currie, B. W., "How the West Dealt With the Industrial Workmen of the West," *Harper's Weekly,* 51, June 22, 1907, pp. 908–10.

Debs, Eugene V., "The Industrial Convention," *International Socialist Review,* 5, August 1905, pp. 85–86.

———, "Industrial Unionism," *International Socialist Review,* 11, August 1910, p. 11.

De Leon, Daniel, "The Preamble of the Industrial Workers of the World," *Miner's Magazine,* 7, October 19, 26, November 2, 9, 1905.

Doherty, Robert, "Thomas J. Hagerty, The Church, and Socialism," *Labor History,* 3, Winter 1962, pp. 39–56.

Dosch, A., "What the I.W.W. Is," *World's Work,* 26, August 1913, pp. 406–20.

Green, Archie, "John Neuhouse: Wobbly Folklorist," *Journal of American Folklore,* 73, 1960, pp. 189–217.

Hagerty, Father Thomas J., "Reasons for Industrial Unionism," *Voice of Labor,* March 1905.

Hamilton, Grant, "A Story of a 'Funny' Unionism," *American Federationist,* 12, March 1905, p. 137.

Haywood, William D., "Industrial Unionism," *Voice of Labor,* June 1905.

Hoxie, R. F., "Truth About the I.W.W.," *Journal of Political Economics,* 21, November 1913, pp. 785–97.

Kellog, Paul U., "The McKees' Rocks Strike," *Survey,* 22, August 7, 1909, pp. 656–65.

McKee, Don K., "Daniel De Leon: A Reappraisal," *Labor History,* 1, Fall 1960, pp. 264–97.

O'Neill, J. M., "Our Comment on the Various Reports of the I.W.W. Convention," *Miner's Magazine,* November 8, 1906, pp. 6–9.

Simons, A. M., "Industrial Workers of the World," *International Socialist Review,* 6, August 1905, pp. 65–77.

Tyler, Robert L., "The Rise and Fall of an American Radicalism: The I.W.W.," *The Historian,* 19, November 1956, pp. 48–65.

———, "The I.W.W. and the West," *American Quarterly,* 12, Summer 1960, pp. 175–87.

Woehlke, W. V., "I.W.W.," *Outlook,* 101, July 6, 1912, pp. 531–36.

Other Sources

Brissenden, Paul F., "The I.W.W.," *Encyclopedia of the Social Sciences,* 8, pp. 13–18.

Unpublished Material

Barnes, Donald M., "The Ideology of the Industrial Workers of the World: 1905–1921." Unpublished Ph.D. thesis, Washington State University, 1962.

Conlin, Joseph R., "The Wobblies: A Study of the I.W.W. before World War I." Unpublished Ph.D. thesis, University of Wisconsin, 1966.

Crow, John E., "Ideology and Organization: A Case Study of the Industrial Workers of the World." Unpublished master's thesis, University of Chicago, 1958.

Tyler, Robert L., "Rebels of the Woods: A Study of the I.W.W. in the Pacific Northwest." Unpublished Ph.D. dissertation, University of Oregon, 1953.

Weintraub, Hyman, "The I.W.W. in California: 1905–1931." Unpublished master's thesis, University of California at Los Angeles, 1947.

Chapter 2. With Folded Arms

Books

Brissenden, Paul F., *The I.W.W.: A Study of American Syndicalism.* New York: Columbia University Press, 1920.

Brooks, J. G., *American Syndicalism, The I.W.W.* New York: Macmillan, 1913.

Crook, Wilfred H., *The General Strike.* Chapel Hill: University of North Carolina Press, 1931.

Groat, George G., *An Introduction to the Study of Organized Labor in America.* New York: Macmillan, 1916.

Hiller, E. T., *The Strike.* Chicago: University of Chicago Press, 1928.

Hoxie, Robert F., *Trade Unionism in the United States.* New York: Appleton, 1917.

Kipnis, Ira A., *The American Socialist Movement, 1897–1912.* New York: Columbia University Press, 1952.

Mathewson, S. B., *Restriction of Output Among Unorganized Workers.* New York: Viking, 1931.

Perlman, Mark, *Labor Union Theories in America.* Evanston and White Plains: Row, Peterson and Co., 1958.

Savage, Marion D., *Industrial Unionism in America*. New York: Ronald, 1922.

Shannon, David A., *The Socialist Party of America: A History*. New York: Macmillan, 1955.

Thompson, Fred, *The I.W.W.: Its First Fifty Years*. Chicago: I.W.W., 1955.

Tridon, Andre, *The New Unionism*. New York: Huebsch, 1917.

Veblen, Thorstein, *The Engineers and the Price System*. New York: Huebsch, 1921.

Ward, Harry F., *The Labor Movement*. New York: Sturgis and Walton, 1917.

Pamphlets

Ebert, Justus, *The I.W.W. in Theory and Practice*. Chicago: I.W.W., n.d.

Flynn, Elizabeth G., *Sabotage, the Conscious Withdrawal of the Workers' Industrial Efficiency*. Cleveland: I.W.W. Publishing Bureau, 1915.

Haywood, William D., *The General Strike*. Chicago: I.W.W. Publicity Bureau, n.d.

———, *Testimony Before the Industrial Relations Commission*. Chicago: I.W.W. Publishing Bureau, n.d.

Pouget, Emile, *Le Sabotage* (Paris, 1910), translated by Arturo Giovannitti. Chicago: I.W.W., 1913.

St. John, Vincent, *The I.W.W.: Its History, Structure, and Methods*. Rev. ed.; Chicago: I.W.W., 1919.

Smith, Walker C., *Sabotage: Its History, Philosophy, and Function*. Spokane: Published by author, 1913.

Trautmann, William E., *Direct Action and Sabotage*. Pittsburgh, 1913.

Articles

Boyle, J., "Syndicalism, the Latest Manifestation of Labor's Unrest," *Forum*, 48, August 1912, pp. 223–33.

"Direct Action as a Weapon," *Independent*, 74, January 9, 1913, pp. 70–71.

"Does the I.W.W. Spell Social Revolution?" *Current Literature*, 52, April 1912, pp. 380–88.

Dosch, A., "What the I.W.W. Is," *Worlds Work*, 26, August 1913, pp. 406–20.

Hoxie, Robert F., "The Truth About the I.W.W.," *Journal of Political Economy*, 21, November 1913, pp. 785–97.

Levine, Louis, "Development of Syndicalism in the United States," *Political Science Quarterly*, 28, September 1913, pp. 451–79.

———, "Direct Action: The Philosophy of the Labor Struggles of Today," *Forum*, 47, May 1912, pp. 577–88.

Tridon, Andre, "Syndicalism and 'Sabotage' and How They Were Originated," *Square Deal*, 10, 1912, pp. 407–14.

———, "The Workers' Only Hope—Direct Action," *Independent*, 74, January 9, 1913, pp. 79–83.

Unpublished Material

Barnes, Donald M., "The Ideology of the Industrial Workers of the World: 1905–1921." Unpublished Ph.D. thesis, Washington State University, 1962.

Chapter 3. Riding the Rails

Books

Anderson, Nels, *The Hobo: The Sociology of the Homeless Man*. Chicago: University of Chicago Press, 1923, 1961.

Kemp, Harry, *The Cry of Youth*. New York: Mitchell, Kennerly, 1914.

———, *Tramping on Life*. New York: Boni and Liveright, 1922.

Knibbs, H. H., *Songs of the Outlands*. New York: Houghton Mifflin, 1914.

London, Jack, *The Road*. New York: Macmillan, 1907.

———, *War on the Classes*. New York: Macmillan, 1905.

Milburn, George, *The Hobo's Hornbook*. New York: I. Washburn, 1930.

Parker, Carleton H., *The Casual Laborer and Other Essays*. New York: Harcourt, Brace and Howe, 1920.

Stiff, Dean (pseud. Nels Anderson), *The Milk and Honey Route*. New York: Vanguard, 1931.

Articles

Ashleigh, Charles, "The Floater," *International Socialist Review*, 15, July 1914, pp. 34–38.

Forbes, J., "Caste in the Jungle," *Outlook*, 98, August 19, 1911, pp. 869–75.

Kemp, Harry, "Lure of the Tramp, *Independent*, 70, January 8, 1911, pp. 1270–71.

Lewis, O. F., "Railway Vagrancy," *Charities*, 21, January 23, 1909, pp. 713–17.

———, "Vagrant and the Railroad," *North American*, 185, July 19, 1907, pp. 603–13.

Lindsay, N. V., "Rules of the Road," *American Magazine*, 74, May 1912, pp. 54–59.

London, Jack, "Hoboes That Pass in the Night," *Cosmopolitan*, 44, December 1907, pp. 190–97.

———, "Adventures With the Police," *Cosmopolitan*, 44, March 1908, pp. 417–23.

———, "Rods and Gunnels," *Bookman*, 44, October 1916, pp. 176–79.

Mullin, Glen, "Adventures of a Scholar Tramp," *Century*, 105, February–March 1923, pp. 507–15, 753–59.

Speek, Peter A., "The Psychology of Floating Workers," *Annals of the American Academy of Political and Social Science*, 69, January 1917, pp. 72–78.

Whiting, F. V., "Trespassers Killed on Railways—Who Are They?" *Scientific America*, 73, May 11, 1912, pp. 303–4.

Other Sources

"The Men We Lodge," Report of the Advisory Social Service Committee of the Municipal Lodging House. New York City: Department of Public Charities, 1915.

Chapter 4.   Soapbox Militants

Books

Flynn, Elizabeth G., *I Speak My Own Piece*. New York: Masses and Mainstream, 1955.

Perlman, Selig and Taft, Philip, *History of Labor in the United States, 1896–1932*, Vol. 4, *Labor Movements*. New York: Macmillan, 1935.

Schroeder, Theodore, *Free Speech for Radicals*. New York: Free Speech League, 1916.

Smith, Walker C., *The Everett Massacre: A History of the Class Struggle in the Lumber Industry*. Chicago: I.W.W. Publishing Bureau, 1918.

Weinstock, Harris, *Report to the Governor of California on the Disturbances in the City and County of San Diego in 1912*. Sacramento: State Printing Office, 1912.

Articles

"Bloodshed at Everett," *Literary Digest*, 53, November 25, 1916, p. 1395.

Botting, David C., Jr., "Bloody Sunday," *Pacific Northwest Quarterly*, 69, October 1958, pp. 162–72.

Coleman, B. S., "I.W.W. and the Law, The Result of Everett's Bloody Sunday," *Sunset*, 39, July 1917, pp. 68–70.

Flynn, Elizabeth G., "The Free Speech Fight at Spokane," *International Socialist Review*, 10, December 1909, p. 483.

———, "The Shame of Spokane," *International Socialist Review*, 10, January 1910, pp. 610–19.

———, "Latest News from Spokane," *International Socialist Review*, 10, March 1910, pp. 828–34.

Goldman, Emma, "The Outrage of San Diego," *Mother Earth*, 7, June 1912, pp. 115–22.

Heslewood, Frank, "Barbarous Spokane," *International Socialist Review*, 10, February 1910, pp. 705–13.

Hill, M. A., "Free Speech Fight at San Diego," *Survey*, 28, May 4, 1912, pp. 192–94.

Payne, C. E., "The Mainspring of Action," *One Big Union Monthly*, 1, March 1919, pp. 29–30.

Reitman, Ben L., "The Respectable Mob," *Mother Earth*, 7, June 1912, pp. 109–14.

"San Diego's Free Speech Troubles," *Literary Digest*, 44, June 1, 1912, p. 1146.

Smith, Walker C., "The Voyage of the Verona," *International Socialist Review*, 17, December 1916, pp. 340–46.

Strong, Anna Louise, "Everett's Bloody Sunday, A Free Speech Fight That Led to a Murder Trial," *Survey*, 37, January 27, 1917, pp. 475–76.

Tyler, Robert L., "The Everett Free Speech Fight," *Pacific Historical Review*, 23, February 1954, pp. 19–30.

Woehlke, Walter, "The I.W.W. and the Golden Rule, Why Everett Used the Club and Gun on the Red Apostles of Direct Action," *Sunset*, 38, February 1917, pp. 16–18.

Chapter 5.   Joe Hill: Wobbly Bard

Books

Blaisdell, Lowell L., *The Desert Revolution*. Madison: University of Wisconsin Press, 1962.

Chaplin, Ralph, *Wobbly: The Rough and Tumble Story of an American Radical*. Chicago: University of Chicago Press, 1948.

Flynn, Elizabeth G., *I Speak My Own Piece*. New York: Masses and Mainstream, 1955.

Foner, Philip S., *The Case of Joe Hill*. New York: International Publishers, 1965.

Greenway, John, *American Folksongs of Protest*. Philadelphia: University of Pennsylvania Press, 1953.

Smith, Gibbs M., *Joe Hill*. Salt Lake City: University of Utah Press, 1968.

Stavis, Barrie, *The Man Who Never Died*. New York: Haven Press, 1951, 1954.

Stavis, Barrie and Harmon, Frank, editors, *The Songs of Joe Hill*. New York: Oak Publishers, 1960.

Stegner, Wallace, *The Preacher and the Slave*. Boston: Houghton Mifflin, 1950.

Articles

"Case of Joe Hill," *New Republic*, 119, November 15, 1948, pp. 18–20.

Chaplin, Ralph, "Joe Hill's Funeral," *International Socialist Review*, 16, December 1915, pp. 400–405.

———, "Joe Hill, A Biography," *Industrial Pioneer*, 1, November 1923, pp. 23–25.

Haywood, William D., "Sentenced to Be Shot—Act Quick," *International Socialist Review*, 16, August 1915, p. 110.

Hilton, Judge O. N., "A Challenge," *International Socialist Review*, 16, December 1915, p. 328.

———, "The Joe Hill Case," *International Socialist Review*, 16, September 1915, pp. 171–72.

———, "Joe Hill," *International Socialist Review*, 16, December 1915, pp. 329–30.

Jensen, Vernon H., "The Legend of Joe Hill," *Industrial and Labor Relations Review*, 4, April 1951, pp. 356–66.

Larkin, Jim, "Murder Most Foul," *International Socialist Review*, 16, December 1915, p. 330–31.

———, "The Execution of the I.W.W. Poet," *Survey*, 35, November 27, 1915, p. 200.

"The Last Letters of Joe Hill," *Industrial Pioneer*, 1, December 1923, pp. 53–56.

Modesto, Zapeta (Barry Nichols), "Joe Hill: Some Notes on an American Culture Hero," *Wobbly*, No. 3 (I.W.W. General Recruiting Union, Berkeley, California), October 1963, pp. 2–11.

Stegner, Wallace, "I Dreamed I Saw Joe Hill Last Night," *Pacific Spectator*, 1, Spring 1947, pp. 184–87.

————, "Joe Hill: The Wobblies' 'Troubadour,'" *New Republic*, 118, January 5, 1948, pp. 20–24. Discussion, 118, February 9, 1948, pp. 38–39.

Van Valkenburgh, W. S., "The Murder of Joseph Hillstrom," *Mother Earth*, 10, December 1915, pp. 326–28.

Waring, John, "Questioned the Executioners," *International Socialist Review*, 16, January 1916, p. 405.

Unpublished Material

Morris, James O., "The Joe Hill Case." Unpublished manuscript in the Labadie Collection, The University of Michigan Library.

Chapter 6.   Bread and Roses

Books

Cahn, Bill, *Milltown*. New York: Cameron and Kahn, 1954.

Cole, Donald B., *Immigrant City: Lawrence, Massachusetts, 1845–1921*. Chapel Hill: University of North Carolina Press, 1963.

Ebert, Justus, *The Trial of a New Society*. Cleveland: I.W.W. Publishing Bureau, 1913.

Yellin, Samuel, *American Labor Struggles*. New York: Harcourt, Brace and Co., 1936.

Pamphlets

Ettor and Giovannitti Before the Jury at Salem, Massachusetts. Cleveland: I.W.W., 1913.

Articles

Baker, Ray Stannard, "Revolutionary Strike," *American Magazine*, 74, May 1912, pp. 18–30C.

Carstens, C. C., "The Children's Exodus from Lawrence," *Survey*, 28, April 6, 1912, pp. 70–71.

Cole, J. N., "The Issue at Lawrence—The Manufacturers' Point of View," *Outlook*, 100, February 24, 1912, pp. 405–6.

Deland, L. F., "The Lawrence Strike; A Study," *Atlantic Monthly*, 109, May 1912, pp. 694–705.

Heaton, J. P., "The Salem Trial," *Survey*, 29, December 7, 1912, pp. 301–4.

————, "The Legal Aftermath of the Lawrence Strike," *Survey*, 28, July 6, 1912, pp. 503–10.

Lauck, W. J., "The Significance of the Situation at Lawrence," *Survey*, 27, February 17, 1912, pp. 1772–74.

Leupp, C. D., "The Lawrence Strike Hearings," *Survey*, 27, March 1912, pp. 1953–54.

Marcy, Leslie H. and Boyd, Frederick S., "One Big Union Wins," *International Socialist Review*, 12, April 1912, pp. 613–30.

Marcy, Mary, "The Battle for Bread at Lawrence," *International Socialist Review*, 12, March 1912, pp. 533–43.

McGowan, Kenneth, "Giovannitti: Poet of the Wop," *Forum*, 52, October 1914, pp. 609–11.

"Poet of the I.W.W.," *Outlook*, 104, July 5, 1913, pp. 504–6.

"Poetry of Syndicalism," *Atlantic*, 3, June 1913, pp. 853–54.

Russell, Phillips, "The Second Battle of Lawrence," *International Socialist Review*, 13, November 1912, pp. 417–23.

————, "Lawrence and the Industrial Workers of the World," *Survey*, 28, April 6, 1912, pp. 79–80.

"Salem Trial of the Lawrence Case," *Outlook*, 102, December 7, 1912, pp. 739–40.

"Social Significance of Arturo Giovannitti," *Current Opinion*, 54, January 1913, pp. 24–26.

Sumner, M. B., "Lyric Singer," *Survey*, 29, November 2, 1912, pp. 163–66.

Vorse, Mary H., "The Troubles at Lawrence," *Harper's Weekly*, 56, March 16, 1912, p. 10.

Weyl, Walter E., "It Is Time to Know," *Survey*, 28, April 6, 1912, pp. 65–67.

————, "The Strikers at Lawrence," *Outlook*, 100, February 10, 1912, pp. 309–12.

Woods, R. A., "The Clod Stirs," *Survey*, 27, March 16, 1912, pp. 1929–32.

————, "The Breadth and Depth of the Lawrence Outcome," *Survey*, 28, April 6, 1912, pp. 67–68.

Government Publications

Report on Strike of Textile Workers in Lawrence, Massachusetts in 1912. 62nd Congress, 2nd Session, Senate Document 870, Washington, 1912.

The Strike at Lawrence, Massachusetts, Hearings Before the Committee on Rules of the House of Representatives . . . 1912. 62nd Congress, 2nd Session, House Document 671. Washington, 1912.

Unpublished Material

Morris, James O., "The Dynamite Conspiracy at Lawrence, Massachusetts." Unpublished manuscript in the Labadie Collection, The University of Michigan Library.

Chapter 7.   Paterson: 1913

Books

Flynn, Elizabeth G., *I Speak My Own Piece*. New York: Masses and Mainstream, 1955.

Haywood, William D., *Bill Haywood's Book*. New York: International Publishers, 1929.

Hicks, Granville, *John Reed: The Making of a Revolutionary*. New York: Macmillan, 1936.

Luhan, Mabel Dodge, *Intimate Memories*, Vol. 3, *Movers and Shakers*. New York: Harcourt, Brace and Co., 1933.

May, Henry F., *The End of American Innocence: A Study of the First Years of Our Own Time, 1912–1917*. New York: Alfred A. Knopf, 1959.

Valentine, Alan C., *1913: America Between Two Worlds*. New York: Macmillan, 1962.

Vorse, Mary H., *Footnote to Folly*. New York: Farrar and Rinehart, 1935.

Articles

"A Double Labor War," *Outlook*, 104, May 3, 1913, p. 11.

"Aftermath of the Paterson Strike, *Outlook*, 105, November 29, 1913, p. 679.

Boyd, Frederick S., "The General Strike in the Silk Industry," *The Pageant of the Paterson Strike*. New York: Success Press, 1913, pp. 3–8.

"City Officials Adopt Repressive Measures," *Survey*, 30, April 19, 1913, pp. 82–83.

"End of the Paterson Strike," *Outlook*, 104, August 9, 1913, p. 780.

Fitch, John A., "I.W.W.: An Outlaw Organization," *Survey*, 30, June 7, 1913, pp. 355–62.

Fitch, John A., "The Paterson Silk Strike: A Year After," *Survey*, 32, June 27, 1914, pp. 339–40.

Haywood, William D., "On the Paterson Picket Line," *International Socialist Review*, 13, June 1913, pp. 847–51.

———, "The Rip in the Silk Industry," *International Socialist Review*, 13, May 1913, pp. 783–88.

———, "Smoothing Out the Wrinkles in Silk," *The Pageant of the Paterson Strikers*. New York: Success Press, 1913, pp. 22–27.

"Haywood's Battle in Paterson," *Literary Digest*, 46, May 10, 1913, pp. 1043–44.

Koettgen, Ewald, "Making Silk," *International Socialist Review*, 14, March 1914, pp. 551–56.

Mannheimer, Leo, "Darkest New Jersey," *Independent*, 74, May 29, 1913, pp. 1190–92.

Mason, Gregory, "Industrial War in Paterson," *Outlook*, 104, June 7, 1913, pp. 283–87.

"New Jersey's Journalistic Perils," *Literary Digest*, 46, June 21, 1913, pp. 1366–67.

"Pageant of the Paterson Strike," *Survey*, 30, June 28, 1913, p. 428.

"Paterson Convictions Again Set Aside," *Survey*, 31, November 22, 1913, pp. 191–92.

"Paterson Strike Leaders in Jersey Prison," *Survey*, 34, April 3, 1915, p. 387.

"Paterson Strike Pageant," *Independent*, 74, June 19, 1913, pp. 1406–7.

Quinlan, Patrick L., "The Paterson Strike and After," *New Review*, 2, January 1914, pp. 26–33.

Reed, John, "War in Paterson," *International Socialist Review*, 14, July 1913, pp. 43–48.

Russell, Phillips, "The Arrest of Haywood and Lessig," *International Socialist Review*, 13, May 1913, pp. 789–92.

"Strike of the Jersey Silk Weavers," *Survey*, 30, April 19, 1913, pp. 81–83.

Sumner, Mary B., "Broad Silk Weavers of Paterson," *Survey*, 27, March 16, 1912, pp. 1932–35.

Wheeler, Robert J., "The Allentown Silk Dyers Strike," *International Socialist Review*, 13, May 1913, pp. 820–21.

"Work of the I.W.W. in Paterson," *Literary Digest*, 47, August 9, 1913, pp. 197–98.

Other Sources

Newman, Philip, "The First I.W.W. Invasion of New Jersey," *New Jersey Historical Society Proceedings*, 58, October 1940, pp. 268–83.

Government Publications

U.S. Commission on Industrial Relations, *Final Report and Testimony on Industrial Relations*. 64th Congress, 1st Session. Washington: Government Printing Office, 1916, pp. 2411–2645.

Unpublished Material

Beffel, John N. "Patrick Quinlan." Manuscript in the Labadie Collection, The University of Michigan Library.

Flynn, Elizabeth G., "The Truth About the Paterson Strike." Manuscript in the Labadie Collection, The University of Michigan Library.

Chapter 8. Organizing the Harvest Stiffs

Books

McWilliams, Carey, *Factories in the Fields*. Boston: Little Brown, 1939.

———, *Ill Fares the Land*. Boston: Little, Brown, 1942.

Parker, Carleton H., *The Casual Laborer and Other Essays*. New York: Harcourt, Brace and Howe, 1920. Appendix 1, "Report on the Wheatland Riot," Official Report of the Commission on Immigration and Housing, 1914.

Pamphlets

Woodruff, Abner E., *Evolution of American Agriculture*. Chicago: Industrial Workers of the World, n.d.

Articles

Bell, G. L., "Wheatland Hop Fields Riot," *Outlook*, 107, May 16, 1914, pp. 118–23.

Downing, Mortimer, "The Case of the Hop Pickers," *International Socialist Review*, 14, October 1913, pp. 210–13.

Gilmore, Inez Haynes, "Marysville Strike," *Harper's Weekly*, 59, April 4, 1914, pp. 18–20.

Krysto, Christine, "California's Labor Camps," *Survey*, 43, November 8, 1919, pp. 70–78.

Lescohier, D. D., "With the I.W.W. in the Wheatlands," *Harpers*, 147, August 1923, pp. 371–78.

———, "The Farm Labor Problem," *Journal of Farm Economics*, 2, March 1921, pp. 10–15.

Nef, W. T., "Job Control in the Harvest Fields," *International Socialist Review*, 17, September 1916, pp. 140–43.

Parker, Carleton H., "The California Casual and His Revolt," *Quarterly Journal of Economics*, 30, November 1915, pp. 110–26.

Ruess, Carl F., "The Farm Labor Problem in Washington: 1917–1918," *Pacific Northwest Quarterly*, 34, October 1943, pp. 339–52.

Taft, Philip, "The I.W.W. in the Grain Belt," *Labor History*, 1, Winter 1960, pp. 53–67.

Whitten, Woodrow C., "The Wheatland Episode," *Pacific Historical Review*, 17, February 1948, pp. 37–42.

Government Publications

Baker, Oliver E., *Seed Time and Harvest*. U.S. Department of Agriculture, Bulletin No. 183. Washington: Government Printing Office, March 1922.

Jamieson, Stuart, *Labor Unionism in American Agriculture*. U.S. Department of Labor, Bureau of Labor Statistics, Bulletin No. 836. Washington: Government Printing Office, 1946.

Lescohier, D. D., *The Harvest Worker*. U.S. Department of Labor, Bulletin No. 1020. Washington: Government Printing Office, 1922.

———, *Conditions Affecting the Demand for Harvest Labor in the Wheat Belt*. U.S. Department of Agriculture, Bulletin No. 1230. Washington: Government Printing Office, 1924.

U.S. Commission on Industrial Relations, *Final Report and Testimony on Industrial Relations*. 64th Congress, 1st Session. Washington: Government Printing Office, 1916, 5, pp. 4911–5027.

Chapter 9.   Lumberjacks: North and South

Books

Allen, Ruth A., *East Texas Lumber Workers: An Economic and Social Picture, 1870–1950*. Austin: University of Texas Press, 1961.

Bing, Alexander M., *War Time Strikes and Their Adjustments*. New York: E. P. Dutton, 1921.

Holbrook, Stewart H., *Holy Old Mackinaw—A Natural History of the American Lumberjack*. New York: Macmillan, 1939.

Jensen, Vernon H., *Lumber and Labor*. New York: Farrar and Rhinehart, 1945.

Smith, Walker C., *The Everett Massacre—A History of the Class Struggle in the Lumber Industry*. Chicago: I.W.W. Publishing Bureau, 1917.

Spero, Sterling D. and Harris, Abram L., *The Black Worker—The Negro and the Labor Movement*. New York: Columbia University Press, 1931.

Todes, Charlotte, *Labor and Lumber*. New York: International Publishers, 1931.

Pamphlets

Chaplin, Ralph, *The Centralia Conspiracy*. Chicago: I.W.W. Publishing Co., 1920.

Federal Council of Churches of Christ in America, *The Centralia Case—A Joint Report on the Armistice Day Tragedy at Centralia, Washington, November 11, 1919*. New York: Department of Research and Education, Federal Council of Churches of Christ in America, 1930.

Lampman, Ben H., *The Centralia Tragedy and Trial*. American Legion, 1920.

The Lumber Industry and Its Workers. Chicago: I.W.W. Publishing Co., n.d.

Articles

Boaz, R. P., "The Loyal Legion of Loggers and Lumbermen," *Atlantic Monthly*, 127, February 1921, pp. 221–26.

Bruere, Robert W., "Following the Trail of the I.W.W.," *New York Evening Post*, beginning February 16, 1918.

Clay, Samuel H., "The Man Who Heads the Spruce Drive," *Review of Reviews*, 57, June 1918, pp. 633–35.

Coleman, B. S., "The I.W.W. and the Law—The Result of Everett's Bloody Sunday," *Sunset*, 39, July 1917, pp. 3, 5, 68–70.

"Colonel Disque and the I.W.W.," *New Republic*, 14, April 6, 1918, pp. 284–85.

"Company Stores and the Scrip System," *Monthly Labor Review*, 61, July 1935, pp. 44–50.

Creel, G., "Feudal Towns of Texas," *Harper's Weekly*, 60, January 23, 1915, p. 76.

Disque, Brice P., "How We Found a Cure for Strikes," *System*, 36, September 1919, pp. 379–83.

Gill, R. S., "The Four L's in Lumber," *Survey*, 44, May 1, 1920, pp. 165–70.

Griffin, C. R., "The Short Log Country," *International Socialist Review*, 17, January 1917, pp. 422–23.

Lockhart, J. W., "The I.W.W. Raid at Centralia," *Current History*, 17, October 1922, pp. 55–57.

McMahon, Teresa S., "Centralia and the I.W.W.," *Survey*, 43, November 29, 1919, pp. 173–74.

Merz, C., "Tying Up Western Lumber," *New Republic*, 12, September 29, 1917, pp. 142–44.

Mittelman, E. B., "The Loyal Legion of Loggers and Lumbermen," *Journal of Political Economy*, 31, June 1923, pp. 313–41.

———, "Gyppo System," *Journal of Political Economy*, 31, December 1923, pp. 840–51.

Mueller, J. R., "Food in the Lumber Camps," *Journal of Home Economics*, 13, June 1921, pp. 241–45.

Payne, C. E., "Captain Coll—Legionnaire," *Nation*, 129, July 10, 1929, pp. 38–39.

Smith, Walker C., "The Voyage of the Verona," *International Socialist Review*, 17, December 1916, pp. 341–46.

Strong, Anna Louise, "Centralia, an Unfinished Story," *Nation*, 110, April 17, 1920, pp. 508–10.

Thompson, E. Bigelow, "The Case of the Lumberjack," *World Outlook*, 6, June 1920, pp. 22–37.

Tugwell, Rexford G., "The Casual of the Woods," *Survey*, 44, July 3, 1920, pp. 472–74.

Tyler, Robert L., "I.W.W. in the Pacific N. W.; Rebels of the Woods," *Oregon Historical Quarterly*, 60, March 1954, pp. 3–44.

——, "Violence at Centralia, 1919," *Pacific Northwest Quarterly*, 65, October 1954, pp. 116–24.

Winstead, Ralph, "Enter a Logger: An I.W.W. Reply to the Four L's," *Survey*, 44, July 3, 1920, pp. 474–77.

Wolff, W. A., "The Northwest Front," *Collier's Weekly*, 61, April 20, 1918, pp. 10 ff., 31 ff.

Government Publications

Howd, Cloice R., *Industrial Relations in the West Coast Lumber Industry*. U.S. Department of Labor, Bureau of Labor Statistics, Bulletin No. 349. Washington: Government Printing Office, 1924.

Report of the President's Mediation Commission to the President of the United States—Unrest in the Lumber Industry. Washington: Government Printing Office, 1918.

U.S. Commission on Industrial Relations, *Final Report and Testimony on Industrial Relations*. Washington: Government Printing Office, 1916. Vol. 5, pp. 4394, 4412.

Unpublished Material

Cox, John H., "Organizations of the Lumber Industry in the Pacific Northwest, 1889–1914." Unpublished Ph.D. thesis, University of California, 1937.

Jensen, Vernon H., "Labor Relations in the Douglas Fir Lumber Industry." Unpublished Ph.D. thesis, University of California, 1939.

McCord, Charles R., "A Brief History of the Brotherhood of Timber Workers." Unpublished master's thesis, University of Texas, 1958.

Chapter 10.   Down in the Mines

Books

Duffy, J. H., *Butte Was Like That*. Butte: Tom Greenfield Press, 1941.

Holbrook, Stewart H., *Iron Brew: A Century of American Ore and Steel*. New York: Macmillan, 1939.

Jensen, Vernon H., *Heritage of Conflict*. Ithaca: Cornell University Press, 1950.

Murdock, A., *Boom Copper*. New York: Macmillan Co., 1943.

Work Projects Administration, *Copper Camp—Stories of the World's Greatest Mining Town, Butte, Montana*. New York: Hastings House, 1943.

Work Projects Administration, *Montana: A State Guide Book*. New York: Hastings House, 1949.

Work Projects Administration, *Nevada: A Guide to the Silver State*, Portland, Oregon: Binford and Mort, 1940.

Articles

Brissenden, Paul F., "The Butte Miners and the Rustling Card," *American Economic Review*, December 1920, pp. 755–75.

Bruere, Robert W., "Copper Camp Patriotism," *Nation*, 106, February 21, 1918, pp. 202–3.

——, "Copper Camp Patriotism," *Nation*, 106, February 28, 1918, pp. 235–36.

——, "Following the Trail of the I.W.W.," *New York Evening Post*, November 14, 17, 24, December 1, 8, 12, 15, 1917, February 13, 16, 23, 30, April 6, 13, 20, 1918.

——, "The Industrial Workers of the World," *Harper's*, 137, July 1918, pp. 250–57.

Currie, B. W., "How the West Dealt with One Labor Union," *Harper's Weekly*, 51, June 22, 1907, pp. 908–10.

Debs, Eugene V., "The Butte Affair Reviewed," *Miners' Magazine*, July 23, 1914, pp. 7–8.

Dennett, T., "The Mining Strike in Minnesota," *Outlook*, 113, August 30, 1916, pp. 1046–48.

Elliott, Russell R., "Labor Troubles in the Mining Camp at Goldfield, Nevada, 1906–1908," *Pacific Historical Review*, 19, November 1950, pp. 369–84.

Hand, Wayland, "The Folklore, Customs, and Traditions of the Butte Miner," *California Folklore Quarterly*, 5, January 1946, pp. 1–25, April 1946, pp. 153–76.

Haywood, William D., "The Revolt at Butte," *International Socialist Review*, 15, August 1914, pp. 89–96.

——, "Butte Better," *International Socialist Review*, 15, February 1915, pp. 473–74.

MacDonald, J., "From Butte to Bisbee," *International Socialist Review*, 17, August 1917, pp. 67–69.

Marcy, L. H., "Calumet," *International Socialist Review*, 14, February 1914, pp. 453–67.

——, "The Iron Heel on the Mesabi Range," *International Socialist Review*, 17, April 1916, pp. 74–77.

Merz, C., "The Issue in Butte," *New Republic*, 12, September 22, 1917, pp. 215–17.

Perry, Grover, "Metal Miners' Riot," *International Socialist Review*, 17, June 1917, p. 730.

Taylor, G. R., "The Clash in the Copper Country," *Survey*, 31, November 1, 1913, pp. 127–35.

——, "Moyer's Story of Why He Left the Copper Country," *Survey*, 31, January 10, 1914, pp. 433–35.

Vorse, Mary H., "The Mining Strike in Minnesota," *Outlook*, 113, August 30, 1916, pp. 1036, 1045–46.

West, George P., "Mesabi Strike," *International Socialist Review*, 17, September 1916, pp. 158–59.

Government Publications

Labor Troubles at Goldfield, Nevada. House Document No. 607, 60th Congress, 1st Session. Washington: Government Printing Office, 1908.

Report on Bisbee Deportations Made by the President's Mediation Commission to the President of the United States, November 6, 1917. Washington: Government Printing Office, 1918.

"Report of the Federal Mediation Commission to the President of the United States, January 9, 1918," *United States Official Bulletin*, 2, February 11, 1918.

U. S. Commission on Industrial Relations, *Final Report and Testimony on Industrial Relations.* 64th Congress, 1st Session. Washington: Government Printing Office, 1916. Vol. 4, pp. 3681–4095.

Unpublished Material

Stegner, Page, "Protest Songs from the Butte Mines." Unpublished manuscript in the library of Mr. Stegner, Stanford University.

White, L. A., "Rise of the Industrial Workers of the World in Goldfield, Nevada." Unpublished master's thesis, University of Nebraska, 1912.

Chapter 11.   Behind Bars: War and Prison

Books

Bing, Alexander M., *War Time Strikes and Their Adjustment.* New York: Dutton, 1921.

Chafee, Jr., Zachariah, *Freedom of Speech.* New York: Harcourt, Brace and Howe, 1920.

———, *Free Speech in the United States.* Cambridge: Harvard University Press, 1941.

Chaplin, Ralph, *Wobbly: The Rough and Tumble Story of an American Radical.* Chicago: University of Chicago Press, 1948.

Dowell, Eldridge F., *A History of Criminal Syndicalism Legislation in the United States.* Baltimore: Johns Hopkins University Press, 1939.

Dunn, Robert W., *The Palmer Raids.* New York: International Publishers, 1948.

Gambs, John S., *The Decline of the I.W.W.* New York: Columbia University Press, 1932.

Hawley, Lowell S., and Potts, Ralph B., *Counsel for the Damned: A Biography of George Francis Vanderveer.* Philadelphia: Lippincott, 1953.

Haywood, William D., *Bill Haywood's Book.* New York: International Publishers, 1929.

Mowry, George E., *The California Progressives.* Berkeley: University of California Press, 1951.

Murray, Robert K., *Red Scare: A Study in National Hysteria 1919–1920.* Minneapolis: University of Minnesota Press, 1955.

Panunzio, Constantine M., *The Deportation Cases of 1919–1920.* New York: Commission on the Church and Social Service, 1921.

Perlman, Selig, and Taft, Philip, *History of Labor in the United States, 1896–1932.* Vol. 4, *Labor Movements.* New York: Macmillan, 1935.

Preston, William, Jr., *Aliens and Dissenters.* Cambridge, Harvard University Press, 1963.

Rand School of Social Science, Department of Labor Research, *The American Labor Year Book.* New York: Rand School of Social Science, Vol. 1 (1916)–Vol. 6 (1925).

Sinclair, Upton, *Singing Jailbirds.* California, published by author, 1924.

Pamphlets

(*Note: The American Civil Liberties Union was an outgrowth of the National Civil Liberties Bureau.*)

American Civil Liberties Union, *Civil Liberty Since the Armistice.* New York: A.C.L.U., 1920.

———, *The Fight for Free Speech.* New York: A.C.L.U., 1921.

———, The "Knights of Liberty" Mob and the I.W.W. Prisoners at Tulsa, Oklahoma. New York: N.C.L.B., 1918.

———, *Memorandum Regarding the Persecution of the Radical Labor Movement in the United States.* New York: N.C.L.B., 1919.

———, *Mob Violence in the United States.* New York: A.C.L.U., 1923.

———, *The Persecution of the I.W.W.* New York: A.C.L.U., 1921.

———, *The Truth About the I.W.W.* New York: N.C.L.B., 1918.

———, *The Truth About the I.W.W. Prisoners.* New York: A.C.L.U., 1923.

———, *Why Two Governors Freed Political Prisoners.* New York: A.C.L.U., 1923.

Amnesty for Political Prisoners. New York: National Civil Federation, 1922.

Brissenden, Paul F., *Justice and the I.W.W.* Chicago: I.W.W. General Defense Committee, n.d.

Duff, Harvey, *The Silent Defenders: Courts and Capitalism in California.* Chicago: I.W.W., n.d.

I.W.W. General Executive Board, *The I.W.W. Reply to The Red Trade Union International.* Chicago: I.W.W., 1922.

Lane, Winthrop D., *Uncle Sam, Jailor.* Chicago: I.W.W., n.d.

Open Letter to President Harding from 52 I.W.W. Prisoners at Leavenworth Penitentiary. Chicago: I.W.W. General Defense Committee, 1922.

Opening Statement of George F. Vanderveer in United States vs. William D. Haywood, et al. Chicago: I.W.W. General Defense Committee, 1918.

U.S.A. vs. William D. Haywood et al., Evidence and Cross Examination. Chicago: I.W.W. General Defense Committee, 1918.

Articles

Callahan, D. F., "Criminal Syndicalism and Sabotage," *Monthly Labor Review*, 14, April 1922, pp. 803–12.

Chafee, Jr., Zachariah, "California Justice," *New Republic*, 36, September 19, 1923, pp. 97–100.

deFord, Miriam, "Injury to All: Criminal Syndicalism Law of California," *Overland*, 82, December 1924, pp. 536–37.

————, "Vacation at San Quentin," *Nation*, 117, August 1, 1923, pp. 114–15.

Eastman, Max, "Bill Haywood, Communist," *Liberator*, 4, April 1921, pp. 13–14.

Elliott, W. Y., "Political Application of Romanticism," *Political Science Quarterly*, 39, June 1924, pp. 234–64.

Ford, Lynn, "The Growing Menace of the I.W.W.," *Forum*, 61, January 1919, pp. 62–70.

Gannett, Lewis, "Bill Haywood in Moscow," *Liberator*, 4, September 1921, pp. 11–12.

————, "The I.W.W." *Nation*, 111, October 20, 1920, pp. 448–49.

George, Harrison, "The Prison Story of the Wobblies," *Workers' Monthly*, 1, pp. 209–11.

Hanson, Ole, "Fighting the Reds in Their Home Town," *World's Work*, 39, December 1919–March, 1920, pp. 123–26, 302–7, 401–8, 484–87.

"Big Bill Haywood," *Outlook*, 149, May 30, 1928, p. 171.

"William D. Haywood, Obituary," *Nation*, 126, May 30, 1928, p. 601.

Hibschmann, Harry, "The I.W.W. Menace Self-Revealed," *Current History*, 16, August 1922, pp. 761–68.

Hofteling, Catherine, "Arbuckle and the I.W.W.," *Nation*, 116, February 14, 1923, pp. 170–71.

————, "Sunkist Prisoners," *Nation*, 113, September 21, 1921, p. 316.

————, "The I.W.W. to Warren G. Harding," *Nation*, 117, August 29, 1923, p. 217.

"Is Civil Liberty Dead?" *Liberator*, 1, November 1918, p. 43.

"I.W.W. Closed the Saloons," *Nation*, 116, May 23, 1923, p. 588.

Keller, Helen, "In Behalf of the I.W.W.," *Liberator*, 1, March 1918, p. 13.

Lanier, A. S., "To the President: Open Letter in Regard to the Case of the U.S. vs. W. D. Haywood, et al.," *New Republic*, 18, April 19, 1919, pp. 383–84.

"Membership in the I.W.W.: A Criminal Offense Under California Statute," *Monthly Labor Review*, 16, February 1923, pp. 471–73.

"Ol' Rags and Bottles," *Nation*, 108, January 25, 1919, pp. 114–16.

Reading, A. B., "California Syndicalism Act, Strong or Wobbly?," *Overland*, 83, March 1925, pp. 117–18.

Reed, Mary, "San Pedro," *Nation*, 119, July 9, 1924, pp. 45–46.

Rowan, James, "Imprisoned I.W.W. at Leavenworth," *Nation*, 113, August 3, 1921, p. 123.

Ryder, D. W., "California: Ashamed and Repentant," *New Republic*, 51, June 1, 1927, pp. 41–44.

"Several Poems by I.W.W. Prisoners," *Liberator*, 5, March 1922, p. 9.

Spargo, John, "Why the I.W.W. Flourishes," *World's Work*, 39, January 1920, pp. 243–47.

Stephens, Daniel, "Fair Play for the I.W.W.," *Current History*, 16, October 1922, p. 58.

Sterling, Jean, "The Silent Defense in Sacramento," *Liberator*, 2, February, 1919, pp. 15–17.

"Syndicalism and the Supreme Court," *Outlook*, 146, May 25, 1927, p. 100.

"Tulsa, November 9th," *Liberator*, 1, April 1918, pp. 15–17.

Vorse, Mary H., "Twenty Years," *Liberator*, 4, January 21, pp. 10–13.

Wetter, Pierce, "Men I Left at Leavenworth," *Survey*, 49, October 1, 1922, pp. 29–31.

Yarros, Victor S., "I.W.W. Trial," *Nation*, 107, August 31, 1918, pp. 220–23.

————, "The Story of the I.W.W. Trial," *Survey*, 40, August 31–September 14, 1918, pp. 603–4, 630–32, 660–63.

Young, Art, and Reed, John, "The Social Revolution in Court," *Liberator*, 1, September 1918, pp. 20–28.

Other Sources

Lorwin, Lewis, "Criminal Syndicalism," *Encyclopedia of the Social Sciences*, 4, pp. 582–84.

Government Publications

Amnesty for Political Prisoners. Hearings Before the Committee on the Judiciary, House of Representatives, 67th Congress, 2nd Session, March 16, 1922. Washington: Government Printing Office, 1922.

Huddleston, George, *For the Release of Political Prisoners.* Speeches of Hon. George Huddleston of Alabama in the House of Representatives, December 11, 1922. Washington: Government Printing Office, 1924.

Revolutionary Radicalism, Its History, Purpose and Tactics. Report of the Joint Legislative Committee Investigating Seditious Activities, filed April 24, 1920, in the Senate of the State of New York. Albany, 1920. 4 vols.

I.W.W. Deportation Cases. Hearings before the Subcommittee, House Committee on Immigration and Naturalization, 66th Congress, 2nd Session, April 27–30, 1920. Washington: Government Printing Office, 1920.

Unpublished Materials

Tulin, Leo, "Digest of Criminal Syndicalism Cases in California." San Francisco, 1926. Manuscript in the Labadie Collection, The University of Michigan Library.

Weintraub, Hyman, "The I.W.W. in California." Unpublished Ph.D. thesis, University of California at Los Angeles, 1947.

Chapter 12.   An I.W.W. Miscellany

Books

Anderson, Nels, *Men On the Move.* Chicago: University of Chicago Press, 1938.

Bernstein, Irving, *The Lean Years: A History of the American Worker 1920–1933.* Boston: Houghton Mifflin, 1960.

Draper, Theodore, *The Roots of American Communism.* New York: Viking Press, 1957.

Dreiser, Theodore, et al., *Harlan Miners Speak.* New York: Harcourt Brace, 1932.

Gambs, John S., *The Decline of the I.W.W.* New York: Columbia University Press, 1932.

Perlman, Selig and Taft, Philip, *History of Labor in the United States, 1896–1932.* Vol. 4, *Labor Movements.* New York: Macmillan, 1935.

Thompson, Fred, *The I.W.W.: Its First Fifty Years.* Chicago: I.W.W., 1955.

Articles

Abel, Herbert, "Gun Rule in Kentucky," *Nation,* 133, September 23, 1931, pp. 306–7.

"Bloody Colorado," *Nation,* 125, November 6, 1927, p. 534.

"Blood Spilling in Colorado," *Literary Digest,* 95, December 3, 1927, pp. 5–7.

Byers, Jr., J. C., "Harlan County—Act of God?" *Nation,* 134, June 15, 1932, pp. 672–74.

"Colorado Coal Battle," *Outlook,* 147, December 7, 1927, p. 422.

Hays, Arthur G., "The Right to Get Shot," *Nation,* 134, June 1, 1932, p. 619.

Holbrook, Stewart H., "Last of the Wobblies," *American Mercury,* 62, April 1946, pp. 462–68.

——, "Wobbly Talk," *American Mercury,* 7, January 1926, pp. 62–65.

"I.W.W. Revives," *Business Week,* January 6, 1945, p. 96.

Johnson, Oakley, "Starvation and the 'Reds' in Kentucky," *Nation,* 134, February 3, 1932, pp. 140–42.

Leighton, G. R., "Seattle, Washington: The Edge of the Last Frontier," *Harper,* 178, March 1939, pp. 422–40.

Lens, Sidney, "The Wobblies—50 Years Later," *Progressive,* 19, August 1955, pp. 20–21.

McClurg, Donald J., "The Colorado Coal Strike of 1927—Tactical Leadership of the I.W.W.," *Labor History,* 4, Winter 1963, pp. 68–92.

Meyer, E. F., "Six Killed, Twenty Wounded," *Survey,* 59, February 15, 1928, pp. 644–46.

North, Cedric, "Brotherhood of Man and the Wobblies," *North American,* 227, April 1929, pp. 487–92.

Oneal, James. "Passing of the I.W.W.," *Current History,* 21, January 1925, pp. 528–34.

Palmer, Fred, "Solidarity in Colorado," *Nation,* 126, February 1, 1928, pp. 118–20.

——, "War in Colorado," *Nation,* 125, December 7, 1927, pp. 623–24.

Putnam, S., "Red Days in Chicago," *American Mercury,* 30, September 1933, pp. 64–71.

Rice, M. M., "Bloody Monday Again in Colorado," *Independent,* 119, December 31, 1927, pp. 655–56.

Spero, S. D., and Aronoff, J. B., "War in the Kentucky Mountains," *American Mercury,* 25, February 1932, pp. 226–33.

"Two Church Views of the Colorado Strike," *Literary Digest,* 95, December 17, 1927, pp. 31–32.

"Wobblies in the Northwest," *Nation,* 145, November 13, 1937, p. 543.

Government Publications

Conditions in the Coal Fields of Harlan and Bell Counties, Kentucky. Hearings on Senate Resolution 178, Senate Subcommittee on Manufacture, 72nd Congress, 1st Session. Washington: Government Printing Office, 1932.